Program Phases ™
A Programming Language and API Translator

Program Phases LLC

Dave Mihalik

Program Phases ™
A Programming Language and API Translator

This book is dedicated to my loving wife Kara.

Contents

Program Phases

Program Phases Overview

Part I. Program Phase Task 1

Part II. Program Phase Task 2

Part III. Program Phase Task 3

Part IV. Program Phase Task 4

Appendix

Preface

Have you ever found yourself extremely frustrated while trying to learn a new programming language or technology? I know I have, especially when the programming task that I was trying to perform was an extremely simple task that I knew how to perform in a different programming language. Tasks such as concatenating two strings or displaying a main window for a GUI based application are simple once you know how to do them, but what basic programming task isn't simple to perform once you have mastered it? I enjoy learning about new programming languages and programming techniques, but I get frustrated at the lack of common documentation and example programs for different programming languages. If you're like me, you can learn a new programming language concept much easier with a clear example program that illustrates the task at hand.

Learning by example is a great way to learn how to program in a new programming language. In order for an example program to be used as an effective learning tool, you must first understand the programming idea being conveyed. Understanding a programming concept or idea being conveyed in an example program written in a programming language you are familiar with is quite easy to do. If you have an example program written in a computer language that you are unfamiliar with, you must read an additional description as to what the example program is doing.

Why not use your existing understanding of the programming concept in the programming language you are familiar with to learn a new programming language? All you need are two example programs, one written in the programming language you have a firm understanding of and an additional example program written in the language that you are trying to learn.

Program Phases provides relevant example programs illustrating real world programming concepts written in multiple programming languages. Each example program is indexed to allow the reader to easily cross reference programming concepts across multiple programming languages.

It is the goal of this book to help you learn new programming languages while avoiding much of the frustration that often accompanies such learning.

Intended Audience

This book is intended for all levels of programmers who are interested in learning how to perform various common programming tasks in multiple programming languages. Program Phases is intended for experienced programmers as well as novice programmers. Experienced programmers can utilize the cross referenced code blocks to efficiently learn how to perform various tasks using different programming language/API combinations. Novices can use this book as a supplement to a beginner's programming book. Program Phases provides novice programmers simple examples of various programming tasks that are documented in a well-ordered fashion.

What You Need to Know

To effectively use this book, you should be learning or have already learned one of the programming languages presented in one of the sections in this book. In addition, you should have a basic understanding of object oriented programming. Examples in this book are targeted at programmers who are familiar with writing console based applications in a programming language such as C or Pascal and want to learn how to write Graphical User Interface (GUI) based applications.

About the Example Code

The driving force behind this book is the indexed and documented example code. Each of the indexed blocks of code describes a specific programming task. These tasks are indexed in such a way that they can be easily cross referenced across different Program Phases.

Acknowledgements

Cover artwork designed and created by Jeff Seevers.

I would like to thank the following people for helping me over the years to learn the technical information needed to write this book:

Lee Hall
Larry Winkles
Dr. John K. Estell
Joe Kiel
Don Bensch
Allen Rioux
Rick Stansley
John Hogan

I would also like to thank Nancy Mihalik (my awesome mom!) for proofreading the entire text. You're the best!

Introduction

Program Phases is a methodology for indexing computer programs called Program Phase Tasks. A Program Phase Task is a specially designed computer program that clearly illustrates specific functionality supported by an operating system, programming language, and application programming interface (API). An implementation of a Program Phase Task is called a Program Phase and is assigned a unique number with respect to other Program Phases. For example, this book describes a computer program called Program Phase Task 1 and illustrates 18 Program Phases of Program Phase Task 1. The first Program Phase of Program Phase Task 1 is called Program Phase 1-1. The second Program Phase of Program Phase Task 1 is called Program Phase 1-2. The third Program Phase of Program Phase Task 1 is called Program Phase 1-3 and so on.

The code in a Program Phase is categorized and indexed by its functionality. Each of the categories is called a Code Block, and each unique index entry is called a Code Block Identifier (CBI). A CBI takes the following form:

```
<Program Phase ID>.<File Number*>.<Function Number>.<Block Number>
```

**Note that a class header file and its corresponding implementation file share a common file number even though they are stored in two separate files.*

Using this numbering scheme, every Code Block will always have a unique index number associated with it. The next section illustrates an example using this numbering scheme.

The Purpose of Program Phases

Program Phases facilitates comparative analysis of Code Blocks for programs that may be written for different platforms using different programming languages, using different APIs. This allows Program Phases to be used as a programming platform/language/API translator. The following Code Blocks are represented in Program Phase 4-1, Program Phase 4-2, and Program Phase 4-3 respectively:

```
CBI: 4-1.1.1.7 - Java using the Active Window Toolkit (AWT) and Swing API
CBI: 4-2.1.1.7 - Visual FoxPro using the Visual FoxPro API
CBI: 4-3.1.1.7 - C using the Win32 API
```

This particular Code Block has the following description:

```
Set the background color of the main window.
```

In Program Phase Task 4, a window is created that serves as the main window for the program. If a programmer wants to know how to set the background color of a window using the Java programming language, CBI: 4-1.1.1.7 illustrates exactly how to do it.

```
CBI: 4-1.1.1.7: Set the background color of the main window. (Java/Swing/AWT)
```

```
loContentPane = this.getContentPane();
loWindowBackColor = new Color(255,255,255);
loContentPane.setBackground(loWindowBackColor);
```

Incrementing the Program Phase ID by one results in CBI: 4-2.1.1.7, which shows how to change the background color of the main window using Visual FoxPro.

CBI: 4-2.1.1.7: Set the background color of the main window. (Visual FoxPro)

```
lnWindowBackColor = RGB(255,255,255)
_SCREEN.BackColor = lnWindowBackColor
```

The C/Win32 implementation is found in CBI: 4-3.1.1.7.

CBI: 4-3.1.1.7: Set the background color of the main window. (C/Win32)

```
lnWindowBackColor = RGB(255,255,255);
lhBrush = CreateSolidBrush(lnWindowBackColor);
loWindowClass.hbrBackground = lhBrush;
```

The preceding examples illustrate how the indexing numbers work. The CBI number is identical for each of these Code Blocks except for the Program Phase ID portion of the Code Block Identifier. Incrementing the Program Phase ID portion of a CBI provides the index for implementing the functionality of the Code Block in a different Program Phase.

Variable Naming Conventions

Program Phases uses a simplified variable naming convention. Each variable is prefaced with two single letter prefixes. The first letter indicates if the variable is a local, global, or function parameter variable.

```
l - local variable
g - global variable
t - parameter variable
```

The second letter provides some information as to the type of value that is stored in the variable. The set of type prefixes is limited to the following:

```
n - number
c - character string
l - logical or Boolean
o - object
a - array
h - Window handle
```

For example, the variable lcMyVariable indicates that the value stored is a character string in a local variable. Different programming languages have various constructs for declaring and accessing a character string. No matter what the string construct is, and no matter if it is a pointer or not, it is prefaced with the character "c". The "n" character is used whether or not the value stored is a float, integer, or long. The purpose of this type of naming convention is to facilitate comparative analysis among differing programming languages. Note that for class properties, the scope variable prefix is omitted. In addition, no variable prefix is used for "main" function parameters.

Book Organization

The sections in this book are numbered according to their Program Phase ID. Each section stands alone from the other sections and as a result, it is not necessary to read the sections in the order presented. There is no traditional index in this book because the information is inherently indexed with the Code Block Identifiers.

Program Phase Task 1

Console Based Hello World! with Strings

- Program Phase Task 1 is an implementation of the classic Hello World program. A Hello World program is a traditional way of learning the constructs of a programming language. It shows the user where the Entry Point of Execution (EPE) is for a particular language. It illustrates how to output the text string "Hello World!", and it shows where the program exits. Even a simple program such as the traditional Hello World program is informative. It shows important syntax information and introduces the user to the programming language in a simple manner. The goal of Program Phase Task 1 is to accomplish the same thing but with a few additional programming ideas illustrated.

- A traditional Hello World program prints the text string "Hello World" in a console and then exits. The following is the output of a traditional Hello World program:

```
C:\helloworld>helloworld.exe
Hello World!
```

- Program Phase Task 1 is slightly more advanced than a traditional Hello World program. Two lines of output are generated each time a Program Phase that implements Program Phase Task 1 is executed. The first line of output is dependent on the number of command line parameters entered by the user at runtime. The second line of output is the text string "Hello World!". If the user enters no command line parameters, a text string indicating such is displayed. The following is the sample output of Program Phase 1-3 launched with no command line parameters:

```
C:\pp1_3\Release>pp1_3.exe
You entered no command line parameters.
Hello World!
```

- If the user enters a single command line parameter, it will be printed to the screen.

```
C:\pp1_3\Release>pp1_3.exe param1
Command line parameter entered: param1
Hello World!
```

- If the user attempts to enter more than one command line parameter, the program outputs an error. The following is the sample output of Program Phase 1-3 with two command line parameters specified:

```
C:\pp1_3\Release>pp1_3.exe param1 param2
The command line is limited to 1 parameter.
Hello World!
```

Program Phase Task 1 and Unicode

- Some of the Program Phase Tasks implemented in this book utilize a particular Unicode encoding for storing character data. The native format for Unicode encoding for Windows 2000/XP/Vista and Mac OS X is UTF-16 encoding. Many Linux distributions use UTF-8 Unicode encoding. UTF stands for Unicode Transformation Format.

- The UTF-16 encoding mechanism uses a single 16 bit word to represent a character in the Basic Multilingual Plane (BMP). There are seventeen Unicode planes in UTF-16 that correspond to different sets of characters. The BMP, also called Plane 0, represents characters represented by the codes 0000 – FFFF. Since the characters found in the 128 US-ASCII table are represented in plane 0, only a single 16 bit word is needed to represent the characters manipulated in the Program Phases implemented in this book. If a character such as a Japanese or Chinese symbol needs to be represented, then a different Plane is used in addition to a single 16 bit word. In this case, two 16 bit words are needed to represent the character. These two words are called surrogate pairs and together represent the encoded character. No surrogate pairs are needed for any of the Program Phases implemented in this book.

- In the UTF-16 encoding scheme, the letter 'a' is represented by the 16 bit word 0x0061.

Hexadecimal 'a'	Binary 'a'
00 61	0000 0000 0110 0001

The value is identical to the value found in the US ASCII table except that it is stored in a 16 bit value. Some data types such as the wide char (wchar_t) data type found in C/C++ use four bytes to store UTF-16 encoded data. When representing the characters found in the 128 US-ASCII table, the extra bytes are set to the value zero.

- The UTF-8 encoding scheme can use one to four bytes to encode a particular character. Only a single byte is needed to encode a character found in the 128 US-ASCII table.

Hexadecimal 'a'	Binary 'a'
61	0110 0001

- More information about the Unicode standard is available at the following URL:

  `http://www.unicode.org`

Program Phase 1-1

Java ▪ Multi-Platform

Console Based Hello World! with Strings

- Program Phase Task 1 is implemented in Program Phase 1-1 using the Java programming language.
- The String class found in the java.lang package is used to implement strings.
- The System.out class is used to output to standard output.

Code Block Features

The Program Phase 1-1 code blocks illustrate the following programming features using the Java programming language:

- **Console Application**
- **Integer and String Variable Declarations**
- **Application Command Line Parameters**
- **Case/Switch Statement**
- **String Literal Assignment and String Concatenation**
- **Console Application Standard Output**

Java
Console Application

- The test1 class in the following example must match the name of the text file it is stored in minus the file extension. The first line of code in the main() function is the Entry Point of Execution (EPE). The main() function supports an optional parameter that is an array of Java String objects that stores any command line parameters entered by the user at runtime.

test1.java: Java Console Application

```
public class test1
{
public static void main(final String argv[])
{
   // Java code goes here.
}}
```

Java
Integer and String Variable Declarations

- The Java String class stores a string of characters as UTF-16 Unicode data.

- The following example declares an integer variable and a string variable:

test2.java: Java Integer and String Variable Declarations

```
public class test2
{
public static void main(final String argv[])
{
   int lnVar1;
   String lcVar2;
}}
```

Java
Application Command Line Parameters

- The following example stores a single command line parameter in a string variable:

test3.java: Java Application Command Line Parameters

```
public class test3
{
public static void main(final String argv[])
{
   String lcCmdLineParam1;

   if (argv.length == 1)
   {
      lcCmdLineParam1 = argv[0];
   }
}}
```

Java
Case/Switch Statement

- The following example implements a "switch" statement:

test4.java: Java Case/Switch Statement

```
public class test4
{
public static void main(final String argv[])
{
   int lnCmdLineParamCount;
   lnCmdLineParamCount = argv.length;

   switch (lnCmdLineParamCount)
   {
      case 0:
         // No command line parameters entered.
         break;
```

test4.java continued on the next page

test4.java: Java Case/Switch Statement continued

```
      case 1:
         // One command line parameter entered.
         break;

      default:
         // More than one command line parameter entered.
   }
}}
```

Java
String Literal Assignment and String Concatenation

- The following example stores two string literals and then concatenates the strings:

test5.java: Java String Literal Assignment and String Concatenation

```
public class test5
{
public static void main(final String argv[])
{
   String lcString1;
   String lcString2;
   String lcString3;

   lcString1 = "Hello";
   lcString2 = "World!";
   lcString3 = lcString1 + " " + lcString2;
}}
```

Java
Console Application Standard Output

- The following example outputs text to standard output:

test6.java: Java Console Application Standard Output

```
public class test6
{
public static void main(final String argv[])
{
   String lcString1;

   lcString1 = "Hello World!";
   System.out.println(lcString1);
}}
```

Source Code Files

- Text files: pp1_1.java

- The reserved section of the pp1_1.java file contains a java package statement indicating that the pp1_1 class is in the programphases.programphase1_1 package. Packages are useful for organizing classes according to their functionality.

- When the pp1_1.java file is compiled into the pp1_1.class byte code file, it will be placed in a folder structure that mimics the package name.

pp1_1.java: Program Phase 1-1 Source Code

```
//*************************************************************************
// Program Phase 1-1 Java Hello World! with Strings                       *
// Programming Tasks Illustrated: Console Application                     *
//                                Integer and String Variable Declarations *
//                                Application Command Line Parameters      *
//                                Case/Switch Statement                    *
//                                String Literal Assignment and Concatenation *
//                                Console Application Standard Output      *
//*************************************************************************

//*************************************************************************
// File: pp1_1.java                                                       *
// Reserved                                                               *
//*************************************************************************

package programphases.programphase1_1;

public class pp1_1
{


//*************************************************************************
// Program Phase 1-1 Main                                                 *
// Define the Entry Point of Execution (EPE) for Program Phase 1-1        *
// CBI:  1-1.1.1.1                                                        *
//*************************************************************************

public static void main(final String argv[])
{


//*************************************************************************
// Program Phase 1-1 Main                                                 *
// Declare the local variables for the "main" program                     *
// CBI:  1-1.1.1.2                                                        *
//*************************************************************************

   int lnCmdLineParamCount;
   String lcString1;
   String lcString2;
   String lcStringOutput1;
   String lcStringOutput2;


//*************************************************************************
// Program Phase 1-1 Main                                                 *
// Store the command line parameters                                      *
// CBI:  1-1.1.1.3                                                        *
//*************************************************************************

   // The local argv array stores the command line parameters.
   lnCmdLineParamCount = argv.length;


//*************************************************************************
// Program Phase 1-1 Main                                                 *
// Parse the command line parameters using a Case/Switch statement        *
// CBI:  1-1.1.1.4                                                        *
//*************************************************************************

   switch (lnCmdLineParamCount)
   {
      case 0:
         lcStringOutput1 = "You entered no command line parameters.";
         break;
```

pp1_1.java continued on the next page

pp1_1.java: Program Phase 1-1 Source Code continued

```
      case 1:
         lcStringOutput1 = "Command line parameter entered: " + argv[0];
         break;

      default:
         lcStringOutput1 = "The command line is limited to 1 parameter.";
   }


//***************************************************************************
// Program Phase 1-1 Main                                                  *
// Concatenate two string variables                                        *
// CBI:  1-1.1.1.5                                                         *
//***************************************************************************

   lcString1 = "Hello";
   lcString2 = "World!";
   lcStringOutput2 = lcString1 + " " + lcString2;


//***************************************************************************
// Program Phase 1-1 Main                                                  *
// Output to standard output                                               *
// CBI:  1-1.1.1.6                                                         *
//***************************************************************************

   System.out.println(lcStringOutput1);
   System.out.println(lcStringOutput2);
}}
```

Windows and Linux – Code Setup and Compilation

- Tools: Java SE Development Kit (JDK) 5.0 (Appendix A), Netbeans IDE (Appendix A)

Windows and Linux Code Setup and Compilation Steps

1: Start the Netbeans IDE program.

2: Netbeans - Activate Menu Item: File → New Project

Select the "Java" category and then select "Java Application" as the project type. Activate the "Next" button.

3: Enter pp1_1 as the "Project Name". Enter the appropriate folder name for the "Project Location". Check the "Set as Main Project" check box. Uncheck the "Create Main Class" check box. Activate the "Finish" button.

4: Create a folder called programphases\programphase1_1 inside the src folder of the pp1_1 folder. Example: `pp1_1\src\programphases\programphase1_1`

5: Netbeans - Activate Menu Item: File → New File

In the "New File" dialog window, select the "Other" category and then select "Empty File" as the file type. Activate the "Next" button. Enter the "File Name" as pp1_1.java and select the src\programphases\programphase1_1 folder as the destination "Folder". Activate the "Finish" button to create the pp1_1.java file.

Steps continued on the next page

Windows and Linux Code Setup and Compilation Steps continued

6: Open the pp1_1.java file in the Netbeans IDE and then enter the source code for Program Phase 1-1.

7: Netbeans - Activate Menu Item: File → "pp1_1" Properties

On the "Project Properties" window, select the "Run" category and then enter programphases.programphase1_1.pp1_1 for the "Main Class". Activate the "OK" button.

8: Netbeans - Activate Menu Item: Build → Build Main Project

```
Output:  pp1_1\build\classes\programphases\programphase1_1\pp1_1.class
         pp1_1\dist\pp1_1.jar
```

Windows and Linux Command Prompt Compilation Steps

1: Update the path to the javac executable file.

```
Windows:   PATH = "C:\Program Files\Java\jdk1.6.0_01\bin";%PATH%

Linux Bash:  export PATH=~/jdk1.6.0_01/bin:$PATH
Linux C shell or the TC shell: setenv PATH ~/jdk1.6.0/bin:$PATH
```

Substitute the path for the version of the JDK installed.

2: Change directories to the pp1_1 folder and then enter the following command:

Windows

```
javac -d "build\classes" "src\programphases\programphase1_1\pp1_1.java"
```

Linux:

```
javac -d "build/classes" "src/programphases/programphase1_1/pp1_1.java"
```

3: Create a text file called manifest in the pp1_1 folder using a text editor and put this line in the file:

```
Main-Class: programphases.programphase1_1.pp1_1
```

Enter a newline at the end of the text.

4: Create the pp1_1.jar "executable" file.

```
jar -cvfm ./dist/pp1_1.jar manifest -C build/classes .
```

This command results in the pp1_1.jar file being placed in the dist folder of the pp1_1 folder. This is the same location that Netbeans places the pp1_1.jar file.

Mac OS X – Code Setup and Compilation

- Tools: Java SE Development Kit (JDK) 5.0 (included with Mac OS X), Xcode IDE (Appendix C)

Mac OS X Code Setup and Compilation Steps

1: Start the Xcode IDE program found in the /Developer/Applications folder.

2: Xcode - Activate Menu Item: File → New Project

3: Select "Java → Java Tool" and then activate the "Next" button.

4: Enter pp1_1 as the "Project Name". Enter the appropriate folder as the "Project Directory". Activate the "Finish" button.

5: Xcode - Activate Menu Item: Project → Set Active Build Configuration → Release

6: A text file called pp1_1.java is automatically created. Delete the entire contents of this file and then enter the source code for Program Phase 1-1.

7: In the Xcode IDE, double-click on the resource file called Manifest. Change the "Main-Class" entry in the Manifest file from pp1_1 to programphases.programphase1_1.pp1_1. Save and close the Manifest file. If using Xcode 3, expand the "Executables" entry and then double click on the "java" entry to display the "Executable 'java' Info" window. Edit the argument to look like this:

```
-cp pp1_1.jar programphases.programphase1_1.pp1_1
```

8: Activate the "Build" button in Xcode to compile the pp1_1.java file.

Mac OS X Command Prompt Compilation Steps

1: Open a terminal window and change directories to the pp1_1 folder.

Xcode 2.4

```
javac -d "build/pp1_1.build/Release/pp1_1.build/JavaClasses" pp1_1.java
```

The destination path (-d) must be created if it does not exist yet. The folder will automatically be created when compiled in the Xcode IDE.

Xcode 3

```
javac -d bin src/pp1_1.java
```

2: Create a text file called Manifest in the pp1_1 folder using a text editor and put this line in the file:

```
Main-Class: programphases.programphase1_1.pp1_1
```

Enter a newline at the end of the text.

3: Create the pp1_1.jar "executable" file. Enter the following on a single line:

Xcode 2.4

```
jar -cvfm build/Release/pp1_1.jar Manifest -C
build/pp1_1.build/Release/pp1_1.build/JavaClasses .
```

Xcode 3

```
jar -cvfm jars/pp1_1.jar Manifest -C bin .
```

Windows and Linux – Program Execution

- Execute Program

```
Netbeans IDE - Activate Menu Item:  Run → Run Main Project
```

- Enter Command Line Parameters

```
Netbeans - Activate Menu Item:  File → pp1_1 properties
```

Select the "Run" category and then specify any command line parameters in the "Arguments" field.

- Debug Program

```
Netbeans IDE - Activate Menu Item:  Run → Step Into Project
```

- Command Prompt Execution

```
   Windows:  java -jar dist\pp1_1.jar
   Linux: java -jar dist/pp1_1.jar

or

   java programphases.programphase1_1.pp1_1
(from the build/classes folder)
```

Mac OS X – Program Execution

- Execute Program

```
Xcode IDE - Activate the "Build and Go" button
```

- Enter Command Line Parameters

```
Xcode IDE - Expand the Executables entry
            Activate Menu Item:  Right click on java → Get Info
```

Select the "Arguments" tab. Specify any command line parameters in the –jar "pp1_1.jar" entry immediately following the pp1_1.jar value. For example, to pass a command line parameter of "test1", the "Argument" entry should look like this:

```
-jar "pp1_1.jar" test1
```

- Debug Program

```
   Xcode 2.4 - Activate Menu Item: Debug → Add Breakpoint at Current Line
   Xcode 3 - Activate Menu Item: Run → Manage Breakpoints → Add
Breakpoint at Current Line

   Xcode - Activate Menu Item: Build → Build and Debug
```

- Command Prompt Execution

```
   java -jar pp1_1.jar (from the pp1_1/build/Release or jars folder)

or

   java programphases.programphase1_1.pp1_1
(from the pp1_1/build/pp1_1.build/Release/pp1_1.build/JavaClasses or bin
folder)
```

Program Phase 1-2

Visual FoxPro ▪ Windows

GUI Based Hello World! with Strings

- Program Phase Task 1 is implemented in Program Phase 1-2 using the Visual FoxPro (VFP) programming language.
- The VFP character string data type is used to implement strings.
- Program Phase 1-2 uses the VFP programming language to create a GUI based application. VFP does not natively support building a console based application. The output for Program Phase 1-2 is performed using the VFP MESSAGEBOX() function to display a dialog window with a single "OK" button.

Code Block Features

The Program Phase 1-2 code blocks illustrate the following programming features using the VFP programming language:

- **GUI Based Application**
- **Integer and String Variable Declarations**
- **Application Command Line Parameters**
- **Case/Switch Statement**
- **String Literal Assignment and String Concatenation**
- **Message Box Output**

Visual FoxPro
GUI Based Application

- The first line of code in a ".prg" text file is the Entry Point of Execution (EPE) for a VFP application.

test1.prg: Visual FoxPro GUI Based Application

```
** Visual FoxPro code goes here.
```

Visual FoxPro
Integer and String Variable Declarations

- VFP variables are loosely typed.
- A VFP variable stores a string of characters as ASCII data.

test2.prg: Visual FoxPro Integer and String Variable Declarations

```
LOCAL lnVar1
LOCAL lcVar2
```

Visual FoxPro
Application Command Line Parameters

- Command line parameters are accessible in the local variables following the "LPARAMETERS" statement at the top of the source code file. The number of command line parameters the user may enter (without generating a runtime error) at runtime is limited by the number of local variables specified after the "LPARAMETERS" statement.

- The following example stores a single command line parameter in a VFP variable:

test3.prg: Visual FoxPro Application Command Line Parameters

```
LPARAMETERS argv1,argv2,argv3,argv4,argv5

LOCAL lcCmdLineParam1

IF PCOUNT() == 1

   lcCmdLineParam1 = argv1

ENDIF
```

Visual FoxPro
Case/Switch Statement

- The following example implements a "CASE" statement:

test4.prg: Visual FoxPro Case/Switch Statement

```
LOCAL lnCmdLineParamCount

lnCmdLineParamCount = PCOUNT()

DO CASE

   CASE lnCmdLineParamCount == 0

      ** No command line parameters entered.

   CASE lnCmdLineParamCount == 1

      ** One command line parameter entered.

   OTHERWISE

      ** More than one command line parameter entered.

ENDCASE
```

Visual FoxPro
String Literal Assignment and String Concatenation

- The following example stores two string literals and then concatenates the strings:

test5.prg: Visual FoxPro String Literal Assignment and String Concatenation

```
LOCAL lcString1
LOCAL lcString2
LOCAL lcString3

lcString1 = "Hello"
lcString2 = "World!"
lcString3 = lcString1 + " " + lcString2
```

Visual FoxPro
Message Box Output

- The following example outputs text in a message box:

test6.prg: Visual FoxPro Message Box Output

```
LOCAL lcString1

lcString1 = "Hello World"
=MESSAGEBOX(lcString1)
```

Source Code Files

- Text Files: pp1_2.prg

pp1_2.prg: Program Phase 1-2 Source Code

```
*****************************************************************************
** Program Phase 1-2 Visual FoxPro Hello World! with Strings               *
** Programming Tasks Illustrated: GUI Based Application                    *
**                                Integer and String Variable Declarations  *
**                                Application Command Line Parameters       *
**                                Case/Switch Statement                     *
**                                String Literal Assignment and Concatenation *
**                                Message Box Output                        *
*****************************************************************************

*****************************************************************************
** File: pp1_2.prg                                                          *
** Reserved                                                                 *
*****************************************************************************

LPARAMETERS argv1,argv2,argv3,argv4,argv5


*****************************************************************************
** Program Phase 1-2 Main                                                   *
** Define the Entry Point of Execution (EPE) for Program Phase 1-2         *
** CBI:  1-2.1.1.1                                                          *
*****************************************************************************

** The first line of the code in the pp1_2.prg file is the EPE.
```

pp1_2.prg continued on the next page

pp1_2.prg: Program Phase 1-2 Source Code continued

```
******************************************************************************
** Program Phase 1-2 Main                                                    *
** Declare the local variables for the "main" program                        *
** CBI:  1-2.1.1.2                                                           *
******************************************************************************

LOCAL lnCmdLineParamCount
LOCAL lcString1
LOCAL lcString2
LOCAL lcStringOutput1
LOCAL lcStringOutput2


******************************************************************************
** Program Phase 1-2 Main                                                    *
** Store the command line parameters                                         *
** CBI:  1-2.1.1.3                                                           *
******************************************************************************

** The command line parameters are stored in the LPARAMETERS variables specified
** in the Reserved code block.

lnCmdLineParamCount = PCOUNT()


******************************************************************************
** Program Phase 1-2 Main                                                    *
** Parse the command line parameters using a Case/Switch statement           *
** CBI:  1-2.1.1.4                                                           *
******************************************************************************

DO CASE

   CASE lnCmdLineParamCount == 0

      lcStringOutput1 = "You entered no command line parameters."

   CASE lnCmdLineParamCount == 1

      lcStringOutput1 = "Command line parameter entered: " + argv1

   OTHERWISE

      lcStringOutput1 = "The command line is limited to 1 parameter."

ENDCASE


******************************************************************************
** Program Phase 1-2 Main                                                    *
** Concatenate two string variables                                          *
** CBI:  1-2.1.1.5                                                           *
******************************************************************************

lcString1 = "Hello"
lcString2 = "World!"
lcStringOutput2 = lcString1 + " " + lcString2


******************************************************************************
** Program Phase 1-2 Main                                                    *
** Output to standard output                                                 *
** CBI:  1-2.1.1.6                                                           *
******************************************************************************

   ** Message box GUI output is used instead of console output.
   =MESSAGEBOX(lcStringOutput1 + chr(13) + lcStringOutput2)
```

Code Setup and Compilation

- Tools: Visual FoxPro

Code Setup and Compilation Steps

1: Create a folder called pp1_2 that will store the source code files for Program Phase 1-2.

2: Start the Visual FoxPro IDE program.

3: VFP - Activate Menu Item: File → New

From the "New" dialog window, select the "Project" radio button and then activate the "New file" button. Save the project as pp1_2.pjx in the pp1_2 folder.

4: VFP - Activate Menu Item: File → New

From the "New" dialog window, select the "Program" radio button and then activate the "New file" button.

5: Enter the Program Phase 1-2 source code into the new program file and save the file as pp1_2.prg in the pp1_2 folder.

6: Add the pp1_2.prg file to the project by selecting the "Code" tab in the "Project Manager" window for the pp1_2 project and then activating the "Add" button. Browse for the pp1_2.prg file to add it to the project.

7: Create a text file called config.fpw in the pp1_2 folder and enter the following text:

```
screen = off
```

8: Click the "Build" button on the "Project Manager" window. Select the "Win32 executable" radio button. Select "Recompile All Files" and "Display Errors". Activate the "OK" button. Use the "Save As" dialog to select a destination for the executable file and then activate the "Save" button.

- VFP does not provide a facility for compiling from a command prompt. The pp1_2.prg source code file can be compiled from the VFP command window. Substitute the appropriate path to the pp1_2.pjx file.

Visual FoxPro Command Window Compilation

From the VFP command window:

```
BUILD EXE "c:\pp1_2\pp1_2.exe" FROM "c:\pp1_2\pp1_2.pjx" RECOMPILE
```

Program Execution

- Execute Program

```
VFP - Activate Menu Item:  Program → Do
```

Navigate to the pp1_2.exe file in the "Do" dialog window and then activate the "Do" button.

- Debug Program

```
VFP - Activate Menu Item:  Tools → Debugger
VFP Debugger window - Activate Menu Item:  Debug → Do
```

Select the pp1_2.prg file found in the pp1_2 folder and then activate the "Do" button on the "Do" dialog window.

- The pp1_2.exe file can also be executed from the Visual FoxPro command window.

```
DO "c:\pp1_2\pp1_2.exe" with "param1" , "param2"
```

Program Phase 1-3

C ▪ Multi-Platform

Console Based Hello World! with Strings

- Program Phase Task 1 is implemented in Program Phase 1-3 using the C programming language.
- The standard C string data type is used to implement strings.
- The fprintf() function is used to output to standard output.

Code Block Features

The Program Phase 1-3 code blocks illustrate the following programming features using the C programming language:

- **Console Application**
- **Integer and String Variable Declarations**
- **Application Command Line Parameters**
- **Case/Switch Statement**
- **String Literal Assignment and String Concatenation**
- **Console Application Standard Output**

C
Console Application

- The first line of code in the main() function is the Entry Point of Execution (EPE) for a C application. The main() function takes an integer parameter and an array of C strings parameter.

test1.c: C Console Application

```
int main(int argc, char* argv[])
{
   // C code goes here.
   return 0;
}
```

C
Integer and String Variable Declarations

- C strings store 8 bit ASCII characters, and the last entry in the array of ASCII characters is always the NUL character.

- The following example declares an integer variable and a string variable:

test2.c: C Integer and String Variable Declarations

```
int main(int argc, char* argv[])
{
   int lnVar1;
   char lcVar2[100];

   return 0;
}
```

C
Application Command Line Parameters

- The following example stores a single command line parameter in a string variable:

test3.c: C Application Command Line Parameters

```
int main(int argc, char* argv[])
{
   char *lcCmdLineParam1;

   if ((argc - 1) == 1)
   {
      lcCmdLineParam1 = argv[1];
   }
   return 0;
}
```

C
Case/Switch Statement

- The following example implements a "switch" statement:

test4.c: C Case/Switch Statement

```
int main(int argc, char* argv[])
{
   int lnCmdLineParamCount;

   lnCmdLineParamCount = argc - 1;

   switch(lnCmdLineParamCount)
   {
      case 0:
         // No command line parameters entered.
         break;

      case 1:
         // One command line parameter entered.
         break;

      default:

         ; // More than one command line parameter entered.
   }

   return 0;
}
```

C
String Literal Assignment and String Concatenation

- C strings allocated on the stack are fixed size. The memory for these strings is statically allocated, and there is no need to de-allocate the memory.

- The following example stores two string literals and then concatenates the strings:

test5.c: C String Literal Assignment and String Concatenation

```
#include <string.h>
#include <stdio.h>

int main(int argc, char* argv[])
{
   char lcString1[5 + 1];
   char lcString2[6 + 1];
   char lcString3[5 + 6 + 1 + 1];

   strcpy(lcString1,"Hello");
   strcpy(lcString2,"World!");
   sprintf(lcString3,"%s %s",lcString1,lcString2);

   return 0;
}
```

- Memory for C strings can also be allocated on the heap using the malloc() function. Each call to the malloc() function must have a corresponding call to the free() function.

test5b.c: C String Literal Assignment and String Concatenation

```
#include <string.h>
#include <stdlib.h>

int main(int argc, char* argv[])
{
   char *lcString1;
   char *lcString2;
   char *lcString3;

   lcString1 = (char *) malloc(5 + 1);
   lcString2 = (char *) malloc(6 + 1);
   lcString3 = (char *) malloc(12 + 1);

   strcpy(lcString1,"Hello");
   strcpy(lcString2,"World!");
   sprintf(lcString3,"%s %s",lcString1,lcString2);

   free(lcString1);
   free(lcString2);
   free(lcString3);
   return 0;
}
```

- The C++ programming language provides the "new" keyword for allocating memory on the heap. When memory is allocated using the "new" keyword, the memory must be de-allocated using the "delete" keyword.

test5c.cpp: C String Literal Assignment and String Concatenation

```
#include <string.h>
#include <stdlib.h>
#include <stdio.h>

int main(int argc, char* argv[])
{
   char *lcString1;
   char *lcString2;
   char *lcString3;

   lcString1 = new char [5 + 1];
   lcString2 = new char [6 + 1];
   lcString3 = new char [12 + 1];

   strcpy(lcString1,"Hello");
   strcpy(lcString2,"World!");
   sprintf(lcString3,"%s %s",lcString1,lcString2);

   delete [] lcString1;
   delete [] lcString2;
   delete [] lcString3;

   return 0;
}
```

C
Console Application Standard Output

- The following example outputs text to standard output:

test6.c: C Console Application Standard Output

```
#include <stdio.h>

int main(int argc, char* argv[])
{
   char lcString1[12 + 1];

   strcpy(lcString1,"Hello World!");
   fprintf(stdout,"%s\n",lcString1);
}
```

Source Code Files

- Text files: pp1_3.c

pp1_3.c: Program Phase 1-3 Source Code

```
//*************************************************************************
// Program Phase 1-3 C Hello World! with Strings                          *
// Programming Tasks Illustrated: Console Application                     *
//                                Integer and String Variable Declarations *
//                                Application Command Line Parameters     *
//                                Case/Switch Statement                   *
//                                String Literal Assignment and Concatenation *
//                                Console Application Standard Output     *
//*************************************************************************
```

pp1_3.c continued on the next page

pp1_3.c: Program Phase 1-3 Source Code continued

```
//****************************************************************************
// File: pp1_3.c                                                              *
// Reserved                                                                   *
//****************************************************************************

#include <stdio.h>
#include <string.h>

//****************************************************************************
// Program Phase 1-3 Main                                                     *
// Define the Entry Point of Execution (EPE) for Program Phase 1-3            *
// CBI:  1-3.1.1.1                                                            *
//****************************************************************************

int main(int argc, char* argv[])
{

//****************************************************************************
// Program Phase 1-3 Main                                                     *
// Declare the local variables for the "main" program                         *
// CBI:  1-3.1.1.2                                                            *
//****************************************************************************

   int lnCmdLineParamCount;
   char lcString1[5 + 1];
   char lcString2[6 + 1];
   char lcStringOutput1[256];
   char lcStringOutput2[5 + 6 + 1 + 1];

//****************************************************************************
// Program Phase 1-3 Main                                                     *
// Store the command line parameters                                          *
// CBI:  1-3.1.1.3                                                            *
//****************************************************************************

   // The laArgv array stores the command line parameters.
   lnCmdLineParamCount = argc - 1;

//****************************************************************************
// Program Phase 1-3 Main                                                     *
// Parse the command line parameters using a Case/Switch statement            *
// CBI:  1-3.1.1.4                                                            *
//****************************************************************************

   switch(lnCmdLineParamCount)
   {
      case 0:
         sprintf(lcStringOutput1,"You entered no command line parameters.");
         break;

      case 1:
         sprintf(lcStringOutput1,"Command line parameter entered: %s",argv[1]);
         break;

      default:
        sprintf(lcStringOutput1,"The command line is limted to 1 parameter.");
   }

//****************************************************************************
// Program Phase 1-3 Main                                                     *
// Concatenate two string variables                                           *
// CBI:  1-3.1.1.5                                                            *
//****************************************************************************
```

pp1_3.c continued on the next page

ppl_3.c: Program Phase 1-3 Source Code continued

```
    strcpy(lcString1,"Hello");
    strcpy(lcString2,"World!");
    sprintf(lcStringOutput2,"%s %s",lcString1,lcString2);

//*****************************************************************************
// Program Phase 1-3 Main                                                     *
// Output to standard output                                                  *
// CBI:   1-3.1.1.6                                                           *
//*****************************************************************************

    fprintf(stdout,"%s \n",lcStringOutput1);
    fprintf(stdout,"%s \n",lcStringOutput2);

    return 0;
}
```

Windows – Code Setup and Compilation

- Tools: MS Visual C++ 2008 Express Edition (msdn.microsoft.com)

Windows Code Setup and Compilation Steps

1: Start the Visual C++ 2008 Express Edition program.

2: VC++ EE - Activate Menu Item: File → New → Project

For the "Project type", select "Win32" and then select the "Win32 Console Application" template. Enter pp1_3 as the project "Name". Enter the appropriate folder as the project "Location". The pp1_3 folder will automatically be created. Make sure that the "Create directory for solution" check box is not checked.

3: Activate the "OK" button to proceed with the "Win32 Application Wizard".

4: Activate the "Next" button of the "Win32 Application Wizard".

5: Select the "Console application" radio button and also check the "Empty project" check box. Activate the "Finish" button of the "Win32 Application Wizard".

6: VC++ EE - Activate Menu Item: Project → Add New Item

On the "Add New Item" dialog window, select the "Visual C++ → Code" category and then select the "C++ File (.cpp)" template. Enter pp1_3.c for the file "Name". Activate the "Add" button.

7: Enter the source code for Program Phase 1-3 into the pp1_3.c text file.

8: VC++ EE - Activate Menu Item: Build → Configuration Manager

Select the "Release" value for the "Active solution configuration". Activate the "Close" button.

Steps continued on the next page

Windows Code Setup and Compilation Steps continued

9: VC++ EE - Activate Menu Item: Project → pp1_3 Properties

Enter the following settings:

Configuration Properties → C/C++ → Code Generation → Runtime Library

For Release Configuration

```
Multi-threaded (/MT) or Multi-threaded DLL (/MD)
```

For Debug Configuration

```
Multi-threaded Debug /MTd or Multi-threaded Debug DLL (/MDd)
```

Configuration Properties → General → Character Set

```
"Use Multi-Byte Character Set"
```

10: VC++ EE - Activate Menu Item: Build → Build pp1_3

After the build is successful, a compiled file called pp1_3.exe will be found in the Release folder in the pp1_3 folder.

Windows Command Prompt Compilation

Open a Visual Studio 2008 command prompt and change directories to the pp1_3 folder.

```
cl.exe /MT pp1_3.c
```

This command compiles and links the pp1_3.c with the C library being statically linked. The pp1_3.exe file is generated and stored in the current directory.

To compile the pp1_3.c file to use the C Library in a shared dll, enter the following two commands:

```
cl.exe /MD pp1_3.c
mt.exe /manifest pp1_3.exe.manifest /outputresource:pp1_3.exe
```

The second command invokes the mt.exe program, which causes the manifest to be embedded into the executable file.

Linux – Code Setup and Compilation

- Tools: GNU GCC, KDevelop (Appendix B)

Linux Code Setup and Compilation Steps

1: Start the KDevelop program.

2: KDevelop - Activate Menu Item: Project → New Project

Select the "C → Simple Hello world program" template. Set the "Application name" to pp1_3. Set the "Location" to the appropriate folder.

Steps continued on the next page

Linux Code Setup and Compilation Steps continued

3: Activate the "Next" button four times and then activate the "Finish" button.

4: Edit the pp1_3.c source code file and remove all of the code in it. Enter the source code for Program Phase 1-3 into the pp1_3.c text file. Save and close the file.

5: KDevelop - Activate Menu Item: Project → Build Configuration → debug

This results in the executable file being placed in the debug/src folder under the pp1_3 source code folder.

6: KDevelop – Activate Menu Item: Build → Build Project

If prompted about a missing Makefile, activate the "Run Them" button.

Linux Command Prompt Compilation

Open a terminal window and then enter the following in the pp1_3/src folder:

```
g++ pp1_3.c -o pp1_3
```

This command uses the GCC C compiler to compile the program to use the C library in a shared dll file. Instructions are only provided for linking dynamically to the C/C++ standard libraries.

Mac OS X – Code Setup and Compilation

- Tools: GNU GCC, Xcode (Appendix C)

Mac OS X Code Setup and Compilation Steps

1: Start the Xcode program.

2: Xcode - Activate Menu Item: File → New Project

3: Select "Command Line Utility → C++ Tool" and then activate the "Next" button.

4: Set the "Project Name" to pp1_3. Set the "Project Directory" to the appropriate folder. Activate the "Finish" button.

5: Right click on the main.cpp file that has been automatically added to the project and rename it to pp1_3.c. Delete the contents of the pp1_3.c file and then enter the source code for Program Phase 1-3. Save and close the file.

6: Compile the program by activating the "Build" button.

Mac OS X Command Prompt Compilation

Open a terminal window and then enter the following in the pp1_3 folder:

```
g++ pp1_3.c -o pp1_3
```

Windows – Program Execution

- Execute Program

```
VC++ EE - Activate Menu Item: Debug → Start Without Debugging
```

- Enter Command Line Parameters

```
VC++ EE - Activate Menu Item: Project → pp1_3 Properties
```

Expand the "Configuration Properties" entry and then click on the "Debugging" item. Command line parameters can be specified in the "Command Arguments" field.

- Debug Program

```
VC++ EE - Activate Menu Item: Project → pp1_3 Properties
```

Expand the "Configuration Properties → Linker" entry and then click on the "Debugging" item. Set the "Generate Debug Info" entry to "Yes". Close the "pp1_3 Properties" window.

```
VC++ EE - Activate Menu Item: Debug → Step Into
```

Linux – Program Execution

- Execute Program

```
KDevelop - Activate Menu Item: Build → Execute Program
```

- Enter Command Line Parameters

```
KDevelop - Activate Menu Item: Project → Project Options
```

On the left side of the dialog window, select the "Run Options" entry. Check the "Main Program" check box. Specify the path to the pp1_3 executable file. The command line parameters can be specified in the "Run Arguments" field. Depending on the currently installed version of KDevelop, this setting may be found in the "Debugger" entry of the "Project Options" dialog window.

- Debug Program

Include the debug information in the program build.

```
KDevelop - Activate Menu Item: Project → Project Options
```

Click on the "Configure Options" item. Select the "debug" configuration and then enter "--enable-debug=full" (without quotes) in the "Configure arguments" field on the "General" tab. Close the "Project Options" dialog window.

```
KDevelop - Activate Menu Item: Project → Build Configuration → Debug
```

Set the cursor position in the source file to the first line of code in the CBI: 1-3.1.1.3 code block and then create a breakpoint.

```
KDevelop - Activate Menu Item: Debug → Toggle Breakpoint
```

After the breakpoint has been created, the program can be debugged.

```
KDevelop - Activate Menu Item: Debug → Start
```

Mac OS X – Program Execution

- Execute Program

  Activate the "Build/Go" button. The output is displayed in the "Run Log" window. If using Xcode 3, the "Debugger Console" displays the program output. This window can be displayed by activating the "Console" menu item from the "Run" menu.

- Enter Command Line Parameters

  ```
  Xcode - Activate Menu Item: Project → Edit Active Executable "pp1_3"
  ```

  On the "pp1_3 Info" window, select the "Arguments" tab. Specify each command line parameter as a separate argument.

- Debug Program

  To debug the pp1_3.c file one line at a time, place the cursor at the first line of code in the CBI: 1-3.1.1.3 code block and then create a breakpoint.

  ```
  Xcode 2.4 - Activate Menu Item: Debug → Add Breakpoint at Current Line

  Xcode 3 - Activate Menu Item: Run → Manage Breakpoints → Add
  Breakpoint at Current Line
  ```

  After the break point has been created, the program can be debugged.

  ```
  Xcode - Activate Menu Item: Build → Build and Debug
  ```

Program Phase 1-4

Visual Basic 6 ▪ Windows

GUI Based Hello World! with Strings

- Program Phase Task 1 is implemented in Program Phase 1-4 using the Visual Basic 6 (VB6) programming language.

- The VB6 string type is used to implement strings.

- Program Phase 1-4 uses the VB6 programming language to create a GUI based application because VB6 does not natively support building a console based application. The output for Program Phase 1-4 is performed using the MsgBox() function to display a dialog window with a single "OK" button.

Code Block Features

The Program Phase 1-4 code blocks illustrate the following programming features using the VB6 programming language:

- **GUI Based Application**

- **Integer and String Variable Declarations**

- **Application Command Line Parameters**

- **Case/Switch Statement**

- **String Literal Assignment and String Concatenation**

- **Message Box Output**

Visual Basic 6
GUI Based Application

- A text file named test1.bas can be added to a "Standard Exe" project that has the "Startup Object" set to "Sub Main". The first line of code in the Main() subroutine is the Entry Point of Execution (EPE) for a VB6 application.

test1.bas: Visual Basic 6 GUI Based Application

```
Sub Main()

    '' Visual Basic 6 code goes here.

End Sub
```

Visual Basic 6
Integer and String Variable Declarations

- A VB6 String stores a string of characters as UTF-16 Unicode data.
- The following example declares an integer variable and a string variable:

test2.bas: Visual Basic 6 Integer and String Variable Declarations

```
Sub Main()

   Dim lnVar1 as Integer
   Dim lcVar2 as String

End Sub
```

Visual Basic 6
Application Command Line Parameters

- The following example stores a single command line parameter in a string variable:

test3.bas: Visual Basic 6 Application Command Line Parameters

```
Sub Main()

   Dim argc As Integer
   Dim laArgv() As String
   Dim lcCmdLineParam1 As String

   argv = Split(Command, " ")
   argc = UBound(argv) + 1

   If (argc = 1) Then

      lcCmdLineParam1 = argv(0)

   End If

End Sub
```

Visual Basic 6
Case/Switch Statement

- The following example implements a "Select Case" statement:

test4.bas: Visual Basic 6 Case/Switch Statement

```
Sub Main()

   Dim lnCmdLineParamCount As Integer
   Dim argv() As String

   argv = Split(Command, " ")
   lnCmdLineParamCount = UBound(argv) + 1

   Select Case lnCmdLineParamCount

      Case 0
```

test4.bas continued on the next page

test4.bas: Visual Basic 6 Case/Switch Statement continued

```
        '' No command line parameters entered.

      Case 1
        '' One command line parameter entered.

      Case Else
        '' More than one command line parameter entered.

   End Select

End Sub
```

Visual Basic 6
String Literal Assignment and String Concatenation

- The following example stores two string literals and then concatenates the strings:

test5.bas: Visual Basic 6 String Literal Assignment and String Concatenation

```
Sub Main()

   Dim lcString1 As String
   Dim lcString2 As String
   Dim lcString3 As String

   lcString1 = "Hello"
   lcString2 = "World!"
   lcString3 = lcString1 & " " & lcString2

End Sub
```

Visual Basic 6
Message Box Output

- The following example outputs text in a message box:

test6.bas: Visual Basic 6 Message Box Output

```
Sub Main()

   Dim lcString1 As String

   lcString1 = "Hello World!"
   MsgBox(lcString1)

End Sub
```

Source Code Files

- Text files: pp1_4.bas

pp1_4.bas: Program Phase 1-4 Source Code

```
''***********************************************************************
'' Program Phase 1-4 Visual Basic 6 Hello World! with Strings           *
'' Programming Tasks Illustrated: GUI Based Application                 *
''                                Integer and String Variable Declarations    *
''                                Application Command Line Parameters   *
''                                Case/Switch Statement                 *
''                                String Literal Assignment and Concatenation *
''                                Message Box Output                    *
''***********************************************************************

''***********************************************************************
'' File: pp1_4.bas                                                      *
'' Reserved                                                             *
''***********************************************************************


''***********************************************************************
'' Program Phase 1-4 Main                                               *
'' Define the Entry Point of Execution (EPE) for Program Phase 1-4      *
'' CBI:  1-4.1.1.1                                                      *
''***********************************************************************

Sub Main()


''***********************************************************************
'' Program Phase 1-4 Main                                               *
'' Declare the local variables for the "main" program                   *
'' CBI:  1-4.1.1.2                                                      *
''***********************************************************************

   Dim argc As Integer
   Dim argv() As String
   Dim lcString1 As String
   Dim lcString2 As String
   Dim lcStringOutput1 As String
   Dim lcStringOutput2 As String


''***********************************************************************
'' Program Phase 1-4 Main                                               *
'' Store the command line parameters                                    *
'' CBI:  1-4.1.1.3                                                      *
''***********************************************************************

   argv = Split(Command, " ")
   argc = UBound(argv) + 1


''***********************************************************************
'' Program Phase 1-4 Main                                               *
'' Parse the command line parameters using a Case/Switch statement      *
'' CBI:  1-4.1.1.4                                                      *
''***********************************************************************

   Select Case argc

      Case 0

         lcStringOutput1 = "You entered no command line parameters."

      Case 1

         lcStringOutput1 = "Command line paramater entered: " + argv(0)

      Case Else
```

pp1_4.bas continued on the next page

pp1_4.bas: Program Phase 1-4 Source Code continued

```
        lcStringOutput1 = "The command line is limited to 1 parameter."

    End Select

''***************************************************************************
'' Program Phase 1-4 Main                                                   *
'' Concatenate two string variables                                         *
'' CBI:  1-4.1.1.5                                                          *
''***************************************************************************

    lcString1 = "Hello"
    lcString2 = "World!"
    lcStringOutput2 = lcString1 & " " & lcString2


''***************************************************************************
'' Program Phase 1-4 Main                                                   *
'' Output to standard output                                                *
'' CBI:  1-4.1.1.6                                                          *
''***************************************************************************

    '' Message box GUI output is used instead of console output.

    MsgBox (lcStringOutput1 & Chr(13) & lcStringOutput2)

End Sub
```

Code Setup and Compilation

- Tools: Visual Basic 6

Code Setup and Compilation Steps

1: Create a folder called pp1_4 that will store the source code files.

2: Open the Visual Basic 6 program.

3: VB6 - Activate Menu Item: File → New Project

Select "Standard EXE" and then activate the "OK" button.

4: Remove the "Form1" Form that is automatically added to the project by right-clicking on the "Form1" Form in the project and activating the "Remove Form1" menu item.

5: VB6 - Activate Menu Item: File → Save Project

Save the project with the name pp1_4 in the pp1_4 source folder. Click on the pp1_4.vbp file in the properties window and then set the name of the project to pp1_4.

6: VB6 - Activate Menu Item: Project → Add Module

Create a new module and then enter the source code for Program Phase 1-4. Save the module file as pp1_4.bas in the pp1_4 folder.

7: VB6 - Activate Menu Item: File → Make pp1_4.exe

Visual Basic 6 Command Prompt Compilation

Change directories to the pp1_4 folder and then enter the following commands:

```
PATH = "C:\Program Files\Microsoft Visual Studio\VB98";%PATH%
vb6.exe /make pp1_4.vbp
```

Program Execution

- Execute Program

  `VB6 - Activate Menu Item: Run → Start`

- Enter Command Line Parameters

  `VB6 - Activate Menu Item: Project → pp1_4 Properties`

  On the "pp1_4 - Project Properties" dialog window, click on the "Make" tab and then enter any command line parameters in the "Command Line Arguments" field.

- Debug Program

  `VB6 - Activate Menu Item: Debug → Step Into`

Program Phase 1-5

Visual C++ ▪ MFC ▪ Windows

Console Based Hello World! with Strings

- Program Phase Task 1 is implemented in Program Phase 1-5 using the C++ programming language and the Microsoft Foundation Classes (MFC) class library. MFC is primarily used to create GUI based applications, but it can also be used to create console based applications.
- The MFC CString class is used to implement strings.
- The fprintf() function is used to output to standard output.

Code Block Features

The Program Phase 1-5 code blocks illustrate the following programming features using the C++ programming language and MFC:

- **Console Application**
- **Integer and String Variable Declarations**
- **Application Command Line Parameters**
- **Case/Switch Statement**
- **String Literal Assignment and String Concatenation**
- **Console Application Standard Output**

C++ MFC
Console Application

- In a typical GUI based MFC application, a function called AfxWinMain() is automatically called by the MFC framework's WinMain() function. The AfxWinMain() function can also be called in a standard main() function.
- The AfxWinMain() function is responsible for calling the InitInstance() member function of the globally declared CWinApp instance. The CWinApp instance is available in the AfxWinMain() function because C++ will create all globally declared instances before the main() function is called.
- In a GUI based MFC application, the "m_pMainWnd" member variable is set to the handle of the main window for the application. Setting the variable to NULL causes the MFC application to exit after the InitInstance() member function ends. Returning a "FALSE" value indicates that some form of error condition has been met and will cause the program to end regardless of the value stored in the "m_pMainWnd" variable. Returning a "TRUE" value indicates that normal processing has occurred in the

InitInstance() member function. The MFC framework exits the application after the InitInstance() method returns a "TRUE" value when it finds that the _pMainWnd member variable is set to the NULL value. See Program Phase 2-5 for information on returning a custom exit status code to the operating system.

test1.cpp: C++ MFC Console Application

```
#include <afxwin.h>

extern int AFXAPI AfxWinMain(HINSTANCE hInstance,HINSTANCE hPrevInstance,
                             LPTSTR lpCmdLine,int nCmdShow);

int main(int argc, char* argv[])
{
   return AfxWinMain(GetModuleHandle(NULL),NULL,GetCommandLine(),SW_SHOW);
}

class test1 : public CWinApp
{
virtual BOOL InitInstance()
{
   // C++ code goes here.

   this->m_pMainWnd = NULL;
   return TRUE;
}};

test1 goTest1;
```

C++ MFC
Integer and String Variable Declarations

- The MFC CString class is used to implement strings for Program Phase 1-5. This class supports ASCII strings and Unicode strings. To enable Unicode string handling with the CString class, install the proper Unicode files for Visual Studio and define the "_UNICODE" symbol for the program build. If the "_UNICODE" symbol is not defined for the program build, the CString class uses standard ASCII strings. Program Phase 1-5 uses ASCII strings with the CString class. More information about enabling Unicode with C++ and MFC can be found at the following URL:

  http://msdn2.microsoft.com/en-us/library/ey142t48.aspx

- The following example declares an integer variable and a string variable:

test2.cpp: C++ MFC Integer and String Variable Declarations

```
#include <afxwin.h>

extern int AFXAPI AfxWinMain(HINSTANCE hInstance,HINSTANCE hPrevInstance,
                             LPTSTR lpCmdLine,int nCmdShow);

int main(int argc, char* argv[])
{
   return AfxWinMain(GetModuleHandle(NULL),NULL,GetCommandLine(),SW_SHOW);
}

class test2 : public CWinApp
{
virtual BOOL InitInstance()
{
   int lnVar1;
```

test2.cpp continued on the next page

test2.cpp: C++ MFC Integer and String Variable Declarations continued

```
   CString lcVar2;

   return TRUE;
}};

test2 goTest2;
```

C++ MFC
Application Command Line Parameters

- Command line parameters are accessible in the argv array that is passed to the main function. The Visual C++ compiler supports the __argc and __argv global variables containing the same data as the argc and argv parameters.

- MFC has an alternate way of accessing command line parameters using the MFC CCmdLine class. The CCmdLine class can help with automating command line parameter parsing. This class is not used in Program Phase 1-5.

- The following example stores a single command line parameter in a string variable:

test3.cpp: C++ MFC Application Command Line Parameters

```
#include <afxwin.h>

extern int AFXAPI AfxWinMain(HINSTANCE hInstance,HINSTANCE hPrevInstance,
                             LPTSTR lpCmdLine,int nCmdShow);

int main(int argc, char* argv[])
{
   return AfxWinMain(GetModuleHandle(NULL),NULL,GetCommandLine(),SW_SHOW);
}

class test3 : public CWinApp
{
virtual BOOL InitInstance()
{
   CString lcCmdLineParam1;

   if ((__argc - 1) == 1)
   {
     lcCmdLineParam1 = __argv[1];
   }

   return TRUE;
}};

test3 goTest3;
```

C++ MFC
Case/Switch Statement

- The following example implements a "switch" statement:

test4.cpp: C++ MFC Case/Switch Statement

```
#include <afxwin.h>

extern int AFXAPI AfxWinMain(HINSTANCE hInstance,HINSTANCE hPrevInstance,
                             LPTSTR lpCmdLine,int nCmdShow);

int main(int argc, char* argv[])
{
   return AfxWinMain(GetModuleHandle(NULL),NULL,GetCommandLine(),SW_SHOW);
}

class test4 : public CWinApp
{
virtual BOOL InitInstance()
{
   int lnCmdLineParamCount;

   lnCmdLineParamCount = __argc - 1;

   switch(lnCmdLineParamCount)
   {
      case 0:
         // No command line parameters entered.
         break;

      case 1:
         // One command line parameter entered.
         break;

      default:
         ; // More than one command line parameter entered.
   }

   return TRUE;
}};

test4 goTest4;
```

C++ MFC
String Literal Assignment and String Concatenation

- The following example stores two string literals and then concatenates the strings:

test5.cpp: C++ MFC String Literal Assignment and String Concatenation

```
#include <afxwin.h>

extern int AFXAPI AfxWinMain(HINSTANCE hInstance,HINSTANCE hPrevInstance,
                             LPTSTR lpCmdLine,int nCmdShow);

int main(int argc, char* argv[])
{
   return AfxWinMain(GetModuleHandle(NULL),NULL,GetCommandLine(),SW_SHOW);
}

class test5 : public CWinApp
{
virtual BOOL InitInstance()
{
   CString lcString1;
   CString lcString2;
   CString lcString3;

   lcString1 = "Hello";
```

test5.cpp continued on the next page

test5.cpp: C++ MFC String Literal Assignment and String Concatenation continued

```
   lcString2 = "World!";
   lcString3 = lcString1 + " " + lcString2;

   return TRUE;
}};

test5 goTest5;
```

C++ MFC
Console Application Standard Output

- The following example outputs text to standard output:

test6.cpp: C++ MFC Console Application Standard Output

```
#include <afxwin.h>

extern int AFXAPI AfxWinMain(HINSTANCE hInstance,HINSTANCE hPrevInstance,
                             LPTSTR lpCmdLine,int nCmdShow);

int main(int argc, char* argv[])
{
   return AfxWinMain(GetModuleHandle(NULL),NULL,GetCommandLine(),SW_SHOW);
}

class test6 : public CWinApp
{
virtual BOOL InitInstance()
{
   CString lcString1;

   lcString1 = "Hello World!";
   fprintf(stdout,"%s \n",lcString1);

   return TRUE;
}};

test6 goTest6;
```

Source Code Files

- Text files: pp1_5.cpp

pp1_5.cpp: Program Phase 1-5 Source Code

```
//*****************************************************************************
// Program Phase 1-5 C++ MFC Hello World! with Strings                        *
// Programming Tasks Illustrated: Console Application                          *
//                                Integer and String Variable Declarations    *
//                                Application Command Line Parameters         *
//                                Case/Switch Statement                        *
//                                String Literal Assignment and Concatenation *
//                                Console Application Standard Output         *
//*****************************************************************************

//*****************************************************************************
// File: pp1_5.cpp                                                            *
// Reserved                                                                   *
//*****************************************************************************
```

pp1_5.cpp continued on the next page

pp1_5.cpp: Program Phase 1-5 Source Code continued

```
#include <afxwin.h>
#include <stdio.h>

extern int AFXAPI AfxWinMain(HINSTANCE hInstance,HINSTANCE hPrevInstance,
                             LPTSTR lpCmdLine,int nCmdShow);

int main(int argc, char* argv[])
{
   // Actual Entry Point of Execution
   return AfxWinMain(GetModuleHandle(NULL),NULL,GetCommandLine(),SW_SHOW);

}

class pp1_5 : public CWinApp
{


//*****************************************************************************
// Program Phase 1-5 Main                                                     *
// Define the Entry Point of Execution (EPE) for Program Phase 1-5            *
// CBI:  1-5.1.1.1                                                            *
//*****************************************************************************

virtual BOOL InitInstance()
{
   this->m_pMainWnd = NULL;


//*****************************************************************************
// Program Phase 1-5 Main                                                     *
// Declare the local variables for the "main" program                         *
// CBI:  1-5.1.1.2                                                            *
//*****************************************************************************

   int lnCmdLineParamCount;
   CString lcString1;
   CString lcString2;
   CString lcStringOutput1;
   CString lcStringOutput2;


//*****************************************************************************
// Program Phase 1-5 Main                                                     *
// Store the command line parameters                                          *
// CBI:  1-5.1.1.3                                                            *
//*****************************************************************************

   // The command line parameters can be accessed from the __argv array.
   lnCmdLineParamCount = __argc - 1;


//*****************************************************************************
// Program Phase 1-5 Main                                                     *
// Parse the command line parameters using a Case/Switch statement            *
// CBI:  1-5.1.1.4                                                            *
//*****************************************************************************

   switch(lnCmdLineParamCount)
   {
      case 0:
         lcStringOutput1 = "You entered no command line parameters.";
         break;

      case 1:
         lcStringOutput1.Format("Command line parameter entered: %s",__argv[1]);
```

pp1_5.cpp continued on the next page

pp1_5.cpp: Program Phase 1-5 Source Code continued

```
            break;

        default:
            lcStringOutput1 = "The command line is limited to 1 parameter.";
    }


//****************************************************************************
// Program Phase 1-5 Main                                                    *
// Concatenate two string variables                                          *
// CBI:  1-5.1.1.5                                                           *
//****************************************************************************

    lcString1 = "Hello";
    lcString2 = "World!";
    lcStringOutput2 = lcString1 + " " + lcString2;


//****************************************************************************
// Program Phase 1-5 Main                                                    *
// Output to standard output                                                 *
// CBI:  1-5.1.1.6                                                           *
//****************************************************************************

   fprintf(stdout,"%s \n",lcStringOutput1);
   fprintf(stdout,"%s \n",lcStringOutput2);

   return TRUE;
}};

pp1_5 goPp1_5;
```

Code Setup and Compilation

- Tools: Microsoft Visual C++ 2008

Code Setup and Compilation Steps

1: Start the Microsoft Visual C++ 2008 program.

2: VC++ - Activate Menu Item: File → New → Project

For the "Project type", select "Win32" and then select the "Win32 Console Application" template. Enter pp1_5 as the project "Name". Enter the appropriate folder as the project "Location". The pp1_5 folder will be automatically created. Make sure that the "Create directory for solution" check box is not checked.

3: Activate the "OK" button to proceed with the "Win32 Application Wizard".

4: Activate the "Next" button of the "Win32 Application Wizard".

5: Select the "Console application" radio button and also check the "Empty project" check box. Activate the "Finish" button of the "Win32 Application Wizard".

6: VC++ - Activate Menu Item: Build → Configuration Manager

Select the "Release" value for the "Active solution configuration".

Steps continued on the next page

Code Setup and Compilation Steps continued

7: VC++ - Activate Menu Item: Project → Add New Item

On the "Add New Item" dialog window, select the "Visual C++ → Code" category and then select the "C++ File (.cpp)" template. Enter pp1_5.cpp for the file "Name". Activate the "Add" button.

8: Enter the source code for Program Phase 1-5 into the pp1_5.cpp text file.

9: VC++ - Activate Menu Item: Project → pp1_5 Properties

Enter the following settings:

Configuration Properties → General → Character Set

```
"Use Multi-Byte Character Set"
```

Configuration Properties → General → Use of MFC

```
"Use MFC in a Static Library" or "Use MFC in a Shared DLL"
```

10: VC++ - Activate Menu Item: Build → Build pp1_5

After the build is successful, a compiled file called pp1_5.exe will be found in the Release folder in the pp1_5 folder.

Command Prompt Compilation

From a Visual Studio 2008 command prompt in the pp1_5 folder, enter the following:

```
cl.exe /MT /EHsc pp1_5.cpp

dynamic library:  cl.exe /MD /D "_AFXDLL" pp1_5.cpp
mt.exe /manifest pp1_5.exe.manifest /outputresource:pp1_5.exe
```

Program Execution

- Execute Program

```
VC++ - Activate Menu Item: Debug → Start Without Debugging
```

- Enter Command Line Parameters:

```
VC++ - Activate Menu Item: Project → pp1_5 Properties
```

Expand the "Configuration Properties" entry and then click on the "Debugging" item. Command line parameters can be specified in the "Command Arguments" field.

- Debug Program

```
VC++ EE - Activate Menu Item: Project → pp1_5 Properties
```

Expand the "Configuration Properties → Linker" entry and then click on the "Debugging" item. Set the "Generate Debug Info" entry to "Yes". Close the "pp1_5 Properties" window.

```
VC++ EE - Activate Menu Item: Debug → Step Into
```

C# ▪ .NET Framework - Mono ▪ Multi-Platform

Console Based Hello World! with Strings

- Program Phase Task 1 is implemented in Program Phase 1-6 using the C# programming language and the Microsoft .NET Framework 2.0 or higher.
- The String class found in the System namespace is used to implement strings.
- The Console class found in the System namespace is used to output to standard output.

Code Block Features

The Program Phase 1-6 code blocks illustrate the following programming features using the C# programming language and the .NET Framework - Mono:

- **Console Application**
- **Integer and String Variable Declarations**
- **Application Command Line Parameters**
- **Case/Switch Statement**
- **String Literal Assignment and String Concatenation**
- **Console Application Standard Output**

C# .NET Framework - Mono
Console Application

- A console application can be a created by defining a class with a Main() function inside of the class. Unlike Java, the name of the class does not need to match the name of the file minus the file extension. In the properties for the C# project, the "Output type" can be set to "Console Application" and the "Startup object" can be set to the name of the class. After the "Startup object" is set, the Main() function becomes the Entry Point of Execution (EPE) for the program.

test1.cs: C# .NET Framework - Mono Console Application

```
class test1
{
static void Main()
{
   // C# code goes here.
}}
```

C# .NET Framework - Mono
Integer and String Variable Declarations

- The "int" keyword is aliased to the System.Int32 structure. The "string" keyword is aliased to the System.String class. The System.String class stores all string data in the UTF-16 Unicode format.

  The following example declares an integer variable and a string variable:

test2.cs: C# .NET Framework - Mono Integer and String Variable Declarations

```
class test2
{
static void Main()
{
   int lnVar1;
   string lcVar2;
}}
```

C# .NET Framework - Mono
Application Command Line Parameters

- The following example stores a single command line parameter in a string variable:

test3.cs: C# .NET Framework - Mono Application Command Line Parameters

```
class test3
{
static void Main()
{
   string[] argv;
   int argc;
   string lcCmdLineParam1;

   argv = System.Environment.GetCommandLineArgs();
   argc = argv.Length;

   if ((argc - 1) == 1)
   {
      lcCmdLineParam1 = argv[1];
   }
}}
```

C# .NET Framework - Mono
Case/Switch Statement

- The following example implements a "switch" statement:

test4.cs: C# .NET Framework - Mono Case/Switch Statement

```
class test4
{
static void Main()
{
   string[] argv;
   int lnCmdLineParamCount;
```

test4.cs continued on the next page

test4.cs: C# .NET Framework - Mono Case/Switch Statement continued

```
    argv = System.Environment.GetCommandLineArgs();
    lnCmdLineParamCount = argv.Length - 1;

    switch (lnCmdLineParamCount)
    {
       case 0:

          // No command line parameters entered.
          break;

       case 1:

          // One command line parameter entered.
          break;

       default:

          // More than one command line parameter entered.
          break;
    }
}}
```

C# .NET Framework - Mono String Literal Assignment and String Concatenation

- The following example stores two string literals and then concatenates the strings:

test5.cs: C# .NET FW - Mono String Literal Assignment and String Concatenation

```
class test5
{
static void Main()
{
   string lcString1;
   string lcString2;
   string lcString3;

   lcString1 = "Hello";
   lcString2 = "World!";
   lcString3 = lcString1 + " " + lcString2;
}}
```

C# .NET Framework - Mono Console Application Standard Output

- The following example outputs text to standard output:

test6.cs: C# .NET Framework - Mono Console Application Standard Output

```
class test6
{
static void Main()
{
   string lcString1;

   lcString1 = "Hello World!";
   System.Console.WriteLine(lcString1);
}}
```

Source Code Files

- Text files: pp1_6.cs
- The "namespace" directive in the Reserved code block places the pp1_6 class in the nspp1_6 namespace. The nspp1_6.pp1_6 class is set as the "Startup object" for the program. When a class is set as the "Startup object", the Main() function defined in the class is the EPE for the program.

pp1_6.cs: Program Phase 1-6 Source Code

```
//*****************************************************************************
// Program Phase 1-6 C# .NET Framework - Mono Hello World! with Strings       *
// Programming Tasks Illustrated: Console Application                         *
//                                Integer and String Variable Declarations    *
//                                Application Command Line Parameters         *
//                                Case/Switch Statement                       *
//                                String Literal Assignment and Concatenation *
//                                Console Application Standard Output         *
//*****************************************************************************

//*****************************************************************************
// File: pp1_6.cs                                                             *
// Reserved                                                                   *
//*****************************************************************************

using System;

namespace nspp1_6
{
class pp1_6
{

//*****************************************************************************
// Program Phase 1-6 Main                                                     *
// Define the Entry Point of Execution (EPE) for Program Phase 1-6            *
// CBI:  1-6.1.1.1                                                            *
//*****************************************************************************

static void Main()
{


//*****************************************************************************
// Program Phase 1-6 Main                                                     *
// Declare the local variables for the "main" program                         *
// CBI:  1-6.1.1.2                                                            *
//*****************************************************************************

   int lnCmdLineParamCount;
   string[] argv;
   string lcString1;
   string lcString2;
   string lcStringOutput1;
   string lcStringOutput2;


//*****************************************************************************
// Program Phase 1-6 Main                                                     *
// Store the command line parameters                                          *
// CBI:  1-6.1.1.3                                                            *
//*****************************************************************************

   argv = Environment.GetCommandLineArgs();
```

pp1_6.cs continued on the next page

pp1_6.cs: Program Phase 1-6 Source Code continued

```
   lnCmdLineParamCount = argv.Length - 1;

//****************************************************************************
// Program Phase 1-6 Main                                                    *
// Parse the command line parameters using a Case/Switch statement           *
// CBI:  1-6.1.1.4                                                           *
//****************************************************************************

   switch (lnCmdLineParamCount)
   {
      case 0:
         lcStringOutput1 = "You entered no command line parameters.";
         break;

      case 1:
         lcStringOutput1 = "Command line parameter entered: " + argv[1];
         break;

      default:
         lcStringOutput1 = "The command line is limited to 1 parameter.";
         break;
   }

//****************************************************************************
// Program Phase 1-6 Main                                                    *
// Concatenate two string variables                                          *
// CBI:  1-6.1.1.5                                                           *
//****************************************************************************

   lcString1 = "Hello";
   lcString2 = "World!";
   lcStringOutput2 = lcString1 + " " + lcString2;

//****************************************************************************
// Program Phase 1-6 Main                                                    *
// Output to standard output                                                 *
// CBI:  1-6.1.1.6                                                           *
//****************************************************************************

   Console.WriteLine(lcStringOutput1);
   Console.WriteLine(lcStringOutput2);
}}}
```

Code Setup and Compilation

- Tools: Microsoft Visual C# 2008 Express Edition (msdn.microsoft.com), Microsoft .NET Framework 2.0 or higher (windowsupdate.microsoft.com), Steps to compile and execute using Mono on the Linux platform (programphases.com/?page_id=589)

Code Setup and Compilation Steps

1: Start the Microsoft Visual C# 2008 Express Edition program.

2: VC# EE - Activate Menu Item: File → New Project

Select the "Empty Project" template. Name the project pp1_6 and then activate the "OK" button.

Steps continued on the next page

Code Setup and Compilation Steps continued

3: VC# EE - Activate Menu Item: File → Save ppl_6

Set the "Location" to the appropriate folder. Verify that the "Create directory for solution" check box is not checked and then activate the "Save" button.

4: VC# EE - Activate Menu Item: Project → Add New Item

On the "Add New Item" dialog window, select the "Code File" template. Enter ppl_6.cs for the file "Name" and then activate the "Add" button. Enter the source code for Program Phase 1-6 into the ppl_6.cs text file.

5: VC# EE - Activate Menu Item: Project → ppl_6 Properties

Verify that the "Output type" is set to "Console Application". Set the "Startup object" to nsppl_6.ppl_6. Close the "ppl_6 Properties" window.

6: VC# EE - Activate Menu Item: File → Save All

7: VC# EE - Activate Menu Item: Build → Build Solution

The resulting ppl_6.exe file will be found in the build or debug folder inside the ppl_6\bin folder.

Command Prompt Compilation

Enter the following commands from the ppl_6 folder to compile Program Phase 1-6:

```
PATH = "%SYSTEMROOT%\microsoft.net\framework\v2.0.50727";%PATH%
csc.exe /out:bin\release\ppl_6.exe ppl_6.cs
```

Program Execution

- Execute Program

  `VC# EE - Activate Menu Item:  Debug → Start Without Debugging`

- Enter Command Line Parameters

  `VC# EE - Activate Menu Item:  Project → ppl_6 Properties`

  Select the "Debug" tab and then enter any command line parameters in the "Command line arguments" field.

- Debug Program

  `VC# EE - Activate Menu Item:  Debug → Step into`

VB .NET ▪ .NET Framework ▪ Windows

Console Based Hello World! with Strings

- Program Phase Task 1 is implemented in Program Phase 1-7 using the Visual Basic .NET (VB.NET) programming language and the Microsoft .NET Framework 2.0 or higher.
- The String class found in the System namespace is used to implement strings.
- The Console class found in the System namespace is used to output to standard output.

Code Block Features

The Program Phase 1-7 code blocks illustrate the following programming features using the VB.NET programming language:

- **Console Application**
- **Integer and String Variable Declarations**
- **Application Command Line Parameters**
- **Case/Switch Statement**
- **String Literal Assignment and String Concatenation**
- **Console Application Standard Output**

Visual Basic .NET Console Application

- A console application can be created in a module that contains a subroutine called Main(). The test1 module can be assigned as the "Startup object" for the application. The Main() subroutine in the test1 module is the Entry Point of Execution (EPE) for the program.

test1.vb: Visual Basic .NET Console Application

```
Module test1
Sub Main()

    '' Visual Basic .NET code goes here.

End Sub
End Module
```

Visual Basic .NET
Integer and String Variable Declarations

- The "int" keyword is aliased to the System.Int32 structure. The "string" keyword is aliased to the System.String class. The System.String class stores all string data in the UTF-16 Unicode format.

test2.vb: Visual Basic .NET Integer and String Variable Declarations

```
Module test2
Sub Main()

   Dim lnVar1 as Integer
   Dim lcVar2 as String

End Sub
End Module
```

Visual Basic .NET
Application Command Line Parameters

- The following example stores a single command line parameter in a string variable:

test3.vb: Visual Basic .NET Application Command Line Parameters

```
Module test3
Sub Main()

   Dim argc as Integer
   Dim argv() As String
   Dim lcCmdLineParam1 as String

   argv = System.Environment.GetCommandLineArgs()
   argc = argv.Length

   If ((argc -1) = 1)

      lcCmdLineParam1 = argv(1)

   End If

End Sub
End Module
```

Visual Basic .NET
Case/Switch Statement

- The following example implements a "Select Case" statement:

test4.vb: Visual Basic .NET Case/Switch Statement

```
Module test4
Sub Main()

   Dim lnCmdLineParamCount As Integer
   Dim laArgv() As String
```

test4.vb continued on the next page

test4.vb: Visual Basic .NET Case/Switch Statement continued

```
   laArgv = System.Environment.GetCommandLineArgs()
   lnCmdLineParamCount = laArgv.Length - 1

   Select Case lnCmdLineParamCount

      Case 0
         '' No command line parameters entered.

      Case 1
         '' One command line parameter entered.

      Case Else
         '' More than one command line parameter entered.

End Select
End Sub
End Module
```

Visual Basic .NET
String Literal Assignment and String Concatenation

- The following example stores two string literals and then concatenates the strings:

test5.vb: String Literal Assignment and String Concatenation

```
Imports System

Module test5
Sub Main()

   Dim lcString1 As String
   Dim lcString2 As String
   Dim lcString3 As String

   lcString1 = "Hello"
   lcString2 = "World!"
   lcString3 = lcString1 & " " & lcString2

End Sub
End Module
```

Visual Basic .NET
Console Application Standard Output

- The following example outputs text to standard output:

test6.vb: Console Application Standard Output

```
Imports System

Module test6
Sub Main()

   Dim lcString1 As System.String

   lcString1 = "Hello World!"
   System.Console.WriteLine(lcString1)

End Sub
End Module
```

Source Code Files

- Text files: pp1_7.vb
- The "namespace" directive in the Reserved code block places the pp1_7 module in the nspp1_7 namespace. The nspp1_7.pp1_7 module can be specified as the "Startup object" for the program. When a module is set as the "Startup object", the "Sub Main" defined in the module is the EPE for the program.

pp1_7.vb: Program Phase 1-7 Source Code

```
''**********************************************************************
'' Program Phase 1-7 VB.NET Hello World! with Strings                  *
'' Programming Tasks Illustrated: Console Application                  *
''                                Integer and String Variable Declarations    *
''                                Application Command Line Parameters  *
''                                Case/Switch Statement                *
''                                String Literal Assignment and Concatenation *
''                                Console Application Standard Output  *
''**********************************************************************

''**********************************************************************
'' File: pp1_7.vb                                                      *
'' Reserved                                                            *
''**********************************************************************

Imports System
Namespace nspp1_7
Module pp1_7

''**********************************************************************
'' Program Phase 1-7 Main                                              *
'' Define the Entry Point of Execution (EPE) for Program Phase 1-7     *
'' CBI:  1-7.1.1.1                                                     *
''**********************************************************************

Sub Main()

''**********************************************************************
'' Program Phase 1-7 Main                                              *
'' Declare the local variables for the "main" program                  *
'' CBI:  1-7.1.1.2                                                     *
''''********************************************************************

    Dim lnCmdLineParamCount As Integer
    Dim argv() As String
    Dim lcString1 As String
    Dim lcString2 As String
    Dim lcStringOutput1 As String
    Dim lcStringOutput2 As String

''**********************************************************************
'' Program Phase 1-7 Main                                              *
'' Store the command line parameters                                   *
'' CBI:  1-7.1.1.3                                                     *
''**********************************************************************

    argv = System.Environment.GetCommandLineArgs()
    lnCmdLineParamCount = argv.Length - 1
```

pp1_7.vb continued on the next page

pp1_7.vb: Program Phase 1-7 Source Code continued

```
''*************************************************************************
'' Program Phase 1-7 Main                                                  *
'' Parse the command line parameters using a Case/Switch statement         *
'' CBI:  1-7.1.1.4                                                         *
''*************************************************************************

   Select Case lnCmdLineParamCount

      Case 0
        lcStringOutput1 = "You entered no command line parameters."

      Case 1
         lcStringOutput1 = "Command line paramater entered:  " + argv(1)

      Case Else
         lcStringOutput1 = "The command line is limted to 1 parameter."

   End Select


''*************************************************************************
'' Program Phase 1-7 Main                                                  *
'' Concatenate two string variables                                        *
'' CBI:  1-7.1.1.5                                                         *
''*************************************************************************

   lcString1 = "Hello"
   lcString2 = "World!"
   lcStringOutput2 = lcString1 & " " & lcString2


''*************************************************************************
'' Program Phase 1-7 Main                                                  *
'' Output to standard output                                               *
'' CBI:  1-7.1.1.6                                                         *
''*************************************************************************

   Console.WriteLine(lcStringOutput1)
   Console.WriteLine(lcStringOutput2)

End Sub
End Module
End Namespace
```

Code Setup and Compilation

- Tools: Microsoft Basic 2008 Express Edition (msdn.microsoft.com), Microsoft .NET Framework 2.0 or higher (windowsupdate.microsoft.com)

Code Setup and Compilation Steps

1: Start the Microsoft Visual Basic 2008 Express Edition program.

2: VB.NET EE - Activate Menu Item: File → New Project

Select "Console Application". Name the project pp1_7 and then activate the "OK" button.

3: Delete the module1.bas file in the "Solution Explorer" window.

Steps continued on the next page

Code Setup and Compilation Steps continued

4: VB.NET EE - Activate Menu Item: File → Save All

On the "Save Project" dialog window, specify pp1_7 for the "Name". Set the "Location" to the appropriate folder. Uncheck the "Create directory for solution" check box and then activate the "Save" button.

5: VB.NET EE - Activate Menu Item: Project → Add New Item

On the "Add New Item" dialog window, select the "Module" template. Enter pp1_7.vb for the file "Name" and then activate the "Add" button. Enter the source code for Program Phase 1-7 into the pp1_7.vb text file.

6: VB.NET EE - Activate Menu Item: Project → pp1_7 Properties

Set the "Startup object" to nspp1_7.pp1_7. Close the "pp1_7 Properties" window.

7: VB.NET EE - Activate Menu Item: File → Save All

8: VB.NET EE - Activate Menu Item: Build → Build pp1_7

The resulting pp1_7.exe file will be found in the pp1_7\build or pp1_7\debug folder.

Command Prompt Compilation

Enter the following commands from the pp1_7 folder to compile Program Phase 1-7:

```
PATH = "%SYSTEMROOT%\microsoft.net\framework\v2.0.50727";%PATH%
vbc.exe /r:system.dll /out:bin\release\pp1_7.exe pp1_7.vb
```

Program Execution

- Execute Program

  Place the cursor at the "End Sub" line of code in the CBI: 1-7.1.1.6 code block.

  ```
  VB.NET EE - Activate Menu Item:  Debug → Toggle Breakpoint
  VB.NET EE - Activate Menu Item:  Debug → Start Debugging
  ```

- Enter Command Line Parameters

  ```
  VB.NET EE - Activate Menu Item:  Project → pp1_7 Properties
  ```

  Select the "Debug" tab and then enter any command line parameters in the "Command line arguments" field.

- Debug Program

  ```
  VB.NET EE - Activate Menu Item:  Debug → Step Into
  ```

Program Phase 1-8
Managed C++ ▪ Windows

Console Based Hello World! with Strings

- Program Phase Task 1 is implemented in Program Phase 1-8 using the C++ programming language and the Microsoft .NET Framework 2.0 or higher.
- The String class found in the System namespace is used to implement strings.
- The Console class found in the System namespace is used to output to standard output.

Code Block Features

The Program Phase 1-8 code blocks illustrate the following programming features using the C++ programming language and the Microsoft .NET Framework:

- **Console Application**
- **Integer and String Variable Declarations**
- **Application Command Line Parameters**
- **Case/Switch Statement**
- **String Literal Assignment and String Concatenation**
- **Console Application Standard Output**

Managed C++
Console Application

- A console application can be created by implementing a main() function. The "#using <mscorlib.dll>" preprocessor directive is required when creating a Managed C++ program.

test1.cpp: Managed C++ Console Application

```
#using <mscorlib.dll>

int main()
{
   // Managed and Unmanaged C++ code goes here.

   return 0;
}
```

Managed C++
Integer and String Variable Declarations

- The "int" data type is aliased to the System.Int32 structure. The String class in the System namespace stores all string data in the UTF-16 Unicode format.

test2.cpp: Managed C++ Integer and String Variable Declarations

```
#using <mscorlib.dll>
using namespace System;

int main()
{
   int lnVar1;
   String^ lcVar2;

   return 0;
}
```

Managed C++
Application Command Line Parameters

- The following example stores a single command line parameter in a string variable:

test3.cpp: Managed C++ Application Command Line Parameters

```
#using <mscorlib.dll>
using namespace System;

int main()
{
   cli::array <String^> ^argv;
   int argc;
   System::String^ lcCmdLineParam1;

   argv = System::Environment::GetCommandLineArgs();
   argc = argv->Length;

   if ((argc - 1) == 1)
   {
      lcCmdLineParam1 = argv[1];
   }
   return 0;
}
```

Managed C++
Case/Switch Statement

- The following example implements a "switch" statement:

test4.cpp: Managed C++ Case/Switch Statement

```
#using <mscorlib.dll>
using namespace System;

int main()
{
   cli::array <String^> ^argv;
```

test4.cpp continued on the next page

test4.cpp: Managed C++ Case/Switch Statement continued

```
   int argc;
   int lnCmdLineParamCount;

   argv = System::Environment::GetCommandLineArgs();
   argc = argv->Length;
   lnCmdLineParamCount = argc - 1;

   switch(lnCmdLineParamCount)
   {
      case 0:
         // No command line parameters entered.
         break;

      case 1:
         // One command line parameter entered.
         break;

      default:
         ; // More than one command line parameter entered.
   }
   return 0;
}
```

Managed C++
String Literal Assignment and String Concatenation

- The following example stores two string literals and then concatenates the strings:

test5.cpp: Managed C++ String Literal Assignment and String Concatenation

```
#using <mscorlib.dll>
using namespace System;

int main()
{
   System::String^ lcString1;
   System::String^ lcString2;
   System::String^ lcString3;

   lcString1 = "Hello";
   lcString2 = "World!";
   lcString3 = System::String::Format("{0} {1}",lcString1,lcString2);
   return 0;
}
```

Managed C++
Console Application Standard Output

- The following example outputs text to standard output:

test6.cpp: Managed C++ Console Application Standard Output

```
#using <mscorlib.dll>
using namespace System;

int main()
{
   System::String^ lcString1;
```

test6.cpp continued on the next page

test6.cpp: Managed C++ Console Application Standard Output continued

```
    lcString1 = "Hello World!";
    System::Console::WriteLine(lcString1);
    return 0;
}
```

Source Code Files

- Text files: pp1_8.cpp

pp1_8.cpp: Program Phase 1-8 Source Code

```
//***************************************************************************
// Program Phase 1-8 Managed C++ Hello World! with Strings                  *
// Programming Tasks Illustrated: Console Application                       *
//                                Integer and String Variable Declarations  *
//                                Application Command Line Parameters       *
//                                Case/Switch Statement                     *
//                                String Literal Assignment and Concatenation *
//                                Console Application Standard Output       *
//***************************************************************************

//***************************************************************************
// File: pp1_8.cpp                                                          *
// Reserved                                                                 *
//***************************************************************************

#using <mscorlib.dll>
using namespace System;

//***************************************************************************
// Program Phase 1-8 Main                                                   *
// Define the Entry Point of Execution (EPE) for Program Phase 1-8          *
// CBI:  1-8.1.1.1                                                          *
//***************************************************************************

int main()
{

//***************************************************************************
// Program Phase 1-8 Main                                                   *
// Declare the local variables for the "main" program                       *
// CBI:  1-8.1.1.2                                                          *
//***************************************************************************

    int lnCmdLineParamCount;
    cli::array <String^> ^laArgv;
    String^ lcString1;
    String^ lcString2;
    String^ lcStringOutput1;
    String^ lcStringOutput2;

//***************************************************************************
// Program Phase 1-8 Main                                                   *
// Store the command line parameters                                        *
// CBI:  1-8.1.1.3                                                          *
//***************************************************************************

    laArgv = Environment::GetCommandLineArgs();
    lnCmdLineParamCount = laArgv->Length - 1;
```

pp1_8.cpp continued on the next page

```
ppl_8.cpp: Program Phase 1-8 Source Code continued
```

```
//****************************************************************************
// Program Phase 1-8 Main                                                    *
// Parse the command line parameters using a Case/Switch statement           *
// CBI:  1-8.1.1.4                                                           *
//****************************************************************************

   switch(lnCmdLineParamCount)
   {
      case 0:
         lcStringOutput1 = "You entered no command line parameters.";
         break;

      case 1:
         lcStringOutput1 = String::Format("Command line parameter entered: {0}",
                                          laArgv[1]);
         break;

      default:
         lcStringOutput1 = "The command line is limited to 1 parameter.";
   }

//****************************************************************************
// Program Phase 1-8 Main                                                    *
// Concatenate two string variables                                          *
// CBI:  1-8.1.1.5                                                           *
//****************************************************************************

   lcString1 = "Hello";
   lcString2 = "World!";
   lcStringOutput2 = String::Format("{0} {1}",lcString1,lcString2);

//****************************************************************************
// Program Phase 1-8 Main                                                    *
// Output to standard output                                                 *
// CBI:  1-8.1.1.6                                                           *
//****************************************************************************

   Console::WriteLine(lcStringOutput1);
   Console::WriteLine(lcStringOutput2);
   return 0;
}
```

Code Setup and Compilation

- Tools: Microsoft Visual C++ 2008 Express Edition (msdn.microsoft.com), Microsoft .NET Framework 2.0 or higher (windowsupdate.microsoft.com)

```
Code Setup and Compilation Steps
```

1: Start the Microsoft Visual C++ 2008 Express Edition program.

2: VC++ EE - Activate Menu Item: File → New → Project

3: Select "Win32" for the "Project" type. Select the "Win32 Console Application" template.

Steps continued on the next page

Code Setup and Compilation Steps continued

4: Set the "Name" of the project "pp1_8". Set the project "Location" to the appropriate folder. Do not check the "Create directory for solution" check box. Activate the "OK" button to proceed with the "Win32 Application Wizard".

5: Activate the "Next" button of the "Win32 Application Wizard".

6: Verify that a "Console Application" is selected and also check the "Empty project" check box. Activate the "Finish" button of the "Win32 Application Wizard".

7: VC++ EE - Activate Menu Item: Project → Add New Item

On the "Add New Item" dialog window, select the "Visual C++ → Code" category and then select the "C++ File" template. Enter pp1_8.cpp for the file "Name" and then activate the "Add" button. Enter the source code for Program Phase 1-8 into the pp1_8.cpp text file.

8: VC++ EE - Activate Menu Item: Project → pp1_8 Properties

Enter the following settings:

Configuration Properties → General → Character Set

```
"Use Multi-Byte Character Set"
```

Configuration Properties → General → Common Language Runtime Support

```
"Common Language Runtime Support (/clr)"
```

9: VC++ EE - Activate Menu Item: Build → Build Solution

Command Prompt Compilation

From a Visual Studio 2008 command prompt, enter the following command in the pp1_8 folder:

```
cl.exe /clr pp1_8.cpp
```

Program Execution

- Execute Program

```
VC++ EE - Activate Menu Item: Debug → Start Without Debugging
```

- Enter Command Line Parameters

```
VC++ EE - Activate Menu Item: Project → pp1_8 Properties
```

Expand the "Configuration Properties" entry and then click on the "Debugging" item. Command line parameters can be specified in the "Command Arguments" field.

- Debug Program

```
VC++ EE - Activate Menu Item: Debug → Step Into
```

Program Phase 1-9

Python ▪ Multi-Platform

Console Based Hello World! with Strings

- Program Phase Task 1 is implemented in Program Phase 1-9 using the Python programming language.
- The character string collection data type is used to implement strings.
- The "print" statement is used to output to standard output.

Code Block Features

The Program Phase 1-9 code blocks illustrate the following programming features using the Python programming language:

- **Console Application**
- **Integer and String Variable Declarations**
- **Application Command Line Parameters**
- **Case/Switch Statement**
- **String Literal Assignment and String Concatenation**
- **Console Application Standard Output**

Python
Console Application

- The Entry Point of Execution (EPE) for a Python console application is the first line of code in a text file ending with the ".py" file extension.

test1.py: Python Console Application

```
## Python code goes here.
```

Python
Integer and String Variable Declarations

- A string variable can be created by assigning a string literal to a loosely typed Python variable. Python supports ASCII strings and Unicode strings. The strings implemented for Program Phase 1-9 are ASCII strings. The variables in the following example are global variables because they are not declared within a function. To access a global variable within a function, declare the variable again inside the function with the global keyword.

test2.py: Python Integer and String Variable Declarations

```
gnVar1 = 0
gcVar2 = ""
```

Python
Application Command Line Parameters

- Variables declared inside a function are locally scoped to the function.
- The following example stores a single command line parameter in a string variable:

test3.py: Python Application Command Line Parameters

```
import sys

def main():

    lcCmdLineParam1 = ""
    argc = 0

    argc = len(sys.argv)

    if (argc - 1) == 1:
       lcCmdLineParam1 = sys.argv[1]

main()
```

Python
Case/Switch Statement

- The functionality of a Case/Switch statement can be implemented using a Python "for loop" combined with "if" statements.

test4.py: Python Case/Switch Statement

```
import sys

def main():

    lnCmdLineParamCount = len(sys.argv) - 1

    for lnCmdLineParamCount in [lnCmdLineParamCount]:

       if lnCmdLineParamCount == 0:

          ## No command line parameters entered.
          break

       if lnCmdLineParamCount == 1:

          ## One command line parameter entered.
          break

       # default

       ## More than one command line parameter entered.
       break

main()
```

Python
String Literal Assignment and String Concatenation

- The following example stores two string literals and then concatenates the strings:

test5.py: Python String Literal Assignment and String Concatenation

```
gcString1 = "Hello"
gcString2 = "World!"
gcString3 = gcString1 + " " + gcString2
```

Python
Console Application Standard Output

- The print() function appends a newline to the text parameter and then internally calls the sys.stdout.write() function.
- The following example outputs text to standard output:

test6.py: Python Console Application Standard Output

```
gcString1 = "Hello World!"
print gcString1
```

Source Code Files

- Text files: pp1_9.py
- The "import" statement in the Reserved code block allows the objects in the sys module to be used without specifying the full path to the object.

pp1_9.py: Program Phase 1-9 Source Code

```
##***************************************************************************
## Program Phase 1-9 Python Hello World! with Strings                        *
## Programming Tasks Illustrated: Console Application                        *
##                                Integer and String Variable Declarations   *
##                                Application Command Line Parameters        *
##                                Case/Switch Statement                      *
##                                String Literal Assignment and Concatenation *
##                                Console Application Standard Output        *
##***************************************************************************

##***************************************************************************
## File: pp1_9.py                                                            *
## Reserved                                                                  *
##***************************************************************************

import sys

##***************************************************************************
## Program Phase 1-9 Main                                                    *
## Define the Entry Point of Execution (EPE) for Program Phase 1-9           *
## CBI:  1-9.1.1.1                                                           *
##***************************************************************************

def main():
```

pp1_9.py continued on the next page

pp1_9.py: Program Phase 1-9 Source Code continued

```
##*************************************************************************
## Program Phase 1-9 Main                                                 *
## Declare the local variables for the "main" program                     *
## CBI:  1-9.1.1.2                                                        *
##*************************************************************************

    lnCmdLineParamCount = 0
    lcString1 = ""
    lcString2 = ""
    lcStringOutput1 = ""
    lcStringOutput2 = ""

##*************************************************************************
## Program Phase 1-9 Main                                                 *
## Store the command line parameters                                      *
## CBI:  1-9.1.1.3                                                        *
##*************************************************************************

    ## The sys.argv list contains the command line parameters.
    lnCmdLineParamCount = len(sys.argv) - 1

##*************************************************************************
## Program Phase 1-9 Main                                                 *
## Parse the command line parameters using a Case/Switch statement        *
## CBI:  1-9.1.1.4                                                        *
##*************************************************************************

    for lnCmdLineParamCount in [lnCmdLineParamCount]:

       if lnCmdLineParamCount == 0:

         lcStringOutput1 = "You entered no command line parameters."
         break

       if lnCmdLineParamCount == 1:

         lcStringOutput1 = "Command line parameter entered:  " + sys.argv[1];
         break

       # default
       lcStringOutput1 = "The command line is limited to 1 parameter."
       break

##*************************************************************************
## Program Phase 1-9 Main                                                 *
## Concatenate two string variables                                       *
## CBI:  1-9.1.1.5                                                        *
##*************************************************************************

    lcString1 = "Hello"
    lcString2 = "World!"
    lcStringOutput2 = lcString1 + " " + lcString2

##*************************************************************************
## Program Phase 1-9 Main                                                 *
## Output to standard output                                              *
## CBI:  1-9.1.1.6                                                        *
##*************************************************************************

    print lcStringOutput1
    print lcStringOutput2

main()
```

Code Setup and Compilation

- Tools: Python distribution (Appendix G), Komodo IDE (Appendix F)

Code Setup and Compilation Steps

1: Create a folder called pp1_9 that will store the source code files.

2: Start the Komodo IDE program.

3: Komodo - Activate Menu Item: File → New → New Project

Set the project name to pp1_9.kpf and then save the new project in the pp1_9 folder.

4: Komodo - Activate Menu Item: File → New → New File

Click on the "Common" category and then select the "Text" template. Set the "Filename" to pp1_9.py. Verify that the "add to pp1_9 project" check box is checked, and the "Directory" is set to the pp1_9 folder. Activate the "Open" button. Enter the source code for Program Phase 1-9 and then save the file.

5: There is no step for compiling the pp1_9.py file. It is compiled at runtime by the Python interpreter.

Program Execution

- Execute Program

  ```
  Komodo - Activate Menu Item: Debug → Run Without Debugging
  ```

  On the "Debugging Options" window, verify that the "Script" is set to the full path to the pp1_9.py file and then activate the "OK" button. The output for Program Phase 1-9 is displayed in the Komodo output window on the "Run Output" tab.

- Enter Command Line Parameters

  On the "Debugging Options" dialog window that is displayed when the "Run Without Debugging" menu item is activated, command line parameters can be specified in the "Script Arguments" field.

- Debug Program

  ```
  Komodo - Activate Menu Item: Debug → Step In
  ```

- To launch the pp1_9.py file from a command prompt, change directories to the pp1_9 folder and then enter the following command:

  ```
  python pp1_9.py
  ```

  The preceding command assumes that the python interpreter is in the path.

Program Phase 1-10

Perl ▪ Multi-Platform

Console Based Hello World! with Strings

- Program Phase Task 1 is implemented in Program Phase 1-10 using the Perl programming language.
- Program Phase 1-10 stores integer and string data in Perl scalar variables.
- The "print" statement is used to output to standard output.

Code Block Features

The Program Phase 1-10 code blocks illustrate the following programming features using the Perl programming language:

- **Console Application**
- **Integer and String Variable Declarations**
- **Application Command Line Parameters**
- **Case/Switch Statement**
- **String Literal Assignment and String Concatenation**
- **Console Application Standard Output**

Perl
Console Application

- A Perl console application begins with the first line of code in a text file ending with the ".pl" file extension.
- A Perl program executed on Unix based platforms often contains the following line of code:

  ```
  #!/usr/bin/perl -w
  ```

  The "#!" is called a shebang . The path after the shebang is the path to the Perl interpreter. This allows a Perl program to be launched by typing in the file name in a Unix terminal window. This indicator is not necessary on the Windows platform since the Perl interpreter can be associated with files having the ".pl" file extension.

`test1.pl: Perl Console Application`

```
## Perl code goes here.
```

Perl
Integer and String Variable Declarations

- Perl is not a strongly typed language and supports only three different data types: scalars, arrays, and hashes. Only scalars and arrays are used in Program Phase 1-10. A scalar variable can hold numeric data and string data. There is no need to declare a particular type for a scalar variable, and it is possible to change the type value of a variable during program execution.

- A string variable can be created by assigning a string literal to a scalar variable. A Perl variable declaration is prefaced with the "my" keyword, and a Perl scalar variable begins with the "$" symbol. String data is stored in Perl's extended UTF-8 Unicode format.

test2.pl: Perl Integer and String Variable Declarations

```
my $lnVar1;
my $lcVar2;
```

Perl
Application Command Line Parameters

- The following example stores a single command line parameter in a string variable:

test3.pl: Perl Application Command Line Parameters

```
my $argc = 0;
my $lcCmdLineParam1 = "";

$argc = scalar(@ARGV);

if ($argc == 1)
{
   $lcCmdLineParam1 = $ARGV[0];
}
```

Perl
Case/Switch Statement

- The functionality of a Case/Switch statement can be implemented with a Perl block.

test4.pl: Perl Case/Switch Statement

```
my $lnCmdLineParamCount = 0;

$lnCmdLineParamCount = scalar(@ARGV);

SWITCH:
{
   if($lnCmdLineParamCount == 0)
   {
      ## No command line parameters entered.
      last SWITCH;
   };

   if($lnCmdLineParamCount == 1)
   {
```

test4.pl continued on the next page

test4.pl: Perl Case/Switch Statement continued

```
        ## One command line parameter entered.
        last SWITCH;
    };

    ## Otherwise

        ## More than one command line parameter entered.
}
```

Perl
String Literal Assignment and String Concatenation

- The following example stores two string literals and then concatenates the strings:

test5.pl: Perl String Literal Assignment and String Concatenation

```
my $lcString1;
my $lcString2;
my $lcString3;

$lcString1 = "Hello";
$lcString2 = "World!";
$lcString3 = sprintf("%s %s\n",$lcString1,$lcString2);
```

Perl
Console Application Standard Output

- The following example outputs text to standard output:

test6.pl: Perl Console Application Standard Output

```
my $lcString1;

$lcString1 = "Hello World!";
print STDOUT $lcString1;
```

Source Code Files

- Text files: pp1_10.pl
- The "use strict" pragma in the Reserved code block causes various code restrictions to be implemented for the program. For Program Phase 1-10, it forces all variables to be declared using the "my" keyword before being used.

pp1_10.pl: Program Phase 1-10 Source Code

```
##*************************************************************************
## Program Phase 1-10 Perl Hello World! with Strings                     *
## Programming Tasks Illustrated: Console Application                    *
##                                Integer and String Variable Declarations    *
##                                Application Command Line Parameters    *
##                                Case/Switch Statement                  *
##                                String Literal Assignment and Concatenation *
##                                Console Application Standard Output    *
##*************************************************************************
```

pp1_10.pl continued on the next page

pp1_10.pl: Program Phase 1-10 Source Code continued

```
##*************************************************************************
## File: pp1_10.pl                                                        *
## Reserved                                                               *
##*************************************************************************

use strict;


##*************************************************************************
## Program Phase 1-10 Main                                                *
## Define the Entry Point of Execution (EPE) for Program Phase 1-10       *
## CBI:  1-10.1.1.1                                                       *
##*************************************************************************

## The first line of the code in the pp1_10.pl file is the EPE.


##*************************************************************************
## Program Phase 1-10 Main                                                *
## Declare the local variables for the "main" program                     *
## CBI:  1-10.1.1.2                                                       *
##*************************************************************************

my $lnCmdLineParamCount;
my $lcString1;
my $lcString2;
my $lcStringOutput1;
my $lcStringOutput2;


##*************************************************************************
## Program Phase 1-10 Main                                                *
## Store the command line parameters                                      *
## CBI:  1-10.1.1.3                                                       *
##*************************************************************************

## The $ARGV array stores the command line parameters.
$lnCmdLineParamCount =  scalar(@ARGV);


##*************************************************************************
## Program Phase 1-10 Main                                                *
## Parse the command line parameters using a Case/Switch statement        *
## CBI:  1-10.1.1.4                                                       *
##*************************************************************************

SWITCH:
{
   if($lnCmdLineParamCount == 0)
   {
      $lcStringOutput1 = "You entered no command line parameters.\n";
      last SWITCH;
   };

   if($lnCmdLineParamCount == 1)
   {

       $lcStringOutput1 = sprintf("Command line paramater entered:  %s\n",
                                  $ARGV[0]);
       last SWITCH;
   };

   ## Otherwise
      $lcStringOutput1 = "The command line is limited to 1 parameter.\n";
}
```

pp1_10.pl continued on the next page

ppl_10.pl: Program Phase 1-10 Source Code continued

```
##**************************************************************************
## Program Phase 1-10 Main                                                *
## Concatenate two string variables                                       *
## CBI:  1-10.1.1.5                                                       *
##**************************************************************************

$lcString1 = "Hello";
$lcString2 = "World!";
$lcStringOutput2 = sprintf("%s %s\n",$lcString1,$lcString2);


##**************************************************************************
## Program Phase 1-10 Main                                                *
## Output to standard output                                              *
## CBI:  1-10.1.1.6                                                       *
##**************************************************************************

print STDOUT $lcStringOutput1;
print STDOUT $lcStringOutput2;
```

Code Setup and Compilation

- Tools: Perl 5 distribution (Appendix H), Komodo IDE (Appendix F)

Code Setup and Compilation Steps

1: Create a folder called pp1_10 that will store the source code files.

2: Start the Komodo IDE program.

3: Komodo - Activate Menu Item: File → New → New Project

Set the project name to pp1_10.kpf and save the new project in the pp1_10 folder.

4: Komodo - Activate Menu Item: File → New → New File

Click on the "Common" category and then select the "Text" template. Set the "Filename" to pp1_10.pl. Verify that the "add to pp1_10 project" check box is checked and the "Directory" is set to the pp1_10 folder. Activate the "Open" button. Enter the source code for Program Phase 1-10 and save the text file as pp1_10.pl.

5: There is no step for compiling the pp1_10.pl file. It is compiled at runtime by the Perl interpreter.

Program Execution

- Execute Program

    Komodo - Activate Menu Item: Debug → Run Without Debugging

On the "Debugging Options" window, verify that the "Script" is set to the full path to the pp1_10.pl file and then activate the "OK" button. The output for Program Phase 1-10 is displayed in the Komodo output window on the "Run Output" tab.

- Enter Command Line Parameters

  On the "Debugging Options" dialog window that is displayed when the "Run Without Debugging" menu item is activated, command line parameters can be specified in the "Script Arguments" field.

- Debug Program

  ```
  Komodo - Activate Menu Item: Debug → Step In
  ```

- To launch the pp1_10.pl file from a command prompt, change directories to the pp1_10 folder and then enter the following command

  ```
  perl pp1_10.pl
  ```

  The preceding command assumes that the perl interpreter is in the path.

Program Phase 1-11
PHP CLI ▪ Multi-Platform
Console Based Hello World! with Strings

- Program Phase Task 1 is implemented in Program Phase 1-11 using PHP (Hypertext Preprocessor). PHP is usually used to create server-side applications, but it can also be used to create a console program such as that specified by Program Phase Task 1. The command line utility to run PHP client programs is called PHP CLI.
- The PHP string data type is used to implement strings.
- The "echo" language construct is used to output to standard output.

Code Block Features

The Program Phase 1-11 code blocks illustrate the following programming features using the PHP programming language:

- **Console Application**
- **Integer and String Variable Declarations**
- **Application Command Line Parameters**
- **Case/Switch Statement**
- **String Literal Assignment and String Concatenation**
- **Console Application Standard Output**

PHP CLI
Console Application

- A PHP console application can be entered into a text file ending with the ".php" file extension. A PHP program must begin with the "<?php" tag and conclude with the "?>" tag.

test1.php: PHP Console Application

```
<?php

   // PHP code goes here.
?>
```

PHP CLI
Integer and String Variable Declarations

- A PHP variable declaration begins with the "$" symbol.

- PHP strings do not support Unicode, but additional libraries are available for implementing Unicode strings. Program Phase 1-11 is implemented with ASCII strings.
- The variables in the following example are global variables because they are not declared within a function. To access a global variable within a function, declare the variable again inside the function with the global keyword.

test2.php: PHP Integer and String Variable Declarations

```
<?php

   $gnVar1 = null;
   $gcVar2 = null;
?>
```

PHP CLI
Application Command Line Parameters

- Variables declared inside a function are locally scoped to the function.
- The following example stores a single command line parameter in a PHP variable:

test3.php: PHP Application Command Line Parameters

```
<?php

main($argc,$argv);

function main($argc,$argv)
{
   $lcCmdLineParam1 = null;

   if (($argc - 1) == 1)
   {
      $lcCmdLineParam1 = $argv[1];
   }
}

?>
```

PHP CLI
Case/Switch Statement

- The following example program implements a "switch" statement:

test4.php: PHP Case/Switch Statement

```
<?php

main($argc,$argv);

function main($argc,$argv)
{

   $lnCmdLineParamCount = null;
   $lnCmdLineParamCount = $argc - 1;
```

test4.php continued on the next page

test4.php: PHP Case/Switch Statement continued

```
   switch ($lnCmdLineParamCount)
   {
      case 0:
         // No command line parameters entered.
         break;

      case 1:
        // One command line parameter entered.
         break;

      default:
         // More than one command line parameter entered.
         break;
   }
}
?>
```

PHP CLI
String Literal Assignment and String Concatenation

- The following example stores two string literals and then concatenates the strings:

test5.php: PHP String Literal Assignment and String Concatenation

```
<?php

$gcString1 = "Hello";
$gcString2 = "World!";
$gcString3 = $gcString1 . " " . $gcString2;

?>
```

PHP CLI
Console Application Standard Output

- The following example outputs text to standard output:

test6.php: PHP Console Application Standard Output

```
<?php

$gcString1 = "Hello World!";
echo $gcString1;

?>
```

Source Code Files

- Text files: pp1_11.php

pp1_11.php: Program Phase 1-11 Source Code

```
<?php

//*****************************************************************************
// Program Phase 1-11 PHP CLI Hello World! with Strings                       *
// Programming Tasks Illustrated: Console Application                          *
//                                Integer and String Variable Declarations    *
//                                Application Command Line Parameters         *
//                                Case/Switch Statement                       *
//                                String Literal Assignment and Concatenation *
//                                Console Application Standard Output         *
//*****************************************************************************

//*****************************************************************************
// File: pp1_11.php                                                           *
// Reserved                                                                   *
//*****************************************************************************


//*****************************************************************************
// Program Phase 1-11 Main                                                    *
// Define the Entry Point of Execution (EPE) for Program Phase 1-11           *
// CBI:  1-11.1.1.1                                                           *
//*****************************************************************************

main($argc,$argv);

function main($argc,$argv)
{

//*****************************************************************************
// Program Phase 1-11 Main                                                    *
// Declare the local variables for the "main" program                         *
// CBI:  1-11.1.1.2                                                           *
//*****************************************************************************

   $lnCmdLineParamCount = null;
   $lcString1 = null;
   $lcString2 = null;
   $lcStringOutput1 = null;
   $lcStringOutput2 = null;


//*****************************************************************************
// Program Phase 1-11 Main                                                    *
// Store the command line parameters                                          *
// CBI:  1-11.1.1.3                                                           *
//*****************************************************************************

   // the $argv array stores the command line parameters.
   $lnCmdLineParamCount = $argc - 1;


//*****************************************************************************
// Program Phase 1-11 Main                                                    *
// Parse the command line parameters using a Case/Switch statement            *
// CBI:  1-11.1.1.4                                                           *
//*****************************************************************************

   switch ($lnCmdLineParamCount)
   {
      case 0:
         $lcStringOutput1 = "You entered no command line parameters.\n";
         break;

      case 1:
       $lcStringOutput1 = "Command line paramater entered:  " . $argv[1] . "\n";
         break;
```

pp1_11.php continued on the next page

ppl_11.php: Program Phase 1-11 Source Code continued

```
      default:
         $lcStringOutput1 = "The command line is limited to 1 parameter.\n";
         break;
}


//***************************************************************************
// Program Phase 1-11 Main                                                  *
// Concatenate two string variables                                         *
// CBI:  1-11.1.1.5                                                         *
//***************************************************************************

   $lcString1 = "Hello";
   $lcString2 = "World!";
   $lcStringOutput2 = $lcString1 . " " . $lcString2;


//***************************************************************************
// Program Phase 1-11 Main                                                  *
// Output to standard output                                                *
// CBI:  1-11.1.1.6                                                         *
//***************************************************************************

   echo $lcStringOutput1;
   echo $lcStringOutput2;
}

?>
```

Code Setup and Compilation

- Tools: PHP CLI (Appendix J), Komodo IDE (Appendix F)

Code Setup and Compilation Steps

1: Create a folder called ppl_11 that will store the source code files.

2: Start the Komodo IDE program.

3: Komodo - Activate Menu Item: File → New → New Project

Set the name of the project to ppl_11.kpf and save the new project in the ppl_11 folder.

4: Komodo - Activate Menu Item: File → New → New File

Click on the "Common" category and then select the "Text" template. Set the "Filename" to ppl_11.php. Verify that the "add to ppl_11 project" check box is checked and the "Directory" is set to the ppl_11 folder. Activate the "Open" button. Enter the source code for Program Phase 1-11 and then save the file.

5: There is no step for compiling the ppl_11.php file. It is compiled at runtime by the PHP CLI interpreter.

Program Execution

- Execute Program

```
Komodo - Activate Menu Item: Debug → Run Without Debugging
```

On the "Debugging Options" window, verify that the "Script" is set to the full path to the pp1_11.php file. Also, verify that the "Use the CLI interpreter" radio button is enabled and then activate the "OK" button. The output for Program Phase 1-11 is displayed in the Komodo output window on the "Run Output" tab.

- Enter Command Line Parameters

On the "Debugging Options" dialog window that is displayed when the "Run Without Debugging" menu item is activated, command line parameters can be specified in the "Script Arguments" field.

- Debug Program

```
Komodo - Activate Menu Item: Debug → Step In
```

- To launch the pp1_11.php file from a command prompt, change directories to the pp1_11 folder and then enter the following command:

```
php pp1_11.php
```

The preceding command assumes that the PHP interpreter is in the path.

Program Phase 1-12
Ruby ▪ Multi-Platform

Console Based Hello World! with Strings

- Program Phase Task 1 is implemented in Program Phase 1-12 using the Ruby programming language.
- The Ruby String class is used to implement strings.
- The puts() method of the main object is used to output to standard output.

Code Block Features

The Program Phase 1-12 code blocks illustrate the following programming features using the Ruby programming language:

- **Console Application**
- **Integer and String Variable Declarations**
- **Application Command Line Parameters**
- **Case/Switch Statement**
- **String Literal Assignment and String Concatenation**
- **Console Application Standard Output**

Ruby
Console Application

- A Ruby console application can be stored in a text file ending with the ".rb" file extension. The first line of code in the ".rb" text file is the Entry Point of Execution (EPE) for the application.

`test1.rb: Ruby Console Application`

```
## Ruby code goes here.
```

Ruby
Integer and String Variable Declarations

- Every variable in a Ruby program is an instance of a class.
- A String class instance can be created by assigning a string literal value to a Ruby loosely typed variable. The strings implemented in Program Phase 1-12 are implemented as ASCII strings.

test2.rb: Ruby Integer and String Variable Declarations

```
lnVar1 = 0
lcVar2 = ''
```

Ruby
Application Command Line Parameters

- The following example stores a single command line parameter in a string variable:

test3.rb: Ruby Application Command Line Parameters

```
lcCmdLineParam1 = '';
argc = 0;

argc = ARGV.length;

if argc == 1 then

   lcCmdLineParam1 = ARGV[0];

end
```

Ruby
Case/Switch Statement

- The following example implements a "case" statement:

test4.rb: Ruby Case/Switch Statement

```
lnCmdLineParamCount = ARGV.length

case lnCmdLineParamCount

   when 0
      ## No command line parameters entered.

   when 1
      ## One command line parameter entered.

   else
      ## More than one command line parameter entered.

end
```

Ruby
String Literal Assignment and String Concatenation

- The following example stores two string literals and then concatenates the strings:

test5.rb: Ruby String Literal Assignment and String Concatenation

```
lcString1 = 'Hello'
lcString2 = 'World!'
lcString3 = lcString1 + " " + lcString2
```

Ruby
Console Application Standard Output

- When a Ruby program starts, a default object called "main" is automatically created. The puts() member function is a private function that must be called implicitly. The "main" Ruby object is the default object when a Ruby program starts and can be referred to using the "self" keyword. Calling self.puts() will fail because puts() is a private method and, thus, cannot be called explicitly. Not specifying the "self" object (which refers to the "main" object) and calling the puts() function works because it is being called implicitly.

- The following example outputs text to standard output:

test6.rb: Ruby Console Application Standard Output

```
lcString1 = "Hello World!"
puts lcString1
```

Source Code Files

- Text files: pp1_12.rb

pp1_12.rb: Program Phase 1-12 Source Code

```
##*************************************************************************
## Program Phase 1-12 Ruby Hello World! with Strings                      *
## Programming Tasks Illustrated: Console Application                     *
##                                Integer and String Variable Declarations *
##                                Application Command Line Parameters     *
##                                Case/Switch Statement                   *
##                                String Literal Assignment and Concatenation *
##                                Console Application Standard Output     *
##*************************************************************************

##*************************************************************************
## File: pp1_12.rb                                                        *
## Reserved                                                               *
##*************************************************************************


##*************************************************************************
## Program Phase 1-12 Main                                                *
## Define the Entry Point of Execution (EPE) for Program Phase 1-12       *
## CBI:  1-12.1.1.1                                                       *
##*************************************************************************

## The first line of the code in the pp1_12.rb file is the EPE.


##*************************************************************************
## Program Phase 1-12 Main                                                *
## Declare the local variables for the "main" program                     *
## CBI:  1-12.1.1.2                                                       *
##*************************************************************************

lnCmdLineParamCount = 0
lcString1 = ''
lcString2 = ''
lcStringOutput1 = ''
lcStringOutput2 = ''
```

pp1_12.rb continued on the next page

ppl_12.rb: Program Phase 1-12 Source Code continued

```
##**************************************************************************
## Program Phase 1-12 Main                                                  *
## Store the command line parameters                                        *
## CBI:  1-12.1.1.3                                                         *
##**************************************************************************

## The ARGV array stores the command line parameters.
lnCmdLineParamCount = ARGV.length


##**************************************************************************
## Program Phase 1-12 Main                                                  *
## Parse the command line parameters using a Case/Switch statement          *
## CBI:  1-12.1.1.4                                                         *
##**************************************************************************

case lnCmdLineParamCount

   when 0
      lcStringOutput1 = "You entered no command line parameters."

   when 1
      lcStringOutput1 = "Command line parameter entered: " + ARGV[0]

   else
      lcStringOutput1 = "The command line is limited to 1 parameter."

end


##**************************************************************************
## Program Phase 1-12 Main                                                  *
## Concatenate two string variables                                         *
## CBI:  1-12.1.1.5                                                         *
##**************************************************************************

lcString1 = "Hello"
lcString2 = "World!"
lcStringOutput2 = lcString1 + " " + lcString2


##**************************************************************************
## Program Phase 1-12 Main                                                  *
## Output to standard output                                                *
## CBI:  1-12.1.1.6                                                         *
##**************************************************************************

puts lcStringOutput1
puts lcStringOutput2
```

Code Setup and Compilation

- Tools: Ruby distribution (Appendix I), Komodo IDE (Appendix F)

Code Setup and Compilation Steps

1: Create a folder called pp1_12 that will store the source code files.

2: Start the Komodo IDE program.

Steps continued on the next page

Code Setup and Compilation Steps continued

3: Komodo - Activate Menu Item: File → New → New Project

Set the project name to pp1_12.kpf and save the new project in the pp1_12 folder.

4: Komodo - Activate Menu Item: File → New → New File

Click on the "Common" category and then select the "Text" template. Set the "Filename" to pp1_12.rb. Verify that the "add to pp1_12 project" check box is checked and the "Directory" is set to the pp1_12 folder. Activate the "Open" button. Enter the source code for Program Phase 1-12 and then save the file.

5: There is no step for compiling the pp1_12.rb file. It is compiled at runtime by the Ruby interpreter.

Program Execution

- Execute Program

  ```
  Komodo - Activate Menu Item: Debug → Run Without Debugging
  ```

  On the "Debugging Options" window, verify that the "Script" is set to the full path to the pp1_12.rb file and then activate the "OK" button. The output for Program Phase 1-12 is displayed in the Komodo output window on the "Run Output" tab.

- Enter Command Line Parameters

  On the "Debugging Options" dialog window that is displayed when the "Run Without Debugging" menu item is activated, command line parameters can be specified in the "Script Arguments" field.

- Debug Program

  ```
  Komodo - Activate Menu Item: Debug → Step In
  ```

- To launch the pp1_12.rb file from a command prompt, change directories to the pp1_12 folder and then enter the following command:

  ```
  ruby pp1_12.rb
  ```

  The preceding command assumes that the ruby interpreter is in the path.

Program Phase 1-13

Tcl ▪ Multi-Platform

Console Based Hello World! with Strings

- Program Phase Task 1 is implemented in Program Phase 1-13 using the Tool Command Language (Tcl - pronounced tickle).
- The Tcl strings manipulated in Program Phase 1-13 are created by assigning a string literal value to a loosely typed Tcl variable using the Tcl "set" command.
- The Tcl "puts" command is used to output to standard output.

Code Block Features

The Program Phase 1-13 code blocks illustrate the following programming features using the Tcl programming language:

- **Console Application**
- **Integer and String Variable Declarations**
- **Application Command Line Parameters**
- **Case/Switch Statement**
- **String Literal Assignment and String Concatenation**
- **Console Application Standard Output**

Tcl
Console Application

- A Tcl console application can be stored in a text file ending with the ".tcl" file extension. The first line of code in the ".tcl" text file is the Entry Point of Execution (EPE) for the application.

test1.tcl: Tcl Console Application

```
## Tcl code goes here.
```

Tcl
Integer and String Variable Declarations

- A Tcl string variable is created by assigning a string literal to a variable using the Tcl "set" command. As of version 8.1, Tcl stores strings internally in the UTF-8 Unicode format.

test2.tcl: Tcl Integer and String Variable Declarations

```
set lnVar1  0
set lcVar2  ""
```

Tcl
Application Command Line Parameters

- When a Tcl program is started by the tclsh interpreter, three special variables are created. The first variable is called $argc. The second variable is a Tcl list called $argv. The third special variable called $argv0 is a string representing the name of the currently running Tcl script.

- The following example stores a single command line parameter in a string variable:

test3.tcl: Tcl Application Command Line Parameters

```
if {$argc == 1} {
   set lcCmdLineParam1 [lindex $argv 0]
}
```

Tcl
Case/Switch Statement

- The following example implements a "switch" statement:

test4.tcl: Tcl Case/Switch Statement

```
set lnCmdLineParamCount $argc

switch $lnCmdLineParamCount {
   0
   {
      ## No command line parameters entered.
   }
   1
   {
      ## One command line parameter entered.
   }
   default
   {
      ## More than one command line parameter entered.
   }
}
```

Tcl
String Literal Assignment and String Concatenation

- The following example stores two string literals and then concatenates the strings:

test5.tcl: Tcl String Literal Assignment and String Concatenation

```
set lcString1 "Hello"
set lcString2 "World!"
set lcString3 "$lcString1 $lcString2"
```

Tcl
Console Application Standard Output

- The following example outputs text to standard output:

test6.tcl: Tcl Console Application Standard Output

```
set lcString1 "Hello World!"
puts $lcString1
```

Source Code Files

- Text files: pp1_13.tcl

pp1_13.tcl: Program Phase 1-13 Source Code

```
##***********************************************************************
## Program Phase 1-13 Tcl Hello World! with Strings                      *
## Programming Tasks Illustrated: Console Application                    *
##                                Integer and String Variable Declarations  *
##                                Application Command Line Parameters    *
##                                Case/Switch Statement                  *
##                                String Literal Assignment and Concatenation *
##                                Console Application Standard Output    *
##***********************************************************************

##***********************************************************************
## File: pp1_13.tcl                                                      *
## Reserved                                                              *
##***********************************************************************


##***********************************************************************
## Program Phase 1-13 Main                                               *
## Define the Entry Point of Execution (EPE) for Program Phase 1-13      *
## CBI:  1-13.1.1.1                                                      *
##***********************************************************************

## The first line of the code in the pp1_13.tcl file is the EPE.


##***********************************************************************
## Program Phase 1-13 Main                                               *
## Declare the local variables for the "main" program                    *
## CBI:  1-13.1.1.2                                                      *
##***********************************************************************

set lnCmdLineParamCount 0
set lcString1 ""
set lcString2 ""
set lcStringOutput1 ""
set lcStringOutput2 ""


##***********************************************************************
## Program Phase 1-13 Main                                               *
## Store the command line parameters                                     *
## CBI:  1-13.1.1.3                                                      *
##***********************************************************************

# The global argv list variable stores the command line arguments.
set lnCmdLineParamCount $argc
```

pp1_13.tcl continued on the next page

ppl_13.tcl: Program Phase 1-13 Source Code continued

```
##**************************************************************************
## Program Phase 1-13 Main                                                  *
## Parse the command line parameters using a Case/Switch statement          *
## CBI:  1-13.1.1.4                                                         *
##**************************************************************************

switch $lnCmdLineParamCount {
   0
   {
      set lcStringOutput1 "You entered no command line parameters."
   }
   1
   {
      set lcStringOutput1 "Command line paramater entered: [lindex $argv 0]"
   }
   default
   {
      set lcStringOutput1 "The command line is limited to 1 parameter."
   }
}

##**************************************************************************
## Program Phase 1-13 Main                                                  *
## Concatenate two string variables                                         *
## CBI:  1-13.1.1.5                                                         *
##**************************************************************************

set lcString1 "Hello"
set lcString2 "World!"
set lcStringOutput2 "$lcString1 $lcString2"


##**************************************************************************
## Program Phase 1-13 Main                                                  *
## Output to standard output                                                *
## CBI:  1-13.1.1.6                                                         *
##**************************************************************************

puts $lcStringOutput1
puts $lcStringOutput2
```

Code Setup and Compilation

- Tools: Tcl distribution (Appendix K), Komodo IDE (Appendix F)

Code Setup and Compilation Steps

1: Create a folder called pp1_13 that will store the source code files.

2: Start the Komodo IDE program.

3: Komodo - Activate Menu Item: File → New → New Project

Set the project name to pp1_13.kpf and save the new project in the pp1_13 folder.

Steps continued on the next page

Code Setup and Compilation Steps continued

4: Komodo - Activate Menu Item: File → New → New File

Click on the "Common" category and then select the "Text" template. Set the "Filename" to pp1_13.tcl. Verify that the "add to pp1_13 project" check box is checked and the "Directory" is set to the pp1_13 folder. Activate the "Open" button. Enter the source code for Program Phase 1-13 and then save the file.

5: There is no step for compiling the pp1_13.tcl file. It is compiled at runtime by the Tcl interpreter.

Program Execution

- Execute Program

  ```
  Komodo - Activate Menu Item: Debug → Run Without Debugging
  ```

  On the "Debugging Options" window, verify that the "Script" is set to the full path to the pp1_13.tcl file and the "Use default tclsh interpreter" radio button is selected. Activate the "OK" button. The output for Program Phase 1-13 is displayed in the Komodo output window on the "Run Output" tab.

- Enter Command Line Parameters

  On the "Debugging Options" dialog window that is displayed when the "Run Without Debugging" menu item is activated, command line parameters can be specified in the "Script Arguments" field.

- Debug Program

  ```
  Komodo - Activate Menu Item: Debug → Step In
  ```

- To launch the pp1_13.tcl file from a command prompt, change directories to the pp1_13 folder and then enter the following command to execute the program:

  ```
  tclsh pp1_13.tcl
  ```

  The preceding command assumes that the tclsh interpreter is in the path.

Program Phase 1-14
Delphi ▪ Windows

Console Based Hello World! with Strings

- Program Phase Task 1 is implemented in Program Phase 1-14 using the Delphi programming language.
- The String data type is used to implement strings.
- The writeln() function is used to output to standard output.

Code Block Features

The Program Phase 1-14 code blocks illustrate the following programming features using the Delphi programming language:

- **Console Application**
- **Integer and String Variable Declarations**
- **Application Command Line Parameters**
- **Case/Switch Statement**
- **String Literal Assignment and String Concatenation**
- **Console Application Standard Output**

Delphi
Console Application

- A ".dpr" source file is called a project file in Delphi. A console application is indicated using the "{$AppType CONSOLE}" statement. In addition, the SysUtils unit is required. The Entry Point of Execution (EPE) is the first line of code following the "begin" statement.

test1.dpr: Delphi Console Application

```
program test1;

{$APPTYPE CONSOLE}

uses
   SysUtils;

var
   //Variable declarations go here.

begin

   // Delphi code goes here.
end.
```

Delphi
Integer and String Variable Declarations

- The Delphi String data type stores ASCII strings. Delphi supports Unicode strings using the "WideString" data type. Program Phase 1-14 is implemented using ASCII strings.

- The following example declares an integer variable and a string variable:

test2.dpr: Delphi Integer and String Variable Declarations

```
program test2;

{$APPTYPE CONSOLE}

uses
   SysUtils;

var
   lnVar1: Integer;
   lcVar2: String;

begin

   // Delphi code goes here.

end.
```

Delphi
Application Command Line Parameters

- The following example stores a single command line parameter in a string variable:

test3.dpr: Delphi Application Command Line Parameters

```
program test3;

{$APPTYPE CONSOLE}

uses
   SysUtils;

var
   argc: Integer;
   lcCmdLineParam1: String;

begin

if argc = 1 then
   begin

      lcCmdLineParam1 := ParamStr(1);

   end;
end.
```

Delphi
Case/Switch Statement

- The following example implements a "Case" statement:

test4.dpr: Delphi Case/Switch Statement

```
program test4;

{$APPTYPE CONSOLE}

uses
   SysUtils;

var
   lnCmdLineParamCount: Integer;

begin

   Case lnCmdLineParamCount of

       0 : begin

             // No command line parameters entered.

           end;
       1 : begin

             // One command line parameter entered.

           end;

       else // More than one command line parameter entered.

   end;
end.
```

Delphi
String Literal Assignment and String Concatenation

- The following example stores two string literals and then concatenates the strings:

test5.dpr: Delphi String Literal Assignment and String Concatenation

```
program test5;

{$APPTYPE CONSOLE}

uses
   SysUtils;

var
  lcString1: String;
  lcString2: String;
  lcString3: String;

begin

   lcString1 := 'Hello';
   lcString2 := 'World!';
   lcString3 := lcString1 + ' ' + lcString2;

end.
```

Delphi
Console Application Standard Output

- The following example outputs text to standard output:

test6.dpr: Delphi Console Application Standard Output

```
program test6;

{$APPTYPE CONSOLE}

uses
   SysUtils;

var
   lcString1: String;

begin

   lcString1 := 'Hello World!';
   Writeln(lcString1);

end.
```

Source Code Files

- Text files: pp1_14.dpr

pp1_14.dpr: Program Phase 1-14 Source Code

```
//*************************************************************************
// Program Phase 1-14 Delphi Hello World! with Strings                    *
// Programming Tasks Illustrated: Console Application                     *
//                                Integer and String Variable Declarations *
//                                Application Command Line Parameters      *
//                                Case/Switch Statement                    *
//                                String Literal Assignment and Concatenation *
//                                Console Application Standard Output      *
//*************************************************************************

//*************************************************************************
// File: pp1_14.dpr                                                       *
// Reserved                                                               *
//*************************************************************************

program pp1_14;

{$APPTYPE CONSOLE}

uses
   SysUtils;


//*************************************************************************
// Program Phase 1-14 Main                                                *
// Declare the local variables for the "main" program                     *
// CBI:  1-14.1.1.2                                                       *
//*************************************************************************

var
  lnCmdLineParamCount: Integer;
  lcString1: String;
  lcString2: String;
  lcStringOutput1: String;
  lcStringOutput2: String;
```

pp1_14.dpr continued on the next page

pp1_14.dpr: Program Phase 1-14 Source Code continued

```
//*****************************************************************************
// Program Phase 1-14 Main                                                    *
// Define the Entry Point of Execution (EPE) for Program Phase 1-14           *
// CBI:  1-14.1.1.1                                                           *
//*****************************************************************************

begin


//*****************************************************************************
// Program Phase 1-14 Main                                                    *
// Store the command line parameters                                          *
// CBI:  1-14.1.1.3                                                           *
//*****************************************************************************

   lnCmdLineParamCount := ParamCount();


//*****************************************************************************
// Program Phase 1-14 Main                                                    *
// Parse the command line parameters using a Case/Switch statement            *
// CBI:  1-14.1.1.4                                                           *
//*****************************************************************************

   Case lnCmdLineParamCount of

       0 : begin

              lcStringOutput1 := 'You entered no command line parameters.';

           end;

       1 : begin

              lcStringOutput1 := 'Command line paramater entered:  ' +
                                 ParamStr(1);
           end;

       else lcStringOutput1 := 'The command line is limited to 1 parameter.';
   end;


//*****************************************************************************
// Program Phase 1-14 Main                                                    *
// Concatenate two string variables                                           *
// CBI:  1-14.1.1.5                                                           *
//*****************************************************************************

   lcString1 := 'Hello';
   lcString2 := 'World!';
   lcStringOutput2 := lcString1 + ' ' + lcString2;


//*****************************************************************************
// Program Phase 1-14 Main                                                    *
// Output to standard output                                                  *
// CBI:  1-14.1.1.6                                                           *
//*****************************************************************************

   Writeln(lcStringOutput1);
   Writeln(lcStringOutput2);

end.
```

Code Setup and Compilation

- Tools: Turbo Delphi Explorer (Appendix M)

`Code Setup and Compilation Steps`

1: Create a folder called pp1_14 that will store the source code files.

2: Start the Delphi IDE program.

3: Delphi - Activate Menu Item: Project → Add New Project

On the "New Items" dialog window, select the "Delphi Projects" item category and then select "Console Application". Activate the "'OK" button. Enter the source code for Program Phase 1-14 into the project source code file.

4: Delphi - Activate Menu Item: File → Save Project As

Save the project as pp1_14.bdsproj in the pp1_14 folder.

5: Delphi - Activate Menu Item: Project → Build pp1_14

Program Execution

- Execute Program

```
Delphi - Activate Menu Item: Run → Run Without Debugging
```

The console output window will disappear. To view the output, create a breakpoint at the last line of code in the file. Place the cursor at the "end." line of code.

```
Delphi - Activate Menu Item: Run → Add Breakpoint → Source Breakpoint
Delphi - Activate Menu Item: Run → Run
```

- Enter Command Line Parameters

```
Delphi - Activate Menu Item: Run → Parameters
```

Enter the command line arguments in the "Parameters" field.

- Debug Program

```
Delphi - Activate Menu Item: Run → Step Over
```

Program Phase 1-15

C++ ▪ QT4 ▪ Multi-Platform

Console Based Hello World! with Strings

- Program Phase Task 1 is implemented in Program Phase 1-15 using the C++ programming language and the QT4 framework.
- The QString class is used to implement strings.
- The standard fprintf() function is used to output to standard output.

Code Block Features

The Program Phase 1-15 code blocks illustrate the following programming features using the C++ programming language and the QT4 framework:

- **Console Application**
- **Integer and String Variable Declarations**
- **Application Command Line Parameters**
- **Case/Switch Statement**
- **String Literal Assignment and String Concatenation**
- **Console Application Standard Output**

C++ with QT4
Console Application

- The QCoreApplication class is created at the beginning of the application and provides services appropriate for a console based application. The QCoreApplication class can be used to access the command line parameters and to create an event loop for a console based application if one is needed.
- The QCoreApplication class instance is not required to create objects such as a QString class instance, but it is generally recommended to create a single QCoreApplication instance at the beginning of a QT4 console based application.

test1.cpp: C++ with QT4 Console Application

```
#include <QCoreApplication>

int main(int argc, char *argv[])
{
   QCoreApplication loApplication(argc, argv);
```

test1.cpp continued on the next page

test1.cpp: C++ with QT4 Console Application continued

```
   // C++ code that accesses the QT4 framework goes here.
   // loApplication.exec();   uncomment to enable a message loop.

   return 0;
}
```

C++ with QT4
Integer and String Variable Declarations

- The QString class internally stores data in the UTF-16 Unicode format.
- The following example declares an integer variable and a QString variable:

test2.cpp: C++ with QT4 Integer and String Variable Declarations

```
#include <QCoreApplication>

int main(int argc, char *argv[])
{
   QCoreApplication loApplication(argc, argv);

   int lnVar1;
   QString lcVar2;

   return 0;
}
```

C++ with QT4
Application Command Line Parameters

- The following example stores a single command line parameter in a QString variable:

test3.cpp: C++ with QT4 Application Command Line Parameters

```
#include <QCoreApplication>
#include <QStringList>

int main(int argc, char *argv[])
{
   QCoreApplication loApplication(argc, argv);

   QString lcCmdLineParam1;

   if ((QCoreApplication::arguments().size() - 1) == 1)
   {
      lcCmdLineParam1 = QCoreApplication::arguments().at(1);
   }

   return 0;
}
```

C++ with QT4
Case/Switch Statement

- The following example implements a "switch" statement:

test4.cpp: C++ with QT4 Case/Switch Statement

```
#include <QCoreApplication>
#include <QStringList>

int main(int argc, char* argv[])
{
   QCoreApplication loApplication(argc, argv);

   int lnCmdLineParamCount;

   lnCmdLineParamCount = QCoreApplication::arguments().size() - 1;

   switch(lnCmdLineParamCount)
   {
      case 0:
         // No command line parameters entered.
         break;

      case 1:
         // One command line parameter entered.
         break;

      default:
         ; // More than one command line parameter entered.
   }

   return 0;
}
```

C++ with QT4
String Literal Assignment and String Concatenation

- The following example stores two string literals and then concatenates the strings:

test5.cpp: C++ with QT4 String Literal Assignment and String Concatenation

```
#include <QCoreApplication>
#include <QStringList>

int main(int argc, char* argv[])
{
   QCoreApplication loApplication(argc, argv);
   QString lcString1;
   QString lcString2;
   QString lcString3;

   lcString1 = "Hello";
   lcString2 = "World!";
   lcString3 = lcString1 + " " + lcString2;
}
```

C++ with QT4
Console Application Standard Output

- The following example outputs text to standard output:

test6.cpp: C++ with QT4 Console Application Standard Output

```
#include <QCoreApplication>
#include <QStringList>

int main(int argc, char* argv[])
{
   QCoreApplication loApplication(argc, argv);
   QString lcString1;

   lcString1 = "Hello World!";
   fprintf(stdout,"%s\n",lcString1.toAscii().constData());
}
```

Source Code Files

- Text files: pp1_15.cpp

pp1_15.cpp: Program Phase 1-15 Source Code

```
//****************************************************************************
// Program Phase 1-15 C++ QT4 Hello World! with Strings                      *
// Programming Tasks Illustrated: Console Application                         *
//                                Integer and String Variable Declarations    *
//                                Application Command Line Parameters         *
//                                Case/Switch Statement                       *
//                                String Literal Assignment and Concatenation *
//                                Console Application Standard Output         *
//****************************************************************************

//****************************************************************************
// File: pp1_15.cpp                                                          *
// Reserved                                                                  *
//****************************************************************************

#include <QCoreApplication>
#include <QStringList>


//****************************************************************************
// Program Phase 1-15 Main                                                   *
// Define the Entry Point of Execution (EPE) for Program Phase 1-15          *
// CBI:  1-15.1.1.1                                                          *
//****************************************************************************

int main(int argc, char *argv[])
{
   QCoreApplication loPp1_15(argc, argv);


//****************************************************************************
// Program Phase 1-15 Main                                                   *
// Declare the local variables for the "main" program                        *
// CBI:  1-15.1.1.2                                                          *
//****************************************************************************

   int lnCmdLineParamCount;
   QString lcString1;
   QString lcString2;
   QString lcStringOutput1;
   QString lcStringOutput2;
```

pp1_15.cpp continued on the next page

pp1_15.cpp: Program Phase 1-15 Source Code continued

```
//***************************************************************************
// Program Phase 1-15 Main                                                  *
// Store the command line parameters                                        *
// CBI:  1-15.1.1.3                                                         *
//***************************************************************************

   lnCmdLineParamCount = QCoreApplication::arguments().size() - 1;


//***************************************************************************
// Program Phase 1-15 Main                                                  *
// Parse the command line parameters using a Case/Switch statement          *
// CBI:  1-15.1.1.4                                                         *
//***************************************************************************

   switch(lnCmdLineParamCount)
   {
      case 0:
         lcStringOutput1 = "You entered no command line parameters.";
         break;

      case 1:
         lcStringOutput1 = "Command line paramater entered: " +
                           QCoreApplication::arguments().at(1).toAscii();
         break;

      default:
         lcStringOutput1 = "The command line is limited to 1 parameter.";
         break;
   }


//***************************************************************************
// Program Phase 1-15 Main                                                  *
// Concatenate two string variables                                         *
// CBI: 1-15.1.1.5                                                          *
//***************************************************************************

   lcString1 = "Hello";
   lcString2 = "World!";
   lcStringOutput2 = lcString1 + " " + lcString2;


//***************************************************************************
// Program Phase 1-15 Main                                                  *
// Output to standard output                                                *
// CBI:  1-15.1.1.6                                                         *
//***************************************************************************

   fprintf(stdout,"%s\n",lcStringOutput1.toAscii().constData());
   fprintf(stdout,"%s\n",lcStringOutput2.toAscii().constData());

   return 0;
}
```

Windows Code Setup and Compilation

- Tools: Mingw compiler and the QT4 library (Appendix E)

Windows Code Setup and Compilation Steps

1: Create a folder called pp1_15 that will store the source code files.

Steps continued on the next page

Windows Code Setup and Compilation Steps continued

2: Using a text editor, enter the source code for Program Phase 1-15 and save the file as pp1_15.cpp in the pp1_15 folder.

3: Open a QT command prompt and change directories to the pp1_15 folder.

4: Enter the following command:

```
qmake -project
```

5: Edit the pp1_15.pro file that has just been generated and add the following:

```
CONFIG += release
CONFIG += qt console
```

6: After editing the pp1_15.pro file, save and close the file and then enter the following commands:

```
qmake pp1_15.pro
make
```

The "qmake" command creates a file called Makefile, and the "make" command compiles the program. The steps detailed here create a release executable file that accesses the QT4 library in a shared dll.

Linux Code Setup and Compilation

- Tools: GNU GCC (Appendix B), QT4 Library (Appendix E)

Linux Code Setup and Compilation Steps

1: Create a folder called pp1_15 that will store the source code files.

2: Using a text editor, enter the source code for Program Phase 1-15 and save the file as pp1_15.cpp in the pp1_15 folder.

3: Open a terminal window and change directories to the pp1_15 folder. Enter the following command:

```
qmake -project
```

4: Edit the pp1_15.pro file that has just been generated and add the following two lines:

```
CONFIG += release
CONFIG += qt console
```

5: After editing the pp1_15.pro file, save and close the file and then enter the following commands:

```
qmake pp1_15.pro
make
```

Mac OS X Code Setup and Compilation

- Tools: Xcode (Appendix C), QT4 Library (Appendix E)

Mac OS X Code Setup and Compilation Steps

1: Create a folder called pp1_15 that will store the source code files.

2: Using a text editor, enter the source code for Program Phase 1-15 and save the file as pp1_15.cpp in the pp1_15 folder.

3: Open a terminal window and change directories to the pp1_15 folder. Enter the following command:

```
qmake -project
```

4: Edit the pp1_15.pro file that has just been generated and add the following two lines:

```
CONFIG += release
CONFIG += qt console
```

5: Enter the following command to create an Xcode project for Program Phase 1-15:

```
qmake -spec macx-xcode pp1_15.pro
```

6: Open the Xcode program and then open the newly created project.

7: Compile the program by activating the "Build" button.

Windows Program Execution

- To execute the pp1_15 program from a command prompt, change directories to pp1_15\release folder and then enter the following:

```
pp1_15.exe
```

Linux Program Execution

- To execute the pp1_15 program from a terminal window, change directories to pp1_15/release folder and then enter the following:

```
./pp1_15
```

Mac OS X Program Execution

- Execute Program

  To execute the pp1_15 program, activate the "Build/Go" button. The program output is displayed in the "Run Log" window. If using Xcode 3, the "Debugger Console" displays the program output. This window can be displayed by activating the "Console" menu item from the "Run" menu.

- Enter Command Line Parameters

```
Xcode - Activate Menu Item: Project → Edit Active Executable "pp1_15"
```

On the "pp1_15 Info" window, select the "Arguments" tab. Specify each command line parameter as a separate argument.

- Debug Program

To debug the pp1_15.cpp file one line at a time, place the cursor at the first line of code in the CBI: 1-15.1.1.3 code block and then create a breakpoint.

```
   Xcode 2.4 - Activate Menu Item: Debug → Add Breakpoint at Current Line
   Xcode 3 - Activate Menu Item: Run → Manage Breakpoints → Add
Breakpoint at Current Line
```

After the break point has been created, the program can be debugged.

```
Xcode - Activate Menu Item: Build → Build and Debug
```

Program Phase 1-16

C++ ▪ wxWidgets ▪ Multi-Platform

Console Based Hello World! with Strings

- Program Phase Task 1 is implemented in Program Phase 1-16 using the C++ programming language and the wxWidgets library. The wxWidgets library is normally used to create cross platform GUI based applications, but it can also be used to create console based applications.
- The wxString class found in the wxWidgets library is used to implement strings.
- The wxFprintf() function is used to output to standard output.

Code Block Features

The Program Phase 1-16 code blocks illustrate the following programming features using the C++ programming language and the wxWidgets library:

- **Console Application**
- **Integer and String Variable Declarations**
- **Application Command Line Parameters**
- **Case/Switch Statement**
- **String Literal Assignment and String Concatenation**
- **Console Application Standard Output**

C++ wxWidgets
Console Application

- The wxInitialize() function initializes the wxWidgets library components for the program. If this function returns a Boolean "false" value, the initialization failed. For each successful call to the wxInitialize() function, a corresponding call to the wxUnitialize() function should be called before exiting the program.

test1.cpp: C++ wxWidgets Console Application

```
#include "wx/wx.h"

int main(int argc, char* argv[])
{
   if (wxInitialize() == false)
   {
      wxFprintf(stderr,wxT("Failed to initialize wxWidgets.\n"));
      return 1;
   }
```

test1.cpp continued on the next page

test1.cpp: C++ wxWidgets Console Application continued

```
   // C++ code that accesses the wxWidgets library goes here.

   wxUninitialize();
   return 0;
}
```

C++ wxWidgets
Integer and String Variable Declarations

- Program Phase 1-16 implements strings with the wxString class. The "wx/wx.h" header file needs to be included in the source file in order to access the wxString class. The wxString class supports ASCII strings and Unicode strings depending on which build of the wxWidgets library is being used.

test2.cpp: C++ wxWidgets Integer and String Variable Declarations

```
#include "wx/wx.h"

int main(int argc, char* argv[])
{
   if (wxInitialize() == false)
   {
      wxFprintf(stderr,wxT("Failed to initialize wxWidgets.\n"));
      return 1;
   }

   int lnVar1;
   wxString lcVar2;
   wxUninitialize();

   return 0;
}
```

C++ wxWidgets
Application Command Line Parameters

- A GUI based wxWidgets application provides the command line parameters as properties of the wxApp object, but since a GUI based application isn't created for Program Phase 1-16, the command line parameters are accessed from the main() function parameters.

test3.cpp: C++ wxWidgets Application Command Line Parameters

```
#include "wx/wx.h"

int main(int argc, char* argv[])
{
   if (wxInitialize() == false)
   {
      wxFprintf(stderr,wxT("Failed to initialize wxWidgets.\n"));
      return 1;
   }

   wxString lcCmdLineParam1;

   if ((argc - 1) == 1)
   {
```

test3.cpp continued on the next page

test3.cpp: C++ wxWidgets Command Line Parameters continued

```
        lcCmdLineParam1.Printf("%s",wxT(argv[1]));
    }

    wxUninitialize();
    return 0;
}
```

C++ wxWidgets
Case/Switch Statement

- The following example implements a "switch" statement:

test4.cpp: C++ wxWidgets Case/Switch Statement

```
#include "wx/wx.h"

int main(int argc, char* argv[])
{
   if (wxInitialize() == false)
   {
      wxFprintf(stderr,wxT("Failed to initialize wxWidgets.\n"));
      return 1;
   }

   int lnCmdLineParamCount;
   lnCmdLineParamCount = argc - 1;

   switch(lnCmdLineParamCount)
   {
      case 0:
         // No command line parameters entered.
         break;

      case 1:
         // One command line parameter entered.
         break;

      default:

         ; // More than one command line parameter entered.
   }

   wxUninitialize();
   return 0;
}
```

C++ wxWidgets
String Literal Assignment and String Concatenation

- The wxT() macro supports ASCII and Unicode string literals.
- The following example stores two string literals and then concatenates the strings:

test5.cpp: C++ wxWidgets String Literal Assignment and String Concatenation

```
#include "wx/wx.h"
int main(int argc, char* argv[])
{
   if (wxInitialize() == false)
   {
      wxFprintf(stderr,wxT("Failed to initialize wxWidgets.\n"));
      return 1;
   }

   wxString lcString1;
   wxString lcString2;
   wxString lcString3;

   lcString1.Printf(wxT("Hello"));
   lcString2.Printf(wxT("World!"));
   lcString3 << lcString1 << wxT(" ") << lcString2;

   wxUninitialize();
   return 0;
}
```

C++ wxWidgets Console Application Standard Output

- The wxFprintf() function can be used to output the text stored in a wxString variable. This function will work with an ANSI or Unicode build of the wxWidgets library.

test6.cpp: C++ wxWidgets Console Application Standard Output

```
#include <stdio.h>
#include "wx/wx.h"

int main(int argc, char* argv[])
{
   if (wxInitialize() == false)
   {
      wxFprintf(stderr,wxT("Failed to initialize wxWidgets.\n"));
      return 1;
   }

   wxString lcString1;
   lcString1.Printf(wxT("Hello World!"));
   wxFprintf(stdout,wxT("%s\n"),lcString1.c_str());

   wxUninitialize();
   return 0;
}
```

Source Code Files

- Text files: pp1_16.cpp

pp1_16.cpp: Program Phase 1-16 Source Code

```
//*****************************************************************************
// Program Phase 1-16 C++ wxWidgets Hello World! with Strings                 *
// Programming Tasks Illustrated: Console Application                         *
//                                Integer and String Variable Declarations    *
//                                Application Command Line Parameters         *
//                                Case/Switch Statement                       *
//                                String Literal Assignment and Concatenation *
//                                Console Application Standard Output         *
//*****************************************************************************

//*****************************************************************************
// File: pp1_16.cpp                                                           *
// Reserved                                                                   *
//*****************************************************************************

#include <stdio.h>
#include "wx/wx.h"


//*****************************************************************************
// Program Phase 1-16 Main                                                    *
// Define the Entry Point of Execution (EPE) for Program Phase 1-16           *
// CBI:  1-16.1.1.1                                                           *
//*****************************************************************************

int main(int argc, char* argv[])
{
   if (wxInitialize() == false)
   {
      wxFprintf(stderr,wxT("Failed to initialize wxWidgets.\n"));
      return 1;
   }


//*****************************************************************************
// Program Phase 1-16 Main                                                    *
// Declare the local variables for the "main" program                         *
// CBI:  1-16.1.1.2                                                           *
//*****************************************************************************

   int lnCmdLineParamCount;
   wxString lcString1;
   wxString lcString2;
   wxString lcStringOutput1;
   wxString lcStringOutput2;


//*****************************************************************************
// Program Phase 1-16 Main                                                    *
// Store the command line parameters                                          *
// CBI:  1-16.1.1.3                                                           *
//*****************************************************************************

   lnCmdLineParamCount = argc - 1;


//*****************************************************************************
// Program Phase 1-16 Main                                                    *
// Parse the command line parameters using a Case/Switch statement           *
// CBI:  1-16.1.1.4                                                           *
//*****************************************************************************

   switch(lnCmdLineParamCount)
   {
      case 0:
        lcStringOutput1.Printf(wxT("You entered no command line parameters."));
        break;
```

pp1_16.cpp continued on the next page

ppl_16.cpp: Program Phase 1-16 Source Code continued

```
      case 1:
         lcStringOutput1.Printf(wxT("Command line parameter entered:  %s"),
                                      wxT(argv[1]));
         break;

      default:

     lcStringOutput1.Printf(wxT("The command line is limted to 1 parameter."));
   }


//************************************************************************
// Program Phase 1-16 Main                                              *
// Concatenate two string variables                                     *
// CBI:  1-16.1.1.5                                                     *
//************************************************************************

   lcString1.Printf(wxT("Hello"));
   lcString2.Printf(wxT("World!"));
   lcStringOutput2 << lcString1 << wxT(" ") << lcString2;


//************************************************************************
// Program Phase 1-16 Main                                              *
// Output to standard output                                            *
// CBI:  1-16.1.1.6                                                     *
//************************************************************************

   wxFprintf(stdout,wxT("%s\n"),lcStringOutput1.c_str());
   wxFprintf(stdout,wxT("%s\n"),lcStringOutput2.c_str());
   wxUninitialize();

   return 0;
}
```

Windows – Code Setup and Compilation

- Tools: Microsoft Visual C++ 2008 Express Edition (msdn.microsoft.com), wxWidgets library (Appendix D)

Windows Code Setup and Compilation Steps

1: Start the Visual C++ 2008 Express Edition program.

2: VC++ EE - Activate Menu Item: File → New → Project

For the "Project type", select "Win32" and then select the "Win32 Console Application" template. Enter ppl_16 as the project "Name". Enter the appropriate folder as the project "Location". Make sure that the "Create directory for solution" check box is not checked. Activate the "OK" button to proceed with the "Win32 Application Wizard".

3: Activate the "Next" button of the "Win32 Application Wizard".

4: Verify that a "Console Application" is selected and also check the "Empty project" check box. Activate the "Finish" button of the "Win32 Application Wizard".

Steps continued on the next page

Windows Code Setup and Compilation Steps continued

5: VC++ EE - Activate Menu Item: Project → Add New Item

On the "Add New Item" dialog window, select the "Visual C++ → Code" category and then select the "C++ File" template. Enter pp1_16.cpp for the file "Name" and then activate the "Add" button. Enter the source code for the pp1_16.cpp file.

6: VC++ EE - Activate Menu Item: Build → Configuration Manager

Select "Release" or "Debug" for the "Active solution configuration". This setting needs to match the setting specified when the wxWidgets library was compiled (Appendix D).

7: VC++ EE - Activate Menu Item: Project → pp1_16 Properties

Enter the following settings:

Configuration Properties → General → Character Set

For ANSI Configuration:

```
"Use Multi-Byte Character Set"
```

For Unicode Configuration:

```
"Use Unicode Character Set"
```

This setting needs to match the setting specified when the wxWidgets library was compiled (Appendix D).

Configuration Properties → C/C++ → General → Additional Include Directories

```
"$(wxwin)\lib\vc_lib\msw";"$(wxwin)\include"
```

Configuration Properties → C/C++ → Preprocessor → Processor Definitions

For Release Configuration:

```
WIN32;__WXMSW__;_CONSOLE;NOPCH
```

For Debug Configuration:

```
WIN32;__WXMSW__;__WXDEBUG__;_CONSOLE;NOPCH
```

This setting needs to match the setting specified when the wxWidgets library was compiled (Appendix D).

Configuration Properties → C/C++ → Code Generation → Runtime Library

For Release Configuration:

```
Multi-threaded (/MT) or Multi-threaded DLL (/MD)
```

For Debug Configuration:

```
Multi-threaded Debug /MTd or Multi-threaded Debug DLL (/MDd)
```

This setting needs to match the setting specified when the wxWidgets library was compiled (Appendix D).

Configuration Properties → Linker → General → Additional Library Directories

```
"$(wxwin)\lib\vc_lib"
```

Steps continued on the next page

Windows Code Setup and Compilation Steps continued

8: Continue entering settings on the "pp1_16 Property Pages" window.

Configuration Properties → Linker → Input → Additional Dependencies

For Release Configuration:

```
wxmsw28_core.lib wxbase28.lib
```

For Debug Configuration:

```
wxmsw28d_core.lib wxbase28d.lib
```

The name of the library files is dependent on the version of wxWidgets installed. Substitute the appropriate version number in the file name to match the version of the wxWidgets library installed on your computer. This setting needs to match the setting specified when the wxWidgets library was compiled (Appendix D).

Configuration Properties → Linker → System → SubSystem

```
Console (/SUBSYSTEM:CONSOLE)
```

9: Close the "pp1_16 Property Pages" window by activating the "OK" button.

10: VC++ EE - Activate Menu Item: Build → Build pp1_16

After the build is successful, a compiled file called pp1_16.exe will be found in either the Release or Debug folder of the pp1_16 folder.

Windows Command Prompt Compilation Steps

1: From a Visual Studio 2008 command prompt, enter one of the following commands on a single line.

For Release Configuration:

```
cl.exe /I "C:\Program Files\Microsoft SDK's\Windows\v6.0A\Include"
 /I "c:\wxWidgets-2.8.6\lib\vc_lib\msw"
 /I "c:\wxWidgets-2.8.6\include"
 /D "WIN32"
 /D "__WXMSW__"
 /D "_CONSOLE"
 /MT /Fo"Release\\" /EHsc /c pp1_16.cpp
```

For Debug Configuration:

```
cl.exe /I "C:\Program Files\Microsoft SDK's\Windows\v6.0A\Include"
 /I "c:\wxWidgets-2.8.6\lib\vc_lib\msw"
 /I "c:\wxWidgets-2.8.6\include"
 /D "WIN32"
 /D "__WXMSW__"
 /D "__WXDEBUG__"
 /D "_CONSOLE"
 /MTd /Fo"Debug\\" /EHsc /c pp1_16.cpp
```

Substitute the appropriate name for the library files that match the version of the wxWidgets library and platform SDK installed. The Runtime Library switch (/MT, MTd, /MD, /MDd) needs to match the setting used to compile the wxWidgets source code (Appendix D).

Steps continued on the next page

Windows Command Prompt Compilation Steps continued

2: Run the linker to create the ppl_16.exe file from the ppl_16.obj file.

For Release Configuration:

```
link.exe /OUT:"Release\ppl_16.exe" /INCREMENTAL:NO
/LIBPATH:"c:\wxWidgets-2.8.6\lib\vc_lib"
/LIBPATH:"C:\Program Files\Microsoft SDK's\Windows\v6.0A\Lib"
/SUBSYSTEM:CONSOLE
wxmsw28_core.lib wxbase28.lib user32.lib advapi32.lib
shell32.lib ole32.lib .\release\ppl_16.obj
```

For Debug Configuration:

```
link.exe /OUT:"Debug\ppl_16.exe" /INCREMENTAL:NO
/LIBPATH:"c:\wxWidgets-2.8.6\lib\vc_lib"
/LIBPATH:"C:\Program Files\Microsoft SDK's\Windows\v6.0A\Lib"
/SUBSYSTEM:CONSOLE
wxmsw28d_core.lib wxbase28d.lib user32.lib advapi32.lib
shell32.lib ole32.lib .\debug\ppl_16.obj
```

Substitute the appropriate name for the path and library files that match the version of the wxWidgets library and platform SDK installed. Each of the preceding commands should be entered on a single line.

Linux – Code Setup and Compilation

- Tools: GNU GCC, KDevelop (Appendix B), wxWidgets library (Appendix D)

Linux Code Setup and Compilation Steps

1: Update the LD_LIBRARY_PATH variable and then start the KDevelop program.

```
export LD_LIBRARY_PATH=/usr/local/lib:$LD_LIBRARY_PATH
kdevelop &
```

2: KDevelop - Activate Menu Item: Project → New Project

Select the "C++ → Simple Hello world program" template. Set the "Application name" to ppl_16. Set the "Location" to the appropriate folder. Activate the "Next" button four times and then activate the "Finish" button.

3: KDevelop - Activate Menu Item: Project → Build Configuration → debug

4: Enter the source code for the ppl_16.cpp file. Replace any existing code in the file.

5: Before compiling the ppl_16.cpp source code file, additional settings for accessing the wxWidgets library need to be entered into the KDevelop project. From a terminal window, enter the following:

For Release Configuration:

```
wx-config --unicode=no --debug=no --static=yes --cxxflags > cxxresults.txt
```

For Debug Configuration:

```
wx-config --unicode=no --debug=yes --static=yes --cxxflags >
cxxresults.txt
```

Steps continued on the next page

Linux Code Setup and Compilation Steps continued

6: Next, run this command:

For Release Configuration

```
wx-config --unicode=no --debug=no --static=yes --libs > libresults.txt
```

For Debug Configuration

```
wx-config --unicode=no --debug=yes --static=yes --libs > libresults.txt
```

7: KDevelop - Activate Menu Item: Project → Project Options

8: Click on the "Configure Options" item on the left pane. Select the "debug" configuration. Click on the "C++" tab. Here you will see the "Compiler flags" text box. The results of running the wx-config utility stored in the cxxresults.txt file must be copied and pasted here. Next, click on the "General" tab and paste the contents of the libresults.txt file in the "Linker flags" text box. You may be prompted to "Re-run configure". Select the "Do Not Run" button.

9: KDevelop - Activate Menu Item: Build → Run automake and friends

10: KDevelop - Activate Menu Item: Build → Run Configure

11: KDevelop - Activate Menu Item: Build → Build Project

If a message is displayed concerning no Makefile, activate the "Run Them" button.

Linux Command Prompt Compilation

The following commands can be used to compile the pp1_16.cpp file:

For Release Configuration

```
g++ pp1_16.cpp `wx-config --unicode=no --debug=no --static=yes --libs`
`wx-config --unicode=no --debug=no --static=yes --cxxflags` -o pp1_16
```

For Debug Configuration

```
g++ pp1_16.cpp `wx-config --unicode=no --debug=yes --static=yes --libs`
`wx-config --unicode=no --debug=yes --static=yes --cxxflags` -o pp1_16
```

The preceding commands should be entered on a single line inside the source code folder (pp1_16/src). The command line settings need to match the settings specified when the wxWidgets library was compiled (Appendix D).

- Mac OS X code setup and compilation steps can be found at the following URL:

  http://www.wxwidgets.org/wiki/index.php/Getting_started_on_OS_X

Windows – Program Execution

- Execute Program

  VC++ EE - Activate Menu Item: Debug → Start Without Debugging

- Enter Command Line Parameters

```
VC++ EE - Activate Menu Item: Project → pp1_16 Properties
```

Expand the "Configuration Properties" entry and then click on the "Debugging" item. Command line parameters can be specified in the "Command Arguments" field.

- Debug Program

Set the "Generate Debug Info" entry in the "pp1_16 Property Pages" to "Yes". This setting is found under the "Configuration Properties → Linker → Debugging" item. After this has been set, the program can be debugged.

```
VC++ EE - Activate Menu Item: Debug → Step Into
```

Linux – Program Execution

- Execute Program

```
KDevelop - Activate Menu Item: Build → Execute Program
```

- Enter Command Line Parameters

```
KDevelop - Activate Menu Item: Project → Project Options
```

On the left side of the dialog window, select the "Run Options" entry. Check the "Main Program" check box. Specify the path to the pp1_16 executable file (pp1_16/debug/src or pp1_16/src). The command line arguments can be specified in the "Run Arguments" field. Depending on the currently installed version of KDevelop, this setting may be found in the "Debugger" options of the "Project Options" dialog window.

- Debug Program

Include the debug information in the program build.

```
KDevelop - Activate Menu Item: Project → Project Options
```

Click on the "Configure Options" item. Select the debug "Configuration" and then enter "--enable-debug=full" (without quotes) in the "Configure arguments" field on the "General" tab. Close the "Project Options" dialog window.

Select the debug configuration for the project.

```
KDevelop - Activate Menu Item: Project → Build Configuration → debug
```

Set the cursor position in the source file to the first line of code in the CBI: 1-16.1.1.3 code block. Create a breakpoint.

```
KDevelop - Activate Menu Item: Debug → Toggle Breakpoint
```

After the breakpoint has been created, the program can be debugged.

```
KDevelop - Activate Menu Item: Debug → Start
```

Program Phase 1-17

C ▪ Core Foundation ▪ Mac OS X

Console Based Hello World! with Strings

- Program Phase Task 1 is implemented in Program Phase 1-17 using the C programming language and the Core Foundation library on the Mac OS X platform.
- The CFString class is used to implement strings.
- The CFSHOW() function is used to output to standard output.

Code Block Features

The Program Phase 1-17 code blocks illustrate the following programming features using the C programming language and the Core Foundation library:

- **Console Application**
- **Integer and String Variable Declarations**
- **Application Command Line Parameters**
- **Case/Switch Statement**
- **String Literal Assignment and String Concatenation**
- **Console Application Standard Output**

C with Core Foundation
Console Application

- The Core Foundation library can be used in a standard C console application.

test1.c: C with Core Foundation Console Application

```
#include <CoreFoundation/CoreFoundation.h>

int main(int argc, char* argv[])
{
   // C code that accesses the Core Foundation library goes here.
   return 0;
}
```

C with Core Foundation
Integer and String Variable Declarations

The CFString class stores data in the UTF-16 Unicode format.

- The following example declares an integer variable and a string variable:

test2.c: C with Core Foundation Integer and String Variable Declarations

```
#include <CoreFoundation/CoreFoundation.h>

int main(int argc, char* argv[])
{
   int lnVar1;
   CFStringRef lcVar2;

   return 0;
}
```

C with Core Foundation Application Command Line Parameters

- The following example stores a single command line parameter in a string variable:

test3.c: C with Core Foundation Application Command Line Parameters

```
#include <CoreFoundation/CoreFoundation.h>

int main(int argc, char* argv[])
{
  CFStringRef lcCmdLineParam1;

  if ((argc - 1) == 1)
  {
      lcCmdLineParam1 = CFStringCreateWithFormat(NULL,NULL,CFSTR("%s"),argv[1]);
  }

   return 0;
}
```

C with Core Foundation Case/Switch Statement

- The following example implements a "switch" statement:

test4.c: C with Core Foundation Case/Switch Statement

```
#include <CoreFoundation/CoreFoundation.h>

int main(int argc, char* argv[])
{
   int lnCmdLineParamCount;
   lnCmdLineParamCount = argc - 1;

   switch(lnCmdLineParamCount)
   {
      case 0:
          // No command line parameters entered.
         break;

      case 1:
         // One command line parameter entered.
         break;
```

test4.c continued on the next page

test4.c: C with Core Foundation Case/Switch Statement

```
      default:
         ; // More than one command line parameter entered.
   }
   return 0;
}
```

C with Core Foundation String Literal Assignment and String Concatenation

- The following example stores two string literals and then concatenates the strings:

test5.c: C with Core Foundation String Literal Assign. and String Concatenation

```
#include <CoreFoundation/CoreFoundation.h>

int main(int argc, char* argv[])
{
   CFStringRef lcString1;
   CFStringRef lcString2;
   CFStringRef lcString3;

   lcString1 = CFSTR("Hello");
   lcString2 = CFSTR("World!");
   lcString3 = CFStringCreateWithFormat(NULL,NULL,CFSTR("%@ %@"),
                                         lcString1,lcString2);

   return 0;
}
```

C with Core Foundation Console Application Standard Output

- The following example outputs text to standard output:

test6.c: C with Core Foundation Console Application Standard Output

```
#include <CoreFoundation/CoreFoundation.h>

int main(int argc, char* argv[])
{
   CFStringRef lcString1;

   lcString1 = CFSTR("Hello World!");
   CFShow(lcString1);

   return 0;
}
```

Source Code Files

- Text files: pp1_17.c

pp1_17.c: Program Phase 1-17 Source Code

```
//****************************************************************************
// Program Phase 1-17 OS X C Core Foundation Hello World! with Strings        *
// Programming Tasks Illustrated: Console Application                         *
//                                Integer and String Variable Declarations    *
//                                Application Command Line Parameters         *
//                                Case/Switch Statement                       *
//                                String Literal Assignment and Concatenation *
//                                Console Application Standard Output         *
//****************************************************************************

//****************************************************************************
// File: pp1_17.c                                                             *
// Reserved                                                                   *
//****************************************************************************

#include <CoreFoundation/CoreFoundation.h>


//****************************************************************************
// Program Phase 1-17 Main                                                    *
// Define the Entry Point of Execution (EPE) for Program Phase 1-17           *
// CBI:  1-17.1.1.1                                                           *
//****************************************************************************

int main (int argc, const char * argv[])
{


//****************************************************************************
// Program Phase 1-17 Main                                                    *
// Declare the local variables for the "main" program                        *
// CBI:  1-17.1.1.2                                                           *
//****************************************************************************

   int lnCmdLineParamCount;
   CFStringRef lcString1;
   CFStringRef lcString2;
   CFStringRef lcStringOutput1;
   CFStringRef lcStringOutput2;


//****************************************************************************
// Program Phase 1-17 Main                                                    *
// Store the command line parameters                                          *
// CBI:  1-17.1.1.3                                                           *
//****************************************************************************

   // The local argv array stores the command line parameters.
   lnCmdLineParamCount = argc - 1;


//****************************************************************************
// Program Phase 1-17 Main                                                    *
// Parse the command line parameters using a Case/Switch statement            *
// CBI:  1-17.1.1.4                                                           *
//****************************************************************************

   switch (lnCmdLineParamCount)
   {
      case 0:
         lcStringOutput1 = CFSTR("You entered no command line parameters.");
         break;

      case 1:
         lcStringOutput1 = CFStringCreateWithFormat(NULL,NULL,
                  CFSTR("Command line parameter entered: %s"),argv[1]);
```

pp1_17.c continued on the next page

pp1_17.c: Program Phase 1-17 Source Code continued

```
            break;

        default:

         lcStringOutput1 = CFSTR("The command line is limited to 1 parameter.");
    }


//*****************************************************************************
// Program Phase 1-17 Main                                                   *
// Concatenate two string variables                                          *
// CBI:   1-17.1.1.5                                                         *
//*****************************************************************************

    lcString1 = CFSTR("Hello");
    lcString2 = CFSTR("World!");

    lcStringOutput2 = CFStringCreateWithFormat(NULL,NULL,CFSTR("%@ %@"),
                                               lcString1,lcString2);


//*****************************************************************************
// Program Phase 1-17 Main                                                   *
// Output to standard output                                                 *
// CBI:   1-17.1.1.6                                                         *
//*****************************************************************************

    CFShow(lcStringOutput1);
    CFShow(lcStringOutput2);

    return 0;
}
```

Code Setup and Compilation

- Tools: Xcode (Appendix C), Core Foundation library

Code Setup and Compilation Steps

1: Start the Xcode program.

2: Xcode - Activate Menu Item: File → New Project

Select "Command Line Utility → Core Foundation Tool" and then activate the "Next" button.

3: Set the "Project Name" to pp1_17. Set the "Project Directory" to the appropriate folder. Activate the "Finish" button.

4: Delete the main.c file that has been automatically added to the project.

5: Xcode - Activate Menu Item: File → New File

Select "Empty File in Project" and then activate the "Next" button. Set the "File name" to pp1_17.c and the "Location" to the pp1_17 folder and then activate the "Finish" button. Enter the source code for Program Phase 1-17 into the pp1_17.c file.

Steps continued on the next page

Code Setup and Compilation Steps continued

6: Compile the program by activating the "Build" button.

Command Prompt Compilation

Enter the following command in the pp1_17 folder:

```
gcc -o pp1_17 pp1_17.c -framework Carbon
```

Program Execution

- Execute Program

To execute the pp1_17 program, activate the "Build/Go" button in the Xcode IDE. The program output is displayed in the "Run Log" window. If using Xcode 3, the "Debugger Console" displays the program output. This window can be displayed by activating the "Console" menu item from the "Run" menu.

- Enter Command Line Parameters

```
Xcode - Activate Menu Item: Project → Edit Active Executable "pp1_17"
```

On the "pp1_17 Info" window, select the "Arguments" tab. Specify each command line parameter as a separate argument.

- Debug Program

Place the cursor in the CBI: 1-17.1.1.3 code block and then activate the following menu items:

```
Xcode 2.4 - Activate Menu Item: Debug → Add Breakpoint at Current Line
Xcode 3 - Activate Menu Item: Run → Manage Breakpoints → Add
Breakpoint at Current Line

Xcode - Activate Menu Item: Build → Build and Debug
```

Program Phase 1-18

Objective-C ▪ Cocoa ▪ Mac OS X

Console Based Hello World! with Strings

- Program Phase Task 1 is implemented in Program Phase 1-18 using the Objective-C programming language and the Cocoa Foundation Kit framework. The Cocoa API is made up of several frameworks including the Application Kit (AppKit) and Foundation Kit frameworks. The Foundation Kit is not the same as the Core Foundation framework. The AppKit is used for creating a GUI for an application while the Foundation Kit framework contains useful classes such as the NSString class that is used in Program Phase 1-18. The AppKit framework is used in Program Phase 3-18 and Program Phase 4-18 to build GUI based applications.

- The NSString class is used to implement strings.

- The writeToFile() method of the NSString class is used to output to standard output.

Code Block Features

The Program Phase 1-18 code blocks illustrate the following programming features using the Objective-C programming language and the Cocoa Foundation framework:

- **Console Application**

- **Integer and String Variable Declarations**

- **Application Command Line Parameters**

- **Case/Switch Statement**

- **String Literal Assignment and String Concatenation**

- **Console Application Standard Output**

Objective-C with Cocoa
Console Application

- The Entry Point of Execution (EPE) in an Objective-C program is a main() function that is defined the same as a C/C++ main() function.

- When an Objective-C class instance (object) is created, it is given a reference count of one. The memory for the object is not de-allocated until its reference count reaches zero. The reference count for an object can be decremented manually by sending the object a release message. If an "autorelease" message is assigned to an object, an NSAutoreleasePool object can automatically send a "release" message to the object in question. The NSAutoreleasePool class is used to keep track of objects that have been sent an "autorelease" message. When a "release" message is received by an NSAutoreleasePool class instance, and its reference count reaches zero, before it is deallocated, it will send a "release" message to each of the objects that have previously been sent an "autorelease" message. An Objective-C application should start by creating an NSAutoreleasePool object, and the program should send a "release" message to the NSAutorelease object before exiting.

test1.m: Objective-C with Cocoa Console Application

```
#import <Foundation/Foundation.h>

int main(int argc, char* argv[])
{
   NSAutoreleasePool * loPool = [[NSAutoreleasePool alloc] init];

   // Objective-C code that accesses the Foundation Framework goes here.

   [loPool release];
   return 0;
}
```

Objective-C with Cocoa
Integer and String Variable Declarations

- The NSString class instance stores string data in the UTF-16 Unicode format.
- The following example declares an integer variable and a string variable:

test2.m: Objective-C with Cocoa Integer and String Variable Declarations

```
#import <Foundation/Foundation.h>

int main(int argc, char* argv[])
{
   NSAutoreleasePool * loPool = [[NSAutoreleasePool alloc] init];
   int lnVar1;
   NSString* lcVar2;
   [loPool release];
   return 0;
}
```

Objective-C with Cocoa
Application Command Line Parameters

- The following example stores a single command line parameter in a string variable:

test3.m: Objective-C with Cocoa Application Command Line Parameters

```
#import <Foundation/Foundation.h>

int main(int argc, char* argv[])
{
   NSAutoreleasePool * loPool = [[NSAutoreleasePool alloc] init];
   NSString* lcCmdLineParam1;

   if ((argc - 1) == 1)
   {
      lcCmdLineParam1 = [NSString stringWithFormat:@"%@",[NSString
stringWithCString:argv[1]]];
   }
   [loPool release];
   return 0;
}
```

Objective-C with Cocoa
Case/Switch Statement

- The following example implements a "switch" statement:

test4.m: Objective-C with Cocoa Case/Switch Statement

```
#import <Foundation/Foundation.h>

int main(int argc, char* argv[])
{
   NSAutoreleasePool * loPool = [[NSAutoreleasePool alloc] init];
   int lnCmdLineParamCount;
   lnCmdLineParamCount = argc - 1;

   switch(lnCmdLineParamCount)
   {
      case 0:
         // No command line parameters entered.
         break;

      case 1:
         // One command line parameter entered.
         break;

      default:
        ;  // More than one command line parameter entered.
   }
   [loPool release];
   return 0;
}
```

Objective-C with Cocoa
String Literal Assignment and String Concatenation

- NSString instances can be created and referenced in an NSString pointer variable by prefacing a string literal with the "@" construct. When instantiating an NSString class instance using the "@" construct, there is no need to send a release message to it in order to release its memory before exiting because such strings are considered constants. If an NSString instance is created using the "alloc" message, a "release" message should be sent to it before exiting in order to release the allocated memory. The stringWithFormat() method returns an NSString object that is automatically assigned to the most recently created NSAutoreleasePool, so no "release" message needs to be manually sent to it.

- The following example stores two string literals and then concatenates the strings:

test5.m: Objective-C w/ Cocoa String Literal Assignment and String Concatenation

```
#import <Foundation/Foundation.h>

int main(int argc, char* argv[])
{
   NSAutoreleasePool * loPool = [[NSAutoreleasePool alloc] init];
   NSString* lcString1;
   NSString* lcString2;
   NSString* lcString3;

   lcString1 = @"Hello";
```

test5.m continued on the next page

test5.m: Objective-C w/ Cocoa String Literal Assign. and String Concat. continued

```
   lcString2 = [[NSString alloc] initWithString:@"World!"];
   lcString3 = [NSString stringWithFormat:@"%@ %@",lcString1,lcString2];
  // equivalent to:
  // lcString3 = [[[NSString alloc] initWithFormat:@"%@ %@",lcString1,lcString2]
  //              autorelease];
   [lcString2 release];
   [loPool release];
   return 0;
}
```

Objective-C with Cocoa Console Application Standard Output

- The following example outputs text to standard output:

test6.m: Objective-C with Cocoa Console Application Standard Output

```
#import <Foundation/Foundation.h>

int main(int argc, char* argv[])
{
   NSAutoreleasePool * loPool = [[NSAutoreleasePool alloc] init];
   NSString* lcString1;

   lcString1 = @"Hello World!";
   lcString1 = [NSString stringWithFormat:@"%@ %@",lcString1,@"\n"];
   [lcString1 writeToFile:@"/dev/stdout" atomically:NO];

   [loPool release];
   return 0;
}
```

Source Code Files

- Text files: pp1_18.m

pp1_18.m: Program Phase 1-18 Source Code

```
//**************************************************************************
// Program Phase 1-18 OS X Objective-C Cocoa Hello World! with Strings     *
// Programming Tasks Illustrated: Console Application                      *
//                                Integer and String Variable Declarations *
//                                Application Command Line Parameters      *
//                                Case/Switch Statement                    *
//                                String Literal Assignment and Concatenation *
//                                Console Application Standard Output      *
//**************************************************************************

//**************************************************************************
// File: pp1_18.m                                                          *
// Reserved                                                                *
//**************************************************************************

#import <Foundation/Foundation.h>

//**************************************************************************
// Program Phase 1-18 Main                                                 *
// Define the Entry Point of Execution (EPE) for Program Phase 1-18        *
// CBI:  1-18.1.1.1                                                        *
//**************************************************************************
```

pp1_18.m continued on the next page

pp1_18.m: Program Phase 1-18 Source Code continued

```
int main (int argc, const char * argv[])
{
   NSAutoreleasePool * loPool = [[NSAutoreleasePool alloc] init];


//*****************************************************************************
// Program Phase 1-18 Main                                                    *
// Declare the local variables for the "main" program                         *
// CBI:  1-18.1.1.2                                                           *
//*****************************************************************************

   int lnCmdLineParamCount;
   NSString* lcString1;
   NSString* lcString2;
   NSString* lcStringOutput1;
   NSString* lcStringOutput2;


//*****************************************************************************
// Program Phase 1-18 Main                                                    *
// Store the command line parameters                                          *
// CBI:  1-18.1.1.3                                                           *
//*****************************************************************************

   // The command line parameters are stored in the argv array.
   lnCmdLineParamCount = argc - 1;


//*****************************************************************************
// Program Phase 1-18 Main                                                    *
// Parse the command line parameters using a Case/Switch statement            *
// CBI:  1-18.1.1.4                                                           *
//*****************************************************************************

   switch (lnCmdLineParamCount)
   {
      case 0:
          lcStringOutput1 = @"You entered no command line parameters.";
         break;

      case 1:
          lcStringOutput1 = [NSString stringWithFormat:@"Command line parameter
entered:  %@",[NSString stringWithCString:argv[1]]];

         break;

      default:
          lcStringOutput1 = @"The command line is limited to 1 parameter.";
   }


//*****************************************************************************
// Program Phase 1-18 Main                                                    *
// Concatenate two string variables                                           *
// CBI:  1-18.1.1.5                                                           *
//*****************************************************************************

   lcString1 = @"Hello";
   lcString2 = @"World!";
   lcStringOutput2 = [NSString stringWithFormat:@"%@ %@",lcString1,lcString2];


//*****************************************************************************
// Program Phase 1-18 Main                                                    *
// Output to standard output                                                  *
// CBI:  1-18.1.1.6                                                           *
//*****************************************************************************
```

pp1_18.m continued on the next page

ppl_18.m: Program Phase 1-18 Source Code continued

```
    lcStringOutput1 = [NSString stringWithFormat:@"%@ %@",lcStringOutput1,@"\n"];
    [lcStringOutput1 writeToFile:@"/dev/stdout" atomically:NO];

    lcStringOutput2 = [NSString stringWithFormat:@"%@ %@",lcStringOutput2,@"\n"];
    [lcStringOutput2 writeToFile:@"/dev/stdout" atomically:NO];

    [loPool release];
    return 0;
}
```

Code Setup and Compilation

- Tools: Xcode (Appendix C), AppKit

Code Setup and Compilation Steps

1: Start the Xcode IDE program.

2: Xcode - Activate Menu Item: File → New Project

Select "Command Line Utility → Foundation Tool" and then activate the "Next" button.

3: Set the "Project Name" to ppl_18 and set the "Project Directory" to the appropriate folder. Activate the "Finish" button.

4: Enter the source code for Program Phase 1-18 into the ppl_18.m file that has been automatically created. Replace any existing code in the file. Compile the program by activating the "Build" button.

Command Prompt Compilation

```
gcc -o ppl_18 ppl_18.m -framework Cocoa
```

Program Execution

- Execute Program

  Activate the "Build/Go" button in the Xcode IDE.

- Enter Command Line Parameters

  `Xcode - Activate Menu Item: Project → Edit Active Executable "ppl_18"`

  On the "ppl_18 Info" window, select the "Arguments" tab. Specify each command line parameter as a separate argument.

- Debug Program

  Place the cursor in the CBI: 1-18.1.1.3 code block

```
   Xcode 2.4 - Activate Menu Item: Debug → Add Breakpoint at Current Line
   Xcode 3 - Activate Menu Item: Run → Manage Breakpoints → Add
Breakpoint at Current Line
   Xcode - Activate Menu Item: Build → Build and Debug
```

Program Phase Task 2

Application Name Console Output

- The program specified by Program Phase Task 2 retrieves the name of the currently running program and stores it in a string variable. Each character in the string is then copied one at a time to an individual array element. A fixed length array of 200 characters is used as the destination for the individual characters in the program. If the program name is greater than 200 characters, an error condition is reported. The length of the program name could possibly be greater than 200 characters because often the program name includes the full path to the program name. A length limit of 200 is an arbitrary value that should not be reached in most circumstances.

- Like Program Phase Task 1, Program Phase Task 2 is implemented as a console application. It illustrates how to implement an "if" statement, "for" loop, and "while" loop. Even a simple program such as that specified by Program Phase Task 2 is informative. It shows important syntax information and introduces the user to important programming language features in a simple manner. Program Phase Task 2 ignores all program parameters passed at the command line.

- Sample output of Program Phase 2-3:

```
C:\pp2_3\Release>pp2_3.exe
Program Name: pp2_3.exe
```

- For some programming languages, the program name includes the path to the program if the program is executed from a different folder. For instance, when Program Phase 2-3 is started from its parent folder, the folder that the pp2_3.exe file resides in is included in the program name.

```
C:\pp2_3>.\Release\pp2_3.exe
Program Name: .\Release\pp2_3.exe
```

- If Program Phase 2-3 is started from the root folder of drive c, the full path to the executable is included in the program name.

```
C:\>c:\pp2_3\Release\pp2_3.exe
Program Name: c:\pp2_3\Release\pp2_3.exe
```

- If the program name including the path exceeds 200 characters, an error message is sent to standard error. In addition to sending an error message to standard error, an error level of "1" is set. To check the error level of the most recently run program in the command prompt, enter the following:

```
Windows:         echo %ERRORLEVEL%

Linux Bash:      echo $?
Linux C shell:   echo $status

Mac OS X Bash:   echo $?
```

Program Phase 2-1

Java ▪ Multi-Platform

Application Name Console Output

- Program Phase Task 2 is implemented in Program Phase 2-1 using the Java programming language (J2SE 5.0).
- The name of the program is stored one character at a time in a Java array.
- The Java "if" statement, "for" loop, and "while" loop are illustrated.
- Program Phase 2-1 is a console application that provides an example for sending output to standard output and standard error.

Code Block Features

The Program Phase 2-1 code blocks illustrate the following programming features in a console application using the Java programming language:

- **Array Variable Declaration and Assignment**
- **Program Name Parsing**
- **If Statement**
- **For Loop**
- **While Loop**
- **Console Application Output to Standard Error**

Java
Array Variable Declaration and Assignment

- The test1.java example stores the string "Hello World!" one character at a time in the array called laArray. This array contains twelve array entries. Each array entry is then outputted to standard output.

test1.java: Java Array Variable Declaration and Assignment

```
public class test1
{
public static void main(final String argv[])
{
   char[] laArray;

   laArray = new char[12];
   laArray[0] = 'H';
   laArray[1] = 'e';
```

test1.java continued on the next page

test1.java: Java Array Variable Declaration and Assignment continued

```
   laArray[2] = 'l';
   laArray[3] = 'l';
   laArray[4] = 'o';
   laArray[5] =  ' ';
   laArray[6] = 'W';
   laArray[7] = 'o';
   laArray[8] = 'r';
   laArray[9] = 'l';
   laArray[10] = 'd';
   laArray[11] = '!';

   System.out.print(laArray[0]);
   System.out.print(laArray[1]);
   System.out.print(laArray[2]);
   System.out.print(laArray[3]);
   System.out.print(laArray[4]);
   System.out.print(laArray[5]);
   System.out.print(laArray[6]);
   System.out.print(laArray[7]);
   System.out.print(laArray[8]);
   System.out.print(laArray[9]);
   System.out.print(laArray[10]);
   System.out.print(laArray[11]);
   System.out.println("");
}}
```

Java
Program Name Parsing

- The getClass().getName() method can be called to get the name of the executing class. In addition, the "user.dir" property provides the full path to the currently executing class.

test2.java: Java Program Name Parsing

```
public class test2
{
public static void main(final String argv[])
{
   test2 loClass;
   String lcProgramName;

   loClass = new test2();

   lcProgramName = System.getProperty("user.dir") + "\\" +
                   loClass.getClass().getName();
}}
```

Java
If Statement

- The "if" statement example presented here is identical in functionality to the Switch/Case statement presented in Program Phase 1-1.

test3.java: Java If Statement

```
public class test3
{
public static void main(final String argv[])
```

test3.java continued on the next page

test3.java: Java If Statement continued

```
{
   int lnCmdLineParamCount;
   lnCmdLineParamCount = argv.length;

   if (lnCmdLineParamCount == 0)
   {
      // No command line parameters entered.
   }
   else
   {
      if (lnCmdLineParamCount == 1)
      {
         // One command line parameter entered.
      }
      else
      {
         // More than one command line parameter entered.
      }
   }
}}
```

Java
For Loop

- The following "for" loop example prints the string "Hello World!" ten times:

test4.java: Java For Loop

```
public class test4
{
public static void main(final String argv[])
{
   int i;

   for (i=0;i < 10;i++)
   {
      System.out.println("Hello World!");
   }
}}
```

Java
While Loop

- The following "while" loop example prints the string "Hello World!" ten times:

test5.java: Java While Loop

```
public class test5
{
public static void main(final String argv[])
{
   int i;
   i = 0;

   while (i < 10)
   {
      System.out.println("Hello World!");
      i++;
   }
}}
```

Java
Console Application Output to Standard Error

- An error code of one is returned to the operating system using the exit() method of the System class. The following example outputs text to standard error:

test6.java: Java Console Application Output to Standard Error

```
public class test6
{
public static void main(final String argv[])
{
    System.err.println("A program error has occurred.");
    System.exit(1);
}}
```

Source Code Files

- Text files: pp2_1.java

pp2_1.java: Program Phase 2-1 Source Code

```
//*****************************************************************************
// Program Phase 2-1 Java Application Name Console Output                    *
// Programming Tasks Illustrated: Console Application                         *
//                                Array Variable Declaration and Assignment   *
//                                Program Name Parsing                        *
//                                If Statement                                *
//                                For Loop                                    *
//                                While Loop                                  *
//                                Console Application Output to Standard Error*
//*****************************************************************************

//*****************************************************************************
// File: pp2_1.java                                                           *
// Reserved                                                                   *
//*****************************************************************************

package programphases.programphase2_1;

public class pp2_1
{


//*****************************************************************************
// Program Phase 2-1 Main                                                     *
// Define the Entry Point of Execution (EPE) for Program Phase 2-1            *
// CBI:  2-1.1.1.1                                                            *
//*****************************************************************************

public static void main(final String taArgv[])
{


//*****************************************************************************
// Program Phase 2-1 Main                                                     *
// Declare the local variables for the "main" program                        *
// CBI:  2-1.1.1.2                                                            *
//*****************************************************************************

   int lnLength;
   int lnIndex;
```

pp2_1.java continued on the next page

pp2_1.java: Program Phase 2-1 Source Code continued

```
   char[] laArray;
   pp2_1 loClass;
   String lcProgramName;

   laArray = new char[200];
   loClass = new pp2_1();


//***************************************************************************
// Program Phase 2-1 Main                                                   *
// Store the program name                                                   *
// CBI:  2-1.1.1.3                                                          *
//***************************************************************************

   lcProgramName = System.getProperty("user.dir") + "\\" +
                   loClass.getClass().getName();


//***************************************************************************
// Program Phase 2-1 Main                                                   *
// Use an if statement to verify the number of characters in the program name *
// CBI:  2-1.1.1.4                                                          *
//***************************************************************************

   lnLength = lcProgramName.length();

   if (lnLength > 200)
   {
      // Output To Standard Error
      System.err.println("The program name is greater than 200 characters.");

      // Error Exit Status Code
      System.exit(1);
   }


//***************************************************************************
// Program Phase 2-1 Main                                                   *
// Use a for loop to store the program name in an array                     *
// CBI:  2-1.1.1.5                                                          *
//***************************************************************************

   for (lnIndex=0;lnIndex < lnLength;lnIndex++)
   {
       laArray[lnIndex] = lcProgramName.charAt(lnIndex);
   }


//***************************************************************************
// Program Phase 2-1 Main                                                   *
// Use a while loop to output to standard output each array character element *
// CBI:  2-1.1.1.6                                                          *
//***************************************************************************

   System.out.print("Program Name: ");
   lnIndex = 0;

   while (lnIndex < lnLength)
   {
      // Output To Standard Output
      System.out.print(laArray[lnIndex]);
      lnIndex++;
   }
   System.out.println("");
}}
```

Windows and Linux – Code Setup and Compilation

- Tools: Java SE Development Kit (JDK) 5.0, Netbeans IDE (Appendix A)

`Windows and Linux Code Setup and Compilation Steps`

1: Start the Netbeans IDE program.

2: Netbeans - Activate Menu Item: File → New Project

Select the "Java" category and then select "Java Application" as the project type. Activate the "Next" button.

3: Enter pp2_1 as the "Project Name". Enter the appropriate folder name for the "Project Location". Check the "Set as Main Project" check box. Uncheck the "Create Main Class" check box. Activate the "Finish" button.

4: Create a folder called programphases\programphase2_1 inside the src folder of the pp2_1 folder. Example: `pp2_1\src\programphases\programphase2_1`

5: Netbeans - Activate Menu Item: File → New File

In the "New File" dialog window, select the "Other" category and then select "Empty File" as the file type. Activate the "Next" button. Enter the "File Name" as pp2_1.java and select the src/programphases/programphase2_1 folder as the destination "Folder". Activate the "Finish" button to create the pp2_1.java file.

6: Open the pp2_1.java file in the Netbeans IDE and then enter the source code for Program Phase 2-1.

7: Netbeans - Activate Menu Item: File → "pp2_1" Properties

On the "Project Properties" window, select the "Run" category and then enter programphases.programphase2_1.pp2_1 for the "Main Class". Activate the "OK" button.

8: Netbeans - Activate Menu Item: Build → Build Main Project

`Windows and Linux Command Prompt Compilation Steps`

1: Update the path to the javac executable file.

```
Windows:  PATH = "C:\Program Files\Java\jdk1.6.0_01\bin";%PATH%

Linux Bash:  export PATH=~/jdk1.6.0_01/bin:$PATH
Linux C shell or the TC shell: setenv PATH ~/jdk1.6.0/bin:$PATH
```

2: Change directories to the pp2_1 folder and then enter the following command:

Windows

```
javac -d "build\classes" "src\programphases\programphase2_1\pp2_1.java"
```

Linux

```
javac -d "build/classes" "src/programphases/programphase2_1/pp2_1.java"
```

Steps continued on the next page

Windows and Linux Command Prompt Compilation Steps continued

3: Create a text file called manifest in the pp2_1 folder using a text editor and put this line in the file.

```
Main-Class: programphases.programphase2_1.pp2_1
```

Enter a newline at the end of the text.

4: Create the pp2_1.jar "executable" file.

```
jar -cvfm ./dist/pp2_1.jar manifest -C build/classes .
```

Mac OS X – Code Setup and Compilation

- Tools: Java SE Development Kit (JDK) 5.0 (included with Mac OS X), Xcode IDE. (Appendix C).

Mac OS X Code Setup and Compilation Steps

1: Start the Xcode IDE program found in the /Developer/Applications folder.

2: Xcode - Activate Menu Item: File → New Project

Select "Java → Tool" and then activate the "Next" button.

3: Enter pp2_1 as the "Project Name". Enter the appropriate folder as the "Project Directory". Activate the "Finish" button.

4: Xcode - Activate Menu Item: Project → Set Active Build Configuration → Release

5: A text file called pp2_1.java is automatically created. Delete the entire contents of this file and then enter the source code for Program Phase 2-1.

6: In the Xcode IDE, double-click on the resource file called Manifest. Change the "Main-Class" entry in the Manifest file from pp2_1 to programphases.programphase2_1.pp2_1. Save and close the Manifest file. If using Xcode 3, expand the "Executables" entry and then double click on the "java" entry to display the "Executable 'java' Info" window. Edit the argument to look like this:

```
-cp pp2_1.jar programphases.programphase2_1.pp2_1
```

7: Activate the "Build" button in Xcode to compile the pp2_1.java file.

Mac OS X Command Prompt Compilation Steps

1: Open a terminal window and change directories to the pp2_1 folder.

Xcode 2.4

```
javac -d "build/pp2_1.build/Release/pp2_1.build/JavaClasses" pp2_1.java
```

Xcode 3

```
javac -d bin src/pp2_1.java
```

Steps continued on the next page

Mac OS X Command Prompt Compilation Steps continued

2: Create a text file called Manifest in the pp2_1 folder using a text editor and put this line in the file:

```
Main-Class: programphases.programphase2_1.pp2_1
```

Enter a newline at the end of the text.

3: Create the pp2_1.jar "executable" file. Enter the following on a single line:

Xcode 2.4

```
   jar -cvfm build/Release/pp2_1.jar Manifest -C
build/pp2_1.build/Release/pp2_1.build/JavaClasses .
```

Xcode 3

```
jar -cvfm jars/pp2_1.jar Manifest -C bin .
```

Windows and Linux – Program Execution

- Execute Program

```
Netbeans IDE - Activate Menu Item:  Run → Run Main Project
```

- Debug Program

```
Netbeans IDE - Activate Menu Item:  Run → Step Into Project
```

- To launch the program using the pp2_1.jar file from a command prompt, enter the following from the pp2_1 folder:

```
Windows:  java -jar dist\pp2_1.jar
Linux: java -jar dist/pp2_1.jar
```

Mac OS X – Program Execution

- Execute Program

```
Xcode IDE - Activate the "Build and Go" button
```

- Debug Program

```
   Xcode 2.4 - Activate Menu Item: Debug → Add Breakpoint at Current Line
   Xcode 3 - Activate Menu Item: Run → Manage Breakpoints → Add
Breakpoint at Current Line

   Xcode - Activate Menu Item: Build → Build and Debug
```

Command Prompt Execution

```
   java -jar pp2_1.jar (from the pp2_1/build/Release or jars folder)

or

   java programphases.programphase2_1.pp2_1
(from the pp2_1/build/pp2_1.build/Release/pp2_1.build/JavaClasses or bin
folder)
```

Program Phase 2-2
Visual FoxPro ▪ Windows

Application Name Message Box Output

- Program Phase Task 2 is implemented in Program Phase 2-2 using the Visual FoxPro (VFP) programming language.
- The name of the program is stored one character at a time in a VFP array.
- The VFP "if" statement, "for" loop, and "while" loop are illustrated.
- Program Phase 2-2 is a GUI based application that provides an example for displaying output in a message box.

Code Block Features

The Program Phase 2-2 code blocks illustrate the following programming features in a GUI application using the VFP programming language:

- **Array Variable Declaration and Assignment**
- **Program Name Parsing**
- **If Statement**
- **For Loop**
- **While Loop**
- **Message Box Error Output**

Visual FoxPro
Array Variable Declaration and Assignment

- The test1.prg example stores the string "Hello World!" one character at a time in the array called laArray. This array contains twelve array entries. Each array entry is then stored in a string that is outputted using a VFP message box.

test1.prg: Visual FoxPro Array Variable Declaration and Assignment

```
DIMENSION laArray(12)
LOCAL lcOutput

laArray[1] = "H"
laArray[2] = "e"
laArray[3] = "l"
```

test1.prg continued on the next page

test1.prg: Visual FoxPro Array Variable Declaration and Assignment continued

```
laArray[4] = "l"
laArray[5] = "o"
laArray[6] = " "
laArray[7] = "W"
laArray[8] = "o"
laArray[9] = "r"
laArray[10] = "l"
laArray[11] = "d"
laArray[12] = "!"

lcOutput = laArray[1]
lcOutput = lcOutput + laArray[2]
lcOutput = lcOutput + laArray[3]
lcOutput = lcOutput + laArray[4]
lcOutput = lcOutput + laArray[5]
lcOutput = lcOutput + laArray[6]
lcOutput = lcOutput + laArray[7]
lcOutput = lcOutput + laArray[8]
lcOutput = lcOutput + laArray[9]
lcOutput = lcOutput + laArray[10]
lcOutput = lcOutput + laArray[11]
lcOutput = lcOutput + laArray[12]

=MessageBox(lcOutput)
```

Visual FoxPro
Program Name Parsing

- The VFP SYS(16) function is called to get the name of the executing program.
- The SYS() function supports many different parameters that return different types of system information. The parameters supported by the SYS() function can vary based on the VFP version. The SYS(16) function is supported in all versions of VFP.

test2.prg: Visual FoxPro Program Name Parsing

```
LOCAL lcProgramName

lcProgramName = SYS(16)
```

Visual FoxPro
If Statement

- The "if" statement example presented here is identical in functionality to the Switch/Case statement presented in Program Phase 1-2.

test3.prg: Visual FoxPro If Statement

```
LOCAL lnCmdLineParamCount

lnCmdLineParamCount = PCOUNT()

IF lnCmdLineParamCount == 0

   ** No command line parameters entered.
```

test3.prg continued on the next page

test3.prg: Visual FoxPro If Statement continued

```
ELSE

   IF lnCmdLineParamCount == 1

      ** One command line parameter entered.

   ELSE

      ** More than one command line parameter entered.

   ENDIF

ENDIF
```

Visual FoxPro For Loop

- The following "for" loop example prints the string "Hello World!" ten times to the automatically created VFP main window:

test4.prg: Visual FoxPro For Loop

```
_SCREEN.WindowState = 2

LOCAL i

FOR i = 1 TO 10

   ? "Hello World!"

ENDFOR

WAIT WINDOW "Press any key to exit"
```

Visual FoxPro While Loop

- The following "while" loop example prints the string "Hello World!" ten times to the automatically created VFP main window:

test5.prg: Visual FoxPro While Loop

```
_SCREEN.WindowState = 2

LOCAL i

i = 0

DO WHILE i < 10

   ? "Hello World!"
   i = i + 1

ENDDO

WAIT WINDOW "Press any key to exit"
```

Visual FoxPro
Message Box Error Output

- The MESSAGEBOX() function can be used to output an error message. To indicate an error message, a stop sign icon is displayed in the message box window. An error code of one is returned to the operating system using the VFP "return" statement.

test6.prg: Visual FoxPro Message Box Error Output

```
=MESSAGEBOX("A program error has occurred.",16)
RETURN 1
```

Source Code Files

- Text files: pp2_2.prg

pp2_2.prg: Program Phase 2-2 Source Code

```
******************************************************************************
** Program Phase 2-2 Visual FoxPro Application Name Message Box Output      *
** Programming Tasks Illustrated: GUI Based Application                     *
**                                Array Variable Declaration and Assignment *
**                                Program Name Parsing                      *
**                                If Statement                              *
**                                For Loop                                  *
**                                While Loop                                *
**                                Message Box Error Output                  *
******************************************************************************

******************************************************************************
** File: pp2_2.prg                                                          *
** Reserved                                                                 *
******************************************************************************


******************************************************************************
** Program Phase 2-2 Main                                                   *
** Define the Entry Point of Execution (EPE) for Program Phase 2-2          *
** CBI:  2-2.1.1.1                                                          *
******************************************************************************

** The first line of the code in the pp2_2.prg file is the EPE.


******************************************************************************
** Program Phase 2-2 Main                                                   *
** Declare the local variables for the "main" program                      *
** CBI:  2-2.1.1.2                                                          *
******************************************************************************

LOCAL lnLength
LOCAL lnIndex
LOCAL lcProgramName
LOCAL lcOuput
DIMENSION laArray(200)
```

pp2_2.prg continued on the next page

pp2_2.prg: Program Phase 2-2 Source Code continued

```
*******************************************************************************
** Program Phase 2-2 Main                                                     *
** Store the program name                                                     *
** CBI:  2-2.1.1.3                                                            *
*******************************************************************************

lcProgramName = SYS(16)

*******************************************************************************
** Program Phase 2-2 Main                                                     *
** Use an if statement to verify the number of characters in the program name *
** CBI:  2-2.1.1.4                                                            *
*******************************************************************************

lnLength = LEN(lcProgramName)

IF (lnLength > 200)

   =MESSAGEBOX("The program name is greater than 200 characters.",16)
   RETURN 1

ENDIF

*******************************************************************************
** Program Phase 2-2 Main                                                     *
** Use a for loop to store the program name in an array                       *
** CBI:  2-2.1.1.5                                                            *
*******************************************************************************

FOR lnIndex = 1 to lnLength

    laArray[lnIndex] = SUBSTR(lcProgramName,lnIndex,1)

ENDFOR

*******************************************************************************
** Program Phase 2-2 Main                                                     *
** Use a while loop to output to standard output each array character element *
** CBI:  2-2.1.1.6                                                            *
*******************************************************************************

lcOutput = "Program Name:  "
lnIndex = 1

DO WHILE lnIndex < lnLength + 1

   lcOutput = lcOutput + laArray[lnIndex]
   lnIndex = lnIndex + 1

ENDDO

=MESSAGEBOX(lcOutput)
```

Code Setup and Compilation

- Tools: Visual FoxPro

Code Setup and Compilation Steps

1: Create a folder called pp2_2 that will store the source code files.

2: Start the Visual FoxPro IDE program.

3: VFP - Activate Menu Item: File → New

From the "New" dialog window, select the "Project" radio button and then activate the "New file" button. Save the project as pp2_2.pjx in the pp2_2 folder.

4: VFP - Activate Menu Item: File → New

From the "New" dialog window, select the "Program" radio button and then activate the "New file" button.

5: Enter the source code into the new program file and save the file as pp2_2.prg in the pp2_2 folder.

6: Add the pp2_2.prg file to the project by selecting the "Code" tab in the "Project Manager" window for the pp2_2 project and then activating the "Add" button. Browse for the pp2_2.prg file to add it to the project.

7: Create a text file called config.fpw in the pp2_2 folder and then enter the following text:

```
screen = off
```

8: Click the "Build" button on the "Project Manager" window. Select the "Win32 executable" radio button. Select "Recompile All Files" and "Display Errors". Activate the "OK" button. Use the "Save As" dialog to select a destination for the executable file and then activate the "Save" button.

Visual FoxPro Command Window Compilation

Enter the following command in the VFP command window:

```
BUILD EXE "c:\pp2_2\pp2_2.exe" FROM "c:\pp2_2\pp2_2.pjx" RECOMPILE
```

Program Execution

- Execute Program

```
VFP - Activate Menu Item:  Program → Do
```

Navigate to the pp2_2.exe file in the "Do" dialog window and then activate the "Do" button.

- Debug Program

```
VFP - Activate Menu Item:  Tools → Debugger
VFP Debugger window - Activate Menu Item:  Debug → Do
```

Select the pp2_2.prg file found in the pp2_2 folder and then activate the "Do" button on the Do dialog window.

Program Phase 2-3
C ▪ Multi-Platform

Application Name Console Output

- Program Phase Task 2 is implemented in Program Phase 2-3 using the C programming language.
- The name of the program is stored one character at a time in a C array.
- The C "if" statement, "for" loop, and "while" loop are illustrated.
- Program Phase 2-3 is a console application that provides an example for sending output to standard output and standard error.

Code Block Features

The Program Phase 2-3 code blocks illustrate the following programming features in a console application using the C programming language:

- **Array Variable Declaration and Assignment**
- **Program Name Parsing**
- **If Statement**
- **For Loop**
- **While Loop**
- **Console Application Output to Standard Error**

C
Array Variable Declaration and Assignment

- The test1.c example stores the string "Hello World!" one character at a time in the array called laArray. This array contains twelve array entries. Each array entry is then outputted to standard output.

test1.c: C Array Variable Declaration and Assignment

```
#include <stdio.h>

int main(int argc, char* argv[])
{
   char laArray[12];
   laArray[0] = 'H';
   laArray[1] = 'e';
   laArray[2] = 'l';
   laArray[3] = 'l';
```

test1.c continued on the next page

test1.c: Array Variable Declaration and Assignment continued

```
   laArray[4] = 'o';
   laArray[5] = ' ';
   laArray[6] = 'W';
   laArray[7] = 'o';
   laArray[8] = 'r';
   laArray[9] = 'l';
   laArray[10] = 'd';
   laArray[11] = '!';

   fprintf(stdout, "%c",laArray[0]);
   fprintf(stdout, "%c",laArray[1]);
   fprintf(stdout, "%c",laArray[2]);
   fprintf(stdout, "%c",laArray[3]);
   fprintf(stdout, "%c",laArray[4]);
   fprintf(stdout, "%c",laArray[5]);
   fprintf(stdout, "%c",laArray[6]);
   fprintf(stdout, "%c",laArray[7]);
   fprintf(stdout, "%c",laArray[8]);
   fprintf(stdout, "%c",laArray[9]);
   fprintf(stdout, "%c",laArray[10]);
   fprintf(stdout, "%c\n",laArray[11]);
   return 0;
}
```

C
Program Name Parsing

- The program name is stored in the first array entry of the argv array.

test2.c: C Program Name Parsing

```
int main(int argc, char* argv[])
{
   char *lcProgramName;

   lcProgramName = argv[0];
   return 0;
}
```

C
If Statement

- The "if" statement example presented here is identical in functionality to the Switch/Case statement presented in Program Phase 1-3:

test3.c: C If Statement

```
int main(int argc, char* argv[])
{
   int lnCmdLineParamCount;

   lnCmdLineParamCount = argc - 1;

   if (lnCmdLineParamCount == 0)
   {
      // No command line parameters entered.
   }
   else
```

test3.c continued on the next page

test3.c: C If Statement continued

```
   {
      if (lnCmdLineParamCount == 1)
      {
         // One command line parameter entered.
      }
      else
      {
         // More than one command line parameter entered.
      }
   }
   return 0;
}
```

C
For Loop

- The following "for" loop example prints the string "Hello World!" ten times:

test4.c: C For Loop

```
#include <stdio.h>

int main(int argc, char* argv[])
{
   int i;

   for (i=0;i < 10;i++)
   {
      fprintf(stdout,"Hello World!\n");
   }

   return 0;
}
```

C
While Loop

- The following "while" loop example prints the string "Hello World!" ten times:

test5.c: C While Loop

```
#include <stdio.h>

int main(int argc, char* argv[])
{
   int i;

   i = 0;

   while (i < 10)
   {
      fprintf(stdout,"Hello World!\n");
      i++;
   }

   return 0;
}
```

C
Console Application Output to Standard Error

- An error code of one is returned to the operating system using the "return" statement. The following example outputs text to standard error:

test6.c: C Console Application Output to Standard Error

```
#include <stdio.h>

int main(int argc, char* argv[])
{
   fprintf(stderr,"A program error has occurred.\n");
   return 1;
}
```

Source Code Files

- Text files: pp2_3.c

pp2_3.c: Program Phase 2-3 Source Code

```
//*****************************************************************************
// Program Phase 2-3 C Application Name Console Output                        *
// Programming Tasks Illustrated: Console Application                         *
//                                Array Variable Declaration and Assignment   *
//                                Program Name Parsing                        *
//                                If Statement                                *
//                                For Loop                                    *
//                                While Loop                                  *
//                                Console Application Output to Standard Error*
//*****************************************************************************

//*****************************************************************************
// File: pp2_3.c                                                              *
// Reserved                                                                   *
//*****************************************************************************

#include <stdio.h>
#include <string.h>


//*****************************************************************************
// Program Phase 2-3 Main                                                     *
// Define the Entry Point of Execution (EPE) for Program Phase 2-3            *
// CBI:  2-3.1.1.1                                                            *
//*****************************************************************************

int main(int argc, char* argv[])
{


//*****************************************************************************
// Program Phase 2-3 Main                                                     *
// Declare the local variables for the "main" program                         *
// CBI:  2-3.1.1.2                                                            *
//*****************************************************************************

   size_t lnLength;
   size_t lnIndex;
   char laArray[200];
   char *lcProgramName;
```

pp2_3.c continued on the next page

pp2_3.c: Program Phase 2-3 Source Code continued

```
//***************************************************************************
// Program Phase 2-3 Main                                                   *
// Store the program name                                                   *
// CBI:  2-3.1.1.3                                                          *
//***************************************************************************

    lcProgramName = argv[0];


//***************************************************************************
// Program Phase 2-3 Main                                                   *
// Use an if statement to verify the number of characters in the program name *
// CBI:  2-3.1.1.4                                                          *
//***************************************************************************

   lnLength = strlen(lcProgramName);

   if (lnLength > 200)
   {
      fprintf(stderr,"The program name is greater than 200 characters.\n");
      return 1;
   }


//***************************************************************************
// Program Phase 2-3 Main                                                   *
// Use a for loop to store the program name in an array                     *
// CBI:  2-3.1.1.5                                                          *
//***************************************************************************

   for (lnIndex=0;lnIndex < lnLength;lnIndex++)
   {
       laArray[lnIndex] = lcProgramName[lnIndex];
   }


//***************************************************************************
// Program Phase 2-3 Main                                                   *
// Use a while loop to output to standard output each array character element *
// CBI:  2-3.1.1.6                                                          *
//***************************************************************************

   fprintf(stdout,"Program Name: ");
   lnIndex = 0;

   while (lnIndex < lnLength)
   {
      printf("%c",laArray[lnIndex]);
      lnIndex++;
   }
   printf("\n");
}
```

Windows – Code Setup and Compilation

- Tools: Microsoft Visual Studio 2008 Express Edition (msdn.microsoft.com)

Windows Code Setup and Compilation Steps

1: Start the Visual C++ 2008 Express Edition program.

2: VC++ EE - Activate Menu Item: File → New → Project

Steps continued on the next page

Windows Code Setup and Compilation Steps continued

3: For the "Project type", select "Win32" and then select the "Win32 Console Application" template. Enter pp2_3 as the project "Name". Enter the appropriate folder as the project "Location". The pp2_3 folder will be automatically created. Make sure that the "Create directory for solution" check box is not checked.

4: Activate the "OK" button to proceed with the "Win32 Application Wizard".

5: Activate the "Next" button of the "Win32 Application Wizard".

6: Verify that a "Console Application" is selected and also check the "Empty project" check box. Activate the "Finish" button of the "Win32 Application Wizard".

7: VC++ EE - Activate Menu Item: Project → Add New Item

On the "Add New Item" dialog window, select the "Visual C++ → Code" category and then select the "C++ File" template. Enter pp2_3.c for the file "Name". Activate the "Add" button.

8: Enter the source code for Program Phase 2-3 into the pp2_3.c text file and save the file.

9: Select the Release configuration for the project.

10: VC++ EE - Activate Menu Item: Project → pp2_3 Properties

Enter the following settings:

Configuration Properties → C/C++ → Code Generation → Runtime Library

For Release Configuration:

```
Multi-threaded (/MT) or Multi-threaded DLL (/MD)
```

For Debug Configuration:

```
Multi-threaded Debug /MTd or Multi-threaded Debug DLL (/MDd)
```

Configuration Properties → General → Character Set

```
"Use Multi-Byte Character Set"
```

11: VC++ EE - Activate Menu Item: Build → Build pp2_3

Windows Command Prompt Compilation

Open a Visual Studio 2008 command prompt and change directories to the pp2_3 folder.

```
   cl.exe /MT pp2_3.c

shared dll:  cl.exe /MD pp2_3.c
             mt.exe /manifest pp2_3.exe.manifest /outputresource:pp2_3.exe
```

Linux – Code Setup and Compilation

- Tools: GNU GCC, KDevelop (Appendix B)

`Linux Code Setup and Compilation Steps`

1: Start the KDevelop program.

2: KDevelop - Activate Menu Item: Project → New Project

Select the "C → Simple Hello world program" template. Set the "Application name" to pp2_3. Set the "Location" to the appropriate folder.

3: Activate the "Next" button four times and then activate the "Finish" button.

4: Edit the pp2_3.c source code file and remove all of the code in it. Enter the source code for Program Phase 2-3 into the pp2_3.c text file.

5: KDevelop - Activate Menu Item: Project → Build Configuration → debug

This results in the executable file being placed in the debug/src folder under the pp2_3 source code folder.

6: KDevelop - Activate Menu Item: Build → Build Project

If prompted about a missing Makefile, choose the "Run Them" button.

`Linux Command Prompt Compilation`

Open a terminal window and then enter the following in the pp2_3/src folder:

```
g++ pp2_3.c -o pp2_3
```

Mac OS X – Code Setup and Compilation

- Tools: GNU GCC, Xcode (Appendix C)

`Mac OS X Code Setup and Compilation Steps`

1: Start the Xcode program.

2: Xcode - Activate Menu Item: File → New Project

3: Select "Command Line Utility → C++ Tool" and then activate the "Next" button.

4: Set the "Project Name" to pp2_3. Set the "Project Directory" to the appropriate folder. Activate the "Finish" button.

5: Right click on the main.cpp file that has been automatically added to the project and rename it to pp2_3.c. Enter the source code for Program Phase 2-3 into the pp2_3.c file.

6: Compile the program by activating the "Build" button.

`Mac OS X Command Prompt Compilation`

Open a terminal window and then enter the following in the pp2_3 folder:

```
g++ pp2_3.c -o pp2_3
```

Windows – Program Execution

- Execute Program

```
VC++ EE - Activate Menu Item: Debug → Start Without Debugging
```

- Debug Program

```
VC++ EE - Activate Menu Item: Project → pp2_3 Properties
```

Expand the "Configuration Properties → Linker" entry and then click on the "Debugging" item. Set the "Generate Debug Info" entry to "Yes". Close the pp2_3 Properties window.

```
VC++ EE - Activate Menu Item: Debug → Step Into
```

Linux – Program Execution

- Execute Program

```
KDevelop - Activate Menu Item: Build → Execute Program
```

- Debug Program

Include the debug information in the program build.

```
KDevelop - Activate Menu Item: Project → Project Options
```

Click on the "Configure Options" item. Select the "debug" configuration and then enter "--enable-debug=full" (without quotes) in the "Configure arguments" field on the "General" tab. Close the "Project Options" dialog window.

```
KDevelop - Activate Menu Item: Project → Build Configuration → Debug
```

Set the cursor position in the source file to the first line of code in the CBI: 2-3.1.1.3 code block.

```
KDevelop - Activate Menu Item: Debug → Toggle Breakpoint
KDevelop - Activate Menu Item: Debug → Start
```

Mac OS X – Program Execution

- Execute Program

Activate the" Build/Go" button. The program output is displayed in the "Run Log" window. This window can be displayed by activating the "Console" menu item from the "Run" menu.

- Debug Program

```
   Xcode 2.4 - Activate Menu Item: Debug → Add Breakpoint at Current Line
   Xcode 3 - Activate Menu Item: Run → Manage Breakpoints → Add
Breakpoint at Current Line
```

```
Xcode - Activate Menu Item: Build → Build and Debug
```

Program Phase 2-4
Visual Basic 6 ▪ Windows

Application Name Message Box Output

- Program Phase Task 2 is implemented in Program Phase 2-4 using the Visual Basic 6 (VB6) programming language.
- The name of the program is stored one character at a time in a VB6 array.
- The VB6 "if" statement, "for" loop, and "while" loop are illustrated.
- Program Phase 2-4 is a GUI based application that provides an example for displaying output in a message box.

Code Block Features

The Program Phase 2-4 code blocks illustrate the following programming features in a GUI application using the VB6 programming language:

- **Array Variable Declaration and Assignment**
- **Program Name Parsing**
- **If Statement**
- **For Loop**
- **While Loop**
- **Message Box Error Output**

Visual Basic 6
Array Variable Declaration and Assignment

- The test1.bas example stores the string "Hello World!" one character at a time in the array called laArray. This array contains twelve array entries. Each array entry is then stored in a string that is outputted using a VB6 message box.

test1.bas: Visual Basic 6 Array Variable Declaration and Assignment

```
Sub Main()

    Dim laArray(1 To 12) As Variant
    Dim lcOutput As String

    laArray(1) = "H"
    laArray(2) = "e"
    laArray(3) = "l"
```

test1.bas continued on the next page

test1.bas: Visual Basic 6 Array Variable Declaration and Assignment continued

```
    laArray(4) = "l"
    laArray(5) = "o"
    laArray(6) = " "
    laArray(7) = "W"
    laArray(8) = "o"
    laArray(9) = "r"
    laArray(10) = "l"
    laArray(11) = "d"
    laArray(12) = "!"

    lcOutput = laArray(1)
    lcOutput = lcOutput & laArray(2)
    lcOutput = lcOutput & laArray(3)
    lcOutput = lcOutput & laArray(4)
    lcOutput = lcOutput & laArray(5)
    lcOutput = lcOutput & laArray(6)
    lcOutput = lcOutput & laArray(7)
    lcOutput = lcOutput & laArray(8)
    lcOutput = lcOutput & laArray(9)
    lcOutput = lcOutput & laArray(10)
    lcOutput = lcOutput & laArray(11)
    lcOutput = lcOutput & laArray(12)

    Call MsgBox(lcOutput)
End Sub
```

Visual Basic 6
Program Name Parsing

- The "EXEName" property of the global "App" object is accessed to get the name of the executing program. The "Path" property contains the path to the program.

test2.bas: Visual Basic 6 Program Name Parsing

```
Sub Main()

    Dim lcProgramName As String

    lcProgramName = App.Path & "\" & App.EXEName & ".exe"

End Sub
```

Visual Basic 6
If Statement

- The Visual Basic "If" statement example presented here is identical in functionality to the Switch/Case statement presented in Program Phase 1-4.

test3.bas: Visual Basic 6 If Statement

```
Sub Main()

    Dim lnCmdLineParamCount As Integer
    Dim argv() As String

    argv = Split(Command, " ")
    lnCmdLineParamCount = UBound(argv) + 1
```

test3.bas continued on the next page

test3.bas: Visual Basic 6 If Statement continued

```
    If (lnCmdLineParamCount = 0) Then

        '' No command line parameters entered.

    Else

        If (lnCmdLineParamCount = 1) Then

            '' One command line parameter entered.

        Else

            '' More than one command line parameter entered.

        End If

    End If

End Sub
```

Visual Basic 6 For Loop

- The test4.frm "For" loop example program prints the string "Hello World!" ten times in a Visual Basic Form created to be the main window. The following example assumes that the test4.frm Form has been added to the Visual Basic project and set to be the "Startup object":

test4.frm: Visual Basic 6 For Loop

```
Private Sub Form_Load()

    Dim i As Integer
    Me.AutoRedraw = True

    For i = 1 To 10

        Print "Hello World!"

    Next i

End Sub

'' Note that additional VB code is found in this file but is hidden when
'' viewed in the Visual Basic 6 IDE.
```

Visual Basic 6 While Loop

- The following "While" loop example prints the string "Hello World!" ten times in a Visual Basic Form created to be the main window:

test5.frm: Visual Basic 6 While Loop

```
Private Sub Form_Load()

    Dim i As Integer
    Me.AutoRedraw = True
    i = 0
```

test5.frm continued on the next page

test5.frm: Visual Basic 6 While Loop continued

```
   Do While i < 10

      Print "Hello World!"
      i = i + 1

   Loop

End Sub

'' Note that additional VB code is found in this file but is hidden when
'' viewed in the Visual Basic 6 IDE.
```

Visual Basic 6 Message Box Error Output

- The VB6 MsgBox() function is used to output an error message. To indicate an error message, a stop sign icon is displayed in the message box window. An error code of one is returned to the operating system using the Win32 API ExitProcess() function.

test6.bas: Visual Basic 6 Message Box Error Output

```
Private Declare Sub ExitProcess Lib "kernel32" (ByVal ExitCode As Long)

Sub Main()

   Call MsgBox("A program error has occurred.", vbCritical)
   ExitProcess 1

End Sub
```

Source Code Files

- Text files: pp2_4.bas

pp2_4.bas: Program Phase 2-4 Source Code

```
''***********************************************************************
'' Program Phase 2-4 Visual Basic 6 Application Name Message Box Output   *
'' Programming Tasks Illustrated: GUI Based Application                   *
''                                Array Variable Declaration and Assignment  *
''                                If Statement                            *
''                                For Loop                                *
''                                While Loop                              *
''                                Message Box Error Output                *
''***********************************************************************

''***********************************************************************
'' File: pp2_4.bas                                                        *
'' Reserved                                                               *
''***********************************************************************

Private Declare Sub ExitProcess Lib "kernel32" (ByVal tnExitCode As Long)

''***********************************************************************
'' Program Phase 2-4 Main                                                 *
'' Define the Entry Point of Execution (EPE) for Program Phase 2-4        *
'' CBI:  2-4.1.1.1                                                        *
''***********************************************************************
```

pp2_4.bas continued on the next page

pp2_4.bas: Program Phase 2-4 Source Code continued

```
   Sub Main()

''***************************************************************************
'' Program Phase 2-4 Main                                                    *
'' Declare the local variables for the "main" program                        *
'' CBI:  2-4.1.1.2                                                           *
''***************************************************************************

   Dim lnLength As Integer
   Dim lnIndex As Integer
   Dim laArray(1 To 200) As Variant
   Dim lcProgramName As String
   Dim lcOutput As String


''***************************************************************************
'' Program Phase 2-4 Main                                                    *
'' Store the program name                                                    *
'' CBI:  2-4.1.1.3                                                           *
''***************************************************************************

   lcProgramName = App.Path & "\" & App.EXEName & ".exe"

''***************************************************************************
'' Program Phase 2-4 Main                                                    *
'' Use an if statement to verify the number of characters in the program name *
'' CBI:  2-4.1.1.4                                                           *
''***************************************************************************

   lnLength = Len(lcProgramName)

   If (lnLength > 200) Then

      MsgBox ("The program name is greater than 200 characters.")
      ExitProcess 1

   End If


''***************************************************************************
'' Program Phase 2-4 Main                                                    *
'' Use a for loop to store the program name in an array                     *
'' CBI:  2-4.1.1.5                                                           *
''***************************************************************************

   For lnIndex = 1 To lnLength

      laArray(lnIndex) = Mid(lcProgramName, lnIndex, 1)

   Next lnIndex


''***************************************************************************
'' Program Phase 2-4 Main                                                    *
'' Use a while loop to output to standard output each array character element *
'' CBI:  2-4.1.1.6                                                           *
''***************************************************************************

   lcOutput = "Program Name: "
   lnIndex = 1

   Do While lnIndex < lnLength + 1
```

pp2_4.bas continued on the next page

pp2_4.bas: Program Phase 2-4 Source Code continued

```
      lcOutput = lcOutput & laArray(lnIndex)
      lnIndex = lnIndex + 1

   Loop

   MsgBox (lcOutput)

End Sub
```

Code Setup and Compilation

- Tools: Visual Basic 6

Code Setup and Compilation Steps

1: Create a folder called pp2_4 that will store the source code files.

2: Open the Visual Basic 6 program.

3: VB6 - Activate Menu Item: File → New Project

Select "Standard EXE" and then activate the "OK" button.

4: Remove the "Form1" Form that is automatically added to the project by right-clicking on the "Form1" Form in the project and activating the "Remove Form1" menu item.

5: VB6 - Activate Menu Item: File → Save Project

Save the project with the name pp2_4 in the pp2_4 source folder. Click on the pp2_4.vbp file in the properties window and then set the name of the project to pp2_4.

6: VB6 - Activate Menu Item: Project → Add Module

Enter the source code for Program Phase 2-4 into this file and save the file as pp2_4.bas.

7: VB6 - Activate Menu Item: File → Make pp2_4.exe

Command Prompt Compilation

Change directories to the pp2_4 folder and then enter the following commands:

```
PATH = "C:\Program Files\Microsoft Visual Studio\VB98";%PATH%
vb6.exe /make pp2_4.vbp
```

Program Execution

- Execute Program

```
VB6 - Activate Menu Item: Run → Start
```

- Debug Program

```
VB6 - Activate Menu Item: Debug → Step Into
```

Program Phase 2-5
Visual C++ ▪ MFC ▪ Windows

Application Name Console Output

- Program Phase Task 4 is implemented in Program Phase 2-5 using the C++ programming language and the Microsoft Foundation Classes (MFC) class library.
- The name of the program is stored one character at a time in a C array.
- The C/C++ "if" statement, "for" loop, and "while" loop are illustrated.
- Program Phase 2-5 is a console application that provides an example for sending output to standard output and standard error.

Code Block Features

The Program Phase 2-5 code blocks illustrate the following programming features in a console application using the C++ programming language and MFC:

- **Array Variable Declaration and Assignment**
- **Program Name Parsing**
- **If Statement**
- **For Loop**
- **While Loop**
- **Console Application Output to Standard Error**

C++ MFC
Array Variable Declaration and Assignment

- The test1.cpp example stores the string "Hello World!" one character at a time in an array called laArray. This array contains twelve array entries. Each array entry is then outputted to standard output.

test1.cpp: C++ MFC Array Variable Declaration and Assignment

```
#include <afxwin.h>

extern int AFXAPI AfxWinMain(HINSTANCE hInstance,HINSTANCE hPrevInstance,
                             LPTSTR lpCmdLine,int nCmdShow);

int main(int argc, char* argv[])
{
   return AfxWinMain(GetModuleHandle(NULL),NULL,GetCommandLine(),SW_SHOW);
}
```

test1.cpp continued on the next page

test1.cpp: C++ MFC Array Variable Declaration and Assignment continued

```
class test1 : public CWinApp
{

virtual BOOL InitInstance()
{
   char laArray[12];

   laArray[0] = 'H';
   laArray[1] = 'e';
   laArray[2] = 'l';
   laArray[3] = 'l';
   laArray[4] = 'o';
   laArray[5] = ' ';
   laArray[6] = 'W';
   laArray[7] = 'o';
   laArray[8] = 'r';
   laArray[9] = 'l';
   laArray[10] = 'd';
   laArray[11] = '!';

   fprintf(stdout, "%c",laArray[0]);
   fprintf(stdout, "%c",laArray[1]);
   fprintf(stdout, "%c",laArray[2]);
   fprintf(stdout, "%c",laArray[3]);
   fprintf(stdout, "%c",laArray[4]);
   fprintf(stdout, "%c",laArray[5]);
   fprintf(stdout, "%c",laArray[6]);
   fprintf(stdout, "%c",laArray[7]);
   fprintf(stdout, "%c",laArray[8]);
   fprintf(stdout, "%c",laArray[9]);
   fprintf(stdout, "%c",laArray[10]);
   fprintf(stdout, "%c\n",laArray[11]);

   return TRUE;
}};

test1 goTest1;
```

C++ MFC
Program Name Parsing

- The program name is stored in the first array entry of the argv array.
- If using the Visual C++ compiler, the __argc and __argv global variables contain the command line parameter count and command line parameters array respectively. These global variables can be used instead of the variables passed to the main() function.

test2.cpp: C++ MFC Program Name Parsing

```
#include <afxwin.h>

extern int AFXAPI AfxWinMain(HINSTANCE hInstance,HINSTANCE hPrevInstance,
                             LPTSTR lpCmdLine,int nCmdShow);

int main(int argc, char* argv[])
{
   return AfxWinMain(GetModuleHandle(NULL),NULL,GetCommandLine(),SW_SHOW);
}

class test2 : public CWinApp
{
```

test2.cpp continued on the next page

test2.cpp: C++ MFC Program Name Parsing continued

```
virtual BOOL InitInstance()
{
   CString lcProgramName;

   lcProgramName = __argv[0];

   return TRUE;
}};

test2 goTest2;
```

C++ MFC
If Statement

- The "if" statement example presented here is identical in functionality to the Switch/Case statement presented in Program Phase 1-5.

test3.cpp: C++ MFC If Statement

```
#include <afxwin.h>

extern int AFXAPI AfxWinMain(HINSTANCE hInstance,HINSTANCE hPrevInstance,
                             LPTSTR lpCmdLine,int nCmdShow);

int main(int argc, char* argv[])
{
   return AfxWinMain(GetModuleHandle(NULL),NULL,GetCommandLine(),SW_SHOW);
}

class test3 : public CWinApp
{

virtual BOOL InitInstance()
{
   int lnCmdLineParamCount;
   lnCmdLineParamCount = __argc - 1;

   if (lnCmdLineParamCount == 0)
   {
      // No command line parameters entered.
   }
   else
   {
      if (lnCmdLineParamCount == 1)
      {
         // One command line parameter entered.
      }
      else
      {
         // More than one command line parameter entered.
      }
   }
   return true;
}};

test3 goTest3;
```

C++ MFC
For Loop

- The following "for" loop example prints the string "Hello World!" ten times:

test4.cpp: C++ MFC For Loop

```
#include <afxwin.h>

extern int AFXAPI AfxWinMain(HINSTANCE hInstance,HINSTANCE hPrevInstance,
                             LPTSTR lpCmdLine,int nCmdShow);

int main(int argc, char* argv[])
{
   return AfxWinMain(GetModuleHandle(NULL),NULL,GetCommandLine(),SW_SHOW);
}

class test4 : public CWinApp
{

virtual BOOL InitInstance()
{
   int i;

   for (i=0;i < 10;i++)
   {
      fprintf(stdout,"Hello World!\n");
   }

   return TRUE;
}};

test4 goTest4;
```

C++ MFC
While Loop

- The following "while" loop example prints the string "Hello World!" ten times:

test5.cpp: C++ MFC While Loop

```
#include <afxwin.h>

extern int AFXAPI AfxWinMain(HINSTANCE hInstance,HINSTANCE hPrevInstance,
                             LPTSTR lpCmdLine,int nCmdShow);

int main(int argc, char* argv[])
{
   return AfxWinMain(GetModuleHandle(NULL),NULL,GetCommandLine(),SW_SHOW);
}

class test5 : public CWinApp
{

virtual BOOL InitInstance()
{
   int i;

   i = 0;

   while (i < 10)
   {
      fprintf(stdout,"Hello World!\n");
      i++;
   }
   return TRUE;
}};

test5 goTest5;
```

C++ MFC
Console Application Output to Standard Error

- The status code returned from the AfxWinMain() function is returned to the operating system. The ExitStatus() member function can be implemented in the application. The value returned from ExitStatus() member function will be returned by the AfxWinMain() function. A custom property called nMyReturnStatus is used to store a custom error status for the program. The code in the ExitStatus() function calls the default implementation of this function. If no custom error has been identified in the nMyReturnStatus property, the value returned from the default implementation of the ExitStatus() function is returned. Otherwise, the value stored in the nMyReturnStatus property is returned.

- The following example outputs text to standard error:

test6.cpp: C++ MFC Console Application Output to Standard Error

```
#include <afxwin.h>

extern int AFXAPI AfxWinMain(HINSTANCE hInstance,HINSTANCE hPrevInstance,
                             LPTSTR lpCmdLine,int nCmdShow);

int main(int argc, char* argv[])
{
   return AfxWinMain(GetModuleHandle(NULL),NULL,GetCommandLine(),SW_SHOW);
}

class test6 : public CWinApp
{
   int nMyReturnStatus;

virtual int ExitInstance()
{
   int lnReturnStatus;

   lnReturnStatus = CWinApp::ExitInstance();

   if (nMyReturnStatus == 0)
   {
      return lnReturnStatus;
   }
   else
   {
      return nMyReturnStatus;
   }
}

virtual BOOL InitInstance()
{
   nMyReturnStatus = 1;
   fprintf(stderr,"A program error has occurred.\n");

   return TRUE;
}};

test6 goTest6;
```

Source Code Files

- Text files: pp2_5.cpp

pp2_5.cpp: Program Phase 2-5 Source Code

```
//***************************************************************************
// Program Phase 2-5 C++ MFC Application Name Console Output               *
// Programming Tasks Illustrated: Console Application                       *
//                                Array Variable Declaration and Assignment *
//                                Program Name Parsing                      *
//                                If Statement                              *
//                                For Loop                                  *
//                                While Loop                                *
//                                Console Application Output to Standard Error*
//***************************************************************************

//***************************************************************************
// File: pp2_5.cpp                                                          *
// Reserved                                                                 *
//***************************************************************************

#include <afxwin.h>
#include <stdio.h>

extern int AFXAPI AfxWinMain(HINSTANCE hInstance,HINSTANCE hPrevInstance,
                             LPTSTR lpCmdLine,int nCmdShow);

int main(int tnArgc, char* taArgv[])
{
   // Actual Entry Point of Execution
   return AfxWinMain(GetModuleHandle(NULL),NULL,GetCommandLine(),SW_SHOW);
}

class pp2_5 : public CWinApp
{
   int nMyReturnStatus;

virtual int ExitInstance()
{
   int lnReturnStatus;

   lnReturnStatus = CWinApp::ExitInstance();

   if (nMyReturnStatus == 0)
   {
      return lnReturnStatus;
   }
   else
   {
      return nMyReturnStatus;
   }
}

//***************************************************************************
// Program Phase 2-5 Main                                                   *
// Define the Entry Point of Execution (EPE) for Program Phase 2-5          *
// CBI:  2-5.1.1.1                                                          *
//***************************************************************************

virtual BOOL InitInstance()
{


//***************************************************************************
// Program Phase 2-5 Main                                                   *
// Declare the local variables for the "main" program                      *
// CBI:  2-5.1.1.2                                                          *
//***************************************************************************

   size_t lnLength;
   size_t lnIndex;
```

pp2_5.cpp continued on the next page

pp2_5.cpp: Program Phase 2-5 Source Code continued

```
    char laArray[200];
    CString lcProgramName;

//***************************************************************************
// Program Phase 2-5 Main                                                   *
// Store the program name                                                   *
// CBI:  2-5.1.1.3                                                          *
//***************************************************************************

    lcProgramName = __argv[0];


//***************************************************************************
// Program Phase 2-5 Main                                                   *
// Use an if statement to verify the number of characters in the program name *
// CBI:  2-5.1.1.4                                                          *
//***************************************************************************

    lnLength = lcProgramName.GetLength();

    if (lnLength > 200)
    {
       fprintf(stderr,"The program name is greater than 200 characters.\n");
       nMyReturnStatus = 1;
       return FALSE;
    }


//***************************************************************************
// Program Phase 2-5 Main                                                   *
// Use a for loop to store the program name in an array                     *
// CBI:  2-5.1.1.5                                                          *
//***************************************************************************

    for (lnIndex=0;lnIndex < lnLength;lnIndex++)
    {
        laArray[lnIndex] = lcProgramName.GetAt(lnIndex);
    }


//***************************************************************************
// Program Phase 2-5 Main                                                   *
// Use a while loop to output to standard output each array character element *
// CBI:  2-5.1.1.6                                                          *
//***************************************************************************

    lnIndex = 0;
    printf("Program Name: ");

    while (lnIndex < lnLength)
    {
       printf("%c",laArray[lnIndex]);
       lnIndex++;
    }
    printf("\n");
    nMyReturnStatus = 0;

    return TRUE;
}};

pp2_5 go2_5;
```

Code Setup and Compilation

- Tools: Microsoft Visual C++ 2008

Code Setup and Compilation Steps

1: Start the Microsoft Visual C++ 2008 program.

2: VC++ - Activate Menu Item: File → New → Project

For the "Project type", select "Win32" and then select the "Win32 Console Application" template. Enter pp2_5 as the project "Name". Enter the appropriate folder as the project "Location". The pp2_5 folder will be automatically created. Make sure that the "Create directory for solution" check box is not checked.

3: Activate the "OK" button to proceed with the "Win32 Application Wizard".

4: Activate the "Next" button of the "Win32 Application Wizard".

5: Select the "Console application" radio button and also check the "Empty project" check box. Activate the "Finish" button of the "Win32 Application Wizard".

6: VC++ - Activate Menu Item: Build → Configuration Manager

Select the "Release" value for the "Active solution configuration".

7: VC++ - Activate Menu Item: Project → Add New Item

On the "Add New Item" dialog window, select the "Visual C++ → Code" category and then select the "C++ File (.cpp)" template. Enter pp2_5.cpp for the file "Name". Activate the "Add" button. Enter the source code for Program Phase 2-5 into the pp2_5.cpp text file.

8: VC++ - Activate Menu Item: Project → pp2_5 Properties

Enter the following settings:

Configuration Properties → General → Character Set

```
"Use Multi-Byte Character Set"
```

Configuration Properties → General → Use of MFC

```
"Use MFC in a Static Library" or "Use MFC in a Shared DLL"
```

9: VC++ - Activate Menu Item: Build → Build pp2_5

Command Prompt Compilation

From a Visual Studio 2008 command prompt in the pp2_5 folder, enter the following:

```
cl.exe /MT /EHsc pp2_5.cpp
```

Program Execution

- Execute Program

```
VC++ - Activate Menu Item: Debug → Start Without Debugging
```

C# ▪ .NET Framework - Mono ▪ Multi-Platform

Application Name Console Output

- Program Phase Task 2 is implemented in Program Phase 2-6 using the C# programming language and the Microsoft .NET Framework 2.0 or higher.
- The name of the program is stored one character at a time in a .NET Framework array.
- The C# "if" statement, "for" loop, and "while" loop are illustrated.
- Program Phase 2-6 is a console application that provides an example for sending output to standard output and standard error.

Code Block Features

The Program Phase 2-6 code blocks illustrate the following programming features in a console application using the C# programming language and the .NET Framework - Mono:

- **Array Variable Declaration and Assignment**
- **Program Name Parsing**
- **If Statement**
- **For Loop**
- **While Loop**
- **Console Application Output to Standard Error**

C# .NET Framework - Mono
Array Variable Declaration and Assignment

- The test1.cs example stores the string "Hello World!" one character at a time in the array called laArray. This array contains twelve array entries. Each array entry is then outputted to standard output.

test1.cs: C# .NET Framework - Mono Array Variable Declaration and Assignment

```
class test1
{
static int Main(string[] args)
{
   char[] laArray;
   laArray = new char[12];

   laArray[0] = 'H';
   laArray[1] = 'e';
```

test1.cs continued on the next page

test1.cs: C# .NET FW - Mono Array Variable Declaration and Assignment continued

```
    laArray[2] = 'l';
    laArray[3] = 'l';
    laArray[4] = 'o';
    laArray[5] = ' ';
    laArray[6] = 'W';
    laArray[7] = 'o';
    laArray[8] = 'r';
    laArray[9] = 'l';
    laArray[10] = 'd';
    laArray[11] = '!';

    System.Console.Write(laArray[0]);
    System.Console.Write(laArray[1]);
    System.Console.Write(laArray[2]);
    System.Console.Write(laArray[3]);
    System.Console.Write(laArray[4]);
    System.Console.Write(laArray[5]);
    System.Console.Write(laArray[6]);
    System.Console.Write(laArray[7]);
    System.Console.Write(laArray[8]);
    System.Console.Write(laArray[9]);
    System.Console.Write(laArray[10]);
    System.Console.Write(laArray[11]);

    System.Console.WriteLine("");
    return 0;
}}
```

C# .NET Framework - Mono Program Name Parsing

- The GetCommandLineArgs() method of the System.Environment class is called statically to get the path of the executing program. The name of the program is stored in the first entry of the argv array.

test2.cs: C# .NET Framework - Mono Program Name Parsing

```
class test2
{
static void Main()
{
    string[] argv;
    string lcProgramName;

    argv = System.Environment.GetCommandLineArgs();
    lcProgramName = argv[0];
}}
```

C# .NET Framework - Mono If Statement

- The "if" statement example presented here is identical in functionality to the Switch/Case statement presented in Program Phase 1-6.

test3.cs: C# .NET Framework - Mono If Statement

```
class test3
{
```

test3.cs continued on the next page

test3.cs: C# .NET Framework - Mono If Statement continued

```
static void Main()
{
   string[] argv;
   int lnCmdLineParamCount;

   argv = System.Environment.GetCommandLineArgs();
   lnCmdLineParamCount = argv.Length - 1;

   if (lnCmdLineParamCount == 0)
   {
      // No command line parameters entered.
   }
   else
   {
      if (lnCmdLineParamCount == 1)
      {
         // One command line parameter entered.
      }
      else
      {
         // More than one command line parameter entered.
      }
   }
}}
```

C# .NET Framework - Mono For Loop

- The following "for" loop example prints the string "Hello World!" ten times:

test4.cs: C# .NET Framework - Mono For Loop

```
using System;
class test4
{
static void Main()
{
   int i;

   for (i=0;i < 10;i++)
   {
      Console.WriteLine("Hello World!");
   }
}}
```

C# .NET Framework - Mono While Loop

- The following "while" loop example prints the string "Hello World!" ten times:

test5.cs: C# .NET Framework - Mono While Loop

```
class test5
{
static void Main()
{
   int i;
   i = 0;
```

test5.cs continued on the next page

test5.cs: C# .NET Framework - Mono While Loop continued

```
   while (i < 10)
   {
      System.Console.WriteLine("Hello World!");
      i++;
   }
}}
```

C# .NET Framework - Mono
Console Application Output to Standard Error

- An error code of one is returned to the operating system using the "return" statement. The following example outputs text to standard error:

test6.cs: C# .NET Framework - Mono Console Application Output to Standard Error

```
class test6
{
static int Main()
{
   System.Console.Error.WriteLine("A program error has occurred.");
   return 1;
}}
```

Source Code Files

- Text files: pp2_6.cs

pp2_6.cs: Program Phase 2-6 Source Code

```
//******************************************************************************
// Program Phase 2-6 C# .NET Framework - Mono Application Name Console Output *
// Programming Tasks Illustrated: Console Application                          *
//                                Array Variable Declaration and Assignment    *
//                                Progam Name Parsing                          *
//                                If Statement                                 *
//                                For Loop                                     *
//                                While Loop                                   *
//                                Console Application Output to Standard Error*
//******************************************************************************

//******************************************************************************
// File: pp2_6.cs                                                              *
// Reserved                                                                    *
//******************************************************************************

using System;
namespace nspp2_6
{
class pp2_6
{


//******************************************************************************
// Program Phase 2-6 Main                                                      *
// Define the Entry Point of Execution (EPE) for Program Phase 2-6             *
// CBI:  2-6.1.1.1                                                             *
//******************************************************************************

static int Main(string[] argv)
{
```

pp2_6.cs continued on the next page

pp2_6.cs: Program Phase 2-6 Source Code continued

```
//***************************************************************************
// Program Phase 2-6 Main                                                   *
// Declare the local variables for the "main" program                       *
// CBI:  2-6.1.1.2                                                          *
//***************************************************************************

   int lnLength;
   int lnIndex;
   char[] laArray;
   string lcProgramName;
   string[] laArgv;
   laArray = new char[200];
   laArgv = Environment.GetCommandLineArgs();


//***************************************************************************
// Program Phase 2-6 Main                                                   *
// Store the program name                                                   *
// CBI:  2-6.1.1.3                                                          *
//***************************************************************************

   lcProgramName = laArgv[0];


//***************************************************************************
// Program Phase 2-6 Main                                                   *
// Use an if statement to verify the number of characters in the program name *
// CBI:  2-6.1.1.4                                                          *
//***************************************************************************

   lnLength = lcProgramName.Length;

   if (lnLength > 200)
   {
    Console.Error.WriteLine("The program name is greater than 200 characters.");

      // Error Exit Status Code
      return 1;
   }


//***************************************************************************
// Program Phase 2-6 Main                                                   *
// Use a for loop to store the program name in an array                     *
// CBI:  2-6.1.1.5                                                          *
//***************************************************************************

   for (lnIndex = 0; lnIndex < lnLength; lnIndex++)
   {
      laArray[lnIndex] = lcProgramName[lnIndex];
   }


//***************************************************************************
// Program Phase 2-6 Main                                                   *
// Use a while loop to output to standard output each array character element *
// CBI:  2-6.1.1.6                                                          *
//***************************************************************************

   Console.Write("Program Name: ");
   lnIndex = 0;

   while (lnIndex < lnLength)
   {
      Console.Write(laArray[lnIndex]);
      lnIndex++;
   }
```

pp2_6.cs continued on the next page

pp2_6.cs: Program Phase 2-6 Source Code continued

```
    Console.Write("\n");
    return 0;
}
}}
```

Code Setup and Compilation

- Tools: Microsoft Visual C# 2008 Express Edition (msdn.microsoft.com), Microsoft .NET Framework 2.0 or higher (windowsupdate.microsoft.com), Steps to compile and execute using Mono on the Linux platform (programphases.com/?page_id=589)

Code Setup and Compilation Steps

1: Start the Microsoft Visual C# 2008 Express Edition program.

2: VC# EE - Activate Menu Item: File → New Project

Select the "Empty Project" template. Name the project pp2_6 and then activate the "OK" button.

3: VC# EE - Activate Menu Item: File → Save pp2_6

Set the "Location" to the appropriate folder. Verify that the "Create directory for solution" check box is not checked and then activate the "Save" button.

4: VC# EE - Activate Menu Item: Project → Add New Item

On the "Add New Item" dialog window, select the "Code File" template. Enter pp2_6.cs for the file "Name" and then activate the "Add" button. Enter the source code for Program Phase 2-6 into the pp2_6.cs text file.

5: VC# EE - Activate Menu Item: Project → pp2_6 Properties

Verify that the "Output type" is set to "Console Application". Set the "Startup object" to nspp2_6.pp2_6. Close the "pp2_6 Properties" window.

6: VC# EE - Activate Menu Item: File → Save All
VC# EE - Activate Menu Item: Build → Build Solution

Command Prompt Compilation

Enter the following commands from the pp2_6 folder to compile Program Phase 2-6:

```
PATH = "c:\windows\microsoft.net\framework\v2.0.50727";%PATH%
csc.exe /out:bin\release\pp2_6.exe pp2_6.cs
```

Program Execution

- Execute Program

  `VC# EE - Activate Menu Item:  Debug → Start Without Debugging`

- Debug Program

  `VC# EE - Activate Menu Item:  Debug → Step into`

Program Phase 2-7

VB .NET ▪ .NET Framework ▪ Windows

Application Name Console Output

- Program Phase Task 2 is implemented in Program Phase 2-7 using the Visual Basic .NET (VB.NET) programming language and the Microsoft .NET Framework 2.0 or higher.
- The name of the program is stored one character at a time in a .NET Framework array.
- The VB.NET "If" statement, "For" loop, and "While" loop are illustrated.
- Program Phase 2-7 is a console application that provides an example for sending output to standard output and standard error.

Code Block Features

The Program Phase 2-7 code blocks illustrate the following programming features in a console application using the Visual Basic .NET programming language:

- **Array Variable Declaration and Assignment**
- **Program Name Parsing**
- **If Statement**
- **For Loop**
- **While Loop**
- **Console Application Output to Standard Error**

Visual Basic .NET
Array Variable Declaration and Assignment

- The test1.vb example stores the string "Hello World!" one character at a time in the array called laArray. This array contains twelve array entries. Each array entry is then outputted to standard output.

test1.vb: Visual Basic .NET Array Variable Declaration and Assignment

```
Imports System

Module test1
Sub Main()

   Dim laArray(200) As Char
```

test1.vb continued on the next page

test1.vb: Visual Basic .NET Array Variable Declaration and Assignment continued

```
    laArray(0) = "H"
    laArray(1) = "e"
    laArray(2) = "l"
    laArray(3) = "l"
    laArray(4) = "o"
    laArray(5) = " "
    laArray(6) = "W"
    laArray(7) = "o"
    laArray(8) = "r"
    laArray(9) = "l"
    laArray(10) = "d"
    laArray(11) = "!"

    System.Console.Write(laArray(0))
    System.Console.Write(laArray(1))
    System.Console.Write(laArray(2))
    System.Console.Write(laArray(3))
    System.Console.Write(laArray(4))
    System.Console.Write(laArray(5))
    System.Console.Write(laArray(6))
    System.Console.Write(laArray(7))
    System.Console.Write(laArray(8))
    System.Console.Write(laArray(9))
    System.Console.Write(laArray(10))
    System.Console.Write(laArray(11))
    Console.WriteLine("")

End Sub
End Module
```

Visual Basic .NET Program Name Parsing

- The GetCommandLineArgs() method of the System.Environment class can be called statically to get the path of the executing program. The name of the program is stored in the first entry of the argv array.

test2.vb: Visual Basic .NET Program Name Parsing

```
Module test2
Sub Main()

    Dim argv() As String
    Dim lcProgramName As String

    argv = System.Environment.GetCommandLineArgs()
    lcProgramName = argv(0)

End Sub
End Module
```

Visual Basic .NET If Statement

- The "If" statement example presented here is identical in functionality to the Switch/Case statement presented in Program Phase 1-7.

test3.vb: Visual Basic .NET If Statement

```
Module test3
Sub Main()

   Dim lnCmdLineParamCount As Integer
   Dim laArgv() As String

   laArgv = System.Environment.GetCommandLineArgs()
   lnCmdLineParamCount = laArgv.Length - 1

   If (lnCmdLineParamCount = 0) Then

      '' No command line parameters entered.

   Else

      If (lnCmdLineParamCount = 1) Then

         '' One command line parameter entered.

      Else

         '' More than one command line parameter entered.

      End If

   End If

End Sub
End Module
```

Visual Basic .NET For Loop

- The following "For" loop example prints the string "Hello World!" ten times:

test4.vb: Visual Basic .NET For Loop

```
Imports System

Module test4
Sub Main()

   Dim i as Integer

   For i = 1 To 10
      System.Console.WriteLine("Hello World!")
   Next i

End Sub
End Module
```

Visual Basic .NET While Loop

- The following "While" loop example prints the string "Hello World!" ten times:

test5.vb: Visual Basic .NET While Loop

```
Module test5
Sub Main()

   Dim i as Integer
   i = 0

   Do While (i < 10)
      System.Console.WriteLine("Hello World!")
      i = i + 1
   Loop

End Sub
End Module
```

Visual Basic .NET
Console Application Output to Standard Error

- An error code of one is returned to the operating system from the Main() function using the "Return" statement. The following example outputs text to standard error:

test6.vb: Visual Basic .NET Console Application Output to Standard Error

```
Imports System

Module test6
Public Function Main() As Integer

   Console.Error.WriteLine("A program error has occurred.")
   Return 1

End Function
End Module
```

Source Code Files

- Text files: pp2_7.vb

pp2_7.vb: Program Phase 2-7 Source Code

```
''*****************************************************************************
'' Program Phase 2-7 VB.NET Application Name Console Output                  *
'' Programming Tasks Illustrated: Console Application                         *
''                                Array Variable Declaration and Assignment   *
''                                Program Name Parsing                        *
''                                If Statement                                *
''                                For Loop                                    *
''                                While Loop                                  *
''                                Console Application Output to Standard Error*
''*****************************************************************************

''*****************************************************************************
'' File: pp2_7.vb                                                             *
'' Reserved                                                                   *
''*****************************************************************************

Imports System
Namespace nspp2_7
Module pp2_7
```

pp2_7.vb continued on the next page

pp2_7.vb: Program Phase 2-7 Source Code continued

```
''*************************************************************************
'' Program Phase 2-7 Main                                                 *
'' Define the Entry Point of Execution (EPE) for Program Phase 2-7        *
'' CBI:  2-7.1.1.1                                                        *
''*************************************************************************

Public Function Main() As Integer


''*************************************************************************
'' Program Phase 2-7 Main                                                 *
'' Declare the local variables for the "main" program                     *
'' CBI:  2-7.1.1.2                                                        *
''*************************************************************************

   Dim lnLength As Integer
   Dim lnIndex As Integer
   Dim laArray(200) As Char
   Dim lcProgramName As String
   Dim argv() As String


''*************************************************************************
'' Program Phase 2-7 Main                                                 *
'' Store the program name                                                 *
'' CBI:  2-7.1.1.3                                                        *
''*************************************************************************

   argv = Environment.GetCommandLineArgs()
   lcProgramName = argv(0)


''*************************************************************************
'' Program Phase 2-7 Main                                                 *
'' Use an if statement to verify the number of characters in the program name *
'' CBI:  2-7.1.1.4                                                        *
''*************************************************************************

   lnLength = lcProgramName.Length

   If (lnLength > 200) Then

     Console.Error.WriteLine("The program name is greater than 200 characters.")

      '' Error Exit Status Code
      Return 1

   End If


''*************************************************************************
'' Program Phase 2-7 Main                                                 *
'' Use a for loop to store the program name in an array                   *
'' CBI:  2-7.1.1.5                                                        *
''*************************************************************************

   For lnIndex = 0 To lnLength - 1

      laArray(lnIndex) = lcProgramName.Chars(lnIndex)

   Next lnIndex
```

pp2_7.vb continued on the next page

pp2_7.vb: Program Phase 2-7 Source Code continued

```
''************************************************************************
'' Program Phase 2-7 Main                                                *
'' Use a while loop to output to standard output each array character element *
'' CBI:  2-7.1.1.6                                                       *
''************************************************************************

   Console.Write("Program Name: ")

   lnIndex = 0

   Do While (lnIndex < lnLength)

      Console.Write(laArray(lnIndex))
      lnIndex = lnIndex + 1

   Loop

   Console.WriteLine("")
   Return 0

End Function
End Module

End Namespace
```

Code Setup and Compilation

- Tools: Microsoft Visual Basic 2008 Express Edition (msdn.microsoft.com), Microsoft .NET Framework 2.0 or higher (windowsupdate.microsoft.com)

Code Setup and Compilation Steps

1: Start the Microsoft Visual Basic 2008 Express Edition program.

2: VB.NET EE - Activate Menu Item: File → New Project

Select "Console Application". Name the project pp2_7 and then activate the "OK" button.

3: Delete the module1.bas file in the "Solution Explorer" window.

4: VB.NET EE - Activate Menu Item: File → Save All

On the "Save Project" dialog window, specify pp2_7 for the "Name". Set the "Location" to the appropriate folder. Uncheck the "Create directory for solution" check box and then activate the "Save" button.

5: VB.NET EE - Activate Menu Item: Project → Add New Item

On the "Add New Item" dialog window, select the "Module" template. Enter pp2_7.vb for the file "Name" and then activate the "Add" button. Enter the source code for Program Phase 2-7 into the pp2_7.vb text file.

Steps continued on the next page

```
Code Setup and Compilation Steps continued
```

6: VB.NET EE - Activate Menu Item: Project → pp2_7 Properties

The "Startup object" should be set to nspp2_7.pp2_7. Close the "pp2_7 Properties" window.

7: VB.NET EE - Activate Menu Item: File → Save All

8: VB.NET EE - Activate Menu Item: Build → Build pp2_7

The resulting pp2_7.exe file will be found in the pp2_7\build or pp2_7\debug folder.

```
Command Prompt Compilation
```

Enter the following commands from the pp2_7 folder to compile Program Phase 2-7:

```
PATH = "c:\windows\microsoft.net\framework\v2.0.50727";%PATH%
vbc.exe /r:system.dll /out:bin\release\pp2_7.exe pp2_7.vb
```

Program Execution

- Execute Program

Place the cursor at the End Function line of code in the CBI: 2-7.1.1.6 code block.

```
VB.NET EE - Activate Menu Item:  Debug → Toggle Breakpoint
VB.NET EE - Activate Menu Item:  Debug → Start Debugging
```

- Debug Program

```
VB.NET EE - Activate Menu Item:  Debug → Step Into
```

Program Phase 2-8
Managed C++ ▪ Windows
Application Name Console Output

- Program Phase Task 2 is implemented in Program Phase 2-8 using the C++ programming language and the Microsoft .NET Framework 2.0 or higher.
- The name of the program is stored one character at a time in a .NET Framework array.
- The C/C++ "if" statement, "for" loop, and "while" loop are illustrated.
- Program Phase 2-8 is a console application that provides an example for sending output to standard output and standard error.

Code Block Features

The Program Phase 2-8 code blocks illustrate the following programming features in a console application using the C++ programming language and the Microsoft .NET Framework:

- **Array Variable Declaration and Assignment**
- **Program Name Parsing**
- **If Statement**
- **For Loop**
- **While Loop**
- **Console Application Output to Standard Error**

Managed C++
Array Variable Declaration and Assignment

- The test1.cpp example stores the string "Hello World!" one character at a time in the array called laArray. This array contains twelve array entries. Each array entry is then outputted to standard output.

test1.cpp: Managed C++ Array Variable Declaration and Assignment

```
#using <mscorlib.dll>
using namespace System;

int main()
{
   cli::array <System::Char> ^laArray;
   laArray = gcnew array<System::Char>(12);
```

test1.cpp continued on the next page

test1.cpp: Managed C++ Array Variable Declaration and Assignment continued

```
    laArray[0] = 'H';
    laArray[1] = 'e';
    laArray[2] = 'l';
    laArray[3] = 'l';
    laArray[4] = 'o';
    laArray[5] = ' ';
    laArray[6] = 'W';
    laArray[7] = 'o';
    laArray[8] = 'r';
    laArray[9] = 'l';
    laArray[10] = 'd';
    laArray[11] = '!';

    System::Console::Write(laArray[0]);
    System::Console::Write(laArray[1]);
    System::Console::Write(laArray[2]);
    System::Console::Write(laArray[3]);
    System::Console::Write(laArray[4]);
    System::Console::Write(laArray[5]);
    System::Console::Write(laArray[6]);
    System::Console::Write(laArray[7]);
    System::Console::Write(laArray[8]);
    System::Console::Write(laArray[9]);
    System::Console::Write(laArray[10]);
    System::Console::Write(laArray[11]);
    System::Console::WriteLine(" ");

    return 0;
}
```

Managed C++
Program Name Parsing

- The GetCommandLineArgs() method of the System::Environment class is called statically to get the path of the executing program. The name of the program is stored in the first entry of the argv array.

test2.cpp: Managed C++ Program Name Parsing

```
#using <mscorlib.dll>
using namespace System;

int main()
{
    cli::array <String^> ^argv;
    System::String^ lcProgramName;

    argv = System::Environment::GetCommandLineArgs();
    lcProgramName = argv[0];
    return 0;
}
```

Managed C++
If Statement

- The "if" statement example presented here is identical in functionality to the Switch/Case statement presented in Program Phase 1-8.

test3.cpp: Managed C++ If Statement

```
#using <mscorlib.dll>
using namespace System;

int main()
{
   cli::array <String^> ^argv;
   int argc;
   int lnCmdLineParamCount;

   argv = System::Environment::GetCommandLineArgs();
   argc = argv->Length;
   lnCmdLineParamCount = argc - 1;

   if (lnCmdLineParamCount == 0)
   {
      // No command line parameters entered.
   }
   else
   {
      if (lnCmdLineParamCount == 1)
      {
         // One command line parameter entered.
      }
      else
      {
         // More than one command line parameter entered.
      }
   }

   return 0;
}
```

Managed C++ For Loop

- The following "for" loop example prints the string "Hello World!" ten times:

test4.cpp: Managed C++ For Loop

```
#using <mscorlib.dll>

int main()
{
   int i;

   for (i=0;i < 10;i++)
   {
      System::Console::WriteLine("Hello World!");
   }
   return 0;
}
```

Managed C++ While Loop

- The following "while" loop example prints the string "Hello World!" ten times:

test5.cpp: Managed C++ While Loop

```
#using <mscorlib.dll>

int main()
{
   int i;

   i = 0;

   while (i < 10)
   {
      System::Console::WriteLine("Hello World!");
      i++;
   }

   return 0;
}
```

Managed C++
Console Application Output to Standard Error

- An error code of one is returned to the operating system using the "return" statement. The following example outputs text to standard error:

test6.cpp: Managed C++ Console Application Output to Standard Error

```
#using <mscorlib.dll>

int main()
{
   System::Console::Error->WriteLine("A program error has occurred.");
   return 1;
}
```

Source Code Files

- Text files: pp2_8.cpp

pp2_8.cpp: Program Phase 2-8 Source Code

```
//*****************************************************************************
// Program Phase 2-8 Managed C++ Application Name Console Output              *
// Programming Tasks Illustrated: Console Application                         *
//                                Array Variable Declaration and Assignment   *
//                                Program Name Parsing                        *
//                                If Statement                                *
//                                For Loop                                    *
//                                While Loop                                  *
//                                Console Application Output to Standard Error*
//*****************************************************************************

//*****************************************************************************
// File: pp2_8.cpp                                                            *
// Reserved                                                                   *
//*****************************************************************************

#using <mscorlib.dll>
using namespace System;
```

pp2_8.cpp continued on the next page

pp2_8.cpp: Program Phase 2-8 Source Code continued

```
//***************************************************************************
// Program Phase 2-8 Main                                                   *
// Define the Entry Point of Execution (EPE) for Program Phase 2-8          *
// CBI:  2-8.1.1.1                                                          *
//***************************************************************************

int main()
{


//***************************************************************************
// Program Phase 2-8 Main                                                   *
// Declare the local variables for the "main" program                       *
// CBI:  2-8.1.1.2                                                          *
//***************************************************************************

   int lnLength;
   int lnIndex;
   cli::array <String^> ^argv;
   String^ lcProgramName;
   cli::array <System::Char> ^laArray;
   laArray = gcnew array<System::Char>(200);


//***************************************************************************
// Program Phase 2-8 Main                                                   *
// Store the program name                                                   *
// CBI:  2-8.1.1.3                                                          *
//***************************************************************************

   argv = Environment::GetCommandLineArgs();
   lcProgramName = argv[0];


//***************************************************************************
// Program Phase 2-8 Main                                                   *
// Use an if statement to verify the number of characters in the program name *
// CBI:  2-8.1.1.4                                                          *
//***************************************************************************

   lnLength = lcProgramName->Length;

   if (lnLength > 200)
   {
 Console::Error->WriteLine("The program name is greater than 200 characters.");
      return 1;
   }


//***************************************************************************
// Program Phase 2-8 Main                                                   *
// Use a for loop to store the program name in an array                     *
// CBI:  2-8.1.1.5                                                          *
//***************************************************************************

   for (lnIndex=0;lnIndex < lnLength;lnIndex++)
   {
      laArray[lnIndex] = lcProgramName->default::get(lnIndex);
   }


//***************************************************************************
// Program Phase 2-8 Main                                                   *
// Use a while loop to output to standard output each array character element *
// CBI:  2-8.1.1.6                                                          *
//***************************************************************************
```

pp2_8.cpp continued on the next page

pp2_8.cpp: Program Phase 2-8 Source Code continued

```
    lnIndex = 0;
    Console::Write("Program Name: ");

    while (lnIndex < lnLength)
    {
        // Output To Standard Output
        Console::Write(laArray[lnIndex]);
        lnIndex++;
    }
    Console::Write("\n");
    return 0;
}
```

Code Setup and Compilation

- Tools: Microsoft Visual C++ 2008 Express Edition (msdn.microsoft.com), Microsoft .NET Framework 2.0 or higher (windowsupdate.microsoft.com)

Code Setup and Compilation Steps

1: Start the Microsoft Visual Studio C++ 2008 Express Edition program.

2: VC++ EE - Activate Menu Item: File → New → Project

3: Select "Win32" for the "Project" type. Select the "Win32 Console Application" template.

4: Set the "Name" of the project to pp2_8. Set the project "Location" to the appropriate folder. Do not check the "Create directory for solution" check box. Activate the "OK" button to proceed with the "Win32 Application Wizard".

5: Activate the "Next" button of the "Win32 Application Wizard".

6: Verify that a "Console Application" is selected and also check the "Empty project" check box. Activate the "Finish" button of the "Win32 Application Wizard".

7: VC++ EE - Activate Menu Item: Project → Add New Item

On the "Add New Item" dialog window, select the "Visual C++ → Code" category and then select the "C++ File" template. Enter pp2_8.cpp for the file "Name" and then activate the "Add" button. Enter the source code for Program Phase 2-8 into the pp2_8.cpp text file.

8: VC++ EE - Activate Menu Item: Project → pp2_8 Properties

Enter the following settings:

Configuration Properties → General → Character Set

```
"Use Multi-Byte Character Set"
```

Configuration Properties → General → Common Language Runtime Support

```
"Common Language Runtime Support (/clr)"
```

9: VC++ EE - Activate Menu Item: Build → Build Solution

Command Prompt Compilation

From a Visual Studio 2008 command prompt, enter the following command from the pp2_8 folder:

```
cl.exe /clr pp2_8.cpp
```

Program Execution

- Execute Program

  `VC++ EE - Activate Menu Item: Debug → Start Without Debugging`

- Debug Program

  `VC++ EE - Activate Menu Item: Debug → Step Into`

Program Phase 2-9
Python ▪ Multi-Platform
Application Name Console Output

- Program Phase Task 2 is implemented in Program Phase 2-9 using the Python programming language.
- The name of the program is stored one character at a time in a Python array.
- The Python "if" statement, "for" loop, and "while" loop are illustrated.
- Program Phase 2-9 is a console application that provides an example for sending output to standard output and standard error.

Code Block Features

The Program Phase 2-9 code blocks illustrate the following programming features in a console application using the Python programming language:

- **Array Variable Declaration and Assignment**
- **Program Name Parsing**
- **If Statement**
- **For Loop**
- **While Loop**
- **Console Application Output to Standard Error**

Python
Array Variable Declaration and Assignment

- The test1.py example stores the string "Hello World!" one character at a time in the array called laArray. This array contains twelve array entries. Each array entry is then outputted to standard output.

test1.py: Python Array Variable Declaration and Assignment

```
import sys

def main():
    laArray = 12 * [0]

    laArray[0] = "H";
    laArray[1] = "e";
    laArray[2] = "l";
    laArray[3] = "l";
    laArray[4] = "o";
```

test1.py continued on the next page

test1.py: Python Array Variable Declaration and Assignment continued

```
    laArray[5] = " ";
    laArray[6] = "W";
    laArray[7] = "o";
    laArray[8] = "r";
    laArray[9] = "l";
    laArray[10] = "d";
    laArray[11] = "!";

    sys.stdout.write(laArray[0])
    sys.stdout.write(laArray[1])
    sys.stdout.write(laArray[2])
    sys.stdout.write(laArray[3])
    sys.stdout.write(laArray[4])
    sys.stdout.write(laArray[5])
    sys.stdout.write(laArray[6])
    sys.stdout.write(laArray[7])
    sys.stdout.write(laArray[8])
    sys.stdout.write(laArray[9])
    sys.stdout.write(laArray[10])
    sys.stdout.write(laArray[11])
    sys.stdout.write("\n")

main()
```

Python
Program Name Parsing

- The first entry in the sys.argv array stores the program name.

test2.py: Python Program Name Parsing

```
import sys

def main():
    lcProgramName =  sys.argv[0]

main()
```

Python
If Statement

- The "if" statement example presented here is identical in functionality to the Switch/Case statement presented in Program Phase 1-9.

test3.py: Python If Statement

```
import sys

def main():
    lnCmdLineParamCount = len(sys.argv) - 1

    if lnCmdLineParamCount == 0:
       print 'No command line parameters entered.'

    elif lnCmdLineParamCount == 1:
       print 'One command line parameter entered.'

    else:
       print 'More than one command line parameter entered.'
main()
```

Python
For Loop

- The test4.py "for" loop example prints the string "Hello World!" ten times. The indent of the sys.stdout.write line is important because it determines the lines of code that are part of the loop.

test4.py: Python For Loop

```
import sys

def main():
    i = 1

    for i in range(10):

        sys.stdout.write("Hello World!\n")

main()
```

Python
While Loop

- The following "while" loop example prints the string "Hello World!" ten times:

test5.py: Python While Loop

```
import sys

def main():
    i = 0

    while i < 10:

        sys.stdout.write("Hello World!\n")
        i += 1

main()
```

Python
Console Application Output to Standard Error

- An error code of one is returned to the operating system using the sys.exit() function. The following example outputs text to standard error:

test6.py: Python Console Application Output to Standard Error

```
import sys

def main():
    sys.stderr.write("A program error has occurred.\n")
    sys.exit(1)

main()
```

Source Code Files

- Text files: pp2_9.py

pp2_9.py: Program Phase 2-9 Source Code

```
##*************************************************************************
## Program Phase 2-9 Python Application Name Console Output              *
## Programming Tasks Illustrated: Console Application                    *
##                                Array Variable Declaration and Assignment *
##                                Program Name Parsing                   *
##                                If Statement                           *
##                                For Loop                               *
##                                While Loop                             *
##                                Console Application Output to Standard Error*
##*************************************************************************

##*************************************************************************
## File: pp2_9.py                                                        *
## Reserved                                                              *
##*************************************************************************

import sys

##*************************************************************************
## Program Phase 2-9 Main                                                *
## Define the Entry Point of Execution (EPE) for Program Phase 2-9       *
## CBI:  2-9.1.1.1                                                       *
##*************************************************************************

def main():

##*************************************************************************
## Program Phase 2-9 Main                                                *
## Declare the local variables for the "main" program                    *
## CBI:  2-9.1.1.2                                                       *
##*************************************************************************

    lnLength = 0
    lnIndex = 0
    laArray = 200 * [0]
    lcProgramName = ""

##*************************************************************************
## Program Phase 2-9 Main                                                *
## Store the program name                                                *
## CBI:  2-9.1.1.3                                                       *
##*************************************************************************

    lcProgramName =  sys.argv[0]
    lnLength = len(lcProgramName)

##*************************************************************************
## Program Phase 2-9 Main                                                *
## Use an if statement to verify the number of characters in the program name *
## CBI:  2-9.1.1.4                                                       *
##*************************************************************************

    if lnLength > 200:

        ## Output To Standard Error
        sys.stderr.write("The program name is greater than 200 characters.\n")

        ## Error Exit Status Code
        sys.exit(1)
```

pp2_9.py continued on the next page

pp2_9.py: Program Phase 2-9 Source Code continued

```
##**********************************************************************
## Program Phase 2-9 Main                                               *
## Use a for loop to store the program name in an array                 *
## CBI:  2-9.1.1.5                                                      *
##**********************************************************************

    lnIndex = 0

    for lnIndex in range(lnLength):

       laArray[lnIndex] = lcProgramName[lnIndex]


##**********************************************************************
## Program Phase 2-9 Main                                               *
## Use a while loop to output to standard output each array character element *
## CBI:  2-9.1.1.6                                                      *
##**********************************************************************

    lnIndex = 0
    sys.stdout.write("Program Name: ")

    while lnIndex < lnLength:

       sys.stdout.write(laArray[lnIndex])
       lnIndex += 1

    sys.stdout.write("\n")

# Actual EPE
main()
```

Code Setup and Compilation

- Tools: Python distribution (Appendix G), Komodo IDE (Appendix F)

Code Setup and Compilation Steps

1: Create a folder called pp2_9 that will store the Program Phase 2-9 source code files.

2: Start the Komodo IDE program.

3: Komodo - Activate Menu Item: File → New → New Project

Set the project name to pp2_9.kpf and save the new project in the pp2_9 folder.

4: Komodo - Activate Menu Item: File → New → New File

Click on the "Common" category and then select the "Text" template. Set the "Filename" to pp2_9.py. Verify that the "add to pp2_9 project" check box is checked and the "Directory" is set to the pp2_9 folder. Activate the "Open" button. Enter the source code for Program Phase 2-9 and then save the file.

5: There is no step for compiling the pp2_9.py file. It is compiled at runtime by the Python interpreter.

Program Execution

- Execute Program

```
Komodo - Activate Menu Item: Debug → Run Without Debugging
```

On the "Debugging Options" window, verify that the "Script" is set to the full path to the pp2_9.py file and then activate the "OK" button. The output for Program Phase 2-9 is displayed in the Komodo output window on the "Run Output" tab.

- Debug Program

```
Komodo - Activate Menu Item: Debug → Step In
```

Program Phase 2-10

Perl ▪ Multi-Platform

Application Name Console Output

- Program Phase Task 2 is implemented in Program Phase 2-10 using the Perl programming language.
- The name of the program is stored one character at a time in a Perl array.
- The Perl "if" statement, "for" loop, and "while" loop are illustrated.
- Program Phase 2-10 is a console application that provides an example for sending output to standard output and standard error.

Code Block Features

The Program Phase 2-10 code blocks illustrate the following programming features in a console application using the Perl programming language:

- **Array Variable Declaration and Assignment**
- **Program Name Parsing**
- **If Statement**
- **For Loop**
- **While Loop**
- **Console Application Output to Standard Error**

Perl
Array Variable Declaration and Assignment

- Perl arrays are declared using the "@" symbol. Each entry in the array can store a scalar value such as a string or number. Individual array scalar entries can be accessed like any other scalar variable by prefacing the variable with the "$" symbol.

test1.pl: Perl Array Variable Declaration and Assignment

```
@laArray = (1 .. 12);

$laArray[0] = "H";
$laArray[1] = "e";
$laArray[2] = "l";
$laArray[3] = "l";
$laArray[4] = "o";
$laArray[5] = " ";
$laArray[6] = "W";
```

test1.pl continued on the next page

test1.pl: Perl Array Variable Declaration and Assignment continued

```
$laArray[7] = "o";
$laArray[8] = "r";
$laArray[9] = "l";
$laArray[10] = "d";
$laArray[11] = "!";

print(STDOUT $laArray[0]);
print(STDOUT $laArray[1]);
print(STDOUT $laArray[2]);
print(STDOUT $laArray[3]);
print(STDOUT $laArray[4]);
print(STDOUT $laArray[5]);
print(STDOUT $laArray[6]);
print(STDOUT $laArray[7]);
print(STDOUT $laArray[8]);
print(STDOUT $laArray[9]);
print(STDOUT $laArray[10]);
print(STDOUT $laArray[11]);
print(STDOUT "\n");
```

Perl
Program Name Parsing

- A Perl application accesses the program name in a special variable called "$0".

test2.pl: Perl Program Name Parsing

```
my $lcProgramName = "";

$lcProgramName = $0;
```

Perl
If Statement

- The "if" statement example presented here is identical in functionality to the Switch/Case statement presented in Program Phase 1-10.

test3.pl: Perl If Statement

```
my $lnCmdLineParalCount = 0;

$lnCmdLineParamCount = scalar(@ARGV);

if($lnCmdLineParamCount == 0)
{
   ## No command line parameters entered.
}
elsif ($lnCmdLineParamCount == 1)
{
   ## One command line parameter entered.
}
else
{
  ## More than one command line parameter entered.
}
```

Perl
For Loop

- The following "for" loop example prints the string "Hello World!" ten times:

test4.pl: Perl For Loop

```
my $i;

for ($i=0; $i<10; $i++)
{
   print(STDOUT "Hello World!\n");
}
```

Perl
While Loop

- The following "while" loop example prints the string "Hello World!" ten times:

test5.pl: Perl While Loop

```
my $i;

while ($i < 10)
{
   print(STDOUT "Hello World!\n");
   $i++;
}
```

Perl
Console Application Output to Standard Error

- An error code of one is returned to the operating system using the Perl "exit" statement. The following example outputs text to standard error:

test6.pl: Perl Console Application Output to Standard Error

```
print(STDERR "A program error has occurred.\n");
exit 1;
```

Source Code Files

- Text files: pp2_10.pl

pp2_10.pl: Program Phase 2-10 Source Code

```
##****************************************************************************
## Program Phase 2-10 Perl Application Name Console Output                   *
## Programming Tasks Illustrated: Console Application                         *
##                                Array Variable Declaration and Assignment   *
##                                Program Name Parsing                        *
##                                If Statement                                *
##                                For Loop                                    *
##                                While Loop                                  *
##                                Console Application Output to Standard Error*
##****************************************************************************

##****************************************************************************
## File: pp2_10.pl                                                           *
## Reserved                                                                  *
##****************************************************************************


##****************************************************************************
## Program Phase 2-10 Main                                                   *
## Define the Entry Point of Execution (EPE) for Program Phase 2-10          *
## CBI:  2-10.1.1.1                                                          *
##****************************************************************************

## The first line of the code in the pp2_10.pl file is the EPE.


##****************************************************************************
## Program Phase 2-10 Main                                                   *
## Declare the local variables for the "main" program                        *
## CBI:  2-10.1.1.2                                                          *
##****************************************************************************

my $lnLength;
my $lnIndex;
@laArray = (1 .. 200);
my $lcProgramName;


##****************************************************************************
## Program Phase 2-10 Main                                                   *
## Store the program name                                                    *
## CBI:  2-10.1.1.3                                                          *
##****************************************************************************

$lcProgramName =  $0;
$lnLength = length($lcProgramName);


##****************************************************************************
## Program Phase 2-10 Main                                                   *
## Use an if statement to verify the number of characters in the program name *
## CBI:  2-10.1.1.4                                                          *
##****************************************************************************

if ($lnLength > 200)
{
   print(STDERR "The program name is greater than 200 characters.\n");
   exit 1;
}


##****************************************************************************
## Program Phase 2-10 Main                                                   *
## Use a for loop to store the program name in an array                      *
## CBI:  2-10.1.1.5                                                          *
##****************************************************************************
```

pp2_10.pl continued on the next page

pp2_10.pl: Program Phase 2-10 Source Code continued

```
for ($lnIndex=0; $lnIndex<$lnLength; $lnIndex++)
{
   $laArray[$lnIndex] = substr($lcProgramName,$lnIndex,1);
}


##*************************************************************************
## Program Phase 2-10 Main                                                *
## Use a while loop to output to standard output each array character element *
## CBI:  2-10.1.1.6                                                       *
##*************************************************************************

print(STDOUT "Program Name: ");

$lnIndex = 0;

while ($lnIndex < $lnLength)
{
   print(STDOUT $laArray[$lnIndex]);
   $lnIndex ++;
}

print(STDOUT "\n");
```

Code Setup and Compilation

- Tools: Perl 5 distribution (Appendix H), Komodo IDE (Appendix F)

Code Setup and Compilation Steps

1: Create a folder called pp2_10 that will store the source code files.

2: Start the Komodo IDE program.

3: Komodo - Activate Menu Item: File → New → New Project

Set the project name to pp2_10.kpf and save the new project in the pp2_10 folder.

4: Komodo - Activate Menu Item: File → New → New File

Click on the "Common" category and then select the "Text" template. Set the "Filename" to pp2_10.pl. Verify that the "add to pp2_10 project" check box is checked and the "Directory" is set to the pp2_10 folder. Activate the "Open" button. Enter the source code for Program Phase 2-10 and then save the file.

5: There is no step for compiling the pp2_10.pl file. It is compiled at runtime by the Perl interpreter.

Program Execution

- Execute Program

```
Komodo - Activate Menu Item: Debug → Run Without Debugging
```

On the "Debugging Options" window, verify that the "Script" is set to the full path to the pp2_10.pl file and then activate the "OK" button. The output for Program Phase 2-10 is displayed in the Komodo output window on the "Run Output" tab.

- Debug Program

```
Komodo - Activate Menu Item: Debug → Step In
```

Program Phase 2-11

PHP CLI ▪ Multi-Platform

Application Name Console Output

- Program Phase Task 2 is implemented in Program Phase 2-11 using the PHP programming language.
- The name of the program is stored one character at a time in a PHP array.
- The PHP "if" statement, "for" loop, and "while" loop are illustrated.
- Program Phase 2-11 is a console application that provides an example for sending output to standard output and standard error.

Code Block Features

The Program Phase 2-11 code blocks illustrate the following programming features in a console application using the PHP programming language:

- **Array Variable Declaration and Assignment**
- **Program Name Parsing**
- **If Statement**
- **For Loop**
- **While Loop**
- **Console Application Output to Standard Error**

PHP CLI
Array Variable Declaration and Assignment

- The test1.php example stores the string "Hello World!" one character at a time in the array called laArray. This array contains twelve array entries. Each array entry is then outputted to standard output.

test1.php: PHP CLI Array Variable Declaration and Assignment

```
<?php

main($argc,$argv);

function main($argc,$argv)
{
   $laArray = array_pad(array(),12, 0);

   $laArray[0] = "H";
```

test1.php continued on the next page

test1.php: PHP CLI Array Variable Declaration and Assignment continued

```
    $laArray[1] = "e";
    $laArray[2] = "l";
    $laArray[3] = "l";
    $laArray[4] = "o";
    $laArray[5] = " ";
    $laArray[6] = "W";
    $laArray[7] = "o";
    $laArray[8] = "r";
    $laArray[9] = "l";
    $laArray[10] = "d";
    $laArray[11] = "!";

    $stdout = fopen("php://stdout","w");

    fwrite($stdout,$laArray[0]);
    fwrite($stdout,$laArray[1]);
    fwrite($stdout,$laArray[2]);
    fwrite($stdout,$laArray[3]);
    fwrite($stdout,$laArray[4]);
    fwrite($stdout,$laArray[5]);
    fwrite($stdout,$laArray[6]);
    fwrite($stdout,$laArray[7]);
    fwrite($stdout,$laArray[8]);
    fwrite($stdout,$laArray[9]);
    fwrite($stdout,$laArray[10]);
    fwrite($stdout,$laArray[11]);
    fwrite($stdout,"\n");

    fclose($stdout);
}
?>
```

PHP CLI
Program Name Parsing

- The program name is accessed in a special variable called $argv. The $argv variable is an array that stores the program name in the first array entry.

test2.php: PHP CLI Program Name Parsing

```
<?php

main($argc,$argv);

function main($argc,$argv)
{
    $lcProgramName = $argv[0];
}
?>
```

PHP CLI
If Statement

- The "if" statement example presented here is identical in functionality to the Switch/Case statement presented in Program Phase 1-11.

test3.php: PHP CLI If Statement

```
<?php

main($argc,$argv);

function main($argc,$argv)
{

   $lnCmdLineParamCount = null;
   $lnCmdLineParamCount = $argc - 1;

   if ($lnCmdLineParamCount == 0)
   {
      // No command line parameters entered.
   }
   elseif ($lnCmdLineParamCount == 1)
   {
      // One command line parameter entered.
   }
   else
   {
      // More than one command line parameter entered.
   }
}
?>
```

PHP CLI For Loop

- The following "for" loop example prints the string "Hello World!" ten times:

test4.php: PHP CLI For Loop

```
<?php

main($argc,$argv);

function main($argc,$argv)
{
   $i = null;
   $stdout = null;

   $stdout = fopen("php://stdout","w");

   for ($i=1;$i<12;$i++)
   {
      fwrite($stdout,"Hello World!\n");
   }

   fclose($stdout);
}
?>
```

PHP CLI While Loop

- The following "while" loop example prints the string "Hello World!" ten times:

test5.php: PHP CLI While Loop

```
<?php
main($argc,$argv);

function main($argc,$argv)
{
   $i = null;
   $stdout = null;
   $stdout = fopen("php://stdout","w");
   $i = 0;

   while ($i < 10)
   {
      fwrite($stdout,"Hello World!\n");
      $i++;
   }
   fclose($stdout);
}
?>
```

PHP CLI
Console Application Output to Standard Error

- An error code of one is returned to the operating system using the exit() function. The following example outputs text to standard error:

test6.php: PHP CLI Console Application Output to Standard Error

```
<?php
main($argc,$argv);

function main($argc,$argv)
{
   $stderr = null;
   $stderr = fopen("php://stderr","w");
   fwrite($stderr,"A program error has occurred.\n");
   fclose($stderr);

   exit(1);
}
?>
```

Source Code Files

- Text files: pp2_11.php

pp2_11.php: Program Phase 2-11 Source Code

```
<?php
//***********************************************************************
// Program Phase 2-11 PHP Application Name Console Output              *
// Programming Tasks Illustrated: Console Application                  *
//                                Array Variable Declaration and Assignment  *
//                                Program Name Parsing                 *
//                                If Statement                         *
//                                For Loop                             *
//                                While Loop                           *
//                                Console Application Output to Standard Error*
//***********************************************************************
```

pp2_11.php continued on the next page

pp2_11.php: Program Phase 2-11 Source Code continued

```
//***************************************************************************
// File: pp2_11.php                                                        *
// Reserved                                                                *
//***************************************************************************


//***************************************************************************
// Program Phase 2-11 Main                                                 *
// Define the Entry Point of Execution (EPE) for Program Phase 2-11        *
// CBI:  2-11.1.1.1                                                        *
//***************************************************************************

main($argc,$argv);

function main($argc,$argv)
{


//***************************************************************************
// Program Phase 2-11 Main                                                 *
// Declare the local variables for the "main" program                      *
// CBI:  2-11.1.1.2                                                        *
//***************************************************************************

   $lnLength = null;
   $lnIndex = null;
   $laArray = array_pad(array(),200,0);
   $lcProgramName = null;


//***************************************************************************
// Program Phase 2-11 Main                                                 *
// Store the program name                                                  *
// CBI:  2-11.1.1.3                                                        *
//***************************************************************************

   $lcProgramName = $argv[0];
   $lnLength = strlen($lcProgramName);


//***************************************************************************
// Program Phase 2-11 Main                                                 *
// Use an if statement to verify the number of characters in the program name *
// CBI:  2-11.1.1.4                                                        *
//***************************************************************************

   if ($lnLength > 200)
   {
      $stderr = fopen("php://stderr","w");
      fwrite($stderr,"The program name is greater than 200 characters.\n");
      fclose($stderr);
      exit(1);
   }


//***************************************************************************
// Program Phase 2-11 Main                                                 *
// Use a for loop to store the program name in an array                    *
// CBI:  2-11.1.1.5                                                        *
//***************************************************************************

   for ($lnIndex=0;$lnIndex < $lnLength;$lnIndex++)
   {
       $laArray[$lnIndex] = substr($lcProgramName,$lnIndex,1);
   }
```

pp2_11.php continued on the next page

pp2_11.php: Program Phase 2-11 Source Code continued

```
//**************************************************************************
// Program Phase 2-11 Main                                                  *
// Use a while loop to output to standard output each array character element *
// CBI:   2-11.1.1.6                                                        *
//**************************************************************************

    $stdout = fopen("php://stdout","w");
    fwrite($stdout,"Program Name: ");
    $lnIndex = 0;

    while ($lnIndex < $lnLength)
    {
       fwrite($stdout,$laArray[$lnIndex]);
       $lnIndex++;
    }
    fwrite($stdout,"\n");
    fclose($stdout);
}
?>
```

Code Setup and Compilation

- Tools: PHP CLI (Appendix J), Komodo IDE (Appendix F)

Code Setup and Compilation Steps

1: Create a folder called pp2_11 that will store the source code files.

2: Start the Komodo IDE program.

3: Komodo - Activate Menu Item: File → New → New Project

Set the name of the project to pp2_11.kpf and save the new project in the pp2_11 folder.

4: Komodo - Activate Menu Item: File → New → New File

Click on the "Common" category and then select the "Text" template. Set the "Filename" to pp2_11.php. Verify that the "add to pp2_11 project" check box is checked and the "Directory" is set to the pp2_11 folder. Activate the "Open" button. Enter the source code for Program Phase 2-11 and then save the file.

5: There is no step for compiling the pp2_11.php file. It is compiled at runtime by the PHP CLI interpreter.

Program Execution

- Execute Program

    Komodo - Activate Menu Item: Debug → Run Without Debugging

  On the "Debugging Options" window, verify that the "Script" is set to the full path to the pp2_11.php file. Also, verify that the "Use the CLI interpreter" radio button is enabled and then activate the "OK" button. The output for Program Phase 2-11 is displayed in the Komodo output window on the "Run Output" tab.

- Debug Program

    Komodo - Activate Menu Item: Debug → Step In

Program Phase 2-12

Ruby ▪ Multi-Platform

Application Name Console Output

- Program Phase Task 2 is implemented in Program Phase 2-12 using the Ruby programming language.
- The name of the program is stored one character at a time in a Ruby array.
- The Ruby "if" statement, "for" loop, and "while" loop are illustrated.
- Program Phase 2-12 is a console application that provides an example for sending output to standard output and standard error.

Code Block Features

The Program Phase 2-12 code blocks illustrate the following programming features in a console application using the Ruby programming language:

- **Array Variable Declaration and Assignment**
- **Program Name Parsing**
- **If Statement**
- **For Loop**
- **While Loop**
- **Console Application Output to Standard Error**

Ruby
Array Variable Declaration and Assignment

- The test1.rb example stores the string "Hello World!" one character at a time in the array called laArray. This array contains twelve array entries. Each array entry is then outputted to standard output.

test1.rb: Ruby Array Variable Declaration and Assignment

```
laArray = Array[1..12]

laArray[0] = "H"[0]
laArray[1] = "e"[0]
laArray[2] = "l"[0]
laArray[3] = "l"[0]
laArray[4] = "o"[0]
laArray[5] = " "[0]
laArray[6] = "W"[0]
```

test1.rb continued on the next page

test1.rb: Ruby Array Variable Declaration and Assignment continued

```
laArray[7] = "o"[0]
laArray[8] = "r"[0]
laArray[9] = "l"[0]
laArray[10] = "d"[0]
laArray[11] = "!"[0]

print (laArray[0].chr)
print (laArray[1].chr)
print (laArray[2].chr)
print (laArray[3].chr)
print (laArray[4].chr)
print (laArray[5].chr)
print (laArray[6].chr)
print (laArray[7].chr)
print (laArray[8].chr)
print (laArray[9].chr)
print (laArray[10].chr)
print (laArray[11].chr)
print "\n"
```

Ruby
Program Name Parsing

- The program name is accessed in a Ruby program using a special variable called "$0".

test2.rb: Ruby Program Name Parsing

```
lcProgramName = $0;
```

Ruby
If Statement

- The "if" statement example presented here is identical in functionality to the Switch/Case statement presented in Program Phase 1-12.

test3.rb: Ruby If Statement

```
lnCmdLineParamCount = ARGV.length

if lnCmdLineParamCount == 0 then

   ## No command line parameters entered.

elsif lnCmdLineParamCount == 1 then

   ## One command line parameter entered.

else

   ## More than one command line parameter entered.

end
```

Ruby
For Loop

- The following "for" loop example prints the string "Hello World!" ten times:

test4.rb: Ruby For Loop

```
for i in 1..12

   print ("Hello World!\n")

end
```

Ruby
While Loop

- The following "while" loop example prints the string "Hello World!" ten times:

test5.rb: Ruby While Loop

```
i = 0

while i < 12

   print ("Hello World!\n")
   i = i + 1

end
```

Ruby
Console Application Output to Standard Error

- An error code of one is returned to the operating system using the "exit" statement. The following example outputs text to standard error:

test6.rb: Ruby Console Application Output to Standard Error

```
$stderr.puts "A program error has occurred.\n"
exit 1
```

Source Code Files

- Text files: pp2_12.rb

pp2_12.rb: Program Phase 2-12 Source Code

```
##***********************************************************************
## Program Phase 2-12 Ruby Application Name Console Output              *
## Programming Tasks Illustrated: Console Application                   *
##                                Array Variable Declaration and Assignment  *
##                                Program Name Parsing                  *
##                                If Statement                          *
##                                For Loop                              *
##                                While Loop                            *
##                                Console Application Output to Standard Error*
##***********************************************************************

##***********************************************************************
## File: pp2_12.rb                                                      *
## Reserved                                                             *
##***********************************************************************
```

pp2_12.rb continued on the next page

pp2_12.rb: Program Phase 2-12 Source Code continued

```
##*************************************************************************
## Program Phase 2-12 Main                                                *
## Define the Entry Point of Execution (EPE) for Program Phase 2-12       *
## CBI:  2-12.1.1.1                                                       *
##*************************************************************************

## The first line of the code in the pp2_12.rb file is the EPE.


##*************************************************************************
## Program Phase 2-12 Main                                                *
## Declare the local variables for the "main" program                     *
## CBI:  2-12.1.1.2                                                       *
##*************************************************************************

lnLength = 0
lnIndex = 0
laArray = Array[1..200]
lcProgramName = ''


##*************************************************************************
## Program Phase 2-12 Main                                                *
## Store the program name                                                 *
## CBI:  2-12.1.1.3                                                       *
##*************************************************************************

lcProgramName = $0
lnLength = lcProgramName.length


##*************************************************************************
## Program Phase 2-12 Main                                                *
## Use an if statement to verify the number of characters in the program name *
## CBI:  2-12.1.1.4                                                       *
##*************************************************************************

if lnLength > 200 then

   $stderr.puts "The program name is greater than 200 characters.\n"
   exit 1

end

##*************************************************************************
## Program Phase 2-12 Main                                                *
## Use a for loop to store the program name in an array                   *
## CBI:  2-12.1.1.5                                                       *
##*************************************************************************

for lnIndex in 0..lnLength

   laArray[lnIndex] = lcProgramName[lnIndex]

end


##*************************************************************************
## Program Phase 2-12 Main                                                *
## Use a while loop to output to standard output each array character element *
## CBI:  2-12.1.1.6                                                       *
##*************************************************************************

lnIndex = 0
print ('Program Name: ')
```

pp2_12.rb continued on the next page

pp2_12.rb: Program Phase 2-12 Source Code continued

```
while lnIndex < lnLength

   ## Output To Standard Output
   print (laArray[lnIndex].chr)
   lnIndex = lnIndex + 1

end
print "\n"
```

Code Setup and Compilation

- Tools: Ruby distribution (Appendix I), Komodo IDE (Appendix F)

Code Setup and Compilation Steps

1: Create a folder called pp2_12 that will store the source code files.

2: Start the Komodo IDE program.

3: Komodo - Activate Menu Item: File → New → New Project

Set the project name to pp2_12.kpf and save the new project in the pp2_12 folder.

4: Komodo - Activate Menu Item: File → New → New File

Click on the "Common" category and then select the "Text" template. Set the "Filename" to pp2_12.rb. Verify that the "add to pp2_12 project" check box is checked and the "Directory" is set to the pp2_12 folder. Activate the "Open" button. Enter the source code for Program Phase 2-12 and then save the file.

5: There is no step for compiling the pp2_12.rb file. It is compiled at runtime by the Ruby interpreter.

Program Execution

- Execute Program

    Komodo - Activate Menu Item: Debug → Run Without Debugging

    On the "Debugging Options" window, verify that the "Script" is set to the full path to the pp2_12.rb file and then activate the "OK" button. The output for Program Phase 2-12 is displayed in the Komodo output window on the "Run Output" tab.

- Debug Program

    Komodo - Activate Menu Item: Debug → Step In

Program Phase 2-13
Tcl ▪ Multi-Platform

Application Name Console Output

- Program Phase Task 2 is implemented in Program Phase 2-13 using the Tcl programming language.
- The name of the program is stored one character at a time in a Tcl array.
- The Tcl "if" statement, "for" loop, and "while" loop are illustrated.
- Program Phase 2-13 is a console application that provides an example for sending output to standard output and standard error.

Code Block Features

The Program Phase 2-13 code blocks illustrate the following programming features in a console application using the Tcl programming language:

- **Array Variable Declaration and Assignment**
- **Program Name Parsing**
- **If Statement**
- **For Loop**
- **While Loop**
- **Console Application Output to Standard Error**

Tcl
Array Variable Declaration and Assignment

- The test1.tcl example stores the string "Hello World!" one character at a time in the array called laArray. This array contains twelve array entries. Each array entry is then outputted to standard output.

test1.tcl: Tcl Array Variable Declaration and Assignment

```
array set laArray {0 "H"}
array set laArray {1 "e"}
array set laArray {2 "l"}
array set laArray {3 "l"}
array set laArray {4 "o"}
array set laArray {5 " "}
array set laArray {6 "W"}
array set laArray {7 "o"}
array set laArray {8 "r"}
```

test1.tcl continued on the next page

test1.tcl: Tcl Array Variable Declaration and Assignment continued

```
array set laArray {9 "l"}
array set laArray {10 "d"}
array set laArray {11 "!"}

puts -nonewline [lindex [array get laArray 0] 1]
puts -nonewline [lindex [array get laArray 1] 1]
puts -nonewline [lindex [array get laArray 2] 1]
puts -nonewline [lindex [array get laArray 3] 1]
puts -nonewline [lindex [array get laArray 4] 1]
puts -nonewline [lindex [array get laArray 5] 1]
puts -nonewline [lindex [array get laArray 6] 1]
puts -nonewline [lindex [array get laArray 7] 1]
puts -nonewline [lindex [array get laArray 8] 1]
puts -nonewline [lindex [array get laArray 9] 1]
puts -nonewline [lindex [array get laArray 10] 1]
puts -nonewline [lindex [array get laArray 11] 1]

puts ""
```

- A Tcl list can also be used to implement array like functionality.

test1b.tcl: Tcl List Variable Declaration and Assignment

```
set laArray [list]

lappend laArray "H"
lappend laArray "e"
lappend laArray "l"
lappend laArray "l"
lappend laArray "o"
lappend laArray " "
lappend laArray "W"
lappend laArray "o"
lappend laArray "r"
lappend laArray "l"
lappend laArray "d"
lappend laArray "!"

puts -nonewline [lindex $laArray 0]
puts -nonewline [lindex $laArray 1]
puts -nonewline [lindex $laArray 2]
puts -nonewline [lindex $laArray 3]
puts -nonewline [lindex $laArray 4]
puts -nonewline [lindex $laArray 5]
puts -nonewline [lindex $laArray 6]
puts -nonewline [lindex $laArray 7]
puts -nonewline [lindex $laArray 8]
puts -nonewline [lindex $laArray 9]
puts -nonewline [lindex $laArray 10]
puts -nonewline [lindex $laArray 11]
puts ""
```

Tcl
Program Name Parsing

- When a Tcl program is started by the Tcl interpreter, a special variable called $argv0 is created and contains a string representing the name of the currently running Tcl script.

test2.tcl: Tcl Program Name Parsing

```
set lcProgramName $argv0
```

Tcl
If Statement

- The "if" statement example presented here is identical in functionality to the Switch/Case statement presented in Program Phase 1-13.

test3.tcl: Tcl If Statement

```
set lnCmdLineParamCount $argc

if {$lnCmdLineParamCount == 0} {

   puts "No command line parameters entered."

} elseif {$lnCmdLineParamCount == 1} {

   puts "One command line parameter entered."

} else {

   puts "More than one command line parameter entered."
}
```

Tcl
For Loop

- The following "for" loop example prints the string "Hello World!" ten times:

test4.tcl: Tcl For Loop

```
for {set i 0} {$i<10} {incr i} {

   puts "Hello World!"
}
```

Tcl
While Loop

- The following "while" loop example prints the string "Hello World!" ten times:

test5.tcl: Tcl While Loop

```
set i 0

while {$i < 10} {

   puts "Hello World!"
   incr i
}
```

Tcl
Console Application Output to Standard Error

- An error code of one is returned to the operating system using the Tcl "exit" statement. The following example outputs text to standard error:

test6.tcl: Tcl Console Application Output to Standard Error

```
puts stderr "A program error has occurred."
exit 1
```

Source Code Files

- Text files: pp2_13.tcl

pp2_13.tcl: Program Phase 2-13 Source Code

```
##**************************************************************************
## Program Phase 2-13 Tcl Application Name Console Output                  *
## Programming Tasks Illustrated: Console Application                      *
##                                Array Variable Declaration and Assignment *
##                                Program Name Parsing                     *
##                                If Statement                             *
##                                For Loop                                 *
##                                While Loop                               *
##                                Console Application Output to Standard Error*
##**************************************************************************

##**************************************************************************
## File: pp2_13.tcl                                                        *
## Reserved                                                                *
##**************************************************************************


##**************************************************************************
## Program Phase 2-13 Main                                                 *
## Define the Entry Point of Execution (EPE) for Program Phase 2-13        *
## CBI:  2-13.1.1.1                                                        *
##**************************************************************************

## The first line of the code in the pp2_13.tcl file is the EPE.


##**************************************************************************
## Program Phase 2-13 Main                                                 *
## Declare the local variables for the "main" program                      *
## CBI:  2-13.1.1.2                                                        *
##**************************************************************************

set lnLength 0
set lnIndex 0
array set laArray {}
set mylist [list]


##**************************************************************************
## Program Phase 2-13 Main                                                 *
## Store the program name                                                  *
## CBI:  2-13.1.1.3                                                        *
##**************************************************************************

set lcProgramName $argv0;


##**************************************************************************
## Program Phase 2-13 Main                                                 *
## Use an if statement to verify the number of characters in the program name *
## CBI:  2-13.1.1.4                                                        *
##**************************************************************************
```

pp2_13.tcl continued on the next page

pp2_13.tcl: Program Phase 2-13 Source Code continued

```
set lnLength [string length $lcProgramName]

if {$lnLength > 200} {

   puts stderr "The program name is greater than 200 characters."
   exit 1
}


##*************************************************************************
## Program Phase 2-13 Main                                                *
## Use a for loop to store the program name in an array                   *
## CBI:  2-13.1.1.5                                                       *
##*************************************************************************

for {set lnIndex 0} {$lnIndex<$lnLength} {incr lnIndex} {

   set mylist $lnIndex
   lappend mylist [string index $lcProgramName $lnIndex]
   array set laArray $mylist
}


##*************************************************************************
## Program Phase 2-13 Main                                                *
## Use a while loop to output to standard output each array character element *
## CBI:  2-13.1.1.6                                                       *
##*************************************************************************

set lnIndex 0
puts -nonewline "Program Name: "

while {$lnIndex < $lnLength} {

   set mylist [array get laArray $lnIndex]
   puts -nonewline [lindex $mylist 1]
   incr lnIndex
}

puts ""
```

- Program Phase 2-13 can be implemented using a Tcl list to store the program name instead of using a Tcl array.

- Text files: pp2_13list.tcl

pp2_13list.tcl: Program Phase 2-13 Source Code (Tcl List)

```
##*************************************************************************
## Program Phase 2-13 Tcl Application Name Console Output                 *
## Programming Tasks Illustrated: Console Application                     *
##                                List Variable Declaration and Assignment *
##                                Program Name Parsing                    *
##                                If Statement                            *
##                                For Loop                                *
##                                While Loop                              *
##                                Console Application Output to Standard Error*
##*************************************************************************

##*************************************************************************
## File: pp2_13list.tcl                                                   *
## Reserved                                                               *
##*************************************************************************
```

pp2_13list.tcl continued on the next page

pp2_13list.tcl: Program Phase 2-13 Source Code (Tcl List) continued

```
##*********************************************************************
## Program Phase 2-13 Main                                            *
## Define the Entry Point of Execution (EPE) for Program Phase 2-13   *
## CBI:  2-13.1.1.1                                                   *
##*********************************************************************

## The first line of the code in the pp2_13list.tcl file is the EPE.


##*********************************************************************
## Program Phase 2-13 Main                                            *
## Declare the local variables for the "main" program                 *
## CBI:  2-13.1.1.2                                                   *
##*********************************************************************

set lnLength 0
set lnIndex 0
set mylist [list]


##*********************************************************************
## Program Phase 2-13 Main                                            *
## Store the program name                                             *
## CBI:  2-13.1.1.3                                                   *
##*********************************************************************

set lcProgramName $argv0


##*********************************************************************
## Program Phase 2-13 Main                                            *
## Use an if statement to verify the number of characters in the program name *
## CBI:  2-13.1.1.4                                                   *
##*********************************************************************

set lnLength [string length $lcProgramName]

if {$lnLength > 200} {

   puts stderr "The program name is greater than 200 characters."
   exit 1
}


##*********************************************************************
## Program Phase 2-13 Main                                            *
## Use a for loop to store the program name in an array               *
## CBI:  2-13.1.1.5                                                   *
##*********************************************************************

for {set lnIndex 0} {$lnIndex<$lnLength} {incr lnIndex} {

   lappend mylist [string index $lcProgramName $lnIndex]
}


##*********************************************************************
## Program Phase 2-13 Main                                            *
## Use a while loop to output to standard output each array character element *
## CBI:  2-13.1.1.6                                                   *
##*********************************************************************

set lnIndex 0
puts -nonewline "Program Name: "
```

pp2_13list.tcl continued on the next page

pp2_13list.tcl: Program Phase 2-13 Source Code (Tcl List) continued

```
while {$lnIndex < $lnLength} {

   puts -nonewline [lindex $mylist $lnIndex]
   incr lnIndex
}

puts ""
```

Code Setup and Compilation

- Tools: Tcl distribution (Appendix K), Komodo IDE (Appendix F)

Code Setup and Compilation Steps

1: Create a folder called pp2_13 that will store the source code files.

2: Start the Komodo IDE program.

3: Komodo - Activate Menu Item: File → New → New Project

Set the project name to pp2_13.kpf and save the new project in the pp2_13 folder.

4: Komodo - Activate Menu Item: File → New → New File

Click on the "Common" category and then select the "Text" template. Set the "Filename" to pp2_13.tcl. Verify that the "add to pp2_13 project" check box is checked and the "Directory" is set to the pp2_13 folder. Activate the "Open" button. Enter the source code for Program Phase 2-13 and then save the file.

5: There is no step for compiling the pp2_13.tcl file. It is compiled at runtime by the Tcl interpreter.

Program Execution

- Execute Program

  `Komodo - Activate Menu Item: Debug → Run Without Debugging`

  On the "Debugging Options" window, verify that the "Script" is set to the full path to the pp2_13.tcl file and that the "Use default tclsh interpreter" radio button is selected. Activate the "OK" button. The output for Program Phase 2-13 is displayed in the Komodo output window on the "Run Output" tab.

- Debug Program

  `Komodo - Activate Menu Item: Debug → Step In`

Program Phase 2-14
Delphi ▪ Windows

Application Name Console Output

- Program Phase Task 2 is implemented in Program Phase 2-14 using the Delphi programming language.
- The name of the program is stored one character at a time in a Delphi array.
- The Delphi "if" statement, "for" loop, and "while" loop are illustrated.
- Program Phase 2-14 is a console application that provides an example for sending output to standard output and standard error.

Code Block Features

The Program Phase 2-14 code blocks illustrate the following programming features in a console application using the Delphi programming language:

- **Array Variable Declaration and Assignment**
- **Program Name Parsing**
- **If Statement**
- **For Loop**
- **While Loop**
- **Console Application Output to Standard Error**

Delphi
Array Variable Declaration and Assignment

- The test1.dpr example stores the string "Hello World!" one character at a time in the array called laArray. This array contains twelve array entries. Each array entry is then outputted to standard output.

test1.dpr: Delphi Array Variable Declaration and Assignment

```
program test1;

{$APPTYPE CONSOLE}

uses
   SysUtils;

var
   laArray: Array[1..12] of Char;
```

test1.dpr continued on the next page

test1.dpr: Delphi Array Variable Declaration and Assignment continued

```
begin

   laArray[1] := 'H';
   laArray[2] := 'e';
   laArray[3] := 'l';
   laArray[4] := 'l';
   laArray[5] := 'o';
   laArray[6] := ' ';
   laArray[7] := 'W';
   laArray[8] := 'o';
   laArray[9] := 'r';
   laArray[10] := 'l';
   laArray[11] := 'd';
   laArray[12] := '!';

   Write(laArray[1]);
   Write(laArray[2]);
   Write(laArray[3]);
   Write(laArray[4]);
   Write(laArray[5]);
   Write(laArray[6]);
   Write(laArray[7]);
   Write(laArray[8]);
   Write(laArray[9]);
   Write(laArray[10]);
   Write(laArray[11]);
   Write(laArray[12]);
   Writeln('');

end.
```

Delphi
Program Name Parsing

- The Delphi ParamStr() function can be used to access the program name.

test2.dpr: Delphi Program Name Parsing

```
program test2;

{$APPTYPE CONSOLE}

uses
   SysUtils;

var
   lcProgramName: String;

begin

   lcProgramName := ParamStr(0);

end.
```

Delphi
If Statement

- The "if" statement example presented here is identical in functionality to the Switch/Case statement presented in Program Phase 1-14.

test3.dpr: Delphi If Statement

```
program test3;

{$APPTYPE CONSOLE}

uses
   SysUtils;

var
   lnCmdLineParamCount: Integer;

begin

   lnCmdLineParamCount := ParamCount();

   if lnCmdLineParamCount = 0 then
   begin

      // No command line parameters entered.

   end
   else
   begin
      if lnCmdLineParamCount = 1 then
      begin

        // One command line parameter entered.

      end
      else
      begin

         // More than one command line parameter entered.

      end;
   end;
end.
```

Delphi
For Loop

- The following "for" loop example prints the string "Hello World!" ten times:

test4.dpr: Delphi For Loop

```
program test4;

{$APPTYPE CONSOLE}

uses
   SysUtils;
var
   i: Integer;

begin

   For i := 1 to 10 do
   begin

      Writeln('Hello World!');

   end;

end.
```

Delphi
While Loop

- The following "while" loop example prints the string "Hello World!" ten times:

test5.dpr: Delphi While Loop

```
program test5;

{$APPTYPE CONSOLE}

uses
   SysUtils;

var
   i: Integer;

begin
   i := 1;

   while i <= 10 do
    begin

      Writeln('Hello World!');
      i := i + 1;

   end;
end.
```

Delphi
Console Application Output to Standard Error

- An error code of one is returned to the operating system using the Halt() function. The following example outputs text to standard error:

test6.dpr: Delphi Console Application Output to Standard Error

```
program test6;

{$APPTYPE CONSOLE}

uses
   SysUtils;

begin

   Writeln(ErrOutput,'A program error has occurred.');
   Halt(1);

end.
```

Source Code Files

- Text files: pp2_14.dpr

pp2_14.dpr: Program Phase 2-14 Source Code

```
//****************************************************************************
// Program Phase 2-14 Delphi Application Name Console Output                 *
// Programming Tasks Illustrated: Console Application                        *
//                                Array Variable Declaration and Assignment  *
//                                Program Name Parsing                       *
//                                If Statement                               *
//                                For Loop                                   *
//                                While Loop                                 *
//                                Console Application Output to Standard Error*
//****************************************************************************

//****************************************************************************
// File: pp2_14.dpr                                                          *
// Reserved                                                                  *
//****************************************************************************

program pp2_14;

{$APPTYPE CONSOLE}

uses
  SysUtils;

//****************************************************************************
// Program Phase 2-14 Main                                                   *
// Declare the local variables for the "main" program                        *
// CBI:  2-14.1.1.2                                                          *
//****************************************************************************

var
   // Variable Declarations
   lnLength: Integer;
   lnIndex: Integer;
   laArray: Array[1..200] of Char;
   lcProgramName: String;

//****************************************************************************
// Program Phase 2-14 Main                                                   *
// Define the Entry Point of Execution (EPE) for Program Phase 2-14          *
// CBI:  2-14.1.1.1                                                          *
//****************************************************************************

begin

//****************************************************************************
// Program Phase 2-14 Main                                                   *
// Store the program name                                                    *
// CBI:  2-14.1.1.3                                                          *
//****************************************************************************

   lcProgramName := ParamStr(0);

//****************************************************************************
// Program Phase 2-14 Main                                                   *
// Use an if statement to verify the number of characters in the program name *
// CBI:  2-14.1.1.4                                                          *
//****************************************************************************

   lnLength := Length(lcProgramName);
```

pp2_14.dpr continued on the next page

pp2_14.dpr: Program Phase 2-14 Source Code continued

```
   if lnLength > 200 then
   begin

      Writeln(ErrOutput,'The program name is greater than 200 characters.');
      Halt(1);

   end;


//****************************************************************************
// Program Phase 2-14 Main                                                   *
// Use a for loop to store the program name in an array                      *
// CBI:  2-14.1.1.5                                                          *
//****************************************************************************

   For lnIndex := 1 to lnLength do
   begin

      laArray[lnIndex] := lcProgramName[lnIndex];

   end;


//****************************************************************************
// Program Phase 2-14 Main                                                   *
// Use a while loop to output to standard output each array character element *
// CBI:  2-14.1.1.6                                                          *
//****************************************************************************

   lnIndex := 1;
   Write('Program Name: ');

   while lnIndex <= lnLength do
   begin

      Write(laArray[lnIndex]);
      lnIndex := lnIndex + 1;

   end;

   Writeln('');

end.
```

Code Setup and Compilation

- Tools: Turbo Delphi Explorer (Appendix M)

Code Setup and Compilation Steps

1: Create a folder called pp2_14 that will store the source code files.

2: Start the Delphi IDE program.

3: Delphi - Activate Menu Item: Project → Add New Project

On the "New Items" dialog window, select the "Delphi Projects" item category and then select "Console Application". Activate the '"OK" button. Enter the source code for Program Phase 2-14 into the project source code file.

Steps continued on the next page

Code Setup and Compilation Steps continued

4: Delphi - Activate Menu Item: File → Save Project As

Save the project as pp2_14.bdsproj in the pp2_14 folder.

5: Delphi - Activate Menu Item: Project → Build pp2_14

Program Execution

- Execute Program

```
Delphi - Activate Menu Item: Run → Run
```

- Debug Program

```
Delphi - Activate Menu Item: Run → Step Over
```

Program Phase 2-15

C++ ▪ QT4 ▪ Multi-Platform

Application Name Console Output

- Program Phase Task 2 is implemented in Program Phase 2-15 using the C++ programming language and the QT4 framework.
- The name of the program is stored one character at a time in the QVector data structure.
- The C/C++ "if" statement, "for" loop, and "while" loop are illustrated.
- Program Phase 2-15 is a console application that provides an example for sending output to standard output and standard error.

Code Block Features

The Program Phase 2-15 code blocks illustrate the following programming features in a console application using the C++ programming language and the QT4 framework:

- **Array Variable Declaration and Assignment**
- **Program Name Parsing**
- **If Statement**
- **For Loop**
- **While Loop**
- **Console Application Output to Standard Error**

C++ with QT4
Array Variable Declaration and Assignment

- The QVector data structure is used to implement array like functionality.

test1.cpp: C++ with QT4 Array Variable Declaration and Assignment

```
#include <QCoreApplication>
#include <QVector>

int main(int argc, char *argv[])
{
   QCoreApplication loApplication(argc, argv);
   QVector<char> laArray(12);

   laArray[0] = 'H';
   laArray[1] = 'e';
```

test1.cpp continued on the next page

test1.cpp: C++ with QT4 Array Variable Declaration and Assignment continued

```
   laArray[2] = 'l';
   laArray[3] = 'l';
   laArray[4] = 'o';
   laArray[5] = ' ';
   laArray[6] = 'W';
   laArray[7] = 'o';
   laArray[8] = 'r';
   laArray[9] = 'l';
   laArray[10] = 'd';
   laArray[11] = '!';

   fprintf(stdout, "%c",laArray[0]);
   fprintf(stdout, "%c",laArray[1]);
   fprintf(stdout, "%c",laArray[2]);
   fprintf(stdout, "%c",laArray[3]);
   fprintf(stdout, "%c",laArray[4]);
   fprintf(stdout, "%c",laArray[5]);
   fprintf(stdout, "%c",laArray[6]);
   fprintf(stdout, "%c",laArray[7]);
   fprintf(stdout, "%c",laArray[8]);
   fprintf(stdout, "%c",laArray[9]);
   fprintf(stdout, "%c",laArray[10]);
   fprintf(stdout, "%c\n",laArray[11]);

   return 0;
}
```

C++ with QT4
Program Name Parsing

- The at() member function of the QStringList object provides access to the individual command line parameters. Passing a value of zero to the at() member function returns the program name.

test2.cpp: C++ with QT4 Program Name Parsing

```
#include <QCoreApplication>
#include <QStringList>

int main(int argc, char *argv[])
{
   QCoreApplication loApplication(argc, argv);
   QString lcProgramName;

   lcProgramName = QCoreApplication::arguments().at(0);

   return 0;
}
```

C++ with QT4
If Statement

- The "if" statement example presented here is identical in functionality to the Switch/Case statement presented in Program Phase 1-15.

test3.cpp: C++ with QT4 If Statement

```
#include <QCoreApplication>
#include <QStringList>

int main(int argc, char* argv[])
{
   QCoreApplication loApplication(argc, argv);

   int lnCmdLineParamCount;

   lnCmdLineParamCount = QCoreApplication::arguments().size() - 1;

   if (lnCmdLineParamCount == 0)
   {
      // No command line parameters entered.
   }
   else
   {
      if (lnCmdLineParamCount == 1)
      {
         // One command line parameter entered.
      }
      else
      {
         // More than one command line parameter entered.
      }
   }
   return 0;
}
```

C++ with QT4
For Loop

- The following "for" loop example prints the string "Hello World!" ten times:

test4.cpp: C++ with QT4 For Loop

```
#include <QCoreApplication>

int main(int argc, char* argv[])
{
   QCoreApplication loApplication(argc, argv);

   int i;

   for (i=0;i < 10;i++)
   {
      fprintf(stdout,"Hello World!\n");
   }

   return 0;
}
```

C++ with QT4
While Loop

- The following "while" loop example prints the string "Hello World!" ten times:

test5.cpp: C++ with QT4 While Loop

```
#include <QCoreApplication>

int main(int argc, char* argv[])
{
   QCoreApplication loApplication(argc, argv);
   int i = 0;

   while (i < 10)
   {
      fprintf(stdout,"Hello World!\n");
      i++;
   }
  return 0;
}
```

C++ with QT4
Console Application Output to Standard Error

- An error code of one is returned to the operating system using the "return" statement. The following example outputs text to standard error:

test6.cpp: C++ with QT4 Console Application Output to Standard Error

```
#include <QCoreApplication>

int main(int argc, char* argv[])
{
   QCoreApplication loApplication(argc, argv);

   fprintf(stderr,"A program error has occurred.\n");
   return 1;
}
```

Source Code Files

- Text files: pp2_15.cpp

pp2_15.cpp: Program Phase 2-15 Source Code

```
//******************************************************************************
// Program Phase 2-15 C++ QT4 Application Name Console Output                  *
// Programming Tasks Illustrated: Console Application                          *
//                                Array Variable Declaration and Assignment    *
//                                Program Name Parsing                         *
//                                If Statement                                 *
//                                For Loop                                     *
//                                While Loop                                   *
//                                Console Application Output to Standard Error*
//******************************************************************************

//******************************************************************************
// File: pp2_15.cpp                                                            *
// Reserved                                                                    *
//******************************************************************************

#include <QCoreApplication>
#include <QStringList>
#include <QVector>
```

pp2_15.cpp continued on the next page

pp2_15.cpp: Program Phase 2-15 Source Code continued

```
//******************************************************************************
// Program Phase 2-15 Main                                                      *
// Define the Entry Point of Execution (EPE) for Program Phase 2-15             *
// CBI:  2-15.1.1.1                                                             *
//******************************************************************************

int main(int argc, char *argv[])
{
   QCoreApplication a(argc, argv);


//******************************************************************************
// Program Phase 2-15 Main                                                      *
// Declare the local variables for the "main" program                           *
// CBI:  2-15.1.1.2                                                             *
//******************************************************************************

   int lnLength;
   int lnIndex;
   QVector<char> laArray(200);
   QString lcProgramName;


//******************************************************************************
// Program Phase 2-15 Main                                                      *
// Store the program name                                                       *
// CBI:  2-15.1.1.3                                                             *
//******************************************************************************

   lcProgramName = QCoreApplication::arguments().at(0);


//******************************************************************************
// Program Phase 2-15 Main                                                      *
// Use an if statement to verify the number of characters in the program name *
// CBI:  2-15.1.1.4                                                             *
//******************************************************************************

   lnLength = lcProgramName.length();

   if (lnLength > 200)
   {
      fprintf(stderr,"The program name is greater than 200 characters.\n");
      return 1;
   }


//******************************************************************************
// Program Phase 2-15 Main                                                      *
// Use a for loop to store the program name in an array                         *
// CBI:  2-15.1.1.5                                                             *
//******************************************************************************

   for (lnIndex=0;lnIndex < lnLength;lnIndex++)
   {
      laArray[lnIndex] = lcProgramName.at(lnIndex).toAscii();
   }


//******************************************************************************
// Program Phase 2-15 Main                                                      *
// Use a while loop to output to standard output each array character element *
// CBI:  2-15.1.1.6                                                             *
//******************************************************************************
```

pp2_15.cpp continued on the next page

pp2_15.cpp: Program Phase 2-15 Source Code continued

```
    fprintf(stdout,"Program Name: ");
    lnIndex = 0;

    while (lnIndex < lnLength)
    {
        fprintf(stdout,"%c",laArray[lnIndex]);
        lnIndex++;
    }

    fprintf(stdout,"\n");
    return 0;
}
```

Windows Code Setup and Compilation

- Tools: Mingw compiler and the QT4 library (Appendix E)

Windows Code Setup and Compilation Steps

1: Create a folder called pp2_15 that will store the source code files.

2: Using a text editor, enter the source code for Program Phase 2-15 and save the file as pp2_15.cpp in the pp2_15 folder.

3: Open a QT command prompt and change directories to the pp2_15 folder.

4: Enter the following command:

```
qmake -project
```

5: Edit the pp2_15.pro file that has just been generated and add the following two lines:

```
CONFIG += release
CONFIG += qt console
```

6: After editing the pp2_15.pro file, save and close the file and then enter the following commands:

```
qmake pp2_15.pro
make
```

The "qmake" command creates a file called Makefile, and the "make" command compiles the program. The steps detailed here create a release executable file that accesses the QT4 library in a shared dll.

Linux Code Setup and Compilation

- Tools: GNU GCC (Appendix B), QT4 Library (Appendix E)

Linux Code Setup and Compilation Steps

1: Create a folder called pp2_15 that will store the source code files.

Steps continued on the next page

Linux Code Setup and Compilation Steps continued

2: Using a text editor, enter the source code for Program Phase 2-15 and save the file as pp2_15.cpp in the pp2_15 folder.

3: Open a terminal window and change directories to the pp2_15 folder.

4: Enter the following command:

```
qmake -project
```

5: Edit the pp2_15.pro file that has just been generated and add the following two lines:

```
CONFIG += release
CONFIG += qt console
```

6: After editing the pp2_15.pro file, save and close the file and then enter the following commands:

```
qmake pp2_15.pro
make
```

Mac OS X Code Setup and Compilation

- Tools: Xcode (See Appendix C), QT4 Library (See Appendix E)

Mac OS X Code Setup and Compilation Steps

1: Create a folder called pp2_15 that will store the source code files.

2: Using a text editor, enter the source code for Program Phase 2-15 and save the file as pp2_15.cpp in the pp2_15 folder.

3: Open a terminal window and change directories to the pp2_15 folder.

4: Edit the pp2_15.pro file that has just been generated and add the following two lines:

```
CONFIG += release
CONFIG += qt console
```

5: Enter the following commands to create an Xcode project for Program Phase 2-15:

```
qmake -project
qmake -spec macx-xcode pp2_15.pro
```

6: Open the Xcode program and then open the newly create project.

7: Compile the program by activating the "Build" button.

Windows Program Execution

- To execute the pp2_15 program from a command prompt, change directories to pp2_15\release folder and then enter the following:

```
pp2_15.exe
```

Linux Program Execution

- To execute the pp2_15 program from a terminal window, change directories to pp2_15/release folder and then enter the following:

```
./pp2_15
```

Mac OS X Program Execution

- Execute Program

  To execute the pp2_15 program, activate the "Build/Go" button. The program output is displayed in the "Run Log" window. If using Xcode 3, the "Debugger Console" displays the program output. This window can be displayed by activating the "Console" menu item from the "Run" menu.

- Debug Program

  To debug the pp2_15.cpp file one line at a time, place the cursor at the first line of code in the CBI: 2-15.1.1.3 code block and then create a breakpoint.

```
   Xcode 2.4 - Activate Menu Item: Debug → Add Breakpoint at Current Line
   Xcode 3 - Activate Menu Item: Run → Manage Breakpoints → Add
Breakpoint at Current Line
```

  After the break point has been created, the program can be debugged.

```
   Xcode - Activate Menu Item: Build → Build and Debug
```

Program Phase 2-16

C++ ▪ wxWidgets ▪ Multi-Platform

Application Name Console Output

- Program Phase Task 2 is implemented in Program Phase 2-16 using the C++ programming language and the wxWidgets library.
- The name of the program is stored one character at a time in a wxWidgets array.
- The C/C++ "if" statement, "for" loop, and "while" loop are illustrated.
- Program Phase 2-16 is a console application that provides an example for sending output to standard output and standard error.

Code Block Features

The Program Phase 2-16 code blocks illustrate the following programming features in a console application using the C++ programming language and the wxWidgets library:

- **Array Variable Declaration and Assignment**
- **Program Name Parsing**
- **If Statement**
- **For Loop**
- **While Loop**
- **Console Application Output to Standard Error**

C++ wxWidgets
Array Variable Declaration and Assignment

- The test1.cpp example stores the string "Hello World!" one character at a time in the array called laArray. This array contains twelve array entries. Each array entry is then outputted to standard output.

test1.cpp: C++ wxWidgets Array Variable Declaration and Assignment

```
#include "wx/wx.h"

WX_DEFINE_ARRAY_CHAR(char,myarray);

int main(int argc, char* argv[])
{
   if (wxInitialize() == false)
   {
      wxFprintf(stderr,"Failed to initialize wxWidgets.\n");
```

test1.cpp continued on the next page

test1.cpp: C++ wxWidgets Array Variable Declaration and Assignment continued

```
        return 1;
    }

    myarray laArray;

    laArray.Add('H');
    laArray.Add('e');
    laArray.Add('l');
    laArray.Add('l');
    laArray.Add('o');
    laArray.Add(' ');
    laArray.Add('W');
    laArray.Add('o');
    laArray.Add('r');
    laArray.Add('l');
    laArray.Add('d');
    laArray.Add('!');

    wxFprintf(stdout, "%c",laArray.Item(0));
    wxFprintf(stdout, "%c",laArray.Item(1));
    wxFprintf(stdout, "%c",laArray.Item(2));
    wxFprintf(stdout, "%c",laArray.Item(3));
    wxFprintf(stdout, "%c",laArray.Item(4));
    wxFprintf(stdout, "%c",laArray.Item(5));
    wxFprintf(stdout, "%c",laArray.Item(6));
    wxFprintf(stdout, "%c",laArray.Item(7));
    wxFprintf(stdout, "%c",laArray.Item(8));
    wxFprintf(stdout, "%c",laArray.Item(9));
    wxFprintf(stdout, "%c",laArray.Item(10));
    wxFprintf(stdout, "%c",laArray.Item(11));
    wxFprintf(stdout, "\n");

    wxUninitialize();
    return 0;
}
```

C++ wxWidgets Program Name Parsing

- A GUI based wxWidgets application provides the command line parameters and program name as properties of a wxApp object. Since a GUI based application is not created for Program Phase 2-16, the program name is accessed from the argv array passed as a parameter to the main() function.

test2.cpp: C++ wxWidgets Program Name Parsing

```
#include "wx/wx.h"

int main(int argc, char* argv[])
{
    if (wxInitialize() == false)
      {
        wxFprintf(stderr,"Failed to initialize wxWidgets.\n");
        return 1;
    }

    wxString lcProgramName;

    lcProgramName.Printf(wxT(argv[0]));
    wxUninitialize();
    return 0;
}
```

C++ wxWidgets
If Statement

- The "if" statement example presented here is identical in functionality to the Switch/Case statement presented in Program Phase 1-16.

test3.cpp: C++ wxWidgets If Statement

```
#include "wx/wx.h"

int main(int argc, char* argv[])
{
   if (wxInitialize() == false)
   {
      wxFprintf(stderr,"Failed to initialize wxWidgets.\n");
      return 1;
   }

   int lnCmdLineParamCount;

   lnCmdLineParamCount = argc - 1;

   if (lnCmdLineParamCount == 0)
   {
      // No command line parameters entered.
   }
   else
   {
      if (lnCmdLineParamCount == 1)
      {
         // One command line parameter entered.
      }

      else
      {
         // More than one command line parameter entered.
      }
   }

   wxUninitialize();
   return 0;
}
```

C++ wxWidgets
For Loop

- The following "for" loop example prints the string "Hello World!" ten times:

test4.cpp: C++ wxWidgets For Loop

```
#include "wx/wx.h"

int main(int argc, char* argv[])
{
   if (wxInitialize() == false)
   {
      wxFprintf(stderr,"Failed to initialize wxWidgets.\n");
      return 1;
   }
```

test4.cpp continued on the next page

test4.cpp: C++ wxWidgets For Loop continued

```
   int i;

   for (i=0;i < 10;i++)
   {
      wxFprintf(stdout,"%s\n","Hello World!");

   }

   wxUninitialize();
   return 0;
}
```

C++ wxWidgets
While Loop

- The following "while" loop example prints the string "Hello World!" ten times:

test5.cpp: C++ wxWidgets While Loop

```
#include <stdio.h>
#include "wx/wx.h"

int main(int argc, char* argv[])
{
   if (wxInitialize() == false)
   {
      wxFprintf(stderr,"Failed to initialize wxWidgets.\n");
      return 1;
   }

   int i;
   i = 0;

   while (i < 10)
   {
      fprintf(stdout,"Hello World!\n");
      i++;
   }
   wxUninitialize();
   return 0;
}
```

C++ wxWidgets
Console Application Output to Standard Error

- An error code of one is returned to the operating system using the "return" statement. The following example outputs text to standard error:

test6.cpp: C++ wxWidgets Console Application Output to Standard Error

```
#include <stdio.h>
#include "wx/wx.h"

int main(int argc, char* argv[])
{
   if (wxInitialize() == false)
   {
      wxFprintf(stderr,"Failed to initialize wxWidgets.\n");
```

test6.cpp continued on the next page

test6.cpp: C++ wxWidgets Console Application Output to Standard Error continued

```
      return 1;
   }

   wxFprintf(stderr,"A program error has occurred.\n");
   wxUninitialize();
   return 1;
}
```

Source Code Files

- Text files: pp2_16.cpp

pp2_16.cpp: Program Phase 2-16 Source Code

```
//****************************************************************************
// Program Phase 2-16 C++ wxWidgets Application Name Console Output         *
// Programming Tasks Illustrated: Console Application                       *
//                                Array Variable Declaration and Assignment *
//                                Program Name Parsing                      *
//                                If Statement                              *
//                                For Loop                                  *
//                                While Loop                                *
//                                Console Application Output to Standard Error*
//****************************************************************************

//****************************************************************************
// File: pp2_16.cpp                                                         *
// Reserved                                                                 *
//****************************************************************************

#include <stdio.h>
#include <string.h>
#include "wx/wx.h"

WX_DEFINE_ARRAY_CHAR(char,myarray);


//****************************************************************************
// Program Phase 2-16 Main                                                  *
// Define the Entry Point of Execution (EPE) for Program Phase 2-16         *
// CBI:  2-16.1.1.1                                                         *
//****************************************************************************

int main(int argc, char* argv[])
{
   if (wxInitialize() == false)
   {
      wxFprintf(stderr,wxT("Failed to initialize wxWidgets.\n"));
      return 1;
   }


//****************************************************************************
// Program Phase 2-16 Main                                                  *
// Declare the local variables for the "main" program                       *
// CBI:  2-16.1.1.2                                                         *
//****************************************************************************

   size_t lnLength;
   size_t lnIndex;
   myarray laArray;
   wxString lcProgramName;
```

pp2_16.cpp continued on the next page

pp2_16.cpp: Program Phase 2-16 Source Code continued

```
//****************************************************************************
// Program Phase 2-16 Main                                                    *
// Store the program name                                                     *
// CBI:  2-16.1.1.3                                                           *
//****************************************************************************

   lcProgramName.Printf(wxT(argv[0]));
   lnLength = lcProgramName.Len();


//****************************************************************************
// Program Phase 2-16 Main                                                    *
// Use an if statement to verify the number of characters in the program name *
// CBI:  2-16.1.1.4                                                           *
//****************************************************************************

   if (lnLength > 200)
   {
   wxFprintf(stderr,wxT("The program name is greater than 200 characters.\n"));
      return 1;
   }


//****************************************************************************
// Program Phase 2-16 Main                                                    *
// Use a for loop to store the program name in an array                       *
// CBI:  2-16.1.1.5                                                           *
//****************************************************************************

   for (lnIndex=0;lnIndex < lnLength;lnIndex++)
   {
      laArray.Add(lcProgramName.GetChar(lnIndex));
   }


//****************************************************************************
// Program Phase 2-16 Main                                                    *
// Use a while loop to output to standard output each array character element *
// CBI:  2-16.1.1.6                                                           *
//****************************************************************************

   wxFprintf(stdout,wxT("Program Name: "));
   lnIndex = 0;

   while (lnIndex < lnLength)
   {
      wxFprintf(stdout,"%c",laArray.Item(lnIndex));
      lnIndex++;
   }

   wxFprintf(stdout,wxT("\n"));
   wxUninitialize();
   return 0;
}
```

Windows – Code Setup and Compilation

- Tools: Microsoft Visual Studio 2008 Express Edition (msdn.microsoft.com), wxWidgets library (Appendix D)

Windows Code Setup and Compilation Steps

1: Start the Visual C++ 2008 Express Edition program.

2: VC++ EE - Activate Menu Item: File → New → Project

For the "Project type", select "Win32" and then select the "Win32 Console Application" template. Enter pp2_16 as the project "Name". Enter the appropriate folder as the project "Location". Make sure that the "Create directory for solution" check box is not checked. Activate the "OK" button to proceed with the "Win32 Application Wizard".

3: Activate the "Next" button of the "Win32 Application Wizard".

4: Verify that a "Console Application" is selected and also check the "Empty project" check box. Activate the "Finish" button of the "Win32 Application Wizard".

5: VC++ EE - Activate Menu Item: Project → Add New Item

On the "Add New Item" dialog window, select the "Visual C++ → Code" category and then select the "C++ File" template. Enter pp2_16.cpp for the file "Name" and then activate the "Add" button. Enter the source code for the pp2_16.cpp file.

6: VC++ EE - Activate Menu Item: Build → Configuration Manager

Select "Release" or "Debug" for the "Active solution configuration". This setting needs to match the setting specified when the wxWidgets library was compiled (Appendix D).

7: VC++ EE - Activate Menu Item: Project → pp2_16 Properties

Enter the following settings:

Configuration Properties → General → Character Set

For ANSI Configuration:

```
"Use Multi-Byte Character Set"
```

For Unicode Configuration:

```
"Use Unicode Character Set"
```

This setting needs to match the setting specified when the wxWidgets library was compiled (Appendix D).

Configuration Properties → C/C++ → General → Additional Include Directories

```
"$(wxwin)\lib\vc_lib\msw";"$(wxwin)\include"
```

Configuration Properties → C/C++ → Preprocessor → Processor Definitions

For Release Configuration:

```
WIN32;__WXMSW__;_CONSOLE;NOPCH
```

For Debug Configuration:

```
WIN32;__WXMSW__;__WXDEBUG__;_CONSOLE;NOPCH
```

This setting needs to match the setting specified when the wxWidgets library was compiled (Appendix D).

Steps continued on the next page

`Windows Code Setup and Compilation Steps continued`

8: Continue entering settings on the "pp2_16 Property Pages" window.

Configuration Properties → C/C++ → Code Generation → Runtime Library

For Release Configuration:

```
Multi-threaded (/MT) or Multi-threaded DLL (/MD)
```

For Debug Configuration:

```
Multi-threaded Debug /MTd or Multi-threaded Debug DLL (/MDd)
```

This setting needs to match the setting specified when the wxWidgets library was compiled (Appendix D).

Configuration Properties → Linker → General → Additional Library Directories

```
"$(wxwin)\lib\vc_lib"
```

Configuration Properties → Linker -> Input → Additional Dependencies

For Release Configuration:

```
wxmsw26_core.lib wxbase26.lib
```

For Debug Configuration:

```
wxmsw26d_core.lib wxbase26d.lib
```

The name of the library files depends on the version of wxWidgets installed. Substitute the appropriate version number in the file name to match the version of the wxWidgets library installed. This setting needs to match the setting specified when the wxWidgets library was compiled (Appendix D).

Configuration Properties → Linker → System → SubSystem

```
Console (/SUBSYSTEM:CONSOLE)
```

9: Close the "pp2_16 Property Pages" window by activating the 'OK" button.

10: VC++ EE - Activate Menu Item: Build → Build pp2_16

After the build is successful, a compiled file called pp2_16.exe will be found in either the Release or Debug folder of the pp2_16 folder.

`Windows Command Prompt Compilation Steps`

1: From a Visual Studio 2008 command prompt, enter one of the following commands on a single line.

For Release Configuration

```
cl.exe /I "C:\Program Files\Microsoft SDK's\Windows\v6.0A\Include"
/I "c:\wxWidgets-2.8.6\lib\vc_lib\msw"
/I "c:\wxWidgets-2.8.6\include"
/D "WIN32"
/D "__WXMSW__"
/D "_CONSOLE"
/MT /Fo"Release\\" /EHsc /c pp2_16.cpp
```

For Debug Configuration:

```
cl.exe /I "C:\Program Files\Microsoft SDK's\Windows\v6.0A\Include"
/I "c:\wxWidgets-2.8.6\lib\vc_lib\msw"
/I "c:\wxWidgets-2.8.6\include"
/D "WIN32"
/D "__WXMSW__"
/D "__WXDEBUG__"
/D "_CONSOLE"
/MTd
/Fo"Debug\\"
/EHsc /c pp2_16.cpp
```

Substitute the appropriate name for the library files that match the version of the wxWidgets library and platform SDK installed. The Runtime Library switch (/MT, MTd, /MD, /MDd) needs to match the setting used to compile the wxWidgets source code (Appendix D).

2: Run the linker to create the pp2_16.exe file from the pp2_16.obj file.

For Release Configuration:

```
link.exe /OUT:"Release\pp2_16.exe"
/INCREMENTAL:NO
/LIBPATH:"c:\wxWidgets-2.8.6\lib\vc_lib"
/LIBPATH:"C:\Program Files\Microsoft SDK's\Windows\v6.0A\Lib"
/SUBSYSTEM:CONSOLE
wxmsw28_core.lib wxbase28.lib user32.lib advapi32.lib
shell32.lib ole32.lib .\release\pp2_16.obj
```

For Debug Configuration:

```
link.exe /OUT:"Debug\pp2_16.exe"
/INCREMENTAL:NO
/LIBPATH:"c:\wxWidgets-2.8.6\lib\vc_lib"
/LIBPATH:"C:\Program Files\Microsoft SDK's\Windows\v6.0A\Lib"
/SUBSYSTEM:CONSOLE
wxmsw28d_core.lib wxbase28d.lib user32.lib advapi32.lib
shell32.lib ole32.lib .\debug\pp2_16.obj
```

Substitute the appropriate name for the path and library files that match the version of the wxWidgets library and platform SDK installed. Each of the preceding commands should be entered on a single line.

Linux – Code Setup and Compilation

- Tools: GNU GCC, KDevelop (Appendix B), wxWidgets library (Appendix D)

Linux Code Setup and Compilation Steps

1: Update the LD_LIBRARY_PATH variable and then start the KDevelop program.

```
export LD_LIBRARY_PATH=/usr/local/lib:$LD_LIBRARY_PATH
kdevelop &
```

2: KDevelop - Activate Menu Item: Project → New Project

Select the "C++ → Simple Hello world program" template. Set the "Application name" to pp2_16. Set the "Location" to the appropriate folder. Activate the "Next" button four times and then activate the "Finish" button.

Steps continued on the next page

Linux Code Setup and Compilation Steps continued

3: KDevelop - Activate Menu Item: Project → Build Configuration → debug

4: Enter the source code for the pp2_16.cpp file. Replace any existing code in the file.

5: Before compiling the pp2_16.cpp source code file, additional settings for accessing the wxWidgets library need to be entered into the KDevelop project. From a terminal window, enter the following:

For Release Configuration:

```
wx-config --unicode=no --debug=no --static=yes --cxxflags > cxxresults.txt
```

For Debug Configuration:

```
wx-config --unicode=no --debug=yes --static=yes --cxxflags >
cxxresults.txt
```

6: Next, run the following command:

For Release Configuration:

```
wx-config --unicode=no --debug=no --static=yes --libs > libresults.txt
```

For Debug Configuration:

```
wx-config --unicode=no --debug=yes --static=yes --libs > libresults.txt
```

7: KDevelop - Activate Menu Item: Project → Project Options

8: Click on the "Configure Options" item on the left pane. Select the "debug" configuration. Click on the "C++" tab. Here you will see the "Compiler flags" text box. The results of running the wx-config utility stored in the cxxresults.txt file must be copied and pasted here. Next, click on the "General" tab and paste the contents of the libresults.txt file in the "Linker flags" text box. You may be prompted to "Re-run configure". Select the "Do Not Run" button.

9: KDevelop - Activate Menu Item: Build → Run automake and friends

10: KDevelop - Activate Menu Item: Build → Run Configure

11: KDevelop - Activate Menu Item: Build → Build Project

If you get a message concerning no Makefile, activate the "Run Them" button.

Linux Command Prompt Compilation

For Release Configuration:

```
g++ pp2_16.cpp `wx-config --unicode=no --debug=no --static=yes --libs`
`wx-config --unicode=no --debug=no --static=yes --cxxflags` -o pp2_16
```

For Debug Configuration:

```
g++ pp2_16.cpp `wx-config --unicode=no --debug=yes --static=yes --libs`
`wx-config --unicode=no --debug=yes --static=yes --cxxflags` -o pp2_16
```

The preceding commands should be entered on a single line inside the source code folder (pp2_16/src).

- Mac OS X code setup and compilation steps can be found at the following URL:

```
http://www.wxwidgets.org/wiki/index.php/Getting_started_on_OS_X
```

Windows – Program Execution

- Execute Program

```
VC++ EE - Activate Menu Item: Debug → Start Without Debugging
```

- Debug Program

  Set the "Generate Debug Info" entry in the "pp2_16 Property Pages" to "Yes". This setting is found under the "Configuration Properties → Linker → Debugging" item. After this has been set, the program can be debugged.

```
VC++ EE - Activate Menu Item: Debug → Step Into
```

Linux – Program Execution

- Execute Program

```
KDevelop - Activate Menu Item: Build → Execute Program
```

- Debug Program

  Include the debug information in the build.

```
KDevelop - Activate Menu Item: Project → Project Options
```

  Click on the "Configure Options" item. Select the debug "Configuration" and then enter "--enable-debug=full" in the "Configure arguments" field on the "General" tab. Close the "Project Options" dialog window.

  Select the debug configuration for the project.

```
KDevelop - Activate Menu Item: Project → Build Configuration → debug
```

  Set the cursor position in the source file to the first line of code in the CBI: 2-16.1.1.3 code block. Create a breakpoint.

```
KDevelop - Activate Menu Item: Debug → Toggle Breakpoint
```

  After the breakpoint has been created, the program can be debugged.

```
KDevelop - Activate Menu Item: Debug → Start
```

Program Phase 2-17

C ▪ Core Foundation ▪ Mac OS X

Application Name Console Output

- Program Phase Task 2 is implemented in Program Phase 2-17 using the C programming language and the Core Foundation library.
- The name of the program is stored one character at a time in a C array.
- The C "if" statement, "for" loop, and "while" loop are illustrated.
- Program Phase 2-17 is a console application that provides an example for sending output to standard output and standard error.

Code Block Features

The Program Phase 2-17 code blocks illustrate the following programming features in a console application using the C programming language and the Core Foundation library:

- **Array Variable Declaration and Assignment**
- **Program Name Parsing**
- **If Statement**
- **For Loop**
- **While Loop**
- **Console Application Output to Standard Error**

C with Core Foundation
Array Variable Declaration and Assignment

- The test1.c example stores the string "Hello World!" one character at a time in an array called laArray. This array contains twelve array entries. Each array entry is then outputted to standard output.
- The "L" prefix indicates that the character is to be treated as a 4 byte Unicode character. Since the UniChar data type is only 16 bits, the extra two bytes are discarded.
- The UniChar data type stores a single 16 bit word representing a UTF-16 character in the Basic Multilingual Plane (BMP) called Plane 0. The CFStringGetCharacterAtIndex() function does not actually retrieve a Unicode character but rather retrieves a single 16 bit value that may or may not correspond to a UTF-16 character. It always corresponds to a Unicode character when the 16 bit value retrieved represents a character in the BMP that includes those characters found in the 128 character ASCII table.

test1.c: C with Core Foundation Array Variable Declaration and Assignment

```
#include <CoreFoundation/CoreFoundation.h>

int main(int argc, char* argv[])
{
   UniChar laArray[12];

   laArray[0]  = L'H';
   laArray[1]  = L'e';
   laArray[2]  = L'l';
   laArray[3]  = L'l';
   laArray[4]  = L'o';
   laArray[5]  = L' ';
   laArray[6]  = L'W';
   laArray[7]  = L'o';
   laArray[8]  = L'r';
   laArray[9]  = L'l';
   laArray[10] = L'd';
   laArray[11] = L'!';

   fwprintf(stdout, L"%lc",laArray[0]);
   fwprintf(stdout, L"%lc",laArray[1]);
   fwprintf(stdout, L"%lc",laArray[2]);
   fwprintf(stdout, L"%lc",laArray[3]);
   fwprintf(stdout, L"%lc",laArray[4]);
   fwprintf(stdout, L"%lc",laArray[5]);
   fwprintf(stdout, L"%lc",laArray[6]);
   fwprintf(stdout, L"%lc",laArray[7]);
   fwprintf(stdout, L"%lc",laArray[8]);
   fwprintf(stdout, L"%lc",laArray[9]);
   fwprintf(stdout, L"%lc",laArray[10]);
   fwprintf(stdout, L"%lc\n",laArray[11]);

   return 0;
}
```

C with Core Foundation
Program Name Parsing

- The program name is stored in the first entry of the argv array.

test2.c: C with Core Foundation Program Name Parsing

```
#include <CoreFoundation/CoreFoundation.h>

int main(int argc, char* argv[])
{
   CFStringRef lcProgramName;

   lcProgramName = CFStringCreateWithFormat(NULL,NULL,CFSTR("%s"),argv[0]);

   return 0;
}
```

C with Core Foundation
If Statement

- The "if" statement example presented here is identical in functionality to the Switch/Case statement presented in Program Phase 1-17.

test3.c: C with Core Foundation If Statement

```
#include <CoreFoundation/CoreFoundation.h>

int main(int argc, char* argv[])
{
   int lnCmdLineParamCount;

   lnCmdLineParamCount = argc - 1;

   if (lnCmdLineParamCount == 0)
   {
      // No command line parameters entered.
   }
   else
   {
      if (lnCmdLineParamCount == 1)
      {
         // One command line parameter entered.
      }
      else
      {
         // More than one command line parameter entered.
      }
   }
   return 0;
}
```

C with Core Foundation For Loop

- The following "for" loop example prints the string "Hello World!" ten times:

test4.c: C with Core Foundation For Loop

```
#include <CoreFoundation/CoreFoundation.h>

int main(int argc, char* argv[])
{
   int i;

   for (i=0;i < 10;i++)
   {
      fprintf(stdout,"Hello World!\n");
   }
   return 0;
}
```

C with Core Foundation While Loop

- The following "while" loop example prints the string "Hello World!" ten times:

test5.c: C with Core Foundation While Loop

```
#include <CoreFoundation/CoreFoundation.h>

int main(int argc, char* argv[])
{
```

test5.c continued on the next page

test5.c: C with Core Foundation While Loop continued

```
    int i;
    i = 0;

    while (i < 10)
    {
        fprintf(stdout,"Hello World!\n");
        i++;
    }
    return 0;
}
```

C with Core Foundation
Console Application Output to Standard Error

- An error code of one is returned to the operating system using the "return" statement. The CFShow() function outputs to the standard error file descriptor. The following example outputs text to standard error:

test6.c: C with Core Foundation Console Application Output to Standard Error

```
#include <CoreFoundation/CoreFoundation.h>

int main(int argc, char* argv[])
{
    CFShow(CFSTR("A program error has occurred."));
    return 1;
}
```

Source Code Files

- Text files: pp2_17.c

pp2_17.c: Program Phase 2-17 Source Code

```
//****************************************************************************
// Program Phase 2-17 OS X C Core Foundation Application Name Console Output  *
// Programming Tasks Illustrated: Console Application                         *
//                                Array Variable Declaration and Assignement  *
//                                Program Name Parsing                        *
//                                If Statement                                *
//                                For Loop                                    *
//                                While Loop                                  *
//                                Console Application Output to Standard Error*
//****************************************************************************

//****************************************************************************
// File: pp2_17.c                                                             *
// Reserved                                                                   *
//****************************************************************************

#include <CoreFoundation/CoreFoundation.h>


//****************************************************************************
// Program Phase 2-17 Main                                                    *
// Define the Entry Point of Execution (EPE) for Program Phase 2-17           *
// CBI:  2-17.1.1.1                                                           *
//****************************************************************************
```

pp2_17.c continued on the next page

pp2_17.c: Program Phase 2-17 Source Code continued

```
int main (int argc, const char * argv[]) {

//**************************************************************************
// Program Phase 2-17 Main                                                 *
// Declare the local variables for the "main" program                      *
// CBI:  2-17.1.1.2                                                        *
//**************************************************************************

   CFIndex lnLength;
   CFIndex lnIndex;
   UniChar laArray[200];
   CFStringRef lcProgramName;

//**************************************************************************
// Program Phase 2-17 Main                                                 *
// Store the program name                                                  *
// CBI:  2-17.1.1.3                                                        *
//**************************************************************************

   lcProgramName = CFStringCreateWithFormat(NULL,NULL, CFSTR("%s"),argv[0]);

//**************************************************************************
// Program Phase 2-17 Main                                                 *
// Use an if statement to verify the number of characters in the program name *
// CBI:  2-17.1.1.4                                                        *
//**************************************************************************

   lnLength = CFStringGetLength(lcProgramName);

   if (lnLength > 200)
   {
      CFShow(CFSTR("The program name is greater than 200 characters."));
      return 1;
   }

//**************************************************************************
// Program Phase 2-17 Main                                                 *
// Use a for loop to store the program name in an array                    *
// CBI:  2-17.1.1.5                                                        *
//**************************************************************************

   for (lnIndex=0;lnIndex < lnLength;lnIndex++)
   {
      laArray[lnIndex] = CFStringGetCharacterAtIndex(lcProgramName,lnIndex);
   }


//**************************************************************************
// Program Phase 2-17 Main                                                 *
// Use a while loop to output to standard output each array character element *
// CBI:  2-17.1.1.6                                                        *
//**************************************************************************

   lnIndex = 0;

   fwprintf(stdout,L"Program Name: ");

   while (lnIndex < lnLength)
   {
      fwprintf(stdout,L"%lc",laArray[lnIndex]);
      lnIndex++;
   }

   fwprintf(stdout,L"\n");
   return 0;
}
```

Code Setup and Compilation

- Tools: Xcode (Appendix C), Core Foundation library

Code Setup and Compilation Steps

1: Start the Xcode program.

2: Xcode - Activate Menu Item: File → New Project

Select "Command Line Utility → Core Foundation Tool" and then activate the "Next" button.

3: Set the "Project Name" to pp2_17. Set the "Project Directory" to the appropriate folder. Activate the "Finish" button.

4: Delete the main.c file that has been automatically added to the project.

5: Xcode - Activate Menu Item: File → New File

Select "Empty File in Project" and then activate the "Next" button. Set the "File name" to pp2_17.c and the "Location" to the pp2_17 folder and then activate the "Finish" button. Enter the source code for Program Phase 2-17 into the pp2_17.c file.

6: Compile the program by activating the "Build" button.

Command Prompt Compilation

Enter the following command in the pp2_17 folder:

```
gcc -o pp2_17 pp2_17.c -framework Carbon
```

Program Execution

- Execute Program

To execute the pp2_17 program, activate the "Build/Go" button in the Xcode IDE. The program output is displayed in the "Run Log" window. If using Xcode 3, the "Debugger Console" displays the program output. This window can be displayed by activating the "Console" menu item from the "Run" menu.

- Debug Program

Place the cursor in the CBI: 2-17.1.1.3 code block and then activate the following menu items:

```
Xcode 2.4 - Activate Menu Item: Debug → Add Breakpoint at Current Line
Xcode 3 - Activate Menu Item: Run → Manage Breakpoints → Add
Breakpoint at Current Line

Xcode - Activate Menu Item: Build → Build and Debug
```

Objective-C ▪ Cocoa ▪ Mac OS X

Application Name Console Output

- Program Phase Task 2 is implemented in Program Phase 2-18 using the Objective-C programming language and the Cocoa Foundation framework.
- The name of the program is stored one character at a time in a C array.
- The Objective-C "if" statement, "for" loop, and "while" loop are illustrated.
- Program Phase 2-18 is a console application that provides an example for sending output to standard output and standard error.

Code Block Features

The Program Phase 2-18 code blocks illustrate the following programming features in a console application using the Objective-C programming language and the Cocoa Foundation framework:

- **Array Variable Declaration and Assignment**
- **Program Name Parsing**
- **If Statement**
- **For Loop**
- **While Loop**
- **Console Application Output to Standard Error**

Objective-C with Cocoa Array Variable Declaration and Assignment

- The "L" prefix indicates that the character is to be treated as a 4 byte Unicode character. Since the UniChar data type is only 16 bits, the extra two bytes are discarded.
- The test1.m example stores the string "Hello World!" one Unicode character at a time in the array called laArray. Each array entry is then outputted to standard output using the fwprintf() function.

test1.m: Objective-C with Cocoa Array Variable Declaration and Assignment

```
#import <Foundation/Foundation.h>
int main(int argc, char* argv[])
{
```

test1.m continued on the next page

test1.m: Objective-C with Cocoa Array Variable Declaration and Assign. continued

```
    NSAutoreleasePool * loPool = [[NSAutoreleasePool alloc] init];

    UniChar laArray[12];

    laArray[0] = L'H';
    laArray[1] = L'e';
    laArray[2] = L'l';
    laArray[3] = L'l';
    laArray[4] = L'o';
    laArray[5] = L' ';
    laArray[6] = L'W';
    laArray[7] = L'o';
    laArray[8] = L'r';
    laArray[9] = L'l';
    laArray[10] = L'd';
    laArray[11] = L'!';

    fwprintf(stdout, L"%lc",laArray[0]);
    fwprintf(stdout, L"%lc",laArray[1]);
    fwprintf(stdout, L"%lc",laArray[2]);
    fwprintf(stdout, L"%lc",laArray[3]);
    fwprintf(stdout, L"%lc",laArray[4]);
    fwprintf(stdout, L"%lc",laArray[5]);
    fwprintf(stdout, L"%lc",laArray[6]);
    fwprintf(stdout, L"%lc",laArray[7]);
    fwprintf(stdout, L"%lc",laArray[8]);
    fwprintf(stdout, L"%lc",laArray[9]);
    fwprintf(stdout, L"%lc",laArray[10]);
    fwprintf(stdout, L"%lc\n",laArray[11]);

    [loPool release];
    return 0;
}
```

Objective-C with Cocoa Program Name Parsing

- The program name is stored in the first entry of the argv array.

test2.m: Objective-C with Cocoa Program Name Parsing

```
#import <Foundation/Foundation.h>

int main(int argc, char* argv[])
{
    NSAutoreleasePool * loPool = [[NSAutoreleasePool alloc] init];
    NSString* lcProgramName;

    lcProgramName = [NSString stringWithFormat:@"%s",argv[0]];

    [loPool release];
    return 0;
}
```

Objective-C with Cocoa If Statement

- The "if" statement example presented here is identical in functionality to the Switch/Case statement presented in Program Phase 1-18.

test3.m: Objective-C with Cocoa If Statement

```
#import <Foundation/Foundation.h>

int main(int argc, char* argv[])
{
   NSAutoreleasePool * loPool = [[NSAutoreleasePool alloc] init];

   int lnCmdLineParamCount;

   lnCmdLineParamCount = argc - 1;

   if (lnCmdLineParamCount == 0)
   {
      // No command line parameters entered.
   }
   else
   {
      if (lnCmdLineParamCount == 1)
      {
         // One command line parameter entered.
      }
      else
      {
         // More than one command line parameter entered.
      }
   }

   [loPool release];
   return 0;
}
```

Objective-C with Cocoa For Loop

- The following "for" loop example prints the string "Hello World!" ten times:

test4.m: Objective-C with Cocoa For Loop

```
#import <Foundation/Foundation.h>

int main(int argc, char* argv[])
{
   NSAutoreleasePool * loPool = [[NSAutoreleasePool alloc] init];
   int i;

   for (i=0;i < 10;i++)
   {
      NSLog(@"Hello World!");
   }

   [loPool release];
   return 0;
}
```

Objective-C with Cocoa While Loop

- The following "while" loop example prints the string "Hello World!" ten times:

test5.m: Objective-C with Cocoa While Loop

```
#import <Foundation/Foundation.h>

int main(int argc, char* argv[])
{
   NSAutoreleasePool * loPool = [[NSAutoreleasePool alloc] init];
   int i;

   i = 0;

   while (i < 10)
   {
      NSLog(@"Hello World!");
      i++;
   }

   [loPool release];
   return 0;
}
```

Objective-C with Cocoa
Console Application Output to Standard Error

- An error code of one is returned to the operating system using the "return" statement. The NSLog() function outputs to standard error.

test6.m: Objective-C with Cocoa Console Application Output to Standard Error

```
#import <Foundation/Foundation.h>

int main(int argc, char* argv[])
{
   NSLog(@"A program error has occurred.");
   return 1;
}
```

Source Code Files

- Text files: pp2_18.m

pp2_18.m: Program Phase 2-18 Source Code

```
//*****************************************************************************
// Program Phase 2-18 OS X Objective-C Cocoa Application Name Console Output  *
// Programming Tasks Illustrated: Console Application                         *
//                                Array Variable Declaration and Assignment   *
//                                Program Name Parsing                        *
//                                If Statement                                *
//                                For Loop                                    *
//                                While Loop                                  *
//                                Console Application Output to Standard Error*
//*****************************************************************************

//*****************************************************************************
// File: pp2_18.m                                                             *
// Reserved                                                                   *
//*****************************************************************************

#import <Foundation/Foundation.h>
```

pp2_18.m continued on the next page

pp2_18: Program Phase 2-18 Source Code continued

```
//******************************************************************************
// Program Phase 2-18 Main                                                      *
// Define the Entry Point of Execution (EPE) for Program Phase 2-18             *
// CBI:  2-18.1.1.1                                                             *
//******************************************************************************

int main (int argc, const char * argv[])
{
    NSAutoreleasePool * loPool = [[NSAutoreleasePool alloc] init];


//******************************************************************************
// Program Phase 2-18 Main                                                      *
// Declare the local variables for the "main" program                           *
// CBI:  2-18.1.1.2                                                             *
//******************************************************************************

   int lnLength;
   int lnIndex;
   UniChar laArray[200];
   NSString* lcProgramName;


//******************************************************************************
// Program Phase 2-18 Main                                                      *
// Store the program name                                                       *
// CBI:  2-18.1.1.3                                                             *
//******************************************************************************

   lcProgramName = [NSString stringWithCString:argv[0]];


//******************************************************************************
// Program Phase 2-18 Main                                                      *
// Use an if statement to verify the number of characters in the program name *
// CBI:  2-18.1.1.4                                                             *
//******************************************************************************

   lnLength = [lcProgramName length];

   if (lnLength > 200)
   {
      NSLog(@"The program name is greater than 200 characters.");
      [loPool release];
      return 1;
   }


//******************************************************************************
// Program Phase 2-18 Main                                                      *
// Use a for loop to store the program name in an array                         *
// CBI:  2-18.1.1.5                                                             *
//******************************************************************************

   for (lnIndex=0;lnIndex < lnLength;lnIndex++)
   {
      laArray[lnIndex] = [lcProgramName characterAtIndex: lnIndex];
   }

//******************************************************************************
// Program Phase 2-18 Main                                                      *
// Use a while loop to output to standard output each array character element *
// CBI:  2-18.1.1.6                                                             *
//******************************************************************************
```

pp2_18.m continued on the next page

pp2_18: Program Phase 2-18 Source Code continued

```
    lnIndex = 0;
    fwprintf(stdout,L"Program Name: ");

    while (lnIndex < lnLength)
    {
        fwprintf(stdout,L"%lc",laArray[lnIndex]);
        lnIndex++;
    }

    fwprintf(stdout,L"\n");

    [loPool release];
    return 0;
}
```

Code Setup and Compilation

- Tools: Xcode (Appendix C), AppKit

Code Setup and Compilation Steps

1: Start the Xcode IDE program.

2: Xcode - Activate Menu Item: File → New Project

Select "Command Line Utility → Foundation Tool" and then activate the "Next" button.

3: Set the "Project Name" to pp2_18 and set the "Project Directory" to the appropriate folder. Activate the "Finish" button.

4: Enter the source code for Program Phase 2-18 into the pp2_18.m file that has been automatically created. Replace any existing code in the file.

5: Compile the program by activating the "Build" button.

Command Prompt Compilation

Enter the following command in the pp2_18 folder:

```
gcc -o pp2_18 pp2_18.m -framework Cocoa
```

Program Execution

- Execute Program

  To execute the pp2_18 program, activate the "Build/Go" button in the Xcode IDE.

- Debug Program

  Place the cursor in the CBI: 2-18.1.1.3 code block.

```
   Xcode 2.4 - Activate Menu Item: Debug → Add Breakpoint at Current Line
   Xcode 3 - Activate Menu Item: Run → Manage Breakpoints → Add
Breakpoint at Current Line

   Xcode - Activate Menu Item: Build → Build and Debug
```

Program Phase Task 3

GUI Based Program with Custom Class Definition and Instantiation

- Program Phase Task 3 is a GUI based program that attempts to instantiate a custom class with data passed to the initialization function of the class. Inside the initialization function of the class, the user is prompted to continue instantiating the class. If the user selects the "Yes" button, the initialization parameters are stored as class data, and the class is then instantiated. If the user selects the "No" button, class instantiation is cancelled. The part of the program that attempted instantiation then checks to see if the class successfully instantiated. If it did, a class instance method is called. If it did not, the user is notified that the class did not instantiate.

- There are two source code files that make up Program Phase Task 3. The first file contains the Entry Point of Execution (EPE) for the GUI based program, and the second file contains the class definition for the custom class to be instantiated. A third file is used as the class header file for programming languages that support separate files for class definition and implementation.

- When the program is started, it attempts to instantiate the myclass custom class. The initialization function for the myclass class displays a prompt in the form of a message box, asking the user to continue instantiating the class.

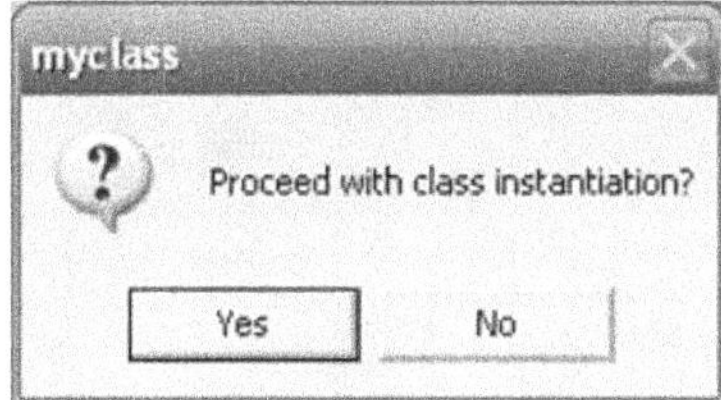

If the user activates the "No" button, the class instantiation is cancelled. The part of the program that attempted instantiation of the myclass class checks to see if the class successfully instantiated. If it did not, the following message box is displayed.

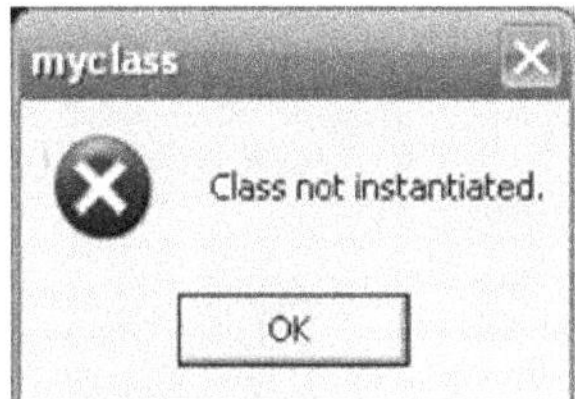

If the user activates the "Yes" button to confirm instantiation of the class, the myclass class is instantiated. When the program confirms that instantiation was successful, a class instance method is called displaying the data stored as class data.

Program Phase 3-1

Java ▪ Multi-Platform

GUI Based Program with Custom Class Definition and Instantiation

- Program Phase Task 3 is implemented in Program Phase 3-1 using the Java programming language and the Swing API.
- The JOptionPane class is used in Program Phase 3-1 to implement input and output for a GUI based application.
- The Entry Point of Execution (EPE) is stored in the pp3_1.java text file. The myclass class is defined and implemented in the myclass.java text file.

Code Block Features

The Program Phase 3-1 code blocks illustrate the following programming features using the Java programming language and the Swing API:

- **GUI Application**
- **Custom Class Definition**
- **Object Variable Declaration**
- **Custom Class Instantiation**
- **Cancel Class Instantiation from the Class Initialization Function**
- **Message Box Input and Output**

Java
GUI Application

- The EPE for a GUI based Java application is no different than a console based Java application.

test1.java: Java GUI Application

```
public class test1
{
   public static void main(final String argv[])
   {
      // GUI based Java code goes here.
   }
}
```

Java
Custom Class Definition

- The following example illustrates defining and implementing a custom class using Java:

testclass1.java: Java Custom Class Definition

```
package programphases.test;

class testclass1
{
   // Class data
   private int nData;
   private String cData;

public testclass1(int tnData,String tcData)
{
   this.nData = tnData;
   this.cData = tcData;
}

public void TestMethod()
{
   // Java code goes here.
}}
```

Java
Object Variable Declaration

- A testclass1 typed variable can store an instance of the testclass1 class. Access to the testclass1 class is necessary when the object variable is declared.

- Since the testclass1 class resides in the same package as the test2 program, the testclass1 class is accessible in the test2 program.

test2.java: Java Object Variable Declaration

```
package programphases.test;

public class test2
{
public static void main(final String argv[])
{
    testclass1 loTestClass = null;
}}
```

Java
Custom Class Instantiation

- The following example creates an instance of the testclass1 class and calls the TestMethod() method:

test3.java: Java Custom Class Instantiation

```
package programphases.test;

public class test3
{
public static void main(final String argv[])
{
   testclass1 loTestClass;

   loTestClass = null;
   loTestClass = new testclass1(12345,"Hello World!");
   loTestClass.TestMethod();
}}
```

Java
Cancel Class Instantiation from the Class Initialization Function

- Class instantiation is cancelled by throwing an exception from the class constructor.

testclass2.java: Java Cancel Class Instantiation from the Class Init Function

```
package programphases.test;

class testclass2
{
   // Class data
   private int nData;
   private String cData;

public testclass2(int tnData,String tcData) throws Exception

{
   Exception loException;

   // Java code goes here.

   //… Some error has occurred so cancel instantiation by
   // throwing an exception.

  loException = new Exception("Class not instantiated because of some error.");
   throw loException;


   // Program execution never gets here.
   this.nData = tnData;
   this.cData = tcData;
}

public void TestMethod()
{
   // Java code goes here.
}}
```

- The class instantiation attempt is placed in a try/catch block that responds to an exception thrown in the testclass2 constructor. If the testclass2 instantiation fails, the loTestClass variable still stores the "null" value previously assigned before the class instantiation was attempted.

test4.java: Java Attempt to Instantiate the testclass2 Class

```
package programphases.test;

public class test4
{
public static void main(final String argv[])
{
   testclass2 loTestClass;
   loTestClass = null;

   try
   {
      loTestClass = new testclass2(12345,"Hello World!");
   }
   catch(Exception loError)
   {
      // The class failed to instantiate.
      // An error message can be retrieved by calling loError.getMessage()
   }

   if (loTestClass == null)
   {
      System.exit(1);
   }

   loTestClass.TestMethod();
}}
```

Java
Message Box Input and Output

- The following example prompts the user to select "Yes" or "No":

test5.java: Java Message Box Input and Output

```
import javax.swing.JOptionPane;

public class test5
{
public static void main(final String argv[])
{
   int lnResult;

   lnResult = JOptionPane.showOptionDialog(null,"Select Yes or No","test",
                                           JOptionPane.YES_NO_OPTION,
                                           JOptionPane.QUESTION_MESSAGE,
                                           null,null,null);

   if (lnResult == JOptionPane.NO_OPTION)
   {
      // No selected
   }
   else
   {
      // Yes selected (JOptionPane.YES_OPTION)
   }
}}
```

Source Code Files

- Text files: pp3_1.java, myclass.java

pp3_1.java: Program Phase 3-1 EPE Source Code

```
//******************************************************************************
// Program Phase 3-1 Java Class Definition/Instantiation                      *
// Programming Tasks Illustrated: Swing GUI Based Application                 *
//                                Custom Class Definition                     *
//                                Object Variable Declaration                 *
//                                Custom Class Instantiation                  *
//                                Cancel Instantiation from the Init Function *
//                                Message Box Input and Output                *
//******************************************************************************

//******************************************************************************
// File: pp3_1.java                                                           *
// Reserved                                                                   *
//******************************************************************************

package programphases.programphase3_1;
import javax.swing.JOptionPane;

public class pp3_1
{

//******************************************************************************
// Program Phase 3-1 Main                                                     *
// Define the Entry Point of Execution (EPE) for Program Phase 3-1            *
// CBI:  3-1.1.1.1                                                            *
//******************************************************************************

public static void main(final String taArgv[])
{

//******************************************************************************
// Program Phase 3-1 Main                                                     *
// Declare the local variables for the "main" program                         *
// CBI:  3-1.1.1.2                                                            *
//******************************************************************************

   myclass loMyClass = null;

//******************************************************************************
// Program Phase 3-1 Main                                                     *
// Attempt to instantiate the myclass class                                   *
// CBI:  3-1.1.1.3                                                            *
//******************************************************************************

   try
   {
      loMyClass = new myclass(12345,"Hello World!");
   }

//******************************************************************************
// Program Phase 3-1 Main                                                     *
// If the myclass class fails to instantiate, notify the user and exit        *
// CBI:  3-1.1.1.4                                                            *
//******************************************************************************

   catch(Exception loError)
   {
      JOptionPane.showMessageDialog(null,loError.getMessage(),
                                  "myclass",JOptionPane.ERROR_MESSAGE,null);
   }
   if (loMyClass == null)
   {
```

pp3_1.java continued on the next page

pp3_1.java: Program Phase 3-1 EPE Source Code continued

```
         System.exit(1);
      }

//*************************************************************************
// Program Phase 3-1 Main                                                 *
// If the myclass class instantiated, call an instance method             *
// CBI:  3-1.1.1.5                                                        *
//*************************************************************************

      loMyClass.DisplayInstanceData();
}}
```

- myclass.java

myclass.java: Class Definition and Implementation for the myclass Class

```
//*************************************************************************
// File: myclass.java                                                     *
// Reserved                                                               *
//*************************************************************************

package programphases.programphase3_1;
import javax.swing.JOptionPane;


//*************************************************************************
// myclass definition                                                     *
// Class definition for the myclass class                                 *
// CBI:  3-1.2.1.1                                                        *
//*************************************************************************

// The myclass class is defined and implemented starting in CBI:  3-1.2.2.1.


//*************************************************************************
// myclass implementation                                                 *
// Class implementation for the myclass class                             *
// CBI:  3-1.2.2.1                                                        *
//*************************************************************************

class myclass
{
   // Class data
   private int nData;
   private String cData;


//*************************************************************************
// myclass implementation                                                 *
// Implement the initialization function for the myclass class            *
// CBI:  3-1.2.3.1                                                        *
//*************************************************************************

public myclass(int tnData,String tcData) throws Exception
{

//*************************************************************************
// myclass implementation                                                 *
// Declare the local variables for the myclass initialization function    *
// CBI:  3-1.2.3.2                                                        *
//*************************************************************************
```

myclass.java continued on the next page

myclass.java: Class Definition and Implementation for the myclass Class continued

```
   int lnResult;
   Exception loException;


//*************************************************************************
// myclass implementation                                                 *
// Prompt the user to continue instantiating the myclass class            *
// CBI:  3-1.2.3.3                                                        *
//*************************************************************************

   lnResult = JOptionPane.showOptionDialog(null,
                                     "Proceed with class instantiation?",
                                     "myclass",JOptionPane.YES_NO_OPTION,
                                     JOptionPane.QUESTION_MESSAGE,
                                     null,null,null);


//*************************************************************************
// myclass implementation                                                 *
// Cancel instantiation of the myclass class if the user selects no       *
// CBI:  3-1.2.3.4                                                        *
//*************************************************************************

   if (lnResult == JOptionPane.NO_OPTION)
   {
      loException = new Exception("Class not instantiated.");
      throw loException;
   }


//*************************************************************************
// myclass implementation                                                 *
// Store the parameters to the initialization function as instance data   *
// CBI:  3-1.2.3.5                                                        *
//*************************************************************************

   this.nData = tnData;
   this.cData = tcData;
}


//*************************************************************************
// myclass implementation                                                 *
// Implement the DisplayInstanceData method of the myclass class          *
// CBI:  3-1.2.4.1                                                        *
//*************************************************************************

public void DisplayInstanceData()
{
   JOptionPane.showMessageDialog(null,"nData: " + this.nData +
                              System.getProperty("line.separator") +
                              "cData: " + this.cData,
                              "myclass instance data",
                              JOptionPane.INFORMATION_MESSAGE,null);
}}
```

Windows and Linux – Code Setup and Compilation

- Tools: Java SE Development Kit (JDK) 5.0, Netbeans IDE (Appendix A)

Windows and Linux Code Setup and Compilation Steps

1: Start the Netbeans IDE program.

Steps continued on the next page

Windows and Linux Code Setup and Compilation Steps continued

2: Netbeans - Activate Menu Item: File → New Project

Select the "Java" category and then select "Java Application" as the project type. Activate the "Next" button.

3: Enter pp3_1 as the "Project Name". Enter the appropriate folder name for the "File Location". Check the "Set as Main Project" check box. Uncheck the "Create Main Class" check box. Activate the "Finish" button.

4: Create a folder called programphases\programphase3_1 inside the src folder of the pp3_1 folder. Example: `pp3_1\src\programphases\programphase3_1`

5: Netbeans - Activate Menu Item: File → New File

In the "New File" dialog window, select the "Other" category and then select "Empty File" as the file type. Activate the "Next" button. Enter the file name as pp3_1.java and select the src/programphases/programphase3_1 folder as the destination "Folder". Activate the "Finish" button to create the pp3_1.java file.

6: Open the pp3_1.java file and then enter the appropriate source code.

7: Netbeans - Activate Menu Item: File → New File

In the "New File" dialog window, select the "Other" category and select "Empty File" as the file type. Activate the "Next" button. Enter the file name as myclass.java and select the src/programphases/programphase3_1 folder as the destination folder. Activate the "Finish" button to create the myclass.java file.

8: Open the myclass.java file and then enter the appropriate source code.

9: Netbeans - Activate Menu Item: File → pp3_1 Properties

On the "Project Properties" window, select the "Run" category and then enter programphases.programphase3_1.pp3_1 for the "Main Class". Activate the "OK" button.

10: Netbeans - Activate Menu Item: Build → Build Main Project

Windows and Linux Command Prompt Compilation Steps

1: Update the path to the javac executable file.

```
Windows:  PATH = %PATH%;"C:\Program Files\Java\jdk1.6.0_01\bin"

Linux Bash:  export PATH=~/jdk1.6.0_01/bin:$PATH
Linux C shell or the TC shell: setenv PATH ~/jdk1.6.0/bin:$PATH
```

Substitute the path for the version of the JDK installed.

Steps continued on the next page

Windows and Linux Command Prompt Compilation Steps continued

2: Change directories to the pp3_1 folder and then enter the following command:

Windows

```
javac -d "build\classes" "src\programphases\programphase3_1\pp3_1.java"
                    "src\programphases\programphase3_1\myclass.java"
```

Linux

```
javac -d "build/classes" "src/programphases/programphase3_1/pp3_1.java"
                    "src/programphases/programphase3_1/myclass.java"
```

3: Create a text file called manifest in the pp3_1 folder using a text editor and put the following in the file:

```
Main-Class: programphases.programphase3_1.pp3_1
```

Enter a newline at the end of the text.

4: Create the pp3_1.jar "executable" file.

```
jar -cvfm ./dist/pp3_1.jar manifest -C build/classes .
```

Mac OS X – Code Setup and Compilation

- Tools: Java SE Development Kit (JDK) 5.0 (included with Mac OS X), Xcode IDE (Appendix C)

Mac OS X Code Setup and Compilation Steps

1: Start the Xcode IDE program found in the /Developer/Applications folder.

2: Xcode - Activate Menu Item: File → New Project

Select "Java Tool" and then activate the "Next" button.

3: Enter pp3_1 as the "Project Name". Enter the appropriate folder as the "Project Directory". Activate the "Finish" button.

4: Xcode - Activate Menu Item: Project → Set Active Build Configuration → Release

5: A text file called pp3_1.java is automatically created. Delete the entire contents of this file and then enter the source code for Program Phase 3-1.

6: Xcode - Activate Menu Item: File → New File

Select "Empty File in Project" and then activate the "Next" button. Enter the source code for the myclass class and save the file as myclass.java.

7: In the Xcode IDE, double-click on the Resource file called Manifest. Change the "Main-Class" entry in the Manifest file from pp3_1 to programphases.programphase3_1.pp3_1. Save and close the Manifest file.

Steps continued on the next page

Mac OS X Code Setup and Compilation Steps continued

8: If using Xcode 3, expand the "Executables" entry and then double-click on the "java" entry to display the "Executable 'java' Info" window. Edit the argument to look like this:

```
-cp pp3_1.jar programphases.programphase3_1.pp3_1
```

9: Activate the Build button in Xcode to compile the pp3_1.java and myclass.java files.

Mac OS X Command Prompt Compilation Steps

1: Open a terminal window and change directories to the pp3_1 folder.

Xcode 2.4: `javac -d "build/pp3_1.build/Release/pp3_1.build/JavaClasses" pp3_1.java myclass.java`

Xcode 3: `javac -d bin src/pp3_1.java src/myclass.java`

2: Create a text file called Manifest in the pp3_1 folder using a text editor and put this line in the file:

```
Main-Class: programphases.programphase3_1.pp3_1
```

Enter a newline at the end of the text.

3: Create the pp3_1.jar "executable" file. Enter the following on a single line:

Xcode 2.4: `jar -cvfm build/Release/pp3_1.jar Manifest -C build/pp3_1.build/Release/pp3_1.build/JavaClasses .`

Xcode 3: `jar -cvfm jars/pp3_1.jar Manifest -C bin .`

Windows and Linux – Program Execution

- Execute Program

```
Netbeans IDE - Activate Menu Item:  Run → Run Main Project
```

- Debug Program

```
Netbeans IDE - Activate Menu Item:  Run → Step Into Project
```

Mac OS X – Program Execution

- Execute Program

```
Xcode IDE - Activate the "Build and Go" button
```

- Debug Program

```
Xcode 2.4 - Activate Menu Item: Debug → Add Breakpoint at Current Line
Xcode 3 - Activate Menu Item: Run → Manage Breakpoints → Add
Breakpoint at Current Line

Xcode - Activate Menu Item: Build → Build and Debug
```

Program Phase 3-2
Visual FoxPro ▪ Windows

GUI Based Program with Custom Class Definition and Instantiation

- Program Phase Task 3 is implemented in Program Phase 3-2 using the Visual FoxPro (VFP) programming language.
- The MESSAGEBOX() function is used in Program Phase 3-2 to implement input and output for a GUI based application.
- The Entry Point of Execution (EPE) is stored in the pp3_2.prg text file. The myclass class is defined and implemented in the myclass.prg text file.

Code Block Features

The Program Phase 3-2 code blocks illustrate the following programming features using the VFP programming language:

- **GUI Application**
- **Custom Class Definition**
- **Object Variable Declaration**
- **Custom Class Instantiation**
- **Cancel Class Instantiation from the Class Initialization Function**
- **Message Box Input and Output**

Visual FoxPro
GUI Application

- VFP only supports creating GUI based applications. See page 13 for example.

Visual FoxPro
Custom Class Definition

- The following example illustrates defining and implementing a custom class using VFP:

testclass1.prg: Visual FoxPro Custom Class Definition

```
DEFINE CLASS testclass1 AS CUSTOM

nData = 0
cData = ""
```

testclass1.prg continued on the next page

testclass1.prg: Visual FoxPro Custom Class Definition continued

```
PROCEDURE INIT
LPARAMETERS tnData,tcData

this.nData = tnData
this.cData = tcData

ENDPROC

PROCEDURE TestMethod()

** Visual FoxPro code goes here.

ENDPROC
ENDDEFINE
```

Visual FoxPro Object Variable Declaration

- A VFP loosely typed variable can store an instance of the testclass1 class. Access to the testclass1 class is not necessary when the object variable is declared.

test2.prg: Visual FoxPro Object Variable Declaration

```
LOCAL loTestClass
```

Visual FoxPro Custom Class Instantiation

- A VFP custom class is instantiated using the CREATEOBJECT() function.

- The "SET PROCEDURE" statement allows the testclass1 class to be accessed in the test3.prg program.

- Assigning an empty string to the class instance variable removes it from memory. The "SET PROCEDURE TO" command closes the testclass1.prg procedure file. The test3.prg and testclass1.prg source files are compiled into a single executable file. When the program executes the "SET PROCEDURE" command, the testclass1.prg file loads from the executable file and not the actual testclass1.prg file found on the file system.

- The following example creates an instance of the testclass1 class and calls the TestMethod() method:

test3.prg: Visual FoxPro Custom Class Instantiation

```
SET PROCEDURE TO testclass1.prg
LOCAL loTestClass

loTestClass = CreateObject("testclass1")
loTestClass.TestMethod()

loTestClass = ""
SET PROCEDURE TO
```

Visual FoxPro
Cancel Class Instantiation from the Class Initialization Function

- Class instantiation is cancelled by returning a Boolean "false" value from the INIT() event of the class.

testclass2.prg: VFP Cancel Class Instantiation from the Class Init Function

```
DEFINE CLASS testclass2 AS CUSTOM

nData = 0
cData = ""

PROCEDURE INIT
LPARAMETERS tnData,tcData

   ** Visual FoxPro code goes here.
   **… Some error has occurred so cancel instantiation by
   ** returning a Boolean false value.

   RETURN .F.

   ** Program execution never gets here.
   this.nData = tnData
   this.cData = tcData

ENDPROC

PROCEDURE TestMethod()

** Visual FoxPro code goes here.

ENDPROC
ENDDEFINE
```

- If the testclass2 instantiation fails, then the TYPE() function does not return the value "O" for the string "loTestclass".

test4.prg: VFP Attempt to Instantiate the testclass2 Class

```
SET PROCEDURE TO testclass2.prg

LOCAL loTestClass

loTestClass = CreateObject("testclass2")

IF TYPE("loTestClass") != "O"

   SET PROCEDURE TO
   RETURN

ENDIF

loTestClass.TestMethod()
SET PROCEDURE TO
```

Visual FoxPro
Message Box Input and Output

- The following example prompts the user to select "Yes" or "No":

test5.prg: Visual FoxPro Message Box Input and Output

```
LOCAL lnResult

lnResult = MESSAGEBOX("Select Yes or No",4 + 32,  "test")

IF lnResult = 7

   ** No Selected
ELSE

   ** Yes Selected (lnResult = 6)
ENDIF
```

Source Code Files

- Text files: pp3_2.prg, myclass.prg

pp3_2.prg: Program Phase 3-2 EPE Source Code

```
******************************************************************************
** Program Phase 3-2 Visual FoxPro Class Definition/Instantiation              *
** Programming Tasks Illustrated: Visual FoxPro GUI Based Application          *
**                                Custom Class Definition                      *
**                                Object Variable Declaration                  *
**                                Custom Class Instantiation                   *
**                                Cancel Instantiation from the Init Function *
**                                Message Box Input and Output                 *
******************************************************************************

******************************************************************************
** File: pp3_2.prg                                                              *
** Reserved                                                                     *
******************************************************************************

SET PROCEDURE TO myclass.prg


******************************************************************************
** Program Phase 3-2 Main                                                       *
** Define the Entry Point of Execution (EPE) for Program Phase 3-2             *
** CBI:  3-2.1.1.1                                                              *
******************************************************************************

** The first line of the code in the pp3_2.prg file is the EPE.


******************************************************************************
** Program Phase 3-2 Main                                                       *
** Declare the local variables for the "main" program                          *
** CBI:  3-2.1.1.2                                                              *
******************************************************************************

LOCAL loMyClass


******************************************************************************
** Program Phase 3-2 Main                                                       *
** Attempt to instantiate the myclass class                                    *
** CBI:  3-2.1.1.3                                                              *
******************************************************************************

loMyClass = CREATEOBJECT("myclass",12345,"Hello World!")
```

pp3_2.prg continued on the next page

pp3_2.prg: Program Phase 3-2 EPE Source Code continued

```
*******************************************************************************
** Program Phase 3-2 Main                                                     *
** If the myclass class fails to instantiate, notify the user and exit        *
** CBI:  3-2.1.1.4                                                            *
*******************************************************************************

IF TYPE("loMyClass") <> "O"

    =MESSAGEBOX("Class not instantiated.",0 + 16,"myclass")
   SET PROCEDURE TO
   RETURN 1

ENDIF


*******************************************************************************
** Program Phase 3-2 Main                                                     *
** If the myclass class instantiated, call an instance method                 *
** CBI:  3-2.1.1.5                                                            *
*******************************************************************************

loMyClass.DisplayInstanceData()

loMyClass = ""
SET PROCEDURE TO
```

- myclass.prg

myclass.prg: Class Definition and Implementation for the myclass Class

```
*******************************************************************************
** myclass.prg                                                                *
** Reserved                                                                   *
*******************************************************************************

*******************************************************************************
** myclass definition                                                         *
** Class definition for the myclass class                                     *
** CBI:  3-2.2.1.1                                                            *
*******************************************************************************

** The myclass class is defined and implemented starting in CBI: 3-2.2.2.1.


*******************************************************************************
** myclass implementation                                                     *
** Class implementation for the myclass class                                 *
** CBI:  3-2.2.2.1                                                            *
*******************************************************************************

DEFINE CLASS myclass AS CUSTOM

   ** class data
   nData = 0
   cData = ""


*******************************************************************************
** myclass implementation                                                     *
** Implement the initialization function for the myclass class                *
** CBI:  3-2.2.3.1                                                            *
*******************************************************************************
```

myclass.prg continued on the next page

myclass.prg: Class Definition and Implementation for the myclass Class continued

```
PROCEDURE INIT
LPARAMETERS tnData,tcData

*****************************************************************************
** myclass implementation                                                   *
** Declare the local variables for the myclass initialization function      *
** CBI:  3-2.2.3.2                                                          *
*****************************************************************************

   LOCAL lnResult

*****************************************************************************
** myclass implementation                                                   *
** Prompt the user to continue instantiating the myclass class              *
** CBI:  3-2.2.3.3                                                          *
*****************************************************************************

   lnResult = MESSAGEBOX("Proceed with class instantiation?",4 + 32,"myclass")

*****************************************************************************
** myclass implementation                                                   *
** Cancel instantiation of the myclass class if the user selects no         *
** CBI:  3-2.2.3.4                                                          *
*****************************************************************************

   IF lnResult = 7

      RETURN .F.

   ENDIF

*****************************************************************************
** myclass implementation                                                   *
** Store the parameters to the initialization function as instance data     *
** CBI:  3-2.2.3.5                                                          *
*****************************************************************************

   this.nData = tnData
   this.cData = tcData

ENDPROC

*****************************************************************************
** myclass implementation                                                   *
** Implement the DisplayInstanceData method of the myclass class            *
** CBI:  3-2.2.4.1                                                          *
*****************************************************************************

PROCEDURE DisplayInstanceData()

   =MESSAGEBOX("nData: " + ALLTRIM(STR(this.nData)) + CHR(13) + "cData: " + ;
            this.cData,0 + 64,"myclass instance data")

ENDPROC

ENDDEFINE
```

Code Setup and Compilation

- Tools: Visual FoxPro

Code Setup and Compilation Steps

1: Create a folder called pp3_2 that will store the source code files.

2: Start the Visual FoxPro IDE program.

3: VFP - Activate Menu Item: File → New

From the "New" dialog window, select the "Project" radio button and then activate the "New file" button. Save the project as pp3_2.pjx in the pp3_2 folder.

4: VFP - Activate Menu Item: File → New

From the "New" dialog window, select the "Program" radio button and then activate the "New file" button.

5: Enter the EPE source code into the new program file and save the file as pp3_2.prg.

6: Add the pp3_2.prg file to the project by selecting the "Code" tab in the "Project Manager" for the pp3_2 project and then activating the "Add" button. Browse for the pp3_2.prg file to add it to the project.

7: VFP - Activate Menu Item: File → New

From the "New" dialog window, select the "Program" radio button and then activate the "New file" button.

8: Enter the source code for the myclass class into the new program file and save the file as myclass.prg.

9: Add the myclass.prg file to the project by selecting the "Code" tab in the "Project Manager" for the pp3_2 project and then activating the "Add" button. Browse for the myclass.prg file to add it to the project.

10: Create a text file called config.fpw in the pp3_2 folder and enter the following text:

```
screen = off
```

11: Right click on the pp3_2.prg file in the "Project Manager" window and activate the "set main" menu item if it does not already have a check mark next to it in the menu.

12: Click the "Build" button on the "Project Manager" window. Select the "Win32 executable" radio button. Select "Recompile All Files" and "Display Errors". Activate the "OK" button. Use the "Save As" dialog to select a destination for the executable file and then activate the "Save" button.

Visual FoxPro Command Window Compilation

Enter the following command in the VFP command window:

```
BUILD EXE "c:\pp3_2\pp3_2.exe" FROM "c:\pp3_2\pp3_2.pjx" RECOMPILE
```

Program Execution

- Execute Program

```
VFP - Activate Menu Item:  Program → Do.
```

Navigate to the pp3_2.exe file in the "Do" dialog window and then activate the "Do" button.

- Debug Program

```
VFP - Activate Menu Item:  Tools → Debugger.
VFP Debugger window - Activate Menu Item:  Debug → Do
```

Select the pp3_2.prg file found in the pp3_2 folder and then activate the "Do" button on the "Do" dialog window.

- The pp3_2.exe file can also be executed from the VFP command window.

```
DO "c:\pp3_2\pp3_2.exe"
```

- VFP automatically reads a text file called config.fpw if it exists in the startup folder. Settings for VFP can be set in this text file. The only setting present in the config.fpw file for Program Phase 3-2 is a setting for hiding the automatically created VFP main window.

```
screen = off
```

The VFP main window can be made visible in the program by setting the visible property of the _SCREEN global object to the Boolean "true" value.

```
_SCREEN.VISIBLE = .T.
```

The VFP main window is never made visible in Program Phase 3-2, but this technique is used in Program Phase 4-2 to make the main window visible. Remember to set the startup folder to the folder containing the config.fpw file when creating Windows shortcuts to executable files created with VFP.

Program Phase 3-3
C++ ▪ Win32 API ▪ Windows

GUI Based Program with Custom Class Definition and Instantiation

- Program Phase Task 3 is implemented in Program Phase 3-3 using the C++ programming language and the Win32 API.
- The Win32 API MessageBox() function is used in Program Phase 3-3 to implement input and output for a GUI based application.
- The Entry Point of Execution (EPE) is stored in the pp3_3.cpp text file. The myclass class is defined in the myclass.h text file and implemented in the myclass.cpp text file.

Code Block Features

The Program Phase 3-3 code blocks illustrate the following programming features using the C++ programming language:

- **GUI Application**
- **Custom Class Definition**
- **Object Variable Declaration**
- **Custom Class Instantiation**
- **Cancel Class Instantiation from the Class Initialization Function**
- **Message Box Input and Output**

C++ with Win32 API
GUI Application

- The EPE for a Win32 GUI based application is a function called WinMain() that takes four parameters. The first parameter is an instance variable that is unique for each running application. The second parameter is a handle to a previous instance of the program. This value is always "NULL". The third parameter is a C string containing any command line parameters entered by the user. The fourth parameter can be specified in the Windows shortcut that started the application. This value indicates the desired state of the main window such as "maximized" or "minimized" when it is displayed. Program Phase 3-3 does not create a main window, so this value is ignored.

testl.cpp: C++ w/ Win32 API GUI Application

```
#include <windows.h>

INT WINAPI WinMain(HINSTANCE thInstance,HINSTANCE thPreviousInstance,
                   CHAR *tcCmdLine, INT tnShowCmd)
{
   // Win32 GUI based C/C++ code goes here.

   return 0;
}
```

C++
Custom Class Definition

- The "#ifndef" stands for "if not defined". Enclosing the class definition in a "#ifndf""#endif" block ensures that only one copy of the class is included in the build even if multiple source code files include the testclass1.h header file.

- The testclass1 class is defined in the testclass1.h file.

testclass1.h: C++ Custom Class Definition

```
#ifndef TESTCLASS1_H
#define TESTCLASS1_H

class testclass1
{
   private:
      // class data
      int nData;
      char *cData;

   public:
      testclass1(int tnData,char *tcData);
      void TestMethod();
};
#endif
```

- The testclass1 class is implemented in the testclass1.cpp file.

testclass1.cpp: C++ Custom Class Implementation

```
#include "testclass1.h"

testclass1::testclass1(int tnData,char *tcData)
{
   this->nData = tnData;
   this->cData = tcData;
}

void testclass1::TestMethod()
{
   // C/C++ code goes here.
}
```

C++ with Win32 API
Object Variable Declaration

- A testclass1 typed pointer variable can store a pointer to an instance of the testclass1 class. Access to the testclass1 class is necessary when the object variable is declared.
- The testclass1 class is accessible in the test2.cpp program because the class definition stored in the testclass1.h file is included at the top of the file.

test2.cpp: C++ w/ Win32 API Object Variable Declaration

```
#include <windows.h>
#include "testclass1.h"

INT WINAPI WinMain(HINSTANCE thInstance,HINSTANCE thPreviousInstance,
                   CHAR *tcCmdLine,INT tnShowCmd)
{
   testclass1* loTestClass;
   return 0;
}
```

C++ with Win32 API
Custom Class Instantiation

- The C++ "new" operator is used to create an instance of the testclass1 class defined in the testclass1.h header file. Since the "new" operator is used, a corresponding "delete" must be issued in order to free the memory used by the testclass1 class instance.
- The following example creates an instance of the testclass1 class and calls the TestMethod() method:

test3.cpp: C++ w/ Win32 API Custom Class Instantiation

```
#include <windows.h>
#include "testclass1.h"

INT WINAPI WinMain(HINSTANCE thInstance,HINSTANCE thPreviousInstance,
                   CHAR *tcCmdLine,INT tnShowCmd)
{
   testclass1* loTestClass;

   loTestClass = new testclass1(12345,"Hello World!");
   loTestClass->TestMethod();

   delete loTestClass;
   return 0;
}
```

C++ with Win32 API
Cancel Class Instantiation from the Initialization Function

- Class instantiation can be cancelled by throwing an exception from the class constructor.

testclass2.h: Class Header File for the testclass2 Class

```
#ifndef TESTCLASS2_H
#define TESTCLASS2_H

class testclass2
{
   private:
      // class data
      int nData;
      char *cData;

   public:
      testclass2(int tnData,char *tcData);
      void TestMethod();
};
#endif
```

testclass2.cpp: C++ Cancel Class Instantiation from the Initialization Function

```
#include "testclass2.h"
#include <exception>

testclass2::testclass2(int tnData,char *tcData)
{
   // C++ code goes here.

   //… Some error has occurred so cancel instantiation by
   // throwing an exception.

   throw "Class not instantiated because of some error.";

   // Program execution never gets here.
   this->nData = tnData;
   this->cData = tcData;
}

void testclass2::TestMethod()
{
   // C/C++ code goes here.
}
```

- A try/catch block is used to check if an exception has been thrown in the class constructor. If the testclass2 instantiation fails, the loTestClass variable will still store the value zero previously assigned before the class instantiation was attempted.

test4.cpp: C++ Attempt to Instantiate the testclass2 Class

```
#include <windows.h>
#include <exception>
#include "testclass2.h"

INT WINAPI WinMain(HINSTANCE thInstance, HINSTANCE thPreviousInstance,
                   CHAR *tcCmdLine,INT tnShowCmd)
{
   testclass2* loTestClass;
   loTestClass = 0;

   try
   {
      loTestClass = new testclass2(12345,"Hello World!");
   }
   catch (char* lcError)
   {
```

test4.cpp continued on the next page

test4.cpp: C++ Attempt to Instantiate the testclass2 Class continued

```
      // The class failed to instantiate.
      // An error message is stored in the lcError C string.
   }

   if (loTestClass == 0)
   {
      return 1;
   }

   loTestClass->TestMethod();
   delete loTestClass;
   return 0;
}
```

C with Win32 API
Message Box Input and Output

- The following example prompts the user to select "Yes" or "No":

test5.cpp: C w/ Win32 API Message Box Input and Output

```
#include <windows.h>

INT WINAPI WinMain(HINSTANCE thInstance,HINSTANCE thPreviousInstance,
                   CHAR *tcCmdLine,INT tnShowCmd)
{
   INT lnResult;

   lnResult = MessageBox(NULL,"Select Yes or No.",
                         "test",MB_YESNO | MB_ICONQUESTION);
   if (lnResult == IDNO)
   {
      // No selected
   }
   else
   {
      // Yes selected (IDYES)
   }
}
```

Source Code Files

- Text files: pp3_3.cpp, myclass.h, myclass.cpp

pp3_3.cpp: Program Phase 3-3 EPE Source Code

```
//*************************************************************************
// Program Phase 3-3 C++ Win32 Class Definition/Instantiation            *
// Programming Tasks Illustrated: Win32 GUI Based Application             *
//                                Custom Class Definition                 *
//                                Object Variable Declaration             *
//                                Custom Class Instantiation              *
//                                Cancel Instantiation from the Init Funtion *
//                                Message Box Input and Output            *
//*************************************************************************

//*************************************************************************
// File: pp3_3.cpp                                                        *
// Reserved                                                               *
//*************************************************************************
```

pp3_3.cpp continued on the next page

pp3_3.cpp: Program Phase 3-3 EPE Source Code continued

```
#include <windows.h>
#include <exception>
#include "myclass.h"


//****************************************************************************
// Program Phase 3-3 Main                                                    *
// Define the Entry Point of Execution (EPE) for Program Phase 3-3           *
// CBI:  3-3.1.1.1                                                           *
//****************************************************************************

INT WINAPI WinMain(HINSTANCE thInstance,HINSTANCE thPreviousInstance,
                   CHAR *tcCmdLine,INT tnShowCmd)
{


//****************************************************************************
// Program Phase 3-3 Main                                                    *
// Declare the local variables for the "main" program                        *
// CBI:  3-3.1.1.2                                                           *
//****************************************************************************

   myclass* loMyClass;


//****************************************************************************
// Program Phase 3-3 Main                                                    *
// Attempt to instantiate the myclass class                                  *
// CBI:  3-3.1.1.3                                                           *
//****************************************************************************

   loMyClass = 0;

   try
   {
      loMyClass = new myclass(12345,"Hello World!");
   }


//****************************************************************************
// Program Phase 3-3 Main                                                    *
// If the myclass class fails to instantiate, notify the user and exit       *
// CBI:  3-3.1.1.4                                                           *
//****************************************************************************

   catch (char* lcError)
   {
       MessageBox(NULL,lcError,"myclass",MB_OK | MB_ICONERROR);
   }

   if (loMyClass == 0)
   {
      return 1;
   }


//****************************************************************************
// Program Phase 3-3 Main                                                    *
// If the myclass class instantiated, call an instance method                *
// CBI:  3-3.1.1.5                                                           *
//****************************************************************************

   loMyClass->DisplayInstanceData();

   delete loMyClass;
   return 0;
}
```

- myclass.h

myclass.h: Class Definition for the myclass Class

```
//****************************************************************************
// myclass.h                                                                 *
// Reserved                                                                  *
//****************************************************************************

//****************************************************************************
// myclass definition                                                        *
// Class definition for the myclass class                                    *
// CBI:  3-3.2.1.1                                                           *
//****************************************************************************

#ifndef MYCLASS_H
#define MTCLASS_H

class myclass
{
   private:

      // class data
      INT nData;
      CHAR *cData;

   public:

     myclass(int tnData,char *tcData);
     VOID DisplayInstanceData();
};

#endif
```

- myclass.cpp

myclass.cpp: Class Implementation for the myclass Class

```
//****************************************************************************
// myclass.cpp                                                               *
// Reserved                                                                  *
//****************************************************************************

#include <windows.h>
#include <exception>
#include <stdio.h>
#include "myclass.h"


//****************************************************************************
// myclass implementation                                                    *
// Class implementation for the myclass class                                *
// CBI:  3-3.2.2.1                                                           *
//****************************************************************************

// The myclass class methods are implemented in CBI: 3-3.2.3.1 and
// CBI: 3-3.2.4.1


//****************************************************************************
// myclass implementation                                                    *
// Implement the initialization function for the myclass class              *
// CBI:  3-3.2.3.1                                                           *
//****************************************************************************
```

myclass.cpp continued on the next page

myclass.cpp: Class Implementation for the myclass Class continued

```
myclass::myclass(INT tnData,CHAR *tcData)
{

//***************************************************************************
// myclass implementation                                                   *
// Declare the local variables for the myclass initialization function     *
// CBI:  3-3.2.3.2                                                          *
//***************************************************************************

   INT lnResult;

//***************************************************************************
// myclass implementation                                                   *
// Prompt the user to continue instantiating the myclass class              *
// CBI:  3-3.2.3.3                                                          *
//***************************************************************************

   lnResult = MessageBox(NULL,"Proceed with class instantiation?",
                         "myclass",MB_YESNO | MB_ICONQUESTION);

//***************************************************************************
// myclass implementation                                                   *
// Cancel instantiation of the myclass class if the user selects no         *
// CBI:  3-3.2.3.4                                                          *
//***************************************************************************

   if (lnResult == IDNO)
   {
      throw "Class not instantiated.";
   }

//***************************************************************************
// myclass implementation                                                   *
// Store the parameters to the initialization function as instance data     *
// CBI:  3-3.2.3.5                                                          *
//***************************************************************************

   this->nData = tnData;
   this->cData = tcData;
}

//***************************************************************************
// myclass implementation                                                   *
// Implement the DisplayInstanceData method of the myclass class            *
// CBI:  3-3.2.4.1                                                          *
//***************************************************************************

VOID myclass::DisplayInstanceData()
{
   char lcString[255];

   sprintf_s(lcString,"nData: %d \ncData: %s",this->nData,this->cData);

   MessageBox(NULL,lcString,"myclass instance data",
              MB_OK | MB_ICONINFORMATION);
}
```

Code Setup and Compilation

- Tools: Microsoft Visual Studio 2008 Express Edition (msdn.microsoft.com)

Code Setup and Compilation Steps

1: Start the Visual C++ 2008 Express Edition program.

2: VC++ EE - Activate Menu Item: File → New → Project

For the "Project type", select "Win32" and then select "Win32 Console Application" as the template. Enter pp3_3 as the project "Name". Enter the appropriate folder as the project "Location". The pp3_3 folder will be automatically created. Make sure that the "Create directory for solution" check box is not checked.

3: Activate the "OK" button to proceed with the "Win32 Application Wizard".

4: Activate the "Next" button of the "Win32 Application Wizard".

5: Verify that a "Console Application" is selected and also check the "Empty project" check box. Activate the "Finish" button of the "Win32 Application Wizard".

6: VC++ EE - Activate Menu Item: Project → Add New Item

On the "Add New Item" dialog window, select the "Visual C++ → Code" category and then select the "C++ File" template. Enter pp3_3.cpp for the file "Name". Activate the "Add" button.

7: Enter the source code for the pp3_3.cpp text file and then save and close the file.

8: VC++ EE - Activate Menu Item: Project → Add New Item

On the "Add New Item" dialog window, select the "Visual C++ → Code" category and then select the "Header File" template. Enter myclass.h for the file name and then activate the "Add" button.

9: Enter the source code for the myclass.h file and then save and close the file.

10: VC++ EE - Activate Menu Item: Project → Add New Item

On the "Add New Item" dialog window, select the "Visual C++ → Code" category and then select the "C++ File" template. Enter myclass.cpp for the file "Name" and then activate the "Add" button.

11: Enter the source code for the myclass.cpp file and then save and close the file.

12: Select the Release configuration for the project.

13: VC++ EE - Activate Menu Item: Project → pp3_3 Properties

Enter the following settings:

Configuration Properties → C/C++ → Code Generation → Runtime Library

For Release Configuration:

```
Multi-threaded (/MT) or Multi-threaded DLL (/MD)
```

For Debug Configuration:

```
Multi-threaded Debug /MTd or Multi-threaded Debug DLL (/MDd)
```

Steps continued on the next page

Code Setup and Compilation Steps continued

14: Continue entering settings on the "pp3_16 Property Pages" window.

Configuration Properties → General → Character Set

```
"Use Multi-Byte Character Set"
```

Configuration Properties → C/C++ → Preprocessor → Preprocessor Definitions

```
remove _CONSOLE
add _WINDOWS
```

Configuration Properties → Linker → System → SubSystem

```
Windows
```

15: VC++ EE - Activate Menu Item: Build → Build pp3_3

Command Prompt Compilation Steps

1: Open a Visual Studio 2008 command prompt and change directories to the pp3_3 folder.

```
cl.exe /MT /c pp3_3.cpp myclass.cpp /EHsc
```

The preceding command compiles the source code into object files. The /MT switch tells the compiler to use the statically linked C/C++ runtime. Use the /MD switch to use the C/C++ library in a shared dll.

2: The following command can be used to link the pp3_3.obj and myclass.obj object files and create the pp3_3.exe program.

```
link.exe pp3_3.obj myclass.obj /OUT:".\Release\pp3_3.exe" /INCREMENTAL:NO
/MANIFEST /SUBSYSTEM:WINDOWS kernel32.lib user32.lib
```

Windows – Program Execution

- Execute Program

```
VC++ EE - Activate Menu Item: Debug → Start Without Debugging
```

- Debug Program

```
VC++ EE - Activate Menu Item: Project → pp3_3 Properties
```

Expand the "Configuration Properties → Linker" entry and then click on the "Debugging" item. Set the "Generate Debug Info" entry to "Yes". Close the "pp3_3 Properties" window.

```
VC++ EE - Activate Menu Item: Debug → Step Into
```

Program Phase 3-4
Visual Basic 6 ▪ Windows

GUI Based Program with Custom Class Definition and Instantiation

- Program Phase Task 3 is implemented in Program Phase 3-4 using the Visual Basic 6 (VB6) programming language.
- The MsgBox() function is used in Program Phase 3-4 to implement input and output for a GUI based application.
- The Entry Point of Execution (EPE) is stored in the pp3_4.bas text file. The myclass class is defined and implemented in the myclass.cls text file.

Code Block Features

The Program Phase 3-4 code blocks illustrate the following programming features using the VB6 programming language:

- **GUI Application**
- **Custom Class Definition**
- **Object Variable Declaration**
- **Custom Class Instantiation**
- **Cancel Class Instantiation from the Class Initialization Function**
- **Message Box Input and Output**

Visual Basic 6
GUI Application

- VB6 natively supports creating GUI based applications only. See page 29 for example.

Visual Basic 6
Custom Class Definition

- The following example illustrates defining and implementing a custom class using VB6:

testclass1.cls: Visual Basic 6 Custom Class Definition

```
Private nData
Private cData

Private Sub Class_Initialize()

'' Visual Basic 6 does not support passing parameters to the
'' class initialization function.  Two phase construction can be
'' used to allow parameters to be sent but this means
'' that the Class_Initialize2 method must be manually called.

End Sub

Sub Class_Initialize2(ByVal tnData As Integer, _
                      ByVal tcData As String)

    nData = tnData
    cData = tcData

End Sub

Sub TestMethod()

    '' Visual Basic 6 code goes here.

End Sub

'' Note that additional VB code is found in this file but is hidden when
'' viewed in the Visual Basic 6 IDE.
```

Visual Basic 6
Object Variable Declaration

- A testclass1 typed variable can store an instance of the testclass1 class. Access to the testclass1 class is necessary when the object variable is declared.
- Since the testclass1 class resides in the same project as the test2 program, the testclass1 class is accessible in the test2 program.

test2.bas: Visual Basic 6 Object Variable Declaration

```
Sub Main()

    Dim loTestClass as testclass1

End Sub
```

Visual Basic 6
Custom Class Instantiation

- A VB6 custom class is instantiated using the "New" keyword. The custom class needs to be in the same VB6 project as the test3.bas file. VB6 does not support passing parameters to the initialization function. Two phase construction is used, which involves creating a special method in the class that is manually called by the program that instantiated the class. This method should be called before any other method.
- The following example creates an instance of the testclass1 class and calls the TestMethod() method:

test3.bas: Visual Basic 6 Custom Class Instantiation

```
Sub Main()

  Dim loTestClass As testclass1

  Set loTestClass = New testclass1
  Call loTestClass.Class_Initialize2(12345, "Hello World!")
  Call loTestClass.TestMethod

End Sub
```

Visual Basic 6
Cancel Class Instantiation from the Class Init Function

- Class instantiation is cancelled by calling the Raise() method of the global "Err" object in the class initialization event.

testclass2.cls: Visual Basic 6 Cancel Class Instantiation from the Init Function

```
Private nData As Integer
Private cData As String

Private Sub Class_Initialize()

   Call Err.Raise(1, , "Class not instantiated because of some error.")

End Sub

Sub Class_Initialize2(ByVal tnData As Integer, _
                      ByVal tcData As String)

   nData = tnData
   cData = tcData

End Sub

Sub TestMethod()

   '' Visual Basic 6 code goes here.

End Sub

'' Note that additional VB code is found in this file but is hidden when
'' viewed in the Visual Basic 6 IDE.
```

- The "On Error" statement is used to check if an error has occurred in the Class_Initialize() event of the testclass2 class.

test4.bas: Visual Basic 6 Attempt to Instantiate the testclass2 Class

```
Sub Main()

   On Error GoTo ErrorHandler
   Dim loTestClass As testclass2

   Set loTestClass = New testclass2
   Call loTestClass.Class_Initialize2(12345, "Hello World!")
```

test4.bas continued on the next page

test4.bas: Visual Basic 6 Attempt to Instantiate the testclass2 Class continued

```
    Call loTestClass.TestMethod

  Exit Sub

ErrorHandler:

'' The class failed to instantiate.
'' An error message can be retrieved by accessing the Err.Description
'' property

End Sub
```

Visual Basic 6
Message Box Input and Output

- The following example prompts the user to select "Yes" or "No":

test5.bas: Visual Basic 6 Message Box Input and Output

```
Sub Main()

   Dim lnResult As Integer

   lnResult = MsgBox("Select Yes or No", _
                     vbYesNo + vbQuestion, _
                     "test")

   If (lnResult = vbNo) Then

      '' No Selected

   Else

      '' Yes Selected (vbYes)

   End If

End Sub
```

Source Code Files

- Text files: pp3_4.bas, myclass.cls

pp3_4.bas: Program Phase 3-4 EPE Source Code

```
''*************************************************************************
'' Program Phase 3-4 Visual Basic 6 Class Definition/Instantiation        *
'' Programming Tasks Illustrated: GUI Based Application                   *
''                                Custom Class Definition                 *
''                                Object Variable Declaration             *
''                                Custom Class Instantiation              *
''                                Cancel Instantiation from the Init Function *
''                                Message Box Input and Output            *
''*************************************************************************

''*************************************************************************
'' File: pp3_4.bas                                                        *
'' Reserved                                                               *
''*************************************************************************
```

pp3_4.bas continued on the next page

pp3_4.bas: Program Phase 3-4 EPE Source Code continued

```
''*************************************************************************
'' Program Phase 3-4 Main                                                  *
'' Define the Entry Point of Execution (EPE) for Program Phase 3-4        *
'' CBI:  3-4.1.1.1                                                         *
''*************************************************************************

Sub Main()

''*************************************************************************
'' Program Phase 3-4 Main                                                  *
'' Declare the local variables for the "main" program                      *
'' CBI:  3-4.1.1.2                                                         *
''*************************************************************************

  Dim loMyClass As myclass
  On Error GoTo ErrorHandler


''*************************************************************************
'' Program Phase 3-4 Main                                                  *
'' Attempt to instantiate the myclass class                                *
'' CBI:  3-4.1.1.3                                                         *
''*************************************************************************

  Set loMyClass = New myclass
  Call loMyClass.Class_Initialize2(12345, "Hello World!")


''*************************************************************************
'' Program Phase 3-4 Main                                                  *
'' If the myclass class instantiated, call an instance method              *
'' CBI:  3-4.1.1.4                                                         *
''*************************************************************************

  Call loMyClass.DisplayInstanceData
  Exit Sub


''*************************************************************************
'' Program Phase 3-4 Main                                                  *
'' If the myclass class fails to instantiate, notify the user and exit     *
'' CBI:  3-4.1.1.5                                                         *
''*************************************************************************

ErrorHandler:

   Call MsgBox(Err.Description, vbCritical, "myclass")

End Sub
```

- myclass.cls

myclass.cls: Class Definition and Implementation for the myclass Class

```
''*************************************************************************
'' myclass.cls                                                             *
'' Reserved                                                                *
''*************************************************************************

''*************************************************************************
'' myclass definition                                                      *
'' Class definition for the myclass class                                  *
'' CBI:  3-4.2.1.1                                                         *
''*************************************************************************
```

myclass.cls continued on the next page

myclass.cls: Class Definition and Implementation for the myclass Class continued

```
'' The myclass class is defined and implemented starting in CBI: 3-4.2.2.1.


''*************************************************************************
'' myclass implementation                                                  *
'' Class implementation for the myclass class                              *
'' CBI:  3-4.2.2.1                                                          *
''*************************************************************************

  '' class data
  Private nData As Integer
  Private cData As String


''*************************************************************************
'' myclass implementation                                                  *
'' Implement the initialization function for the myclass class            *
'' CBI:  3-4.2.3.1                                                          *
''*************************************************************************

Private Sub Class_Initialize()


''*************************************************************************
'' myclass implementation                                                  *
'' Declare the local variables for the myclass initialization function     *
'' CBI:  3-4.2.3.2                                                          *
''*************************************************************************

   Dim lnResult As Integer


''*************************************************************************
'' myclass implementation                                                  *
'' Prompt the user to continue instantiating the myclass class            *
'' CBI:  3-4.2.3.3                                                          *
''*************************************************************************

   lnResult = MsgBox("Proceed with class instantiation?", _
                     vbYesNo + vbQuestion,"myclass")


''*************************************************************************
'' myclass implementation                                                  *
'' Cancel instantiation of the myclass class if the user selects no       *
'' CBI:  3-4.2.3.4                                                          *
''*************************************************************************

   If (lnResult = vbNo) Then

     Call Err.Raise(1, , "Class not instantiated.")

   End If

End Sub


''*************************************************************************
'' myclass implementation                                                  *
'' Store the parameters to the initialization function as instance data   *
'' CBI:  3-4.2.3.5                                                          *
''*************************************************************************

Sub Class_Initialize2(ByVal tnData As Integer, ByVal tcData As String)

   nData = tnData
```

myclass.cls continued on the next page

myclass.cls: Class Definition and Implementation for the myclass Class continued

```
   cData = tcData

End Sub

''*****************************************************************************
'' myclass implementation                                                     *
'' Implement the DisplayInstanceData method of the myclass class              *
'' CBI:  3-4.2.4.1                                                            *
''*****************************************************************************

Sub DisplayInstanceData()

   Call MsgBox("nData: " & Str(nData) & Chr(13) & "cData: " & cData,
vbInformation, "myclass instance data")

End Sub

'' Note that additional VB code is found in this file but is hidden when
'' viewed in the Visual Basic 6 IDE.
```

Code Setup and Compilation

- Tools: Visual Basic 6

Code Setup and Compilation Steps

1: Create a folder called pp3_4 that will store the source code files.

2: Open the Visual Basic 6 program.

3: VB6 - Activate Menu Item: File → New Project

Select "Standard EXE" and then activate the "OK" button.

4: Remove the "Form1" Form that is automatically added to the project by right-clicking the "Form1" Form in the project and then activating the "Remove Form1" menu item.

5: VB6 - Activate Menu Item: File → Save Project

Save the project with the name pp3_4 in the pp3_4 source folder. Click on the pp3_4.vbp file in the properties window and then set the name of the project to pp3_4.

6: VB6 - Activate Menu Item: Project → Add Module

Enter the EPE source code for Program Phase 3-4 into this file and save the file as pp3_4.bas.

7: VB6 - Activate Menu Item: Project → Add Class Module

Select "Class Module" from the "New" tab and then activate the "Open" button. Enter the source code for the myclass class into this file and then save the file as myclass.cls. In the "Solution Explorer", click on the myclass.cls file and then change the class name in the properties window from "class1" to "myclass".

8: VB6 - Activate Menu Item: File → Make pp3_4.exe

Command Prompt Compilation

Change directories to the pp3_4 folder and then enter the following commands:

```
PATH = "C:\Program Files\Microsoft Visual Studio\VB98";%PATH%
vb6.exe /make pp3_4.vbp
```

Program Execution

- Execute Program

```
VB6 - Activate Menu Item: Run → Start
```

- Debug Program

```
VB6 - Activate Menu Item: Debug → Step Into
```

Program Phase 3-5
Visual C++ ▪ MFC ▪ Windows

GUI Based Program with Custom Class Definition and Instantiation

- Program Phase Task 3 is implemented in Program Phase 3-5 using the C++ programming language and the Microsoft Foundation Classes (MFC) class library.
- The Win32 API MessageBox() function is used in Program Phase 3-5 to implement input and output for a GUI based application. MFC provides the AfxMessageBox() function, but since there is no way to set the caption of the displayed dialog using it, the Win32 API MessageBox() function is used instead.
- The Entry Point of Execution (EPE) is stored in the pp3_5.cpp text file. The myclass class is defined in the myclass.h text file and implemented in the myclass.cpp text file.

Code Block Features

The Program Phase 3-5 code blocks illustrate the following programming features using the C++ programming language and MFC:

- **GUI Application**
- **Custom Class Definition**
- **Object Variable Declaration**
- **Custom Class Instantiation**
- **Cancel Class Instantiation from the Class Initialization Function**
- **Message Box Input and Output**

C++ MFC
GUI Application

- In a GUI based MFC application, a global CWinApp instance is declared. When the CWinApp class is implemented, the InitInstance() function serves as the EPE for the program. The MFC framework will automatically call this function when the program starts.

test1.cpp: C++ MFC GUI Application

```
#include <afxwin.h>

class test1 : public CWinApp
{
virtual BOOL InitInstance()
{
```

test1.cpp continued on the next page

testl.cpp: C++ MFC GUI Based Application continued

```
    // C/C++ MFC GUI based code goes here.

    return TRUE;
}};
test1 goTest1;
```

C++ MFC
Custom Class Definition

- The testclass1 class is defined in the testclass1.h file.

testclass1.h: C++ MFC Custom Class Definition

```
#ifndef TESTCLASS1_H
#define TESTCLASS1_H

#include <afxwin.h>

class testclass1
{
   private:
      // class data
      int nData;
      char *cData;

   public:
     testclass1(int tnData,char *tcData);
     VOID TestMethod();
};

#endif
```

- The testclass1 class is implemented in the testclass1.cpp file.

testclass1.cpp: Class Implementation for the testclass1 Class

```
#include <afxwin.h>
#include "testclass1.h"

testclass1::testclass1(int tnData,char *tcData)
{
   this->nData = tnData;
   this->cData = tcData;
}

VOID testclass1::TestMethod()
{
   // C++ code goes here.
}
```

C++ MFC
Object Variable Declaration

- A testclass1 typed pointer variable can store a pointer to an instance of the testclass1 class. Access to the testclass1 class is necessary when the object variable is declared.

- The testclass1 class is accessible in the test2.cpp program because the class definition stored in the testclass1.h file is included at the top of the file.

test2.cpp: C++ MFC Object Variable Declaration

```
#include <afxwin.h>
#include "testclass1.h"

class test2 : public CWinApp
{
virtual BOOL InitInstance()
{
   testclass1* loTestClass;
   return true;
}};

test2 goTest2;
```

C++ MFC
Custom Class Instantiation

- The C++ "new" operator is used to create an instance of the testclass1 class defined in the testclass1.h header file. Since the "new" operator is used, a corresponding "delete" must be issued in order to free the memory used by the testclass1 class instance.

- The following example creates an instance of the testclass1 class and calls the TestMethod() method:

test3.cpp: C++ MFC Custom Class Instantiation

```
#include <afxwin.h>
#include "testclass1.h"

class test3 : public CWinApp
{
virtual BOOL InitInstance()
{
   testclass1* loTestClass;

   loTestClass = new testclass1(12345,"Hello World!");
   loTestClass->TestMethod();
   delete loTestClass;

   return true;
}};

test3 goTest3;
```

C++ MFC
Cancel Class Instantiation from the Class Initialization Function

- Class instantiation is cancelled by calling the AfxThrowUserException() function from the class constructor.

testclass2.h: Class Header File for the testclass2 Class

```
#ifndef TESTCLASS2_H
#define TESTCLASS2_H

#include <afxwin.h>

class testclass2
```

testclass2.h continued on the next page

testclass2.h: Class Header File for the testclass2 Class

```
{
   private:
      // class data
      int nData;
      char *cData;

   public:
      testclass2(int tnData,char *tcData);
      VOID TestMethod();
};

#endif
```

testclass2.cpp: C++ MFC Cancel Class Instantiation from the Init Function

```
#include <afxwin.h>
#include "testclass2.h"

testclass2::testclass2(INT tnData,CHAR *tcData)
{
   AfxThrowUserException();

   // Program execution never gets here.
   this->nData = tnData;
   this->cData = tcData;
}

VOID testclass2::TestMethod()
{
   // C++ code goes here.
}
```

- The class instantiation attempt is placed in a TRY/CATCH block that responds to an exception thrown in the testclass2 constructor. If the testclass2 instantiation fails, the loTestClass variable still stores the value zero previously assigned before the class instantiation was attempted. No error message is provided by the AfxThrowUserException() MFC function.

test4.cpp: C++ MFC Attempt to Instantiate the testclass2 Class

```
#include <afxwin.h>
#include "testclass2.h"

class test4 : public CWinApp
{
virtual BOOL InitInstance()
{
   testclass2* loTestClass;
   loTestClass = 0;

   TRY
   {
      loTestClass = new testclass2(12345,"Hello World!");
   }
   CATCH (CUserException,loException)
   {
      // The class failed to instantiate.
   }
   END_CATCH
```

test4.cpp continued on the next page

test4.cpp: C++ MFC Attempt to Instantiate the testclass2 Class continued

```
   if (loTestClass == 0)
   {
      // If the testclass2 class did not instantiate then exit.
      return FALSE;
   }

   loTestClass->TestMethod();

   return true;

}};
test4 goTest4;
```

C++ MFC
Message Box Input and Output

- The MFC AfxMessageBox() function can display a message box, but it is not used in Program Phase 3-5 because of the inability to set the message box caption. Instead, the Win32 MessageBox() function is used. The "::" in front of the MessageBox() function indicates that the Win32 API MessageBox() function is being called instead of the MFC version.

  The following example prompts the user to select "Yes" or "No":

test5.cpp: C++ MFC Message Box Input and Output

```
#include <afxwin.h>

class test5 : public CWinApp
{
virtual BOOL InitInstance()
{
   int lnResult;

   lnResult = ::MessageBox(NULL,"Select Yes or No.",
                           "test",
                           MB_YESNO | MB_ICONQUESTION);

   if (lnResult == IDNO)
   {
      // No Selected.
   }
   else
   {
      // Yes Selected. (IDYES)
   }

   return TRUE;
}};

test5 goTest5;
```

Source Code Files

- Text files: pp3_5.cpp, myclass.h, myclass.cpp

pp3_5.cpp: Program Phase 3-5 EPE Source Code

```
//***********************************************************************
// Program Phase 3-5 C++ MFC Class Definition/Instantiation             *
// Programming Tasks Illustrated: MFC GUI Based Application             *
//                                Custom Class Definition               *
//                                Object Variable Declaration           *
//                                Custom Class Instantiation            *
//                                Cancel Instantiation from the Init Funtion  *
//                                Message Box Input and Output          *
//***********************************************************************

//***********************************************************************
// File: pp3_5.cpp                                                      *
// Reserved                                                             *
//***********************************************************************

#include <afxwin.h>
#include "myclass.h"

class pp3_5 : public CWinApp
{


//***********************************************************************
// Program Phase 3-5 Main                                               *
// Define the Entry Point of Execution (EPE) for Program Phase 3-5      *
// CBI:  3-5.1.1.1                                                      *
//***********************************************************************

virtual BOOL InitInstance ()
{


//***********************************************************************
// Program Phase 3-5 Main                                               *
// Declare the local variables for the "main" program                   *
// CBI:  3-5.1.1.2                                                      *
//***********************************************************************

   myclass* loMyClass;


//***********************************************************************
// Program Phase 3-5 Main                                               *
// Attempt to instantiate the myclass class                             *
// CBI:  3-5.1.1.3                                                      *
//***********************************************************************

   loMyClass = 0;

   TRY
   {
      loMyClass = new myclass(12345,"Hello World!");
   }


//***********************************************************************
// Program Phase 3-5 Main                                               *
// If the myclass class fails to instantiate, notify the user and exit  *
// CBI:  3-5.1.1.4                                                      *
//***********************************************************************

   CATCH (CUserException,loException)
   {
      ::MessageBox(NULL,"Class not instantiated.",
                   "myclass",MB_OK | MB_ICONERROR);
   }
   END_CATCH
```

pp3_5.cpp continued on the next page

pp3_5.cpp: Program Phase 3-5 EPE Source Code continued

```
   if (loMyClass == 0)
   {
      // If the myclass class did not instantiate then exit.
      return FALSE;
   }


//******************************************************************************
// Program Phase 3-5 Main                                                      *
// If the myclass class instantiated, call an instance method                  *
// CBI:  3-5.1.1.5                                                             *
//******************************************************************************

   loMyClass->DisplayInstanceData();
   delete loMyClass;

   return TRUE;
}
};

pp3_5 go3_5;
```

- myclass.h

myclass.h: Class Definition for the myclass Class

```
//******************************************************************************
// myclass.h                                                                   *
// Reserved                                                                    *
//******************************************************************************

//******************************************************************************
// myclass definition                                                          *
// Class definition for the myclass class                                      *
// CBI:  3-5.2.1.1                                                             *
//******************************************************************************

#ifndef MYCLASS_H
#define MTCLASS_H

class myclass
{
   private:

      // class data
      INT nData;
      CString cData;

   public:

     myclass(int tnData,CString tcData);
     VOID DisplayInstanceData();
};
#endif
```

- myclass.cpp

myclass.cpp: Class Implementation for the myclass Class

```
//**************************************************************************
// myclass.cpp                                                             *
// Reserved                                                                *
//**************************************************************************

#include <afxwin.h>
#include "myclass.h"


//**************************************************************************
// myclass implementation                                                  *
// Class implementation for the myclass class                              *
// CBI:  3-5.2.2.1                                                         *
//**************************************************************************

// The myclass class methods are implemented in CBI: 3-5.2.3.1 and
// CBI: 3-5.2.4.1


//**************************************************************************
// myclass implementation                                                  *
// Implement the initialization function for the myclass class             *
// CBI:  3-5.2.3.1                                                         *
//**************************************************************************

myclass::myclass(int tnData,CString tcData)
{


//**************************************************************************
// myclass implementation                                                  *
// Declare the local variables for the myclass initialization function     *
// CBI:  3-5.2.3.2                                                         *
//**************************************************************************

   int lnResult;


//**************************************************************************
// myclass implementation                                                  *
// Prompt the user to continue instantiating the myclass class             *
// CBI:  3-5.2.3.3                                                         *
//**************************************************************************

   lnResult = ::MessageBox(NULL,"Proceed with class instantiation?",
                           "myclass",MB_YESNO | MB_ICONQUESTION);


//**************************************************************************
// myclass implementation                                                  *
// Cancel instantiation of the myclass class if the user selects no        *
// CBI:  3-5.2.3.4                                                         *
//**************************************************************************

   if (lnResult == IDNO)
   {
      AfxThrowUserException();
   }


//**************************************************************************
// myclass implementation                                                  *
// Store the parameters to the initialization function as instance data    *
// CBI:  3-5.2.3.5                                                         *
//**************************************************************************
```

myclass.cpp continued on the next page

myclass.cpp: Class Implementation for the myclass Class continued

```
   this->nData = tnData;
   this->cData = tcData;
}

//*****************************************************************************
// myclass implementation                                                     *
// Implement the DisplayInstanceData method of the myclass class             *
// CBI:  3-5.2.4.1                                                            *
//*****************************************************************************

VOID myclass::DisplayInstanceData()
{
   CString lcString;

   lcString.Format("nData: %d \ncData: %s",this->nData,this->cData);
   MessageBox(NULL,lcString,"myclass instance data",MB_OK | MB_ICONINFORMATION);
}
```

Code Setup and Compilation

- Tools: Microsoft Visual C++ 2008

Code Setup and Compilation Steps

1: Start the Microsoft Visual C++ 2008 program.

2: VC++ - Activate Menu Item: File → New → Project

For the "Project type", select "Win32" and then select the "Win32 Console Application" template. Enter pp3_5 as the project "Name". Enter the appropriate folder as the project "Location". The pp3_5 folder will be automatically created. Make sure that the "Create directory for solution" check box is not checked.

3: Activate the "OK" button to proceed with the "Win32 Application Wizard".

4: Activate the "Next" button of the "Win32 Application Wizard".

5: Select the "Console application" radio button and also check the "Empty project" check box. Activate the "Finish" button of the "Win32 Application Wizard".

6: VC++ - Activate Menu Item: Build → Configuration Manager

Select the "Release" value for the "Active solution configuration".

7: VC++ - Activate Menu Item: Project → Add New Item

On the "Add New Item" dialog window, select the "Visual C++ → Code" category and then select the "C++ File (.cpp)" template. Enter pp3_5.cpp for the file "Name". Activate the "Add" button. Enter the source code for the pp3_5.cpp file.

8: VC++ - Activate Menu Item: Project → Add New Item

On the "Add New Item" dialog window, select the "Visual C++ → Code" category and then select the "Header File" template. Enter myclass.h for the file name and then activate the "Add" button. Enter the source code for the myclass.h file.

Steps continued on the next page

Code Setup and Compilation Steps continued

9: VC++ - Activate Menu Item: Project → Add New Item

On the "Add New Item" dialog window, select the "Visual C++ → Code" category and then select the "C++ File" template. Enter myclass.cpp for the file "Name" and then activate the "Add" button. Enter the source code for the myclass.cpp file.

10: VC++ - Activate Menu Item: Project → pp3_5 Properties

Enter the following settings:

Configuration Properties → General → Character Set

```
"Use Multi-Byte Character Set"
```

Configuration Properties → General → Use of MFC

```
"Use MFC in a Static Library" or "Use MFC in a Shared DLL"
```

11: VC++ - Activate Menu Item: Build → Build pp3_5

Command Prompt Compilation

From a Visual Studio 2008 command prompt in the pp3_5 folder, enter the following:

```
cl.exe /c /MT /EHsc pp3_5.cpp myclass.cpp
link.exe /SUBSYSTEM:WINDOWS pp3_5.obj myclass.obj

dynamic library:  cl.exe /c /MD /EHsc /D "_AFXDLL" pp3_5.cpp myclass.cpp
                  link.exe /SUBSYSTEM:WINDOWS pp3_5.obj myclass.obj
             mt.exe /manifest pp3_5.exe.manifest /outputresource:pp3_5.exe
```

Program Execution

- Execute Program

```
VC++ - Activate Menu Item: Debug → Start Without Debugging
```

- Debug Program

```
VC++ EE - Activate Menu Item: Project → pp3_5 Properties
```

Expand the "Configuration Properties → Linker" entry and then click on the "Debugging" item. Set the "Generate Debug Info" entry to "Yes". Close the "pp3_5 Properties" window.

```
VC++ EE - Activate Menu Item: Debug → Step Into
```

C# ▪ .NET Framework - Mono ▪ Multi-Platform

GUI Based Program with Custom Class Definition and Instantiation

- Program Phase Task 3 is implemented in Program Phase 3-6 using the C# programming language and the Microsoft .NET Framework 2.0 or higher.
- The .NET Framework MessageBox class is used in Program Phase 3-6 to implement input and output for a GUI based application.
- The Entry Point of Execution (EPE) is stored in the pp3_6.cs text file. The myclass class is defined and implemented in the myclass.cs text file.

Code Block Features

The Program Phase 3-6 code blocks illustrate the following programming features using the C# programming language and the .NET Framework - Mono:

- **GUI Application**
- **Custom Class Definition**
- **Object Variable Declaration**
- **Custom Class Instantiation**
- **Cancel Class Instantiation from the Class Initialization Function**
- **Message Box Input and Output**

C# .NET Framework - Mono
GUI Application

- The EPE for a GUI based C# application is no different than a console based C# application.

test1.cs: C# .NET Framework - Mono GUI Application

```
namespace testns
{
class test1
{
static void Main()
{
   // GUI based C# code goes here.
}
}}
```

C# .NET Framework - Mono
Custom Class Definition

- The following example illustrates defining and implementing a custom class using C#:

testclass1.cs: C# .NET Framework - Mono Custom Class Definition

```
namespace testns
{
class testclass1
{
   // class data
   private int nData;
   private string cData;

public testclass1(int tnData,string tcData)
{
   this.nData = tnData;
   this.cData = tcData;
}

public void TestMethod()
{
   // C# code goes here.
}
}}
```

C# .NET Framework - Mono
Object Variable Declaration

- A testclass1 typed variable can store an instance of the testclass1 class. Access to the testclass1 class is necessary when the object variable is declared.

- Since the testclass1 class resides in the same namespace as the test2 class, the testclass1 class is accessible in the test2 program.

test2.cs: C# .NET Framework - Mono Object Variable Declaration

```
namespace testns
{
class test2
{
static void Main()
{
   testclass1 loTestClass = null;
}
}}
```

C# .NET Framework - Mono
Custom Class Instantiation

- A custom class is instantiated using the "new" keyword. There is no need to unload or delete the testclass1 instance stored in the loTestClass variable. The .NET Framework garbage collector automatically releases the memory used by the testclass1 instance after the variable goes out of scope.

- The following example creates an instance of the testclass1 class and calls the TestMethod() method:

test3.cs: C# .NET Framework - Mono Custom Class Instantiation

```
namespace testns
{
class test3
{
static void Main()
{
   testclass1 loTestClass = null;
   loTestClass = new testclass1(12345,"Hello World!");
}
}}
```

C# .NET Framework - Mono
Cancel Class Instantiation from the Class Initialization Function

- Class instantiation is cancelled by throwing an exception from the class constructor.

testclass2.cs: C# .NET FW - Mono Cancel Class Instantiation from the Init Func.

```
namespace testns
{
class testclass2
{
   // class data
   private int nData;
   private string cData;

public testclass2(int tnData,string tcData)
{
   // C# code goes here.
   //… Some error has occurred so cancel instantiation by
   // throwing an exception.

   throw new System.Exception("Class not instantiated because of some error.");

   this.nData = tnData;
   this.cData = tcData;
}

public void TestMethod()
{
   // C# code goes here.
}
}}
```

- The class instantiation attempt is placed in a try/catch block that responds to an exception thrown in the testclass2 constructor. If the testclass2 instantiation fails, the loTestClass variable will still store the "null" value previously assigned before the class instantiation was attempted.

test4.cs: C# .NET Framework - Mono Attempt to Instantiate the testclass2 Class

```
namespace testns
{
class test4
{
static int Main()
{
   testclass2 loTestClass = null;

   try
```

test4.cs continued on the next page

test4.cs: C# .NET FW - Mono Attempt to Instantiate the testclass2 Class continued

```
   {
      loTestClass = new testclass2(12345,"Hello World!");
   }
   catch (System.Exception loException)
   {
      // The class failed to instantiate.
      // The error message is stored in loException.Message
   }

   if (loTestClass == null)
   {
      return 1;
   }

   loTestClass.TestMethod();
   return 0;
}
}}
```

C# .NET Framework - Mono Message Box Input and Output

- The following example prompts the user to select "Yes" or "No":

test5.cs: C# .NET Framework - Mono Message Box Input and Output

```
// Add reference to the System.Windows.Forms namespace in the Solution Explorer
using System.Windows.Forms;

namespace testns
{
class test5
{
static int Main()
{
   DialogResult lnResult;

   lnResult = System.Windows.Forms.MessageBox.Show("Select Yes or No.","test",
                              MessageBoxButtons.YesNo,MessageBoxIcon.Question);

   if (lnResult == DialogResult.No)
   {
      // No selected.
   }
   else
   {
      // Yes selected. (DialogResult.Yes)
   }

   return 0;
}
}}
```

Source Code Files

- Text Files: pp3_6.cs, myclass.cs

pp3_6.cs: Program Phase 3-6 EPE Source Code

```
//*****************************************************************************
// Program Phase 3-6 C# .NET Framework - Mono Class Definition/Instantiation  *
// Programming Tasks Illustrated: .NET Framework - Mono GUI Based Application *
//                                Custom Class Definition                     *
//                                Object Variable Declaration                 *
//                                Custom Class Instantiation                  *
//                                Cancel Instantiation from the Init Function *
//                                Message Box Input and Output                *
//*****************************************************************************

//*****************************************************************************
// File: pp3_6.cs                                                             *
// Reserved                                                                   *
//*****************************************************************************

using System;
using System.Windows.Forms;

namespace nspp3_6
{
class pp3_6
{


//*****************************************************************************
// Program Phase 3-6 Main                                                     *
// Define the Entry Point of Execution (EPE) for Program Phase 3-6            *
// CBI:  3-6.1.1.1                                                            *
//*****************************************************************************

public static int Main()
{


//*****************************************************************************
// Program Phase 3-6 Main                                                     *
// Declare the local variables for the "main" program                         *
// CBI:  3-6.1.1.2                                                            *
//*****************************************************************************

   myclass loMyClass = null;


//*****************************************************************************
// Program Phase 3-6 Main                                                     *
// Attempt to instantiate the myclass class                                   *
// CBI:  3-6.1.1.3                                                            *
//*****************************************************************************

   try
   {
      loMyClass = new myclass(12345,"Hello World!");
   }


//*****************************************************************************
// Program Phase 3-6 Main                                                     *
// If the myclass class fails to instantiate, notify the user and exit        *
// CBI:  3-6.1.1.4                                                            *
//*****************************************************************************

   catch (Exception loException)
   {
      MessageBox.Show(loException.Message,"myclass",MessageBoxButtons.OK,
                      MessageBoxIcon.Error);
   }
```

pp3_6.cs continued on the next page

pp3_6.cs: Program Phase 3-6 EPE Source Code continued

```
   if (loMyClass == null)
   {
      return 1;
   }


//*****************************************************************************
// Program Phase 3-6 Main                                                     *
// If the myclass class instantiated, call an instance method                 *
// CBI:  3-6.1.1.5                                                            *
//*****************************************************************************

   loMyClass.DisplayInstanceData();
   return 0;
}
}}
```

myclass.cs: Class Definition and Implementation for the myclass Class

```
//*****************************************************************************
// myclass.cs                                                                 *
// Reserved                                                                   *
//*****************************************************************************

using System;
using System.Windows.Forms;


//*****************************************************************************
// myclass definition                                                         *
// Class definition for the myclass class                                     *
// CBI:  3-6.2.1.1                                                            *
//*****************************************************************************

// The myclass class is defined and implemented starting in CBI: 3-6.2.2.1.


//*****************************************************************************
// myclass implementation                                                     *
// Class implementation for the myclass class                                 *
// CBI:  3-6.2.2.1                                                            *
//*****************************************************************************

namespace nspp3_6
{
public class myclass
{
   // class data
   private int nData;
   private string cData;


//*****************************************************************************
// myclass implementation                                                     *
// Implement the initialization function for the myclass class                *
// CBI:  3-6.2.3.1                                                            *
//*****************************************************************************

public myclass(int tnData,string tcData)
{
```

myclass.cs continued on the next page

myclass.cs: Class Definition and Implementation for the myclass Class continued

```
//*************************************************************************
// myclass implementation                                                 *
// Declare the local variables for the myclass initialization function   *
// CBI:  3-6.2.3.2                                                        *
//*************************************************************************

   DialogResult lnResult;


//*************************************************************************
// myclass implementation                                                 *
// Prompt the user to continue instantiating the myclass class           *
// CBI:  3-6.2.3.3                                                        *
//*************************************************************************

   lnResult = MessageBox.Show("Proceed with class instantiation?","myclass",
                              MessageBoxButtons.YesNo,MessageBoxIcon.Question);


//*************************************************************************
// myclass implementation                                                 *
// Cancel instantiation of the myclass class if the user selects no      *
// CBI:  3-6.2.3.4                                                        *
//*************************************************************************

   if (lnResult == DialogResult.No)
   {
      throw new Exception("Class not instantiated.");
   }


//*************************************************************************
// myclass implementation                                                 *
// Store the parameters to the initialization function as instance data  *
// CBI:  3-6.2.3.5                                                        *
//*************************************************************************

   this.nData = tnData;
   this.cData = tcData;
}


//*************************************************************************
// myclass implementation                                                 *
// Implement the DisplayInstanceData method of the myclass class         *
// CBI:  3-6.2.4.1                                                        *
//*************************************************************************

public void DisplayInstanceData()
{
   MessageBox.Show("nData: " + this.nData + "\n" + "cData: " + this.cData,
                   "myclass instance data",MessageBoxButtons.OK,
                   MessageBoxIcon.Information);
}
}}
```

Code Setup and Compilation

- Tools: Microsoft Visual C# 2008 Express Edition (msdn.microsoft.com), Microsoft .NET Framework 2.0 or higher (windowsupdate.microsoft.com), Steps to compile and execute using Mono on the Linux platform (programphases.com/?page_id=589)

Code Setup and Compilation Steps

1: Start the Microsoft Visual C# 2008 Express Edition program.

2: VC# EE - Activate Menu Item: File → New Project

Select "Empty Project". Name the project pp3_6 and then activate the "OK" button.

3: VC# EE - Activate Menu Item: File → Save pp3_6

Set the "Location" to the appropriate folder. Verify that the "Create directory for solution" check box is not checked and then activate the "Save" button.

4: VC# EE - Activate Menu Item: Project → Add New Item

On the "Add New Item" dialog window, select the "Code File" template. Enter pp3_6.cs for the file name and then activate the "Add" button. Enter the source code for the pp3_6.cs file.

5: VC# EE - Activate Menu Item: Project → Add New Item

On the "Add New Item" dialog window, select the "Code File" template. Enter myclass.cs for the file name and then activate the "Add" button. Enter the appropriate source code into the myclass.cs text file.

6: Add the following references to the project by right-clicking on the "References" item in the "Solution Explorer" window and then activating the "Add Reference" menu item:

```
System
System.Windows.Forms
```

7: VC# EE - Activate Menu Item: Project → pp3_6 Properties

Verify that the "Output type" is set to "Windows Application". Set the "Startup object" to nspp3_6.pp3_6. Close the "pp3_6 Properties" window.

8: VC# EE - Activate Menu Item: File → Save All

9: VC# EE - Activate Menu Item: Build → Build Solution

Command Prompt Compilation

Enter the following commands from the pp3_6 folder to compile Program Phase 3-6:

```
PATH = "c:\windows\microsoft.net\framework\v2.0.50727";%PATH%
csc.exe /t:winexe /out:bin\release\pp3_6.exe pp3_6.cs myclass.cs
```

Program Execution

- Execute Program

```
VC# EE - Activate Menu Item:  Debug → Start Without Debugging
```

- Debug Program

```
VC# EE - Activate Menu Item:  Debug → Step into
```

Program Phase 3-7

VB .NET ▪ .NET Framework ▪ Windows

GUI Based Program with Custom Class Definition and Instantiation

- Program Phase Task 3 is implemented in Program Phase 3-7 using the Visual Basic .NET (VB.NET) programming language and the Microsoft .NET Framework 2.0 or higher.

- The .NET Framework MessageBox class is used in Program Phase 3-7 to implement input and output for a GUI based application.

- The Entry Point of Execution (EPE) is stored in the pp3_7.vb text file. The myclass class is defined and implemented in the myclass.vb text file.

Code Block Features

The Program Phase 3-7 code blocks illustrate the following programming features using the Visual Basic .NET programming language:

- **GUI Application**

- **Custom Class Definition**

- **Object Variable Declaration**

- **Custom Class Instantiation**

- **Cancel Class Instantiation from the Class Initialization Function**

- **Message Box Input and Output**

Visual Basic .NET
GUI Application

- The EPE for a GUI based VB.NET application is no different than a console based VB.NET application. The application type setting on the project properties dialog window needs to be set to "Windows Application".

test1.vb: Visual Basic .NET GUI Application

```
Module test1

Sub Main()

   '' Visual Basic .NET code goes here.

End Sub
End Module
```

Visual Basic .NET
Custom Class Definition

- The following example illustrates defining and implementing a custom class using VB.NET:

testclass1.vb: Visual Basic .NET Custom Class Definition

```
Namespace testns

Public Class testclass1

   '' Class Data
   Private nData As Integer
   Private cData As String

Public Sub New(ByVal tnData As Integer, ByVal tcData As String)

   Me.nData = tnData
   Me.cData = tcData

End Sub

Public Sub TestMethod()

   '' VB.NET code goes here.

End Sub
End Class
End Namespace
```

Visual Basic .NET
Object Variable Declaration

- A testclass1 typed variable can store an instance of the testclass1 class. Access to the testclass1 class is necessary when the object variable is declared.

- Since the testclass1 class resides in the same namespace as the test2 class, the testclass1 class is accessible in the test2 program.

test2.vb: Visual Basic .NET Object Variable Declaration

```
Namespace testns

Module test2

Sub Main()

   Dim loTestClass as testclass1

End Sub
End Module
End Namespace
```

Visual Basic .NET
Custom Class Instantiation

- A custom class is instantiated using the "New" keyword. There is no need to unload or delete the testclass1 instance stored in the loTestClass variable. The .NET Framework garbage collector will automatically release the memory used by the testclass1 instance after the variable goes out of scope.

- The following example creates an instance of the testclass1 class and calls the TestMethod() method:

test3.vb: Visual Basic .NET Custom Class Instantiation

```
Namespace testns

Module test3

Sub Main()

   Dim loTestClass as testclass1
   loTestClass = New testclass1(12345, "Hello World!")

End Sub
End Module
End Namespace
```

Visual Basic .NET
Cancel Class Instantiation from the Class Initialization Function

- Class instantiation is cancelled by throwing an exception from the class constructor.

testclass2.vb: Visual Basic .NET Cancel Class Instantiation from the Init Func.

```
Imports System

Namespace testns

Public Class testclass2

   '' Class Data
   Private nData As Integer
   Private cData As String

Public Sub New(ByVal tnData As Integer, ByVal tcData As String)

   '' vb.net code goes here.

   ''… Some error has occurred so cancel instantiation by
   '' throwing an exception.

   Throw New Exception("Class not instantiated because of some error.")

   Me.nData = tnData
   Me.cData = tcData

End Sub

Public Sub TestMethod()

   '' VB.NET code goes here.

End Sub
End Class
End Namespace
```

- The class instantiation attempt is placed in a try/catch block that responds to an exception thrown in the testclass2 constructor. If the testclass2 instantiation fails, the loTestClass variable will still store the "Nothing" value previously assigned before the class instantiation was attempted.

test4.vb: Visual Basic .NET Attempt to Instantiate the testclass2 Class

```
Imports System

Namespace testns

Module test4
Public Function Main() As Integer

   Dim loTestClass As testclass2
   loTestClass = Nothing

   Try

      loTestClass = New testclass2(12345, "Hello World!")

   Catch loException As Exception

      '' The class failed to instantiate.
      '' The error message is stored in loException.Message

   End Try

   If loTestClass Is Nothing Then

      Return 1

   End If

   Return 0

End Function
End Module
End Namespace
```

Visual Basic .NET Message Box Input and Output

- The following example prompts the user to select "Yes" or "No":

test5.vb: Visual Basic .NET Message Box Input and Output

```
'' Add reference to the System.Windows.Forms namespace in the project properties

Imports System.Windows.Forms

Module test5
Sub Main()

   Dim lnResult As DialogResult

   lnResult = MessageBox.Show("Select Yes or No","test", _
                              MessageBoxButtons.YesNo, _
                              MessageBoxIcon.Question)

   If lnResult = DialogResult.No Then

      '' No Selected

   Else

      '' Yes Selected (DialogResult.Yes)
```

test5.vb continued on the next page

test5.vb: Visual Basic .NET Message Box Input and Output continued

```
   End If

End Sub
End Module
```

Source Code Files

- Text files: pp3_7.vb, myclass.vb

pp3_7.vb: Program Phase 3-7 EPE Source Code

```
''**************************************************************************
'' Program Phase 3-7 VB.NET Class Definition/Instantiation                 *
'' Programming Tasks Illustrated: VB.NET GUI Based Application             *
''                                Custom Class Definition                  *
''                                Object Variable Declaration              *
''                                Custom Class Instantiation               *
''                                Cancel Instantiation from the Init Function *
''                                Message Box Input and Output             *
''**************************************************************************

''**************************************************************************
'' File: pp3_7.vb                                                          *
'' Reserved                                                                *
''**************************************************************************

Imports System
Imports System.Windows.Forms

Namespace nspp3_7

Class pp3_7


''**************************************************************************
'' Program Phase 3-7 Main                                                  *
'' Define the Entry Point of Execution (EPE) for Program Phase 3-7        *
'' CBI:  3-7.1.1.1                                                         *
''**************************************************************************

Public Shared Function Main() As Integer


''**************************************************************************
'' Program Phase 3-7 Main                                                  *
'' Declare the local variables for the "main" program                     *
'' CBI:  3-7.1.1.2                                                         *
''**************************************************************************

   Dim loMyClass As _myclass


''**************************************************************************
'' Program Phase 3-7 Main                                                  *
'' Attempt to instantiate the myclass class                                *
'' CBI:  3-7.1.1.3                                                         *
''**************************************************************************

   loMyClass = Nothing
   Try

      loMyClass = New _myclass(12345, "Hello World!")
```

pp3_7.vb continued on the next page

pp3_7.vb: Program Phase 3-7 EPE Source Code continued

```
''*************************************************************************
'' Program Phase 3-7 Main                                                 *
'' If the myclass class fails to instantiate, notify the user and exit   *
'' CBI:  3-7.1.1.4                                                        *
''*************************************************************************

   Catch loException As Exception

      MessageBox.Show(loException.Message,"myclass", _
                      MessageBoxButtons.OK,MessageBoxIcon.Error)

   End Try

   If loMyClass Is Nothing Then

      Return 1

   End If

''*************************************************************************
'' Program Phase 3-7 Main                                                 *
'' If the myclass class instantiated, call an instance method             *
'' CBI:  3-7.1.1.5                                                        *
''*************************************************************************

   Call loMyClass.DisplayInstanceData()
   Return 0

End Function
End Class
End Namespace
```

myclass.vb: Class Definition and Implementation for the myclass Class

```
''*************************************************************************
'' myclass.vb                                                             *
'' Reserved                                                               *
''*************************************************************************

Imports System
Imports System.Windows.Forms
Imports Microsoft.VisualBasic

Namespace nspp3_7

''*************************************************************************
'' myclass definition                                                     *
'' Class definition for the myclass class                                 *
'' CBI:  3-7.2.1.1                                                        *
''*************************************************************************

'' The myclass class is defined and implemented starting in CBI: 3-7.2.2.1.

''*************************************************************************
'' myclass implementation                                                 *
'' Class implementation for the myclass class                             *
'' CBI:  3-7.2.2.1                                                        *
''*************************************************************************

Public Class _myclass

   '' Class Data
   Private nData As Integer
```

myclass.vb continued on the next page

myclass.vb: Class Definition and Implementation for the myclass Class continued

```
   Private cData As String

''***************************************************************************
'' myclass implementation                                                   *
'' Implement the initialization function for the myclass class              *
'' CBI:  3-7.2.3.1                                                          *
''***************************************************************************

Public Sub New(ByVal tnData As Integer, ByVal tcData As String)

''***************************************************************************
'' myclass implementation                                                   *
'' Declare the local variables for the myclass initialization function     *
'' CBI:  3-7.2.3.2                                                          *
''***************************************************************************

   Dim lnResult As DialogResult

''***************************************************************************
'' myclass implementation                                                   *
'' Prompt the user to continue instantiating the myclass class              *
'' CBI:  3-7.2.3.3                                                          *
''***************************************************************************

   lnResult = MessageBox.Show("Proceed with class instantiation?","myclass", _
                              MessageBoxButtons.YesNo,MessageBoxIcon.Question)

''***************************************************************************
'' myclass implementation                                                   *
'' Cancel instantiation of the myclass class if the user selects no         *
'' CBI:  3-7.2.3.4                                                          *
''***************************************************************************

   If lnResult = DialogResult.No Then

      Throw New Exception("Class not instantiated.")

   End If

''***************************************************************************
'' myclass implementation                                                   *
'' Store the parameters to the initialization function as instance data     *
'' CBI:  3-7.2.3.5                                                          *
''***************************************************************************

   Me.nData = tnData
   Me.cData = tcData

End Sub

''***************************************************************************
'' myclass implementation                                                   *
'' Implement the DisplayInstanceData method of the myclass class            *
'' CBI:  3-7.2.4.1                                                          *
''***************************************************************************

Public Sub DisplayInstanceData()

MessageBox.Show("nData: " & Str(Me.nData) & Chr(13) & "cData: " & Me.cData, _
                "myclass instance data",MessageBoxButtons.OK, _
                MessageBoxIcon.Information)
End Sub
End Class
End Namespace
```

Code Setup and Compilation

- Tools: Microsoft Visual Basic 2008 Express Edition (msdn.microsoft.com), Microsoft .NET Framework 2.0 or higher (windowsupdate.microsoft.com).

Code Setup and Compilation Steps

1: Start the Microsoft Visual Basic 2008 Express Edition program.

2: VB.NET EE - Activate Menu Item: File → New Project

Select "Console Application". Name the project pp3_7 and then activate the "OK" button.

3: Delete the module1.bas file in the "Solution Explorer" window.

4: VB.NET EE - Activate Menu Item: File → Save All

On the "Save Project" dialog window, specify pp3_7 for the "Name". Set the "Location" to the appropriate folder. Uncheck the "Create directory for solution" check box and then activate the "Save" button.

5: VB.NET EE - Activate Menu Item: Project → Add New Item

On the "Add New Item" dialog window, select the "Module" template. Enter pp3_7.vb for the file name and then activate the "Add" button. Enter the source code for the pp3_7.vb file.

6: VB.NET EE - Activate Menu Item: Project → Add New Item

On the "Add New Item" dialog window, select the "Class" template. Enter myclass.vb for the file "Name" and then activate the "Add" button. Enter the source code for the myclass class into the myclass.vb text file.

7: VB.NET EE - Activate Menu Item: Project → pp3_7 Properties

Select the "Application" tab on the left side of the window and then enter the following:

```
uncheck "Enable application framework"
Assembly name:  pp3_7
Default namespace nspp3_7
Output type:  Windows Forms Application
Startup object nspp3_7.pp3_7
```

8: On the left side of the project properties window, select the "References" tab. In the "References" list, add the System and System.Windows.Forms namespaces.

9: VB.NET EE - Activate Menu Item: File → Save All

10: VB.NET EE - Activate Menu Item: Build → Build pp3_7

The resulting pp3_7.exe file will be found in the build or debug folder inside the pp3_7\bin folder.

```
Command Prompt Compilation Steps
```

Enter the following commands from the pp3_7 folder to compile Program Phase 3-7:

```
PATH = "c:\windows\microsoft.net\framework\v2.0.50727";%PATH%

vbc.exe /r:system.dll /r:system.windows.forms.dll
/r:microsoft.visualbasic.dll /out:bin\release\pp3_7.exe pp3_7.vb
myclass.vb

The preceding command needs to be entered on a single line.
```

Program Execution

- Execute Program

```
VB.NET EE - Activate Menu Item:  Debug → Start Debugging
```

- Debug Program

```
VB.NET EE - Activate Menu Item:  Debug → Step Into
```

Program Phase 3-8
Managed C++ ▪ Windows

GUI Based Program with Custom Class Definition and Instantiation

- Program Phase Task 3 is implemented in Program Phase 3-8 using the C++ programming language and the Microsoft .NET Framework 2.0 or higher.
- The .NET Framework MessageBox class is used in Program Phase 3-8 to implement input and output for a GUI based application.
- The Entry Point of Execution (EPE) is stored in the pp3_8.cpp text file. The myclass class is defined in the myclass.h text file and implemented in the myclass.cpp text file.

Code Block Features

The Program Phase 3-8 code blocks illustrate the following programming features using the C++ programming language and the .NET Framework:

- **GUI Application**
- **Custom Class Definition**
- **Object Variable Declaration**
- **Custom Class Instantiation**
- **Cancel Class Instantiation from the Class Initialization Function**
- **Message Box Input and Output**

Managed C++
GUI Application

- The EPE for a GUI based Managed C++ application is no different than a console based Managed C++ application.

test1.cpp: Managed C++ GUI Application

```
#using <mscorlib.dll>

int main(void)
{
   // Managed C++ GUI based code goes here.

   return 0;
}
```

Managed C++
Custom Class Definition

- The testclass1 class is defined in the testclass1.h file.

testclass1.h: Managed C++ Custom Class Definition

```
#ifndef TESTCLASS1_H
#define TESTCLASS1_H

#using <mscorlib.dll>
using namespace System;

ref class testclass1
{
private:

   // class data
   int nData;
   String^ cData;

public:

   testclass1(int tnData,String^ tcData);
   void TestMethod();
};
#endif
```

- The testclass1 class is implemented in the testclass1.cpp file.

testclass1.cpp: Managed C++ Custom Class Implementation

```
#include "testclass1.h"

testclass1::testclass1(int tnData,String^ tcData)
{
   this->nData = tnData;
   this->cData = tcData;
}

void testclass1::TestMethod()
{
   // Managed and Unmanaged C++ code goes here.
}
```

Managed C++
Object Variable Declaration

- A testclass1 typed pointer variable can store a pointer to an instance of the testclass1 class. Access to the testclass1 class is necessary when the object variable is declared.

- The testclass1 class is accessible in the test2.cpp program because the class definition stored in the testclass1.h file is included at the top of the file.

test2.cpp: Managed C++ Object Variable Declaration

```
#include "testclass1.h"
#using <mscorlib.dll>

int main(void)
{
    testclass1^ loTestClass = nullptr;
    return 0;
}
```

Managed C++ Custom Class Instantiation

- The "gcnew" keyword is used to instantiate a custom class that is managed by the .NET Framework runtime.
- The following example creates an instance of the testclass1 class and calls the TestMethod() method:

test3.cpp: Managed C++ Custom Class Instantiation

```
#include "testclass1.h"
#using <mscorlib.dll>

int main(void)
{
   testclass1^ loTestClass = nullptr;

   loTestClass = gcnew testclass1(12345,"Hello World!");
   return 0;
}
```

Managed C++ Cancel Class Instantiation from the Class Initialization Function

- Class instantiation is cancelled by throwing an exception from the class constructor.

testclass2.h: Class Definition for the testclass2 Class

```
#ifndef TESTCLASS2_H
#define TESTCLASS2_H

#using <mscorlib.dll>
using namespace System;

ref class testclass2
{
private:

   // class data
   int nData;
   String^ cData;

public:

   testclass2(int tnData,String^ tcData);
   void TestMethod();
};
#endif
```

testclass2.cpp: Managed C++ Class Implementation for the testclass2 Class

```
#include "testclass2.h"

testclass2::testclass2(int tnData,String^ tcData)
{
   // Managed and Unmanaged C++ code goes here.

   //… Some error has occurred so cancel instantiation by
   // throwing an exception.

   throw gcnew Exception("Class not instantiated because of some error.");

   // Program execution never gets here.
   this->nData = tnData;
   this->cData = tcData;
}

void testclass2::TestMethod()
{
   // Managed and Unmanaged C++ code goes here.
}
```

- The class instantiation attempt is placed in a try/catch block that responds to an exception thrown in the testclass2 constructor. If the testclass2 instantiation fails, the loTestClass variable will still store the "nullptr" value previously assigned before the class instantiation was attempted.

test4.cpp: Managed C++ Attempt to Instantiate the testclass2 Class

```
#include "testclass2.h"
#using <mscorlib.dll>

int main(void)
{
   testclass2^ loTestClass = nullptr;

   try
   {
      loTestClass = gcnew testclass2(12345,"Hello World!");
   }
   catch (Exception^ loException)
   {
      // The class failed to instantiate.
      // An error message is stored in loException->Message.
   }

   if (loTestClass == nullptr)
   {
      return 1;
   }

   loTestClass->TestMethod();
   return 0;
}
```

Managed C++
Message Box Input and Output

- The following example prompts the user to select "Yes" or "No":

test5.cpp: Managed C++ Message Box Input and Output

```
#using <mscorlib.dll>
using namespace System::Windows::Forms;

int main(void)
{
   DialogResult lnResult;

   lnResult = MessageBox::Show("Select Yes or No.","test",
                               MessageBoxButtons::YesNo,
                               MessageBoxIcon::Question);

   if (lnResult == DialogResult::No)
   {
      // No Selected
   }
   else
   {
      // Yes Selected (DialogResult::Yes)
   }
   return 0;
}
```

Source Code Files

- Text files: pp3_8.cpp, myclass.h, myclass.cpp

pp3_8.cpp: Program Phase 3-8 EPE Source Code

```
//*************************************************************************
// Program Phase 3-8 Managed C++ Class Definition/Instantiation          *
// Programming Tasks Illustrated: .NET Framework GUI Based Application    *
//                                Custom Class Definition                 *
//                                Object Variable Declaration             *
//                                Custom Class Instantiation              *
//                                Cancel Instantiation from the Init Funtion  *
//                                Message Box Input and Output            *
//*************************************************************************

//*************************************************************************
// File: pp3_8.cpp                                                        *
// Reserved                                                               *
//*************************************************************************

#include "myclass.h"

#using <mscorlib.dll>
using namespace System;
using namespace System::Windows::Forms;


//*************************************************************************
// Program Phase 3-8 Main                                                 *
// Define the Entry Point of Execution (EPE) for Program Phase 3-8        *
// CBI:  3-8.1.1.1                                                        *
//*************************************************************************

int main(void)
{
```

pp3_8.cpp continued on the next page

pp3_8.cpp: Program Phase 3-8 EPE Source Code continued

```
//******************************************************************************
// Program Phase 3-8 Main                                                      *
// Declare the local variables for the "main" program                          *
// CBI:  3-8.1.1.2                                                             *
//******************************************************************************

   myclass^ loMyClass = nullptr;


//******************************************************************************
// Program Phase 3-8 Main                                                      *
// Attempt to instantiate the myclass class                                    *
// CBI:  3-8.1.1.3                                                             *
//******************************************************************************

   try
   {
      loMyClass = gcnew myclass(12345,"Hello World!");
   }


//******************************************************************************
// Program Phase 3-8 Main                                                      *
// If the myclass class fails to instantiate, notify the user and exit         *
// CBI:  3-8.1.1.4                                                             *
//******************************************************************************

   catch (Exception^ loException)
   {
      MessageBox::Show(loException->Message,"myclass",
                       MessageBoxButtons::OK,MessageBoxIcon::Error);
   }

   if (loMyClass == nullptr)
   {
      return 1;
   }


//******************************************************************************
// Program Phase 3-8 Main                                                      *
// If the myclass class instantiated, call an instance method                  *
// CBI:  3-8.1.1.5                                                             *
//******************************************************************************

   loMyClass->DisplayInstanceData();
   return 0;
}
```

- myclass.h

myclass.h: Class Definition for the myclass Class

```
//******************************************************************************
// myclass.h                                                                   *
// Reserved                                                                    *
//******************************************************************************

//******************************************************************************
// myclass definition                                                          *
// Class definition for the myclass class                                      *
// CBI:  3-8.2.1.1                                                             *
//******************************************************************************
```

myclass.h continued on the next page

myclass.h: Class Definition for the myclass Class continued

```
#ifndef MYCLASS_H
#define MYCLASS_H

#using <mscorlib.dll>

using namespace System;
using namespace System::Windows::Forms;

ref class myclass
{
private:

   // class data
   int nData;
   String^ cData;

public:

   myclass(int tnData,String^ tcData);
   void DisplayInstanceData();
};

#endif
```

- myclass.cpp

myclass.cpp: Class Implementation for the myclass Class

```
//**********************************************************************
// myclass.cpp                                                         *
// Reserved                                                            *
//**********************************************************************

#include "myclass.h"


//**********************************************************************
// myclass implementation                                              *
// Class implementation for the myclass class                          *
// CBI:  3-8.2.2.1                                                     *
//**********************************************************************

// The myclass class methods are implemented in CBI: 3-8.2.3.1 and
// CBI: 3-8.2.4.1


//**********************************************************************
// myclass implementation                                              *
// Implement the initialization function for the myclass class         *
// CBI:  3-8.2.3.1                                                     *
//**********************************************************************

myclass::myclass(int tnData,String^ tcData)
{


//**********************************************************************
// myclass implementation                                              *
// Declare the local variables for the myclass initialization function *
// CBI:  3-8.2.3.2                                                     *
//**********************************************************************

   DialogResult lnResult;
```

myclass.cpp continued on the next page

myclass.cpp: Class Implementation for the myclass Class continued

```
//****************************************************************************
// myclass implementation                                                    *
// Prompt the user to continue instantiating the myclass class               *
// CBI:  3-8.2.3.3                                                           *
//****************************************************************************

   lnResult = MessageBox::Show("Proceed with class instantiation?","myclass",
                               MessageBoxButtons::YesNo,
                               MessageBoxIcon::Question);


//****************************************************************************
// myclass implementation                                                    *
// Cancel instantiation of the myclass class if the user selects no          *
// CBI:  3-8.2.3.4                                                           *
//****************************************************************************

   if (lnResult == DialogResult::No)
   {
       throw gcnew Exception("Class not instantiated.");
   }


//****************************************************************************
// myclass implementation                                                    *
// Store the parameters to the initialization function as instance data      *
// CBI:  3-8.2.3.5                                                           *
//****************************************************************************

   this->nData = tnData;
   this->cData = tcData;
}


//****************************************************************************
// myclass implementation                                                    *
// Implement the DisplayInstanceData method of the myclass class             *
// CBI:  3-8.2.4.1                                                           *
//****************************************************************************

void myclass::DisplayInstanceData()
{
   MessageBox::Show(String::Format("nData:  {0}\ncData: {1}",
                                   this->nData,this->cData),
                                   "myclass instance data",
                                   MessageBoxButtons::OK,
                                   MessageBoxIcon::Information);
}
```

Code Setup and Compilation

- Tools: Microsoft Visual Studio 2008 Express Edition (msdn.microsoft.com)

Code Setup and Compilation Steps

1: Start the Microsoft Visual Studio C++ 2008 Express Edition program.

2: VC++ EE - Activate Menu Item: File → New → Project

Steps continued on the next page

Code Setup and Compilation Steps continued

3: Select "Win32" for the "Project type". Select the "Win32 Application" template.

4: Name the project pp3_8. Set the "Project Location" to the appropriate folder. Do not check the "Create directory for solution" check box. Activate the "OK" button to proceed with the "Win32 Application Wizard".

5: Activate the "Next" button of the "Win32 Application Wizard".

6: Verify that a "Windows application" is selected and also check the "Empty project" check box. Activate the "Finish" button of the "Win32 Application Wizard".

7: VC++ EE - Activate Menu Item: Project → Add New Item

On the "Add New Item" dialog window, select the "Visual C++ → Code" category and then select the "C++ File" template. Enter pp3_8.cpp for the file "Name" and then activate the "Add" button. Enter the source code for the pp3_8.cpp file.

8: VC++ EE - Activate Menu Item: Project → Add New Item

On the "Add New Item" dialog window, select the "Visual C++ → Code" category and then select the "Header File" template. Enter myclass.h for the file name and then activate the "Add" button. Enter the source code for the myclass.h file.

9: VC++ EE - Activate Menu Item: Project → Add New Item

On the "Add New Item" dialog window, select the "Visual C++ → Code" category and then select the "C++ File" template. Enter myclass.cpp for the file name. Activate the "Add" button. Enter the source code for the myclass.cpp file.

10: VC++ EE - Activate Menu Item: Build → Configuration Manager

Select the "Release" value for the "Active solution configuration". Activate the "Close" button.

11: VC++ EE - Activate Menu Item: Project → pp3_8 Properties

Enter the following settings:

Configuration Properties → General → Character Set

`"Use Multi-Byte Character Set"`

Configuration Properties → General → Common Language Runtime Support

`"Common Language Runtime Support (/clr)"`

Configuration Properties → Linker → Advanced → Entry Point

`"main"`

Activate the "Apply" button.

12: Click on the "Common Properties → Frameworks and References" item. Add a reference for System and System.Windows.Forms and then close the window.

13: VC++ EE - Activate Menu Item: Build → Build Solution

```
Command Prompt Compilation
```

From a Visual Studio 2008 command prompt, change directories to the pp3_8 folder and then enter the following command:

```
   cl.exe /clr /FU
"%SYSTEMROOT%\Microsoft.NET\Framework\v2.0.50727\System.dll" /FU
"%SYSTEMROOT%\Microsoft.NET\Framework\v2.0.50727\System.Windows.Forms.dll"
pp3_8.cpp myclass.cpp
```

The preceding command needs to be entered on a single line.

Program Execution

- Execute Program

```
VC++ EE - Activate Menu Item: Debug → Start Without Debugging
```

- Debug Program

```
VC++ EE - Activate Menu Item: Debug → Step Into
```

Program Phase 3-9

Python ▪ Tk ▪ Multi-Platform

GUI Based Program with Custom Class Definition and Instantiation

- Program Phase Task 3 is implemented in Program Phase 3-9 using the Python programming language and the Tk library.
- The tkMessageBox class is used in Program Phase 3-9 to implement input and output for a GUI based application.
- The Entry Point of Execution (EPE) is stored in the pp3_9.py text file. The myclass class is defined and implemented in the myclass.py text file.

Code Block Features

The Program Phase 3-9 code blocks illustrate the following programming features using the Python programming language and the Tk module:

- **GUI Application**
- **Custom Class Definition**
- **Object Variable Declaration**
- **Custom Class Instantiation**
- **Cancel Class Instantiation from the Class Initialization Function**
- **Message Box Input and Output**

Python Tk
GUI Application

- The Tk library can be accessed in a Python program with the "from Tkinter import *" statement.

test1.py: Python Tk GUI Application

```
from Tkinter import *

## Python code that accesses the Tk library goes here.
```

Python
Custom Class Definition

- The testclass1.py example illustrates defining and implementing a custom class using Python. The class and method start and finish are delimited by indentation.

testclass1.py: Python Custom Class Definition

```
class testclass1:

    nData = 0
    cData = ""

    def __init__(self,tnData,tcData):

        self.nData = tnData
        self.cData = tcData

    def TestMethod(self):

        # Python code goes here.
```

Python
Object Variable Declaration

- A Python loosely typed variable can store an instance of the testclass1 class. Access to the testclass1 class is not necessary when the object variable is declared.

test2.py: Python Object Variable Declaration

```
import testclass1

goTestClass = 0
```

Python
Custom Class Instantiation

- The Python "import" statement is used to access the testclass1 class in the testclass1.py file.

- The following example creates an instance of the testclass1 class and calls the TestMethod() method:

test3.py: Python Custom Class Instantiation

```
import testclass1

goTestClass = 0;

goTestClass = testclass1.testclass1(12345,"Hello World!")
goTestClass.TestMethod()
```

Python
Cancel Class Instantiation from the Class Initialization Function

- Instantiation of a Python custom class is cancelled by raising an exception from the initialization function called "__init__".

testclass2.py: Python Cancel Class Instantiation from the Class Init Function

```
class testclass2:

    nData = 0
    cData = ""

    def __init__(self,tnData,tcData):

        raise Exception('Class not instantiated because of some error.')

        ## Program execution never gets here

        self.nData = tnData
        self.cData = tcData

    def TestMethod(self):

        ## Python code goes here.
```

- The class instantiation attempt is placed in a try/except block that responds to an exception raised in the testclass2 constructor. If the testclass2 instantiation fails, the loTestClass variable will still store the value zero previously assigned before the class instantiation was attempted.

test4.py: Python Attempt to Instantiate the testclass2 Class

```
import sys
import testclass2
goTestClass = 0

try:

    goTestClass = testclass2.testclass2(12345,"Hello World!")

except Exception,lcError:

    ## The class failed to instantiate.
    ## An error message can be retrieved from lcError.args[0]
    ## Python code the responds to the exception goes here.

if goTestClass == 0:
    sys.exit(1)

goTestClass.TestMethod()
```

Python Tk
Message Box Input and Output

- The following example prompts the user to select "Yes" or "No":

test5.py: Python Tk Message Box Input and Output

```
from Tkinter import *
import tkMessageBox

goMainWindow = 0
gcResult = ""

goMainWindow = Tk()
goMainWindow.withdraw()
```

test5.py continued on the next page

test5.py: Python Tk Message Box Input and Output continued

```
gcResult = tkMessageBox._show(title='test',type='yesno',
                              icon='question',message='Select Yes or No.')
goMainWindow.destroy()

if gcResult == 'no':
    ## No selected
    ## Python code that responds to the no button being clicked goes here.

else:
    ## Yes selected (lcResult = 'Yes')
    ## Python code that responds to the yes button being clicked goes here.
```

Source Code Files

- Text Files: pp3_9.py, myclass.py

pp3_9.py: Program Phase 3-9 EPE Source Code

```
##***********************************************************************
## Program Phase 3-9 Python Class Definition/Instantiation              *
## Programming Tasks Illustrated: Tk GUI Based Application              *
##                                Custom Class Definition               *
##                                Object Variable Declaration           *
##                                Custom Class Instantiation            *
##                                Cancel Instantiation from the Init Funtion  *
##                                Message Box Input and Output          *
##***********************************************************************

##***********************************************************************
## File: pp3_9.py                                                       *
## Reserved                                                             *
##***********************************************************************

from Tkinter import *
import tkMessageBox
import myclass

##***********************************************************************
## Program Phase 3-9 Main                                               *
## Define the Entry Point of Execution (EPE) for Program Phase 3-9      *
## CBI:  3-9.1.1.1                                                      *
##***********************************************************************

def main():


##***********************************************************************
## Program Phase 3-9 Main                                               *
## Declare the local variables for the "main" program                   *
## CBI:  3-9.1.1.2                                                      *
##***********************************************************************

    loMyClass = 0
    loError = ""


##***********************************************************************
## Program Phase 3-9 Main                                               *
## Attempt to instantiate the myclass class                             *
## CBI:  3-9.1.1.3                                                      *
##***********************************************************************

    try:
       loMyClass = myclass.myclass(12345,"Hello World!")
```

pp3_9.py continued on the next page

pp3_9.py: Program Phase 3-9 EPE Source Code continued

```
##****************************************************************************
## Program Phase 3-9 Main                                                    *
## If the myclass class fails to instantiate, notify the user and exit.     *
## CBI:  3-9.1.1.4                                                           *
##****************************************************************************

    except Exception,goError:

        ## Inform the user that the class has not instantiated.
        loMainWindow = Tk()
        loMainWindow.withdraw()

        tkMessageBox._show(title='myclass',type='ok',icon='error',
                           message=goError.args[0])

        loMainWindow.destroy()

    ## If the myclass class did not instantiate then exit.
    if loMyClass == 0:
        sys.exit(1)

##****************************************************************************
## Program Phase 3-9 Main                                                    *
## If the myclass class instantiated, call an instance method                *
## CBI:  3-9.1.1.5                                                           *
##****************************************************************************

    loMyClass.DisplayInstanceData()

# Actual EPE
main()
```

- myclass.py

myclass.py: myclass Class Definition and Implementation

```
##****************************************************************************
## myclass.py                                                                *
## Reserved                                                                  *
##****************************************************************************

from Tkinter import *
import tkMessageBox


##****************************************************************************
## myclass definition                                                        *
## Class definition for the myclass class                                    *
## CBI:  3-9.2.1.1                                                           *
##****************************************************************************

## The myclass class is defined and implemented starting in CBI: 3-9.2.2.1.

##****************************************************************************
## myclass implementation                                                    *
## Class implementation for the myclass class                                *
## CBI:  3-9.2.2.1                                                           *
##****************************************************************************

class myclass:

    nData = 0
    cData = ""
```

myclass.py continued on the next page

myclass.py: myclass Class Definition and Implementation continued

```
##***************************************************************************
## myclass implementation                                                   *
## Implement the initialization function for the myclass class             *
## CBI:  3-9.2.3.1                                                          *
##***************************************************************************

    def __init__(self,tnData,tcData):


##***************************************************************************
## myclass implementation                                                   *
## Declare the local variables for the myclass initialization function     *
## CBI:  3-9.2.3.2                                                          *
##***************************************************************************

        loMainWindow = 0
        lcResult = ''


##***************************************************************************
## myclass implementation                                                   *
## Prompt the user to continue instantiating the myclass class             *
## CBI:  3-9.2.3.3                                                          *
##***************************************************************************

        loMainWindow = Tk()
        loMainWindow.withdraw()

        lcResult = tkMessageBox._show(title='myclass',
                                      type='yesno',
                                      icon='question',
                           message='Proceed with class instantiation?')

        loMainWindow.destroy()


##***************************************************************************
## myclass implementation                                                   *
## Cancel instantiation of the myclass class if the user selects no        *
## CBI:  3-9.2.3.4                                                          *
##***************************************************************************

        if lcResult == 'no':
           raise Exception('Class not instantiated.')


##***************************************************************************
## myclass implementation                                                   *
## Store the parameters to the initialization function as instance data    *
## CBI:  3-9.2.3.5                                                          *
##***************************************************************************

        self.nData = tnData
        self.cData = tcData


##***************************************************************************
## myclass implementation                                                   *
## Implement the DisplayInstanceData method of the myclass class           *
## CBI:  3-9.2.4.1                                                          *
##***************************************************************************

    def DisplayInstanceData(self):

        loMainWindow = Tk()
        loMainWindow.withdraw()
```

myclass.py continued on the next page

myclass.py: myclass Class Definition and Implementation continued

```
        tkMessageBox._show(title='myclass instance data',
                           type='ok',
                           icon='info',
                           message = 'nData: ' + str(self.nData) +
                                     chr(13) + 'cData: ' + self.cData)
        loMainWindow.destroy()
```

Code Setup and Compilation

- Tools: Python distribution (Appendix G), Komodo IDE (Appendix F)

Code Setup and Compilation Steps

1: Create a folder called pp3_9 that will store the source code files.

2: Start the Komodo IDE program.

3: Komodo - Activate Menu Item: File → New → New Project

Set the project name to pp3_9.kpf and then save the new project in the pp3_9 folder.

4: Komodo - Activate Menu Item: File → New → New File

Click on the "Common" category and then select the "Text" template. Set the "Filename" to pp3_9.py. Verify that the "add to pp3_9 project" check box is checked and the "Directory" is set to the pp3_9 folder. Activate the "Open" button. Enter the source code for the pp3_9.py file and then save the file.

5: Komodo - Activate Menu Item: File → New → New File

Click on the "Common" category and then select the "Text "template. Set the "Filename" to myclass.py. Verify that the "add to pp3_9 project" check box is checked and the "Directory" is set to the pp3_9 folder. Activate the "Open" button. Enter the source code for the myclass class and then save the file.

6: There is no step for compiling the source code files. They are compiled at runtime by the Python interpreter.

Program Execution

- Execute Program

  `Komodo - Activate Menu Item: Debug → Run Without Debugging`

- Debug Program

  `Komodo - Activate Menu Item: Debug → Step In`

Program Phase 3-10

Perl ▪ Tk ▪ Multi-Platform

GUI Based Program with Custom Class Definition and Instantiation

- Program Phase Task 3 is implemented in Program Phase 3-10 using the Perl programming language and the Tk library.
- The messageBox() method of the main window object is used in Program Phase 3-10 to implement input and output for a GUI based application.
- The Entry Point of Execution (EPE) is stored in the pp3_10.pl text file. The myclass class is defined and implemented in the myclass.pm text file.

Code Block Features

The Program Phase 3-10 code blocks illustrate the following programming features using the Perl programming language and the Tk module:

- **GUI Application**
- **Custom Class Definition**
- **Object Variable Declaration**
- **Custom Class Instantiation**
- **Cancel Class Instantiation from the Class Initialization Function**
- **Message Box Input and Output**

Perl Tk
GUI Application

- The Tk library is accessed in a Perl program with the "use Tk" statement.

test1.pl: Perl Tk GUI Application

```
use strict;
use warnings;

use Tk;

## Perl code that accesses the Tk library goes here.
```

Perl
Custom Class Definition

- A custom class is declared and implemented in a Perl package.

- A Perl class instance is created by using the bless() function. The bless() function takes two parameters. The first parameter is the variable that will hold a reference to the class instance. The variable can be a Perl scalar, array, or hash. If a hash is used, each entry in the hash becomes a property (class data) of the class when it is blessed. The second parameter to the bless() function is the name of the class passed as a string value. A method in a Perl package is a Perl subroutine. The "1;" specified at the end of the file is returned to the "use" statement that accesses the package.

testclass1.pm: Perl Custom Class Definition

```
package testclass1;

use strict;
use warnings;

sub new()
{
   my ($testclass1,
       $tnData,
       $tcData) = @_;

   my $this =
   {
      nData => undef,
      cData => undef,
   };

   bless($this,$testclass1);
   $this->{nData} = $tnData;
   $this->{cData} = $tcData;

   return $this;
}

sub TestMethod()
{
   my ($this) = @_;
   # Perl code goes here.
}
1;
```

Perl Object Variable Declaration

- A Perl scalar variable can store an instance of the testclass1 class. Access to the testclass1 class is not necessary when the object variable is declared.

test2.pl: Perl Object Variable Declaration

```
my $loTestClass = 0;
```

Perl Custom Class Instantiation

- The "use" statement is used to access the testclass1 class in the testclass1.pl file.

- A Perl custom class is instantiated by calling the new() function of the testclass1 package. The new() function returns an instance of the testclass1 class.

- The following example creates an instance of the testclass1 class and calls the TestMethod() method:

test3.pl: Perl Custom Class Instantiation

```
use strict;
use warnings;
use testclass1;

my $loTestClass = 0;

$loTestClass = testclass1->new(12345,"Hello World!");
$loTestClass->TestMethod();
```

Perl
Cancel Class Instantiation from the Class Initialization Function

- Class instantiation is cancelled by not returning an object from the new() function.

testclass2.pm: Perl Cancel Class Instantiation from the Class Init Function

```
package testclass2;

use strict;
use warnings;

sub new()
{
   my ($testclass2,$tnData,$tcData) = @_;

   my $this =
   {
      nData => undef,
      cData => undef,
   };

   ## Perl code goes here.

   ##… Some error has occurred so cancel instantiation by
   ##  by not returning a blessed referent.

   return 1;

   ## Program execution never gets here.

   bless($this,$testclass2);

   $this->{nData} = $tnData;
   $this->{cData} = $tcData;
   return $this;
}

sub TestMethod()
{
   my ($this) = @_;
   # Perl code goes here.
}
1;
```

- If the testclass2 instantiation fails, the ref() function does not return the value "testclass2" for the string "loTestclass".

test4.pl: Perl Attempt to Instantiate the testclass2 Class

```
use strict;
use warnings;
use testclass2;

my $loTestClass = 0;
my $lcResult;

$loTestClass = testclass2->new(12345,"Hello World!");
$lcResult = ref($loTestClass);

if (!($lcResult eq "testclass2"))
{
   exit;
}
$loTestClass->TestMethod();
```

Perl Tk
Message Box Input and Output

- The following example prompts the user to select "Yes" or "No":

test5.pl: Perl Tk Message Box Input and Output

```
use strict;
use warnings;
use Tk;

my $loMainWindow;
my $lcResult;
my $loMessageBox;

$loMessageBox = MainWindow->new();
$loMessageBox->withdraw();
$lcResult = $loMessageBox->messageBox(-icon => 'question',
                                      -message => 'Select Yes or No.',
                                      -title => 'test',-type => 'YesNo');
$loMessageBox->destroy();

if ($lcResult eq "No")
{
   ## No selected
}
else
{
   ## Yes selected ($lcResult = "Yes")
}
```

Source Code Files

- Text files: pp3_10.pl, myclass.pm

pp3_10.pl: Program Phase 3-10 EPE Source Code

```
##*************************************************************************
## Program Phase 3-10 Perl Class Definition/Instantiation                 *
## Programming Tasks Illustrated: Tk GUI Based Application                *
##                                Custom Class Definition                 *
##                                Object Variable Declaration             *
##                                Custom Class Instantiation              *
##                                Cancel Instantiation from the Init Funtion *
##                                Message Box Input and Output            *
##*************************************************************************

##*************************************************************************
## File: pp3_10.pl                                                        *
## Reserved                                                               *
##*************************************************************************

use strict;
use warnings;
use Tk;
use myclass;


##*************************************************************************
## Program Phase 3-10 Main                                                *
## Define the Entry Point of Execution (EPE) for Program Phase 3-10       *
## CBI:  3-10.1.1.1                                                       *
##*************************************************************************

## The first line of the code in the pp3_10.pl file is the EPE.


##*************************************************************************
## Program Phase 3-10 Main                                                *
## Declare the local variables for the "main" program                     *
## CBI:  3-10.1.1.2                                                       *
##*************************************************************************

my $loMyClass;
my $lcResult;
my $loMessageBox;


##*************************************************************************
## Program Phase 3-10 Main                                                *
## Attempt to instantiate the myclass class                               *
## CBI:  3-10.1.1.3                                                       *
##*************************************************************************

$loMyClass = myclass->new(12345,"Hello World!");


##*************************************************************************
## Program Phase 3-10 Main                                                *
## If the myclass class fails to instantiate, notify the user and exit    *
## CBI:  3-10.1.1.4                                                       *
##*************************************************************************

$lcResult = ref($loMyClass);

if (!($lcResult eq "myclass"))
{
   $loMessageBox = MainWindow->new();
   $loMessageBox->withdraw();

   ## Inform the user that class instantiation has failed.
   $loMessageBox->messageBox(-icon => 'error',
                             -message => 'Class not instantiated.',
                             -title => 'myclass',-type => 'Ok');
```

pp3_10.pl continued on the next page

pp3_10.pl: Program Phase 3-10 EPE Source Code continued

```
   $loMessageBox->destroy();

   ## If the myclass class did not instantiate then exit.
   exit;
}


##****************************************************************************
## Program Phase 3-10 Main                                                  *
## If the myclass class instantiated, call an instance method              *
## CBI:  3-10.1.1.5                                                         *
##****************************************************************************

$loMyClass->DisplayInstanceData();
```

- myclass.pm

myclass.pm: Class Definition and Implementation for the myclass Class

```
##****************************************************************************
## myclass.pm                                                               *
## Reserved                                                                 *
##****************************************************************************

##****************************************************************************
## myclass definition                                                       *
## Class definition for the myclass class                                   *
## CBI:  3-10.2.1.1                                                         *
##****************************************************************************

## The myclass class is defined and implemented starting in CBI: 3-10.2.2.1.


##****************************************************************************
## myclass implementation                                                   *
## Class implementation for the myclass class                               *
## CBI:  3-10.2.2.1                                                         *
##****************************************************************************

package myclass;

use strict;
use warnings;
use Tk;


##****************************************************************************
## myclass implementation                                                   *
## Implement the initialization function for the myclass class             *
## CBI:  3-10.2.3.1                                                         *
##****************************************************************************

sub new()
{
   my ($MyClass,
       $tnData,
       $tcData) = @_;

   my $this =
   {
      nData => undef,
      cData => undef,
   };
```

myclass.pm continued on the next page

myclass.pm: Class Definition and Implementation for the myclass Class continued

```
##*************************************************************************
## myclass implementation                                                  *
## Declare the local variables for the myclass initialization function     *
## CBI:  3-10.2.3.2                                                        *
##*************************************************************************

   my $loMainWindow;
   my $lcResult;
   my $loMessageBox;


##*************************************************************************
## myclass implementation                                                  *
## Prompt the user to continue instantiating the myclass class             *
## CBI:  3-10.2.3.3                                                        *
##*************************************************************************

$loMessageBox = MainWindow->new();
$loMessageBox->withdraw();
$lcResult = $loMessageBox->messageBox(-icon => 'question',
                               -message => 'Proceed with class instantiation?',
                                      -title => 'myclass',
                                      -type => 'YesNo');
$loMessageBox->destroy();

##*************************************************************************
## myclass implementation                                                  *
## Cancel instantiation of the myclass class if the user selects no        *
## CBI:  3-10.2.3.4                                                        *
##*************************************************************************

if ($lcResult eq "No")
{
   return 1;
}

##*************************************************************************
## myclass implementation                                                  *
## Store the parameters to the initialization function as instance data    *
## CBI:  3-10.2.3.5                                                        *
##*************************************************************************

   bless($this,$MyClass);
   $this->{nData} = $tnData;
   $this->{cData} = $tcData;

   return $this;
}

##*************************************************************************
## myclass implementation                                                  *
## Implement the DisplayInstanceData method of the myclass class           *
## CBI:  3-10.2.4.1                                                        *
##*************************************************************************

sub DisplayInstanceData()
{
   my ($this) = @_;
   my $loMessageBox;

   $loMessageBox = MainWindow->new();
   $loMessageBox->withdraw();

   $loMessageBox->messageBox(-icon => 'info',
```

myclass.pm continued on the next page

myclass.pm: Class Definition and Implementation for the myclass Class continued

```
                                    -message => sprintf('nData: %d %scData: %s',
                                                        $this->{nData},
                                                        chr(13),
                                                        $this->{cData}),
                                    -title => 'myclass instance data',
                                    -type => 'Ok');
   $loMessageBox->destroy();
}

1;
```

Code Setup and Compilation

- Tools: Perl 5 distribution (Appendix H), Komodo IDE (Appendix F)

Code Setup and Compilation Steps

1: Create a folder called pp3_10 that will store the source code files.

2: Start the Komodo IDE program.

3: Komodo - Activate Menu Item: File → New → New Project

Set the project name to pp3_10.kpf and then save the new project in the pp3_10 folder.

4: Komodo - Activate Menu Item: File → New → New File

Click on the "Common" category and then select the "Text" template. Set the "Filename" to pp3_10.pl. Verify that the "add to pp3_10 project" check box is checked and the "Directory" is set to the pp3_10 folder. Activate the "Open" button. Enter the source code for the pp3_10.pl file and then save the file.

5: Komodo - Activate Menu Item: File → New → New File

Click on the "Common" category and then select the "Text" template. Set the "Filename" to myclass.pm. Verify that the "add to pp3_10 project" check box is checked and the "Directory" is set to the pp3_10 folder. Activate the "Open" button. Enter the source code for the myclass class and then save the file.

6: There is no step for compiling the source code files. They are compiled at runtime by the Perl interpreter.

Program Execution

- Execute Program

  `Komodo - Activate Menu Item: Debug → Run Without Debugging`

- Debug Program

  `Komodo - Activate Menu Item: Debug → Step In`

Program Phase 3-11

PHP CLI ▪ Gtk ▪ Multi-Platform

GUI Based Program with Custom Class Definition and Instantiation

- Program Phase Task 3 is implemented in Program Phase 3-11 using the PHP programming language and the Gtk library.
- The GtkMessageDialog class is used in Program Phase 3-11 to implement input and output for a GUI based application.
- The Entry Point of Execution (EPE) is stored in the pp3_11.php text file. The myclass class is defined and implemented in the myclass.php text file.

Code Block Features

The Program Phase 3-11 code blocks illustrate the following programming features using the PHP programming language and the Gtk library:

- **GUI Application**
- **Custom Class Definition**
- **Object Variable Declaration**
- **Custom Class Instantiation**
- **Cancel Class Instantiation from the Class Initialization Function**
- **Message Box Input and Output**

PHP CLI Gtk
GUI Application

- There is no need for an "include" statement to access the Gtk library. The php.ini file contains a reference to the Gtk library (Appendix J).

test1.php: PHP CLI GUI Application

```
<?php

   // PHP code that accesses the Gtk library goes here.

?>
```

PHP CLI
Custom Class Definition

- The following example illustrates defining and implementing a custom class using PHP:

testclass1.php: PHP CLI Custom Class Definition

```
<?php

class testclass1
{
   var $nData = null;
   var $cData = null;

function __construct($tnData,$tcData)
{
   $this->nData = $tnData;
   $this->cData = $tcData;
}

function TestMethod()
{
   // PHP code goes here.
}}

?>
```

PHP CLI
Object Variable Declaration

- A PHP loosely typed variable can store an instance of the testclass1 class. Access to the testclass1 class is not necessary when the object variable is declared.

test2.php: PHP CLI Object Variable Declaration

```
<?php

include 'testclass1.php';

$goTestClass = null;

?>
```

PHP CLI
Custom Class Instantiation

- The PHP "include" statement is used to access the testclass1 class in the testclass1.php file.

- The following example creates an instance of the testclass1 class and calls the TestMethod() method:

test3.php: PHP CLI Custom Class Instantiation

```
<?php

include 'testclass1.php';

$goTestClass = null;

$goTestClass = new testclass1(12345,"Hello World!");
$goTestClass->TestMethod();

?>
```

PHP CLI
Cancel Class Instantiation from the Class Initialization Function

- Class instantiation is cancelled by throwing an exception from the initialization function called "__construct()".

testclass2.php: PHP CLI Cancel Class Instantiation from the Class Init Function

```
<?php

class testclass2
{
   var $nData = null;
   var $cData = null;

function __construct($tnData,$tcData)
{
   // PHP code goes here.
   //… Some error has occurred so cancel instantiation by
   // throwing an exception.

   throw new Exception('Class not instantiated because of some error.');

   // Program execution never gets here.
   $this->nData = $tnData;
   $this->cData = $tcData;
}

function TestMethod()
{
   // PHP code goes here.
}}
?>
```

- The class instantiation attempt is placed in a try/except block that responds to an exception raised in the testclass2 constructor. If the testclass2 instantiation fails, the loTestClass variable will still store the "null" value previously assigned before the class instantiation was attempted.

test4.php: PHP CLI Attempt to Instantiate the testclass2 Class

```
<?php

include 'testclass2.php';

$goTestClass = null;

try
{
   $goTestClass = new testclass2(12345,"Hello World!");
}
catch(Exception $goException)
{
   // The class failed to instantiate.
   // An error message can be retrieved by calling $goException->getMessage()
}

if ($goTestClass == null)
{
   return 1;
}

$goTestClass->TestMethod();
?>
```

PHP CLI Gtk
Message Box Input and Output

- The following example prompts the user to select "Yes" or "No":

test5.php: PHP CLI Gtk Message Box Input and Output

```
<?php

$gnResult = null;
$goMessageBox = null;

$goMessageBox = new GtkMessageDialog(null,0,
                                     Gtk::MESSAGE_QUESTION,Gtk::BUTTONS_YES_NO,
                                     'Select Yes or No.');
$gnResult = $goMessageBox->run();
$goMessageBox->destroy();

if ($gnResult == Gtk::RESPONSE_NO)
{
   // No Selected
}
else
{
   // Yes Selected ($lnResult =  Gtk::RESPONSE_YES)
}
?>
```

Source Code Files

- Text files: pp3_11.php, myclass.php

pp3_11.php: Program Phase 3-11 EPE Source Code

```
<?php

//**************************************************************************
// Program Phase 3-11 PHP Class Definition/Instantiation                   *
// Programming Tasks Illustrated: Gtk GUI Based Application                *
//                                Custom Class Definition                  *
//                                Object Variable Declaration              *
//                                Custom Class Instantiation               *
//                                Cancel Instantiation from the Init Funtion *
//                                Message Box Input and Output             *
//**************************************************************************

//**************************************************************************
// File: pp3_11.php                                                        *
// Reserved                                                                *
//**************************************************************************

include 'myclass.php';


//**************************************************************************
// Program Phase 3-11 Main                                                 *
// Define the Entry Point of Execution (EPE) for Program Phase 3-11        *
// CBI:  3-11.1.1.1                                                        *
//**************************************************************************

main($argc,$argv);
```

pp3_11.php continued on the next page

pp3_11.php: Program Phase 3-11 EPE Source Code continued

```
function main($argc,$argv)
{


//***************************************************************************
// Program Phase 3-11 Main                                                  *
// Declare the local variables for the "main" program                       *
// CBI:  3-11.1.1.2                                                         *
//***************************************************************************

   $loMyClass = null;


//***************************************************************************
// Program Phase 3-11 Main                                                  *
// Attempt to instantiate the myclass class                                 *
// CBI:  3-11.1.1.3                                                         *
//***************************************************************************

   try
   {
      $loMyClass = new myclass(12345,"Hello World!");
   }


//***************************************************************************
// Program Phase 3-11 Main                                                  *
// If the myclass class fails to instantiate, notify the user and exit      *
// CBI:  3-11.1.1.4                                                         *
//***************************************************************************

   catch(Exception $loException)
   {
      $loMessageBox = new GtkMessageDialog(null,0,
                                           Gtk::MESSAGE_ERROR,Gtk::BUTTONS_OK,
                                           $loException->getMessage());
      $loMessageBox->run();
      $loMessageBox->destroy();

   }

   if ($loMyClass == null)
   {
      return 1;
   }


//***************************************************************************
// Program Phase 3-11 Main                                                  *
// If the myclass class instantiated, call an instance method               *
// CBI:  3-11.1.1.5                                                         *
//***************************************************************************

   $loMyClass->DisplayInstanceData();
}
?>
```

- myclass.php

myclass.php: Class Definition and Implementation for the myclass Class

```
<?php

//*****************************************************************************
// myclass.php                                                               *
// Reserved                                                                  *
//*****************************************************************************

//*****************************************************************************
// myclass definition                                                        *
// Class definition for the myclass class                                    *
// CBI:  3-11.2.1.1                                                          *
//*****************************************************************************

// The myclass class is defined and implemented starting in CBI: 3-11.2.2.1.


//*****************************************************************************
// myclass implementation                                                    *
// Class implementation for the myclass class                                *
// CBI:  3-11.2.2.1                                                          *
//*****************************************************************************

class myclass
{
   var $nData = null;
   var $cData = null;


//*****************************************************************************
// myclass implementation                                                    *
// Implement the initialization function for the myclass class               *
// CBI:  3-11.2.3.1                                                          *
//*****************************************************************************

function __construct($tnData,$tcData)
{


//*****************************************************************************
// myclass implementation                                                    *
// Declare the local variables for the myclass initialization function       *
// CBI:  3-11.2.3.2                                                          *
//*****************************************************************************

   $lnResult = null;
   $loMessageBox = null;


//*****************************************************************************
// myclass implementation                                                    *
// Prompt the user to continue instantiating the myclass class               *
// CBI:  3-11.2.3.3                                                          *
//*****************************************************************************

   $loMessageBox = new GtkMessageDialog(null,0,
                                        Gtk::MESSAGE_QUESTION,
                                        Gtk::BUTTONS_YES_NO,
                                        'Proceed with class instantiation?');

   $lnResult = $loMessageBox->run();
   $loMessageBox->destroy();
```

myclass.php continued on the next page

myclass.php: Class Definition and Implementation for the myclass Class continued

```
//***************************************************************************
// myclass implementation                                                  *
// Cancel instantiation of the myclass class if the user selects no        *
// CBI:  3-11.2.3.4                                                         *
//***************************************************************************

   if ($lnResult == Gtk::RESPONSE_NO)
   {
      throw new Exception('Class not instantiated.');
   }


//***************************************************************************
// myclass implementation                                                  *
// Store the parameters to the initialization function as instance data    *
// CBI:  3-11.2.3.5                                                         *
//***************************************************************************

   $this->nData = $tnData;
   $this->cData = $tcData;
}


//***************************************************************************
// myclass implementation                                                  *
// Implement the DisplayInstanceData method of the myclass class          *
// CBI:  3-11.2.4.1                                                         *
//***************************************************************************

function DisplayInstanceData()
{
   $loMessageBox = new GtkMessageDialog(null,0,
                                        Gtk::MESSAGE_INFO,
                                        Gtk::BUTTONS_OK,
                                        "nData: " . $this->nData .
                                        "\n" . "cData: " . $this->cData);
   $loMessageBox->run();
   $loMessageBox->destroy();
}}

?>
```

Code Setup and Compilation

- Tools: PHP CLI (Appendix J), Komodo IDE (Appendix F)

Code Setup and Compilation Steps

1: Create a folder called pp3_11 that will store the source code files.

2: Start the Komodo IDE program.

3: Komodo - Activate Menu Item: File → New → New Project

Set the name of the project to pp3_11.kpf and then save the project in the pp3_11 folder.

Steps continued on the next page

Code Setup and Compilation Steps continued

4: Komodo - Activate Menu Item: File → New → New File

Click on the "Common" category and then select the "Text" template. Set the "Filename" to pp3_11.php. Verify that the "add to pp3_11 project" check box is checked and the "Directory" is set to the pp3_11 folder. Activate the "Open" button. Enter the source code for the pp3_11.php file and then save the file.

5: Komodo - Activate Menu Item: File → New → New File

Click on the "Common" category and then select the "Text" template. Set the "Filename" to myclass.php. Verify that the "add to pp3_11 project" check box is checked and the "Directory" is set to the pp3_11 folder. Activate the "Open" button. Enter the source code for the myclass class and then save the file.

6: There is no step for compiling the source code files. They are compiled at runtime by the PHP CLI interpreter.

Program Execution

- Execute Program

```
Komodo - Activate Menu Item: Debug → Run Without Debugging
```

On the "Debugging Options" window, verify that the "Script" is set to the full path to the pp3_11.php file. Also, verify that the "Use the CLI interpreter" radio button is enabled and then activate the "OK" button.

- Debug Program

```
Komodo - Activate Menu Item: Debug → Step In
```

Program Phase 3-12

Ruby ▪ Tk ▪ Multi-Platform

GUI Based Program with Custom Class Definition and Instantiation

- Program Phase Task 3 is implemented in Program Phase 3-12 using the Ruby programming language and the Tk library.
- The messageBox() method of the main window object is used in Program Phase 3-12 to implement input and output for a GUI based application.
- The Entry Point of Execution (EPE) is stored in the pp3_12.rb text file. The myclass class is defined and implemented in the myclass.rb text file.

Code Block Features

The Program Phase 3-12 code blocks illustrate the following programming features using the Ruby programming language and the Tk library:

- **GUI Application**
- **Custom Class Definition**
- **Object Variable Declaration**
- **Custom Class Instantiation**
- **Cancel Class Instantiation from the Class Initialization Function**
- **Message Box Input and Output**

Ruby Tk
GUI Application

- The Tk library is accessed in a Ruby program with the "require 'tk'" statement.

test1.rb: Ruby Tk GUI Application

```
require 'tk'

## Ruby code goes here.
```

Ruby
Custom Class Definition

- The following example illustrates defining and implementing a custom class using Ruby:

testclass1.rb: Ruby Custom Class Definition

```
class Testclass1

   attr_accessor :nData
   attr_accessor :cData

   def initialize(tnData,tcData)

      self.nData = tnData
      self.cData = tcData

   end

   def TestMethod()

      # Ruby code goes here.

   end

end
```

Ruby
Object Variable Declaration

- A Ruby loosely typed variable can store an instance of the testclass1 class. Access to the testclass1 class is not necessary when the object variable is declared.

test2.rb: Ruby Object Variable Declaration

```
loTestClass = 0;
```

Ruby
Custom Class Instantiation

- The "load" statement is used to access the testclass1 class in the testclass1.rb file.

- The following example creates an instance of the testclass1 class and calls the TestMethod() method:

test3.rb: Ruby Custom Class Instantiation

```
load "testclass1.rb"

loTestClass = 0;
loTestClass = Testclass1.new(12345,"Hello World!")

loTestClass.TestMethod()
```

Ruby
Cancel Class Instantiation from the Class Initialization Function

- Class instantiation is cancelled by using the "raise" command from the initialization function called "initialize".

testclass2.rb: Ruby Cancel Class Instantiation from the Class Init Function

```
class Testclass2

   attr_accessor :nData
   attr_accessor :cData

   def initialize(tnData,tcData)

      ## Ruby code goes here.

      ##... Some error has occurred so cancel instantiation by
      ##  by using the Ruby raise command.

      raise "Class not instantiated because of some error."

      ## Program execution never gets here.
      self.nData = tnData
      self.cData = tcData

   end

   def TestMethod()

      ## Ruby code goes here.

   end

end
```

- In the following example, the "begin" and "end" statements must enclose the class instantiation and the "rescue" statement.

test4.rb: Ruby Attempt to Instantiate the testclass2 Class

```
load "testclass2.rb"

begin

   loTestClass = 0;
   loTestClass = Testclass2.new(12345,"Hello World!")

   rescue Exception => lcException

   ## The class failed to instantiate.
   ## An error message is stored in the lcException variable.

end

if loTestClass == 0 then

   exit 1

end

loTestClass.TestMethod()
```

Ruby Tk
Message Box Input and Output

- The following example prompts the user to select "Yes" or "No":

test5.rb: Ruby Tk Message Box Input and Output

```
require 'tk'

loMainWindow = 0
lcResult = ''

loMainWindow = TkRoot.new
loMainWindow.withdraw

lcResult = loMainWindow.messageBox('icon' => 'question',
                                   'message' => 'Select Yes or No.',
                                   'title' => 'myclass','type' => 'yesno');

if lcResult == "no" then

   ## No Selected

else

   ## Yes Selected (lcResult = "Yes")

end
```

Source Code Files

- Text files: pp3_12.rb, myclass.rb

pp3_12.rb: Program Phase 3-12 EPE Source Code

```
##*************************************************************************
## Program Phase 3-12 Ruby Class Definition/Instantiation                 *
## Programming Tasks Illustrated: Tk GUI Based Application               *
##                                Custom Class Definition                 *
##                                Object Variable Declaration             *
##                                Custom Class Instantiation              *
##                                Cancel Instantiation from the Init Funtion  *
##                                Message Box Input and Output            *
##*************************************************************************

##*************************************************************************
## File: pp3_12.rb                                                        *
## Reserved                                                               *
##*************************************************************************

require 'tk'
load "myclass.rb"


##*************************************************************************
## Program Phase 3-12 Main                                                *
## Define the Entry Point of Execution (EPE) for Program Phase 3-12       *
## CBI:  3-12.1.1.1                                                       *
##*************************************************************************

begin


##*************************************************************************
## Program Phase 3-12 Main                                                *
## Declare the local variables for the "main" program                     *
## CBI:  3-12.1.1.2                                                       *
##*************************************************************************
```

pp3_12.rb continued on the next page

pp3_12.rb: Program Phase 3-12 EPE Source Code continued

```
   loMyClass = 0;
   lcException = '';


##***************************************************************************
## Program Phase 3-12 Main                                                  *
## Attempt to instantiate the myclass class                                 *
## CBI:  3-12.1.1.3                                                         *
##***************************************************************************

   loMyClass = Myclass.new(12345,"Hello World!")


##***************************************************************************
## Program Phase 3-12 Main                                                  *
## If the myclass class fails to instantiate, notify the user and exit      *
## CBI:  3-12.1.1.4                                                         *
##***************************************************************************

   rescue Exception => lcException

      ## Inform the user that class instantiation has failed.
      loMainWindow = TkRoot.new
      loMainWindow.withdraw
      lcResult = loMainWindow.messageBox('icon' => 'error',
                                         'message' => lcException,
                                         'title' => 'myclass','type' => 'ok');
      loMainWindow.destroy
end

if loMyClass == 0 then

   exit 1

end


##***************************************************************************
## Program Phase 3-12 Main                                                  *
## If the myclass class instantiated, call an instance method               *
## CBI:  3-12.1.1.5                                                         *
##***************************************************************************

loMyClass.displayinstancedata()
```

- myclass.rb

myclass.rb: Class Definition and Implementation for the myclass Class

```
##***************************************************************************
## myclass.rb                                                               *
## Reserved                                                                 *
##***************************************************************************

require 'tk'


##***************************************************************************
## myclass definition                                                       *
## Class definition for the myclass class                                   *
## CBI:  3-12.2.1.1                                                         *
##***************************************************************************

## The myclass class is defined and implemented starting in CBI: 3-12.2.2.1.
```

myclass.rb continued on the next page

myclass.rb: Class Definition and Implementation for the myclass Class continued

```
##*****************************************************************************
## myclass implementation                                                      *
## Class implementation for the myclass class.                                 *
## CBI:  3-12.2.2.1                                                            *
##*****************************************************************************

class Myclass

   attr_accessor :nData
   attr_accessor :cData


##*****************************************************************************
## myclass implementation                                                      *
## Implement the initialization function for the myclass class                 *
## CBI:  3-12.2.3.1                                                            *
##*****************************************************************************

   def initialize(tnData,tcData)


##*****************************************************************************
## myclass implementation                                                      *
## Declare the local variables for the myclass initialization function         *
## CBI:  3-12.2.3.2                                                            *
##*****************************************************************************

      loMainWindow = 0
      lcResult = ''


##*****************************************************************************
## myclass implementation                                                      *
## Prompt the user to continue instantiating the myclass class                 *
## CBI:  3-12.2.3.3                                                            *
##*****************************************************************************

      loMainWindow = TkRoot.new
      loMainWindow.withdraw

      lcResult = loMainWindow.messageBox('icon' => 'question',
             'message' => 'Proceed with class instantiation?',
                                         'title' => 'myclass',
                                         'type' => 'yesno');


##*****************************************************************************
## myclass implementation                                                      *
## Cancel instantiation of the myclass class if the user selects no            *
## CBI:  3-12.2.3.4                                                            *
##*****************************************************************************

      if lcResult == "no" then

         raise "Class not instantiated."

      end


##*****************************************************************************
## myclass implementation                                                      *
## Store the parameters to the initialization function as instance data        *
## CBI:  3-12.2.3.5                                                            *
##*****************************************************************************

      self.nData = tnData
```

myclass.rb continued on the next page

myclass.rb: Class Definition and Implementation for the myclass Class continued

```
        self.cData = tcData

    end


##*************************************************************************
## myclass implementation                                                 *
## Implement the DisplayInstanceData method of the myclass class          *
## CBI:  3-12.2.4.1                                                       *
##*************************************************************************

    def displayinstancedata()

        loMainWindow = TkRoot.new
        loMainWindow.withdraw

        lcResult = loMainWindow.messageBox('icon' => 'info',
                                           'message' => sprintf('nData: %d%scData:
%s',self.nData,13.chr,self.cData),
                                           'title' => 'myclass instance data',
                                           'type' => 'ok');

        loMainWindow.destroy

    end

end
```

Code Setup and Compilation

- Tools: Ruby distribution (Appendix I), Komodo IDE (Appendix F)

Code Setup and Compilation Steps

1: Create a folder called pp3_12 that will store the source code files.

2: Start the Komodo IDE program.

3: Komodo - Activate Menu Item: File → New → New Project

Set the project name to pp3_12.kpf and then save the new project in the pp3_12 folder.

4: Komodo - Activate Menu Item: File → New → New File

Click on the "Common" category and then select the "Text" template. Set the "Filename" to pp3_12.rb. Verify that the "add to pp3_12 project" check box is checked and the "Directory" is set to the pp3_12 folder. Activate the "Open" button. Enter the source code for the pp3_12.rb file and then save the file.

5: Komodo - Activate Menu Item: File → New → New File

Click on the "Common" category and then select the "Text" template. Set the "Filename" to myclass.rb. Verify that the "add to pp3_12 project" check box is checked and the "Directory" is set to the pp3_12 folder. Activate the "Open" button. Enter the source code for the myclass class and then save the file.

Steps continued on the next page

Code Setup and Compilation Steps continued

6: There is no step for compiling the source code files. They are compiled at runtime by the Ruby interpreter.

Program Execution

- Execute Program

```
Komodo - Activate Menu Item: Debug → Run Without Debugging
```

On the "Debugging Options" window, verify that the "Script" is set to the full path to the pp3_12.rb file and then activate the "OK" button.

- Debug Program

```
Komodo - Activate Menu Item: Debug → Step In
```

Program Phase 3-13
Tcl ▪ Tk ▪ Multi-Platform

GUI Based Program with Custom Class Definition and Instantiation

- Program Phase Task 3 is implemented in Program Phase 3-13 using the Tcl programming language and the Tk library.

  The "tk_messageBox" command is used in Program Phase 3-13 to implement input and output for a GUI based application.

- The Entry Point of Execution (EPE) for Program Phase 3-13 is stored in the pp3_13.tcl text file. The myclass class is defined and implemented in the myclass.tcl text file.

Code Block Features

The Program Phase 3-13 code blocks illustrate the following programming features using the Tcl programming language and the Tk library:

- **GUI Application**
- **Custom Class Definition**
- **Object Variable Declaration**
- **Custom Class Instantiation**
- **Cancel Class Instantiation from the Class Initialization Function**
- **Message Box Input and Output**

Tcl Tk
GUI Application

- The Tk library is accessed in a Tcl program with the "package require Tk" statement.
- A Tcl Tk GUI program is launched using the tclsh interpreter. The "." window references the default "toplevel" window, created when the Tcl/Tk program is started. The "withdraw" command hides the window, and the "destroy" command is used to remove the window completely.

test1.tcl: Tcl Tk GUI Application

```
package require Tk

## Tcl code that accesses the Tk library goes here.

wm withdraw .
destroy .
```

Tcl
Custom Class Definition

- XOTcl is an extension to Tcl that allows for defining and implementing classes and methods. XOTcl is included with the ActiveState distribution of Tcl. The following example defines and implements a class called testclass1 using the XOTcl package:

testclass1.tcl: Tcl Custom Class Definition

```
package require XOTcl
namespace import ::xotcl::*

Class testclass1 -parameter {nData cData}

testclass1 instproc init {} \
{
   ## The parameters to the class are automatically stored
   ## as properties of the class.
}

testclass1 instproc TestMethod {} \
{
   # Tcl code goes here.
}
```

Tcl
Object Variable Declaration

- A Tcl loosely typed variable can store an instance of the testclass1 class. Access to the testclass1 class is not necessary when the object variable is declared.

test2.tcl: Tcl Object Variable Declaration

```
source "testclass1.tcl"

set loTestClass 0
```

Tcl
Custom Class Instantiation

- The Tcl "source" statement is used to access the testclass1 class in the testclass1.tcl file.

- The following example creates an instance of the testclass1 class and calls the TestMethod() method:

test3.tcl: Tcl Custom Class Instantiation

```
source "testclass1.tcl"

set loTestClass 0
set loTestClass [testclass1 new -nData 12345 -cData "Hello World!"]

$loTestClass TestMethod
```

Tcl
Cancel Class Instantiation from the Class Initialization Function

- Class instantiation is cancelled by using the "error" command in the initialization function called "init".

testclass2.tcl: Tcl Cancel Class Instantiation from the Class Init Function

```
package require XOTcl
namespace import ::xotcl::*

Class testclass2 -parameter {nData cData}

testclass2 instproc init {} \
{
   ## Tcl code goes here.

   ##... Some error has occurred so cancel instantiation by
   ##  by using the Tcl error command.

   error "Class not instantiated because of some error."
}

testclass2 instproc TestMethod {} \
{
   ## Tcl code goes here.
}
```

- The Tcl "catch" command is used to check if the Tcl "error" command has been used in the class initialization function.

test4.tcl: Tcl Attempt to Instantiate the testclass2 Class

```
source "testclass2.tcl"

package require Tk

wm withdraw .

set loTestClass 0
set lcError ""

if {[catch {set loTestClass [testclass2 new -nData 12345 -cData "Hello World!"]}
lcError]} \
{
   ## The class failed to instantiate.
   ## An error message is stored in the lcError variable.
}

if {$loTestClass == 0} \
{
   destroy .
   return
}

$loTestClass TestMethod

destroy .
```

Tcl Tk
Message Box Input and Output

- The following example prompts the user to select "Yes" or "No":

test5.tcl: Tcl Tk Message Box Input and Output

```
package require Tk

wm withdraw .
set lnResult [tk_messageBox -parent . \
                            -message "Select Yes or No." \
                            -icon "question" \
                            -type "yesno" \
                            -title "test"]

if {[string compare $lnResult "no"] == 0} \
{
   ## No Selected
} \
else \
{
   ## Yes Selected (lnResult = "Yes")
}

destroy .
```

Source Code Files

- Text files: pp3_13.tcl, myclass.tcl

pp3_13.tcl: Program Phase 3-13 EPE Source Code

```
##**************************************************************************
## Program Phase 3-13 Tcl Class Definition/Instantiation                   *
## Programming Tasks Illustrated: Tk GUI Based Application                 *
##                                Custom Class Definition                  *
##                                Object Variable Declaration              *
##                                Custom Class Instantiation               *
##                                Cancel Instantiation from the Init Funtion  *
##                                Message Box Input and Output             *
##**************************************************************************

##**************************************************************************
## File: pp3_13.tcl                                                        *
## Reserved                                                                *
##**************************************************************************

source "myclass.tcl"
package require Tk


##**************************************************************************
## Program Phase 3-13 Main                                                 *
## Define the Entry Point of Execution (EPE) for Program Phase 3-13        *
## CBI:  3-13.1.1.1                                                        *
##**************************************************************************

## The first line of the code in the pp3_13.tcl file is the EPE.

## Hide the automatically created toplevel window referenced by "."
wm withdraw .
```

pp3_13.tcl continued on the next page

pp3_13.tcl: Program Phase 3-13 EPE Source Code continued

```
##***************************************************************************
## Program Phase 3-13 Main                                                   *
## Declare the local variables for the "main" program                        *
## CBI:  3-13.1.1.2                                                          *
##***************************************************************************

set loMyClass 0


##***************************************************************************
## Program Phase 3-13 Main                                                   *
## Attempt to instantiate the myclass class                                  *
## CBI:  3-13.1.1.3                                                          *
##***************************************************************************

if {[catch {set loMyClass [myclass new -nData 12345 -cData "Hello World!"]}
lcError]} \
{


##***************************************************************************
## Program Phase 3-13 Main                                                   *
## If the myclass class fails to instantiate, notify the user and exit       *
## CBI:  3-13.1.1.4                                                          *
##***************************************************************************

   toplevel .mainwindow
   wm withdraw .mainwindow
   tk_messageBox -parent .mainwindow \
                 -message $lcError \
                 -icon "error" \
                 -type "ok" \
                 -title "myclass"

   destroy .mainwindow
}

## If the myclass class did not instantiate then exit.
if {$loMyClass == 0} \
{
   destroy .
   return
}


##***************************************************************************
## Program Phase 3-13 Main                                                   *
## If the myclass class instantiated, call an instance method                *
## CBI:  3-13.1.1.5                                                          *
##***************************************************************************

$loMyClass DisplayInstanceData
destroy .
```

- myclass.tcl

myclass.tcl: Class Definition and Implementation for the myclass Class

```
##***************************************************************************
## myclass.tcl                                                               *
## Reserved                                                                  *
##***************************************************************************

package require Tk
```

myclass.tcl continued on the next page

myclass.tcl: Class Definition and Implementation for the myclass Class continued

```
package require XOTcl
namespace import ::xotcl::*


##*************************************************************************
## myclass definition                                                      *
## XOTcl class definition for the myclass class.                           *
## CBI:  3-13.2.1.1                                                        *
##*************************************************************************

## The myclass class is defined and implemented starting in CBI: 3-13.2.2.1.


##*************************************************************************
## myclass implementation                                                  *
## XOTcl class implementation for the myclass class                        *
## CBI:  3-13.2.2.1                                                        *
##*************************************************************************

## Class data
Class myclass -parameter {nData cData}


##*************************************************************************
## myclass implementation                                                  *
## Implement the initialization function for the myclass class             *
## CBI:  3-13.2.3.1                                                        *
##*************************************************************************

myclass instproc init {} \
{


##*************************************************************************
## myclass implementation                                                  *
## Declare the local variables for the myclass initialization function     *
## CBI:  3-13.2.3.2                                                        *
##*************************************************************************

   set lnResult 0


##*************************************************************************
## myclass implementation                                                  *
## Prompt the user to continue instantiating the myclass class             *
## CBI:  3-13.2.3.3                                                        *
##*************************************************************************

   toplevel .mainwindow
   wm withdraw .mainwindow

   set lnResult [tk_messageBox -parent .mainwindow \
              -message "Proceed with class instantiation?" \
              -icon "question" \
              -type "yesno" \
              -title "myclass"]

   destroy .mainwindow


##*************************************************************************
## myclass implementation                                                  *
## Cancel instantiation of the myclass class if the user selects no        *
## CBI:  3-13.2.3.4                                                        *
##*************************************************************************
```

myclass.tcl continued on the next page

myclass.tcl: Class Definition and Implementation for the myclass Class continued

```
   if {[string compare $lnResult "no"] == 0} \
   {
      error "Class not instantiated."
   }


##**************************************************************************
## myclass implementation                                                  *
## Store the parameters to the initialization function as instance data    *
## CBI:  3-13.2.3.5                                                        *
##**************************************************************************

   ## This is done automatically when the class is instantiated.
}


##**************************************************************************
## myclass implementation                                                  *
## Implement the DisplayInstanceData method of the myclass class           *
## CBI:  3-13.2.4.1                                                        *
##**************************************************************************

myclass instproc DisplayInstanceData {} \
{
   toplevel .mainwindow
   wm withdraw .mainwindow
   tk_messageBox -parent .mainwindow \
                 -message "nData: [my nData]\ncData: [my cData]" \
                 -icon "info" \
                 -type "ok" \
                 -title "myclass"

   destroy .mainwindow
}
```

Code Setup and Compilation

- Tools: Tcl distribution version 8.4. (Appendix K), Komodo IDE (Appendix F)

Code Setup and Compilation Steps

1: Create a folder called pp3_13 that will store the source code files.

2: Start the Komodo IDE program.

3: Komodo - Activate Menu Item: File → New → New Project

Set the project name to pp3_13.kpf and then save the new project in the pp3_13 folder.

4: Komodo - Activate Menu Item: File → New → New File

Click on the "Common" category and then select the "Text" template. Set the "Filename" to pp3_13.tcl. Verify that the "add to pp3_13 project" check box is checked and the "Directory" is set to the pp3_13 folder. Activate the "Open" button. Enter the source code for the pp3_13.tcl file and then save the file.

Steps continued on the next page

Code Setup and Compilation Steps continued

5: Komodo - Activate Menu Item: File → New → New File

Click on the "Common" category and then select the "Text" template. Set the "Filename" to myclass.tcl. Verify that the "add to pp3_13 project" check box is checked and the "Directory" is set to the pp3_13 folder. Activate the "Open" button. Enter the source code for the myclass class and then save the file.

6: There is no step for compiling the source code files. They are compiled at runtime by the Tcl interpreter.

Program Execution

- Execute Program

    ```
    Komodo - Activate Menu Item: Debug → Run Without Debugging
    ```

    On the "Debugging Options" window, verify that the "Script" is set to the full path to the pp3_13.tcl file and then activate the "OK" button.

- Debug Program

    ```
    Komodo - Activate Menu Item: Debug → Step In
    ```

Program Phase 3-14
Delphi ▪ Windows

GUI Based Program with Custom Class Definition and Instantiation

- Program Phase Task 3 is implemented in Program Phase 3-14 using the Delphi programming language.
- The MessageDlg() function is used in Program Phase 3-14 to implement input and output for a GUI based application.
- The Entry Point of Execution (EPE) for Program Phase 3-14 is stored in the pp3_14.dpr text file. The myclass class is defined and implemented in the myclassunit.pas text file.

Code Block Features

The Program Phase 3-14 code blocks illustrate the following programming features using the Delphi programming language:

- **GUI Application**
- **Custom Class Definition**
- **Object Variable Declaration**
- **Custom Class Instantiation**
- **Cancel Class Instantiation from the Class Initialization Function**
- **Message Box Input and Output**

Delphi
GUI Application

- A GUI based application is indicated in a Delphi program using the "{$AppType GUI}" statement near the top of the source file following the program statement.

test1.dpr: Delphi GUI Based Application

```
program test1;

{$APPTYPE GUI}

uses
   SysUtils;

var
   // Variable declarations go here.

begin
   // Delphi code goes here.

end.
```

Delphi
Custom Class Definition

- The following example illustrates defining and implementing a custom class using Delphi:

testunit1.pas: Delphi Custom Class Definition

```
unit testunit1;

interface

uses
  SysUtils;

type

   testclass1 = class(TObject)

   nData : Integer;
   cData : String;
   procedure TestMethod();
   constructor Create(tnData : Integer; tcData : String);

end;

implementation
constructor testclass1.Create(tnData : Integer; tcData : String);
begin

   nData := tnData;
   cData := tcData;

end;

procedure testclass1.TestMethod();
begin

   // Delphi code goes here.

end;

end.
```

Delphi
Object Variable Declaration

- A testclass1 typed variable can store an instance of the testclass1 class. Access to the testclass1 class is necessary when the object variable is declared.

- Since the testclass1 class is specified in the "uses" statement, the testclass1 class is accessible in the test2 program.

test2.dpr: Delphi Object Variable Declaration

```
program test2;

{$APPTYPE GUI}
```

test2.dpr continued on the next page

test2.dpr: Delphi Object Variable Declaration continued

```
uses
   SysUtils,
   testunit1 in 'testunit1.pas';

var
   loTestClass : testclass1;

begin

   // Delphi code goes here.

end.
```

Delphi
Custom Class Instantiation

- The following example creates an instance of the testclass1 class and calls the TestMethod() method:

test3.dpr: Delphi Custom Class Instantiation

```
program test3;

{$APPTYPE GUI}

uses
  SysUtils,
  testunit1 in 'testunit1.pas';

var
   loTestClass : testclass1;

begin

   loTestClass := nil;

   loTestClass := testclass1.Create(12345,'Hello World!');
   loTestClass.TestMethod();
   loTestClass.Free();

end.
```

Delphi
Cancel Class Instantiation from the Class Initialization Function

- Class instantiation is cancelled by using the "Raise" command from the class initialization function.

testunit2.pas: Delphi Cancel Class Instantiation from the Class Init Function

```
unit testunit2;
interface

uses
  SysUtils;

var
   lnResult : Integer;
```

testunit2.pas continued on the next page

testunit2.pas: Delphi Cancel Class Instantiation from Class Init Func. continued

```
type

   testclass2 = class(TObject)

   nData : Integer;
   cData : String;
   procedure TestMethod();
   constructor Create(tnData : Integer; tcData : String);

end;

implementation

constructor testclass2.Create(tnData : Integer; tcData : String);
begin

   // Delphi code goes here.

   //… Some error has occurred so cancel instantiation by
   // raising an exception.

   Raise Exception.Create('Class not instantiated because of some error.');

   nData := tnData;
   cData := tcData;

end;

procedure testclass2.TestMethod();
begin

   // Delphi code goes here.

end;
end.
```

- The class instantiation attempt is placed in a try/except block that responds to an exception raised in the testclass2 constructor. If the testclass2 instantiation fails, the loTestClass variable will still store the "nil" value previously assigned before the class instantiation was attempted.

test4.dpr: Delphi Attempt to Instantiate the testclass2 Class

```
program test4;

{$APPTYPE GUI}

uses
  SysUtils,testunit2 in 'testunit2.pas';

var
   loTestClass : testclass2;

begin
      loTestClass := nil;

   try
      loTestClass := testclass2.Create(12345,'Hello World!');

   except

        On loException : Exception do
```

test4.dpr continued on the next page

test4.dpr: Delphi Attempt to Instantiate the testclass2 Class continued

```
         // The class failed to instantiate.
         // An error message can be retrieved from loException.Message

      end;

   if loTestClass = nil then
   begin

      Exit;

   end;

   loTestClass.TestMethod();
   loTestClass.Free();

end.
```

Delphi
Message Box Input and Output

- The following example prompts the user to select "Yes" or "No":

test5.dpr: Delphi Message Box Input and Output

```
program test5;

{$APPTYPE GUI}

uses
    SysUtils,Controls,Forms,Dialogs;

var
   lnResult : Integer;

begin

   lnResult := MessageDlg('Select Yes or No.',mtConfirmation,[mbYes,mbNo],0);

   if lnResult = mrNo then
   begin

      // No selected

   end
   else
   begin

      // Yes selected (lnResult = mrYes)

   end;
end.
```

Source Code Files

- Text files: pp3_14.dpr, myclassunit.pas

pp3_14.dpr: Program Phase 3-14 EPE Source Code

```
//******************************************************************************
// Program Phase 3-14 Delphi Class Definition/Instantiation                    *
// Programming Tasks Illustrated: Delphi GUI Based Application                 *
//                                Custom Class Definition                      *
//                                Object Variable Declaration                  *
//                                Custom Class Instantiation                   *
//                                Cancel Instantiation from the Init Funtion   *
//                                Message Box Input and Output                 *
//******************************************************************************

//******************************************************************************
// File: pp3_14.dpr                                                            *
// Reserved                                                                    *
//******************************************************************************

program pp3_14;
{$APPTYPE GUI}

uses
  SysUtils,Controls,Forms,Dialogs,
  myclassunit in 'myclassunit.pas';


//******************************************************************************
// Program Phase 3-14 Main                                                     *
// Declare the local variables for the "main" program                          *
// CBI:  3-14.1.1.2                                                            *
//******************************************************************************

var

   loMyClass : myclass;


//******************************************************************************
// Program Phase 3-14 Main                                                     *
// Define the Entry Point of Execution (EPE) for Program Phase 3-14            *
// CBI:  3-14.1.1.1                                                            *
//******************************************************************************

begin


//******************************************************************************
// Program Phase 3-14 Main                                                     *
// Attempt to instantiate the myclass class                                    *
// CBI:  3-14.1.1.3                                                            *
//******************************************************************************

   loMyClass := nil;

   try

      loMyClass := myclass.Create(12345,'Hello World!');


//******************************************************************************
// Program Phase 3-14 Main                                                     *
// If the myclass class fails to instantiate, notify the user and exit         *
// CBI:  3-14.1.1.4                                                            *
//******************************************************************************

   except

      On loException : Exception do
      MessageDlg(loException.Message,mtError,[mbOK],0);
```

pp3_14.dpr continued on the next page

pp3_14.dpr: Program Phase 3-14 EPE Source Code continued

```
   end;

   // If the myclass class did not instantiate then exit.
   if loMyClass = nil then
   begin

      Exit;

   end;

//****************************************************************************
// Program Phase 3-14 Main                                                  *
// If the myclass class instantiated, call an instance method               *
// CBI:  3-14.1.1.5                                                         *
//****************************************************************************

   loMyClass.DisplayInstanceData();
   loMyClass.Free();

end.
```

- myclassunit.pas

myclassunit.pas: Class Definition and Implementation for the myclass Class

```
//****************************************************************************
// myclass.pas                                                              *
// Reserved                                                                 *
//****************************************************************************

//****************************************************************************
// myclass definition                                                       *
// Class definition for the myclass class                                   *
// CBI:  3-14.2.1.1                                                         *
//****************************************************************************

unit myclassunit;

interface

uses
  SysUtils,Forms,Controls,Dialogs;


//****************************************************************************
// myclass implementation                                                   *
// Declare the local variables for the myclass initialization function      *
// CBI:  3-14.2.3.2                                                         *
//****************************************************************************

var
   lnResult : Integer;

type

    myclass = class(TObject)

   // myclass data
   nData : Integer;
   cData : String;
   procedure DisplayInstanceData();
   constructor Create(tnData : Integer; tcData : String);
```

myclassunit.pas continued on the next page

myclassunit.pas: Class Def. and Implementation for the myclass Class continued

```
end;


//****************************************************************************
// myclass implementation                                                    *
// Class implementation for the myclass class                                *
// CBI:  3-14.2.2.1                                                          *
//****************************************************************************

implementation


//****************************************************************************
// myclass implementation                                                    *
// Implement the initialization function for the myclass class               *
// CBI:  3-14.2.3.1                                                          *
//****************************************************************************

constructor myclass.Create(tnData : Integer; tcData : String);
begin


//****************************************************************************
// myclass implementation                                                    *
// Prompt the user to continue instantiating the myclass class               *
// CBI:  3-14.2.3.3                                                          *
//****************************************************************************

   lnResult := MessageDlg('Proceed with class instantiation?',
                          mtConfirmation,[mbYes,mbNo],0);


//****************************************************************************
// myclass implementation                                                    *
// Cancel instantiation of the myclass class if the user selects no          *
// CBI:  3-14.2.3.4                                                          *
//****************************************************************************

   if lnResult = mrNo then
   begin

      Raise Exception.Create('Class not instantiated.');

   end;

//****************************************************************************
// myclass implementation                                                    *
// Store the parameters to the initialization function as instance data      *
// CBI:  3-14.2.3.5                                                          *
//****************************************************************************

   nData := tnData;
   cData := tcData;

end;


//****************************************************************************
// myclass implementation                                                    *
// Implement the DisplayInstanceData method of the myclass class             *
// CBI:  3-14.2.4.1                                                          *
//****************************************************************************
```

myclassunit.pas continued on the next page

myclassunit.pas: Class Def. and Implementation for the myclass Class continued

```
procedure myclass.DisplayInstanceData();
begin

   MessageDlg('nData: ' + IntToStr(nData) + chr(13) +
              'cData: ' + cData,
              mtInformation,
              [mbOK],
              0);
end;
end.
```

Code Setup and Compilation

- Tools: Turbo Delphi Explorer (Appendix M)

Code Setup and Compilation Steps

1: Create a folder called pp3_14 that will store the source code files.

2: Start the Delphi IDE program.

3: Delphi - Activate Menu Item: Project → Add New Project

On the "New Items" dialog window, select the "Delphi Projects" item category and then select "Console Application". Activate the "'OK" button. Enter the source code for the pp3_14.dpr file into the project source code file. Replace any existing code in the file.

4: Delphi - Activate Menu Item: File → Save Project As

Save the project as pp3_14.bdsproj in the pp3_14 folder.

5: Since the Delphi IDE will automatically update the reference to the myclassunit unit, change the following line of code:

From

```
SysUtils,Controls,Forms,Dialogs,
myclassunit in 'myclassunit.pas';
```

To

```
SysUtils,Controls,Forms,Dialogs;
```

6: Delphi - Activate Menu Item: File → New -> Unit

Enter the source code for the myclass unit and then save the file as myclassunit.pas in the pp3_14 folder.

7: Delphi - Activate Menu Item: Project → Build pp3_14

Alternate Code Setup and Compilation Steps

1: Create a folder called pp3_14 that will store the source code files.

2: Create the pp3_14.dpr file using a text editor and then enter the appropriate source code. Save the file in the pp3_14 folder.

3: Create the myclassunit.pas file using a text editor and then enter the appropriate source code. Save the file in the pp3_14 folder.

4: Start the Borland Delphi IDE program.

5: Delphi - Activate Menu Item: File → Open Project

Select the pp3_14.dpr file in the pp3_14 folder and then activate the "Open" button.

6: Delphi - Activate Menu Item: Project → Build pp3_14

Program Execution

- Execute Program

  `Delphi - Activate Menu Item: Run → Run`

- Debug Program

  `Delphi - Activate Menu Item: Run → Step Over`

Program Phase 3-15

C++ ▪ QT4 ▪ Multi-Platform

GUI Based Program with Custom Class Definition and Instantiation

- Program Phase Task 3 is implemented in Program Phase 3-15 using the C++ programming language and the QT4 framework.

- The QMessageBox class is used in Program Phase 3-15 to implement input and output for a GUI based application.

- The Entry Point of Execution (EPE) is stored in the pp3_15.cpp text file. The myclass class is defined in the myclass.h text file and implemented in the myclass.cpp text file.

Code Block Features

The Program Phase 3-15 code blocks illustrate the following programming features using the C++ programming language and the QT4 framework:

- **GUI Application**

- **Custom Class Definition**

- **Object Variable Declaration**

- **Custom Class Instantiation**

- **Cancel Class Instantiation from the Class Initialization Function**

- **Message Box Input and Output**

C++ with QT4
GUI Application

- In a QT4 GUI based application, a QApplication object is created instead of the QCoreApplication object. The QApplication object is responsible for managing resources for the application.

test1.cpp: C++ with QT4 GUI Application

```
#include <QApplication>

int main(int argc, char *argv[])
{
   QApplication loApplication(argc, argv);

   // C++ GUI based code that accesss the QT4 framework goes here.

   return 0;
}
```

C++ with QT4
Custom Class Definition

- The testclass1 class is defined in the testclass1.h file.

testclass1.h: C++ with QT4 Custom Class Definition

```
#ifndef TESTCLASS1_H
#define TESTCLASS1_H

class testclass1
{
   private:
      int nData;
      char *cData;

   public:
     testclass1(int tnData,char *tcData);
     void TestMethod();
};
#endif
```

- The testclass1 class is implemented in the testclass1.cpp file.

testclass1.cpp: C++ with QT4 Custom Class Implementation

```
#include "testclass1.h"

testclass1::testclass1(int tnData,char *tcData)
{
   this->nData = tnData;
   this->cData = tcData;
}

void testclass1::TestMethod()
{
   // C++ code goes here.
}
```

C++ with QT4
Object Variable Declaration

- A testclass1 typed pointer variable can store a pointer to an instance of the testclass1 class. Access to the testclass1 class is necessary when the object variable is declared.

- The testclass1 class is accessible in the test2.cpp program because the class definition stored in the testclass1.h file is included at the top of the file.

test2.cpp: C++ with QT4 Object Variable Declaration

```
#include <QApplication>
#include "testclass1.h"

int main(int argc, char *argv[])
{
   QApplication loApplication(argc, argv);
   testclass1* loTestClass;

   return 0;
}
```

C++ with QT4
Custom Class Instantiation

- The following example creates an instance of the testclass1 class and calls the TestMethod() method:

test3.cpp: C++ with QT4 Custom Class Instantiation

```
#include <QApplication.h>
#include "testclass1.h"

int main(int argc, char *argv[])
{
   QApplication loApplication(argc, argv);
   testclass1* loTestClass;

   loTestClass = new testclass1(12345,"Hello World!");
   loTestClass->TestMethod();

   delete loTestClass;
   return 0;
}
```

C++ with QT4
Cancel Class Instantiation from the Class Initialization Function

- Class instantiation is cancelled by throwing an exception from the class constructor.

testclass2.h: Class Header File for the testclass2 Class

```
#ifndef TESTCLASS2_H
#define TESTCLASS2_H

class testclass2
{
   private:
      int nData;
      char *cData;

   public:
     testclass2(int tnData,char *tcData);
     void TestMethod();
};
#endif
```

testclass2.cpp: C++ with QT4 Cancel Class Instantiation from the Init Function

```
#include "testclass2.h"

testclass2::testclass2(int tnData,char *tcData)
{
   // C++ QT4 code goes here.

   //… Some error has occurred so cancel instantiation by
   // throwing an exception.

   throw "Class not instantiated because of some error.";

   // Program execution never gets here.
```

testclass2.cpp continued on the next page

testclass2.cpp: C++ with QT4 Cancel Class Instantiation from Init Func continued

```
    this->nData = tnData;
    this->cData = tcData;
}

void testclass2::TestMethod()
{
    // C++ code goes here.
}
```

- A try/catch block is used to check if an exception has been thrown in the class constructor. If the testclass2 instantiation fails, the loTestClass variable will still store the value zero previously assigned before the class instantiation was attempted.

test4.cpp: C++ with QT4 Attempt to Instantiate the testclass2 Class

```
#include <QApplication>
#include "testclass2.h"

int main(int argc, char *argv[])
{
    QApplication loApplication(argc, argv);

    testclass2* loTestClass;
    loTestClass = 0;

    try
    {
        loTestClass = new testclass2(12345,"Hello World!");
    }
    catch (const char* lcError)
    {
        // The class failed to instantiate.
        // An error message is stored in the lcError C string.
    }

    if (loTestClass == 0)
    {
        return 1;
    }

    loTestClass->TestMethod();

    delete loTestClass;
    return 0;
}
```

C++ with QT4
Message Box Input and Output

- The following example prompts the user to select "Yes" or "No":

test5.cpp: C++ with QT4 Message Box Input and Output

```
#include <QApplication>
#include <QMessageBox>

int main(int argc, char *argv[])
{
    QApplication loApplication(argc, argv);
    int lnResult;
```

test5.cpp continued on the next page

test5.cpp: C++ with QT4 Message Box Input and Output continued

```
   lnResult = QMessageBox::question(0,"test","Select Yes or No.",
                                    QMessageBox::Yes,QMessageBox::No,
                                    QMessageBox::NoButton);

   if (lnResult == QMessageBox::No)
   {
      // No Selected
   }
   else
   {
      // Yes Selected (lnResult = QMessageBox::Yes)
   }
   return 0;
}
```

Source Code Files

- Text files: pp3_15.cpp, myclass.h, myclass.cpp

pp3_15.cpp: Program Phase 3-15 EPE Source Code

```
//******************************************************************************
// Program Phase 3-15 C++ QT4 Class Definition/Instantiation                   *
// Programming Tasks Illustrated: QT4 GUI Based Application                    *
//                                Custom Class Definition                      *
//                                Object Variable Declaration                  *
//                                Custom Class Instantiation                   *
//                                Cancel Instantiation from the Init Funtion   *
//                                Message Box Input and Output                 *
//******************************************************************************

//******************************************************************************
// File: pp3_15.cpp                                                            *
// Reserved                                                                    *
//******************************************************************************

#include <QApplication>
#include <QMessageBox>
#include <myclass.h>


//******************************************************************************
// Program Phase 3-15 Main                                                     *
// Define the Entry Point of Execution (EPE) for Program Phase 3-15            *
// CBI:  3-15.1.1.1                                                            *
//******************************************************************************

int main(int argc, char *argv[])
{


//******************************************************************************
// Program Phase 3-15 Main                                                     *
// Declare the local variables for the "main" program                          *
// CBI:  3-15.1.1.2                                                            *
//******************************************************************************

   myclass* loMyClass;
   QApplication loApplication(argc, argv);
```

pp3_15.cpp continued on the next page

pp3_15.cpp: Program Phase 3-15 EPE Source Code continued

```
//****************************************************************************
// Program Phase 3-15 Main                                                   *
// Attempt to instantiate the myclass class                                  *
// CBI:  3-15.1.1.3                                                          *
//****************************************************************************

   loMyClass = 0;

   try
   {
      loMyClass = new myclass(12345,"Hello World!");
   }


//****************************************************************************
// Program Phase 3-15 Main                                                   *
// If the myclass class fails to instantiate, notify the user and exit      *
// CBI:  3-15.1.1.4                                                          *
//****************************************************************************

   catch (const char *lcException)
   {
      QMessageBox::critical(0,"myclass",
                            lcException,QMessageBox::Ok,
                            QMessageBox::NoButton,QMessageBox::NoButton);
   }

   if (loMyClass == 0)
   {
      return 1;
   }


//****************************************************************************
// Program Phase 3-15 Main                                                   *
// If the myclass class instantiated, call an instance method               *
// CBI:  3-15.1.1.5                                                          *
//****************************************************************************

   loMyClass->DisplayInstanceData();

   delete loMyClass;
   return 0;
}
```

- myclass.h

myclass.h: Class Definition for the myclass Class

```
//****************************************************************************
// myclass.h                                                                 *
// Reserved                                                                  *
//****************************************************************************

//****************************************************************************
// myclass definition                                                        *
// Class definition for the myclass class                                    *
// CBI:  3-15.2.1.1                                                          *
//****************************************************************************

#ifndef MYCLASS_H
#define MYCLASS_H

#include <QStringList>
```

myclass.h continued on the next page

myclass.h: Class Definition for the myclass Class continued

```
class myclass
{

   private:

      int nData;
      QString cData;

   public:

      myclass(int tnData,QString tcData);
      void DisplayInstanceData();
};

#endif
```

- myclass.cpp

myclass.cpp: Class Implementation for the myclass Class

```
//***************************************************************************
// myclass.cpp                                                              *
// Reserved                                                                 *
//***************************************************************************

#include <exception>
#include "myclass.h"
#include <QMessageBox>
#include <QStringList>


//***************************************************************************
// myclass implementation                                                   *
// Class implementation for the myclass class                               *
// CBI:  3-15.2.2.1                                                         *
//***************************************************************************

// The myclass class methods are implemented in CBI: 3-15.2.3.1 and
// CBI: 3-15.2.4.1


//***************************************************************************
// myclass implementation                                                   *
// Implement the initialization function for the myclass class              *
// CBI:  3-15.2.3.1                                                         *
//***************************************************************************

myclass::myclass(int tnData,QString tcData)
{


//***************************************************************************
// myclass implementation                                                   *
// Declare the local variables for the myclass initialization function      *
// CBI:  3-15.2.3.2                                                         *
//***************************************************************************

   int lnResult;


//***************************************************************************
// myclass implementation                                                   *
// Prompt the user to continue instantiating the myclass class              *
// CBI:  3-15.2.3.3                                                         *
//***************************************************************************
```

myclass.cpp continued on the next page

myclass.cpp: Class Implementation for the myclass Class continued

```
   lnResult = QMessageBox::question(0,"myclass",
                                    "Proceed with class instantiation?",
                                    QMessageBox::Yes,QMessageBox::No,
                                    QMessageBox::NoButton);


//*****************************************************************************
// myclass implementation                                                     *
// Cancel instantiation of the myclass class if the user selects no           *
// CBI:  3-15.2.3.4                                                           *
//*****************************************************************************

   if (lnResult == QMessageBox::No)
   {
      throw "Class not instantiated.";
   }


//*****************************************************************************
// myclass implementation                                                     *
// Store the parameters to the initialization function as instance data       *
// CBI:  3-15.2.3.5                                                           *
//*****************************************************************************

   this->nData = tnData;
   this->cData = tcData;
}


//*****************************************************************************
// myclass implementation                                                     *
// Implement the DisplayInstanceData method of the myclass class              *
// CBI:  3-15.2.4.1                                                           *
//*****************************************************************************

void myclass::DisplayInstanceData()
{
   QMessageBox::information(0,
                            "myclass instance data",
  "nData: " + QString::number(this->nData,10) + "\ncData: " + this->cData,
                            QMessageBox::Ok,
                            QMessageBox::NoButton,
                            QMessageBox::NoButton);
}
```

Windows Code Setup and Compilation

- Tools: Mingw compiler and the QT4 library (Appendix E)

Windows Code Setup and Compilation Steps

1: Create a folder called pp3_15 that will store the source code files.

2: Using a text editor, enter the EPE source code for Program Phase 3-15 and then save the file as pp3_15.cpp in the pp3_15 folder. Also, create the myclass.h and myclass.cpp source code files and then enter the source code for each of them.

Steps continued on the next page

Windows Code Setup and Compilation Steps continued

3: From a QT 4 command prompt, change directories to the pp3_15 folder and then enter the following:

```
qmake -project
```

4: Edit the pp3_15.pro file that has just been generated and then add the following two lines:

```
CONFIG += release
QT += gui
```

5: After editing the pp3_15.pro file, save and close it and then enter the following commands:

```
qmake pp3_15.pro
make
```

Linux Code Setup and Compilation

- Tools: GNU GCC (Appendix B), QT4 Library (Appendix E)

Linux Code Setup and Compilation Steps

1: Create a folder called pp3_15 that will store the source code files.

2: Using a text editor, enter the EPE source code for Program Phase 3-15 and then save the file as pp3_15.cpp in the pp3_15 folder. Also, create the myclass.h and myclass.cpp source code files and enter the source code for each of them.

3: Open a terminal window and then change directories to the pp3_15 folder.

4: Enter the following command:

```
qmake -project
```

5: Edit the pp3_15.pro file that has just been generated and then add the following two lines:

```
CONFIG += release
QT += gui
```

6: After editing the pp3_15.pro file, save and close the file and then enter the following commands:

```
qmake pp3_15.pro
make
```

Mac OS X Code Setup and Compilation

- Tools: Xcode (Appendix C), QT4 Library (Appendix E)

Mac OS X Code Setup and Compilation Steps

1: Create a folder called pp3_15 that will store the source code files.

2: Using a text editor, enter the EPE source code for Program Phase 3-15 and then save the file as pp3_15.cpp in the pp3_15 folder. Also, create the myclass.h and myclass.cpp source code files and enter the source code for each of them.

3: Open a terminal window and then change directories to the pp3_15 folder.

4: Enter the following command to create an Xcode project for Program Phase 3-15:

```
qmake -spec macx-xcode
```

5: Open the Xcode program and then open the newly created project.

6: Compile the program by activating the "Build" button.

Windows Program Execution

- To execute the pp3_15 program from a command prompt, change directories to pp3_15\release folder and then enter the following:

```
pp3_15.exe
```

Linux Program Execution

- To execute the pp3_15 program from a terminal window, change directories to pp3_15/release folder and then enter the following:

```
./pp3_15
```

Mac OS X Program Execution

- Execute Program

  To execute the pp3_15 program, activate the "Build/Go" button.

- Debug Program

  To debug the pp3_15.cpp file one line at a time, place the cursor at the first line of code in the CBI: 3-15.1.1.3 code block and then create a breakpoint.

```
Xcode 2.4 - Activate Menu Item: Debug → Add Breakpoint at Current Line
Xcode 3 - Activate Menu Item: Run → Manage Breakpoints → Add
Breakpoint at Current Line
```

  After the break point has been created, the program can be debugged.

```
Xcode - Activate Menu Item: Build → Build and Debug
```

C++ ▪ wxWidgets ▪ Multi-Platform

GUI Based Program with Custom Class Definition and Instantiation

- Program Phase Task 3 is implemented in Program Phase 3-16 using the C++ programming language and the wxWidgets library.
- The wxMessageBox() function is used in Program Phase 3-16 to implement input and output for a GUI based application.
- The Entry Point of Execution (EPE) is stored in the pp3_16.cpp text file. The myclass class is defined in the myclass.h text file and implemented in the myclass.cpp text file.

Code Block Features

The Program Phase 3-16 code blocks illustrate the following programming features using the C++ programming language and the wxWidgets library:

- **GUI Application**
- **Custom Class Definition**
- **Object Variable Declaration**
- **Custom Class Instantiation**
- **Cancel Class Instantiation from the Class Initialization Function**
- **Message Box Input and Output**

C++ with wxWidgets
GUI Application

- The DECLARE_APP() and IMPLEMENT_APP() macros are called run-time type identification (RTTI) macros and are responsible for creating the custom class based on the wxApp class.
- The OnInit() member function of the wxApp class is automatically called by the wxWidgets framework when the program starts. This function is used as the EPE for the program. Returning a Boolean "false" value from the OnInit() function prevents the application event loop from starting. For Program Phase 3-16, the application needs to exit when the OnInit() function ends, so a Boolean "false" value is returned. In Program Phase 4-16, a main window is created, and the OnInit() function returns a Boolean "true" value, so the event loop can be used to process events for the main window.

testl.cpp: C++ wxWidgets GUI Application

```
#include "wx/wx.h"

class test1 : public wxApp
{
public:
    virtual bool OnInit();
};

DECLARE_APP(test1)
IMPLEMENT_APP(test1)

bool test1::OnInit()
{
   // C++ code that access the wxWidget library goes here.

   // returning a Boolean false value prevents the event loop from starting.
   return false;
}
```

C++ wxWidgets Custom Class Definition

- The testclass1 class is defined in the testclass1.h file.

testclass1.h: C++ wxWidgets Custom Class Definition

```
#ifndef TESTCLASS1_H
#define TESTCLASS1_H

class testclass1
{
   private:

      // class data
      int nData;
      char *cData;

   public:
     testclass1(int tnData,char *tcData);
     void TestMethod();
};
#endif
```

- The testclass1 class is implemented in the testclass1.cpp file.

testclass1.cpp: C++ wxWidgets Custom Class Implementation

```
#include "testclass1.h"

testclass1::testclass1(int tnData,char *tcData)
{
   this->nData = tnData;
   this->cData = tcData;
}

void testclass1::TestMethod()
{
   // C++ code goes here.
}
```

C++ wxWidgets
Object Variable Declaration

- A testclass1 typed pointer variable can store a pointer to an instance of the testclass1 class. Access to the testclass1 class is necessary when the object variable is declared.
- The testclass1 class is accessible in the test2.cpp program because the class definition stored in the testclass1.h file is included at the top of the file.

test2.cpp: C++ wxWidgets Object Variable Declaration

```
#include "wx/wx.h"
#include "testclass1.h"

class test2 : public wxApp
{
public:
   virtual bool OnInit();
};

DECLARE_APP(test2)
IMPLEMENT_APP(test2)

bool test2::OnInit()
{
   testclass1* loTestClass;

   return false;
}
```

C++ wxWidgets
Custom Class Instantiation

- The following example creates an instance of the testclass1 class and calls the TestMethod() method:

test3.cpp: C++ wxWidgets Custom Class Instantiation

```
#include "wx/wx.h"
#include "testclass1.h"

class test3 : public wxApp
{
public:
    virtual bool OnInit();
};

DECLARE_APP(test3)
IMPLEMENT_APP(test3)

bool test3::OnInit()
{
   testclass1* loTestClass;

   loTestClass = new testclass1(12345,"Hello World!");
   loTestClass->TestMethod();

   delete loTestClass;
   return false;
}
```

C++ wxWidgets
Cancel Class Instantiation from the Class Initialization Function

- Class instantiation is cancelled from the class constructor by throwing an exception.

testclass2.h: C++ wxWidgets Class Header File for the testclass2 Class

```
#ifndef TESTCLASS2_H
#define TESTCLASS2_H

class testclass2
{
   private:
      // class data
      int nData;
      char *cData;

   public:
      testclass2(int tnData,char *tcData);
      void TestMethod();
};
#endif
```

testclass2.cpp: C++ wxWidgets Cancel Class Instantiation from the Init Function

```
#include "testclass2.h"
#include <exception>

testclass2::testclass2(int tnData,char *tcData)
{
   // C++ code that accesses the wxWidgets library goes here.

   //… Some error has occurred so cancel instantiation by
   // throwing an exception.

   throw "Class not instantiated because of some error.";

   // Program execution never gets here.
   this->nData = tnData;
   this->cData = tcData;
}

void testclass2::TestMethod()
{
   // C++ code goes here.
}
```

- A try/catch block is used to check if an exception has been thrown in the class constructor. If the testclass2 instantiation fails, the loTestClass variable will still store the value zero previously assigned before the class instantiation was attempted.

test4.cpp: C++ wxWidgets Attempt to Instantiate the testclass2 Class

```
#include <exception>
#include "wx/wx.h"
#include "testclass2.h"

class test4 : public wxApp
{
public:
    virtual bool OnInit();
};
```

test4.cpp continued on the next page

test4.cpp: C++ wxWidgets Attempt to Instantiate the testclass2 Class continued

```
DECLARE_APP(test4)
IMPLEMENT_APP(test4)

bool test4::OnInit()
{
   testclass2* loTestClass;
   loTestClass = 0;

   try
   {
      loTestClass = new testclass2(12345,"Hello World!");
   }

   catch (char* lcError)
   {
      // The class failed to instantiate.
      // An error message is stored in the lcError C string.
   }

   if (loTestClass == 0)
   {
      return false;
   }

   loTestClass->TestMethod();

   delete loTestClass;
   return false;
}
```

C++ wxWidgets Message Box Input and Output

- The following example prompts the user to select "Yes" or "No":

test5.cpp: C++ wxWidgets Message Box Input and Output

```
#include "wx/wx.h"

class test5 : public wxApp
{
public:
    virtual bool OnInit();
};

DECLARE_APP(test5)
IMPLEMENT_APP(test5)

bool test5::OnInit()
{
   wxMessageDialog* loMessageBox;
   int lnResult;

   loMessageBox = new wxMessageDialog(NULL,"Select Yes or No.","test",wxYES_NO);

   lnResult = loMessageBox->ShowModal();
   loMessageBox->Destroy();

   if (lnResult == wxID_NO)
   {
      // No selected
   }
```

test5.cpp continued on the next page

test5.cpp: C++ wxWidgets Message Box Input and Output continued

```
   else
   {
      // Yes selected (lnResult = wxID_YES)
   }

   // returning false prevents the event loop from starting.
   return false;
}
```

Source Code Files

- Text files: pp3_16.cpp, myclass.cpp, myclass.h

pp3_16.cpp: Program Phase 3-16 EPE Source Code

```
//*************************************************************************
// Program Phase 3-16 wxWidgets C++ Class Definition/Instantiation        *
// Programming Tasks Illustrated: wxWidgets GUI Based Application         *
//                                Custom Class Definition                  *
//                                Object Variable Declaration              *
//                                Custom Class Instantiation               *
//                                Cancel Instantiation from the Init Funtion *
//                                Message Box Input and Output             *
//*************************************************************************

//*************************************************************************
// File: pp3_16.cpp                                                        *
// Reserved                                                                *
//*************************************************************************

#include "wx/wx.h"
#include "myclass.h"

class pp3_16 : public wxApp
{
public:
    virtual bool OnInit();
};

DECLARE_APP(pp3_16)
IMPLEMENT_APP(pp3_16)


//*************************************************************************
// Program Phase 3-16 Main                                                 *
// Define the Entry Point of Execution (EPE) for Program Phase 3-16       *
// CBI:  3-16.1.1.1                                                        *
//*************************************************************************

bool pp3_16::OnInit()
{


//*************************************************************************
// Program Phase 3-16 Main                                                 *
// Declare the local variables for the "main" program                     *
// CBI:  3-16.1.1.2                                                        *
//*************************************************************************

   myclass* loMyClass;
```

pp3_16.cpp continued on the next page

pp3_16.cpp: Program Phase 3-16 EPE Source Code continued

```
//****************************************************************************
// Program Phase 3-16 Main                                                   *
// Attempt to instantiate the myclass class                                  *
// CBI:  3-16.1.1.3                                                          *
//****************************************************************************

   loMyClass = 0;

   try
   {
      loMyClass = new myclass(12345,"Hello World!");
   }


//****************************************************************************
// Program Phase 3-16 Main                                                   *
// If the myclass class fails to instantiate, notify the user and exit       *
// CBI:  3-16.1.1.4                                                          *
//****************************************************************************

   catch (char* lcError)
   {
      wxMessageBox(wxT(lcError),wxT("myclass"),
                   wxOK | wxICON_ERROR,NULL);
   }

   if (loMyClass == 0)
   {
      return false;
   }

//****************************************************************************
// Program Phase 3-16 Main                                                   *
// If the myclass class instantiated, call an instance method                *
// CBI:  3-16.1.1.5                                                          *
//****************************************************************************

   loMyClass->DisplayInstanceData();
   delete loMyClass;
   return false;
}
```

- myclass.h

myclass.h: Class Definition for the myclass Class

```
//****************************************************************************
// myclass.h                                                                 *
// Reserved                                                                  *
//****************************************************************************


//****************************************************************************
// myclass definition                                                        *
// Class definition for the myclass class                                    *
// CBI:  3-16.2.1.1                                                          *
//****************************************************************************

#ifndef MYCLASS_H
#define MYCLASS_H

class myclass
{
```

myclass.h continued on the next page

myclass.h: Class Definition for the myclass Class continued

```
   private:
      // class data
      int nData;
      char *cData;

   public:
      myclass(int tnData,char *tcData);
      void DisplayInstanceData();
};
#endif
```

- myclass.cpp

myclass.cpp: Class Implementation for the myclass Class

```
//*****************************************************************************
// myclass.cpp                                                                *
// Reserved                                                                   *
//*****************************************************************************

#include <exception>
#include "wx/wx.h"
#include "myclass.h"


//*****************************************************************************
// myclass implementation                                                     *
// Class implementation for the myclass class                                 *
// CBI:  3-16.2.2.1                                                           *
//*****************************************************************************

// The myclass class methods are implemented in CBI: 3-16.2.3.1 and
// CBI: 3-16.2.4.1


//*****************************************************************************
// myclass implementation                                                     *
// Implement the initialization function for the myclass class                *
// CBI:  3-16.2.3.1                                                           *
//*****************************************************************************

myclass::myclass(int tnData,char *tcData)
{


//*****************************************************************************
// myclass implementation                                                     *
// Declare the local variables for the myclass initialization function        *
// CBI:  3-16.2.3.2                                                           *
//*****************************************************************************

   wxMessageDialog* loMessageBox;
   int lnResult;


//*****************************************************************************
// myclass implementation                                                     *
// Prompt the user to continue instantiating the myclass class                *
// CBI:  3-16.2.3.3                                                           *
//*****************************************************************************

   loMessageBox = new wxMessageDialog(NULL,"Proceed with class instantiation?",
                                      "myclass",wxYES_NO);

   lnResult = loMessageBox->ShowModal();
```

myclass.cpp continued on the next page

myclass.cpp: Class Implementation for the myclass Class continued

```
   loMessageBox->Destroy();

//****************************************************************************
// myclass implementation                                                    *
// Cancel instantiation of the myclass class if the user selects no          *
// CBI:  3-16.2.3.4                                                           *
//****************************************************************************

   if (lnResult == wxID_NO)
   {
      throw "Class not instantiated.";
   }


//****************************************************************************
// myclass implementation                                                    *
// Store the parameters to the initialization function as instance data      *
// CBI:  3-16.2.3.5                                                           *
//****************************************************************************

   this->nData = tnData;
   this->cData = tcData;
}


//****************************************************************************
// myclass implementation                                                    *
// Implement the DisplayInstanceData method of the myclass class             *
// CBI:  3-16.2.4.1                                                           *
//****************************************************************************

void myclass::DisplayInstanceData()
{
   wxString lcString;

   lcString.Printf(wxT("nData: %d\ncData: %s"),this->nData,this->cData);

   wxMessageBox(lcString,wxT("myclass instance data"),
                wxOK | wxICON_INFORMATION,NULL);
}
```

Windows – Code Setup and Compilation

- Tools: Microsoft Visual Studio 2008 Express Edition (msdn.microsoft.com), wxWidgets library (Appendix D)

Windows Code Setup and Compilation Steps

1: Start the Visual C++ 2008 Express Edition program.

2: VC++ EE - Activate Menu Item: File → New → Project

For the "Project type", select "Win32" and then select the "Win32 Console Application" template. Enter pp3_16 as the project "Name". Enter the appropriate folder as the "Project Location". Make sure that the "Create directory for solution" check box is not checked. Activate the "OK" button to proceed with the "Win32 Application Wizard".

3: Activate the "Next" button of the Win32 Application Wizard.

Steps continued on the next page

Windows Code Setup and Compilation Steps continued

4: Verify that a "Console Application" is selected and also check the "Empty project" check box. Activate the "Finish" button of the "Win32 Application Wizard".

5: VC++ EE - Activate Menu Item: Project → Add New Item

On the "Add New Item" dialog window, select the "Visual C++ → Code" category and then select the "C++ File" template. Enter pp3_16.cpp for the file "Name" and then activate the "Add" button.

6: Enter the source code for the pp3_16.cpp file.

7: VC++ EE - Activate Menu Item: Project → Add New Item

On the "Add New Item" dialog window, select the "Visual C++ → Code" category and then select the "Header File" template. Enter myclass.h for the file name and then activate the "Add" button.

8: Enter the source code for the myclass.h file.

9: VC++ EE - Activate Menu Item: Project → Add New Item

On the "Add New Item" dialog window, select the "Visual C++ -> Code" category and then select the "C++ File" template. Enter myclass.cpp for the file name and then activate the "Add" button.

10: Enter the source code for the myclass.cpp file.

11: VC++ EE - Activate Menu Item: Build → Configuration Manager

Select "Release" or "Debug" for the "Active solution configuration". This setting needs to match the setting specified when the wxWidgets library was compiled (Appendix D).

12: VC++ EE - Activate Menu Item: Project → pp3_16 Properties

Enter the following settings:

Configuration Properties → General → Character Set

For ANSI Configuration:

```
"Use Multi-Byte Character Set"
```

For Unicode Configuration:

```
"Use Unicode Character Set"
```

This setting needs to match the setting specified when the wxWidgets library was compiled (Appendix D).

Configuration Properties → C/C++ → General → Additional Include Directories

```
"$(wxwin)\lib\vc_lib\msw";"$(wxwin)\include"
```

Configuration Properties → C/C++ → Preprocessor → Processor Definitions

For Release Configuration: `WIN32;__WXMSW__;_WINDOWS;NOPCH`

For Debug Configuration: `WIN32;__WXMSW__;_WINDOWS;__WXDEBUG__;NOPCH`

Steps continued on the next page

Windows Code Setup and Compilation Steps continued

13: Continue entering settings on the "pp3_16 Property Pages" window.

Configuration Properties → C/C++ → Code Generation → Runtime Library

For Release Configuration:

```
Multi-threaded (/MT) or Multi-threaded DLL (/MD)
```

For Debug Configuration:

```
Multi-threaded Debug /MTd or Multi-threaded Debug DLL (/MDd)
```

This setting needs to match the setting specified when the wxWidgets library was compiled (Appendix D).

Configuration Properties → Linker → General → Additional Library Directories

```
"$(wxwin)\lib\vc_lib"
```

Configuration Properties → Linker → Input → Additional Dependencies

For Release Configuration:

```
wxmsw28_core.lib wxbase28.lib comctl32.lib rpcrt4.lib
```

For Debug Configuration:

```
wxmsw28d_core.lib wxbase28d.lib comctl32.lib rpcrt4.lib
```

Substitute the appropriate version number in the file name to match the version of the wxWidgets library installed on your computer.

Configuration Properties → Linker → System → SubSystem

```
Windows (/SUBSYSTEM:WINDOWS)
```

14: Close the "pp3_16 Property Pages" by activating the "OK" button.

15: VC++ EE - Activate Menu Item: Build → Build pp3_16

Windows Command Prompt Compilation Steps

1: From a Visual Studio 2008 command prompt, enter the following command:

For Release Configuration:

```
cl.exe /I "C:\Program Files\Microsoft SDK's\Windows\v6.0A\Include"
  /I "c:\wxWidgets-2.8.6\lib\vc_lib\msw"
  /I "c:\wxWidgets-2.8.6\include"
  /D "WIN32"
  /D "__WXMSW__"
  /D "_WINDOWS"
  /MT
  /Fo"Release\\"
  /EHsc
  /c pp3_16.cpp myclass.cpp
```

Steps continued on the next page

Windows Command Prompt Compilation Steps continued

For Debug Configuration:

```
cl.exe /I "C:\Program Files\Microsoft SDK's\Windows\v6.0A\Include"
  /I "c:\wxWidgets-2.8.6\lib\vc_lib\msw"
  /I "c:\wxWidgets-2.8.6\include"
  /D "WIN32"
  /D "__WXMSW__"
  /D "__WXDEBUG__"
  /D "_WINDOWS"
  /MTd /Fo"Debug\\" /EHsc /c pp3_16.cpp myclass.cpp
```

The preceding commands need to be entered on a single line.

2: Run the linker to create the pp3_16.exe file from the pp3_16.obj file.

For Release Configuration:

```
link.exe /OUT:"pp3_16.exe"
/INCREMENTAL:NO
/LIBPATH:"c:\wxWidgets-2.8.6\lib\vc_lib"
/LIBPATH:"C:\Program Files\Microsoft SDK's\Windows\v6.0A\Lib"
/SUBSYSTEM:WINDOWS
wxmsw28_core.lib wxbase28.lib winmm.lib comctl32.lib rpcrt4.lib
wsock32.lib oleacc.lib  kernel32.lib user32.lib gdi32.lib winspool.lib
comdlg32.lib advapi32.lib shell32.lib ole32.lib oleaut32.lib uuid.lib
.\release\pp3_16.obj .\release\myclass.obj
```

For Debug Configuration:

```
link.exe /OUT:"pp3_16.exe"
/INCREMENTAL:NO
/LIBPATH:"c:\wxWidgets-2.8.6\lib\vc_lib"
//LIBPATH:"C:\Program Files\Microsoft SDK's\Windows\v6.0A\Lib"
/SUBSYSTEM:WINDOWS
wxmsw28d_core.lib wxbase28d.lib winmm.lib comctl32.lib rpcrt4.lib
wsock32.lib oleacc.lib  kernel32.lib user32.lib gdi32.lib winspool.lib
comdlg32.lib advapi32.lib shell32.lib ole32.lib oleaut32.lib uuid.lib
.\debug\pp3_16.obj .\debug\myclass.obj
```

Linux – Code Setup and Compilation

- Tools: GNU GCC, KDevelop (Appendix B), wxWidgets library (Appendix D)

Linux Code Setup and Compilation Steps

1: Update the LD_LIBRARY_PATH variable and then start the KDevelop program.

```
export LD_LIBRARY_PATH=/usr/local/lib:$LD_LIBRARY_PATH
kdevelop &
```

2: KDevelop - Activate Menu Item: Project → New Project

Select the "C++ → Simple Hello world program" template. Set the "Application name" to pp3_16. Set the "Location" to the appropriate folder. Activate the "Next" button four times and then activate the "Finish" button.

3: KDevelop - Activate Menu Item: Project → Build Configuration → debug

Steps continued on the next page

Linux Code Setup and Compilation Steps continued

4: Enter the source code for the pp3_16.cpp file. Replace any existing code in the file.

5: KDevelop - Activate Menu Item: File → New

Select the "Blank File" template and name the file myclass.h. Verify that the "Add to project" check box is checked and then activate the "OK" button.

6: Enter the source code for the myclass class definition in the myclass.h file.

7: KDevelop - Activate Menu Item: File → New

Select the "Blank File" template and name the file myclass.cpp. Verify that the "Add to project" check box is checked and then activate the "OK" button.

8: Enter the source code for the myclass class implementation in the myclass.cpp file.

9: Before the source code files are compiled, additional settings for accessing the wxWidgets library need to be entered into the KDevelop project. From a terminal window, enter the following:

For Release Configuration:

```
   wx-config --unicode=no --debug=no --static=yes --cxxflags >
cxxresults.txt
```

For Debug Configuration:

```
   wx-config --unicode=no --debug=yes --static=yes --cxxflags >
cxxresults.txt
```

10: Next, run this command:

For Release Configuration:

```
wx-config --unicode=no --debug=no --static=yes --libs > libresults.txt
```

For Debug Configuration:

```
wx-config --unicode=no --debug=yes --static=yes --libs > libresults.txt
```

11: Click on the "Configure Options" item on the left pane. Select the "debug" configuration. Click on the "C++" tab. Here you will see the "Compiler flags" text box. The results of running the wx-config utility stored in the cxxresults.txt file must be copied and pasted here. Next, click on the "General" tab and paste the contents of the libresults.txt file in the "Linker flags" text box. You may be prompted to "Re-run configure". Select the "Do Not Run" button.

12: KDevelop - Activate Menu Item: Build → Run automake and friends

13: KDevelop - Activate Menu Item: Build → Run Configure

14: KDevelop - Activate Menu Item: Build → Build Project

If you get a message concerning no Makefile, activate the "Run Them" button.

Linux Command Prompt Compilation

For Release Configuration:

```
g++ pp3_16.cpp myclass.cpp `wx-config --unicode=no --debug=no --static=yes
--libs` `wx-config --unicode=no --debug=no --static=yes --cxxflags` -o
pp3_16
```

For Debug Configuration:

```
g++ pp3_16.cpp myclass.cpp `wx-config --unicode=no --debug=yes --
static=yes --libs` `wx-config --unicode=no --debug=yes --static=yes --
cxxflags` -o pp3_16
```

The preceding commands should be entered on a single line inside the source code folder (pp3_16/src). The command line settings need to match the settings specified when the wxWidgets library was compiled (Appendix D).

- Mac OS X code setup and compilation steps can be found at the following URL:

  `http://www.wxwidgets.org/wiki/index.php/Getting_started_on_OS_X`

Windows – Program Execution

- Execute Program

  `VC++ EE - Activate Menu Item: Debug → Start Without Debugging`

- Debug Program

  Set the "Generate Debug Info" entry in the "pp3_16 Property Pages" to "Yes". This setting is found under the "Configuration Properties → Linker → Debugging" item. After this has been set, the program can be debugged.

  `VC++ EE - Activate Menu Item: Debug → Step Into`

Linux – Program Execution

- Execute Program

  `KDevelop - Activate Menu Item: Build → Execute Program`

- Debug Program

  `KDevelop - Activate Menu Item: Project → Project Options`

  Click on the "Configure Options" item. Select the debug "Configuration" and then enter "--enable-debug=full" in the "Configure arguments" field on the "General" tab. Close the "Project Options" dialog window.

  Select the debug configuration for the project.

  `KDevelop - Activate Menu Item: Project → Build Configuration → debug`

  Set the cursor position in the source file to the first line of code in the CBI: 3-16.1.1.3 code block. Create a breakpoint.

  ```
  KDevelop - Activate Menu Item: Debug → Toggle Breakpoint
  KDevelop - Activate Menu Item: Debug → Start
  ```

Program Phase 3-17
C++ ▪ Carbon ▪ Mac OS X

GUI Based Program with Custom Class Definition and Instantiation

- Program Phase Task 3 is implemented in Program Phase 3-17 using the C++ programming language and the Carbon API.
- The Carbon StandardAlert() function is used in Program Phase 3-17 to implement input and output for a GUI based application.
- The Entry Point of Execution (EPE) is stored in the pp3_17.cpp text file. The myclass class is defined in the myclass.h text file and implemented in the myclass.cpp text file.

Code Block Features

The Program Phase 3-17 code blocks illustrate the following programming features using the C++ programming language and the Carbon API:

- **GUI Application**
- **Custom Class Definition**
- **Object Variable Declaration**
- **Custom Class Instantiation**
- **Cancel Class Instantiation from the Class Initialization Function**
- **Message Box Input and Output**

C++ with Carbon
GUI Application

- The Carbon.h header file provides access to the Carbon data types and functions used in Program Phase 3-17.

test1.cpp: C++ with Carbon GUI Application

```
#include <Carbon/Carbon.h>

int main(int argc, char* argv[])
{
   // C/C++ code that accesss the Carbon API goes here.
}
```

C++ with Carbon
Custom Class Definition

- The testclass1 class is defined in the testclass1.h file.

testclass1.h: C++ with Carbon Custom Class Definition

```
#ifndef TESTCLASS1_H
#define TESTCLASS1_H

class testclass1
{
   private:

      // class data
      int nData;
      char *cData;

   public:

      testclass1(int tnData,char *tcData);
      void TestMethod();
};

#endif
```

- The testclass1 class is implemented in the testclass1.cpp file.

testclass1.cpp: C++ with Carbon Custom Class Implementation

```
#include "testclass1.h"

testclass1::testclass1(int tnData,char *tcData)
{
   this->nData = tnData;
   this->cData = tcData;
}

void testclass1::TestMethod()
{
   // C/C++ code goes here.
}
```

C++ with Carbon Object Variable Declaration

- A testclass1 typed pointer variable can store a pointer to an instance of the testclass1 class. Access to the testclass1 class is necessary when the object variable is declared.

- The testclass1 class is accessible in the test2.cpp program because the class header stored in the testclass1.h file is included at the top of the file.

test2.cpp: C++ with Carbon Object Variable Declaration

```
#include <Carbon/Carbon.h>
#include "testclass1.h"

int main(int argc, char* argv[])
{
   testclass1* loTestClass;
   return 0;
}
```

C++ with Carbon
Custom Class Instantiation

- The following example creates an instance of the testclass1 class and calls the TestMethod() method:

test3.cpp: C++ with Carbon Custom Class Instantiation

```
#include <Carbon/Carbon.h>
#include "testclass1.h"

int main(int argc, char* argv[])
{
   testclass1* loTestClass;

   loTestClass = 0;
   loTestClass = new testclass1(12345,"Hello World!");
   loTestClass->TestMethod();

   delete loTestClass;

   return 0;
}
```

C++ with Carbon
Cancel Class Instantiation from the Class Initialization Function

- Class instantiation is cancelled by throwing an exception from the class constructor.

testclass2.h: Class Header File for the testclass2 Class

```
#ifndef TESTCLASS2_H
#define TESTCLASS2_H

#include <Carbon/Carbon.h>
#include <iostream>

class testclass2
{
   private:

      // class data
      int nData;
      char *cData;

   public:

      testclass2(int tnData,char *tcData);
      void TestMethod();
};
#endif
```

testclass2.cpp: C++ w/ Carbon Cancel Class Instantiation from the Init Function

```
#include <Carbon/Carbon.h>
#include "testclass2.h"
#include <exception>

using namespace std;
```

testclass2.cpp continued on the next page

testclass2.cpp: C++ w/ Carbon Cancel Class Instantiation from Init Func continued

```
class myexception : public exception
{
  virtual const char* what() const throw()
  {
    return "Class not instantiated because of some error.";
  }
} goException;


testclass2::testclass2(int tnData,char *tcData)
{
   // C++ code goes here.

   //… Some error has occurred so cancel instantiation by
   // throwing an exception.

   throw goException;

   // Program execution never gets here.
   this->nData = tnData;
   this->cData = tcData;
}

void testclass2::TestMethod()
{
   // C/C++ code goes here.
}
```

- A try/catch block is used to check if an exception has been thrown in the class constructor. If the testclass2 instantiation fails, the loTestClass variable will still store the value zero previously assigned before the class instantiation was attempted.

test4.cpp: C++ w/ Carbon Attempt to Instantiate the testclass2 Class

```
#include <Carbon/Carbon.h>
#include "testclass2.h"
using namespace std;

int main(int argc, char* argv[])
{
   testclass2* loTestClass;

   try
   {
      loTestClass = new testclass2(12345,"Hello World!");
   }
   catch (exception& loException)
   {
      // The class failed to instantiate.
      // An error message can be retrieved by calling loException.what().
   }

   if (loTestClass == 0)
   {
      return 1;
   }

   loTestClass->TestMethod();
   delete loTestClass;
   return 0;
}
```

C++ with Carbon Message Box Input and Output

- The following example prompts the user to select "Yes" or "No":

test5.cpp: C++ with Carbon Message Box Input and Output

```
#include <Carbon/Carbon.h>

int main(int argc, char* argv[])
{
   short lnResult;
   AlertStdAlertParamRec loMessageBoxRec = {};

   loMessageBoxRec.defaultText = "\pYes";
   loMessageBoxRec.cancelText = "\pNo";
   loMessageBoxRec.defaultButton = kStdOkItemIndex;
   loMessageBoxRec.cancelButton = kStdCancelItemIndex;
   loMessageBoxRec.position = kWindowAlertPositionParentWindowScreen;

   StandardAlert(kAlertPlainAlert,
                 "\ptest",
                 "\pSelect Yes or No.",
                 &loMessageBoxRec,
                 &lnResult);

   if (lnResult = kAlertStdAlertCancelButton)
   {
      // No Selected
   }
   else
   {
      // Yes Selected (lnResult = kAlertStdAlertOKButton)
   }
}
```

Source Code Files

- Text files: pp3_17.cpp, myclass.h, myclass.cpp

pp3_17.cpp: Program Phase 3-17 EPE Source Code

```
//******************************************************************************
// Program Phase 3-17 C++ Class Definition/Instantiation                       *
// Programming Tasks Illustrated: Carbon GUI Based Application                 *
//                                Custom Class Definition                      *
//                                Object Variable Declaration                  *
//                                Custom Class Instantiation                   *
//                                Cancel Instantiation from the Init Funtion   *
//                                Message Box Input and Output                 *
//******************************************************************************

//******************************************************************************
// File: pp3_17.cpp                                                            *
// Reserved                                                                    *
//******************************************************************************

#include <Carbon/Carbon.h>
#include "myclass.h"

using namespace std;
```

pp3_17.cpp continued on the next page

pp3_17.cpp: Program Phase 3-17 EPE Source Code continued

```
//*************************************************************************
// Program Phase 3-17 Main                                                *
// Define the Entry Point of Execution (EPE) for Program Phase 3-17       *
// CBI:  3-17.1.1.1                                                       *
//*************************************************************************

int main(int tnArgc, char* taArgv[])
{


//*************************************************************************
// Program Phase 3-17 Main                                                *
// Declare the local variables for the "main" program                     *
// CBI:  3-17.1.1.2                                                       *
//*************************************************************************

   myclass* loMyClass;
   short lnResult;
   AlertStdAlertParamRec loMessageBoxRec = {};
   Str255 lcString;


//*************************************************************************
// Program Phase 3-17 Main                                                *
// Attempt to instantiate the myclass class                               *
// CBI:  3-17.1.1.3                                                       *
//*************************************************************************

   loMyClass = 0;

   try
   {
      loMyClass = new myclass(12345,CFSTR("Hello World!"));
   }


//*************************************************************************
// Program Phase 3-17 Main                                                *
// If the myclass class fails to instantiate, notify the user and exit    *
// CBI:  3-17.1.1.4                                                       *
//*************************************************************************

   catch (exception& loException)
   {
      loMessageBoxRec.defaultText = "\pOK";
      loMessageBoxRec.cancelText = nil;
      loMessageBoxRec.defaultButton = kStdOkItemIndex;
      loMessageBoxRec.position = kWindowAlertPositionParentWindowScreen;
      CopyCStringToPascal(loException.what(),lcString);

      StandardAlert(kAlertCautionAlert,"\pProgram Phase 3-17",
                    lcString,&loMessageBoxRec,&lnResult);
   }

   if (loMyClass == 0)
   {
      return 1;
   }


//*************************************************************************
// Program Phase 3-17 Main                                                *
// If the myclass class instantiated, call an instance method             *
// CBI:  3-17.1.1.5                                                       *
//*************************************************************************
```

pp3_17.cpp continued on the next page

pp3_17.cpp: Program Phase 3-17 EPE Source Code continued

```
   loMyClass->DisplayInstanceData();

   delete loMyClass;
   return 0;
}
```

- myclass.h

myclass.h: Class Definition for the myclass Class

```
//****************************************************************************
// myclass.h                                                                *
// Reserved                                                                 *
//****************************************************************************

#include <Carbon/Carbon.h>
#include <iostream>
using namespace std;


//****************************************************************************
// myclass definition                                                       *
// Class definition for the myclass class                                   *
// CBI:  3-17.2.1.1                                                         *
//****************************************************************************

class myclass
{
   private:

      // class data
      int nData;
      CFStringRef cData;

   public:

     myclass(int tnData,CFStringRef tcData);
     void DisplayInstanceData();
};
```

- myclasss.cpp

myclass.cpp: Class Implementation for the myclass Class

```
//****************************************************************************
// myclass.cpp                                                              *
// Reserved                                                                 *
//****************************************************************************

#include <Carbon/Carbon.h>
#include "myclass.h"
#include <exception>

using namespace std;

class myexception : public exception
{
  virtual const char* what() const throw()
  {
    return "Class not instantiated.";
  }
} goException;
```

myclass.cpp continued on the next page

myclass.cpp: Class Implementation for the myclass Class continued

```
//****************************************************************************
// myclass implementation                                                    *
// Class implementation for the myclass class                                *
// CBI:  3-17.2.2.1                                                          *
//****************************************************************************

// The myclass class methods are implemented in CBI: 3-17.2.3.1 and
// CBI: 3-17.2.4.1


//****************************************************************************
// myclass implementation                                                    *
// Implement the initialization function for the myclass class               *
// CBI:  3-17.2.3.1                                                          *
//****************************************************************************

myclass::myclass(int tnData,CFStringRef tcData)
{


//****************************************************************************
// myclass implementation                                                    *
// Declare the local variables for the myclass initialization function       *
// CBI:  3-17.2.3.2                                                          *
//****************************************************************************

   short lnResult;
   AlertStdAlertParamRec loMessageBoxRec = {};


//****************************************************************************
// myclass implementation                                                    *
// Prompt the user to continue instantiating the myclass class               *
// CBI:  3-17.2.3.3                                                          *
//****************************************************************************

   loMessageBoxRec.defaultText = "\pYes";
   loMessageBoxRec.cancelText = "\pNo";
   loMessageBoxRec.defaultButton = kStdOkItemIndex;
   loMessageBoxRec.cancelButton = kStdCancelItemIndex;
   loMessageBoxRec.position = kWindowAlertPositionParentWindowScreen;

   StandardAlert(kAlertPlainAlert,"\pmyclass instance",
              "\pProceed with class instantiation?",
              &loMessageBoxRec,&lnResult);


//****************************************************************************
// myclass implementation                                                    *
// Cancel instantiation of the myclass class if the user selects no          *
// CBI:  3-17.2.3.4                                                          *
//****************************************************************************

   if (lnResult != kAlertStdAlertOKButton)
   {
      throw goException;
   }


//****************************************************************************
// myclass implementation                                                    *
// Store the parameters to the initialization function as instance data      *
// CBI:  3-17.2.3.5                                                          *
//****************************************************************************

   this->nData = tnData;
```

myclass.cpp continued on the next page

myclass.cpp: Class Implementation for the myclass Class continued

```
   this->cData = tcData;
}

//*****************************************************************************
// myclass implementation                                                      *
// Implement the DisplayInstanceData method of the myclass class             *
// CBI:  3-17.2.4.1                                                            *
//*****************************************************************************

void myclass::DisplayInstanceData()
{
   short lnResult;
   AlertStdAlertParamRec loMessageBoxRec = {};
   CFStringRef lcString1;
   Str255 lcString2;
   Boolean llResult;

   loMessageBoxRec.defaultText = "\pOK";
   loMessageBoxRec.cancelText = nil;
   loMessageBoxRec.defaultButton = kStdOkItemIndex;
   loMessageBoxRec.position = kWindowAlertPositionParentWindowScreen;

   lcString1 = CFStringCreateWithFormat(NULL,NULL,
                                    CFSTR("nData: %d \ncData: %@"),
                                    this->nData,this->cData);

   llResult = CFStringGetPascalString(lcString1,lcString2,256,
                                    kCFStringEncodingMacRoman);

   StandardAlert(kAlertNoteAlert,"\pmyclass instance data",
                 lcString2,&loMessageBoxRec,&lnResult);
}
```

Code Setup and Compilation

- Tools: Xcode (Appendix C), Carbon API

Code Setup and Compilation Steps

1: Start the Xcode program.

2: Xcode - Activate Menu Item: File → New Project

Select "Application → Carbon Application" and then activate the "Next" button.

3: Set the "Project Name" to pp3_17 and set the "Project Directory" to the appropriate folder. Activate the "Finish" button.

4: Delete the main.c and main.nib files that have been automatically added to the project.

5: Xcode - Activate Menu Item: File → New File

Select "Empty File in Project" and then activate the "Next" button. Set the "File name" to pp3_17.cpp and the "Location" to the pp3_17 folder and then activate the "Finish" button.

6: Enter the source code for the pp3_17.cpp file and then save the file.

Steps continued on the next page

```
Code Setup and Compilation Steps continued
```

7: Xcode - Activate Menu Item: File → New File

Select "Empty File in Project" and then activate the "Next" button. Set the "File name" to myclass.h and the "Location" to the pp3_17 folder and then activate the "Finish" button.

8: Enter the source code for the myclass.h file and then save the file.

9: Xcode - Activate Menu Item: File → New File

Select "Empty File in Project" and then activate the "Next" button. Set the "File name" to myclass.cpp and the "Location" to the pp3_17 folder and then activate the "Finish" button.

10: Enter the source code for the myclass.cpp file and then save the file.

11: Compile the program by activating the "Build" button.

```
Command Prompt Compilation
```

Enter the following in the pp3_17 folder:

```
xcodebuild
```

Program Execution

- Execute Program

To execute the pp3_17 program, activate the "Build/Go" button in the Xcode IDE.

- Debug Program

Place the cursor in the CBI: 3-17.1.1.3 code block and then activate the following menu items:

```
   Xcode 2.4 - Activate Menu Item: Debug → Add Breakpoint at Current Line
   Xcode 3 - Activate Menu Item: Run → Manage Breakpoints → Add
Breakpoint at Current Line

   Xcode - Activate Menu Item: Build → Build and Debug
```

Objective-C ▪ Cocoa ▪ Mac OS X

GUI Based Program with Custom Class Definition and Instantiation

- Program Phase Task 3 is implemented in Program Phase 3-18 using the Objective-C programming language and the Cocoa Foundation framework.
- The NSRunAlert() function is used in Program Phase 3-18 to implement input and output for a GUI based application.
- The Entry Point of Execution (EPE) is stored in the pp3_18.m text file. The myclass class is defined in the myclass.h text file and implemented in the myclass.m text file.

Code Block Features

The Program Phase 3-18 code blocks illustrate the following programming features using the Objective-C programming language and the Cocoa Foundation framework:

- **GUI Application**
- **Custom Class Definition**
- **Object Variable Declaration**
- **Custom Class Instantiation**
- **Cancel Class Instantiation from the Class Initialization Function**
- **Message Box Input and Output**

Objective-C with Cocoa
GUI Application

- Every Appkit application needs to have a single instance of the NSApplication class. The NSApplication class manages the event loop and resources for the application.

test1.m: Objective-C with Cocoa GUI Application

```
#import <Foundation/Foundation.h>

int main(int argc, char* argv[])
{
   NSAutoreleasePool * loPool = [[NSAutoreleasePool alloc] init];
   NSApp = [[NSApplication alloc] init];

   // Objective-C code goes here.

   [NSApp release];
   [loPool release];
   return 0;
}
```

Objective-C with Cocoa
Custom Class Definition

- The testclass1 class is defined in the testclass1.h file.

testclass1.h: Objective-C with Cocoa Custom Class Definition

```
#import <Cocoa/Cocoa.h>

@interface testclass1 : NSObject
{
  // testclass1 data
  int nData;
  NSString *cData;
}

-(id)init:(int)tnData :(NSString *)tcData;
-(void)TestMethod;

@end
```

- The testclass1 class is implemented in the testclass1.cpp file.

testclass1.m: Objective-C Custom Class Implementation

```
#import "testclass1.h"

@implementation testclass1

-(id)init:(int)tnData :(NSString *)tcData
{
   [super init];

   nData = tnData;
   cData = tcData;

   return self;
}

-(void)TestMethod
{
   // Objective-C code goes here.
}
@end
```

Objective-C with Cocoa
Object Variable Declaration

- A testclass1 typed pointer variable can store a pointer to an instance of the testclass1 class. Access to the testclass1 class is necessary when the object variable is declared.

- The testclass1 class is accessible in the test2.cpp program because the class header stored in the testclass1.h file is included at the top of the file.

test2.m: Objective-C with Cocoa Object Variable Declaration

```
#import <Foundation/Foundation.h>
#import "testclass1.h"

int main(int argc, char* argv[])
{
   NSAutoreleasePool * loPool = [[NSAutoreleasePool alloc] init];
   NSApp = [[NSApplication alloc] init];

   testclass1* loTestClass;

   [NSApp release];
   [loPool release];
   return 0;
}
```

Objective-C with Cocoa
Custom Class Instantiation

- The following example creates an instance of the testclass1 class and calls the TestMethod() method:

test3.m: Objective-C with Cocoa Custom Class Instantiation

```
#import <Foundation/Foundation.h>
#import "testclass1.h"

int main(int argc, char* argv[])
{
   NSAutoreleasePool * loPool = [[NSAutoreleasePool alloc] init];
   NSApp = [[NSApplication alloc] init];

   testclass1* loTestClass;
   loTestClass = [[testclass1 alloc] init:12345 :@"Hello World!"];

   [NSApp release];
   [loPool release];
   return 0;
}
```

Objective-C with Cocoa
Cancel Class Instantiation from the Class Initialization Function

- Class instantiation is cancelled by returning the "nil" value from the class constructor.

testclass2.h: Class Header File for the testclass2 Class

```
#import <Cocoa/Cocoa.h>

@interface testclass2 : NSObject
{
  // testclass2 data
  int nData;
  NSString *cData;
}

-(id)init:(int)tnData :(NSString *)tcData;
-(void)TestMethod;

@end
```

testclass2.m: Obj-C w/ Cocoa Cancel Class Instantiation from the Init Function

```
#import "testclass2.h"

@implementation testclass2

-(id)init:(int)tnData :(NSString *)tcData
{
   // Objective-C code goes here.

   //… Some error has occurred so cancel instantiation by
   // returning the nil value.

   return nil;

   // Program execution never gets here.
   [super init];

   nData = tnData;
   cData = tcData;
   return self;
}

-(void)TestMethod
{
   // Objective-C code goes here.
}
@end
```

- If the testclass2 instantiation fails, the loTestClass variable will still store the "nil" value previously assigned before the class instantiation was attempted.

test4.m: Objective-C with Cocoa Attempt to Instantiate the testclass2 Class

```
#import <Foundation/Foundation.h>
#import "testclass2.h"

int main(int argc, char* argv[])
{
   NSAutoreleasePool * loPool = [[NSAutoreleasePool alloc] init];
   NSApp = [[NSApplication alloc] init];

   testclass2* loTestClass;
   loTestClass = nil;

   loTestClass = [[testclass2 alloc] init:12345 :@"Hello World!"];

   if (loTestClass == nil)
   {
      // The class failed to instantiate.
      return 1;
   }

   [loTestClass TestMethod];

   [NSApp release];
   [loPool release];
   return 0;
}
```

Objective-C with Cocoa
Message Box Input and Output

- The following example prompts the user to select "Yes" or "No":

test5.m: Objective-C with Cocoa Message Box Input and Output

```
#import <Foundation/Foundation.h>

int main(int argc, char* argv[])
{
   NSAutoreleasePool * loPool = [[NSAutoreleasePool alloc] init];
   NSApp = [[NSApplication alloc] init];

   int lnResult;

   lnResult = NSRunAlertPanel(@"test",@"Select Yes or No.",
                              @"No",@"Yes",nil,NULL);

   if (lnResult == NSAlertDefaultReturn)
   {
      // Yes Selected
   }
   else
   {
      // No Selected (lnResult = NSAlertAlternateReturn)
   }

   [NSApp release];
   [loPool release];
   return 0;
}
```

Source Code Files

- Text files: pp3_18.m, myclass.h, myclass.m

pp3_18.m: Program Phase 3-18 EPE Source Code

```
//*************************************************************************
// Program Phase 3-18 Objective-C Class Definition/Instantiation         *
// Programming Tasks Illustrated: Cocoa GUI Based Application            *
//                                Custom Class Definition                *
//                                Object Variable Declaration            *
//                                Custom Class Instantiation             *
//                                Cancel Instantiation from the Init Funtion  *
//                                Message Box Input and Output           *
//*************************************************************************

//*************************************************************************
// File: pp3_18.m                                                         *
// Reserved                                                               *
//*************************************************************************

#import <Cocoa/Cocoa.h>
#import "myclass.h"


//*************************************************************************
// Program Phase 3-18 Main                                                *
// Define the Entry Point of Execution (EPE) for Program Phase 3-18       *
// CBI:  3-18.1.1.1                                                       *
//*************************************************************************

int main(int argc, char *argv[])
{
   NSAutoreleasePool * loPool = [[NSAutoreleasePool alloc] init];
   NSApp = [[NSApplication alloc] init];
```

pp3_18.m continued on the next page

pp3_18.m: Program Phase 3-18 EPE Source Code continued

```
//***************************************************************************
// Program Phase 3-18 Main                                                  *
// Declare the local variables for the "main" program                       *
// CBI:  3-18.1.1.2                                                         *
//***************************************************************************

   myclass * loMyClass;


//***************************************************************************
// Program Phase 3-18 Main                                                  *
// Attempt to instantiate the myclass class                                 *
// CBI:  3-18.1.1.3                                                         *
//***************************************************************************

   loMyClass = [[myclass alloc] init:12345 :@"Hello World!"];


//***************************************************************************
// Program Phase 3-18 Main                                                  *
// If the myclass class fails to instantiate, notify the user and exit      *
// CBI:  3-18.1.1.4                                                         *
//***************************************************************************

   if (loMyClass == nil)
   {
      NSRunCriticalAlertPanel(@"myclass",@"Class not instantiated.",
                              @"OK",nil,nil);
      [loPool release];
      return 1;
   }


//***************************************************************************
// Program Phase 3-18 Main                                                  *
// If the myclass class instantiated, call an instance method               *
// CBI:  3-18.1.1.5                                                         *
//***************************************************************************

   [loMyClass DisplayInstanceData];

   [NSApp release];
   [loPool release];
   return 0;
}
```

- myclass.h

myclass.h: Class Definition for the myclass Class

```
//***************************************************************************
// myclass.h                                                                *
// Reserved                                                                 *
//***************************************************************************

#import <Cocoa/Cocoa.h>


//***************************************************************************
// myclass definition                                                       *
// Class definition for the myclass class                                   *
// CBI:  3-18.2.1.1                                                         *
//***************************************************************************
```

myclass.h continued on the next page

myclass.h: Class Definition for the myclass Class continued

```
@interface myclass : NSObject
{
   // myclass data
   int nData;
   NSString *cData;
}

-(id)init:(int)tnData :(NSString *)tcData;
-(void)DisplayInstanceData;

@end
```

- myclass.m

myclass.m: Class Implementation for the myclass Class

```
//**************************************************************************
// myclass.m                                                               *
// Reserved                                                                *
//**************************************************************************

#import "myclass.h"


//**************************************************************************
// myclass implementation                                                  *
// Class implementation for the myclass class                              *
// CBI:  3-18.2.2.1                                                        *
//**************************************************************************

@implementation myclass


//**************************************************************************
// myclass implementation                                                  *
// Implement the initialization function for the myclass class             *
// CBI:  3-18.2.3.1                                                        *
//**************************************************************************

-(id)init:(int)tnData :(NSString *)tcData
{


//**************************************************************************
// myclass implementation                                                  *
// Declare the local variables for the myclass initialization function     *
// CBI:  3-18.2.3.2                                                        *
//**************************************************************************

   int lnResult;


//**************************************************************************
// myclass implementation                                                  *
// Prompt the user to continue instantiating the myclass class             *
// CBI:  3-18.2.3.3                                                        *
//**************************************************************************

   lnResult = NSRunAlertPanel(@"myclass",@"Proceed with class instantiation?",
                          @"No",@"Yes",nil,nil);
```

myclass.m continued on the next page

myclass.m: Class Implementation for the myclass Class continued

```
//***************************************************************************
// myclass implementation                                                   *
// Cancel instantiation of the myclass class if the user selects no         *
// CBI:  3-18.2.3.4                                                         *
//***************************************************************************

   if (lnResult == NSAlertDefaultReturn)
   {
      return nil;
   }


//***************************************************************************
// myclass implementation                                                   *
// Store the parameters to the initialization function as instance data     *
// CBI:  3-18.2.3.5                                                         *
//***************************************************************************

   [super init];

   nData = tnData;
   cData = tcData;

   return self;
}


//***************************************************************************
// myclass implementation                                                   *
// Implement the DisplayInstanceData method of the myclass class            *
// CBI:  3-18.2.4.1                                                         *
//***************************************************************************

-(void)DisplayInstanceData
{
   NSRunInformationalAlertPanel(@"myclass",
     [NSString stringWithFormat:@"nData: %d \ncData: %@",nData,cData],
                                @"OK",
                                nil,nil);
}
@end
```

Code Setup and Compilation

- Tools: Xcode (Appendix C), AppKit

Code Setup and Compilation Steps

1: Start the Xcode IDE program.

2: Xcode - Activate Menu Item: File → New Project

Select "Application → Cocoa Application" and then activate the "Next" button.

3: Set the "Project Name" to pp3_18 and set the "Project Directory" to the appropriate folder. Activate the "Finish" button.

4: Delete the main.m and MainMenu.nib files that have been automatically added to the project.

Steps continued on the next page

Code Setup and Compilation Steps continued

5: Xcode - Activate Menu Item: File → New File

Select "Empty File in Project" and then activate the "Next" button. Name the file pp3_18.m and set the "Location" to the pp3_18 folder. Activate the "Finish" button.

6: Enter the source code for the pp3_18.m file and then save the file.

7: Xcode - Activate Menu Item: File → New File

Select "Empty File in Project" and then activate the "Next" button. Name the file myclass.h and set the "Location" to the pp3_18 folder. Activate the "Finish" button.

8: Enter the source code for the myclass.h file and then save the file.

9: Xcode - Activate Menu Item: File → New File

Select "Empty File in Project" and then activate the "Next" button. Name the file myclass.m and set the "Location" to the pp3_18 folder. Activate the "Finish" button.

10: Enter the source code for the myclass.m file and then save the file.

11: Compile the program by activating the "Build" button.

Command Prompt Compilation

Enter the following in the pp3_18 folder:

```
xcodebuild
```

Program Execution

- Execute Program

  To execute the pp3_18 program, activate the "Build/Go" button.

- Debug Program

  Place the cursor in the CBI: 3-18.1.1.3 code block

```
   Xcode 2.4 - Activate Menu Item: Debug → Add Breakpoint at Current Line
   Xcode 3 - Activate Menu Item: Run → Manage Breakpoints → Add
Breakpoint at Current Line

   Xcode - Activate Menu Item: Build → Build and Debug
```

Program Phase Task 4

GUI Based Program with Main Window

- Program Phase Task 4 specifies a GUI based application that creates a main window. The program sets the window icon, caption, menu, background color, and mouse cursor. In addition, the window is created as a sizeable window. After the window is created, it is displayed in a maximized state. After the main window is displayed, a message loop is started that dispatches events for the window.

- The main window contains a "File" menu with two menu items. The first menu item of the "File" menu contains the caption "Hello World!". The second menu item contains the caption "Exit". Both menu items can be activated with the mouse or by using keyboard hotkeys. The control-h keyboard combination activates the "Hello World!" menu item. The control-x keyboard combination activates the "Exit" menu item.

- The following is the sample execution of Program Phase 4-3:

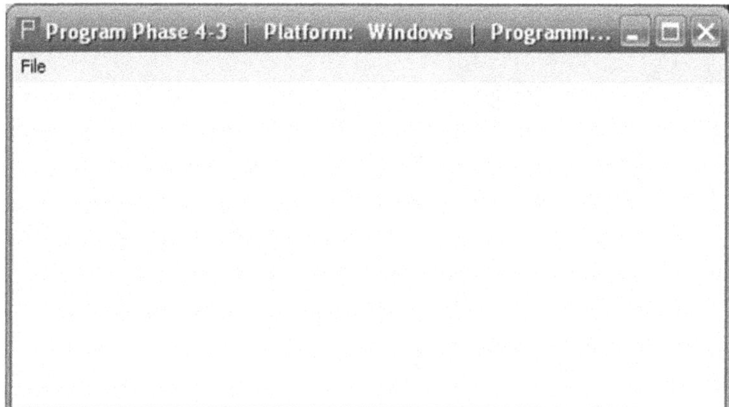

- When the "Hello World!" menu item is activated, the following message box is displayed:

- If the user activates the "Exit" menu item, the main window is closed. The application always exits after the main window is closed. If the user attempts to close the main window by any means other than the "Exit" menu item, the user is prompted to confirm the closing of the main window.

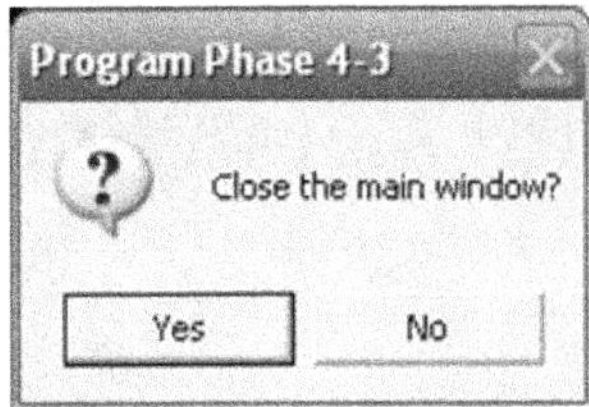

- If the user activates the "Yes" button, the main window is closed and the program exits. Otherwise, the program continues running.

Program Phase 4-1

Java ▪ Swing/AWT ▪ Multi-Platform

GUI Based Program with Main Window

- Program Phase Task 4 is implemented in Program Phase 4-1 using the Java programming language with the Swing API and Active Window Toolkit (AWT).

- Program Phase 4-1 contains a single source code file named pp4_1.java. In addition to the pp4_1.java text file, a gif image file called phase16x16.gif is used to represent the icon for the main window.

Code Block Features

The Program Phase 4-1 code blocks illustrate the following programming features using the Java programming language with Swing and the Active Window Toolkit:

- **Create a Resizable Main Window for a GUI Based Application**

- **Set the Main Window Icon and Caption**

- **Set the Main Window Menu**

- **Set the Main Window Background Color and Mouse Cursor**

- **Prompt to Exit the Application when the Main Window is Closed**

Java Swing/AWT
Create a Main Window for a GUI Based Application

- The JFrame class found in the javax.swing package is used to create a main window in a Java application. After the main window is displayed, there is no need to run an event loop that dispatches events for the main window. When the MainWindow window is displayed, it is said to be "realized". When a JFrame is "realized", any code that accesses or modifies it should be done in the event-dispatching thread. The Java runtime automatically creates two threads when using AWT and Swing. The first thread is the main() execution thread. This thread is started when the main() EPE function is started. The second thread is called the event dispatching thread. Once a JFrame is displayed using the setVisible() method, all interaction with the JFrame occurs in the event-dispatching thread. The JFrame is created in the main() thread, but once displayed, it is accessed and modified in the event-dispatching thread.

- After the JFrame is made visible with the setVisible() method, processing continues in the main() thread. When the last line of code is reached in the main() thread, the program does not exit because the JFrame is still visible and programmatically accessible in the event-dispatching thread. When the main window JFrame is disposed, the program exits because there are no more "realized" components running in the event-dispatching thread, and the last line of code processing in the main() thread has already been reached. The setDefaultCloseOperation() method of the instantiated JFrame class is called with the JFrame.DISPOSE_ON_CLOSE parameter. This indicates that when the user closes the window by clicking on the "x" button in the upper right corner of the window or by activating the "Close" menu item from the window icon menu, the window is disposed.

- The "final" keyword in the JFrame declaration indicates that the variable can only be assigned a value one time.

- The setResizable() method is called with a Boolean "true" parameter to allow the main window to be resized by the user.

test1.java: Java Swing/AWT Create a Resizable Main Window for a GUI Based App.

```
import javax.swing.JFrame;

public class test1
{
public static void main(final String taArgv[])
{
   final JFrame loMainWindow;

   // Create the main window
   loMainWindow = new JFrame();
   loMainWindow.setDefaultCloseOperation(JFrame.DISPOSE_ON_CLOSE);
   loMainWindow.setResizable(true);

   // Maximize and display the main window
   loMainWindow.setExtendedState(JFrame.MAXIMIZED_BOTH);
   loMainWindow.setVisible(true);
}}
```

Java Swing/AWT Set the Main Window Icon and Caption

- The main window icon is assigned from a 16 x 16 pixel gif image.

- The caption of the main window is set by calling the setTitle() method of the main window JFrame instance.

test2.java: Java Swing/AWT Set the Main Window Icon and Caption

```
import javax.swing.JFrame;
import java.net.URL;
import java.net.URLClassLoader;
import java.awt.Toolkit;
import java.awt.Image;

public class test2
{
public static void main(final String taArgv[])
{
   final JFrame loMainWindow;
   Image loIcon;
   URL loURL;

   // Create the main window
   loMainWindow = new JFrame();
   loMainWindow.setDefaultCloseOperation(JFrame.DISPOSE_ON_CLOSE);
   loMainWindow.setResizable(true);
```

test2.java continued on the next page

test2.java: Java Swing/AWT Set the Main Window Icon and Caption continued

```
   // Set the main window icon
   loURL = null;

   loURL = URLClassLoader.getSystemResource("phase16x16.gif");

   if (loURL != null)
   {
      loIcon = Toolkit.getDefaultToolkit().getImage(loURL);
      loMainWindow.setIconImage(loIcon);
   }

   // Set the main window caption
   loMainWindow.setTitle("Hello World!");

   // Maximize and display the main window
   loMainWindow.setExtendedState(JFrame.MAXIMIZED_BOTH);
   loMainWindow.setVisible(true);
}}
```

Java Swing/AWT
Set the Main Window Menu

- The following example creates a "File" menu with a "Hello World!" menu item and "Exit" menu item:

test3.java: Java Swing/AWT Set the Main Window Menu

```
import javax.swing.JOptionPane;
import javax.swing.JFrame;
import javax.swing.JMenu;
import javax.swing.JMenuBar;
import javax.swing.JMenuItem;
import javax.swing.AbstractAction;
import javax.swing.KeyStroke;
import java.awt.event.KeyEvent;
import java.awt.event.ActionEvent;
import java.awt.event.ActionListener;
import java.awt.event.WindowAdapter;
import java.awt.event.WindowEvent;

public class test3
{
public static void main(final String taArgv[])
{
   final JFrame loMainWindow;
   JMenuBar loMenuBar;      JMenu loFileMenu;
   JMenuItem loMenuItem1;  JMenuItem loMenuItem2;
   KeyStroke loKeyStroke1; KeyStroke loKeyStroke2;
   MenuItemActivated loMenuItemActivated;

   // Create the main window
   loMainWindow = new JFrame();

   loMainWindow.setDefaultCloseOperation(JFrame.DISPOSE_ON_CLOSE);
   loMainWindow.setResizable(true);

   // Setup the menu bar
   loMenuBar = new JMenuBar();

   // Create the file menu
   loFileMenu = new JMenu("File");
   loFileMenu.setMnemonic(KeyEvent.VK_F);
```

test3.java continued on the next page

test3.java: Java Swing/AWT Set the Main Window Menu continued

```
    loMenuBar.add(loFileMenu);
    loMenuItemActivated = new MenuItemActivated(loMainWindow);

    // Create the Hello World! menu item
    loMenuItem1 = new JMenuItem("Hello World!",KeyEvent.VK_H);
    loMenuItem1.addActionListener(loMenuItemActivated);
    loKeyStroke1 = KeyStroke.getKeyStroke(KeyEvent.VK_H,ActionEvent.CTRL_MASK);
    loMenuItem1.setAccelerator(loKeyStroke1);
    loFileMenu.add(loMenuItem1);

    // Create the Exit menu item
    loMenuItem2 = new JMenuItem("Exit",KeyEvent.VK_X);
    loMenuItem2.addActionListener(loMenuItemActivated);
    loKeyStroke2 = KeyStroke.getKeyStroke(KeyEvent.VK_X,ActionEvent.CTRL_MASK);

    loMenuItem2.setAccelerator(loKeyStroke2);
    loFileMenu.add(loMenuItem2);

    // Assign the File menu to the main window
    loMainWindow.setJMenuBar(loMenuBar);

    // Maximize and display the main window
    loMainWindow.setExtendedState(JFrame.MAXIMIZED_BOTH);
    loMainWindow.setVisible(true);
}}

// Callback class with a member function that responds to the menu events

class MenuItemActivated extends AbstractAction
{
    JFrame oMainWindow;

    public MenuItemActivated(JFrame toMainWindow)
    {
        this.oMainWindow = toMainWindow;
    }

    public void actionPerformed(ActionEvent toActionEvent)
    {
        String lcActionCommand;
        lcActionCommand = toActionEvent.getActionCommand();

        // Display a message box if the user activates the Hello World! menu item
        if (lcActionCommand ==  "Hello World!")
        {
            JOptionPane.showMessageDialog(null,"Hello World!","test",
                                          JOptionPane.INFORMATION_MESSAGE,null);
        }

        // Exit the program if the user activates the Exit menu item
        if (lcActionCommand == "Exit")
        {
            this.oMainWindow.dispose();
        }
    }
}
```

Java Swing/AWT
Set the Main Window Background Color and Mouse Cursor

- The following example sets the main window background color and mouse cursor:

test4.java: Java Swing/AWT Set the Main Window Background Color and Mouse Cursor

```
import javax.swing.JFrame;
import java.awt.Cursor;
import java.awt.Container;
import java.awt.Color;

public class test4
{
public static void main(final String taArgv[])
{
   final JFrame loMainWindow;

   Container loContentPane;
   Color loWindowBackColor;
   Cursor loMouseCursor;

   // Create the main window
   loMainWindow = new JFrame();
   loMainWindow.setDefaultCloseOperation(JFrame.DISPOSE_ON_CLOSE);
   loMainWindow.setResizable(true);

   // Set the main window background color
   loContentPane = loMainWindow.getContentPane();
   loWindowBackColor = new Color(255,255,255);
   loContentPane.setBackground(loWindowBackColor);

   // Set the main window mouse cursor
   loMouseCursor = new Cursor(Cursor.DEFAULT_CURSOR);
   loMainWindow.setCursor(loMouseCursor);

   // Maximize and display the main window
   loMainWindow.setExtendedState(JFrame.MAXIMIZED_BOTH);
   loMainWindow.setVisible(true);
}}
```

Java Swing/AWT
Prompt to Exit the Application when the Main Window is Closed

- A class based on the WindowAdapter class is instantiated and then assigned to the JFrame main window by calling the addWindowListener() method. A method called WindowClosing is implemented in the WindowAdapter derived class that automatically is called when the user attempts to close the main window by clicking on the "x" button in the upper right corner of the window or by selecting the "Close" menu item from the window icon menu in the upper left corner of the window. Since the setDefaultCloseOperation() method of the main window JFrame instance is called with the JFrame.DO_NOTHING_ON_CLOSE parameter, the window is not automatically disposed when the user attempts to close it. The window can be programmatically closed by calling the dispose() method of the main window JFrame instance in the WindowClosing() event.

test5.java: Prompt to Exit the Application when the Main Window is Closed

```
import javax.swing.JOptionPane;
import javax.swing.JFrame;
import java.awt.event.WindowAdapter;
import java.awt.event.WindowEvent;

public class test5
{
public static void main(final String taArgv[])
{
```

test5.java continued on the next page

test5.java: Prompt to Exit the App. when the Main Window is Closed continued

```
   final JFrame loMainWindow;
   MainWindow_WindowAdapter loWindowAdapter;

   // Create the main window
   loMainWindow = new JFrame();
   loMainWindow.setDefaultCloseOperation(JFrame.DO_NOTHING_ON_CLOSE);
   loMainWindow.setResizable(true);
   loWindowAdapter = new MainWindow_WindowAdapter(loMainWindow);
   loMainWindow.addWindowListener(loWindowAdapter);

   loMainWindow.setExtendedState(JFrame.MAXIMIZED_BOTH);
   loMainWindow.setVisible(true);
}}

class MainWindow_WindowAdapter extends WindowAdapter
{
   JFrame oMainWindow;

   public MainWindow_WindowAdapter(JFrame toMainWindow)
   {
      this.oMainWindow = toMainWindow;
   }

   public void windowClosing(WindowEvent toWindowEvent)
   {
      int lnResult;

      // Prompt the user to continue closing the main window
      lnResult = JOptionPane.showOptionDialog(null,"Close the main window?",
                                              "test5",
                                              JOptionPane.YES_NO_OPTION,
                                              JOptionPane.QUESTION_MESSAGE,
                                              null,null,null);

      if (lnResult == JOptionPane.YES_OPTION)
      {
         this.oMainWindow.dispose();
      }
   }
}
```

Source Code Files

- Text files: pp4_1.java
- Image files: phase16x16.gif (Appendix O)

pp4_1.java: Program Phase 4-1 Source Code

```
//***************************************************************************
// Program Phase 4-1 Java Main Window with File menu                        *
// Programming Tasks Illustrated: Swing/AWT GUI based application           *
//                                Main window                               *
//                                Window icon                               *
//                                Window caption                            *
//                                Window menu with hotkeys                  *
//                                Window background color                   *
//                                Window mouse cursor                       *
//                                User sizable window                       *
//                                Message box input/output                  *
//***************************************************************************
```

pp4_1.java continued on the next page

pp4_1.java: Program Phase 4-1 Source Code continued

```
//***************************************************************************
// File: pp4_1.java                                                         *
// Reserved                                                                 *
//***************************************************************************

package programphases.programphase4_1;

import javax.swing.JOptionPane;
import javax.swing.JFrame;
import javax.swing.JMenu;
import javax.swing.JMenuBar;
import javax.swing.JMenuItem;
import javax.swing.KeyStroke;
import javax.swing.AbstractAction;
import java.awt.event.KeyEvent;
import java.awt.event.ActionEvent;
import java.awt.event.ActionListener;
import java.awt.Image;
import java.awt.Toolkit;
import java.awt.event.WindowAdapter;
import java.awt.event.WindowEvent;
import java.awt.Cursor;
import java.awt.Container;
import java.awt.Color;
import java.net.URL;
import java.net.URLClassLoader;

public class pp4_1
{


//***************************************************************************
// Program Phase 4-1 Main                                                   *
// Define the Entry Point of Execution (EPE) for Program Phase 4-1          *
// CBI:  4-1.1.1.1                                                          *
//***************************************************************************

public static void main(final String taArgv[])
{


//***************************************************************************
// Program Phase 4-1 Main                                                   *
// Declare the local variables for the "main" program                       *
// CBI:  4-1.1.1.2                                                          *
//***************************************************************************

   // Main window
   final JFrame loMainWindow;
   MainWindow_WindowAdapter loWindowAdapter;

   // Main window icon
   Image loIcon;
   URL loURL;

   // Main window menu
   JMenuBar loMenuBar;
   JMenu loFileMenu;
   JMenuItem loMenuItem1;
   JMenuItem loMenuItem2;
   KeyStroke loKeyStroke1;
   KeyStroke loKeyStroke2;
   MenuItemActivated loMenuItemActivated;

   // Main window background color
   Container loContentPane;
```

pp4_1.java continued on the next page

pp4_1.java: Program Phase 4-1 Source Code continued

```
   Color loWindowBackColor;

   // Main window mouse cursor
   Cursor loMouseCursor;


//*************************************************************************
// Program Phase 4-1 Main                                                 *
// Create the main window                                                 *
// CBI:  4-1.1.1.3                                                        *
//*************************************************************************

   loMainWindow = new JFrame();
   loMainWindow.setDefaultCloseOperation(JFrame.DO_NOTHING_ON_CLOSE);
   loWindowAdapter = new MainWindow_WindowAdapter(loMainWindow);
   loMainWindow.addWindowListener(loWindowAdapter);


//*************************************************************************
// Program Phase 4-1 Main                                                 *
// Set the icon for the main window                                       *
// CBI:  4-1.1.1.4                                                        *
//*************************************************************************

   loURL = null;
   loURL = URLClassLoader.getSystemResource(
                           "programphases/programphase4_1/phase16x16.gif");

   if (loURL == null)
   {
      JOptionPane.showOptionDialog(null,
                            "Window icon file (phase16x16.gif) not found.",
                               "Program Phase 4-1",
                               JOptionPane.DEFAULT_OPTION,
                               JOptionPane.ERROR_MESSAGE,
                               null,null,null);
   }
   else
   {
      loIcon = Toolkit.getDefaultToolkit().getImage(loURL);
      loMainWindow.setIconImage(loIcon);
   }


//*************************************************************************
// Program Phase 4-1 Main                                                 *
// Set the caption of the main window                                     *
// CBI:  4-1.1.1.5                                                        *
//*************************************************************************

   loMainWindow.setTitle("Program Phase 4-1  |  " +
                         "Platform:  Multi-Platform  |  " +
                         "Programming Language:  Java  |  " +
                         "GUI API:  Swing/AWT");


//*************************************************************************
// Program Phase 4-1 Main                                                 *
// Create the menu for the main window                                    *
// CBI:  4-1.1.1.6                                                        *
//*************************************************************************

   // Menu bar
   loMenuBar = new JMenuBar();

   // File menu
   loFileMenu = new JMenu("File");
```

pp4_1.java continued on the next page

pp4_1.java: Program Phase 4-1 Source Code continued

```
    loFileMenu.setMnemonic(KeyEvent.VK_F);
    loMenuBar.add(loFileMenu);

    // Hello World! menu item
    loMenuItem1 = new JMenuItem("Hello World!",KeyEvent.VK_H);
    loKeyStroke1 = KeyStroke.getKeyStroke(KeyEvent.VK_H,ActionEvent.CTRL_MASK);
    loMenuItem1.setAccelerator(loKeyStroke1);

    loMenuItemActivated = new MenuItemActivated(loMainWindow);
    loMenuItem1.addActionListener(loMenuItemActivated);
    loFileMenu.add(loMenuItem1);

    // Exit menu item
    loMenuItem2 = new JMenuItem("Exit",KeyEvent.VK_X);
    loKeyStroke2 = KeyStroke.getKeyStroke(KeyEvent.VK_X,ActionEvent.CTRL_MASK);
    loMenuItem2.setAccelerator(loKeyStroke2);
    loMenuItem2.addActionListener(loMenuItemActivated);
    loFileMenu.add(loMenuItem2);

    // Assign the menu to the main window
    loMainWindow.setJMenuBar(loMenuBar);

//******************************************************************************
// Program Phase 4-1 Main                                                      *
// Set the background color of the main window                                 *
// CBI:  4-1.1.1.7                                                             *
//******************************************************************************

    loContentPane = loMainWindow.getContentPane();
    loWindowBackColor = new Color(255,255,255);
    loContentPane.setBackground(loWindowBackColor);


//******************************************************************************
// Program Phase 4-1 Main                                                      *
// Set the mouse cursor displayed when positioned over the main window         *
// CBI:  4-1.1.1.8                                                             *
//******************************************************************************

    loMouseCursor = new Cursor(Cursor.DEFAULT_CURSOR);
    loMainWindow.setCursor(loMouseCursor);


//******************************************************************************
// Program Phase 4-1 Main                                                      *
// Allow resizing of the main window                                           *
// CBI:  4-1.1.1.9                                                             *
//******************************************************************************

    loMainWindow.setResizable(true);


//******************************************************************************
// Program Phase 4-1 Main                                                      *
// Maximize and display the main window                                        *
// CBI:  4-1.1.1.10                                                            *
//******************************************************************************

    loMainWindow.setExtendedState(JFrame.MAXIMIZED_BOTH);
    loMainWindow.setVisible(true);


//******************************************************************************
// Program Phase 4-1 Main                                                      *
// Start the event loop                                                        *
// CBI:  4-1.1.1.11                                                            *
//******************************************************************************
```

pp4_1.java continued on the next page

pp4_1.java: Program Phase 4-1 Source Code continued

```
//******************************************************************************
// Program Phase 4-1 Main                                                      *
// Cleanup the resources used by the main window                               *
// CBI:  4-1.1.1.12                                                            *
//******************************************************************************

// Memory allocation and de-allocation is handled automatically by the Java
// runtime.  The Java runtime will determines if an object is no longer needed
// and will release the memory automatically.  The program does not need to
// explicitly release any memory in Program Phase 4-1.

}}

// Callback Functions

class MenuItemActivated extends AbstractAction
{
   JFrame oMainWindow;

   public MenuItemActivated(JFrame toMainWindow)
   {
      this.oMainWindow = toMainWindow;
   }

   public void actionPerformed(ActionEvent toActionEvent)
   {

      String lcActionCommand;
      lcActionCommand = toActionEvent.getActionCommand();

//******************************************************************************
// Callback Functions                                                          *
// Implement the callback function for the Hello World! menu item              *
// CBI:  4-1.1.2.1                                                             *
//******************************************************************************

      if (lcActionCommand ==  "Hello World!")
      {
         JOptionPane.showMessageDialog(null,"Hello World!",
                                       "Program Phase 4-1",
                                       JOptionPane.INFORMATION_MESSAGE,null);
      }


//******************************************************************************
// Callback Functions                                                          *
// Implement the callback function for the Exit menu item                      *
// CBI:  4-1.1.3.1                                                             *
//******************************************************************************

      // Exit the program if the user activates the Exit menu item
      if (lcActionCommand == "Exit")
      {
         this.oMainWindow.dispose();
      }
   }
}


//******************************************************************************
// Callback Functions                                                          *
// Implement the callback function that fires when the main window is closed  *
// CBI:  4-1.1.4.1                                                             *
//******************************************************************************
```

pp4_1.java continued on the next page

pp4_1.java: Program Phase 4-1 Source Code continued

```
class MainWindow_WindowAdapter extends WindowAdapter
{
   JFrame oMainWindow;

   public MainWindow_WindowAdapter(JFrame toMainWindow)
   {
      this.oMainWindow = toMainWindow;
   }

   public void windowClosing(WindowEvent toWindowEvent)
   {
      int lnResult;

      // Prompt the user to continue closing the main window
      lnResult = JOptionPane.showOptionDialog(null,"Close the main window?",
                                              "Program Phase 4-1",
                                              JOptionPane.YES_NO_OPTION,
                                              JOptionPane.QUESTION_MESSAGE,
                                              null,null,null);

      if (lnResult == JOptionPane.YES_OPTION)
      {
         this.oMainWindow.dispose();
      }
   }
}
```

Windows and Linux – Code Setup and Compilation

- Tools: Java SE Development Kit (JDK) 5.0, Netbeans IDE (Appendix A)

Windows and Linux Code Setup and Compilation Steps

1: Start the Netbeans IDE program.

2: Netbeans - Activate Menu Item: File → New Project

Select the "Java" category and then select "Java Application" as the project type. Activate the "Next" button.

3: Enter pp4_1 as the "Project Name". Enter the appropriate folder name for the "File Location". Check the "Set as Main Project" check box. Uncheck the "Create Main Class" check box. Activate the "Finish" button.

4: Create a folder called programphases\programphase4_1 inside the src folder of the pp4_1 folder:

```
pp4_1\src\programphases\programphase4_1
```

5: Netbeans - Activate Menu Item: File → New File

In the "New File" dialog window, select the "Other" category and then select "Empty File" as the file type. Activate the "Next" button. Enter the file name as pp4_1.java and select the src\programphases\programphase4_1 folder as the destination "Folder". Activate the "Finish" button to create the pp4_1.java file.

Steps continued on the next page

Windows and Linux Code Setup and Compilation Steps continued

6: Open the pp4_1.java file in the Netbeans IDE and then enter the source code for Program Phase 4-1.

7: Netbeans - Activate Menu Item: File → pp4_1 Properties

On the "Project Properties" window, select the "Run" category and then enter programphases.programphase4_1.pp4_1 for the "Main Class". Activate the "OK" button.

8: Create the phase16x16.gif image file according to the instructions in Appendix O. Save the phase16x16.gif image to the pp4_1/src/programphases/programphase4_1 folder.

9: Netbeans - Activate Menu Item: Build → Build Main Project

```
Output:  pp4_1\build\classes\programphases\programphase4_1\pp4_1.class
         pp4_1\dist\pp4_1.jar
```

Windows and Linux Command Prompt Compilation Steps

1: Update the path to the javac executable file, substituting the appropriate path for the version of the J2SE that is installed.

```
Windows:  PATH = %PATH%;"C:\Program Files\Java\jdk1.6.0_01\bin"

Linux:  PATH=~/jdk1.6.0_01/bin:$PATH
        export PATH

Linux C shell or TC shell: setenv PATH ~/jdk1.6.0/bin:$PATH
```

2: Change directories to the pp4_1 folder and then enter the following command:

Windows

```
javac -d "build\classes" "src\programphases\programphase4_1\pp4_1.java"
```

Linux

```
javac -d "build/classes" "src/programphases/programphase4_1/pp4_1.java"
```

3: Create a text file called manifest in the pp4_1 folder and then put this line in the file:

```
Main-Class: programphases.programphase4_1.pp4_1
```

Enter a newline at the end of the text.

4: Create the pp4_1.jar "executable" file:

```
jar -cvfm ./dist/pp4_1.jar manifest -C build/classes .
```

This command results in the pp4_1.jar file being placed in the dist folder of the pp4_1 folder. This is the same location that Netbeans places the pp4_1.jar file.

Mac OS X – Code Setup and Compilation

- Tools: Java SE Development Kit (JDK) 5.0 (included with Mac OS X), Xcode IDE. (Appendix C)

Mac OS X Code Setup and Compilation Steps

1: Start the Xcode IDE program found in the /Developer/Applications folder.

2: Xcode - Activate Menu Item: File → New Project

3: Select "Java Tool" and then activate the "Next" button.

4: Enter pp4_1 as the "Project Name". Enter the appropriate folder as the "Project Directory". Activate the "Finish" button.

5: Xcode - Activate Menu Item: Project → Set Active Build Configuration → Release

6: A text file called pp4_1.java is automatically created. Delete the entire contents of this file and then enter the source code for Program Phase 4-1.

7: In the Xcode IDE, double-click on the file called Manifest. Change the "Main-Class" entry in the Manifest file from pp4_1 to programphases.programphase4_1.pp4_1. Save and close the Manifest file. If using Xcode 3, expand the "Executables" entry and then double click on the "java" entry to display the "Executable 'java' Info" window. Edit the argument to look like this:

```
-cp pp4_1.jar programphases.programphase4_1.pp4_1
```

8: Create the phase16x16.gif image file according to the instructions in Appendix O. Save the phase16x16.gif image to the pp4_1 folder.

9: Activate the Build button in Xcode to compile the pp4_1.java file.

10: When the pp4_1.jar file is created, it may not have the phase16x16 gif image embedded in the file, or it may not be in the proper location in the file. A .jar file is stored in the .zip format. Rename the pp4_1.jar file to pp4_1.zip. Open the zip file and then copy the phase16x16.gif image file to the programphases/programphase4_1/pp4_1 folder inside the pp4_1.zip file. Save and close the file and then rename the file to pp4_1.jar.

Mac OS X Command Prompt Compilation Steps

1: Open a terminal window and then change directories to the pp4_1 folder.

Xcode 2.4

```
javac -d "build/pp4_1.build/Release/pp4_1.build/JavaClasses" pp4_1.java
```

The destination path (-d) must be created if it does not yet exist. The folder will automatically be created when compiled in the Xcode IDE.

Xcode 3

```
javac -d bin src/pp4_1.java
```

2: Using a text editor, create a text file called Manifest (if it does not already exist) in the pp4_1 folder and then put this line in the file:

```
Main-Class: programphases.programphase4_1.pp4_1
```

Enter a newline at the end of the text.

Steps continued on the next page

Mac OS X Command Prompt Compilation Steps continued

3: Create the pp4_1.jar "executable" file. Enter the following on a single line:

Xcode 2.4:

```
   jar -cvfm build/Release/pp4_1.jar Manifest -C
build/pp4_1.build/Release/pp4_1.build/JavaClasses .
```

Xcode 3:

```
   jar -cvfm jars/pp4_1.jar Manifest -C bin .
```

4: Proceed to step 10 of the Mac OS X Code Setup and Compilation Steps.

Windows and Linux – Program Execution

- Execute Program

```
Netbeans IDE - Activate Menu Item:  Run → Run Main Project
```

- Debug Program

```
Netbeans IDE - Activate Menu Item:  Run → Step Into Project
```

Mac OS X – Program Execution

- Execute Program

```
Xcode IDE - Activate the "Build and Go" button
```

- Debug Program

```
   Xcode 2.4 - Activate Menu Item: Debug → Add Breakpoint at Current Line
   Xcode 3 - Activate Menu Item: Run → Manage Breakpoints → Add
Breakpoint at Current Line

   Xcode - Activate Menu Item: Build → Build and Debug
```

Program Phase 4-2

Visual FoxPro ▪ Windows

GUI Based Program with Main Window

- Program Phase Task 4 is implemented in Program Phase 4-2 using the Visual FoxPro (VFP) programming language.

- Program Phase 4-2 contains a single source code file named pp4_2.prg. In addition to the pp4_2.prg text file, an icon image file called phase.ico is used in Program Phase 4-2 as the window icon for the main window and the application icon for the pp4_2.exe executable file.

Code Block Features

The Program Phase 4-2 code blocks illustrate the following programming features using the Visual FoxPro programming language:

- **Create a Resizable Main Window for a GUI Based Application**

- **Set the Main Window Icon and Caption**

- **Set the Main Window Menu**

- **Set the Main Window Background Color and Mouse Cursor**

- **Prompt to Exit the Application when the Main Window is Closed**

Visual FoxPro
Create a Resizable Main Window for a GUI Based Application

- The VFP runtime automatically creates a main window for the application when the program starts. This main window is not visible in Program Phase 1-2, 2-2, and 3-2 because it is hidden, using a config.fpw file. When this file is present in the same folder as the executable file and has the setting "SCREEN=OFF", the automatically created main window is not displayed when the executable file is started. The main window is made visible by setting the "visible" property of the global _SCREEN object to the Boolean "true" value.

- Setting the "borderstyle" property of the global "_SCREEN" object to the value 3 allows the window to be resized by the user. The main window is maximized by setting the "windowstate" property of the "_SCREEN" object to the value 2.

- The "READ EVENTS" command causes the VFP runtime to enter an event loop that dispatches events to the appropriate event handlers. The "READ EVENTS" command "pauses" program execution until the "CLEAR EVENTS" command is issued. By using the "ON SHUTDOWN" command, the EXITPROCEDURE() procedure will automatically be called when the user attempts to exit the application by clicking on the "x" button in the upper right corner of the window or by activating the "Close" menu item from the window icon menu. The "ON SHUTDOWN" command with no parameters prevents the EXITPROCEDURE() procedure from being called when the program exits.

test1.prg: Visual FoxPro Create a Resizable Main Window for a GUI Based App.

```
#DEFINE SW_SHOWMAXIMIZED 2

** The main window is automatically created by the VFP runtime
_SCREEN.BORDERSTYLE = 3

** Maximize and display the main window
_SCREEN.WINDOWSTATE = SW_SHOWMAXIMIZED
_SCREEN.VISIBLE = .T.

ON SHUTDOWN DO EXITPROCEDURE
READ EVENTS
ON SHUTDOWN

PROCEDURE EXITPROCEDURE

  CLEAR EVENTS

ENDPROC
```

Visual FoxPro
Set the Main Window Icon and Caption

- The icon for the main window is set by assigning the icon file name to the "ICON" property of the "_SCREEN" object. This can be a file system path or the name of an icon embedded in the executable file.

- The caption for the main window is assigned by setting the "CAPTION" property of the "_SCREEN" object.

test2.prg: Visual FoxPro Set the Main Window Icon and Caption

```
#DEFINE SW_SHOWMAXIMIZED 2

** The main window is automatically created by the VFP runtime
_SCREEN.BORDERSTYLE = 3
_SCREEN.WINDOWSTATE = SW_SHOWMAXIMIZED
_SCREEN.VISIBLE = .T.

** Set the main window icon
_SCREEN.ICON = "phase.ico"

** Set the main window caption
_SCREEN.CAPTION = "Hello World!"

ON SHUTDOWN DO EXITPROCEDURE
READ EVENTS
ON SHUTDOWN
_SCREEN.ICON = ""

PROCEDURE EXITPROCEDURE

  CLEAR EVENTS

ENDPROC
```

Visual FoxPro
Set the Main Window Menu

- When a Visual FoxPro program starts, a main window is automatically created with a default menu. The menu is referenced with the "_MSYSMENU" variable. Use the "PUSH MENU" command to save the menu before it is erased. It is helpful to save the current menu at the start of the program and restore it at the end of the program when executing the program in the VFP IDE. If the menu is not saved and then restored, the VFP IDE menu will not be displayed after the program finishes execution.

- The default main window menu is erased with the "SET SYSMENU TO" command. The "SET SYSMENU AUTOMATIC" ensures that the main window menu is visible.

- The "DEFINE PAD" command allows the "File" menu label to be created in the "_MSYSMENU". The "DEFINE POPUP" command is used to display a list of menu items when the "File" menu is activated. The "ON PAD" command is used to link the "File" menu label to the popup menu, defined with the "DEFINE POPUP" command. The "DEFINE BAR" command allows menu items to be added to the "File" menu. The "KEY" entry specifies the keyboard shortcut that is used to activate the menu item. The command that executes when the menu item is activated by the user is set with the "ON SELECTION BAR" command.

- The following example creates a "File" menu with a "Hello World!" menu item and "Exit" menu item:

test3.prg: Visual FoxPro Set the Main Window Menu

```
#DEFINE SW_SHOWMAXIMIZED 2

** The main window is automatically created by the VFP runtime
_SCREEN.BORDERSTYLE = 3
_SCREEN.WINDOWSTATE = SW_SHOWMAXIMIZED
_SCREEN.VISIBLE = .T.

** Setup the menu bar
PUSH MENU _MSYSMENU
SET SYSMENU TO
SET SYSMENU AUTOMATIC

** Create the file menu
DEFINE PAD pad1 OF _MSYSMENU PROMPT "File" COLOR SCHEME 3 KEY ALT+F, ""
DEFINE POPUP filepopup MARGIN RELATIVE SHADOW COLOR SCHEME 4
ON PAD pad1 OF _MSYSMENU ACTIVATE POPUP filepopup

** Create the Hello World! menu item
DEFINE BAR 1 OF filepopup PROMPT "\<Hello World!" KEY CTRL+H, "Ctrl+H"
ON SELECTION BAR 1 OF filepopup MenuItem1_Activate()

** Create the Exit menu item
DEFINE BAR 2 OF filepopup PROMPT "E\<xit" KEY CTRL+X, "Ctrl+X"
ON SELECTION BAR 2 OF filepopup MenuItem2_Activate()

ON SHUTDOWN DO EXITPROCEDURE
READ EVENTS
ON SHUTDOWN
POP MENU _MSYSMENU

PROCEDURE EXITPROCEDURE
```

test3.prg continued on the next page

test3.prg: Visual FoxPro Set the Main Window Menu continued

```
   CLEAR EVENTS

ENDPROC


PROCEDURE MenuItem1_Activate

   =MESSAGEBOX("Hello World!")

ENDPROC

PROCEDURE MenuItem2_Activate

   CLEAR EVENTS

ENDPROC
```

Visual FoxPro
Set the Main Window Background Color and Mouse Cursor

- The following example sets the main window background color and mouse cursor:

test4.prg: Visual FoxPro Set the Main Window Background Color and Mouse Cursor

```
#DEFINE SW_SHOWMAXIMIZED 2

local lnWindowBackColor

** The main window is automatically created by the VFP runtime
_SCREEN.BORDERSTYLE = 3
_SCREEN.WINDOWSTATE = SW_SHOWMAXIMIZED
_SCREEN.VISIBLE = .T.

** Set the main window background color
lnWindowBackColor = RGB(255,255,255)
_SCREEN.BACKCOLOR = lnWindowBackColor

** Set the main window mouse cursor - 1:Arrow
_SCREEN.MOUSEPOINTER = 1

ON SHUTDOWN DO EXITPROCEDURE
READ EVENTS
ON SHUTDOWN

PROCEDURE EXITPROCEDURE

  CLEAR EVENTS

ENDPROC
```

Visual FoxPro
Prompt to Exit the Application when the Main Window is Closed

- The procedure specified as the "ON SHUTDOWN" procedure is used to display a message box, prompting the user to continue closing the main window. If the user selects the "Yes" button, the "CLEAR EVENTS" command is issued, and processing continues with the first line of code following the "READ EVENTS" command. If the user selects the "No" button, no action is taken, resulting in processing still being "paused" at "READ EVENTS".

test5.prg: VFP Prompt to Exit the Application when the Main Window is Closed

```
#DEFINE SW_SHOWMAXIMIZED 2

** The main window is automatically created by the VFP runtime
_SCREEN.BORDERSTYLE = 3
_SCREEN.WINDOWSTATE = SW_SHOWMAXIMIZED
_SCREEN.VISIBLE = .T.

ON SHUTDOWN DO EXITPROCEDURE
READ EVENTS
ON SHUTDOWN

PROCEDURE EXITPROCEDURE

   LOCAL lnResult

   lnResult = MESSAGEBOX("Close the main window?",4 + 32,"test")

   IF lnResult = 6

       CLEAR EVENTS

   ENDIF

ENDPROC
```

Source Code Files

- Text files: pp4_2.prg
- Image files: phase.ico (Multi-image icon file, Appendix O)

pp4_2.prg: Program Phase 4-2 Source Code

```
*******************************************************************************
** Program Phase 4-2 Visual FoxPro Main Window with File Menu                *
** Programming Tasks Illustrated: Visual FoxPro GUI based application        *
**                                Main window                                 *
**                                Window icon                                 *
**                                Window caption                              *
**                                Window menu with hotkeys                    *
**                                Window background color                     *
**                                Window mouse cursor                         *
**                                User sizable window                         *
**                                Message box input/output                    *
*******************************************************************************

*******************************************************************************
** File: p4_2.prg                                                             *
** Reserved                                                                   *
*******************************************************************************

#DEFINE SW_SHOWMAXIMIZED 2
SET TALK OFF
SET STATUS BAR OFF


*******************************************************************************
** Program Phase 4-2 Main                                                     *
** Define the Entry Point of Execution (EPE) for Program Phase 4-2            *
** CBI:  4-2.1.1.1                                                            *
*******************************************************************************
```

pp4_2.prg continued on the next page

pp4_2.prg: Program Phase 4-2 Source Code continued

```
*****************************************************************************
** Program Phase 4-2 Main                                                   *
** Declare the local variables for the "main" program                       *
** CBI:  4-2.1.1.2                                                          *
*****************************************************************************

** Main window
LOCAL loMainWindow

** Main window background color
LOCAL lnWindowBackColor


*****************************************************************************
** Program Phase 4-2 Main                                                   *
** Create the main window                                                   *
** CBI:  4-2.1.1.3                                                          *
*****************************************************************************

** The main window is automatically created by the VFP runtime.
loMainWindow = _SCREEN


*****************************************************************************
** Program Phase 4-2 Main                                                   *
** Set the icon for the main window                                         *
** CBI:  4-2.1.1.4                                                          *
*****************************************************************************

loMainWindow.ICON = "phase.ico"


*****************************************************************************
** Program Phase 4-2 Main                                                   *
** Set the caption of the main window                                       *
** CBI:  4-2.1.1.5                                                          *
*****************************************************************************

loMainWindow.CAPTION = "Program Phase 4-2  |  " + ;
                       "Platform:  Windows  |  " + ;
                       "Programming Language:  Visual FoxPro  |  " + ;
                       "GUI API:  Visual FoxPro"


*****************************************************************************
** Program Phase 4-2 Main                                                   *
** Create the menu for the main window                                      *
** CBI:  4-2.1.1.6                                                          *
*****************************************************************************

** Menu bar
PUSH MENU _MSYSMENU
SET SYSMENU TO
*SET SYSMENU AUTOMATIC

** File Menu
DEFINE PAD pad1 OF _MSYSMENU PROMPT "File" COLOR SCHEME 3 KEY ALT+F, ""
DEFINE POPUP filepopup MARGIN RELATIVE SHADOW COLOR SCHEME 4
ON PAD pad1 OF _MSYSMENU ACTIVATE POPUP filepopup

** Hello World! menu item
DEFINE BAR 1 OF filepopup PROMPT "\<Hello World!" KEY CTRL+H, "Ctrl+H"
ON SELECTION BAR 1 OF filepopup MenuItem1_Activate()
```

pp4_2.prg continued on the next page

pp4_2.prg: Program Phase 4-2 Source Code continued

```
** Exit Menu Item
DEFINE BAR 2 OF filepopup PROMPT "E\<xit" KEY CTRL+X, "Ctrl+X"
ON SELECTION BAR 2 OF filepopup MenuItem2_Activate()

** Assign the File menu to the main window
** This is done in the preceding "DEFINE PAD pad1 of _MSYSMENU…" command.


*****************************************************************************
** Program Phase 4-2 Main                                                   *
** Set the background color of the main window                              *
** CBI:  4-2.1.1.7                                                          *
*****************************************************************************

lnWindowBackColor = RGB(255,255,255)
loMainWindow.BACKCOLOR = lnWindowBackColor


*****************************************************************************
** Program Phase 4-2 Main                                                   *
** Set the mouse cursor displayed when positioned over the main window      *
** CBI:  4-2.1.1.8                                                          *
*****************************************************************************

loMainWindow.MOUSEPOINTER = 1


*****************************************************************************
** Program Phase 4-2 Main                                                   *
** Allow resizing of the main window                                        *
** CBI:  4-2.1.1.9                                                          *
*****************************************************************************

loMainWindow.BORDERSTYLE = 3


*****************************************************************************
** Program Phase 4-2 Main                                                   *
** Maximize and display the main window                                     *
** CBI:  4-2.1.1.10                                                         *
*****************************************************************************

loMainWindow.WINDOWSTATE = SW_SHOWMAXIMIZED
loMainWindow.VISIBLE = .T.


*****************************************************************************
** Program Phase 4-2 Main                                                   *
** Start the  event loop                                                    *
** CBI:  4-2.1.1.11                                                         *
*****************************************************************************

ON SHUTDOWN DO EXITPROCEDURE
READ EVENTS


*****************************************************************************
** Program Phase 4-2 Main                                                   *
** Cleanup the resources used by the main window                            *
** CBI:  4-2.1.1.12                                                         *
*****************************************************************************

ON SHUTDOWN
POP MENU _MSYSMENU
_SCREEN.ICON = ""
```

pp4_2.prg continued on the next page

pp4_2.prg: Program Phase 4-2 Source Code continued

```
** Callback Functions/Procedures

*******************************************************************************
** Callback Functions                                                         *
** Implement the callback function for the Hello World! menu item             *
** CBI:  4-2.1.2.1                                                            *
*******************************************************************************

PROCEDURE MenuItem1_Activate

   =MESSAGEBOX("Hello World!")

ENDPROC


*******************************************************************************
** Callback Functions                                                         *
** Implement the callback function for the Exit menu item                     *
** CBI:  4-2.1.3.1                                                            *
*******************************************************************************

PROCEDURE MenuItem2_Activate

   CLEAR EVENTS

ENDPROC


*******************************************************************************
** Callback Functions                                                         *
** Implement the callback function that fires when the main window is closed  *
** CBI:  4-2.1.4.1                                                            *
*******************************************************************************

PROCEDURE EXITPROCEDURE

  LOCAL lnResult

  lnResult = MESSAGEBOX("Close the main window?",;
                        4 + 32,;
                        "Program Phase 4-2")
   IF lnResult = 6

       CLEAR EVENTS

   ENDIF

ENDPROC
```

Code Setup and Compilation

- Tools: Visual FoxPro

Code Setup and Compilation Steps

1: Create a folder called pp4_2 that will store the source code files.

2: Start the Visual FoxPro IDE program.

Steps continued on the next page

Code Setup and Compilation Steps continued

3: VFP - Activate Menu Item: File → New

From the "New" dialog window, select the "Project" radio button and then activate the "New file" button. Save the project as pp4_2.pjx in the pp4_2 folder.

4: VFP - Activate Menu Item: File → New

From the "New" dialog window, select the "Program" radio button and then activate the "New file" button.

5: Enter the source code into the new program file and then save the file as pp4_2.prg in the pp4_2 folder.

6: Add the pp4_2.prg file to the project by selecting the "Code" tab in the "Project Manager" for the pp4_2 project and then activating the "Add" button. Browse for the pp4_2.prg file in the pp4_2 folder to add it to the project.

7: Create a text file called config.fpw in the pp4_2 folder and then enter the following text:

```
screen = off
```

8: Right click on the pp4_2.prg file in the "Project Manager" window and then activate the "set main" menu item if it does not already have a check mark next to it in the menu.

9: Create the phase.ico image file according to the instructions in Appendix O. Copy the image file to the pp4_2 folder. Select the "Other" tab in the pp4_2 "Project Manager" window and click on the "Other Files" item. Activate the "Add" button to display the "Open" dialog window. Change the "Files of type" to "Icon (*.ico)" and then select the phase.ico file stored in the pp4_2 folder. This causes the phase.ico image file to be embedded into the executable file when it is built. When the main window icon is set at runtime, it can be retrieved from the executable file instead of being read from the file system. One more step needs to be performed to indicate that the phase.ico file needs to be set as the application icon. Activate the "Project Info" menu item from the "Project" menu to display the "Project Information" dialog window. Check the "Attach icon" check box to display the "Open" dialog window. Select the phase.ico file and then activate the "OK" button. Activate the "OK" button to close the "Project Information" window. This causes the phase.ico image file to be set as the icon file for the generated pp4_2.exe file.

10: Click the "Build" button on the "Project Manager" window. Select the "Win32 executable" radio button. Select "Recompile All Files" and "Display Errors". Activate the "OK" button. Use the "Save As" dialog to select a destination for the executable file and then activate the "Save" button.

Visual FoxPro Command Window Compilation

Enter the following command in the VFP command window:

```
BUILD EXE "c:\pp4_2\pp4_2.exe" FROM "c:\pp4_2\pp4_2.pjx" RECOMPILE
```

Program Execution

- Execute Program

```
VFP - Activate Menu Item:  Program → Do
```

Navigate to the pp4_2.exe file in the Do dialog window and then activate the "Do" button.

- Debug Program

```
VFP - Activate Menu Item:  Tools → Debugger
VFP Debugger window - Activate Menu Item:  Debug → Do
```

Select the pp4_2.prg file found in the pp4_2 folder and then activate the "Do" button on the Do dialog window.

Program Phase 4-3

C ▪ Win32 API ▪ Windows

GUI Based Program with Main Window

- Program Phase Task 4 is implemented in Program Phase 4-3 using the C programming language and the Win32 API.

- Program Phase 4-3 contains a main source code file named pp4_3.c. In addition to the pp4_3.c text file, an icon image file called phase.ico is used in Program Phase 4-3. The phase.ico file contains the icon that is used as the window icon for the main window and the application icon for the pp4_3.exe executable file. The resources for the program are referenced in the resource.rc and resource.h text files.

Code Block Features

The Program Phase 4-3 code blocks illustrate the following programming features using the C programming language and the Win32 API:

- **Create a Resizable Main Window for a GUI Based Application**

- **Set the Main Window Icon and Caption**

- **Set the Main Window Menu**

- **Set the Main Window Background Color and Mouse Cursor**

- **Prompt to Exit the Application when the Main Window is Closed**

C with Win32 API
Create a Resizable Main Window for a GUI Based Application

- The "WNDCLASS" structure stores information about the main window. This structure is passed as a parameter to the Win32 RegisterClass() function. The callback function that handles events for the main window is specified in the "lpfnWndProc" property of the "WNDCLASS". The "lpszClassName" property is a string identifier for the registered class. This identifier is used when the main window is created by using the Win32 CreateWindow() function. The main window is created as a resizable window because the "WS_OVERLAPPED" constant is specified as a paramater to the CreateWindow() function. The handle returned by the CreateWindow() function is passed to the Win32 ShowWindow() function that displays the main window. The ShowWindow() function displays the window in the maximized state by passing the "SW_SHOWMAXIMIZED" constant as a parameter.

- An infinite "while" loop is the event loop for the application. This infinite loop is what prevents the WinMain() function from automatically ending, which would result in the application terminating. The messages for the application are processed in this loop. The Win32 DispatchMessage() function will ensure that the MainWindowProcedure() window function automatically is called when a message for the main window is received. The infinite event loop breaks when the GetMessage() function returns the value zero, which happens when the "WM_QUIT" message is sent. When the user attempts to close the main window, the "WM_CLOSE" message is sent. This message is processed in the MainWindowProcedure callback function. When this message is processed, the main window is hidden, and then the "WM_QUIT" message is sent by using the Win32 PostQuitMessage() function.

test1.c: C w/ Win32 API Create a Resizable Main Window for a GUI Based App.

```
#include <windows.h>

LRESULT CALLBACK MainWindowProcedure(HWND thWindow,UINT tnWindowMessage,
                                     WPARAM tnWParam,LPARAM tnLParam);

INT WINAPI WinMain(HINSTANCE thInstance,HINSTANCE thPreviousInstance,
                   CHAR *tcCmdLine,INT tnShowCmd)
{
   // Main window
   HWND lhMainWindow;
   WNDCLASS loWindowClass;
   MSG loWindowMessage;
   LRESULT lnResult;

   loWindowClass.style = CS_HREDRAW | CS_VREDRAW;
   loWindowClass.cbClsExtra = 0;
   loWindowClass.cbWndExtra = 0;
   loWindowClass.hInstance = thInstance;
   loWindowClass.lpszClassName = "MainWindowClass";
   loWindowClass.lpfnWndProc = (WNDPROC)MainWindowProcedure;
   loWindowClass.hIcon = NULL;
   loWindowClass.lpszMenuName = NULL;
   loWindowClass.hbrBackground = (HBRUSH) GetStockObject(WHITE_BRUSH);
   loWindowClass.hCursor = LoadCursor(NULL,IDC_ARROW);

   lnResult = RegisterClass(&loWindowClass);

   if(lnResult == 0)
   {
      return 1;
   }

   // Create the main window
   lhMainWindow = CreateWindow("MainWindowClass",NULL,

                              // Make the window resizable
                              WS_OVERLAPPEDWINDOW,
                              CW_USEDEFAULT,CW_USEDEFAULT,CW_USEDEFAULT,
                              CW_USEDEFAULT,NULL,NULL,thInstance,NULL);

   if (lhMainWindow == 0)
   {
      return 1;
   }

   // Maximize and display the main window
   ShowWindow(lhMainWindow,SW_SHOWMAXIMIZED);

   while (1)
   {
      lnResult = GetMessage(&loWindowMessage,NULL,0,0);
      if (lnResult == 0)
      {
         break;
      }
```

test1.c continued on the next page

test1.c: C w/ Win32 API Create a Resizable Main Window for a GUI App. continued

```
        lnResult = TranslateMessage(&loWindowMessage);
        lnResult = DispatchMessage(&loWindowMessage);
    }

    DestroyWindow(lhMainWindow);
    UnregisterClass("MainWindowClass",thInstance);
    return 0;
}

// Window Procedure

LRESULT CALLBACK MainWindowProcedure(HWND thWindow,UINT tnWindowMessage,
                                     WPARAM tnWParam,LPARAM tnLParam)
{
    switch (tnWindowMessage)
    {
        case WM_CLOSE:

            ShowWindow(thWindow,SW_HIDE);
            PostQuitMessage(0);
            break;

        default:
        {
            return (DefWindowProc(thWindow,tnWindowMessage,tnWParam,tnLParam));
        }
    }
    return 0;
}
```

C with Win32 API
Set the Main Window Icon and Caption

- A multi-image icon file is used for the main window icon. A reference to this icon file is stored in a text file ending with the ".rc" file extension. When the project is compiled, the icon file is embedded into the executable file. An identifier for the icon is defined with a constant. The following example uses "IDI_ICON1" as the constant for the icon used as the main window icon. The icon file contains multiple representations of the image. Usually, a 16 x 16 pixel image and 32 x 32 pixel image are created in the icon image file. The Win32 LoadIcon() function is used to obtain a handle to the icon. This handle is stored in the "hIcon" property of the "WNDCLASS" structure.

- The main window caption is specified in the second parameter to the CreateWindow() function.

test2.c: C with Win32 API Set the Main Window Icon and Caption

```
#include <windows.h>
#include "resource.h"

LRESULT CALLBACK MainWindowProcedure(HWND thWindow,UINT tnWindowMessage,
                                     WPARAM tnWParam,LPARAM tnLParam);

INT WINAPI WinMain(HINSTANCE thInstance,HINSTANCE thPreviousInstance,
                   CHAR *tcCmdLine,INT tnShowCmd)
{
```

test2.c continued on the next page

test2.c: C with Win32 API Set the Main Window Icon and Caption continued

```
   // Main window
   HWND lhMainWindow;
   WNDCLASS loWindowClass;
   MSG loWindowMessage;
   LRESULT lnResult;

   loWindowClass.style = CS_HREDRAW | CS_VREDRAW;
   loWindowClass.cbClsExtra = 0;
   loWindowClass.cbWndExtra = 0;
   loWindowClass.hInstance = thInstance;
   loWindowClass.lpszClassName = "MainWindowClass";
   loWindowClass.lpfnWndProc = (WNDPROC)MainWindowProcedure;

   // Set the main window icon
   loWindowClass.hIcon = LoadIcon(thInstance,MAKEINTRESOURCE(IDI_ICON1));

   loWindowClass.lpszMenuName = NULL;
   loWindowClass.hbrBackground = (HBRUSH) GetStockObject(WHITE_BRUSH);
   loWindowClass.hCursor = LoadCursor(NULL,IDC_ARROW);

   lnResult = RegisterClass(&loWindowClass);

   if(lnResult == 0)
   {
      return 1;
   }

   // Create the main window
   lhMainWindow = CreateWindow("MainWindowClass",

                               // Set the main window caption
                               "Hello World!",
                               WS_OVERLAPPEDWINDOW,CW_USEDEFAULT,
                               CW_USEDEFAULT,
                               CW_USEDEFAULT,CW_USEDEFAULT,
                               NULL,NULL,thInstance,NULL);

   if (lhMainWindow == 0)
   {
      return 1;
   }

   // Maximize and display the main window
   ShowWindow(lhMainWindow,SW_SHOWMAXIMIZED);

   while (1)
   {
      lnResult = GetMessage(&loWindowMessage,NULL,0,0);

      if (lnResult == 0)
      {
         break;
      }

      lnResult = TranslateMessage(&loWindowMessage);
      lnResult = DispatchMessage(&loWindowMessage);
   }

   DestroyWindow(lhMainWindow);
   UnregisterClass("MainWindowClass",thInstance);

   return 0;
}
```

test2.c continued on the next page

test2.c: C with Win32 API Set the Main Window Icon and Caption continued

```
// Window Procedure

LRESULT CALLBACK MainWindowProcedure(HWND thWindow,UINT tnWindowMessage,
                                     WPARAM tnWParam,LPARAM tnLParam)
{
   switch (tnWindowMessage)
   {
         case WM_CLOSE:
            ShowWindow(thWindow,SW_HIDE);
            PostQuitMessage(0);
            break;

      default:
      {
         return (DefWindowProc(thWindow,tnWindowMessage,tnWParam,tnLParam));
      }
   }
   return 0;
}
```

resource.h: Header File for the Icon Resource

```
#define IDI_ICON1                        100
```

resource.rc: Resource File for the Icon Resource

```
#include "resource.h"
IDI_ICON1               ICON                    "phase.ico"
```

C with Win32 API
Set the Main Window Menu

- The Win32 CreateMenu() and AppendMenu() functions are used to create a menu for the main window. When the menu handle is created by using the CreateMenu() function, it is assigned to the main window in the ninth parameter to the CreateWindow() function. The menu for the main window can also be defined in a resource file. The "lpszMenuName" property of the "WNDCLASS" structure is used if assigning a menu reference obtained from a resource file (not shown). The example presented uses the CreateMenu() and AppendMenu() functions to create the main window menu.

- Keyboard shortcuts for the main window menu items are defined in the resource file by using accelerators. The keyboard accelerators are created from the resource file by using the MAKEINTRESOURCE() macro and the Win32 LoadAccelerators() function. The Win32 TranslateAccelerator() function is used in the event loop to process the keyboard shortcuts.

- The following example creates a "File" menu with a "Hello World!" menu item and "Exit" menu item:

test3.c: C with Win32 API Set the Main Window Menu

```
#include <windows.h>
#include "resource.h"

LRESULT CALLBACK MainWindowProcedure(HWND thWindow,UINT tnWindowMessage,
                                     WPARAM tnWParam,LPARAM tnLParam);
```

test3.c continued on the next page

test3.c: C with Win32 API Set the Main Window Menu continued

```
INT WINAPI WinMain(HINSTANCE thInstance,HINSTANCE thPreviousInstance,
                   CHAR *tcCmdLine,INT tnShowCmd)
{
   // Main window
   HWND lhMainWindow;
   WNDCLASS loWindowClass;
   MSG loWindowMessage;
   LRESULT lnResult;
   HMENU lhMenuBar;
   HMENU lhFileMenu;
   CHAR *lcAcceleratorName;
   HACCEL lhAccelerator;

   loWindowClass.style = CS_HREDRAW | CS_VREDRAW;
   loWindowClass.cbClsExtra = 0;
   loWindowClass.cbWndExtra = 0;
   loWindowClass.hInstance = thInstance;
   loWindowClass.lpszClassName = "MainWindowClass";
   loWindowClass.lpfnWndProc = (WNDPROC)MainWindowProcedure;
   loWindowClass.hIcon = NULL;
   loWindowClass.lpszMenuName = NULL;
   loWindowClass.hbrBackground = (HBRUSH) GetStockObject(WHITE_BRUSH);
   loWindowClass.hCursor = LoadCursor(NULL,IDC_ARROW);

   // Setup the menu bar
   lhMenuBar = CreateMenu();

   // Create the file menu
   lhFileMenu = CreateMenu();

   // Create the Hello World! menu item
   AppendMenu(lhFileMenu, MF_STRING, IDM_MENUITEM1,"&Hello World!\tCtrl+H");

   // Create the Exit menu item
   AppendMenu(lhFileMenu, MF_STRING, IDM_MENUITEM2,"E&xit\tCtrl+X");

   // Assign the File menu to the main window
   AppendMenu(lhMenuBar, MF_POPUP,(UINT)lhFileMenu,"&File");

   lnResult = RegisterClass(&loWindowClass);
   if(lnResult == 0)
   {
      return 1;
   }

   // Create the main window
   lhMainWindow = CreateWindow("MainWindowClass",NULL,WS_OVERLAPPEDWINDOW,
                               CW_USEDEFAULT,CW_USEDEFAULT,
                               CW_USEDEFAULT,CW_USEDEFAULT,NULL,

                               // Assign the File menu to the main window
                               lhMenuBar,
                               thInstance,NULL);
   if (lhMainWindow == 0)
   {
      return 1;
   }

   // Maximize and display the main window
   ShowWindow(lhMainWindow,SW_SHOWMAXIMIZED);
   lcAcceleratorName = MAKEINTRESOURCE(IDR_ACCELERATOR1);
   lhAccelerator = LoadAccelerators(thInstance,lcAcceleratorName);

   while (1)
   {
      lnResult = GetMessage(&loWindowMessage,NULL,0,0);
```

test3.c continued on the next page

test3.c: C with Win32 API Set the Main Window Menu continued

```
      if (lnResult == 0)
      {
         break;
      }

      lnResult = TranslateAccelerator(lhMainWindow,lhAccelerator,
                                      &loWindowMessage);
      if (lnResult == 0)
      {
         lnResult = TranslateMessage(&loWindowMessage);
         lnResult = DispatchMessage(&loWindowMessage);
      }
   }
   DestroyWindow(lhMainWindow);
   UnregisterClass("MainWindowClass",thInstance);
   return 0;
}

// Window Procedure

LRESULT CALLBACK MainWindowProcedure(HWND thWindow,UINT tnWindowMessage,
                                     WPARAM tnWParam,LPARAM tnLParam)
{
   INT lnWindowMessageCommand;

   switch (tnWindowMessage)
   {
      case WM_COMMAND:

         lnWindowMessageCommand = LOWORD(tnWParam);

         switch(lnWindowMessageCommand)
         {
            case IDM_MENUITEM1:

               MessageBox(NULL,"Hello World!","test",
                          MB_OK | MB_ICONINFORMATION);
               break;

            case IDM_MENUITEM2:

               ShowWindow(thWindow,SW_HIDE);
               PostQuitMessage(0);
               break;
         }
         break;

      case WM_CLOSE:

        ShowWindow(thWindow,SW_HIDE);
        PostQuitMessage(0);
        break;

      default:
      {
         return (DefWindowProc(thWindow,tnWindowMessage,tnWParam,tnLParam));
      }
   }
   return 0;
}
```

resource.h: Header File for the Menu Resources

```
#define IDR_ACCELERATOR1                101
#define IDM_MENUITEM1                   102
#define IDM_MENUITEM2                   103
```

resource.rc: Resource File for the Menu Resources

```
#include "resource.h"

IDR_ACCELERATOR1 ACCELERATORS
BEGIN
    "H",            IDM_MENUITEM1,          VIRTKEY, CONTROL, NOINVERT
    "X",            IDM_MENUITEM2,          VIRTKEY, CONTROL, NOINVERT
END
```

C with Win32 API
Set the Main Window Background Color and Mouse Cursor

- The main window background color is set with an RGB value by creating a "brush" with the Win32 CreateSolidBrush() function. A handle to a "brush" is returned from this function and is assigned to the "hbrBackground" property of the "WNDCLASS" structure. It is important to delete the "brush" before the program exits by using the Win32 DeleteObject() function.

  The Win32 LoadCursor() function is used to retrieve a handle to a mouse cursor. This handle is assigned to the "hcursor" property of the "WNDCLASS" structure.

test4.c: C with Win32 API Set the Main Window Background Color and Mouse Cursor

```
#include <windows.h>

LRESULT CALLBACK MainWindowProcedure(HWND thWindow,UINT tnWindowMessage,
                                     WPARAM tnWParam,LPARAM tnLParam);

INT WINAPI WinMain(HINSTANCE thInstance,HINSTANCE thPreviousInstance,
                   CHAR *tcCmdLine,INT tnShowCmd)
{
   // Main window
   HWND lhMainWindow;
   WNDCLASS loWindowClass;
   MSG loWindowMessage;
   LRESULT lnResult;
   COLORREF lnWindowBackColor;
   HBRUSH lhBrush;

   loWindowClass.style = CS_HREDRAW | CS_VREDRAW;
   loWindowClass.cbClsExtra = 0;
   loWindowClass.cbWndExtra = 0;
   loWindowClass.hInstance = thInstance;
   loWindowClass.lpszClassName = "MainWindowClass";
   loWindowClass.lpfnWndProc = (WNDPROC)MainWindowProcedure;
   loWindowClass.hIcon = NULL;
   loWindowClass.lpszMenuName = NULL;

   lnWindowBackColor = RGB(255,255,255);
   lhBrush = CreateSolidBrush(lnWindowBackColor);

   if (lhBrush == NULL)
   {
      return 1;
   }

  // Set the main window background color
   loWindowClass.hbrBackground = lhBrush;

   // Set the main window mouse cursor
   loWindowClass.hCursor = LoadCursor(NULL,IDC_ARROW);
```

test4.c continued on the next page

test4.c: C w/ Win32 API Set the Main Window BG Color and Mouse Cursor continued

```
   lnResult = RegisterClass(&loWindowClass);

   if(lnResult == 0)
   {
      return 1;
   }

   // Create the main window
   lhMainWindow = CreateWindow("MainWindowClass",NULL,
                               WS_OVERLAPPEDWINDOW,
                               CW_USEDEFAULT,CW_USEDEFAULT,
                               CW_USEDEFAULT,CW_USEDEFAULT,
                               NULL,NULL,thInstance,NULL);

   if (lhMainWindow == 0)
   {
      return 1;
   }

   // Maximize and display the main window
   ShowWindow(lhMainWindow,SW_SHOWMAXIMIZED);

   while (1)
   {
      lnResult = GetMessage(&loWindowMessage,NULL,0,0);

      if (lnResult == 0)
      {
         break;
      }

      lnResult = TranslateMessage(&loWindowMessage);
      lnResult = DispatchMessage(&loWindowMessage);
   }

   DeleteObject(lhBrush);
   DestroyWindow(lhMainWindow);
   UnregisterClass("MainWindowClass",thInstance);

   return 0;
}

// Window Procedure
LRESULT CALLBACK MainWindowProcedure(HWND thWindow,UINT tnWindowMessage,
                                     WPARAM tnWParam,LPARAM tnLParam)
{
   switch (tnWindowMessage)
   {
      case WM_CLOSE:

        ShowWindow(thWindow,SW_HIDE);
        PostQuitMessage(0);
        break;

      default:
      {
         return (DefWindowProc(thWindow,tnWindowMessage,tnWParam,tnLParam));
      }
   }
   return 0;
}
```

C with Win32 API
Prompt to Exit the Application when the Main Window is Closed

- The Win32 MessageBox() function is used in the window procedure to prompt the user to continue closing the main window. If the user selects "No", the "switch" statement is exited using the "break" statement. Otherwise, the window is hidden, and the PostQuitMessage() function is called.

test5.c: C with Win32 API Prompt to Exit the App. when the Main Window is Closed

```
#include <windows.h>

LRESULT CALLBACK MainWindowProcedure(HWND thWindow,UINT tnWindowMessage,
                                     WPARAM tnWParam,LPARAM tnLParam);

INT WINAPI WinMain(HINSTANCE thInstance,HINSTANCE thPreviousInstance,
                   CHAR *tcCmdLine,INT tnShowCmd)
{
   // Main window
   HWND lhMainWindow;
   WNDCLASS loWindowClass;
   MSG loWindowMessage;
   LRESULT lnResult;

   loWindowClass.style = CS_HREDRAW | CS_VREDRAW;
   loWindowClass.cbClsExtra = 0;
   loWindowClass.cbWndExtra = 0;
   loWindowClass.hInstance = thInstance;
   loWindowClass.lpszClassName = "MainWindowClass";
   loWindowClass.lpfnWndProc = (WNDPROC)MainWindowProcedure;
   loWindowClass.hIcon = NULL;
   loWindowClass.lpszMenuName = NULL;
   loWindowClass.hbrBackground = (HBRUSH) GetStockObject(WHITE_BRUSH);
   loWindowClass.hCursor = LoadCursor(NULL,IDC_ARROW);

   lnResult = RegisterClass(&loWindowClass);

   if(lnResult == 0)
   {
      return 1;
   }

   // Create the main window
   lhMainWindow = CreateWindow("MainWindowClass",NULL,
                               WS_OVERLAPPEDWINDOW,
                               CW_USEDEFAULT,CW_USEDEFAULT,
                               CW_USEDEFAULT,CW_USEDEFAULT,
                               NULL,NULL,thInstance,NULL);

   if (lhMainWindow == 0)
   {
      return 1;
   }

   // Maximize and display the main window
   ShowWindow(lhMainWindow,SW_SHOWMAXIMIZED);

   while (1)
   {
      lnResult = GetMessage(&loWindowMessage,NULL,0,0);

      if (lnResult == 0)
      {
         break;
      }
```

test5.c continued on the next page

test5.c: C w/ Win32 API Prompt to Exit when the Main Window is Closed continued

```
      lnResult = TranslateMessage(&loWindowMessage);
      lnResult = DispatchMessage(&loWindowMessage);
   }

   DestroyWindow(lhMainWindow);
   UnregisterClass("MainWindowClass",thInstance);

   return 0;
}

// Window Procedure

LRESULT CALLBACK MainWindowProcedure(HWND thWindow,UINT tnWindowMessage,
                                     WPARAM tnWParam,LPARAM tnLParam)
{
   INT lnResult;

   switch (tnWindowMessage)
   {
      case WM_CLOSE:

        // Prompt the user to continue closing the main window
        lnResult = MessageBox(NULL,"Close the main window?",
                              "test",MB_YESNO | MB_ICONQUESTION);

        if (lnResult == IDNO)
        {
           break;
        }

        ShowWindow(thWindow,SW_HIDE);
        PostQuitMessage(0);
        break;

      default:
      {
         return (DefWindowProc(thWindow,tnWindowMessage,tnWParam,tnLParam));
      }
   }
   return 0;
}
```

Source Code Files

- Text files: pp4_3.c, resource.h, resource.rc
- Image files: phase.ico (Multi-image icon file, Appendix O)

pp4_3.c: Program Phase 4-3 Source Code

```
//****************************************************************************
// Program Phase 4-3 C Main Window with File Menu                            *
// Programming Tasks Illustrated: Win32 GUI based application               *
//                                Main window                                *
//                                Window icon                                *
//                                Window caption                             *
//                                Window menu with hotkeys                   *
//                                Window background color                    *
//                                Window mouse cursor                        *
//                                User sizable window                        *
//                                Message box input/output                   *
//****************************************************************************
```

pp4_3.c continued on the next page

pp4_3.c: Program Phase 4-3 Source Code continued

```
//**************************************************************************
// File: pp4_3.c                                                          *
// Reserved                                                               *
//**************************************************************************

#include <windows.h>
#include "stdio.h"
#include "resource.h"

LRESULT CALLBACK MainWindowProcedure(HWND thWindow,UINT tnWindowMessage,
                                     WPARAM tnWParam,LPARAM tnLParam);


//**************************************************************************
// Program Phase 4-3 Main                                                 *
// Define the Entry Point of Execution (EPE) for Program Phase 4-3        *
// CBI:  4-3.1.1.1                                                        *
//**************************************************************************

INT WINAPI WinMain(HINSTANCE thInstance,HINSTANCE thPreviousInstance,
                   CHAR *tcCmdLine,INT tnShowCmd)
{


//**************************************************************************
// Program Phase 4-3 Main                                                 *
// Declare the local variables for the "main" program                     *
// CBI:  4-3.1.1.2                                                        *
//**************************************************************************

   // Main window
   HWND lhMainWindow;
   WNDCLASSEX loWindowClass;
   MSG loWindowMessage;

   // Main window icon
   CHAR *lcIcon;
   HICON lhIcon;

   // Main window caption
   CHAR lcWindowCaption[256];

   // Main window menu
   HMENU lhMenuBar;
   HMENU lhFileMenu;
   CHAR *lcAcceleratorName;
   HACCEL lhAccelerator;

   // Main window background color
   COLORREF lnWindowBackColor;
   HBRUSH lhBrush;

   // Main window mouse cursor
   HCURSOR lhMouseCursor;

   // Resize main window
   INT lnWindowStyle;

   // Function results
   INT lnBytesStored;
   LRESULT lnResult;
```

pp4_3.c continued on the next page

pp4_3.c: Program Phase 4-3 Source Code continued

```
//*************************************************************************
// Program Phase 4-3 Main                                                 *
// Create the main window                                                 *
// CBI:  4-3.1.1.3                                                        *
//*************************************************************************

   loWindowClass.cbSize = sizeof(WNDCLASSEX);
   loWindowClass.style = CS_HREDRAW | CS_VREDRAW;
   loWindowClass.cbClsExtra = 0;
   loWindowClass.cbWndExtra = 0;
   loWindowClass.hInstance = thInstance;
   loWindowClass.lpszClassName = "MainWindowClass";
   loWindowClass.lpfnWndProc = (WNDPROC)MainWindowProcedure;

   // The main window is created in CBI: 4-3.1.1.10.


//*************************************************************************
// Program Phase 4-3 Main                                                 *
// Set the icon for the main window                                       *
// CBI:  4-3.1.1.4                                                        *
//*************************************************************************

   lcIcon = MAKEINTRESOURCE(IDI_ICON1);
   lhIcon = LoadIcon(thInstance,lcIcon);

   if (lhIcon == NULL)
   {
      MessageBoxA(NULL,
                  "The LoadIcon Win32 API function failed.",
                  "CBI:  4-3.1.1.4",
                  MB_OK | MB_ICONERROR);

      return TRUE;
   }

   loWindowClass.hIcon = lhIcon;
   loWindowClass.hIconSm = NULL;


//*************************************************************************
// Program Phase 4-3 Main                                                 *
// Set the caption of the main window                                     *
// CBI:  4-3.1.1.5                                                        *
//*************************************************************************

   lnBytesStored = sprintf(lcWindowCaption,"Program Phase 4-3  |  "
                                           "Platform:  Windows  |  "
                                           "Programming Language:  C  |  "
                                           "GUI API:  Win32");

   if (lnBytesStored == -1)
   {
      MessageBox(NULL,"The sprintf function failed.",
                 "CBI:  4-3.1.1.5",MB_OK | MB_ICONERROR);

      return TRUE;
   }


//*************************************************************************
// Program Phase 4-3 Main                                                 *
// Create the menu for the main window                                    *
// CBI:  4-3.1.1.6                                                        *
//*************************************************************************
```

pp4_3.c continued on the next page

pp4_3.c: Program Phase 4-3 Source Code continued

```
   // Menu bar
   lhMenuBar = CreateMenu();

   // Hello World! menu item
   lhFileMenu = CreateMenu();

   AppendMenu(lhFileMenu, MF_STRING, IDM_MENUITEM1, "&Hello World!\tCtrl+H");

   // Exit menu item
   AppendMenu(lhFileMenu, MF_STRING, IDM_MENUITEM2, "E&xit\tCtrl+X");

   // File menu
   AppendMenu(lhMenuBar, MF_POPUP,(UINT)lhFileMenu, "&File");

   // Assign the File menu to the main window
   loWindowClass.lpszMenuName = NULL;

   // The File menu is assigned in CBI:  4-3.1.1.10 as the ninth parameter
   // to the CreateWindow() function.  The lpszMenuName property of the
   // WNDCLASSEX structure is used if assigning a menu reference obtained
   // from a resource file.


//***************************************************************************
// Program Phase 4-3 Main                                                   *
// Set the background color of the main window                              *
// CBI:  4-3.1.1.7                                                          *
//***************************************************************************

   lnWindowBackColor = RGB(255,255,255);
   lhBrush = CreateSolidBrush(lnWindowBackColor);

   if (lhBrush == NULL)
   {
      MessageBox(NULL,"The CreateSolidBrush Win32 API function failed.",
                 "CBI:  4-3.1.1.7",MB_OK | MB_ICONERROR);

      return TRUE;
   }

   loWindowClass.hbrBackground = lhBrush;


//***************************************************************************
// Program Phase 4-3 Main                                                   *
// Set the mouse cursor displayed when positoned over the main window       *
// CBI:  4-3.1.1.8                                                          *
//***************************************************************************

   lhMouseCursor = LoadCursor(NULL,IDC_ARROW);

   if (lhMouseCursor == NULL)
   {
      MessageBox(NULL,"The LoadCursor Win32 API function failed.",
                 "CBI:  4-3.1.1.8",MB_OK | MB_ICONERROR);

      lnResult = DeleteObject(lhBrush);

      if (lnResult == 0)
      {
         MessageBox(NULL,"The DeleteObject Win32 API function failed.",
                    "CBI:  4-3.1.1.8",MB_OK | MB_ICONERROR);
      }

      return TRUE;
   }
```

pp4_3.c continued on the next page

pp4_3.c: Program Phase 4-3 Source Code continued

```
   loWindowClass.hCursor = lhMouseCursor;


//*************************************************************************
// Program Phase 4-3 Main                                                 *
// Allow resizing of the main window                                      *
// CBI:  4-3.1.1.9                                                        *
//*************************************************************************

   // The lnWindowStyle variable is used in the third parameter to the
   // CreateWindow() function in CBI: 4-3.1.1.10.
   lnWindowStyle = WS_OVERLAPPEDWINDOW;


//*************************************************************************
// Program Phase 4-3 Main                                                 *
// Maximize and display the main window                                   *
// CBI:  4-3.1.1.10                                                       *
//*************************************************************************

   lnResult = RegisterClassEx(&loWindowClass);

   if(lnResult == 0)
   {
      MessageBox(NULL,"The RegisterClassEx Win32 API function failed.",
                 "CBI:  4-3.1.1.10",MB_OK | MB_ICONERROR);

      lnResult = DeleteObject(lhBrush);

      if (lnResult == 0)
      {
         MessageBox(NULL,"The DeleteObject Win32 API function failed.",
                    "CBI:  4-3.1.1.10",MB_OK | MB_ICONERROR);
      }

      return TRUE;
   }

   lhMainWindow = CreateWindow("MainWindowClass",
                               lcWindowCaption,
                               lnWindowStyle,
                               CW_USEDEFAULT,
                               CW_USEDEFAULT,
                               CW_USEDEFAULT,
                               CW_USEDEFAULT,
                               NULL,lhMenuBar,thInstance,NULL);

   if (lhMainWindow == 0)
   {
      MessageBox(NULL,
                 "The CreateWindow Win32 API function failed.",
                 "CBI:  4-3.1.1.10",
                 MB_OK | MB_ICONERROR);

      return TRUE;
   }

   ShowWindow(lhMainWindow,SW_SHOWMAXIMIZED);


//*************************************************************************
// Program Phase 4-3 Main                                                 *
// Start the event loop                                                   *
// CBI:  4-3.1.1.11                                                       *
//*************************************************************************
```

pp4_3.c continued on the next page

pp4_3.c: Program Phase 4-3 Source Code continued

```
   lcAcceleratorName = MAKEINTRESOURCE(IDR_ACCELERATOR1);
   lhAccelerator = LoadAccelerators(thInstance,lcAcceleratorName);

   if (lhAccelerator == NULL)
   {
      MessageBox(NULL,"The LoadAccelerators function failed.",
                 "CBI:  4-3.1.1.11",MB_OK | MB_ICONERROR);

      return TRUE;
   }

   // Infinite loop that prevents the program from exiting.
   while (1)
   {
      lnResult = GetMessage(&loWindowMessage,NULL,0,0);

      if (lnResult == 0)
      {
         break;
      }

   lnResult = TranslateAccelerator(lhMainWindow,lhAccelerator,
                                   &loWindowMessage);

   if (lnResult == 0)
      {
         lnResult = TranslateMessage(&loWindowMessage);
         lnResult = DispatchMessage(&loWindowMessage);
      }
   }


//***************************************************************************
// Program Phase 4-3 Main                                                   *
// Cleanup the resources used by the main window                            *
// CBI:  4-3.1.1.12                                                         *
//***************************************************************************

   lnResult = DeleteObject(lhBrush);

   if (lnResult == 0)
   {
      MessageBoxA(NULL,"The DeleteObject Win32 API function failed.",
                  "CBI:  4-3.1.1.12",
                  MB_OK | MB_ICONERROR);
   }

   lnResult = DestroyWindow(lhMainWindow);

   if (lnResult == 0)
   {
      MessageBox(NULL,"The DestroyWindow Win32 API function failed.",
                 "CBI:  4-3.1.1.12",
                 MB_OK | MB_ICONERROR);
   }

   lnResult = UnregisterClass("MainWindowClass",thInstance);

   if (lnResult == 0)
   {
      MessageBox(NULL,"The UnregisterClass Win32 API function failed.",
                 "CBI:  4-3.1.1.12",
                 MB_OK | MB_ICONERROR);
   }
   return 0;
}
```

pp4_3.c continued on the next page

pp4_3.c: Program Phase 4-3 Source Code continued

```
// Callback Functions
// The MainWindowProcedure() function is the only callback function
// for the main window.

LRESULT CALLBACK MainWindowProcedure(HWND thWindow,UINT tnWindowMessage,
                                     WPARAM tnWParam,LPARAM tnLParam)
{
   INT lnResult;
   INT lnWindowMessageCommand;

   switch (tnWindowMessage)
   {
      case WM_COMMAND:

         lnWindowMessageCommand = LOWORD(tnWParam);

         switch(lnWindowMessageCommand)
         {

//***********************************************************************
// Callback Functions                                                   *
// Implement the callback function for the Hello World! menu item       *
// CBI:  4-3.1.2.1                                                      *
//***********************************************************************

            case IDM_MENUITEM1:

               // Display the Hello World! message box dialog if the user
               // activates the Hello World! menu item
               MessageBox(NULL,"Hello World!",
                          "Program Phase 4-3",
                          MB_OK | MB_ICONINFORMATION);

               break;

//***********************************************************************
// Callback Functions                                                   *
// Implement the callback function for the Exit menu item               *
// CBI:  4-3.1.3.1                                                      *
//***********************************************************************

            case IDM_MENUITEM2:

               // Exit the program if the user activates the Exit menu item
               lnResult = ShowWindow(thWindow,SW_HIDE);

               PostQuitMessage(0);
               break;
         }

         break;

//***********************************************************************
// Callback Functions                                                   *
// Implement the callback function that fires when the main window is closed  *
// CBI:  4-3.1.4.1                                                      *
//***********************************************************************

      case WM_CLOSE:

         // Prompt the user to continue closing the main window
         lnResult = MessageBox(NULL,"Close the main window?",
                               "Program Phase 4-3",MB_YESNO | MB_ICONQUESTION);
```

pp4_3.c continued on the next page

pp4_3.c: Program Phase 4-3 Source Code continued

```
         if (lnResult == IDNO)
         {
            break;
         }

         lnResult = ShowWindow(thWindow,SW_HIDE);
         PostQuitMessage(0);
         break;

      default:
      {
         return (DefWindowProc(thWindow,tnWindowMessage,tnWParam,tnLParam));
      }
   }
   return 0;
}
```

resource.h: Header File for the Program Resources

```
#define IDI_ICON1                           100
#define IDR_ACCELERATOR1                    101
#define IDM_MENUITEM1                       102
#define IDM_MENUITEM2                       103
```

resource.rc: Resource File for the Program Resources

```
#include "resource.h"
IDI_ICON1               ICON                    "phase.ico"

IDR_ACCELERATOR1 ACCELERATORS
BEGIN
    "H",            IDM_MENUITEM1,          VIRTKEY, CONTROL, NOINVERT
    "X",            IDM_MENUITEM2,          VIRTKEY, CONTROL, NOINVERT
END
```

Code Setup and Compilation

- Tools: Microsoft Visual Studio 2008 Express Edition (msdn.microsoft.com)

Code Setup and Compilation Steps

1: Start the Visual C++ 2008 Express Edition program.

2: VC++ EE - Activate Menu Item: File → New → Project

For the "Project type", select "Win32", and then select the "Win32 Console Application" template. Enter pp4_3 as the project "Name". Enter the appropriate folder as the project "Location". The pp4_3 folder will be created automatically. Make sure that the "Create directory for solution" check box is not checked.

3: Activate the "OK" button to proceed with the "Win32 Application Wizard".

4: Activate the "Next" button of the "Win32 Application Wizard".

Steps continued on the next page

Code Setup and Compilation Steps continued

5: Verify that a "Console Application" is selected and also check the "Empty project" check box. Activate the "Finish" button of the "Win32 Application Wizard".

6: VC++ EE - Activate Menu Item: Project → Add New Item

On the "Add New Item" dialog window, select the "Visual C++ → Code" category and then select the "C++ File" template. Enter pp4_3.c for the file "Name". Activate the "Add" button.

7: Enter the source code for the pp4_3.c text file and then save and close the file.

8: Create the phase.ico image file according to the instructions in Appendix O. Copy the image file to the pp4_3 folder.

9: Using a text editor, create the resource.h and resource.rc files and then enter the appropriate source code. Copy the resource.h and resource.rc files to the pp4_3 folder.

10: VC++ EE - Activate Menu Item: Project → Add Existing Item

Select the resource.h file in the pp4_3 folder and then activate the Add button.

11: VC++ EE - Activate Menu Item: Project → Add Existing Item

Select the resource.rc file in the pp4_3 folder and then activate the "Add" button.

12: VC++ EE - Activate Menu Item: Build → Configuration Manager

Select the "Release" value for the "Active solution configuration". Activate the "Close" button.

13: VC++ EE - Activate Menu Item: Project → pp4_3 Properties

Enter the following settings:

Configuration Properties → C/C++ → Code Generation → Runtime Library

For Release Configuration:

```
Multi-threaded (/MT) or Multi-threaded DLL (/MD)
```

For Debug Configuration:

```
Multi-threaded Debug /MTd or Multi-threaded Debug DLL (/MDd)
```

Configuration Properties → General → Character Set

```
"Use Multi-Byte Character Set"
```

Configuration Properties → C/C++ → Preprocessor → Preprocessor Definitions

```
remove _CONSOLE
add _WINDOWS
```

Configuration Properties → Linker → System → SubSystem

```
Windows
```

Steps continued on the next page

Code Setup and Compilation Steps continued

14: VC++ EE - Activate Menu Item: Build → Build pp4_3

Command Prompt Compilation Steps

1: From the Visual Studio 2008 command prompt, change to the pp4_3 folder and then enter the following:

```
cl.exe /MT /c pp4_3.c
```

This command compiles the source code into an object file. The /MT switch tells the compiler to use the statically linked C/C++ runtime. Use the /MD switch to use the C/C++ library in a shared dll.

2: Compile the resource file into the resource.res file.

```
rc.exe resource.rc
```

3: The following command can be used to link the pp4_3.obj file and resource.res file to create the pp4_3.exe program:

```
link.exe pp4_3.obj resource.res /INCREMENTAL:NO /MANIFEST
/SUBSYSTEM:WINDOWS kernel32.lib user32.lib gdi32.lib
```

4: The mt.exe program can be run to embed the manifest into the executable file. This is necessary so that the C library runtime dlls will be properly accessed at runtime. This step is automatically done when compiling using the IDE to create the pp4_3.exe.

```
mt.exe /manifest pp4_3.exe.manifest /outputresource:pp4_3.exe
```

Windows – Program Execution

- Execute Program

    VC++ EE - Activate Menu Item: Debug → Start Without Debugging

- Debug Program

    VC++ EE - Activate Menu Item: Project → pp4_3 Properties

    Expand the "Configuration Properties → Linker" entry and then click on the "Debugging" item. Set the "Generate Debug Info" entry to "Yes". Close the "pp4_3 Properties" window.

    VC++ EE - Activate Menu Item: Debug → Step Into

Visual Basic 6 ▪ Windows

GUI Based Program with Main Window

- Program Phase Task 4 is implemented in Program Phase 4-4 using the Visual Basic 6 (VB6) programming language.
- Program Phase 4-4 contains a main source code file named pp4_4.bas. Source code for the main window is stored in the mainwindow.frm file. In addition, an icon image file called phase.ico is used as the window icon for the main window and the application icon for the pp4_4.exe executable file.

Code Block Features

The Program Phase 4-4 code blocks illustrate the following programming features using the VB6 programming language:

- **Create a Resizable Main Window for a GUI Based Application**
- **Set the Main Window Icon and Caption**
- **Set the Main Window Menu**
- **Set the Main Window Background Color and Mouse Cursor**
- **Prompt to Exit the Application when the Main Window is Closed**

Visual Basic 6
Create a Resizable Main Window for a GUI Based Application

- The main window is implemented with a VB6 Form. A Form is added to the project by activating the "Add Form" menu item from the "Project" menu. The examples presented in this section assume that a Form named mainwindow has been added to the project.

test1.bas: VB6 Create a Resizable Main Window for a GUI Based Application

```
Private Declare Sub ExitProcess Lib "kernel32" (ByVal tnExitCode As Long)

Sub Main()

   Dim loMainWindow As mainwindow

   '' Create the main window
   Set loMainWindow = Nothing
   Set loMainWindow = New mainwindow

   If loMainWindow Is Nothing Then
      ExitProcess 1
   End If
```

test1.bas continued on the next page

test1.bas: VB 6 Create a Resizable Main Window for a GUI Based App. continued

```
    loMainWindow.BorderStyle = vbSizeable

    '' Maximize and display the main window
    loMainWindow.WindowState = vbMaximized
    loMainWindow.Show

End Sub
```

Visual Basic 6
Set the Main Window Icon and Caption

- The icon for the main window is set in the "Icon" property of the main window Form.
- The "Caption" property of the main window allows the caption of the main window to be set.
- The test2.bas example assumes that the VB6 resource editor has been used to create the ".res" file that stores the icon image. The resource editor is discussed in more detail in the Code Setup and Compilation instructions for Program Phase 4-4.

test2.bas: Visual Basic 6 Set the Main Window Icon and Caption

```
Private Declare Sub ExitProcess Lib "kernel32" (ByVal tnExitCode As Long)

Sub Main()

    Dim loMainWindow As mainwindow

    '' Create the main window
    Set loMainWindow = Nothing
    Set loMainWindow = New mainwindow

    If loMainWindow Is Nothing Then

        ExitProcess 1

    End If

    '' The main window icon can be set in the Icon property of the
    '' main window form.

    '' Set the main window caption
    loMainWindow.Caption = "Hello World!"

    loMainWindow.BorderStyle = vbSizeable

    '' Maximize and display the main window
    loMainWindow.WindowState = vbMaximized
    loMainWindow.Show

End Sub
```

Visual Basic 6
Set the Main Window Menu

- The menu and menu items of the main window are set by using the VB6 IDE. Create a new Form file called mainwindow.frm in a "Standard EXE" project. Open the mainwindow.frm file and then activate the "Menu Editor" item from the "Tools" menu.

The menu editor allows a menu to be generated that is automatically created when the Form is created. The name of the menu is important because the name of the callback procedure that is called when the menu item is activated is based on the name of the menu item.

- For the next example, a "File" menu has been created with two menu items. The menu items in the "File" menu are named MenuItem1 and MenuItem2. The callback procedure that is called when the menu item is activated is the name of the menu with the text "_click" appended to it. The callback procedures are implemented in the mainwindow.frm file. The Code Setup and Compilation instructions for Program Phase 4-4 contain detailed information for creating the menu and menu items. The "Menu Editor" is used to assign keyboard shortcuts to the menu items for the main window. This is also illustrated in the Code Setup and Compilation instructions.

test3.bas: Visual Basic 6 Set the Main Window Menu

```
Private Declare Sub ExitProcess Lib "kernel32" (ByVal tnExitCode As Long)

Sub Main()

   Dim loMainWindow As mainwindow

   '' Create the main window
   Set loMainWindow = Nothing
   Set loMainWindow = New mainwindow

   If loMainWindow Is Nothing Then

      ExitProcess 1

   End If

   loMainWindow.BorderStyle = vbSizeable

   '' Maximize and display the main window
   loMainWindow.WindowState = vbMaximized
   loMainWindow.Show

End Sub
```

mainwindow.frm: Callback Functions for the Main Window Menu Items

```
Private Sub MenuItem1_Click(Index As Integer)

   Call MsgBox("Hello World!", vbInformation, "test")

End Sub

Private Sub MenuItem2_Click(Index As Integer)

   Unload Me

End Sub

'' Note that additional VB code is found in this file but is hidden when
'' viewed in the Visual Basic 6 IDE.
```

Visual Basic 6
Set the Main Window Background Color and Mouse Cursor

- The following example sets the main window background color and mouse cursor:

test4.bas: Visual Basic 6 Set the Main Window Background Color and Mouse Cursor

```
Private Declare Sub ExitProcess Lib "kernel32" (ByVal tnExitCode As Long)

Sub Main()

   Dim loMainWindow As mainwindow
   Dim lnWindowBackColor As Long

   '' Create the main window
   Set loMainWindow = Nothing
   Set loMainWindow = New mainwindow

   If loMainWindow Is Nothing Then

      ExitProcess 1

   End If

   loMainWindow.BorderStyle = vbSizeable

   '' Set the main window background color
   lnWindowBackColor = RGB(255, 255, 255)
   loMainWindow.BackColor = lnWindowBackColor

   '' Set the main window mouse cursor
   loMainWindow.MousePointer = vbArrow

   '' Maximize and display the main window
   loMainWindow.WindowState = vbMaximized
   loMainWindow.Show

End Sub
```

Visual Basic 6
Prompt to Exit the Application when the Main Window is Closed

- The Form_QueryUnload() event of the main window Form is used to prompt the user to continue closing the main window. Setting the "Cancel" parameter to the Boolean "true" value prevents the Form from closing.

test5.bas: VB 6 Prompt to Exit the Application when the Main Window is Closed

```
Private Declare Sub ExitProcess Lib "kernel32" (ByVal tnExitCode As Long)

Sub Main()

   Dim loMainWindow As mainwindow

   '' Create the main window
   Set loMainWindow = Nothing
   Set loMainWindow = New mainwindow

   If loMainWindow Is Nothing Then

      ExitProcess 1

   End If

   loMainWindow.BorderStyle = vbSizeable

    '' Maximize and display the main window
   loMainWindow.WindowState = vbMaximized
   loMainWindow.Show

End Sub
```

mainwindow.frm: Callback Functions for the Main Window Form

```
Private Sub Form_QueryUnload(Cancel As Integer, UnloadMode As Integer)

   Dim lnResult As Integer

   If (UnloadMode = vbFormControlMenu) Then

      '' Prompt the user to continue closing the main window
      lnResult = MsgBox("Close the main window?",vbYesNo + vbQuestion,"test")

      If (lnResult = vbNo) Then
         Cancel = True
      End If

   End If

End Sub

'' Note that additional VB code is found in this file but is hidden when
'' viewed in the Visual Basic 6 IDE.
```

Source Code Files

- Text files: pp4_4.bas, mainwindow.frm
- Image files: phase.ico (Multi-image icon file, Appendix O)

pp4_4.bas: Program Phase 4-4 EPE Source Code

```
''***************************************************************************
'' Program Phase 4-4 Visual Basic 6 Main Window with File Menu             *
'' Programming Tasks Illustrated: Visual Basic 6 GUI based application     *
''                                Main window                              *
''                                Window icon                              *
''                                Window caption                           *
''                                Window menu with hotkeys                 *
''                                Window background color                  *
''                                Window mouse cursor                      *
''                                User sizable window                      *
''                                Message box input/output                 *
''***************************************************************************

''***************************************************************************
'' File: pp4_4.bas                                                         *
'' Reserved                                                                *
''***************************************************************************

Private Declare Sub ExitProcess Lib "kernel32" (ByVal tnExitCode As Long)


''***************************************************************************
'' Program Phase 4-4 Main                                                  *
'' Define the Entry Point of Execution (EPE) for Program Phase 4-4         *
'' CBI:  4-4.1.1.1                                                         *
''***************************************************************************

Sub Main()

''***************************************************************************
'' Program Phase 4-4 Main                                                  *
'' Declare the local variables for the "main" program                      *
'' CBI:  4-4.1.1.2                                                         *
''***************************************************************************
```

pp4_4.bas continued on the next page

pp4_4.bas: Program Phase 4-4 EPE Source Code

```
   '' Main window
   Dim loMainWindow As mainwindow

   '' Main window background color
   Dim lnWindowBackColor As Long


''*****************************************************************************
'' Program Phase 4-4 Main                                                     *
'' Create the main window                                                     *
'' CBI:  4-4.1.1.3                                                            *
''*****************************************************************************

   Set loMainWindow = Nothing
   Set loMainWindow = New mainwindow

   If loMainWindow Is Nothing Then

      Call MsgBox("The MainWindow class failed to instantiate.", _
                  vbOKOnly + vbCritical,"CBI:  4-4.1.1.3")

      ExitProcess 1

   End If


''*****************************************************************************
'' Program Phase 4-4 Main                                                     *
'' Set the icon for the main window                                           *
'' CBI:  4-4.1.1.4                                                            *
''*****************************************************************************

   '' The main window icon can be set in the Icon property of the mainwindow
   '' Form.

''*****************************************************************************
'' Program Phase 4-4 Main                                                     *
'' Set the caption of the main window                                         *
'' CBI:  4-4.1.1.5                                                            *
''*****************************************************************************

   loMainWindow.Caption = "Program Phase 4-4  |  " & _
                          "Platform:  Windows  |  " & _
                          "Programming Language:  Visual Basic 6 |  " & _
                          "GUI API:  Visual Basic 6"


''*****************************************************************************
'' Program Phase 4-4 Main                                                     *
'' Create the menu for the main window                                        *
'' CBI:  4-4.1.1.6                                                            *
''*****************************************************************************

'' The menu is created using the VB6 IDE and is stored in the mainwindow.frm
'' file.


''*****************************************************************************
'' Program Phase 4-4 Main                                                     *
'' Set the background color of the main window                                *
'' CBI:  4-4.1.1.7                                                            *
''*****************************************************************************

   lnWindowBackColor = RGB(255, 255, 255)
   loMainWindow.BackColor = lnWindowBackColor
```

pp4_4.bas continued on the next page

pp4_4.bas: Program Phase 4-4 EPE Source Code continued

```
''*************************************************************************
'' Program Phase 4-4 Main                                                 *
'' Set the mouse cursor displayed when positioned over the main window    *
'' CBI:  4-4.1.1.8                                                        *
''*************************************************************************

   loMainWindow.MousePointer = vbArrow


''*************************************************************************
'' Program Phase 4-4 Main                                                 *
'' Allow resizing of the main window                                      *
'' CBI:  4-4.1.1.9                                                        *
''*************************************************************************

   loMainWindow.BorderStyle = vbSizeable


''*************************************************************************
'' Program Phase 4-4 Main                                                 *
'' Maximize and display the main window                                   *
'' CBI:  4-4.1.1.10                                                       *
''*************************************************************************

   loMainWindow.WindowState = vbMaximized
   loMainWindow.Show


''*************************************************************************
'' Program Phase 4-4 Main                                                 *
'' Start the event loop                                                   *
'' CBI:  4-4.1.1.11                                                       *
''*************************************************************************


''*************************************************************************
'' Program Phase 4-4 Main                                                 *
'' Cleanup the resources used by the main window                          *
'' CBI:  4-4.1.1.12                                                       *
''*************************************************************************

End Sub
```

mainwindow.frm: Callback Functions for the Main Window

```
''*************************************************************************
'' Callback Functions                                                     *
'' Implement the callback function for the Hello World! menu item         *
'' CBI:  4-4.1.2.1                                                        *
''*************************************************************************

Private Sub MenuItem1_Click(Index As Integer)

   Call MsgBox("Hello World!",vbInformation,"Program Phase 4-4")

End Sub


''*************************************************************************
'' Callback Functions                                                     *
'' Implement the callback function for the Exit menu item                 *
'' CBI:  4-4.1.3.1                                                        *
''*************************************************************************
```

mainwindow.frm continued on the next page

mainwindow.frm: Callback Functions for the Main Window continued

```
'' Exit the program if the user activates the Exit menu item
Private Sub MenuItem2_Click(Index As Integer)

   Unload Me

End Sub


''*****************************************************************************
'' Callback Functions                                                          *
'' Implement the callback function that fires when the main window is closed  *
'' CBI:  4-4.1.4.1                                                             *
''*****************************************************************************

Private Sub Form_QueryUnload(Cancel As Integer, UnloadMode As Integer)

   Dim lnResult As Integer

   If (UnloadMode = vbFormControlMenu) Then

      '' Prompt the user to continue closing the main window
      lnResult = MsgBox("Close the main window?",vbYesNo + vbQuestion, _
                        "Program Phase 4-4")

      If (lnResult = vbNo) Then

         Cancel = True

      End If

   End If

End Sub
'' Note that additional VB code is found in this file but is hidden when
'' viewed in the Visual Basic 6 IDE.
```

Code Setup and Compilation

- Tools: Visual Basic 6

Code Setup and Compilation Steps

1: Create a folder called pp4_4 that will store the source code files for Program Phase 4-4.

2: Open the Visual Basic 6 program.

3: VB6 - Activate Menu Item: File → New Project

Select "Standard EXE" and then activate the "OK" button.

4: Remove the "Form1" Form that is automatically created and added to the project by right-clicking the "Form1" Form in the project and activating the "Remove Form1" menu item.

5: VB6 - Activate Menu Item: File → Save Project

Save the project with the name pp4_4 in the pp4_4 source folder. Click on the pp4_4.vbp file in the properties window and then set the name of the project to pp4_4.

Steps continued on the next page

Code Setup and Compilation Steps continued

6: VB6 - Activate Menu Item: Project → Add Module

Enter the source code for Program Phase 4-4 and save the file as pp4_4.bas

7: VB6 - Activate Menu Item: Project → Add Form

Save the Form as mainwindow.frm in the pp4_4 folder. Change the name property of the Form to mainwindow in the properties window for the Form.

8: Open the mainwindow.frm Form and then view the code for the Form by activating the "Code" menu item from the "View" menu. Enter the source code for the mainwindow.frm file.

9: Open the mainwindow.frm Form and then display the menu editor by activating the "Menu Editor" menu item from the "Tools" menu. Enter the following to create the "File" menu:

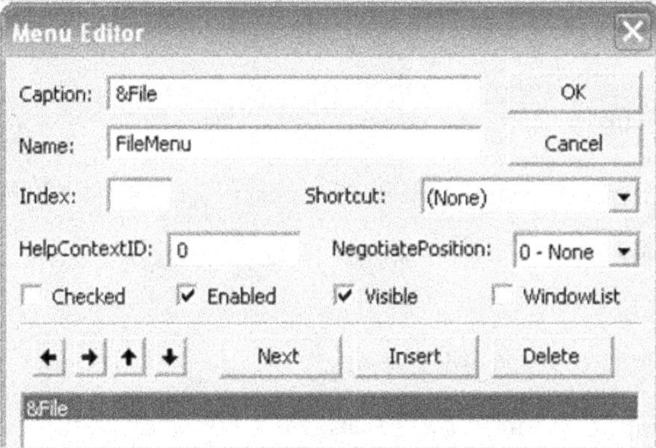

Activate the "Next" button and then activate the "right arrow" to indent the next menu item for the "File" menu. Enter the following for the "Hello World!" menu item:

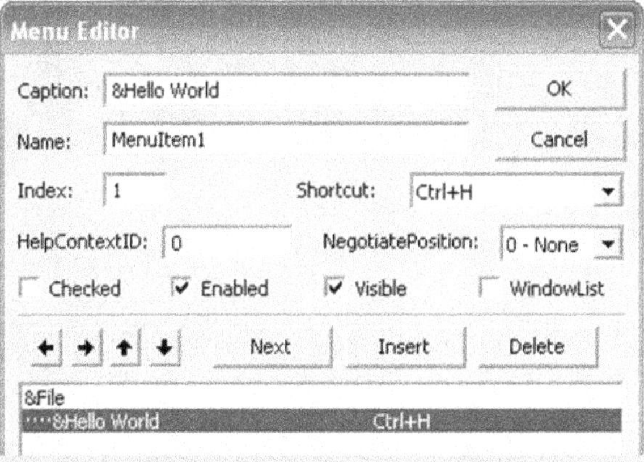

Activate the "Next" button to create the "Exit" menu item for the "File" menu. Enter the following for the "Exit" menu item:

Steps continued on the next page

Code Setup and Compilation Steps continued

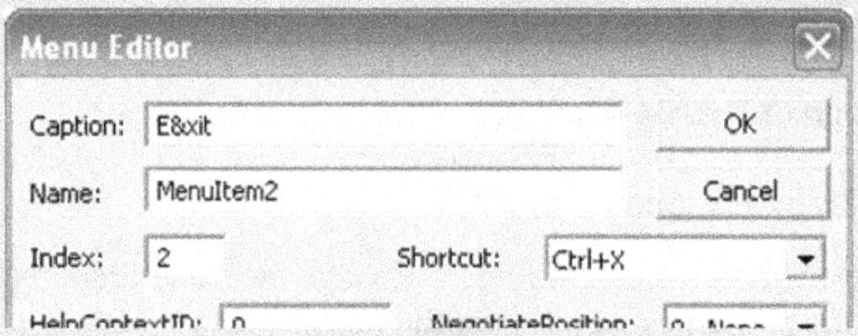

Menu Editor

Caption: E&xit OK

Name: MenuItem2 Cancel

Index: 2 Shortcut: Ctrl+X

10: Create the phase.ico image file according to the instructions in Appendix O. Copy the image file to the pp4_4 folder.

11: Open the mainwindow.frm file and then set the "Icon" property of the Form to the path to the phase.ico file. Save and close the mainwindow Form.

12: Specify the VB 6 Resource Editor in the VB6 Add-In Manager. Display the Add-In Manager by activating the "Add-In Manager" menu item from the "Add-Ins" menu. Click on the VB 6 Resource Editor in the list box and then select "Load On Startup" and "Loaded/Unloaded" and then activate the "OK" button.

13: VB6 - Activate Menu Item: Tools → Resource Editor

Click on the "New" toolbar button and then click on the "Add Icon" toolbar button. Browse for the phase.ico file and select it. Right-click on the icon and then activate the "Properties" menu item. Set the "Id" for the icon to "APPICON" (Enter the quotes). Save the resource file as resource.res.

14: VB6 - Activate Menu Item: Project → pp4_4 Properties

On the "Make" tab, set the icon to "mainwindow". Close the "Project Properties" window.

15: VB6 - Activate Menu Item: File → Make pp4_4.exe

Command Prompt Compilation

Change directories to the folder containing the pp4_4.vbp file and then enter the following commands:

```
PATH = "C:\Program Files\Microsoft Visual Studio\VB98";%PATH%
vb6.exe /make pp4_4.vbp
```

Program Execution

- Execute Program

```
VB6 - Activate Menu Item: Run → Start
```

- Debug Program

```
VB6 - Activate Menu Item: Debug → Step Into
```

Program Phase 4-5

Visual C++ ▪ MFC ▪ Windows

GUI Based Program with Main Window

- Program Phase Task 4 is implemented in Program Phase 4-5 using the C++ programming language and the Microsoft Foundation Classes (MFC) class library.

- Program Phase 4-5 contains a main source code file named pp4_5.cpp. In addition to the pp4_5.cpp text file, an icon image file called phase.ico is used as the window icon for the main window and the application icon for the pp4_5.exe executable file. The resources for the program are referenced in the resource.rc and resource.h text files.

Code Block Features

The Program Phase 4-5 code blocks illustrate the following programming features using the C++ programming language and MFC:

- **Create a Resizable Main Window for a GUI Based Application**

- **Set the Main Window Icon and Caption**

- **Set the Main Window Menu**

- **Set the Main Window Background Color and Mouse Cursor**

- **Prompt to Exit the Application when the Main Window is Closed**

C++ MFC
Create a Resizable Main Window for a GUI Based Application

- A class based on the MFC CFrameWnd class is instantiated and used as the main window for an MFC application. Similar to steps taken in Program Phase 4-3, a window class is registered, but this time there is no "WNDCLASS" structure, and the MFC AfxRegisterWndClass() function is used. Instead of calling the CreateWindow() function, the Create() method of the "CFrameWnd" instance is called to create the main window. The WS_OVERLAPPEDWINDOW constant is passed as the third parameter to the Create() method to set the "borderstyle" of the window to be resizable. The ShowWindow() method is called to maximize and display the main window. The UpdateWindow() method is called to redraw the main window on the screen. Lastly, the "CFrameWnd" instance is assigned to the "m_pMainWnd" property of the "CWinApp" instance.

- What happens when the InitInstance() method returns? If a Boolean "false" value is returned, the MFC AfxWinMain() function assumes that an error has occurred and then exits. If a Boolean "true" value is returned, the AfxWinMain() function will internally call the Run() method of the "CWinApp" instance.

- The Run() method implements the event loop for the application and will exit when a "WM_QUIT" message has been sent. The AfxWinMain() function is hidden from the user and does not need to be edited. To view the AfxWinMain() source code, open the appmodul.cpp file found in the src folder for MFC.

  Example

  ```
  C:\Program Files\Microsoft Visual Studio 9.0\VC\atlmfc\src\mfc
  ```

test1.cpp: C++ MFC Create a Resizable Main Window for a GUI Based Application

```
#include <afxwin.h>

class MainWindow : public CFrameWnd
{
};

class test1 : public CWinApp
{
virtual BOOL InitInstance ()
{
   // Main window
   MainWindow *loMainWindow;
   CString lcWindowClass;

   loMainWindow = new MainWindow();

   lcWindowClass = AfxRegisterWndClass(CS_HREDRAW | CS_VREDRAW,
                                       this->LoadStandardCursor(IDC_ARROW),
                                       (HBRUSH) ::GetStockObject(WHITE_BRUSH),
                                       NULL);

   // Create the main window
   loMainWindow->Create(lcWindowClass,NULL,WS_OVERLAPPEDWINDOW,
                        loMainWindow->rectDefault,
                        NULL,NULL,NULL,NULL);

   loMainWindow->ModifyStyleEx(WS_EX_CLIENTEDGE | WS_EX_WINDOWEDGE,NULL,NULL);


   // Maximize and display the main window
   loMainWindow->ShowWindow(SW_SHOWMAXIMIZED);

   loMainWindow->UpdateWindow();
   this->m_pMainWnd = loMainWindow;

   return TRUE;
}
};

test1 goTest1;
```

C++ MFC
Set the Main Window Icon and Caption

- A multi-image icon file is used as the icon for the main window and application. An icon referenced in a ".rc" resource file is accessed with the LoadIcon() method to load the icon for the main window. The handle returned by the LoadIcon() method is used as the fourth parameter to the AfxRegisterWndClass() function.

- The window caption is specified in the second parameter to the Create() method.

test2.cpp: C++ MFC Set the Main Window Icon and Caption

```
#include <afxwin.h>
#include "resource.h"

class MainWindow : public CFrameWnd
{
};

class test2 : public CWinApp
{
virtual BOOL InitInstance ()
{
   // Main window
   MainWindow *loMainWindow;
   CString lcWindowClass;

   loMainWindow = new MainWindow();

   lcWindowClass = AfxRegisterWndClass(CS_HREDRAW | CS_VREDRAW,
                                        this->LoadStandardCursor(IDC_ARROW),
                                       (HBRUSH) ::GetStockObject(WHITE_BRUSH),
                                        // Set the main window icon
                                        this->LoadIcon(IDI_ICON1));

   // Create the main window
   loMainWindow->Create(lcWindowClass,

                         // Set the main window caption
                        "Hello World!",

                        WS_OVERLAPPEDWINDOW,
                        loMainWindow->rectDefault,
                        NULL,NULL,NULL,NULL);

   loMainWindow->ModifyStyleEx(WS_EX_CLIENTEDGE | WS_EX_WINDOWEDGE,NULL,NULL);

   // Maximize and display the main window
   loMainWindow->ShowWindow(SW_SHOWMAXIMIZED);

   loMainWindow->UpdateWindow();
   this->m_pMainWnd = loMainWindow;

   return TRUE;
}
};

test2 goTest2;
```

resource.h: Header File for the Icon Resource

```
#define IDI_ICON1                       100
```

resource.rc: Resource File for the Icon Resource

```
#include "resource.h"
IDI_ICON1               ICON                    "phase.ico"
```

C++ MFC
Set the Main Window Menu

- The menu for the main window is setup by using the CMenu class.
- The menu bar is assigned to the main window by using the SetMenu() method of the

"CFrameWnd" instance. The Detach() method of the file menu "CMenu" instance is called after it has been assigned to the menu bar with the AppendMenu() method. This is done in order to disassociate the menu with the instance variable. If the Detach() method is not called, the menu is destroyed when the "CMenu" instance variable goes out of scope. The Detach() method of the menu bar "CMenu" instance is also called after it is assigned to the "CFrameWnd" main window instance by using the SetMenu() method. The menu assigned to a "CFrameWnd" instance is recursively destroyed when the main window is closed.

- The DECLARE_MESSAGE_MAP() macro indicates that the "MainWindow" class contains a message map that links callback functions to window messages. The BEGIN_MESSAGE_MAP() and END_MESSAGE_MAP() macros delimit the message map entries. The ON_MESSAGE() macro is used to link the menu item constants to callback methods of the "MainWindow" class. The constants for the menu items are stored in the text file resource.h.

- The keyboard shortcuts for the menu items are stored in a ".rc" resource file and are loaded by using the MAKEINTRESOURCE() macro. The LoadAccelTable() method is used to assign the keyboard shortcuts to the main window.

- Menus can also be setup in a resource file and then assigned to a main window, but this technique is not illustrated in Program Phase 4-5.

test3.cpp: C++ MFC Set the Main Window Menu

```
#include <afxwin.h>
#include "resource.h"

class MainWindow : public CFrameWnd
{
   private:

      void MenuItem1_Activate();
      void MenuItem2_Activate();
      DECLARE_MESSAGE_MAP ()
};

BEGIN_MESSAGE_MAP (MainWindow, CFrameWnd)

   ON_COMMAND (IDM_MENUITEM1, MenuItem1_Activate)
   ON_COMMAND (IDM_MENUITEM2, MenuItem2_Activate)

END_MESSAGE_MAP ()

class test3 : public CWinApp
{
virtual BOOL InitInstance ()
{
   // Main window
   MainWindow *loMainWindow;
   CString lcWindowClass;
   CMenu loMenuBar;
   CMenu loFileMenu;
   CHAR *lcAcceleratorName;

   loMainWindow = new MainWindow();

   lcWindowClass = AfxRegisterWndClass(CS_HREDRAW | CS_VREDRAW,
                                       this->LoadStandardCursor(IDC_ARROW),
                                      (HBRUSH) ::GetStockObject(WHITE_BRUSH),
                                      NULL);
```

test3.cpp continued on the next page

test3.cpp: C++ MFC Set the Main Window Menu continued

```
   // Create the main window
   loMainWindow->Create(lcWindowClass,NULL,WS_OVERLAPPEDWINDOW,
                        loMainWindow->rectDefault,NULL,NULL,NULL,NULL);

   loMainWindow->ModifyStyleEx(WS_EX_CLIENTEDGE | WS_EX_WINDOWEDGE,NULL,NULL);

   // Setup the menu bar
   loMenuBar.CreateMenu();

   // Create the file menu
   loFileMenu.CreatePopupMenu();

   // Create the Hello World! menu item
   loFileMenu.AppendMenu(MF_STRING,IDM_MENUITEM1,"&Hello World!\tCtrl+H");

   // Create the Exit menu item
   loFileMenu.AppendMenu(MF_STRING,IDM_MENUITEM2,"E&xit\tCtrl+X");

   // Assign the File menu to the menu bar
   loMenuBar.AppendMenu(MF_POPUP,(UINT) loFileMenu.m_hMenu,"&File");

   loFileMenu.Detach();

   lcAcceleratorName = MAKEINTRESOURCE(IDR_ACCELERATOR1);
   loMainWindow->LoadAccelTable(lcAcceleratorName);

   // Assign the File menu to the main window
   loMainWindow->SetMenu(&loMenuBar);
   loMenuBar.Detach();

   // Maximize and display the main window
   loMainWindow->ShowWindow(SW_SHOWMAXIMIZED);

   loMainWindow->UpdateWindow();
   this->m_pMainWnd = loMainWindow;

   return TRUE;
}
}; test3 goTest3;

void MainWindow::MenuItem1_Activate()
{
   this->MessageBox("Hello World!","Program Phase 4-5",
                    MB_OK | MB_ICONINFORMATION);
}

void MainWindow::MenuItem2_Activate ()
{
   this->DestroyWindow();
}
```

resource.h: Header File for the Menu Resources

```
#define IDR_ACCELERATOR1                101
#define IDM_MENUITEM1                   102
#define IDM_MENUITEM2                   103
```

resource.rc: Resource File for the Menu Resources

```
#include "resource.h"
IDR_ACCELERATOR1 ACCELERATORS
BEGIN
    "H",            IDM_MENUITEM1,          VIRTKEY, CONTROL, NOINVERT
    "X",            IDM_MENUITEM2,          VIRTKEY, CONTROL, NOINVERT
END
```

C++ MFC
Set the Main Window Background Color and Mouse Cursor

- The background color for the main window is set in a similar fashion as Program Phase 4-3. The Win32 CreateSolidBrush() function is used to obtain a handle to a "brush" that is then passed as the third parameter to the MFC AfxRegisterWndClass() function. A handle to the "brush" is stored as a property of the class and then deleted in the class destructor.

- The main window cursor is set by calling the LoadStandardCursor() method and passing the resulting handle as the second parameter to the AfxRegisterWndClass() function.

test4.cpp: C++ MFC Set the Main Window Background Color and Mouse Cursor

```
#include <afxwin.h>

class MainWindow : public CFrameWnd
{
   public:
      HBRUSH hBrush;

   private:
      ~MainWindow();
};

class test4 : public CWinApp
{
virtual BOOL InitInstance ()
{
   // Main window
   MainWindow *loMainWindow;
   CString lcWindowClass;

   loMainWindow = new MainWindow();
   loMainWindow->hBrush = ::CreateSolidBrush(RGB(255,255,255));

   lcWindowClass = AfxRegisterWndClass(CS_HREDRAW | CS_VREDRAW,
                                       // Set the main window mouse cursor
                                       this->LoadStandardCursor(IDC_ARROW),
                                       // Set the main window background color
                                       (HBRUSH) loMainWindow->hBrush,
                                       NULL);
   // Create the main window
   loMainWindow->Create(lcWindowClass,NULL,WS_OVERLAPPEDWINDOW,
                        loMainWindow->rectDefault,
                        NULL,NULL,NULL,NULL);

   loMainWindow->ModifyStyleEx(WS_EX_CLIENTEDGE | WS_EX_WINDOWEDGE,NULL,NULL);

   // Maximize and display the main window
   loMainWindow->ShowWindow(SW_SHOWMAXIMIZED);

   loMainWindow->UpdateWindow();

   this->m_pMainWnd = loMainWindow;
   return TRUE;
}};

test4 goTest4;

MainWindow::~MainWindow()
{
   ::DeleteObject(this->hBrush);
}
```

C++ MFC
Prompt to Exit the Application when the Main Window is Closed

- In the test5.cpp example, the "ON_WM_CLOSE" message is specified in the message map, and the OnClose() method of the MainWindow CFrameWnd class is implemented. The user is prompted in this event to continue closing the main window. If the user selects "Yes", the DestroyWindow() method is called. If the users selects "No", nothing further is done in the OnClose() event, and the main window remains visible.

test5.cpp: C++ MFC Prompt to Exit the Application when the Main Window is Closed

```
#include <afxwin.h>

class MainWindow : public CFrameWnd
{
 private:

      afx_msg void OnClose();
      DECLARE_MESSAGE_MAP ()
};

BEGIN_MESSAGE_MAP (MainWindow, CFrameWnd)

   ON_WM_CLOSE()

END_MESSAGE_MAP ()

class test5 : public CWinApp
{
virtual BOOL InitInstance ()
{
   // Main window
   MainWindow *loMainWindow;
   CString lcWindowClass;

   loMainWindow = new MainWindow();

   lcWindowClass = AfxRegisterWndClass(CS_HREDRAW | CS_VREDRAW,
                                       this->LoadStandardCursor(IDC_ARROW),
                                       (HBRUSH) ::GetStockObject(WHITE_BRUSH),
                                       NULL);

   // Create the main window
   loMainWindow->Create(lcWindowClass,NULL,WS_OVERLAPPEDWINDOW,
                        loMainWindow->rectDefault,
                        NULL,NULL,NULL,NULL);

   loMainWindow->ModifyStyleEx(WS_EX_CLIENTEDGE | WS_EX_WINDOWEDGE,NULL,NULL);

   // Maximize and display the main window
   loMainWindow->ShowWindow(SW_SHOWMAXIMIZED);

   loMainWindow->UpdateWindow();
   this->m_pMainWnd = loMainWindow;

   return TRUE;
}};

test5 goTest5;

afx_msg void MainWindow::OnClose()
{
   int lnResult;
```

test5.cpp continued on the next page

test5.cpp: C++ MFC Prompt to Exit App. when the Main Window is Closed continued

```
   // Prompt the user to continue closing the main window
   lnResult = ::MessageBox(NULL,"Close the main window?",
                           "test",MB_YESNO | MB_ICONQUESTION);

   if (lnResult == IDYES)
   {
      this->DestroyWindow();
   }
}
```

Source Code Files

- Text files: pp4_5.cpp, resource.h, resource.rc
- Image files: phase.ico (Multi-image icon file, Appendix O)

pp4_5.cpp: Program Phase 4-5 Source Code

```
//******************************************************************************
// Program Phase 4-5 C++ MFC Main Window with File Menu                       *
// Programming Tasks Illustrated: MFC GUI based application                   *
//                                Main window                                 *
//                                Window icon                                 *
//                                Window caption                              *
//                                Window menu with hotkeys                    *
//                                Window background color                     *
//                                Window mouse cursor                         *
//                                User sizable window                         *
//                                Message box input/output                    *
//******************************************************************************

//******************************************************************************
// File: pp4_5.cpp                                                            *
// Reserved                                                                   *
//******************************************************************************

#include <afxwin.h>
#include "resource.h"

class MainWindow : public CFrameWnd
{
   public:

      HBRUSH hBrush;

   private:

      void MenuItem1_Activate();
      void MenuItem2_Activate();
      afx_msg void OnClose();
      ~MainWindow();
      DECLARE_MESSAGE_MAP ()
};

BEGIN_MESSAGE_MAP (MainWindow, CFrameWnd)

   ON_COMMAND (IDM_MENUITEM1, MenuItem1_Activate)
   ON_COMMAND (IDM_MENUITEM2, MenuItem2_Activate)
   ON_WM_CLOSE()

END_MESSAGE_MAP ()
```

pp4_5.cpp continued on the next page

pp4_5.cpp: Program Phase 4-5 Source Code continued

```
class pp4_5 : public CWinApp
{

//*************************************************************************
// Program Phase 4-5 Main                                                 *
// Define the Entry Point of Execution (EPE) for Program Phase 4-5       *
// CBI:  4-5.1.1.1                                                        *
//*************************************************************************

virtual BOOL InitInstance ()
{

//*************************************************************************
// Program Phase 4-5 Main                                                 *
// Declare the local variables for the "main" program                    *
// CBI:  4-5.1.1.2                                                        *
//*************************************************************************

   // Main window
   MainWindow *loMainWindow;
   INT lnWindowStyle;
   CString lcWindowClass;

   // Main window icon
   HICON lhIcon;

   // Main window caption
   CString lcWindowCaption;

   // Main window menu
   CMenu loMenuBar;
   CMenu loFileMenu;
   CHAR *lcAcceleratorName;

   // Main window background color
   COLORREF lnWindowBackColor;

   // Main window mouse cursor
   HCURSOR lhMouseCursor;

   // Function results
   INT lnResult;

//*************************************************************************
// Program Phase 4-5 Main                                                 *
// Create the main window                                                 *
// CBI:  4-5.1.1.3                                                        *
//*************************************************************************

   loMainWindow = new MainWindow();

//*************************************************************************
// Program Phase 4-5 Main                                                 *
// Set the icon for the main window                                      *
// CBI:  4-5.1.1.4                                                        *
//*************************************************************************

   lhIcon = this->LoadIcon(IDI_ICON1);
```

pp4_5.cpp continued on the next page

pp4_5.cpp: Program Phase 4-5 Source Code continued

```
   if (lhIcon == NULL)
   {
      loMainWindow->MessageBox("The LoadIcon function failed.",
                               "CBI:  4-5.1.1.4",
                               MB_OK | MB_ICONERROR);

      return FALSE;
   }

// The icon is assigned in CBI: 4-5.1.1.10 in the fourth parameter to the
// AfxRegisterWndClass() function


//****************************************************************************
// Program Phase 4-5 Main                                                    *
// Set the caption of the main window                                        *
// CBI:  4-5.1.1.5                                                           *
//****************************************************************************

   lcWindowCaption = "Program Phase 4-5  |  "
                     "Platform:  Windows  |  "
                     "Programming Language:  C++  |  "
                     "GUI API:  MFC";


//****************************************************************************
// Program Phase 4-5 Main                                                    *
// Create the menu for the main window                                       *
// CBI:  4-5.1.1.6                                                           *
//****************************************************************************

   // Menu bar
   loMenuBar.CreateMenu();
   loFileMenu.CreatePopupMenu();

   // Hello World! menu item
   loFileMenu.AppendMenu(MF_STRING,IDM_MENUITEM1,"&Hello World!\tCtrl+H");

   // Exit menu item
   loFileMenu.AppendMenu(MF_STRING,IDM_MENUITEM2,"E&xit\tCtrl+X");

   // File menu
   loMenuBar.AppendMenu(MF_POPUP,(UINT) loFileMenu.m_hMenu,"&File");
   loFileMenu.Detach();


//****************************************************************************
// Program Phase 4-5 Main                                                    *
// Set the background color of the main window                               *
// CBI:  4-5.1.1.7                                                           *
//****************************************************************************

   lnWindowBackColor = RGB(255,255,255);
   loMainWindow->hBrush = ::CreateSolidBrush(lnWindowBackColor);

   if (loMainWindow->hBrush == NULL)
   {
      loMainWindow->MessageBox("The CreateSolidBrush function failed.",
                               "CBI:  4-5.1.1.7",
                               MB_OK | MB_ICONERROR);

      return TRUE;
   }
```

pp4_5.cpp continued on the next page

pp4_5.cpp: Program Phase 4-5 Source Code continued

```
//****************************************************************************
// Program Phase 4-5 Main                                                    *
// Set the mouse cursor displayed when positioned over the main window       *
// CBI:  4-5.1.1.8                                                           *
//****************************************************************************

   lhMouseCursor = this->LoadStandardCursor(IDC_ARROW);

   if (lhMouseCursor == NULL)
   {
      loMainWindow->MessageBox("The LoadStandardCursor method of the "
                               "CWinApp class failed.",
                               "CBI:  4-5.1.1.8",
                               MB_OK | MB_ICONERROR);
         return TRUE;
   }


//****************************************************************************
// Program Phase 4-5 Main                                                    *
// Allow resizing of the main window                                         *
// CBI:  4-5.1.1.9                                                           *
//****************************************************************************

   lnWindowStyle = WS_OVERLAPPEDWINDOW;


//****************************************************************************
// Program Phase 4-5 Main                                                    *
// Maximize and display the main window                                      *
// CBI:  4-5.1.1.10                                                          *
//****************************************************************************

   lcWindowClass = AfxRegisterWndClass(CS_HREDRAW | CS_VREDRAW,lhMouseCursor,
                                        loMainWindow->hBrush,lhIcon);

   loMainWindow->Create(lcWindowClass,lcWindowCaption,lnWindowStyle,
                        loMainWindow->rectDefault,NULL,NULL,NULL,NULL);

   loMainWindow->ModifyStyleEx(WS_EX_CLIENTEDGE | WS_EX_WINDOWEDGE,NULL,NULL);

   loMainWindow->SetMenu(&loMenuBar);
   loMenuBar.Detach();

   lcAcceleratorName = MAKEINTRESOURCE(IDR_ACCELERATOR1);
   lnResult = loMainWindow->LoadAccelTable(lcAcceleratorName);

   if (lnResult == 0)
   {
      loMainWindow->MessageBox("The LoadAccelTable method of the CFrameWnd"
                               "class failed.","CBI:  4-5.1.1.10",
                               MB_OK | MB_ICONERROR);
      return TRUE;
   }

   loMainWindow->ShowWindow(SW_SHOWMAXIMIZED);
   loMainWindow->UpdateWindow();
   this->m_pMainWnd = loMainWindow;


//****************************************************************************
// Program Phase 4-5 Main                                                    *
// Start the event loop                                                      *
// CBI:  4-5.1.1.11                                                          *
//****************************************************************************
```

pp4_5.cpp continued on the next page

pp4_5.cpp: Program Phase 4-5 Source Code continued

```
   // The AfxWinMain() function will internally call the Run() method of the
   // "CWinApp" instance to start the event loop.


//******************************************************************************
// Program Phase 4-5 Main                                                      *
// Cleanup the resources used by the main window                               *
// CBI:  4-5.1.1.12                                                            *
//******************************************************************************

   // The main window brush is deleted in the MainWindow class destructor.
   return TRUE;
}};

pp4_5 go4_5;

// Callback Functions

//******************************************************************************
// Callback Functions                                                          *
// Implement the callback function for the Hello World! menu item             *
// CBI:  4-5.1.2.1                                                             *
//******************************************************************************

void MainWindow::MenuItem1_Activate()
{
   this->MessageBox("Hello World!","Program Phase 4-5",
                    MB_OK | MB_ICONINFORMATION);
}


//******************************************************************************
// Callback Functions                                                          *
// Implement the callback function for the Exit menu item                      *
// CBI:  4-5.1.3.1                                                             *
//******************************************************************************

void MainWindow::MenuItem2_Activate ()
{
   this->DestroyWindow();
}


//******************************************************************************
// Callback Functions                                                          *
// Implement the callback function that fires when the main window is closed  *
// CBI:  4-5.1.4.1                                                             *
//******************************************************************************

afx_msg void MainWindow::OnClose()
{
   int lnResult;

   // Prompt the user to continue closing the main window
   lnResult = ::MessageBox(NULL,"Close the main window?",
                           "Program Phase 4-5",MB_YESNO | MB_ICONQUESTION);

   if (lnResult == IDYES)
   {
      this->DestroyWindow();
   }
}

MainWindow::~MainWindow()
{
   ::DeleteObject(this->hBrush);
}
```

resource.h: Header File for the Program Resources

```
#define IDI_ICON1                      100
#define IDR_ACCELERATOR1               101
#define IDM_MENUITEM1                  102
#define IDM_MENUITEM2                  103
```

resource.rc: Resource File for the Program Resources

```
#include "resource.h"
IDI_ICON1              ICON                    "phase.ico"

IDR_ACCELERATOR1 ACCELERATORS
BEGIN
    "H",           IDM_MENUITEM1,          VIRTKEY, CONTROL, NOINVERT
    "X",           IDM_MENUITEM2,          VIRTKEY, CONTROL, NOINVERT
END
```

Code Setup and Compilation

- Tools: Microsoft Visual C++ 2008

Code Setup and Compilation Steps

1: Start the Microsoft Visual C++ 2008 program.

2: VC++ - Activate Menu Item: File → New → Project

For the "Project type", select "Win32" and then select the "Win32 Console Application" template. Enter pp4_5 as the project "Name". Enter the appropriate folder as the project "Location". The pp4_5 folder will be automatically created. Make sure that the "Create directory for solution" check box is not checked.

3: Activate the "OK" button to proceed with the "Win32 Application Wizard".

4: Activate the "Next" button of the "Win32 Application Wizard".

5: Select the "Console application" radio button and also check the "Empty project" check box. Activate the "Finish" button of the "Win32 Application Wizard".

6: VC++ - Activate Menu Item: Project → Add New Item

On the "Add New Item" dialog window, select the "Visual C++ → Code" category and then select the "C++ File (.cpp)" template. Enter pp4_5.cpp for the file "Name". Activate the "Add" button. Enter the source code for the pp4_5.cpp file.

7: Create the phase.ico image file according to the instructions in Appendix O. Copy the image file to the pp4_5 folder.

8: Using a text editor, create the resource.h and resource.rc files and enter the appropriate source code. Copy the resource.h and resource.rc files to the pp4_5 folder.

9: VC++ - Activate Menu Item: Project → Add Existing Item

Select the resource.h file in the pp4_5 folder and then activate the Add button.

Steps continued on the next page

Code Setup and Compilation Steps continued

10: VC++ - Activate Menu Item: Project → Add Existing Item

Select the resource.rc file in the pp4_5 folder and then activate the "Add" button.

11: VC++ - Activate Menu Item: Project → pp4_5 Properties

Enter the following settings:

Configuration Properties → General → Character Set

```
"Use Multi-Byte Character Set"
```

Configuration Properties → General → Use of MFC

```
"Use MFC in a Static Library" or "Use MFC in a Shared DLL"
```

12: VC++ - Activate Menu Item: Build → Build pp4_5

Command Prompt Compilation

From a Visual Studio 2008 command prompt in the pp4_5 folder, enter the following:

```
cl.exe /c /MT /EHsc pp4_5.cpp
rc.exe resource.rc
link.exe /SUBSYSTEM:WINDOWS pp4_5.obj resource.res
```

dynamic library:

```
cl.exe /c /MD /EHsc /D "_AFXDLL" pp4_5.cpp
rc.exe resource.rc
link.exe /SUBSYSTEM:WINDOWS pp4_5.obj resource.res
mt.exe /manifest pp4_5.exe.manifest /outputresource:pp4_5.exe
```

Program Execution

- Execute Program

```
VC++ - Activate Menu Item: Debug → Start Without Debugging
```

- Debug Program

```
VC++ EE - Activate Menu Item: Project → pp4_5 Properties
```

Expand the "Configuration Properties → Linker" entry and then click on the "Debugging" item. Set the "Generate Debug Info" entry to "Yes". Close the "pp4_5 Properties" window.

```
VC++ EE - Activate Menu Item: Debug → Step Into
```

Program Phase 4-6

C# ▪ .NET Framework - Mono ▪ Multi-Platform

GUI Based Program with Main Window

- Program Phase Task 4 is implemented in Program Phase 4-6 using the C# programming language and the Microsoft .NET Framework 2.0 or higher.

- Program Phase 4-6 contains a single source code file named pp4_6.cs. In addition to the pp4_6.cs text file, an icon image file called phase.ico is used as the window icon for the main window and the application icon for the pp4_6.exe executable file.

Code Block Features

The Program Phase 4-6 code blocks illustrate the following programming features using the C# programming language:

- **Create a Resizable Main Window for a GUI Based Application**

- **Set the Main Window Icon and Caption**

- **Set the Main Window Menu**

- **Set the Main Window Background Color and Mouse Cursor**

- **Prompt to Exit the Application when the Main Window is Closed**

C# .NET Framework - Mono
Create a Resizable Main Window for a GUI Based Application

- The main window is implemented with the.NET Framework Form class found in the System.Windows.Forms namespace.

- The code in the constructor for the MainWindow class specifies the MainWindow_Closed() method as the event handler for the Closed() event.

- The border of the main window is set to be resizeable by specifying the "FormBorderStyle.Sizable" value for the "FormBorderStyle" property of the main window.

- The Application.Run() method is called to start the event loop for the program. This loop prevents the Main() function from automatically exiting. The Application.Exit() method is called when the main window is closed. When this happens, processing continues with the line of code immediately following the Application.Run() method.

test1.cs: C# .NET FW - Mono Create a Resizable Main Window for a GUI Based App.

```
using System;
using System.Windows.Forms;

namespace nstest1
{
class test1
{
public static int Main()
{
   MainWindow loMainWindow;

   // Create the main window
   loMainWindow = new MainWindow();
   loMainWindow.FormBorderStyle = FormBorderStyle.Sizable;

   // Maximize and display the main window
   loMainWindow.WindowState = FormWindowState.Maximized;
   loMainWindow.Show();

   Application.Run();
   return 0;
}}

public class MainWindow : System.Windows.Forms.Form
{
public MainWindow()
{
   this.Closed += new EventHandler(this.MainWindow_Closed);
}

private void MainWindow_Closed(object toSender,EventArgs toEventArgs)
{
   Application.Exit();
}
}}
```

C# .NET Framework - Mono
Set the Main Window Icon and Caption

- The phase.ico file is embedded into the executable file and accessed at runtime. The GetManifestResourceStream() method of the currently executing assembly is used to obtain a resource stream object that represents the phase.ico icon. An icon object is obtained from the stream object and then assigned to the "Icon" property of the main window.

- If the program is compiled in the Visual C# 2008 Express Edition IDE, the path to the icon is "nstest2.phase.ico". If the program is compiled at the command line, the path to the phase.ico icon is "phase.ico".

- The main window caption can be set with the "Text" property.

test2.cs: C# .NET Framework - Mono Set the Main Window Icon and Caption

```
using System;
using System.Drawing;
using System.Windows.Forms;
using System.Reflection;
using System.IO;
```

test2.cs continued on the next page

test2.cs: C# .NET Framework - Mono Set the Main Window Icon and Caption continued

```
namespace nstest2
{
class test2
{
public static int Main()
{
   MainWindow loMainWindow;
   System.Drawing.Icon loIcon;
   Stream loStream; Assembly loAssembly;

   // Create the main window
   loMainWindow = new MainWindow();
   loMainWindow.FormBorderStyle = FormBorderStyle.Sizable;

   // Set the main window icon
   loAssembly = Assembly.GetExecutingAssembly();
   loStream = null;
   loStream = loAssembly.GetManifestResourceStream("nstest2.phase.ico");

   if(loStream == null)
   {
      loStream = loAssembly.GetManifestResourceStream("phase.ico");
   }

   if(loStream != null)
   {
      loIcon = new Icon(loStream);
      loMainWindow.Icon = loIcon ;
   }

   // Set the main window caption
   loMainWindow.Text = "Hello World!";

   // Maximize and display the main window
   loMainWindow.WindowState = FormWindowState.Maximized;
   loMainWindow.Show();

   Application.Run();
   return 0;
}
}

public class MainWindow : System.Windows.Forms.Form
{
public MainWindow()
{
   this.Closed += new EventHandler(this.MainWindow_Closed);
}


private void MainWindow_Closed(object toSender,EventArgs toEventArgs)
{
   Application.Exit();
}
}}
```

C# .NET Framework - Mono
Set the Main Window Menu

- The following example creates a "File" menu with a "Hello World!" menu item and "Exit" menu item:

test3.cs: C# .NET Framework - Mono Set the Main Window Menu

```
using System;
using System.Windows.Forms;

namespace nstest3
{
class test3
{
public static int Main()
{
   MainWindow loMainWindow;
   MainMenu loMenuBar;
   MenuItem loFileMenu;
   MenuItem loMenuItem1;
   MenuItem loMenuItem2;
   EventHandler loMenuItem1EventHandler;
   EventHandler loMenuItem2EventHandler;

    // Create the main window
   loMainWindow = new MainWindow();

   loMainWindow.FormBorderStyle = FormBorderStyle.Sizable;

   // Menu bar
   loMenuBar = new MainMenu();

   // File Menu
   loFileMenu = new MenuItem("&File");
   loMenuBar.MenuItems.Add(loFileMenu);

   // Hello World! Menu Item
   loMenuItem1 = new MenuItem("&Hello World!");
   loMenuItem1EventHandler = new EventHandler(loMainWindow.MenuItem1_Activate);
   loMenuItem1.Click += loMenuItem1EventHandler;

   loMenuItem1.Shortcut = Shortcut.CtrlH;
   loFileMenu.MenuItems.Add(loMenuItem1);

   // Exit Menu Item
   loMenuItem2 = new MenuItem("&Exit");
   loMenuItem2EventHandler = new EventHandler(loMainWindow.MenuItem2_Activate);
   loMenuItem2.Click += loMenuItem2EventHandler;
   loMenuItem2.Shortcut = Shortcut.CtrlX;
   loFileMenu.MenuItems.Add(loMenuItem2);

   // Assign the File menu to the main window
   loMainWindow.Menu = loMenuBar;

   // Maximize and display the main window
   loMainWindow.WindowState = FormWindowState.Maximized;
   loMainWindow.Show();

   Application.Run();
   return 0;
}}

public class MainWindow : System.Windows.Forms.Form
{
public MainWindow()
{
   this.Closed += new EventHandler(this.MainWindow_Closed);
}

private void MainWindow_Closed(object toSender,EventArgs toEventArgs)
{
   Application.Exit();
}
```

test3.cs continued on the next page

test3.cs: C# .NET Framework - Mono Set the Main Window Menu continued

```
public void MenuItem1_Activate(System.Object sender, System.EventArgs e)
{
    MessageBox.Show("Hello World!","test",MessageBoxButtons.OK,
                    MessageBoxIcon.Information);
}

public void MenuItem2_Activate(System.Object sender, System.EventArgs e)
{
    this.Dispose();
    Application.Exit();
}}
}
```

C# .NET Framework - Mono
Set the Main Window Background Color and Mouse Cursor

- The following example sets the main window background color and mouse cursor:

test4.cs: C# .NET FW - Mono Set the Main Window Background Color and Mouse Cursor

```
using System;
using System.Drawing;
using System.Windows.Forms;

namespace nstest4
{
class test4
{
public static int Main()
{
   MainWindow loMainWindow;

   // Create the main window
   loMainWindow = new MainWindow();
   loMainWindow.FormBorderStyle = FormBorderStyle.Sizable;

   // Set the main window background color
   loMainWindow.BackColor = Color.FromArgb(255,255,255);

   // Set the main window mouse cursor
   loMainWindow.Cursor = Cursors.Arrow;

   // Maximize and display the main window
   loMainWindow.WindowState = FormWindowState.Maximized;
   loMainWindow.Show();

   Application.Run();

   return 0;
}}

public class MainWindow : System.Windows.Forms.Form
{
public MainWindow()
{
      this.Closed += new EventHandler(this.MainWindow_Closed);
}

private void MainWindow_Closed(object toSender,EventArgs toEventArgs)
{
   Application.Exit();
}
}}
```

C# .NET Framework - Mono
Prompt to Exit the Application when the Main Window is Closed

- The main window Closing event is setup for the MainWindow_Closing() method using the EventHandler class found in the System namespace. If the "Cancel" property of the event argument parameter is set to the Boolean "true" value, the main window does not close. The user is prompted with a message box to continue closing the main window in the MainWindow_Closing() method. If the user selects "No", the "Cancel" property of the event argument parameter is set to the Boolean "true" value.

test5.cs: C# .NET FW - Mono Prompt to Exit the App when the Main Window is Closed

```
using System;
using System.ComponentModel;
using System.Windows.Forms;

namespace nstest5
{
class test5
{
public static int Main()
{
   MainWindow loMainWindow;

   // Create the main window
   loMainWindow = new MainWindow();
   loMainWindow.FormBorderStyle = FormBorderStyle.Sizable;

   // Maximize and display the main window
   loMainWindow.WindowState = FormWindowState.Maximized;
   loMainWindow.Show();

   Application.Run();
   return 0;
}}

public class MainWindow : System.Windows.Forms.Form
{
public MainWindow()
{
   this.Closed += new EventHandler(this.MainWindow_Closed);
   this.Closing += new CancelEventHandler(this.MainWindow_Closing);
}

private void MainWindow_Closed(object toSender,EventArgs toEventArgs)
{
   Application.Exit();
}

private void MainWindow_Closing(object toSender,
                            System.ComponentModel.CancelEventArgs toEventArgs)
{
   DialogResult lnResult;

   lnResult = MessageBox.Show("Close the main window?","test",
                              MessageBoxButtons.YesNo);


   if (lnResult == DialogResult.No)
   {
      toEventArgs.Cancel = true;
   }
}
}}
```

Source Code Files

- Text files: pp4_6.cs
- Image files: phase.ico (Multi-image icon file, Appendix O)

pp4_6.cs: Program Phase 4-6 Source Code

```
//******************************************************************************
// Program Phase 4-6 C# .NET Framework - Mono Main Window with File Menu      *
// Programming Tasks Illustrated: .NET Framework - Mono GUI based application *
//                                Main window                                  *
//                                Window icon                                  *
//                                Window caption                               *
//                                Window menu with hotkeys                     *
//                                Window background color                      *
//                                Window mouse cursor                          *
//                                User sizable window                          *
//                                Message box input/output                     *
//******************************************************************************

//******************************************************************************
// File: pp4_6.cs                                                              *
// Reserved                                                                    *
//******************************************************************************

using System;
using System.Drawing;
using System.Collections;
using System.ComponentModel;
using System.Windows.Forms;
using System.Reflection;
using System.IO;

namespace nspp4_6
{
class pp4_6
{

//******************************************************************************
// Program Phase 4-6 Main                                                      *
// Define the Entry Point of Execution (EPE) for Program Phase 4-6             *
// CBI:  4-6.1.1.1                                                             *
//******************************************************************************

public static int Main()
{


//******************************************************************************
// Program Phase 4-6 Main                                                      *
// Declare the local variables for the "main" program                          *
// CBI:  4-6.1.1.2                                                             *
//******************************************************************************

   // Main window
   MainWindow loMainWindow;

   // Main window icon
   System.Drawing.Icon loIcon;
   Stream loStream;
   Assembly loAssembly;

   // Main window menu
   MainMenu loMenuBar;
```

pp4_6.cs continued on the next page

pp4_6.cs: Program Phase 4-6 Source Code continued

```
   MenuItem loFileMenu;
   MenuItem loMenuItem1;
   MenuItem loMenuItem2;
   EventHandler loMenuItem1EventHandler;
   EventHandler loMenuItem2EventHandler;

   // Main window background color
   System.Drawing.Color loWindowBackColor;

   // Main window mouse cursor
   System.Windows.Forms.Cursor loMouseCursor;


//***************************************************************************
// Program Phase 4-6 Main                                                   *
// Create the main window                                                   *
// CBI:  4-6.1.1.3                                                          *
//***************************************************************************

   loMainWindow = new MainWindow();


//***************************************************************************
// Program Phase 4-6 Main                                                   *
// Set the icon for the main window                                         *
// CBI:  4-6.1.1.4                                                          *
//***************************************************************************

   loAssembly = Assembly.GetExecutingAssembly();

   loStream = null;
   loStream = loAssembly.GetManifestResourceStream("nspp4_6.phase.ico");

   if(loStream == null)
   {
      loStream = loAssembly.GetManifestResourceStream("phase.ico");
   }

   if(loStream != null)
   {
      loIcon = new Icon(loStream);
      loMainWindow.Icon = loIcon ;
   }


//***************************************************************************
// Program Phase 4-6 Main                                                   *
// Set the caption of the main window                                       *
// CBI:  4-6.1.1.5                                                          *
//***************************************************************************

   loMainWindow.Text = "Program Phase 4-6  |  " +
                       "Platform:  Multi-Platform  |  " +
              "Programming Language:  C#  | GUI API:  .NET Framework - Mono";


//***************************************************************************
// Program Phase 4-6 Main                                                   *
// Create the menu for the main window                                      *
// CBI:  4-6.1.1.6                                                          *
//***************************************************************************

   // Menu bar
   loMenuBar = new MainMenu();

   // File Menu
   loFileMenu = new MenuItem("&File");
```

pp4_6.cs continued on the next page

pp4_6.cs: Program Phase 4-6 Source Code continued

```
   loMenuBar.MenuItems.Add(loFileMenu);

   // Hello World! Menu Item
   loMenuItem1 = new MenuItem("&Hello World!");
   loMenuItem1EventHandler = new EventHandler(loMainWindow.MenuItem1_Activate);
   loMenuItem1.Click += loMenuItem1EventHandler;
   loMenuItem1.Shortcut = Shortcut.CtrlH;
   loFileMenu.MenuItems.Add(loMenuItem1);

   // Exit Menu Item
   loMenuItem2 = new MenuItem("&Exit");
   loMenuItem2EventHandler = new EventHandler(loMainWindow.MenuItem2_Activate);
   loMenuItem2.Click += loMenuItem2EventHandler;
   loMenuItem2.Shortcut = Shortcut.CtrlX;
   loFileMenu.MenuItems.Add(loMenuItem2);

   // Assign the File menu to the main window
   loMainWindow.Menu = loMenuBar;


//******************************************************************************
// Program Phase 4-6 Main                                                      *
// Set the background color of the main window                                 *
// CBI:  4-6.1.1.7                                                             *
//******************************************************************************

   loWindowBackColor = Color.FromArgb(255,255,255);
   loMainWindow.BackColor = loWindowBackColor;


//******************************************************************************
// Program Phase 4-6 Main                                                      *
// Set the mouse cursor displayed when positioned over the main window         *
// CBI:  4-6.1.1.8                                                             *
//******************************************************************************

   loMouseCursor = Cursors.Arrow;
   loMainWindow.Cursor = loMouseCursor;


//******************************************************************************
// Program Phase 4-6 Main                                                      *
// Allow resizing of the main window                                           *
// CBI:  4-6.1.1.9                                                             *
//******************************************************************************

   loMainWindow.FormBorderStyle = FormBorderStyle.Sizable;


//******************************************************************************
// Program Phase 4-6 Main                                                      *
// Maximize and display the main window                                        *
// CBI:  4-6.1.1.10                                                            *
//******************************************************************************

   loMainWindow.WindowState = FormWindowState.Maximized;
   loMainWindow.Show();


//******************************************************************************
// Program Phase 4-6 Main                                                      *
// Start the event loop                                                        *
// CBI:  4-6.1.1.11                                                            *
//******************************************************************************

   Application.Run();
```

pp4_6.cs continued on the next page

pp4_6.cs: Program Phase 4-6 Source Code continued

```
//****************************************************************************
// Program Phase 4-6 Main                                                    *
// Cleanup the resources used by the main window                            *
// CBI:  4-6.1.1.12                                                          *
//****************************************************************************

   //  Resources allocated for the main window will automatically be freed at
   //  the appropriate time by the .NET Framework garbage collector.

   return 0;
}}

// callback functions
public class MainWindow : System.Windows.Forms.Form
{


//****************************************************************************
// Callback Functions                                                        *
// Implement the callback function for the Hello World! menu item           *
// CBI:  4-6.1.2.1                                                           *
//****************************************************************************

public void MenuItem1_Activate(Object toSender,EventArgs toEventArgs)
{
   MessageBox.Show("Hello World!","Program Phase 4-6",
                   MessageBoxButtons.OK,MessageBoxIcon.Information);
}


//****************************************************************************
// Callback Functions                                                        *
// Implement the callback function for the Exit menu item                   *
// CBI:  4-6.1.3.1                                                           *
//****************************************************************************

public void MenuItem2_Activate(Object toSender, EventArgs toEventArgs)
{
   this.Dispose();
   Application.Exit();
}


//****************************************************************************
// Callback Functions                                                        *
// Implement the callback function that fires when the main window is closed *
// CBI:  4-6.1.4.1                                                           *
//****************************************************************************

public MainWindow()
{
   this.Closed += new System.EventHandler(this.MainWindow_Closed);
   this.Closing += new CancelEventHandler(this.MainWindow_Closing);
}

private void MainWindow_Closed(object toSender, System.EventArgs toEventArgs)
{
   Application.Exit();
}

private void MainWindow_Closing(object toSender,CancelEventArgs toEventArgs)
{
   DialogResult lnResult;

   lnResult = MessageBox.Show("Close the main window?","Program Phase 4-6",
                              MessageBoxButtons.YesNo);
```

pp4_6.cs continued on the next page

pp4_6.cs: Program Phase 4-6 Source Code continued

```
    if (lnResult == DialogResult.No)
    {
       toEventArgs.Cancel = true;
    }
}
}}
```

Code Setup and Compilation

- Tools: Microsoft Visual C# 2008 Express Edition (msdn.microsoft.com), Microsoft .NET Framework 2.0 or higher (windowsupdate.microsoft.com), Steps to compile and execute using Mono on the Linux platform (programphases.com/?page_id=589)

Code Setup and Compilation Steps

1: Start the Microsoft Visual C# 2008 Express Edition program.

2: VC# EE - Activate Menu Item: File → New Project

Select "Empty Project". Name the project p4_6 and then activate the "OK" button.

3: VC# EE - Activate Menu Item: File → Save pp4_6

Set the "Location" to the appropriate folder. Verify that the "Create directory for solution" check box is not checked and then activate the "Save" button.

4: VC# EE - Activate Menu Item: Project → Add New Item

On the "Add New Item" dialog window, select the "Code File" template. Enter pp4_6.cs for the file name and then activate the "Add" button. Enter the source code for the pp4_6.cs file.

5: Add the following references to the project by right-clicking on the "References" item in the "Solution Explorer" window and then activating the "Add Reference" menu item:

```
System
System.Drawing
System.Windows.Forms
```

6: Create the phase.ico image file according to the instructions in Appendix O. Copy the image file to the pp4_6 folder.

7: VC# EE - Activate Menu Item: Project → pp4_6 Properties

Select the "Application" tab and then enter the following settings:

```
Assembly name:  pp4_6
Default namespace:  nspp4_6
Output type:  Windows Application
Startup object:  nspp4_6.pp4_6
```

Steps continued on the next page

Code Setup and Compilation Steps continued

8: Activate the button next to the icon text box and then select the phase.ico image file found in the pp4_6 folder. This sets the application icon and also adds the phase.ico file to the project. Close the "pp4_6 Properties" window.

9: For the properties of the phase.ico file, set the "Build Action" to be an "embedded resource". This causes the image file to be embedded into the pp4_6.exe file.

10: VC# EE - Activate Menu Item: File → Save All

11: VC# EE - Activate Menu Item: Build → Build Solution

Command Prompt Compilation

Enter the following commands from the pp4_6 folder to compile Program Phase 4-6:

```
PATH = c:\windows\microsoft.net\framework\v2.0.50727;%PATH%

csc.exe /out:bin\release\pp4_6.exe /t:winexe pp4_6.cs
/win32icon:phase.ico /resource:phase.ico
```

The preceding command needs to be entered on a single line.

Program Execution

- Execute Program

  `VC# EE - Activate Menu Item:  Debug → Start Without Debugging`

- Debug Program

  `VC# EE - Activate Menu Item:  Debug → Step into`

Program Phase 4-7

VB .NET ▪ .NET Framework ▪ Windows

GUI Based Program with Main Window

- Program Phase Task 4 is implemented in Program Phase 4-7 using the Visual Basic .NET (VB.NET) programming language and the Microsoft .NET Framework 2.0 or higher.

- Program Phase 4-7 contains a single source code file named pp4_7.vb. In addition to the pp4_7.vb text file, an icon image file called phase.ico is used as the window icon for the main window and the application icon for the pp4_7.exe executable file.

Code Block Features

The Program Phase 4-7 code blocks illustrate the following programming features using the Visual Basic .NET programming language:

- **Create a Resizable Main Window for a GUI Based Application**

- **Set the Main Window Icon and Caption**

- **Set the Main Window Menu**

- **Set the Main Window Background Color and Mouse Cursor**

- **Prompt to Exit the Application when the Main Window is Closed**

Visual Basic .NET
Create a Resizable Main Window for a GUI Based Application

- The main window is implemented with the .NET Framework Form class found in the System.Windows.Forms namespace.

- The code in the constructor for the MainWindow class specifies the MainWindow_Closed() method as the event handler for the Closed() event.

- The border of the main window is set to be resizable by specifying the "FormBorderStyle.Sizable" value for the "FormBorderStyle" property of the main window.

- The Application.Run() method is called to start the event loop for the program. This loop prevents the Main() function from automatically exiting. The Application.Exit() method is called when the main window is closed. When this happens, processing continues with the line of code immediately following the Application.Run() method.

test1.vb: VB.NET Create a Resizable Main Window for a GUI Based Application

```
Imports System
Imports System.Windows.Forms

Namespace test1ns
Class test1

Public Shared Function Main() As Integer

   Dim loMainWindow As MainWindow

   '' Create the main window
   loMainWindow = New MainWindow
   loMainWindow.FormBorderStyle = FormBorderStyle.Sizable

   '' Maximize and display the main window
   loMainWindow.WindowState = FormWindowState.Maximized
   loMainWindow.Show()

   Application.Run()

   Return 0

End Function
End Class

Public Class MainWindow
Inherits System.Windows.Forms.Form

Private Sub MainWindow_Closed(ByVal toSender As Object, ByVal toEventArgs As
EventArgs) Handles MyBase.Closed

   Application.Exit()

End Sub
End Class
End Namespace
```

Visual Basic .NET
Set the Main Window Icon and Caption

- The phase.ico file is embedded into the executable file and accessed at runtime. The GetManifestResourceStream() method of the currently executing assembly is used to obtain a resource stream object that represents the phase.ico icon. An icon object is obtained from the stream object and then assigned to the "Icon" property of the main window.

- If the program is compiled in the VB.NET IDE, the path to the icon is "nstest2.phase.ico". If the program is compiled at the command line, the path to the phase.ico icon is "phase.ico".

- The main window caption can be set with the "Text" property.

test2.vb: VB.NET Set the Main Window Icon and Caption

```
Imports System
Imports System.Windows.Forms
Imports System.Reflection
Imports System.IO
Imports System.Drawing
```

test2.vb continued on the next page

test2.vb: VB.NET Set the Main Window Icon and Caption continued

```
Namespace test2ns
Class test2

Public Shared Function Main() As Integer

   Dim loMainWindow As MainWindow
   Dim loIcon As System.Drawing.Icon
   Dim loStream As Stream
   Dim loAssembly As [Assembly]

   '' Create the main window
   loMainWindow = New MainWindow
   loMainWindow.FormBorderStyle = FormBorderStyle.Sizable

   loAssembly = System.Reflection.Assembly.GetExecutingAssembly()
   loStream = Nothing
   loStream = loAssembly.GetManifestResourceStream("test2ns.phase.ico")

   If (loStream Is Nothing) Then

      loStream = loAssembly.GetManifestResourceStream("phase.ico")

   End If

   If Not (loStream Is Nothing) Then

      loIcon = New Icon(loStream)

      '' Set the main window icon
      loMainWindow.Icon = loIcon

   End If

   '' Set the window caption
   loMainWindow.Text = "Hello World!"

   '' Maximize and display the main window
   loMainWindow.WindowState = FormWindowState.Maximized
   loMainWindow.Show()

   Application.Run()
   Return 0

End Function

End Class

Public Class MainWindow
Inherits System.Windows.Forms.Form

Private Sub MainWindow_Closed(ByVal toSender As Object, ByVal toEventArgs As
EventArgs) Handles MyBase.Closed

   Application.Exit()

End Sub
End Class
End Namespace
```

Visual Basic .NET
Set the Main Window Menu

- The following example creates a "File" menu with a "Hello World!" menu item and "Exit" menu item:

test3.vb: VB.NET Set the Main Window Menu

```
Imports System
Imports System.Windows.Forms

Namespace test3ns
Class test3

Public Shared Function Main() As Integer

   Dim loMainWindow As MainWindow
   Dim loMenuBar As MainMenu
   Dim loFileMenu As MenuItem
   Dim loMenuItem1 As MenuItem
   Dim loMenuItem2 As MenuItem

   '' Create the main window
   loMainWindow = New MainWindow
   loMainWindow.FormBorderStyle = FormBorderStyle.Sizable

   '' Menu bar
   loMenuBar = New MainMenu

   '' File Menu
   loFileMenu = New MenuItem("&File")

   '' Hello World! Menu Item
   loMenuItem1 = New MenuItem("&Hello World!")
   AddHandler loMenuItem1.Click, AddressOf loMainWindow.MenuItem1_Activate
   loMenuItem1.Shortcut = Shortcut.CtrlH
   loFileMenu.MenuItems.Add(loMenuItem1)

   '' Exit Menu Item
   loMenuItem2 = New MenuItem("&Exit")

   AddHandler loMenuItem2.Click, AddressOf loMainWindow.MenuItem2_Activate
   loMenuItem2.Shortcut = Shortcut.CtrlX
   loFileMenu.MenuItems.Add(loMenuItem2)

   '' Assign the File menu to the main window
   loMenuBar.MenuItems.Add(loFileMenu)
   loMainWindow.Menu = loMenuBar

   '' Maximize and display the main window
   loMainWindow.WindowState = FormWindowState.Maximized

   loMainWindow.Show()
   Application.Run()
   Return 0

End Function
End Class

Public Class MainWindow
Inherits System.Windows.Forms.Form

Private Sub MainWindow_Closed(ByVal toSender As Object, ByVal toEventArgs As
EventArgs) Handles MyBase.Closed

   Application.Exit()

End Sub

Sub MenuItem1_Activate(ByVal toSender As Object, ByVal toEventArgs As EventArgs)

   MessageBox.Show("Hello World!","test",MessageBoxButtons.OK, _
                   MessageBoxIcon.Information)

End Sub
```

test3.vb continued on the next page

test3.vb: VB.NET Set the Main Window Menu continued

```
Sub MenuItem2_Activate(ByVal toSender As Object, ByVal toEventArgs As EventArgs)

   Me.Dispose()
   Application.Exit()

End Sub
End Class
End Namespace
```

Visual Basic .NET
Set the Main Window Background Color and Mouse Cursor

- The following example sets the main window background color and mouse cursor:

test4.vb: VB.NET Set the Main Window Background Color and Mouse Cursor

```
Imports System
Imports System.Windows.Forms
Imports System.Drawing

Namespace test4ns
Class test4

Public Shared Function Main() As Integer

   Dim loMainWindow As MainWindow

   '' Create the main window
   loMainWindow = New MainWindow

   loMainWindow.FormBorderStyle = FormBorderStyle.Sizable

   '' Set the main window background color
   loMainWindow.BackColor = Color.FromArgb(255, 255, 255)

   '' Set the main window mouse cursor
   loMainWindow.Cursor = Cursors.Arrow

   '' Maximize and display the main window
   loMainWindow.WindowState = FormWindowState.Maximized

   loMainWindow.Show()
   Application.Run()
   Return 0

End Function

End Class

Public Class MainWindow
Inherits System.Windows.Forms.Form

Private Sub MainWindow_Closed(ByVal toSender As Object, ByVal toEventArgs As
EventArgs) Handles MyBase.Closed

   Application.Exit()

End Sub
End Class
End Namespace
```

Visual Basic .NET
Prompt to Exit the Application when the Main Window is Closed

- The MainWindow_Closing() event occurs right before the main window is closed.
- If the "Cancel" property of the "CancelEventArgs" parameter is set to the Boolean "True" value in the MainWindow_Closing() event, the main window is not closed.

test5.vb: VB.NET Prompt to Exit the Application when the Main Window is Closed

```
Imports System
Imports System.Windows.Forms

Namespace test5ns
Class test5

Public Shared Function Main() As Integer

   Dim loMainWindow As MainWindow

   '' Create the main window
   loMainWindow = New MainWindow
   loMainWindow.FormBorderStyle = FormBorderStyle.Sizable

   '' Maximize and display the main window
   loMainWindow.WindowState = FormWindowState.Maximized
   loMainWindow.Show()

   Application.Run()

Return 0

End Function
End Class

Public Class MainWindow
Inherits System.Windows.Forms.Form

Private Sub MainWindow_Closed(ByVal toSender As Object, ByVal toEventArgs As
EventArgs) Handles MyBase.Closed

   Application.Exit()

End Sub

Private Sub MainWindow_Closing(ByVal toSender As Object, ByVal toEventArgs As
System.ComponentModel.CancelEventArgs) Handles MyBase.Closing

   Dim lnResult As DialogResult

'' Prompt the user to continue closing the main window
   lnResult = MessageBox.Show("Close the main window?","test", _
                              MessageBoxButtons.YesNo)

   If (lnResult = Windows.Forms.DialogResult.No) Then

      toEventArgs.Cancel = True

   End If

End Sub
End Class
End Namespace
```

Source Code Files

- Text files: pp4_7.vb
- Image files: phase.ico (Multi-image icon file, Appendix O)

pp4_7.vb: Program Phase 4-7 Source Code

```
''*****************************************************************************
'' Program Phase 4-7 VB.NET Main Window with File Menu                       *
'' Programming Tasks Illustrated: .NET Framework GUI based application       *
''                                Main window                                *
''                                Window icon                                *
''                                Window caption                             *
''                                Window menu with hotkeys                   *
''                                Window background color                    *
''                                Window mouse cursor                        *
''                                User sizable window                        *
''                                Message box input/output                   *
''*****************************************************************************

''*****************************************************************************
'' File: pp4_7.vb                                                            *
'' Reserved                                                                  *
''*****************************************************************************

Imports System
Imports System.Windows.Forms
Imports System.Drawing
Imports System.Collections
Imports System.ComponentModel
Imports System.Reflection
Imports System.IO

Namespace nspp4_7
Class pp4_7


''*****************************************************************************
'' Program Phase 4-7 Main                                                    *
'' Define the Entry Point of Execution (EPE) for Program Phase 4-7           *
'' CBI:  4-7.1.1.1                                                           *
''*****************************************************************************

Public Shared Function Main() As Integer


''*****************************************************************************
'' Program Phase 4-7 Main                                                    *
'' Declare the local variables for the "main" program                        *
'' CBI:  4-7.1.1.2                                                           *
''*****************************************************************************

   '' Main window
   Dim loMainWindow As MainWindow

   '' Main window icon
   Dim loIcon As System.Drawing.Icon
   Dim loStream As Stream
   Dim loAssembly As [Assembly]

   '' Main window menu
   Dim loMenuBar As MainMenu
   Dim loFileMenu As MenuItem
   Dim loMenuItem1 As MenuItem
```

pp4_7.vb continued on the next page

pp4_7.vb: Program Phase 4-7 Source Code continued

```
   Dim loMenuItem2 As MenuItem

   '' Main window background color
   Dim loWindowBackColor As System.Drawing.Color

   '' Main window mouse cursor
   Dim loMouseCursor As System.Windows.Forms.Cursor


''**************************************************************************
'' Program Phase 4-7 Main                                                  *
'' Create the main window                                                  *
'' CBI:  4-7.1.1.3                                                         *
''**************************************************************************

   loMainWindow = New MainWindow


''**************************************************************************
'' Program Phase 4-7 Main                                                  *
'' Set the icon for the main window                                        *
'' CBI:  4-7.1.1.4                                                         *
''**************************************************************************

   loAssembly = System.Reflection.Assembly.GetExecutingAssembly()

   loStream = Nothing
   loStream = loAssembly.GetManifestResourceStream("nspp4_7.phase.ico")

   If (loStream Is Nothing) Then

      loStream = loAssembly.GetManifestResourceStream("phase.ico")

   End If

   If Not (loStream Is Nothing) Then

      loIcon = New Icon(loStream)
      loMainWindow.Icon = loIcon

   End If


''**************************************************************************
'' Program Phase 4-7 Main                                                  *
'' Set the caption of the main window                                      *
'' CBI:  4-7.1.1.5                                                         *
''**************************************************************************

   loMainWindow.Text = "Program Phase 4-7  |  " + _
                       "Platform:  Windows  |  " + _
                       "Programming Language:  Visual Basic .NET  |  " + _
                       "GUI API:  .NET Framework"


''**************************************************************************
'' Program Phase 4-7 Main                                                  *
'' Create the menu for the main window                                     *
'' CBI:  4-7.1.1.6                                                         *
''**************************************************************************

   '' Menu bar
   loMenuBar = New MainMenu

   '' File Menu
   loFileMenu = New MenuItem("&File")
```

pp4_7.vb continued on the next page

pp4_7.vb: Program Phase 4-7 Source Code continued

```
    '' Hello World! Menu Item
    loMenuItem1 = New MenuItem("&Hello World!")

    AddHandler loMenuItem1.Click, AddressOf loMainWindow.MenuItem1_Activate
    loMenuItem1.Shortcut = Shortcut.CtrlH
    loFileMenu.MenuItems.Add(loMenuItem1)

    '' Exit Menu Item
    loMenuItem2 = New MenuItem("&Exit")
    AddHandler loMenuItem2.Click, AddressOf loMainWindow.MenuItem2_Activate
    loMenuItem2.Shortcut = Shortcut.CtrlX
    loFileMenu.MenuItems.Add(loMenuItem2)

    '' Assign the File menu to the main window
    loMenuBar.MenuItems.Add(loFileMenu)
    loMainWindow.Menu = loMenuBar

''*************************************************************************
'' Program Phase 4-7 Main                                                 *
'' Set the background color of the main window                            *
'' CBI:  4-7.1.1.7                                                        *
''*************************************************************************

    loWindowBackColor = Color.FromArgb(255, 255, 255)
    loMainWindow.BackColor = loWindowBackColor


''*************************************************************************
'' Program Phase 4-7 Main                                                 *
'' Set the mouse cursor displayed when positoned over the main window     *
'' CBI:  4-7.1.1.8                                                        *
''*************************************************************************

    loMouseCursor = Cursors.Arrow
    loMainWindow.Cursor = loMouseCursor


''*************************************************************************
'' Program Phase 4-7 Main                                                 *
'' Allow resizing of the main window                                      *
'' CBI:  4-7.1.1.9                                                        *
''*************************************************************************

    loMainWindow.FormBorderStyle = FormBorderStyle.Sizable


''*************************************************************************
'' Program Phase 4-7 Main                                                 *
'' Maximize and display the main window                                   *
'' CBI:  4-7.1.1.10                                                       *
''*************************************************************************

    loMainWindow.WindowState = FormWindowState.Maximized
    loMainWindow.Show()


''*************************************************************************
'' Program Phase 4-7 Main                                                 *
'' Start the event loop                                                   *
'' CBI:  4-7.1.1.11                                                       *
''*************************************************************************

    Application.Run()
```

pp4_7.vb continued on the next page

pp4_7.vb: Program Phase 4-7 Source Code continued

```
''*************************************************************************
'' Program Phase 4-7 Main                                                 *
'' Cleanup the resources used by the main window                          *
'' CBI:  4-7.1.1.12                                                       *
''*************************************************************************

   ''  Resources allocated for the main window will automatically be freed at
   ''  the appropriate time by the .NET Framework garbage collector.

   Return 0

End Function
End Class

'' Callback Functions

Public Class MainWindow
Inherits System.Windows.Forms.Form


''*************************************************************************
'' Callback Functions                                                     *
'' Implement the callback function for the Hello World! menu item         *
'' CBI:  4-7.1.2.1                                                        *
''*************************************************************************

Sub MenuItem1_Activate(ByVal toSender As Object, ByVal toEventArgs As
System.EventArgs)

   '' Display the Hello World! message box dialog if the user activates the
   '' Hello World! menu item

   MessageBox.Show("Hello World!","Program Phase 4-7", _
                   MessageBoxButtons.OK,MessageBoxIcon.Information)

End Sub


''*************************************************************************
'' Callback Functions                                                     *
'' Implement the callback function for the Exit menu item                 *
'' CBI:  4-7.1.3.1                                                        *
''*************************************************************************

Sub MenuItem2_Activate(ByVal toSender As Object, ByVal toEventArgs As
System.EventArgs)

   '' Exit the program if the user activates the Exit menu item
   Me.Dispose()
   Application.Exit()

End Sub


''*************************************************************************
'' Callback Functions                                                     *
'' Implement the callback function that fires when the main window is closed  *
'' CBI:  4-7.1.4.1                                                        *
''*************************************************************************

Private Sub MainWindow_Closed(ByVal toSender As System.Object, ByVal toEventArgs
As System.EventArgs) Handles MyBase.Closed

   Application.Exit()

End Sub
```

pp4_7.vb continued on the next page

pp4_7.vb: Program Phase 4-7 Source Code continued

```
Private Sub MainWindow_Closing(ByVal toSender As Object, ByVal toEventArgs As
System.ComponentModel.CancelEventArgs) Handles MyBase.Closing

   Dim lnResult As DialogResult

   '' Prompt the user to continue closing the main window
   lnResult = MessageBox.Show("Close the main window?","Program Phase 4-7", _
                              MessageBoxButtons.YesNo)


   If (lnResult = Windows.Forms.DialogResult.No) Then

      toEventArgs.Cancel = True

   End If

End Sub
End Class
End Namespace
```

Code Setup and Compilation

- Tools: Microsoft Visual Basic 2008 Express Edition (msdn.microsoft.com), Microsoft .NET Framework 2.0 or higher (windowsupdate.microsoft.com)

Code Setup and Compilation Steps

1: Start the Microsoft Visual Basic 2008 Express Edition program.

2: VB.NET EE - Activate Menu Item: File → New Project

Select "Console Application". Name the project pp4_7 and then activate the "OK" button.

3: Delete the module1.bas file in the "Solution Explorer" window.

4: VB.NET EE - Activate Menu Item: File → Save All

On the "Save Project" dialog window, specify pp4_7 for the "Name". Set the "Location" to the appropriate folder. Uncheck the "Create directory for solution" check box and then activate the "Save" button.

5: VB.NET EE - Activate Menu Item: Project → Add New Item

On the "Add New Item" dialog window, select the "Module" template. Enter pp4_7.vb for the file name and then activate the "Add" button. Enter the source code for the pp4_7.vb file.

6: Create the phase.ico image file according to the instructions in Appendix O. Copy the image file to the pp4_7 folder.

Steps continued on the next page

Code Setup and Compilation Steps continued

7: VB.NET EE - Activate Menu Item: Project → pp4_7 Properties

Click on the "Application" tab and then enter the following settings:

```
uncheck:  "Enable application framework"
Assembly name:  pp4_7
Root namespace:  nspp4_7
Output type:  Windows Forms Application
Startup object:  nspp4_7.pp4_7
```

8: Using the icon combo box, select the phase.ico image file found in the pp4_7 folder. This sets the application icon and also adds the phase.ico file to the project. Close the "pp4_7 Properties" window.

9: Click on the "References" tab and then add the following references:

```
System
System.Drawing
System.Windows.Forms
```

10: For the properties of the phase.ico file, set the "Build Action" to be an "Embedded Resource". This causes the image file to be embedded into the pp4_7.exe file.

11: VB.NET EE - Activate Menu Item: File → Save All

12: VB.NET EE - Activate Menu Item: Build → Build pp4_7

Command Prompt Compilation

Enter the following commands from the pp4_7 folder to compile Program Phase 4-7:

```
PATH = "c:\windows\microsoft.net\framework\v2.0.50727";%PATH%

  vbc.exe /r:system.dll /r:system.windows.forms.dll /r:system.drawing.dll
/out:bin\release\pp4_7.exe /t:winexe /win32icon:phase.ico
/resource:phase.ico pp4_7.vb
```

The preceding command needs to be entered on a single line.

Program Execution

- Execute Program

```
VB.NET EE - Activate Menu Item:  Debug → Start Debugging
```

- Debug Program

```
VB.NET EE - Activate Menu Item:  Debug → Step Into
```

Program Phase 4-8
Managed C++ ▪ Windows

GUI Based Program with Main Window

- Program Phase Task 4 is implemented in Program Phase 4-8 using the C++ programming language and the Microsoft .NET Framework.
- Program Phase 4-8 contains a main source code file named pp4_8.cpp. In addition to the pp4_8.cpp text file, an icon image file called phase.ico is used as the window icon for the main window and the application icon for the pp4_8.exe executable file. The resources for the program are referenced in the resource.rc and resource.h text files.

Code Block Features

The Program Phase 4-8 code blocks illustrate the following programming features using the C++ programming language and the Microsoft .NET Framework:

- **Create a Resizable Main Window for a GUI Based Application**
- **Set the Main Window Icon and Caption**
- **Set the Main Window Menu**
- **Set the Main Window Background Color and Mouse Cursor**
- **Prompt to Exit the Application when the Main Window is Closed**

Managed C++
Create a Resizable Main Window for a GUI Based Application

- The main window is implemented with the.NET Framework Form class found in the System.Windows.Forms namespace.
- The code in the constructor for the MainWindow class specifies the MainWindow_Closed() method as the event handler for the Closed() event.
- The border of the main window is set to be resizable by specifying the "FormBorderStyle.Sizable" value for the "FormBorderStyle" property of the main window.
- The Application::Run() method is called to start the event loop for the program. This loop prevents the main() function from automatically exiting. The Application::Exit() method is called when the main window is closed. When this happens, processing continues with the line of code immediately following the Application::Run() method.

test1.cpp: Managed C++ Create a Resizable Main Window for a GUI Based Application

```
#using <mscorlib.dll>
using namespace System;
using namespace System::Windows::Forms;

ref class MainWindow : public Form
{
public:
   MainWindow();
   void MainWindow_Closed(Object^  toSender, EventArgs^  toEventArgs);
};

int main(void)
{
   MainWindow^ loMainWindow;

   // Create the main window
   loMainWindow = gcnew MainWindow();
   loMainWindow->FormBorderStyle = FormBorderStyle::Sizable;

   // Maximize and display the main window
   loMainWindow->WindowState = FormWindowState::Maximized;
   loMainWindow->Show();

   Application::Run();
   return 0;
}

MainWindow::MainWindow()
{
   this->Closed += gcnew EventHandler(this,&MainWindow::MainWindow_Closed);
}

void MainWindow::MainWindow_Closed(Object^ toSender,EventArgs^ toEventArgs)
{
    Application::Exit();
}
```

Managed C++
Set the Main Window Icon and Caption

- The phase.ico file is embedded into the executable file and accessed at runtime. The GetManifestResourceStream() method of the currently executing assembly is used to obtain a resource stream object that represents the phase.ico icon. An icon object is obtained from the stream object and then assigned to the "Icon" property of the main window.

- The application icon is set using a resource file.

- The main window caption is set with the "Text" property.

test2.cpp: Managed C++ Set the Main Window Icon and Caption

```
#using <mscorlib.dll>
using namespace System;
using namespace System::Drawing;
using namespace System::Windows::Forms;
using namespace System::Reflection;
using namespace System::IO;
```

test2.cpp continued on the next page

test2.cpp: Managed C++ Set the Main Window Icon and Caption continued

```
ref class MainWindow : public Form
{
public:

   MainWindow();
   void MainWindow_Closed(Object^  toSender, EventArgs^  toEventArgs);
};

int main(void)
{
   MainWindow^ loMainWindow;
   Stream^ loStream;

   Assembly^ loAssembly;

   loMainWindow = gcnew MainWindow();
   loMainWindow->FormBorderStyle = FormBorderStyle::Sizable;

   loStream = nullptr;
   loAssembly = Assembly::GetExecutingAssembly();
   loStream = loAssembly->GetManifestResourceStream("phase.ico");

   if (loStream != nullptr)
   {
      // Set the main window icon
      loMainWindow->Icon = gcnew Icon(loStream);
   }

   // Set the main window caption
   loMainWindow->Text = "Hello World!";

   loMainWindow->WindowState = FormWindowState::Maximized;
   loMainWindow->Show();
   Application::Run();
   return 0;
}

MainWindow::MainWindow()
{
   this->Closed += gcnew EventHandler(this,&MainWindow::MainWindow_Closed);
}

void MainWindow::MainWindow_Closed(Object^ toSender,EventArgs^ toEventArgs)
{
    Application::Exit();
}
```

resource.h: Header File for the Program Resources

```
#define IDI_ICON1                          100
```

resource.rc: Resource File for the Program Resources

```
#include "resource.h"
IDI_ICON1               ICON                    "phase.ico"
```

Managed C++
Set the Main Window Menu

- The following example creates a "File" menu with a "Hello World!" menu item and "Exit" menu item:

test3.cpp: Managed C++ Set the Main Window Menu

```
#using <mscorlib.dll>
using namespace System;
using namespace System::Windows::Forms;

ref class MainWindow : public Form
{
public:

   MainWindow();
   void MainWindow_Closed(Object^  toSender, EventArgs^  toEventArgs);
   void MenuItem1_Activate(Object^ toSender,EventArgs^ toEventArgs);
   void MenuItem2_Activate(Object^ toSender,EventArgs^ toEventArgs);
};

int main(void)
{
   MainWindow^ loMainWindow;
   MainMenu^ loMenuBar;
   MenuItem^ loFileMenu;
   MenuItem^ loMenuItem1;
   MenuItem^ loMenuItem2;

   EventHandler^ loMenuItem1EventHandler;
   EventHandler^ loMenuItem2EventHandler;

   // Create the main window
   loMainWindow = gcnew MainWindow();
   loMainWindow->FormBorderStyle = FormBorderStyle::Sizable;

   // Menu Bar
   loMenuBar = gcnew MainMenu();

   // File menu
   loFileMenu = gcnew MenuItem("&File");

   // Hello World! menu item
   loMenuItem1 = gcnew MenuItem("&Hello World!");
   loMenuItem1EventHandler = gcnew EventHandler(loMainWindow,
                                             &MainWindow::MenuItem1_Activate);

   loMenuItem1->Click += loMenuItem1EventHandler;
   loMenuItem1->Shortcut = Shortcut::CtrlH;
   loFileMenu->MenuItems->Add(loMenuItem1);

   // Exit menu item
   loMenuItem2 = gcnew MenuItem("&Exit");
   loMenuItem2EventHandler = gcnew EventHandler(loMainWindow,
                                             &MainWindow::MenuItem2_Activate);

   loMenuItem2->Click += loMenuItem2EventHandler;
   loMenuItem2->Shortcut = Shortcut::CtrlX;

   // Assign the menu to the main window
   loFileMenu->MenuItems->Add(loMenuItem2);
   loMenuBar->MenuItems->Add(loFileMenu);

   loMainWindow->Menu = loMenuBar;

   loMainWindow->WindowState = FormWindowState::Maximized;
   loMainWindow->Show();

   Application::Run();
   return 0;
}
```

test3.cpp continued on the next page

test3.cpp: Managed C++ Set the Main Window Menu continued

```
MainWindow::MainWindow()
{
   this->Closed += gcnew EventHandler(this,&MainWindow::MainWindow_Closed);
}

void MainWindow::MainWindow_Closed(Object^ toSender,EventArgs^ toEventArgs)
{
    Application::Exit();
}

void MainWindow::MenuItem1_Activate(Object^ toSender,EventArgs^ toEventArgs)
{
   MessageBox::Show("Hello World!","test",
                    MessageBoxButtons::OK,MessageBoxIcon::Information);
}

void MainWindow::MenuItem2_Activate(Object^ toSender,EventArgs^ toEventArgs)
{
   delete this;
   Application::Exit();
}
```

Managed C++
Set the Main Window Background Color and Mouse Cursor

- The following example sets the main window background color and mouse cursor:

test4.cpp: Set the Main Window Background Color and Mouse Cursor

```
#using <mscorlib.dll>
using namespace System;
using namespace System::Drawing;
using namespace System::Windows::Forms;

ref class MainWindow : public Form
{
public:

   MainWindow();
   void MainWindow_Closed(Object^  toSender, EventArgs^  toEventArgs);
};

int main(void)
{
   MainWindow^ loMainWindow;

   // Create the main window
   loMainWindow = gcnew MainWindow();
   loMainWindow->FormBorderStyle = FormBorderStyle::Sizable;

   // Set the main window background color
   loMainWindow->BackColor = Color::FromArgb(255,255,255);
   loMainWindow->Cursor = Cursors::Arrow;

   // Set the main window mouse cursor
   loMainWindow->WindowState = FormWindowState::Maximized;
   loMainWindow->Show();

   Application::Run();
   return 0;
}
```

test4.cpp continued on the next page

test4.cpp: Set the Main Window Background Color and Mouse Cursor continued

```
MainWindow::MainWindow()
{
   this->Closed += gcnew EventHandler(this,&MainWindow::MainWindow_Closed);
}

void MainWindow::MainWindow_Closed(Object^ toSender,EventArgs^ toEventArgs)
{
    Application::Exit();
}
```

Manage C++
Prompt to Exit the Application when the Main Window is Closed

- The main window Closing event is setup for the MainWindow_Closing() method by using the EventHandler class found in the System namespace. If the "Cancel" property of the event argument parameter is set to the Boolean "true" value, the main window does not close. The user is prompted with a message box to continue closing the main window in the MainWindow_Closing() method. If the user selects "No", the "Cancel" property of the event argument parameter is set to "true".

test5.cpp: Managed C++ Prompt to Exit the App. when the Main Window is Closed

```
#using <mscorlib.dll>
using namespace System;
using namespace System::Drawing;
using namespace System::ComponentModel;
using namespace System::Windows::Forms;

ref class MainWindow : public Form
{
public:

   MainWindow();
   void MainWindow_Closed(Object^  toSender, EventArgs^  toEventArgs);
 void MainWindow_Closing(Object^  toSender,CancelEventArgs^ toCancelEventArgs);

};

int main(void)
{
   MainWindow^ loMainWindow;

   // Create the main window
   loMainWindow = gcnew MainWindow();
   loMainWindow->FormBorderStyle = FormBorderStyle::Sizable;
   loMainWindow->WindowState = FormWindowState::Maximized;
   loMainWindow->Show();
   Application::Run();

   return 0;
}

MainWindow::MainWindow()
{
   this->Closed += gcnew EventHandler(this,&MainWindow::MainWindow_Closed);

   this->Closing += gcnew CancelEventHandler(this,
                                          &MainWindow::MainWindow_Closing);
}
```

test5.cpp continued on the next page

test5.cpp: Managed C++ Prompt to Exit when the Main Window is Closed continued

```
void MainWindow::MainWindow_Closed(Object^ toSender,EventArgs^ toEventArgs)
{
    Application::Exit();
}

void MainWindow::MainWindow_Closing(Object^ toSender,CancelEventArgs^
toCancelEventArgs)
{
   System::Windows::Forms::DialogResult lnResult;

   // Prompt the user to continue closing the main window
   lnResult = MessageBox::Show("Close the main window?",
                               "test",
                               MessageBoxButtons::YesNo,
                               MessageBoxIcon::Question);

   if (lnResult == System::Windows::Forms::DialogResult::No)
   {
       toCancelEventArgs->Cancel = true;
   }
}
```

Source Code Files

- Text files: pp4_8.cpp, resource.h, resource.rc
- Image files: phase.ico (Multi-image icon file, Appendix O)

pp4_8.cpp: Program Phase 4-8 Source Code

```
//*************************************************************************
// Program Phase 4-8 Managed C++ Main Window with File Menu               *
// Programming Tasks Illustrated: .NET Framework GUI Based Application    *
//                                Main window                             *
//                                Window icon                             *
//                                Window caption                          *
//                                Window menu with hotkeys                *
//                                Window background color                 *
//                                Window mouse cursor                     *
//                                User sizable window                     *
//                                Message box input/output                *
//*************************************************************************

//*************************************************************************
// File: pp4_8.cpp                                                        *
// Reserved                                                               *
//*************************************************************************

#using <mscorlib.dll>
using namespace System;
using namespace System::Drawing;
using namespace System::Collections;
using namespace System::ComponentModel;
using namespace System::Windows::Forms;
using namespace System::Reflection;
using namespace System::IO;

ref class MainWindow : public Form
{
public:

   MainWindow();
```

pp4_8.cpp continued on the next page

pp4_8.cpp: Program Phase 4-8 Source Code continued

```
   void MainWindow_Closed(Object^ toSender, EventArgs^  toEventArgs);
   void MainWindow_Closing(Object^ toSender,
                           CancelEventArgs^ toCancelEventArgs);

   void MenuItem1_Activate(Object^ toSender,EventArgs^ toEventArgs);
   void MenuItem2_Activate(Object^ toSender,EventArgs^ toEventArgs);
};


//**************************************************************************
// Program Phase 4-8 Main                                                 *
// Define the Entry Point of Execution (EPE) for Program Phase 4-8        *
// CBI:  4-8.1.1.1                                                        *
//**************************************************************************

int main(void)
{


//**************************************************************************
// Program Phase 4-8 Main                                                 *
// Declare the local variables for the "main" program                     *
// CBI:  4-8.1.1.2                                                        *
//**************************************************************************

   // Main window
   MainWindow^ loMainWindow;

   // Main window icon
   System::IO::Stream^ loStream;
   System::Reflection::Assembly^ loAssembly;
   Drawing::Icon^ loIcon;

   // Main window menu
   MainMenu^ loMenuBar;
   MenuItem^ loFileMenu;
   MenuItem^ loMenuItem1;
   MenuItem^ loMenuItem2;
   EventHandler^ loMenuItem1EventHandler;
   EventHandler^ loMenuItem2EventHandler;

   // Main window background color
   Drawing::Color loWindowBackColor;

   // Main window mouse cursor
   System::Windows::Forms::Cursor^ loCursor;


//**************************************************************************
// Program Phase 4-8 Main                                                 *
// Create the main window                                                 *
// CBI:  4-8.1.1.3                                                        *
//**************************************************************************

   loMainWindow = gcnew MainWindow();


//**************************************************************************
// Program Phase 4-8 Main                                                 *
// Set the icon for the main window                                       *
// CBI:  4-8.1.1.4                                                        *
//**************************************************************************

   loStream = nullptr;
   loAssembly = System::Reflection::Assembly::GetExecutingAssembly();
   loStream = loAssembly->GetManifestResourceStream("phase.ico");
```

pp4_8.cpp continued on the next page

pp4_8.cpp: Program Phase 4-8 Source Code continued

```
   if(loStream == nullptr)
   {
      MessageBox::Show("The GetManifestResourceStream method of the "
                       "Assembly class failed.","CBI:  4-8.1.1.4",
                       MessageBoxButtons::OK,MessageBoxIcon::Error);
   }

   if (loStream != nullptr)
   {
      loIcon = gcnew Drawing::Icon(loStream);
      loMainWindow->Icon = loIcon;
 }


//*************************************************************************
// Program Phase 4-8 Main                                                 *
// Set the caption of the main window                                     *
// CBI:  4-8.1.1.5                                                        *
//*************************************************************************

   loMainWindow->Text = "Program Phase 4-8  |  "
                        "Platform:  Windows  |  "
                        "Programming Language:  C++  |  "
                        "GUI API:  .NET Framework 2.0";


//*************************************************************************
// Program Phase 4-8 Main                                                 *
// Create the menu for the main window                                    *
// CBI:  4-8.1.1.6                                                        *
//*************************************************************************

   // Menu Bar
   loMenuBar = gcnew MainMenu();

   // File menu
   loFileMenu = gcnew MenuItem("&File");

   // Hello World! menu item
   loMenuItem1 = gcnew MenuItem("&Hello World!");
   loMenuItem1EventHandler = gcnew EventHandler(loMainWindow,
                                      &MainWindow::MenuItem1_Activate);

   loMenuItem1->Click += loMenuItem1EventHandler;
   loMenuItem1->Shortcut = Shortcut::CtrlH;

   loFileMenu->MenuItems->Add(loMenuItem1);

   // Exit menu item
   loMenuItem2 = gcnew MenuItem("&Exit");
   loMenuItem2EventHandler = gcnew EventHandler(loMainWindow,
                                      &MainWindow::MenuItem2_Activate);

   loMenuItem2->Click += loMenuItem2EventHandler;
   loMenuItem2->Shortcut = Shortcut::CtrlX;

   // Assign the menu to the main window
   loFileMenu->MenuItems->Add(loMenuItem2);
   loMenuBar->MenuItems->Add(loFileMenu);
   loMainWindow->Menu = loMenuBar;


//*************************************************************************
// Program Phase 4-8 Main                                                 *
// Set the background color of the main window                            *
// CBI:  4-8.1.1.7                                                        *
//*************************************************************************
```

pp4_8.cpp continued on the next page

pp4_8.cpp: Program Phase 4-8 Source Code continued

```
  loWindowBackColor = Drawing::Color::FromArgb(255,255,255);
  loMainWindow->BackColor = loWindowBackColor;


//*************************************************************************
// Program Phase 4-8 Main                                                 *
// Set the mouse cursor displayed when positoned over the main window     *
// CBI:  4-8.1.1.8                                                        *
//*************************************************************************

  loCursor = Cursors::Arrow;
  loMainWindow->Cursor = loCursor;


//*************************************************************************
// Program Phase 4-8 Main                                                 *
// Allow resizing of the main window                                      *
// CBI:  4-8.1.1.9                                                        *
//*************************************************************************

  loMainWindow->FormBorderStyle = FormBorderStyle::Sizable;


//*************************************************************************
// Program Phase 4-8 Main                                                 *
// Maximize and display the main window                                   *
// CBI:  4-8.1.1.10                                                       *
//*************************************************************************

   loMainWindow->WindowState = FormWindowState::Maximized;
   loMainWindow->Show();


//*************************************************************************
// Program Phase 4-8 Main                                                 *
// Start the event loop                                                   *
// CBI:  4-8.1.1.11                                                       *
//*************************************************************************

   Application::Run();


//*************************************************************************
// Program Phase 4-8 Main                                                 *
// Cleanup the resources used by the main window                          *
// CBI:  4-8.1.1.12                                                       *
//*************************************************************************

   //  Resources allocated for the main window will automatically be freed at
   //  the appropriate time by the .NET Framework garbage collector.

   return 0;
}

// Callback Functions

//*************************************************************************
// Callback Functions                                                     *
// Implement the callback function for the Hello World! menu item         *
// CBI:  4-8.1.2.1                                                        *
//*************************************************************************
```

pp4_8.cpp continued on the next page

pp4_8.cpp: Program Phase 4-8 Source Code continued

```
void MainWindow::MenuItem1_Activate(Object^ toSender,EventArgs^ toEventArgs)
{
   MessageBox::Show("Hello World!","Program Phase 4-8",
                  MessageBoxButtons::OK,MessageBoxIcon::Information);
}


//**************************************************************************
// Callback Functions                                                      *
// Implement the callback function for the Exit menu item                  *
// CBI:  4-8.1.3.1                                                         *
//**************************************************************************

void MainWindow::MenuItem2_Activate(Object^ toSender,EventArgs^ toEventArgs)
{
   delete this;
   Application::Exit();

}


//**************************************************************************
// Callback Functions                                                      *
// Implement the callback function that fires when the main window is closed  *
// CBI:  4-8.1.4.1                                                         *
//**************************************************************************

MainWindow::MainWindow()
{
   this->Closed += gcnew
System::EventHandler(this,&MainWindow::MainWindow_Closed);

   this->Closing += gcnew
CancelEventHandler(this,&MainWindow::MainWindow_Closing);
}

void MainWindow::MainWindow_Closed(Object^ toSender,EventArgs^ toEventArgs)
{
    Application::Exit();
}

void MainWindow::MainWindow_Closing(Object^ toSender,
                                    CancelEventArgs^ toCancelEventArgs)
{
   System::Windows::Forms::DialogResult lnResult;

   // Prompt the user to continue closing the main window
   lnResult = MessageBox::Show("Close the main window?","Program Phase 4-8",
                              MessageBoxButtons::YesNo,
                              MessageBoxIcon::Question);

   if (lnResult == System::Windows::Forms::DialogResult::No)
   {
       toCancelEventArgs->Cancel = true;
   }
}
```

resource.h: Header File for the Program Resources

```
#define IDI_ICON1                        100
```

resource.rc: Resource File for the Program Resources

```
#include "resource.h"
IDI_ICON1                 ICON                       "phase.ico"
```

Code Setup and Compilation

- Tools: Microsoft Visual Studio 2008 Express Edition (msdn.microsoft.com)

Code Setup and Compilation Steps

1: Start the Microsoft Visual C++ 2008 Express Edition program.

2: VC++ EE - Activate Menu Item: File → New → Project

3: Select "Win32" for the "Project type". Select the "Win32 Console Application" template.

4: Name the project pp4_8. Set the "Project Location" to the appropriate folder. Do not check the "Create directory for solution" check box. Activate the "OK" button to proceed with the "Win32 Application Wizard".

5: Activate the "Next" button of the Win32 Application Wizard.

6: Verify that a "Console Application" is selected and also check the "Empty project" check box. Activate the "Finish" button of the "Win32 Application Wizard".

7: VC++ EE - Activate Menu Item: Project → Add New Item

On the "Add New Item" dialog window, select the "Visual C++ → Code" category and then select the "C++ File" template. Enter pp4_8.cpp for the file name and then activate the "Add" button.

8: Enter the source code for the pp4_8.cpp text file.

9: Create the phase.ico image file according to the instructions in Appendix O. Copy the image file to the pp4_8 folder.

10: Using a text editor, create the resource.h and resource.rc files and then enter the appropriate source code. Copy the resource.h and resource.rc files to the pp4_8 folder.

11: VC++ EE - Activate Menu Item: Project → Add Existing Item

Select the resource.h file in the pp4_8 folder and then activate the "Add" button.

12: VC++ EE - Activate Menu Item: Project → Add Existing Item

Select the resource.rc file in the pp4_8 folder and then activate the "Add" button.

13: VC++ EE - Activate Menu Item: Build → Configuration Manager

Select the "Release" value for the "Active solution configuration". Activate the "Close" button.

14: VC++ EE - Activate Menu Item: Project → pp4_8 Properties

Enter the following settings:

Configuration Properties → General → Character Set

"Use Multi-Byte Character Set"

Steps continued on the next page

Code Setup and Compilation Steps continued

15: Continue entering settings on the "pp4_8 Property Pages" window.

Configuration Properties → General → Common Language Runtime Support

"Common Language Runtime Support (/clr)"

Configuration Properties → Linker → Advanced → Entry Point

"main"

Configuration Properties → Frameworks and References

Specify the System, System.Drawing, and System.Windows.Forms namespace references.

Configuration Properties → Linker → Input → Embed Managed Resource File

phase.ico

Activate the "Apply" button.

16: VC++ EE - Activate Menu Item: Build → Build Solution

Command Prompt Compilation Steps

1: From a Visual Studio 2008 command prompt, enter the following command on a single line:

```
cl.exe /clr /FU
"%SYSTEMROOT%\Microsoft.NET\Framework\v2.0.50727\System.dll" /FU
"%SYSTEMROOT%\Microsoft.NET\Framework\v2.0.50727\System.Drawing.dll" /FU
"%SYSTEMROOT%\Microsoft.NET\Framework\v2.0.50727\System.Windows.Forms.dll"
pp4_8.cpp /c
```

2: The rc.exe program can be used to compile the resource.rc file into the resource.res file.

```
rc.exe resource.rc
```

3: The link.exe program can be used to create the pp4_8.exe file from the pp4_8.obj, resource.res, and phase.ico files.

```
link.exe pp4_8.obj resource.res /ASSEMBLYRESOURCE:phase.ico /ENTRY:main
```

Program Execution

- Execute Program

  VC++ EE - Activate Menu Item: Debug → Start Without Debugging

- Debug Program

  VC++ EE - Activate Menu Item: Project → pp4_8 Properties

  Expand the "Configuration Properties → Linker" entry and then click on the "Debugging" item. Set the "Generate Debug Info" entry to "Yes". Close the "pp4_8 Properties" window.

  VC++ EE - Activate Menu Item: Debug → Step Into

Program Phase 4-9

Python ▪ Tk ▪ Multi-Platform

GUI Based Program with Main Window

- Program Phase Task 4 is implemented in Program Phase 4-9 using the Python programming language and the Tk module.
- Program Phase 4-9 contains a single source code file named pp4_9.py. In addition to the pp4_9.py text file, an icon image file called phase16x16.ico is used as the window icon for the main window.

Code Block Features

The Program Phase 4-9 code blocks illustrate the following programming features using the Python programming language and the Tk module:

- **Create a Resizable Main Window for a GUI Based Application**
- **Set the Main Window Icon and Caption**
- **Set the Main Window Menu**
- **Set the Main Window Background Color and Mouse Cursor**
- **Prompt to Exit the Application when the Main Window is Closed**

Python Tk
Create a Resizable Main Window for a GUI Based Application

- A Tk main window is referred to as a "Toplevel" window.
- The border of the main window is set to be resizable by calling the resizable() method of the main window object. The first parameter indicates the resize condition of the left and right borders of the window, and the second parameter indicates the resize condition of the top and bottom borders of the window.
- The mainloop() method of the main window object is called to start the event loop for the program. This loop prevents the Python program from automatically exiting. The mainloop() function exits when the main window object is destroyed. In the following example, the main window object is destroyed when the user closes the window:

test1.py: Python Tk Create a Resizable Main Window for a GUI Based Application

```
from Tkinter import *

def main():

    global goMainWindow
```

test1.py continued on the next page

test1.py: Python Tk Create a Resizable Main Window for a GUI Based App. continued

```
    ## Create the main window
    goMainWindow = Tk()
    goMainWindow.resizable(1,1)

    ## Maximize and display the main window
    goMainWindow.state(newstate="zoomed")  # Win only, disable for Linux/OSX
    goMainWindow.update

    ## Start the event loop
    goMainWindow.mainloop()

goMainWindow = None
main()
```

Python Tk
Set the Main Window Icon and Caption

- The iconbitmap() method of the main window object is used to assign the phase16x16.ico file to the main window. The phase16x16.ico file needs to be copied to the same folder as the test2.py file and accessible on the file system at runtime.

- The title() method of the main window object is used to set the caption of the main window.

test2.py: Python Tk Set the Main Window Icon and Caption

```
from Tkinter import *

def main():

    global goMainWindow

    ## Create the main window
    goMainWindow = Tk()
    goMainWindow.resizable(1,1)

    ## Set the main window icon
    goMainWindow.iconbitmap('phase16x16.ico')  # Win only, disable for Linux/OSX

    ## Set the main window caption
    goMainWindow.title("Hello World!")

    ## Maximize and display the main window
    goMainWindow.state(newstate="zoomed")  # Win only, disable for Linux/OSX
    goMainWindow.update

    # Start the event loop
    goMainWindow.mainloop()

goMainWindow = None
main()
```

Python Tk
Set the Main Window Menu

- The following example creates a "File" menu with a "Hello World!" menu item and "Exit" menu item:

test3.py: Python Tk Set the Main Window Menu

```
from Tkinter import *
import tkMessageBox

def MenuItem1_Activate(toEvent):
    tkMessageBox._show(title='test',type='ok',
                       icon='info',message = 'Hello World!')

def MenuItem2_Activate(toEvent):
    sys.exit(1)

def main():

    ## Main Window
    global goMainWindow

    ## Create the main window
    goMainWindow = Tk()
    goMainWindow.resizable(1,1)

    ## Menu Bar
    loMenuBar = Menu(goMainWindow)
    goMainWindow.config(menu=loMenuBar)

    ## File Menu
    loFileMenu = Menu(loMenuBar, tearoff = 0)
    loMenuBar.add_cascade(label="File", menu=loFileMenu, underline = 0)

    ## Hello World! Menu Item
    loFileMenu.add_command(label="Hello World!",
                           command=lambda: MenuItem1_Activate(None),
                           underline = 0,accelerator = "Ctrl+H")

    goMainWindow.bind('<Control-h>', MenuItem1_Activate)

    ## Exit Menu Item
    loFileMenu.add_command(label="Exit",
                           command=lambda: MenuItem2_Activate(None),
                           underline = 1,accelerator = "Ctrl+X")

    goMainWindow.bind('<Control-x>', MenuItem2_Activate)

    ## Maximize and display the main window
    goMainWindow.state(newstate="zoomed")  # Win only, disable for Linux/OSX
    goMainWindow.update
    goMainWindow.mainloop()

goMainWindow = None
main()
```

Python Tk
Set the Main Window Background Color and Mouse Cursor

- The following example sets the main window background color and mouse cursor:

test4.py: Python Tk Set the Main Window Background Color and Mouse Cursor

```
from Tkinter import *

def main():

    global goMainWindow
    lcWindowBackColor = None
```

test4.py continued on the next page

test4.py: Python Tk Set the Main Window BG Color and Mouse Cursor continued

```
    ## Create the main window
    goMainWindow = Tk()
    goMainWindow.resizable(1,1)

    ## Set the main window background color
    lcWindowBackColor = '#%02x%02x%02x' % (255,255,255)
    goMainWindow.configure(background=lcWindowBackColor)

    ## Set the main window mouse cursor
    goMainWindow.configure(cursor="arrow")

    ## Maximize and display the main window
    goMainWindow.state(newstate="zoomed")  # Win only, disable for Linux/OSX
    goMainWindow.update

    goMainWindow.mainloop()

goMainWindow = None
main()
```

Python Tk
Prompt to Exit the Application when the Main Window is Closed

- The MainWindow_WindowClosing() callback function is assigned to the main window object using the protocol() method.

- The tkMessageBox object is used to prompt the user to continue closing the main window. If the user selects the "Yes" button, the destroy() method of the main window object is called. If the user selects the "No" button, no action is taken, and the main window is not destroyed.

test5.py: Python Tk Prompt to Exit the Application when the Main Window is Closed

```
from Tkinter import *
import tkMessageBox

def MainWindow_WindowClosing():
    lcResult = ""
    global goMainWindow

    lcResult = tkMessageBox._show(title='test',type='yesno',icon='question',
                                  message='Close the main window?')
    if lcResult == 'yes':
       goMainWindow.destroy()

def main():
    global goMainWindow
    lcWindowBackColor = None

    ## Create the main window
    goMainWindow = Tk()
    goMainWindow.resizable(1,1)
    goMainWindow.protocol("WM_DELETE_WINDOW",MainWindow_WindowClosing)

    ## Maximize and display the main window
    goMainWindow.state(newstate="zoomed")  # Win only, disable for Linux/OSX
    goMainWindow.update
    goMainWindow.mainloop()

goMainWindow = None
main()
```

Source Code Files

- Text files: pp4_9.py
- Image files: phase16x16.ico (Single-image icon file, Appendix O)

pp4_9.py: Program Phase 4-9 Source Code

```
##*****************************************************************************
## Program Phase 4-9 Python Main Window with File Menu                        *
## Programming Tasks Illustrated: Tk GUI based application                    *
##                                Main window                                 *
##                                Window icon                                 *
##                                Window caption                              *
##                                Window menu with hotkeys                    *
##                                Window background color                     *
##                                Window mouse cursor                         *
##                                User sizable window                         *
##                                Message box input/output                    *
##*****************************************************************************

##*****************************************************************************
## File: pp4_9.py                                                             *
## Reserved                                                                   *
##*****************************************************************************

from Tkinter import *
import tkMessageBox

## Callback functions

##*****************************************************************************
## Callback Functions                                                         *
## Implement the callback function for the Hello World! menu item             *
## CBI:  4-9.1.2.1                                                            *
##*****************************************************************************

def MenuItem1_Activate(toEvent):
    tkMessageBox._show(title='Program Phase 4-9',type='ok',icon='info',
                       message = 'Hello World!')


##*****************************************************************************
## Callback Functions                                                         *
## Implement the callback function for the Exit menu item                     *
## CBI:  4-9.1.3.1                                                            *
##*****************************************************************************

def MenuItem2_Activate(toEvent):
    sys.exit(1)


##*****************************************************************************
## Callback Functions                                                         *
## Implement the callback function that fires when the main window is closed *
## CBI:  4-9.1.4.1                                                            *
##*****************************************************************************

def MainWindow_WindowClosing():

    lcResult = ""
    global goMainWindow

    lcResult = tkMessageBox._show(title='Program Phase 4-9',
                                  type='yesno',icon='question',
                                  message='Close the main window?')
```

pp4_9.py continued on the next page

pp4_9.py: Program Phase 4-9 Source Code continued

```
    if lcResult == 'yes':
       goMainWindow.destroy()

##*************************************************************************
## Program Phase 4-9 Main                                                  *
## Define the Entry Point of Execution (EPE) for Program Phase 4-9         *
## CBI:  4-9.1.1.1                                                         *
##*************************************************************************

def main():

##*************************************************************************
## Program Phase 4-9 Main                                                  *
## Declare the local variables for the "main" program                      *
## CBI:  4-9.1.1.2                                                         *
##*************************************************************************

    ## Main window
    global goMainWindow

    ## Main window icon
    loIcon = None

    ## Main window menu
    loFileMenu = None
    loMenuBar = None

    ## Main window background color
    lcWindowBackColor = None

##*************************************************************************
## Program Phase 4-9 Main                                                  *
## Create the main window                                                  *
## CBI:  4-9.1.1.3                                                         *
##*************************************************************************

    goMainWindow = Tk()
    goMainWindow.protocol("WM_DELETE_WINDOW",MainWindow_WindowClosing)

##*************************************************************************
## Program Phase 4-9 Main                                                  *
## Set the icon for the main window                                        *
## CBI:  4-9.1.1.4                                                         *
##*************************************************************************

    goMainWindow.iconbitmap('phase16x16.ico')  # Win only,disable for Linux/OSX

##*************************************************************************
## Program Phase 4-9 Main                                                  *
## Set the caption of the main window                                      *
## CBI:  4-9.1.1.5                                                         *
##*************************************************************************

    goMainWindow.title("Program Phase 4-9  " + "| Platform:  Multi-Platform  " +
                       "|  Programming Language:  Python  " +
                       "|  GUI API:  Tk")

##*************************************************************************
## Program Phase 4-9 Main                                                  *
## Create the menu for the main window                                     *
## CBI:  4-9.1.1.6                                                         *
##*************************************************************************
```

pp4_9.py continued on the next page

pp4_9.py: Program Phase 4-9 Source Code continued

```
    ## Menu Bar
    loMenuBar = Menu(goMainWindow)
    goMainWindow.config(menu=loMenuBar)

    ## File Menu
    loFileMenu = Menu(loMenuBar, tearoff = 0)
    loMenuBar.add_cascade(label="File", menu=loFileMenu, underline = 0)

    ## Hello World! Menu Item
    loFileMenu.add_command(label="Hello World!",
                           command=lambda: MenuItem1_Activate(None),
                           underline = 0,accelerator = "Ctrl+H")

    goMainWindow.bind('<Control-h>', MenuItem1_Activate)

    ## Exit Menu Item
    loFileMenu.add_command(label="Exit",
                           command=lambda: MenuItem2_Activate(None),
                          underline = 1,accelerator = "Ctrl+X")

    goMainWindow.bind('<Control-x>', MenuItem2_Activate)

##****************************************************************************
## Program Phase 4-9 Main                                                    *
## Set the background color of the main window                               *
## CBI:  4-9.1.1.7                                                           *
##****************************************************************************

    lcWindowBackColor = '#%02x%02x%02x' % (255,255,255)
    goMainWindow.configure(background=lcWindowBackColor)


##****************************************************************************
## Program Phase 4-9 Main                                                    *
## Set the mouse cursor displayed when positioned over the main window       *
## CBI:  4-9.1.1.8                                                           *
##****************************************************************************

    goMainWindow.configure(cursor="arrow")


##****************************************************************************
## Program Phase 4-9 Main                                                    *
## Allow resizing of the main window                                         *
## CBI:  4-9.1.1.9                                                           *
##****************************************************************************

    goMainWindow.resizable(1,1)


##****************************************************************************
## Program Phase 4-9 Main                                                    *
## Maximize and display the main window                                      *
## CBI:  4-9.1.1.10                                                          *
##****************************************************************************

    goMainWindow.state(newstate="zoomed")  # Win only, disable for Linux/OSX
    goMainWindow.update


##****************************************************************************
## Program Phase 4-9 Main                                                    *
## Start the event loop                                                      *
## CBI:  4-9.1.1.11                                                          *
##****************************************************************************
```

pp4_9.py continued on the next page

pp4_9.py: Program Phase 4-9 Source Code continued

```
    goMainWindow.mainloop()

##***********************************************************************
## Program Phase 4-9 Main                                               *
## Cleanup the resources used by the main window                        *
## CBI:  4-9.1.1.12                                                     *
##***********************************************************************

## Main window
goMainWindow = None

main()
```

Code Setup and Compilation

- Tools: Python distribution (Appendix G), Komodo IDE (Appendix F)

Code Setup and Compilation Steps

1: Create a folder called pp4_9 that will store the source code files.

2: Start the Komodo IDE program.

3: Komodo - Activate Menu Item: File → New → New Project

Set the project name to pp4_9.kpf and then save the new project in the pp4_9 folder.

4: Komodo - Activate Menu Item: File → New → New File

Click on the "Common" category and then select the "Text" template. Set the "Filename" to pp4_9.py. Verify that the "add to pp4_9 project" check box is checked and the "Directory" is set to the pp4_9 folder. Activate the "Open" button. Enter the source code for the pp4_9.py file and then save the file.

5: Create the phase16x16.ico image file according to the instructions found in Appendix O. Save the icon file to the pp4_9 folder.

6: There is no step for compiling the source code file. It is compiled at runtime by the Python interpreter.

Program Execution

- Execute Program

  `Komodo - Activate Menu Item: Debug → Run Without Debugging`

  On the "Debugging Options" window, verify that the "Script" is set to the full path to the pp4_9.py file and then activate the "OK" button.

- Debug Program

  `Komodo - Activate Menu Item: Debug → Step In`

Program Phase 4-10

Perl ▪ Tk ▪ Multi-Platform

GUI Based Program with Main Window

- Program Phase Task 4 is implemented in Program Phase 4-10 using the Perl programming language and the Tk module.
- Program Phase 4-10 contains a single source code file named pp4_10.pl. In addition to the pp4_10.pl text file, an icon image file called phase32x32.gif is used as the window icon for the main window.

Code Block Features

The Program Phase 4-10 code blocks illustrate the following programming features using the Perl programming language:

- **Create a Resizable Main Window for a GUI Based Application**
- **Set the Main Window Icon and Caption**
- **Set the Main Window Menu**
- **Set the Main Window Background Color and Mouse Cursor**
- **Prompt to Exit the Application when the Main Window is Closed**

Perl Tk
Create a Resizable Main Window for a GUI Based Application

- A Tk main window is referred to as a "Toplevel" window.
- The border of the main window is set to be resizable by calling the resizable() method of the main window object. The first parameter indicates the resize condition of the left and right borders of the window, and the second parameter indicates the resize condition of the top and bottom borders of the window.
- The MainLoop() function is called to start the event loop for the program. This loop prevents the Perl program from automatically exiting. The MainLoop() function exits when the main window object is destroyed. In the following example, the main window object is destroyed when the user closes the window:

test1.pl: Perl Tk Create a Resizable Main Window for a GUI Based Application

```
use strict;
use warnings;
use Tk;
my $loMainWindow;
```

test1.pl continued on the next page

test1.pl: Perl Tk Create a Resizable Main Window for a GUI Based App. continued

```
## Create the main window
$loMainWindow = MainWindow->new();
$loMainWindow->resizable(1,1);

## Maximize and display the main window
$loMainWindow->state('zoomed');  # Win only, disable for Linux and OSX
$loMainWindow->update;

MainLoop();
```

Perl Tk
Set the Main Window Icon and Caption

- The Photo() method of the main window object is used to obtain a reference to the phase32x32.gif image. The iconimage() method is used to set the icon for the top level window.

- The phase32x32.gif file needs to be copied to the same folder as the test2.pl file and accessible on the file system at runtime.

- The "title" property of the main window object is used with the configure() method to set the caption of the main window.

test2.pl: Perl Tk Set the Main Window Icon and Caption

```
use strict;
use warnings;
use Tk;

my $loMainWindow;
my $loIcon;

## Create the main window
$loMainWindow = MainWindow->new();
$loMainWindow->resizable(1,1);

## Set the main window icon
$loIcon = $loMainWindow->Photo(-file=>"phase32x32.gif");
$loMainWindow->iconimage($loIcon);

## Set the main window caption
$loMainWindow->configure(-title=>"Hello World!");

## Maximize and display the main window
$loMainWindow->state('zoomed');  # Win only, disable for Linux and OSX
$loMainWindow->update;

MainLoop();
```

Perl Tk
Set the Main Window Menu

- The following example creates a "File" menu with a "Hello World!" menu item and "Exit" menu item:

test3.pl: Perl Tk Set the Main Window Menu

```
use strict;
use warnings;
use Tk;

my $loMainWindow;
my $loFileMenu;
my $loMenuBar;

## Create the main window
$loMainWindow = MainWindow->new();
$loMainWindow->resizable(1,1);

## Menu Bar
$loMenuBar = $loMainWindow->Menu();

$loMainWindow->configure(-menu => $loMenuBar);

## File Menu
$loFileMenu = $loMenuBar->cascade(-label => '~File',
                                   -tearoff => 0);

## Hello World! Menu Item
$loFileMenu->command(-label => "~Hello World!",
                     -accelerator => "Ctrl+H",
                     -command =>[\&MenuItem1_Activate,$loMainWindow]);

$loMainWindow->bind('<Control-h>',[\&MenuItem1_Activate]);

## Exit Menu Item
$loFileMenu->command(-label => "E~xit",
                     -accelerator => "Ctrl+X",
                     -command => [\&MenuItem2_Activate,$loMainWindow]);

$loMainWindow->bind('<Control-x>',[\&MenuItem2_Activate]);

## Maximize and display the main window
$loMainWindow->state('zoomed');  # Win only, disable for Linux and OSX
$loMainWindow->update;

MainLoop();

sub MenuItem1_Activate()
{
   my $toMainWindow = $_[0];
   $toMainWindow->messageBox(-icon => 'info',-message => 'Hello World!',
                             -title => 'test',-type => 'Ok');
}

sub MenuItem2_Activate()
{
   my $toMainWindow = $_[0];
   $toMainWindow->destroy();
}
```

Perl Tk
Set the Main Window Background Color and Mouse Cursor

- The following example sets the main window background color and mouse cursor:

test4.pl: Perl Tk Set the Main Window Background Color and Mouse Cursor

```
use strict;
use warnings;
use Tk;

my $loMainWindow;
my $lcWindowBackColor;

## Create the main window
$loMainWindow = MainWindow->new();
$loMainWindow->resizable(1,1);

## Set the main window background color
$lcWindowBackColor = sprintf("#%02x%02x%02x",255,255,255);
$loMainWindow->configure(-background => $lcWindowBackColor);

## Set the main window mouse cursor
$loMainWindow->configure(-cursor=>'arrow');

## Maximize and display the main window
$loMainWindow->state('zoomed');  # Win only, disable for Linux and OSX
$loMainWindow->update;

MainLoop();
```

Perl Tk
Prompt to Exit the Application when the Main Window is Closed

- The MainWindow_WindowClosing() callback function is assigned to the main window object by using the protocol() method.

- The tkMessageBox object is used to prompt the user to continue closing the main window. If the user selects the "Yes" button, the destroy() method of the main window object is called. If the user selects the "No" button, no action is taken and the main window is not destroyed.

test5.pl: Perl Tk Prompt to Exit the Application when the Main Window is Closed

```
use strict;
use warnings;
use Tk;

my $loMainWindow;
my $lcWindowBackColor;

## Create the main window
$loMainWindow = MainWindow->new();

$loMainWindow->resizable(1,1);
$loMainWindow->protocol('WM_DELETE_WINDOW'=>[\&MainWindow_WindowClosing,
                        $loMainWindow]);

## Maximize and display the main window
$loMainWindow->state('zoomed');  # Win only, disable for Linux and OSX
$loMainWindow->update;

MainLoop();

sub MainWindow_WindowClosing
{
   my $toMainWindow = $_ [0];
```

test5.pl continued on the next page

test5.pl: Perl Tk Prompt to Exit the App. when the Window is Closed continued

```
   my $lcResult;

   $lcResult = $toMainWindow->messageBox(-icon => 'question',
                                          -message => 'Close the main window?',
                                          -title => 'test',-type => 'YesNo');

   if ($lcResult eq "Yes")
   {
      $toMainWindow->destroy();
   }
}
```

Source Code Files

- Text files: pp4_10.pl
- Image files: phase32x32.gif (Single-image icon file, Appendix O)

pp4_10.pl: Program Phase 4-10 Source Code

```
##************************************************************************
## Program Phase 4-10 Perl Main Window with File Menu                    *
## Programming Tasks Illustrated: Tk GUI based application               *
##                                Main window                            *
##                                Window icon                            *
##                                Window caption                         *
##                                Window menu with hotkeys               *
##                                Window background color                *
##                                Window mouse cursor                    *
##                                User sizable window                    *
##                                Message box input/output               *
##************************************************************************

##************************************************************************
## File: pp4_10.pl                                                       *
## Reserved                                                              *
##************************************************************************

use strict;
use warnings;
use Tk;


##************************************************************************
## Program Phase 4-10 Main                                               *
## Define the Entry Point of Execution (EPE) for Program Phase 4-10      *
## CBI:  4-10.1.1.1                                                      *
##************************************************************************

## The first line of the code in the pp4_10.pl file is the EPE.


##************************************************************************
## Program Phase 4-10 Main                                               *
## Declare the local variables for the "main" program                    *
## CBI:  4-10.1.1.2                                                      *
##************************************************************************

## Main window
my $loMainWindow;

## Main window icon
my $loIcon;
```

pp4_10.pl continued on the next page

pp4_10.pl: Program Phase 4-10 Source Code continued

```
## Main window menu
my $loFileMenu;
my $loMenuBar;

## Main window background color
my $lcWindowBackColor;


##*************************************************************************
## Program Phase 4-10 Main                                                *
## Create the main window                                                 *
## CBI:  4-10.1.1.3                                                       *
##*************************************************************************

$loMainWindow = MainWindow->new();

$loMainWindow->protocol('WM_DELETE_WINDOW'=>[\&MainWindow_WindowClosing,
                        $loMainWindow]);


##*************************************************************************
## Program Phase 4-10 Main                                                *
## Set the icon for the main window                                       *
## CBI:  4-10.1.1.4                                                       *
##*************************************************************************

$loIcon = $loMainWindow->Photo(-file=>"phase32x32.gif");
$loMainWindow->iconimage($loIcon);


##*************************************************************************
## Program Phase 4-10 Main                                                *
## Set the caption of the main window                                     *
## CBI:  4-10.1.1.5                                                       *
##*************************************************************************

$loMainWindow->configure(-title=>
"Program Phase 4-10  |  Platform:  Multi-Platform  |  Programming Language:
Perl  |  GUI API:  Tk");


##*************************************************************************
## Program Phase 4-10 Main                                                *
## Create the menu for the main window                                    *
## CBI:  4-10.1.1.6                                                       *
##*************************************************************************

## Menu Bar
$loMenuBar = $loMainWindow->Menu();
$loMainWindow->configure(-menu => $loMenuBar);

## File Menu
$loFileMenu = $loMenuBar->cascade(-label => '~File',-tearoff => 0);

## Hello World! Menu Item
$loFileMenu->command(-label => "~Hello World!",
                     -accelerator => "Ctrl+H",
                     -command =>[\&MenuItem1_Activate,$loMainWindow]);

$loMainWindow->bind('<Control-h>',
                    [\&MenuItem1_Activate]);

## Exit Menu Item
$loFileMenu->command(-label => "E~xit",
                     -accelerator => "Ctrl+X",
                     -command => [\&MenuItem2_Activate,$loMainWindow]);
```

pp4_10.pl continued on the next page

pp4_10.pl: Program Phase 4-10 Source Code continued

```
$loMainWindow->bind('<Control-x>',[\&MenuItem2_Activate]);


##***********************************************************************
## Program Phase 4-10 Main                                              *
## Set the background color of the main window                          *
## CBI:  4-10.1.1.7                                                     *
##***********************************************************************

$lcWindowBackColor = sprintf("#%02x%02x%02x",255,255,255);
$loMainWindow->configure(-background => $lcWindowBackColor);


##***********************************************************************
## Program Phase 4-10 Main                                              *
## Set the mouse cursor displayed when positioned over the main window  *
## CBI:  4-10.1.1.8                                                     *
##***********************************************************************

$loMainWindow->configure(-cursor=>'arrow');


##***********************************************************************
## Program Phase 4-10 Main                                              *
## Allow resizing of the main window                                    *
## CBI:  4-10.1.1.9                                                     *
##***********************************************************************

$loMainWindow->resizable(1,1);


##***********************************************************************
## Program Phase 4-10 Main                                              *
## Maximize and display the main window                                 *
## CBI:  4-10.1.1.10                                                    *
##***********************************************************************

$loMainWindow->state('zoomed');  # Win only, disable for Linux and OSX
$loMainWindow->update;


##***********************************************************************
## Program Phase 4-10 Main                                              *
## Start the event loop                                                 *
## CBI:  4-10.1.1.11                                                    *
##***********************************************************************

MainLoop();


##***********************************************************************
## Program Phase 4-10 Main                                              *
## Cleanup the resources used by the main window                        *
## CBI:  4-10.1.1.12                                                    *
##***********************************************************************

## Callback Functions

##***********************************************************************
## Callback Functions                                                   *
## Implement the callback function for the Hello World! menu item       *
## CBI:  4-10.1.2.1                                                     *
##***********************************************************************
```

pp4_10.pl continued on the next page

pp4_10.pl: Program Phase 4-10 Source Code continued

```
sub MenuItem1_Activate()
{
   my $toMainWindow = $_[0];
   $toMainWindow->messageBox(-icon => 'info',
                              -message => 'Hello World!',
                              -title => 'Program Phase 4-10',
                              -type => 'Ok');
}


##**************************************************************************
## Callback Functions                                                      *
## Implement the callback function for the Exit menu item                  *
## CBI:  4-10.1.3.1                                                        *
##**************************************************************************

sub MenuItem2_Activate()
{
   my $toMainWindow = $_[0];
   $toMainWindow->destroy();
}


##**************************************************************************
## Callback Functions                                                      *
## Implement the callback function that fires when the main window is closed  *
## CBI:  4-10.1.4.1                                                        *
##**************************************************************************

sub MainWindow_WindowClosing
{
   my $toMainWindow = $_ [0];

   my $lcResult;
   $lcResult = $toMainWindow->messageBox(-icon => 'question',
                                         -message => 'Close the main window?',
                                         -title => 'Program Phase 4-10',
                                         -type => 'YesNo');

   if ($lcResult eq "Yes")
   {
      $toMainWindow->destroy();
   }
}
```

Code Setup and Compilation

- Tools: Perl 5 distribution (Appendix H), Komodo IDE (Appendix F)

Code Setup and Compilation Steps

1: Create a folder called pp4_10 that will store the source code files.

2: Start the Komodo IDE program.

3: Komodo - Activate Menu Item: File → New → New Project

Set the project name to pp4_10.kpf and then save the new project in the pp4_10 folder.

Steps continued on the next page

Code Setup and Compilation Steps continued

4: Komodo - Activate Menu Item: File → New → New File

Click on the "Common" category and then select the "Text" template. Set the "Filename" to pp4_10.pl. Verify that the "add to pp4_10 project" check box is checked and the "Directory" is set to the pp4_10 folder. Activate the "Open" button. Enter the source code for the pp4_10.pl file and then save the file.

5: Create the phase32x32.gif image file according to the instructions found in Appendix O. Save the image file to the pp4_10 folder.

6: There is no step for compiling the source code file. It is compiled at runtime by the Perl interpreter.

Program Execution

- Execute Program

```
Komodo - Activate Menu Item: Debug → Run Without Debugging
```

On the "Debugging Options" window, verify that the "Script" is set to the full path to the pp4_10.pl file and then activate the "OK" button.

- Debug Program

```
Komodo - Activate Menu Item: Debug → Step In
```

Program Phase 4-11

PHP CLI ▪ Gtk ▪ Multi-Platform

GUI Based Program with Main Window

- Program Phase Task 4 is implemented in Program Phase 4-11 using the PHP programming language and the Gtk library.
- Program Phase 4-11 contains a single source code file named pp4_11.php. In addition to the pp4_11.php text file, an icon image file called phase16x16.xpm is used as the window icon for the main window.

Code Block Features

The Program Phase 4-11 code blocks illustrate the following programming features using the PHP programming language and the Gtk library:

- **Create a Resizable Main Window for a GUI Based Application**
- **Set the Main Window Icon and Caption**
- **Set the Main Window Menu**
- **Set the Main Window Background Color and Mouse Cursor**
- **Prompt to Exit the Application when the Main Window is Closed**

PHP CLI Gtk
Create a Resizable Main Window for a GUI Based Application

- The main window object is created by using the GtkWindow() class.
- The border of the main window is set to be resizable by calling the the set_resizable() method of the GtkWindow instance with a parameter value of one.
- The GTK::main() method is called to start the event loop for the program. This loop prevents the PHP program from automatically exiting. The connect_simple_after() method is used to tell the GTK::main() function to quit when the main window object is destroyed. In the following example, the main window object is destroyed when the user closes the window:

test1.php: PHP CLI Gtk Create a Resizable Main Window for a GUI Based Application

```
<?php

main($argc,$argv);

function main($argc,$argv)
{
```

test1.php continued on the next page

test1.php: PHP CLI Gtk Create a Resizable Main Window for a GUI App. continued

```
    $loMainWindow = null;

    // Create the main window
    $loMainWindow = new GtkWindow();
    $loMainWindow->connect_simple_after('destroy', array('Gtk', 'main_quit'));
    $loMainWindow->set_resizable(1);

    // Maximize and display the main window
    $loMainWindow->maximize();
    $loMainWindow->show_all();

    Gtk::main();
}
?>
```

PHP CLI Gtk
Set the Main Window Icon and Caption

- The GdkPixbuf class is used to obtain an object representing the phase16x16.xpm file. This object is then passed to the set_icon() method of the GtkWindow instance.
- The set_title() method of the GtkWindow instance is used to set the window caption.

test2.php: PHP CLI Gtk Set the Main Window Icon and Caption

```
<?php

main($argc,$argv);

function main($argc,$argv)
{
    $loMainWindow = null;
    $loIcon = null;

    // Create the main window
    $loMainWindow = new GtkWindow();
    $loMainWindow->connect_simple_after('destroy', array('Gtk', 'main_quit'));
    $loMainWindow->set_resizable(1);

    // Set the main window icon
    $loIcon = GdkPixbuf::new_from_file('phase16x16.xpm');
    $loMainWindow->set_icon($loIcon);

    // Set the main window caption
    $loMainWindow->set_title('Hello World!');

    // Maximize and display the main window
    $loMainWindow->maximize();
    $loMainWindow->show_all();

    Gtk::main();
}
?>
```

PHP CLI Gtk
Set the Main Window Menu

- The following example creates a "File" menu with a "Hello World!" menu item and "Exit" menu item:

test3.php: PHP CLI Gtk Set the Main Window Menu

```
<?php

main($argc,$argv);

function main($argc,$argv)
{
   $loMainWindow = null;
   $loMenuBar = null;
   $loFileMenu = null;
   $loSubMenu = null;
   $loMenuItem1 = null;
   $loMenuItem2 = null;
   $loVbox = null;

   $loAccelGroup = null;
   $loAcceleratorLabel = null;
   $loAcceleratorKey1 = null;
   $loAcceleratorKey2 = null;

   // Create the main window
   $loMainWindow = new GtkWindow();
   $loMainWindow->connect_simple_after('destroy', array('Gtk', 'main_quit'));
   $loMainWindow->set_resizable(1);

   // Menu Bar
   $loMenuBar = new GtkMenuBar();
   $loVbox = new GtkVBox();
   $loVbox->pack_start($loMenuBar, false, false);
   $loAccelGroup = new gtkaccelgroup();
   $loMainWindow->add_accel_group($loAccelGroup);

   // File Menu
   $loFileMenu = new GtkMenuItem('_File');
   $loMenuBar->append($loFileMenu);
   $loSubMenu = new GtkMenu();
   $loFileMenu->set_submenu($loSubMenu);

   // Hello World! menu item
   $loMenuItem1 = new GtkMenuItem('_Hello World!');
   $loMenuItem1->connect_simple('activate',
                              'MenuItem1_Activate',$loMainWindow);

   $loSubMenu->append($loMenuItem1);
   $loAcceleratorLabel1 = $loMenuItem1->child;
   $loAcceleratorKey1 = $loAcceleratorLabel1->parse_uline("_Hello World!");

   $loMenuItem1->add_accelerator('activate',
                                 $loAccelGroup,
                                 $loAcceleratorKey1,
                                 Gdk::CONTROL_MASK,
                                 Gtk::ACCEL_VISIBLE);

   // Exit menu item
   $loMenuItem2 = new GtkMenuItem('E_xit');
   $loMenuItem2->connect_simple('activate',
                                 'MenuItem2_Activate',$loMainWindow);

   $loSubMenu->append($loMenuItem2);
   $loAcceleratorLabel2 = $loMenuItem2->child;
   $loAcceleratorKey2 = $loAcceleratorLabel2->parse_uline("E_xit");

   $loMenuItem2->add_accelerator('activate',
                                 $loAccelGroup,
                                 $loAcceleratorKey2,
                                 Gdk::CONTROL_MASK,Gtk::ACCEL_VISIBLE);
```

test3.php continued on the next page

test3.php: PHP CLI Gtk Set the Main Window Menu continued

```
    // Assign the menu to the main window
    $loMainWindow->add($loVbox);

    // Maximize and display the main window
    $loMainWindow->maximize();
    $loMainWindow->show_all();

    Gtk::main();
}

function MenuItem1_Activate()
{
    $loMessageBox = null;

    $loMessageBox = new GtkMessageDialog(null,0,
                                         Gtk::MESSAGE_INFO,
                                         Gtk::BUTTONS_OK,
                                         "Hello World!");

    $loMessageBox->set_position(Gtk::WIN_POS_CENTER_ALWAYS);

    $loMessageBox->run();
    $loMessageBox->destroy();
}

function MenuItem2_Activate()
{
    // Exit the program if the user activates the Exit menu item
    Gtk::main_quit();
}
?>
```

PHP CLI Gtk
Set the Main Window Background Color and Mouse Cursor

- The following example sets the main window background color and mouse cursor:

test4.php: PHP CLI Gtk Set the Main Window Background Color and Mouse Cursor

```
<?php

main($argc,$argv);

function main($argc,$argv)
{
    $loMainWindow = null;
    $loGdkWindow = null;
    $loStyle = null;
    $loBackColor = null;
    $loMouseCursor = null;

    // Create the main window
    $loMainWindow = new GtkWindow();

    $loMainWindow->set_resizable(1);
    $loMainWindow->connect_simple_after('destroy', array('Gtk', 'main_quit'));

    //Set the main window background color
    $loStyle = $loMainWindow->style->copy();
    $loBackColor = new GdkColor();
    $loStyle->bg[Gtk::STATE_NORMAL] = $loBackColor->parse('#FFFFFF');
```

test4.php continued on the next page

test4.php: PHP CLI Gtk Set the Main Window BG Color and Mouse Cursor continued

```
   $loMainWindow->set_style($loStyle);

   // Set the main window mouse cursor
   $loMouseCursor = new GdkCursor(Gdk::LEFT_PTR);
   $loMainWindow->realize();
   $loGdkWindow = $loMainWindow->window;
   $loGdkWindow->set_cursor($loMouseCursor);

   // Maximize and display the main window
   $loMainWindow->maximize();
   $loMainWindow->show_all();

   Gtk::main();
}
?>
```

PHP CLI Gtk
Prompt to Exit the Application when the Main Window is Closed

- The connect_simple() method is used to assign the MainWindow_Delete() function to be called when the main window delete event occurs. If a Boolean "true" value is returned from the function implementing this event, the main window is not closed.

test5.php: PHP CLI Gtk Prompt to Exit the App. when the Main Window is Closed

```
<?php

main($argc,$argv);

function main($argc,$argv)
{
   $loMainWindow = null;

   // Create the main window
   $loMainWindow = new GtkWindow();
   $loMainWindow->set_resizable(1);

   $loMainWindow->connect_simple_after('destroy', array('Gtk', 'main_quit'));
   $loMainWindow->connect_simple('delete-event', 'MainWindow_Delete');

   // Maximize and display the main window
   $loMainWindow->maximize();
   $loMainWindow->show_all();

   Gtk::main();
}

function MainWindow_Delete()
{
   $lnResult = null;
   $loMessageBox = null;

   $loMessageBox = new GtkMessageDialog(null,0,Gtk::MESSAGE_QUESTION,
                                        Gtk::BUTTONS_YES_NO,
                                        'Close the main window?');

   $loMessageBox->set_position(Gtk::WIN_POS_CENTER_ALWAYS);
   $lnResult = $loMessageBox->run();
   $loMessageBox->destroy();
```

test5.php continued on the next page

test5.php: PHP CLI Gtk Prompt to Exit when the Main Window is Closed continued

```
   if ($lnResult == Gtk::RESPONSE_NO)
   {
      return true;
   }
}
?>
```

Source Code Files

- Text files: pp4_11.php
- Image files: phase16x16.xpm (Appendix O)

pp4_11.php: Program Phase 4-11 Source Code

```
<?php

//*************************************************************************
// Program Phase 4-11 PHP Main Window with File Menu                     *
// Programming Tasks Illustrated: Gtk GUI based application              *
//                                Main window                            *
//                                Window icon                            *
//                                Window caption                         *
//                                Window menu with hotkeys               *
//                                Window background color                *
//                                Window mouse cursor                    *
//                                User sizable window                    *
//                                Message box input/output               *
//*************************************************************************

//*************************************************************************
// File: pp4_11.php                                                      *
// Reserved                                                              *
//*************************************************************************

//*************************************************************************
// Program Phase 4-11 Main                                               *
// Define the Entry Point of Execution (EPE) for Program Phase 4-11      *
// CBI:  4-11.1.1.1                                                      *
//*************************************************************************

main($argc,$argv);

function main($argc,$argv)
{

//*************************************************************************
// Program Phase 4-11 Main                                               *
// Declare the local variables for the "main" program                    *
// CBI:  4-11.1.1.2                                                      *
//*************************************************************************

   // Main window
   $loMainWindow = null;

   // Main window icon
   $loIcon = null;

   // Main window menu
   $loMenuBar = null;
   $loFileMenu = null;
```

pp4_11.php continued on the next page

pp4_11.php: Program Phase 4-11 Source Code continued

```
   $loSubMenu = null;
   $loMenuItem1 = null;
   $loMenuItem2 = null;
   $loVbox = null;
   $loAccelGroup = null;
   $loAcceleratorLabel = null;
   $loAcceleratorKey1 = null;
   $loAcceleratorKey2 = null;

   // Main window background color
   $loStyle = null;
   $loBackColor = null;

   // Main window mouse cursor
   $loMouseCursor = null;
   $loGdkwindow = null;

//*************************************************************************
// Program Phase 4-11 Main                                               *
// Create the main window                                                *
// CBI:  4-11.1.1.3                                                      *
//*************************************************************************

   $loMainWindow = new GtkWindow();
   $loMainWindow->connect_simple_after('destroy', array('Gtk', 'main_quit'));
   $loMainWindow->connect_simple('delete-event', 'MainWindow_Delete');


//*************************************************************************
// Program Phase 4-11 Main                                               *
// Set the icon for the main window                                      *
// CBI:  4-11.1.1.4                                                      *
//*************************************************************************

   $loIcon = GdkPixbuf::new_from_file('phase16x16.xpm');
   $loMainWindow->set_icon($loIcon);


//*************************************************************************
// Program Phase 4-11 Main                                               *
// Set the caption of the main window                                    *
// CBI:  4-11.1.1.5                                                      *
//*************************************************************************

   $loMainWindow->set_title('Program Phase 4-12  |  Platform:  Multi-Platform  |
Programming Language:  PHP  |  GUI API:  GTk');


//*************************************************************************
// Program Phase 4-11 Main                                               *
// Create the menu for the main window                                   *
// CBI:  4-11.1.1.6                                                      *
//*************************************************************************

   // Menu Bar
   $loMenuBar = new GtkMenuBar();
   $loVbox = new GtkVBox();

   $loVbox->pack_start($loMenuBar, false, false);
   $loAccelGroup = new gtkaccelgroup();
   $loMainWindow->add_accel_group($loAccelGroup);

   // File Menu
   $loFileMenu = new GtkMenuItem('_File');
   $loMenuBar->append($loFileMenu);
```

pp4_11.php continued on the next page

pp4_11.php: Program Phase 4-11 Source Code continued

```
    $loSubMenu = new GtkMenu();
    $loFileMenu->set_submenu($loSubMenu);

    // Hello World! menu item
    $loMenuItem1 = new GtkMenuItem('_Hello World!');
    $loMenuItem1->connect_simple('activate',
                                'MenuItem1_Activate', $loMainWindow);
    $loSubMenu->append($loMenuItem1);
    $loAcceleratorLabel1 = $loMenuItem1->child;
    $loAcceleratorKey1 = $loAcceleratorLabel1->parse_uline("_Hello World!");

    $loMenuItem1->add_accelerator('activate',$loAccelGroup,$loAcceleratorKey1,
                                 Gdk::CONTROL_MASK,Gtk::ACCEL_VISIBLE);

    // Exit menu item
    $loMenuItem2 = new GtkMenuItem('E_xit');
    $loMenuItem2->connect_simple('activate',
                                'MenuItem2_Activate', $loMainWindow);
    $loSubMenu->append($loMenuItem2);

    $loAcceleratorLabel2 = $loMenuItem2->child;
    $loAcceleratorKey2 = $loAcceleratorLabel2->parse_uline("E_xit");

    $loMenuItem2->add_accelerator('activate',$loAccelGroup,$loAcceleratorKey2,
                                 Gdk::CONTROL_MASK,Gtk::ACCEL_VISIBLE);

    // Assign the menu to the main window
    $loMainWindow->add($loVbox);


//*****************************************************************************
// Program Phase 4-11 Main                                                    *
// Set the background color of the main window                                *
// CBI:  4-11.1.1.7                                                           *
//*****************************************************************************

    $loStyle = $loMainWindow->style->copy();
    $loBackColor = new GdkColor(255,255,255);
    $loStyle->bg[Gtk::STATE_NORMAL] = $loBackColor->parse('#FFFFFF');
    $loMainWindow->set_style($loStyle);


//*****************************************************************************
// Program Phase 4-11 Main                                                    *
// Set the mouse cursor displayed when positioned over the main window        *
// CBI:  4-11.1.1.8                                                           *
//*****************************************************************************

    $loMouseCursor = new GdkCursor(Gdk::LEFT_PTR);
    $loMainWindow->realize();
    $loGdkwindow = $loMainWindow->window;
    $loGdkwindow->set_cursor($loMouseCursor);


//*****************************************************************************
// Program Phase 4-11 Main                                                    *
// Allow resizing of the main window                                          *
// CBI:  4-11.1.1.9                                                           *
//*****************************************************************************

    $loMainWindow->set_resizable(1);


//*****************************************************************************
// Program Phase 4-11 Main                                                    *
// Maximize and display the main window                                       *
// CBI:  4-11.1.1.10                                                          *
//*****************************************************************************
```

pp4_11.php continued on the next page

pp4_11.php: Program Phase 4-11 Source Code continued

```
   $loMainWindow->maximize();
   $loMainWindow->show_all();


//*************************************************************************
// Program Phase 4-11 Main                                                *
// Start the event loop                                                   *
// CBI:  4-11.1.1.11                                                      *
//*************************************************************************

   Gtk::main();


//*************************************************************************
// Program Phase 4-11 Main                                                *
// Cleanup the resources used by the main window                          *
// CBI:  4-11.1.1.12                                                      *
//*************************************************************************

}

// Callback Functions

//*************************************************************************
// Callback Functions                                                     *
// Implement the callback function for the Hello World! menu item         *
// CBI:  4-11.1.2.1                                                       *
//*************************************************************************

function MenuItem1_Activate()
{
   $loMessageBox = null;

   $loMessageBox = new GtkMessageDialog(null,0,Gtk::MESSAGE_INFO,
                                        Gtk::BUTTONS_OK,"Hello World!");

   $loMessageBox->set_position(Gtk::WIN_POS_CENTER_ALWAYS);
   $loMessageBox->run();
   $loMessageBox->destroy();
}


//*************************************************************************
// Callback Functions                                                     *
// Implement the callback function for the Exit menu item                 *
// CBI:  4-11.1.3.1                                                       *
//*************************************************************************

function MenuItem2_Activate()
{
   // Exit the program if the user activates the Exit menu item
   Gtk::main_quit();
}


//*************************************************************************
// Callback Functions                                                     *
// Implement the callback function that fires when the main window is closed  *
// CBI:  4-11.1.4.1                                                       *
//*************************************************************************

function MainWindow_Delete()
{
   $lnResult = null;
   $loMessageBox = null;
```

pp4_11.php continued on the next page

pp4_11.php: Program Phase 4-11 Source Code continued

```
    $loMessageBox = new GtkMessageDialog(null,0,Gtk::MESSAGE_QUESTION,
                                          Gtk::BUTTONS_YES_NO,
                                          'Close the main window?');

    $loMessageBox->set_position(Gtk::WIN_POS_CENTER_ALWAYS);
    $lnResult = $loMessageBox->run();
    $loMessageBox->destroy();

    if ($lnResult == Gtk::RESPONSE_NO)
    {
       return true;
    }
}
?>
```

Code Setup and Compilation

- Tools: PHP CLI (Appendix J), Komodo IDE (Appendix F)

Code Setup and Compilation Steps

1: Create a folder called pp4_11 that will store the source code files.

2: Start the Komodo IDE program.

3: Komodo - Activate Menu Item: File → New → New Project

Set the name of the project to pp4_11.kpf and then save the new project in the pp4_11 folder.

4: Komodo - Activate Menu Item: File → New → New File

Click on the "Common" category and then select the "Text" template. Set the "Filename" to pp4_11.php. Verify that the "add to pp4_11 project" check box is checked and the "Directory" is set to the pp4_11 folder. Activate the "Open" button. Enter the source code for the pp4_11.php file and then save the file.

5: Create the phase16x16.xpm image file according to the instructions found in Appendix O. Save the image file to the pp4_11 folder.

6: There is no step for compiling the pp4_11.php file. It is compiled at runtime by the PHP CLI interpreter.

Program Execution

- Execute Program

    Komodo - Activate Menu Item: Debug → Run Without Debugging

    On the "Debugging Options" window, verify that the "Script" is set to the full path to the pp4_11.php file. Also, verify that the "Use the CLI interpreter" radio button is enabled and then activate the "OK" button.

- Debug Program

    Komodo - Activate Menu Item: Debug → Step In

Program Phase 4-12

Ruby ▪ Tk ▪ Multi-Platform

GUI Based Program with Main Window

- Program Phase Task 4 is implemented in Program Phase 4-12 using the Ruby programming language and the Tk module.
- Program Phase 4-12 contains a single source code file named pp4_12.rb. In addition to the pp4_12.rb text file, an icon image file called phase16x16.ico is used as the window icon for the main window.

Code Block Features

The Program Phase 4-12 code blocks illustrate the following programming features using the Ruby programming language and the Tk module:

- **Create a Resizable Main Window for a GUI Based Application**
- **Set the Main Window Icon and Caption**
- **Set the Main Window Menu**
- **Set the Main Window Background Color and Mouse Cursor**
- **Prompt to Exit the Application when the Main Window is Closed**

Ruby Tk
Create a Resizable Main Window for a GUI Based Application

- A Tk main window is referred to as a "Toplevel" window.
- The border of the main window is set to be resizable by calling the resizable() method of the main window object. The first parameter indicates the resize condition of the left and right borders of the window, and the second parameter indicates the resize condition of the top and bottom borders of the window.
- The mainloop() function is called to start the event loop for the program. This loop prevents the Ruby program from automatically exiting. The mainloop() function exits when the main window object is destroyed. The main window object is destroyed in the following example when the user closes the window:

test1.rb: Ruby Tk Create a Resizable Main Window for a GUI Based Application

```
require 'tk'

loMainWindow = nil
```

test1.rb continued on the next page

test1.rb: Ruby Tk Create a Resizable Main Window for a GUI Based App. continued

```
## Create the main window
loMainWindow = TkRoot.new()
loMainWindow.resizable(1,1)

## Maximize and display the main window
loMainWindow.state "zoomed"  # Win only, disable for Linux and OSX
loMainWindow.update()

Tk.mainloop()
```

Ruby Tk
Set the Main Window Icon and Caption

- The iconbitmap() method of the main window object is used to assign the phase16x16.ico file as the icon for the main window. The phase16x16.ico file needs to be copied to the same folder as the test2.rb file and accessible on the file system at runtime.

- The title() method of the main window object is used to set the caption of the main window.

test2.rb: Ruby Tk Set the Main Window Icon and Caption

```
require 'tk'

loMainWindow = nil

## Create the main window
loMainWindow = TkRoot.new()
loMainWindow.resizable(1,1)

## Set the main window icon
loMainWindow.iconbitmap "phase16x16.ico"  # Win only, disable for Linux and OSX

## Set the main window caption
loMainWindow.title "Hello World!"

## Maximize and display the main window
loMainWindow.state "zoomed"  # Win only, disable for Linux and OSX
loMainWindow.update()

Tk.mainloop()
```

Ruby Tk
Set the Main Window Menu

- The following example creates a "File" menu with a "Hello World!" menu item and "Exit" menu item:

test3.rb: Ruby Tk Set the Main Window Menu

```
require 'tk'
def MenuItem1_Activate(toMainWindow)
   lcResult = toMainWindow.messageBox('icon' => 'info',
                                      'message' => 'Hello World!',
                                      'title' => 'test','type' => 'ok');
end
```

test3.rb continued on the next page

test3.rb: Ruby Tk Set the Main Window Menu continued

```
def MenuItem2_Activate(toMainWindow)

   toMainWindow.destroy

end

loMainWindow = nil
loFileMenu = nil
loMenuBar = nil

## Create the main window
loMainWindow = TkRoot.new()
loMainWindow.resizable(1,1)

## Menu bar
loMenuBar = TkMenu.new()

## File menu
loFileMenu = TkMenu.new(loMenuBar) {tearoff false}
loMenuBar.add('cascade', 'menu'=>loFileMenu, 'label'=>"File",'underline' => 0)

## Hello World! menu item
loFileMenu.add('command','label'=>"Hello World!",
               'command'=>proc {MenuItem1_Activate(loMainWindow)},
               'underline' => 0,'accel' => 'Ctrl+H')

loMainWindow.bind('Control-h', proc { MenuItem1_Activate(loMainWindow) })

## Exit menu item
loFileMenu.add('command','label'=>"Exit",
               'command'=>proc { MenuItem2_Activate(loMainWindow) },
               'underline' => 1,'accel' => 'Ctrl+X')

loMainWindow.bind('Control-x', proc { MenuItem2_Activate(loMainWindow) })

## Assign the File menu to the main window
loMainWindow.menu(loMenuBar)

## Maximize and display the main window
loMainWindow.state "zoomed"  # Win only, disable for Linux and OSX
loMainWindow.update()

Tk.mainloop()
```

Ruby Tk
Set the Main Window Background Color and Mouse Cursor

- The following example sets the main window background color and mouse cursor:

test4.rb: Ruby Tk Set the Main Window Background Color and Mouse Cursor

```
require 'tk'

loMainWindow = nil
lcWindowBackColor = nil

## Create the main window
loMainWindow = TkRoot.new()

## Set the main window background color
lcWindowBackColor = sprintf("#%02x%02x%02x",255,255,255)
loMainWindow.configure('background' => lcWindowBackColor)
```

test4.rb continued on the next page

test4.rb: Ruby Tk Set the Main Window Background Color and Mouse Cursor continued

```
## Set the main window mouse cursor
loMainWindow.configure('cursor'=>'arrow')

## Maximize and display the main window
loMainWindow.state "zoomed"  # Win only, disable for Linux and OSX
loMainWindow.update()

Tk.mainloop()
```

Ruby Tk
Prompt to Exit the Application when the Main Window is Closed

- The MainWindow_WindowClosing() callback function is assigned to the main window object using the protocol() method.
- The tkMessageBox is displayed using the messageBox() method of the main window object. The message box is used to prompt the user to continue closing the main window. If the user selects the "Yes" button, the destroy() method of the main window object is called. If the user selects the "No" button, no action is taken, and the main window remains visible.

test5.rb: Ruby Tk Prompt to Exit the Application when the Main Window is Closed

```
require 'tk'

def MainWindow_WindowClosing(toMainWindow)

   ## Prompt the user to continue closing the main window
   lcResult = toMainWindow.messageBox('icon' => 'question',
                                      'message' => 'Close the main window?',
                                      'title' => 'test','type' => 'yesno');
  if lcResult == "yes" then

     toMainWindow.destroy()

   end
end

loMainWindow = nil
lcWindowBackColor = nil

## Create the main window
loMainWindow = TkRoot.new()

loMainWindow.protocol('WM_DELETE_WINDOW',
                      proc{MainWindow_WindowClosing(loMainWindow)})

## Maximize and display the main window
loMainWindow.state "zoomed"  # Win only, disable for Linux and OSX
loMainWindow.update()

Tk.mainloop()
```

Source Code Files

- Text files: pp4_12.rb
- Image files: phase16x16.ico (Single-image icon file, Appendix O)

pp4_12.rb: Program Phase 4-12 Source Code

```
##*************************************************************************
## Program Phase 4-12 Ruby Main Window with File Menu                    *
## Programming Tasks Illustrated: Tk GUI based application               *
##                               Main window                             *
##                               Window icon                             *
##                               Window caption                          *
##                               Window menu with hotkeys                *
##                               Window background color                 *
##                               Window mouse cursor                     *
##                               User sizable window                     *
##                               Message box input/output                *
##*************************************************************************

##*************************************************************************
## File: pp4_12.rb                                                       *
## Reserved                                                              *
##*************************************************************************

require 'tk'


##*************************************************************************
## Callback Functions                                                    *
## Implement the callback function for the Hello World! menu item        *
## CBI:  4-12.1.2.1                                                      *
##*************************************************************************

def MenuItem1_Activate(toMainWindow)

   lcResult = toMainWindow.messageBox('icon' => 'info',
                                      'message' => 'Hello World!',
                                      'title' => 'Program Phase 4-12',
                                      'type' => 'ok');
end


##*************************************************************************
## Callback Functions                                                    *
## Implement the callback function for the Exit menu item                *
## CBI:  4-12.1.3.1                                                      *
##*************************************************************************

def MenuItem2_Activate(toMainWindow)

   toMainWindow.destroy

end


##*************************************************************************
## Callback Functions                                                    *
## Implement the callback function that fires when the main window is closed  *
## CBI:  4-12.1.4.1                                                      *
##*************************************************************************

def MainWindow_WindowClosing(toMainWindow)

   ## Prompt the user to continue closing the main window
   lcResult = toMainWindow.messageBox('icon' => 'question',
                                      'message' => 'Close the main window?',
                                      'title' => 'Program Phase 4-12',
                                      'type' => 'yesno');

   if lcResult == "yes" then

      toMainWindow.destroy()
```

pp4_12.rb continued on the next page

pp4_12.rb: Program Phase 4-12 Source Code continued

```
   end
end

##*****************************************************************************
## Program Phase 4-12 Main                                                     *
## Define the Entry Point of Execution (EPE) for Program Phase 4-12            *
## CBI:  4-12.1.1.1                                                            *
##*****************************************************************************

## The first line of the code not found in a function in pp4_12.rb is the EPE.

##*****************************************************************************
## Program Phase 4-12 Main                                                     *
## Declare the local variables for the "main" program                          *
## CBI:  4-12.1.1.2                                                            *
##*****************************************************************************

## Main window
loMainWindow = nil

## Main window menu
loFileMenu = nil
loMenuBar = nil

## Main window background color
lcWindowBackColor = nil

##*****************************************************************************
## Program Phase 4-12 Main                                                     *
## Create the main window                                                      *
## CBI:  4-12.1.1.3                                                            *
##*****************************************************************************

loMainWindow = TkRoot.new()

loMainWindow.protocol('WM_DELETE_WINDOW',
                      proc{MainWindow_WindowClosing(loMainWindow)})

##*****************************************************************************
## Program Phase 4-12 Main                                                     *
## Set the icon for the main window                                            *
## CBI:  4-12.1.1.4                                                            *
##*****************************************************************************

loMainWindow.iconbitmap "phase16x16.ico"  # Win only, disable for Linux and OSX

##*****************************************************************************
## Program Phase 4-12 Main                                                     *
## Set the caption of the main window                                          *
## CBI:  4-12.1.1.5                                                            *
##*****************************************************************************

loMainWindow.title "Program Phase 4-12  |  " +
                   "Platform:  Multi-Platform  |  " +
                   "Programming Language:  Ruby  |  " +
                   "GUI API:  Tk"

##*****************************************************************************
## Program Phase 4-12 Main                                                     *
## Create the menu for the main window                                         *
## CBI:  4-12.1.1.6                                                            *
##*****************************************************************************
```

pp4_12.rb continued on the next page

pp4_12.rb: Program Phase 4-12 Source Code continued

```
## Menu bar
loMenuBar = TkMenu.new()

## File menu
loFileMenu = TkMenu.new(loMenuBar) {tearoff false}
loMenuBar.add('cascade', 'menu'=>loFileMenu, 'label'=>"File",'underline' => 0)

## Hello World! menu item
loFileMenu.add('command',
              'label'=>"Hello World!",
              'command'=>proc {MenuItem1_Activate(loMainWindow)},
              'underline' => 0,
              'accel' => 'Ctrl+H')

loMainWindow.bind('Control-h', proc { MenuItem1_Activate(loMainWindow) })

## Exit menu item
loFileMenu.add('command',
              'label'=>"Exit",
              'command'=>proc { MenuItem2_Activate(loMainWindow) },
              'underline' => 1,
             'accel' => 'Ctrl+X')

loMainWindow.bind('Control-x', proc { MenuItem2_Activate(loMainWindow) })

## Assign the File menu to the main window
loMainWindow.menu(loMenuBar)


##***************************************************************************
## Program Phase 4-12 Main                                                  *
## Set the background color of the main window                              *
## CBI:  4-12.1.1.7                                                         *
##***************************************************************************

lcWindowBackColor = sprintf("#%02x%02x%02x",255,255,255)
loMainWindow.configure('background' => lcWindowBackColor)


##***************************************************************************
## Program Phase 4-12 Main                                                  *
## Set the mouse cursor displayed when positioned over the main window      *
## CBI:  4-12.1.1.8                                                         *
##***************************************************************************

loMainWindow.configure('cursor'=>'arrow')


##***************************************************************************
## Program Phase 4-12 Main                                                  *
## Allow resizing of the main window                                        *
## CBI:  4-12.1.1.9                                                         *
##***************************************************************************

loMainWindow.resizable(1,1)


##***************************************************************************
## Program Phase 4-12 Main                                                  *
## Maximize and display the main window                                     *
## CBI:  4-12.1.1.10                                                        *
##***************************************************************************

loMainWindow.state "zoomed"  # Win only, disable for Linux and OSX
loMainWindow.update()
```

pp4_12.rb continued on the next page

pp4_12.rb: Program Phase 4-12 Source Code continued

```
##*************************************************************************
## Program Phase 4-12 Main                                                *
## Start the event loop                                                   *
## CBI:  4-12.1.1.11                                                      *
##*************************************************************************

Tk.mainloop()


##*************************************************************************
## Program Phase 4-12 Main                                                *
## Cleanup the resources used by the main window                          *
## CBI:  4-12.1.1.12                                                      *
##*************************************************************************
```

Code Setup and Compilation

- Tools: Ruby distribution (Appendix I), Komodo IDE (Appendix F)

Code Setup and Compilation Steps

1: Create a folder called pp4_12 that will store the source code files.

2: Start the Komodo IDE program.

3: Komodo - Activate Menu Item: File → New → New Project

Set the project name to pp4_12.kpf and then save the new project in the pp4_12 folder.

4: Komodo - Activate Menu Item: File → New → New File

Click on the "Common" category and then select the "Text" template. Set the "Filename" to pp4_12.rb. Verify that the "add to pp4_12 project" check box is checked and the "Directory" is set to the pp4_12 folder. Activate the "Open" button. Enter the source code for the pp4_12.rb file and then save the file.

5: Create the phase16x16.ico image file according to the instructions found in Appendix O. Save the icon file to the pp4_12 folder.

6: There is no step for compiling the source code file. It is compiled at runtime by the Ruby interpreter.

Program Execution

- Execute Program

  `Komodo - Activate Menu Item: Debug → Run Without Debugging`

  On the "Debugging Options" window, verify that the "Script" is set to the full path to the pp4_12.rb file and then activate the "OK" button.

- Debug Program

  `Komodo - Activate Menu Item: Debug → Step In`

Program Phase 4-13

Tcl ▪ Tk ▪ Multi-Platform

GUI Based Program with Main Window

- Program Phase Task 4 is implemented in Program Phase 4-13 using the Tcl programming language and the Tk library.
- Program Phase 4-13 contains a single source code file named pp4_13.tcl. In addition to the pp4_13.tcl text file, an icon image file called phase16x16.ico is used as the window icon for the main window.

Code Block Features

The Program Phase 4-13 code blocks illustrate the following programming features using the Tcl programming language and the Tk library:

- **Create a Resizable Main Window for a GUI Based Application**
- **Set the Main Window Icon and Caption**
- **Set the Main Window Menu**
- **Set the Main Window Background Color and Mouse Cursor**
- **Prompt to Exit the Application when the Main Window is Closed**

Tcl Tk
Create a Resizable Main Window for a GUI Based Application

- A Tk main window is referred to as a "Toplevel" window.
- The "wm" command communicates with the window manager managing the "." "Toplevel" window.
- The border of the main window is set to be resizable by calling the resizable() method of the main window object. The first parameter indicates the resize condition of the left and right borders of the window, and the second parameter indicates the resize condition of the top and bottom borders of the window.
- A main window object referenced by the "." symbol is automatically created when the Tcl program begins. When the main window object is destroyed in the following example, the application exits:

test1.tcl: Tcl Tk Create a Resizable Main Window for a GUI Based Application

```
package require Tk

## Create the main window.

## The main window is automatically created and referenced as "."
wm resizable . 1 1

## Maximize and display the main window
wm state . "zoomed" ;# Windows only, disable this line for Linux and OSX

# The main window is automatically displayed
```

Tcl Tk
Set the Main Window Icon and Caption

- The "wm" command with the "iconbitmap" option is used to assign the phase16x16.ico file as the icon for the main window. The phase16x16.ico file needs to be copied to the same folder as the test2.tcl file and accessible on the file system at runtime.

- The "wm" command with the "title" option can be used to set the caption of the main window.

test2.tcl: Tcl Tk Set the Main Window Icon and Caption

```
package require Tk

## Create the main window.
## The main window is automatically created and referenced as "."

wm resizable . 1 1

## Set the main window icon
wm iconbitmap . phase16x16.ico ;# Win only, disable this line for Linux and OSX

## Set the main window caption
wm title . "Hello World!"

## Maximize and display the main window
wm state . "zoomed" ;# Windows only, disable this line for Linux and OSX

# The main window is automatically displayed
```

Tcl Tk
Set the Main Window Menu

- The following example creates a "File" menu with a "Hello World!" menu item and "Exit" menu item:

test3.tcl: Tcl Tk Set the Main Window Menu

```
package require Tk

## Create the main window.
## The main window is automatically created and referenced as "."

wm resizable . 1 1
```

test3.tcl continued on the next page

test3.tcl: Tcl Tk Set the Main Window Menu continued

```
## Menu Bar
menu .loMenuBar

## File menu
menu .loFileMenu -tearoff 0
.loMenuBar add cascade -label "File" -menu .loFileMenu -underline 0

## Hello World! menu item
.loFileMenu add command -label "Hello World!" \
                        -accelerator "Ctrl+H" -underline 0 \
                        -command MenuItem1_Activate

bind . "<Control-h>" {MenuItem1_Activate}

## Exit menu item
.loFileMenu add command -label "Exit" \
                        -accelerator "Ctrl+X" -underline 1 \
                        -command [list MenuItem2_Activate .]

bind . "<Control-x>" {MenuItem2_Activate .}

## Assign the menu to the main window
. configure -menu .loMenuBar -width 200 -height 150

## Maximize and display the main window (Windows only)
wm state . "zoomed" ;# Windows only, disable this line for Linux and OSX

# The main window is automatically displayed

proc MenuItem1_Activate {} {

     tk_messageBox -message "Hello World!" -parent . -title "test"
}

proc MenuItem2_Activate {toMainWindow} {

     destroy $toMainWindow
}
```

Tcl Tk
Set the Main Window Background Color and Mouse Cursor

- The following example sets the main window background color and mouse cursor:

test4.tcl: Tcl Tk Set the Main Window Background Color and Mouse Cursor

```
package require Tk

## Create the main window.
wm resizable . 1 1

## Set the main window background color
set lcWindowBackColor [format "#%02x%02x%02x" 255 255 255]
. configure -background $lcWindowBackColor

## Set the main window mouse cursor
. configure -cursor "arrow"

## Maximize and display the main window (Windows only)
wm state . "zoomed"
```

Tcl Tk
Prompt to Exit the Application when the Main Window is Closed

- The MainWindow_WindowClosing() callback function is assigned to the main window object by using the "wm" command with the "protocol" option.

- The tk_messageBox object is used to prompt the user to continue closing the main window. If the user selects the "Yes" button, the destroy() method of the main window object is called. If the user select the "No" button, no action is taken, and the main window is not destroyed.

test5.tcl: Tcl Tk Prompt to Exit the Application when the Main Window is Closed

```
package require Tk

## Create the main window.
wm resizable . 1 1
wm protocol . WM_DELETE_WINDOW [list MainWindow_WindowClosing .]

## Maximize and display the main window
wm state . "zoomed" ;# Windows only, disable this line for Linux and OSX

proc MainWindow_WindowClosing {toMainWindow} {

     ## Prompt the user to continue closing the main window
     set lnResult [tk_messageBox -parent $toMainWindow \
                                 -message "Close the main window?" \
                                 -icon "question" -type "yesno" -title "test"]

      if {[string compare $lnResult "yes"] == 0} \
      {
         destroy $toMainWindow
      }
}
```

Source Code Files

- Text files: pp4_13.tcl

- Image files: phase16x16.ico (Single-image icon file, Appendix O)

pp4_13.tcl: Program Phase 4-13 Source Code

```
##****************************************************************************
## Program Phase 4-13 Tcl Main Window with File Menu                        *
## Programming Tasks Illustrated: Tk GUI based application                  *
##                                Main window                               *
##                                Window icon                               *
##                                Window caption                            *
##                                Window menu with hotkeys                  *
##                                Window background color                   *
##                                Window mouse cursor                       *
##                                User sizable window                       *
##                                Message box input/output                  *
##****************************************************************************

##****************************************************************************
## File: pp4_13.tcl                                                         *
## Reserved                                                                 *
##****************************************************************************
```

pp4_13.tcl continued on the next page

pp4_13.tcl: Program Phase 4-13 Source Code continued

```
package require Tk


##***************************************************************************
## Program Phase 4-13 Main                                                  *
## Define the Entry Point of Execution (EPE) for Program Phase 4-13        *
## CBI:  4-13.1.1.1                                                         *
##***************************************************************************

## The first line of the code in the pp4_13.tcl file is the EPE.


##***************************************************************************
## Program Phase 4-13 Main                                                  *
## Declare the local variables for the "main" program                      *
## CBI:  4-13.1.1.2                                                         *
##***************************************************************************

## No local variables are needed in Program Phase 4-13.


##***************************************************************************
## Program Phase 4-13 Main                                                  *
## Create the main window                                                   *
## CBI:  4-13.1.1.3                                                         *
##***************************************************************************

# The "." main window object is automatically created.
wm protocol . WM_DELETE_WINDOW [list MainWindow_WindowClosing .]


##***************************************************************************
## Program Phase 4-13 Main                                                  *
## Set the icon for the main window                                         *
## CBI:  4-13.1.1.4                                                         *
##***************************************************************************

wm iconbitmap . phase16x16.ico ;# Win only, disable this line for Linux and OSX


##***************************************************************************
## Program Phase 4-13 Main                                                  *
## Set the caption of the main window                                       *
## CBI:  4-13.1.1.5                                                         *
##***************************************************************************

wm title . "Program Phase 4-13  |  Platform:  Multi-Platform  | \
Programming Language:  Tcl  |  GUI API:  Tk"


##***************************************************************************
## Program Phase 4-13 Main                                                  *
## Create the menu for the main window                                      *
## CBI:  4-13.1.1.6                                                         *
##***************************************************************************

## Menu Bar
menu .loMenuBar

## File menu
menu .loFileMenu -tearoff 0
.loMenuBar add cascade -label "File" -menu .loFileMenu -underline 0

## Hello World! menu item
.loFileMenu add command -label "Hello World!" \
                        -accelerator "Ctrl+H" -underline 0 \
                        -command MenuItem1_Activate
```

pp4_13.tcl continued on the next page

pp4_13.tcl: Program Phase 4-13 Source Code continued

```
bind . "<Control-h>" {MenuItem1_Activate}

## Exit menu item
.loFileMenu add command -label "Exit" -accelerator "Ctrl+X" -underline 1 \
                                      -command [list MenuItem2_Activate .]

bind . "<Control-x>" {MenuItem2_Activate .}

## Assign the menu to the main window
. configure -menu .loMenuBar -width 200 -height 150


##***************************************************************************
## Program Phase 4-13 Main                                                  *
## Set the background color of the main window                              *
## CBI:  4-13.1.1.7                                                         *
##***************************************************************************

set lcWindowBackColor [format "#%02x%02x%02x" 255 255 255]
. configure -background $lcWindowBackColor


##***************************************************************************
## Program Phase 4-13 Main                                                  *
## Set the mouse cursor displayed when positioned over the main window      *
## CBI:  4-13.1.1.8                                                         *
##***************************************************************************

. configure -cursor "arrow"


##***************************************************************************
## Program Phase 4-13 Main                                                  *
## Allow resizing of the main window                                        *
## CBI:  4-13.1.1.9                                                         *
##***************************************************************************

wm resizable . 1 1


##***************************************************************************
## Program Phase 4-13 Main                                                  *
## Maximize and display the main window                                     *
## CBI:  4-13.1.1.10                                                        *
##***************************************************************************

wm state . "zoomed" ;# Windows only, disable this line for Linux and OSX


##***************************************************************************
## Program Phase 4-13 Main                                                  *
## Start the event loop                                                     *
## CBI:  4-13.1.1.11                                                        *
##***************************************************************************

## The event loop is managed internally by Tk.


##***************************************************************************
## Program Phase 4-13 Main                                                  *
## Cleanup the resources used by the main window                            *
## CBI:  4-13.1.1.12                                                        *
##***************************************************************************
```

pp4_13.tcl continued on the next page

pp4_13.tcl: Program Phase 4-13 Source Code continued

```
## Callback functions

##*************************************************************************
## Callback Functions                                                     *
## Implement the callback function for the Hello World! menu item         *
## CBI:  4-13.1.2.1                                                       *
##*************************************************************************

proc MenuItem1_Activate {} {

    tk_messageBox -message "Hello World!" -parent . \
                  -title "Program Phase 4-13"
}


##*************************************************************************
## Callback Functions                                                     *
## Implement the callback function for the Exit menu item                 *
## CBI:  4-13.1.3.1                                                       *
##*************************************************************************

proc MenuItem2_Activate {toMainWindow} {

     ## Exit the program if the user activates the Exit menu item
     destroy $toMainWindow
}


##*************************************************************************
## Callback Functions                                                     *
## Implement the callback function that fires when the main window is closed  *
## CBI:  4-13.1.4.1                                                       *
##*************************************************************************

proc MainWindow_WindowClosing {toMainWindow} {

     ## Prompt the user to continue closing the main window
     set lnResult [tk_messageBox -parent $toMainWindow \
                                 -message "Close the main window?" \
                                 -icon "question" \
                                 -type "yesno" \
                                 -title "Program Phase 4-13"]

      if {[string compare $lnResult "yes"] == 0} \
      {
          destroy $toMainWindow
      }
}
```

Code Setup and Compilation

- Tools: Tcl distribution (Appendix K), Komodo IDE (Appendix F)

Code Setup and Compilation Steps

1: Create a folder called pp4_13 that will store the source code files.

2: Start the Komodo IDE program.

Steps continued on the next page

Code Setup and Compilation Steps continued

3: Komodo - Activate Menu Item: File → New → New Project

Set the project name to pp4_13.kpf and then save the new project in the pp4_13 folder.

4: Komodo - Activate Menu Item: File → New → New File

Click on the "Common" category and then select the "Text" template. Set the "Filename" to pp4_13.tcl. Verify that the "add to pp4_13 project" check box is checked and the "Directory" is set to the pp4_13 folder. Activate the "Open" button. Enter the source code for the pp4_13.tcl file and then save the file.

5: Create the phase16x16.ico image file according to the instructions found in Appendix O. Save the icon file to the pp4_13 folder.

6: There is no step for compiling the source code file. It is compiled at runtime by the Tcl interpreter.

Program Execution

- Execute Program

```
Komodo - Activate Menu Item: Debug → Run Without Debugging
```

On the "Debugging Options" window, verify that the "Script" is set to the full path to the pp4_13.tcl file and then activate the "OK" button.

- Debug Program

```
Komodo - Activate Menu Item: Debug → Step In
```

Program Phase 4-14

Delphi ▪ Windows

GUI Based Program with Main Window

- Program Phase Task 4 is implemented in Program Phase 4-14 using the Delphi programming language.

- Program Phase 4-14 contains four source code files: pp4_14.dpr, mainwindowunit.pas, mainwindowunit.dfm, and resource.rc. In addition to the source code files, an icon image file called phase.ico is used as the window icon for the main window and the application icon for the pp4_14.exe executable file.

Code Block Features

The Program Phase 4-14 code blocks illustrate the following programming features using the Delphi programming language:

- **Create a Resizable Main Window for a GUI Based Application**

- **Set the Main Window Icon and Caption**

- **Set the Main Window Menu**

- **Set the Main Window Background Color and Mouse Cursor**

- **Prompt to Exit the Application when the Main Window is Closed**

Delphi
Create a Resizable Main Window for a GUI Based Application

- The main window is defined as a Delphi unit in the mainwindowunit.pas file. The mainwindowunit.pas file contains source code for the main window form.

- Delphi executes the initialization section for any units specified in the "uses" statement of the test1.dpr file. There is no initialization section of the mainwindowunit.dpr file, so the first line of code after the "begin" statement in the test1.dpr file is considered the EPE for the program.

- Properties of the main window are set in the mainwindowunit.dfm file. The mainwindowunit.dfm file is paired with the mainwindowunit.pas file to complete the definition for the main window form.

- The mainwindowunit.pas file is specified in the "uses" statement at the top of the test1.dpr file. This allows the unit defined in the mainwindowunit.pas file to be accessible in the test1.dpr file.

- The main window form object is created by using the CreateForm() method of the TApplication object. The first Delphi form created in the EPE function is automatically designated as the "MainForm".
- The event loop is handled internally by the TApplication instance. The Delphi TApplication object instance referenced as "Application" is automatically created when the program starts. The TApplication instance manages low level Win32 tasks for the application. The Application.Run() method starts the event loop. This loop is responsible for keeping the program running until the user closes the form designated as the "MainForm".
- When the "MainForm" form is closed, the application automatically terminates.
- The "{$R *.dfm}" compiler directive indicates that the mainwindowunit.pas file is using the mainwindowunit.dfm to set properties for the window.

test1.dpr: Delphi Create a Resizable Main Window for a GUI Based Application

```
program test1;

uses
   Forms,
   mainwindowunit in 'mainwindowunit.pas' {MainWindow};

var
  loMainWindow : TMainWindow;

begin

   // Create the main window
   Application.CreateForm(TMainWindow, loMainWindow);
   Application.Initialize;
   loMainWindow.BorderStyle := bsSizeable;

   // Maximize and display the main window
   loMainWindow.WindowState := wsMaximized;
   loMainWindow.Visible := true;

   // Start the event loop
   Application.Run;

end.
```

mainwindowunit.pas: Main Window Code File for test1.dpr

```
unit mainwindowunit;

interface

uses
   Forms;

type
   TMainWindow = class(TForm)

end;

implementation

{$R *.dfm}

end.
```

mainwindowunit.dfm: Main Window Properties File for test1.dpr

```
object MainWindow: TMainWindow

end
```

Delphi
Set the Main Window Icon and Caption

- The phase.ico file is a multi-image icon file referenced in the resource.rc file as "MAINICON". The "MAINICON" icon resource is automatically assigned as the icon for the main window.

- The "caption" property of the main window form is used to set the caption of the main window.

test2.dpr: Delphi Set the Main Window Icon and Caption

```
program test2;

uses
  Forms,
  mainwindowunit in 'mainwindowunit.pas' {MainWindow};

  // Set the main window and application icon
  {$R resource.res}

var
  loMainWindow : TMainWindow;

begin

   // Create the main window
   Application.CreateForm(TMainWindow, loMainWindow);
   Application.Initialize;
   loMainWindow.BorderStyle := bsSizeable;

   // Set the main window icon
   // This is automatically set from the icon called MAINICON in the
   // resource.res file.

   // Set the main window caption
   loMainWindow.Caption := 'Hello World';

   // Maximize and display the main window
   loMainWindow.WindowState := wsMaximized;
   loMainWindow.Visible := true;

   // Start the event loop
   Application.Run;

end.
```

mainwindowunit.pas: Main Window Code File for test2.dpr

```
unit mainwindowunit;

interface

uses
   Forms;
```

mainwindowunit.pas continued on the next page

mainwindowunit.pas: Main Window Code File for test2.dpr continued

```
type
   TMainWindow = class(TForm)

end;

implementation

{$R *.dfm}

end.
```

mainwindowunit.dfm: Main Window Properties File for test2.dpr

```
object MainWindow: TMainWindow

end
```

resource.rc: Resource File for Creating the resource.res File for test2.dpr

```
MAINICON ICON "phase.ico"
```

Delphi
Set the Main Window Menu

- The menu for the main window is defined in the mainwindowunit.dfm file. This menu can be built using the Delphi GUI. Open the mainwindowunit.dfm file and then drag the "TMainMenu" item from the tools palette onto the form. Double click the mouse on the menu object that is on the form and use the graphical editor to add the appropriate menu items.

- The main window menu and menu items are defined as variables in the "var" section of the mainwindowunit.pas file.

- The callback functions for the menu items are defined in the mainwindowunit.pas file.

test3.dpr: Delphi Set the Main Window Menu

```
program test3;

uses
  Forms,
  mainwindowunit in 'mainwindowunit.pas' {MainWindow};

var
  loMainWindow : TMainWindow;

begin

   // Create the main window
   Application.CreateForm(TMainWindow, loMainWindow);
   Application.Initialize;
   loMainWindow.BorderStyle := bsSizeable;

   // The main window menu is specified in the mainwindowunit.dfm file

   // Maximize and display the main window
   loMainWindow.WindowState := wsMaximized;
   loMainWindow.Visible := true;
```

test3.dpr continued on the next page

test3.dpr: Delphi Set the Main Window Menu continued

```
   // Start the event loop
   Application.Run;

end.
```

mainwindowunit.pas: Main Window Code File for test3.dpr

```
unit mainwindowunit;

interface

uses
   Forms, Menus, Classes, Dialogs;

type
   TMainWindow = class(TForm)
   MainMenu1: TMainMenu;
   File1: TMenuItem;
   HelloWorld1: TMenuItem;
   Exit1: TMenuItem;
   procedure HelloWorld1Click(Sender: TObject);
   procedure Exit1Click(Sender: TObject);
end;

implementation

{$R *.dfm}

procedure TMainWindow.HelloWorld1Click(Sender: TObject);
begin

   MessageDlg('Hello World!',mtInformation,[mbOK],0);

end;

procedure TMainWindow.Exit1Click(Sender: TObject);
begin

   Application.Terminate;

end;

end.
```

mainwindowunit.dfm: Main Window Properties File for test3.dpr

```
object MainWindow: TMainWindow
  Menu = MainMenu1
  object MainMenu1: TMainMenu
    object File1: TMenuItem
      Caption = '&File'
      object HelloWorld1: TMenuItem
        Caption = '&Hello World!'
        ShortCut = 16456
        OnClick = HelloWorld1Click
      end
      object Exit1: TMenuItem
        Caption = 'E&xit'
        ShortCut = 16472
        OnClick = Exit1Click
      end
    end
  end
end
```

Delphi
Set the Main Window Background Color and Mouse Cursor

- The following example sets the main window background color and mouse cursor:

test4.dpr: Set the Main Window Background Color and Mouse Cursor

```
program test4;

uses
  Forms,  Windows, mainwindowunit in 'mainwindowunit.pas' {MainWindow};

var
  loMainWindow : TMainWindow;
  lnWindowBackColor : Integer;

const
  crArrow = -2;

  begin

   // Create the main window
   Application.CreateForm(TMainWindow, loMainWindow);
   Application.Initialize;
   loMainWindow.BorderStyle := bsSizeable;

   // Set the main window background color
   lnWindowBackColor := RGB(255,255,255);
   loMainWindow.Color := lnWindowBackColor;

   // Set the main window mouse cursor
   loMainWindow.Cursor := crArrow;

   // Maximize and display the main window
   loMainWindow.WindowState := wsMaximized;
   loMainWindow.Visible := true;

   // Start the event loop
   Application.Run;

end.
```

mainwindowunit.pas: Main Window Code File for test4.dpr

```
unit mainwindowunit;

interface

uses
   Forms;

type
   TMainWindow = class(TForm)

end;

implementation

{$R *.dfm}

end.
```

mainwindowunit.dfm: Main Window Properties File for test4.dpr

```
object MainWindow: TMainWindow

end
```

Delphi
Prompt to Exit the Application when the Main Window is Closed

- The FormCloseQuery() method is designated as the OnCloseQuery event for the main window in the mainwindowunit.dfm file.

- Specifying the Boolean "false" value for the "CanClose" parameter in the FormCloseQuery() method prevents the main window from closing.

test5.dpr: Prompt to Exit the Application when the Main Window is Closed

```
program test5;

uses
  Forms, mainwindowunit in 'mainwindowunit.pas' {MainWindow};

var
  loMainWindow : TMainWindow;

  begin

   // Create the main window
   Application.CreateForm(TMainWindow, loMainWindow);
   Application.Initialize;
   loMainWindow.BorderStyle := bsSizeable;

   // Maximize and display the main window
   loMainWindow.WindowState := wsMaximized;
   loMainWindow.Visible := true;

   // Start the event loop
   Application.Run;

end.
```

mainwindowunit.pas: Main Window Code File for test5.dpr

```
unit mainwindowunit;

interface

uses
   Controls, Forms, Dialogs;

var
   lnResult : Integer;

type
   TMainWindow = class(TForm)
   procedure FormCloseQuery(Sender: TObject; var CanClose: Boolean);

end;

implementation

{$R *.dfm}
```

mainwindowunit.pas continued on the next page

mainwindowunit.pas: Main Window Code File for test5.dpr continued

```
procedure TMainWindow.FormCloseQuery(Sender: TObject;
                                     var CanClose: Boolean);
begin

   // Prompt the user to continue closing the main window
   lnResult := MessageDlg('Close the main window?',
                          mtConfirmation,[mbYes, mbNo], 0);

   if lnResult = mrNo then
   begin

      CanClose := False;

   end;

end;

end.
```

mainwindowunit.dfm: Main Window Properties File for test5.dpr

```
object MainWindow: TMainWindow

   OnCloseQuery = FormCloseQuery

end
```

Source Code Files

- Text files: pp4_14.dpr, mainwindowunit.pas, mainwindowunit.dfm, resource.rc
- Image files: phase.ico (Multi-image icon file, Appendix O)

pp4_14.dpr: Program Phase 4-14 source code

```
//***************************************************************************
// Program Phase 4-14 Delphi Main Window with File Menu                     *
// Programming Tasks Illustrated: Win32 GUI based application               *
//                                Main window                               *
//                                Window icon                               *
//                                Window caption                            *
//                                Window menu with hotkeys                  *
//                                Window background color                   *
//                                Window mouse cursor                       *
//                                User sizable window                       *
//                                Message box input/output                  *
//***************************************************************************

//***************************************************************************
// File: pp4_14.dpr                                                         *
// Reserved                                                                 *
//***************************************************************************

program pp4_14;

uses
   Windows, Forms, mainwindowunit in 'mainwindowunit.pas' {MainWindow};

   // Main window icon
   {$R resource.res}
```

pp4_14.dpr continued on the next page

pp4_14.dpr: Program Phase 4-14 Source Code continued

```
//***************************************************************************
// Program Phase 4-14 Main                                                  *
// Declare the local variables for the "main" program                      *
// CBI:  4-14.1.1.2                                                         *
//***************************************************************************

var
   // Main window
   loMainWindow : TMainWindow;

   // Main window background color
   lnWindowBackColor : Integer;

const
   // Main window mouse cursor
   crArrow = -2;


//***************************************************************************
// Program Phase 4-14 Main                                                  *
// Define the Entry Point of Execution (EPE) for Program Phase 4-14         *
// CBI:  4-14.1.1.1                                                         *
//***************************************************************************

begin


//***************************************************************************
// Program Phase 4-14 Main                                                  *
// Create the main window                                                   *
// CBI:  4-14.1.1.3                                                         *
//***************************************************************************

   Application.CreateForm(TMainWindow, loMainWindow);
   Application.Initialize;


//***************************************************************************
// Program Phase 4-14 Main                                                  *
// Set the icon for the main window                                         *
// CBI:  4-14.1.1.4                                                         *
//***************************************************************************

   // The icon is set from the MAINICON resource in the resource.res file.


//***************************************************************************
// Program Phase 4-14 Main                                                  *
// Set the caption of the main window                                       *
// CBI:  4-14.1.1.5                                                         *
//***************************************************************************

   loMainWindow.Caption := 'Program Phase 4-14  |  ' +
                           'Platform:  Windows  |  ' +
                           'Programming Language:  Delphi  |  ' +
                           'GUI API:  Delphi Win32';


//***************************************************************************
// Program Phase 4-14 Main                                                  *
// Create the menu for the main window                                      *
// CBI:  4-14.1.1.6                                                         *
//***************************************************************************

   // The menu is assigned to the main window in the mainwindowunit.dfm file.
   // The mainwindowunit.dfm file can be generated using the Delphi IDE.
```

pp4_14.dpr continued on the next page

pp4_14.dpr: Program Phase 4-14 Source Code continued

```
//******************************************************************************
// Program Phase 4-14 Main                                                      *
// Set the background color of the main window                                  *
// CBI:  4-14.1.1.7                                                             *
//******************************************************************************

   lnWindowBackColor := RGB(255,255,255);
   loMainWindow.Color := lnWindowBackColor;


//******************************************************************************
// Program Phase 4-14 Main                                                      *
// Set the mouse cursor displayed when positioned over the main window          *
// CBI:  4-14.1.1.8                                                             *
//******************************************************************************

   loMainWindow.Cursor := crArrow;


//******************************************************************************
// Program Phase 4-14 Main                                                      *
// Allow resizing of the main window                                            *
// CBI:  4-14.1.1.9                                                             *
//******************************************************************************

   loMainWindow.BorderStyle := bsSizeable;


//******************************************************************************
// Program Phase 4-14 Main                                                      *
// Maximize and display the main window                                         *
// CBI:  4-14.1.1.10                                                            *
//******************************************************************************

   loMainWindow.WindowState := wsMaximized;
   loMainWindow.Visible := true;


//******************************************************************************
// Program Phase 4-14 Main                                                      *
// Start the event loop                                                         *
// CBI:  4-14.1.1.11                                                            *
//******************************************************************************

   Application.Run;


//******************************************************************************
// Program Phase 4-14 Main                                                      *
// Cleanup the resources used by the main window                                *
// CBI:  4-14.1.1.12                                                            *
//******************************************************************************

end.
```

mainwindowunit.pas: Main Window Code File

```
//******************************************************************************
// File: mainwindowunit.pas                                                     *
// Reserved                                                                     *
//******************************************************************************

unit mainwindowunit;

interface
```

mainwindowunit.pas continued on the next page

mainwindowunit.pas: Main Window Code File continued

```
uses
    Classes, Controls, Forms, Dialogs, Menus;

var
   lnResult : Integer;

type
    TMainWindow = class(TForm)
    MainMenu1: TMainMenu;
    File1: TMenuItem;
    HelloWorld1: TMenuItem;
    Exit1: TMenuItem;
    procedure HelloWorld1Click(Sender: TObject);
    procedure Exit1Click(Sender: TObject);
    procedure FormCloseQuery(Sender: TObject; var CanClose: Boolean);
end;

implementation
{$R *.dfm}


//***********************************************************************
// Callback Functions                                                   *
// Implement the callback function for the Hello World! menu item       *
// CBI:  4-14.1.2.1                                                     *
//***********************************************************************

procedure TMainWindow.HelloWorld1Click(Sender: TObject);
begin

   MessageDlg('Hello World!',mtInformation,[mbOK],0);

end;


//***********************************************************************
// Callback Functions                                                   *
// Implement the callback function for the Exit menu item               *
// CBI:  4-14.1.3.1                                                     *
//***********************************************************************

procedure TMainWindow.Exit1Click(Sender: TObject);
begin

   Application.Terminate;

end;


//***********************************************************************
// Callback Functions                                                   *
// Implement the callback function that fires when the main window is closed  *
// CBI:  4-14.1.4.1                                                     *
//***********************************************************************

procedure TMainWindow.FormCloseQuery(Sender: TObject; var CanClose: Boolean);
begin

lnResult := MessageDlg('Close the main window?',mtConfirmation,[mbYes, mbNo],0);

   if lnResult = mrNo then
   begin

      CanClose := False;

   end;
end;
end.
```

mainwindowunit.dfm: Main Window Properties File

```
object MainWindow: TMainWindow
  Menu = MainMenu1

  OnCloseQuery = FormCloseQuery
  object MainMenu1: TMainMenu
    object File1: TMenuItem
      Caption = '&File'
      object HelloWorld1: TMenuItem
        Caption = '&Hello World!'
        ShortCut = 16456
        OnClick = HelloWorld1Click
      end
      object Exit1: TMenuItem
        Caption = 'E&xit'
        ShortCut = 16472
        OnClick = Exit1Click
      end
    end
  end
end
```

resource.rc: Resource File for Creating the resource.res File

```
MAINICON ICON "phase.ico"
```

Code Setup and Compilation

- Tools: Turbo Delphi Explorer (Appendix M)

Code Setup and Compilation Steps

1: Create a folder called pp4_14 that will store the source code files.

2: Start the Borland Delphi IDE program.

3: Delphi - Activate Menu Item: Project → Add New Project

On the "New Items" dialog window, select the "Delphi Projects" item category and then select "Console Application". Activate the '"OK" button.

4: Enter the source code for the pp4_14.dpr file into the project source code file replacing any existing code in the file. Change the following line of code found in the Reserved section of the pp4_14.dpr file:

From

```
Windows, Forms, mainwindowunit in 'mainwindowunit.pas' {MainWindow};
```

To

```
Windows, Forms;
```

5: Delphi - Activate Menu Item: File → Save Project As

Enter pp4_14.bdsproj as the file name when prompted to save. Save the project to the pp4_14 folder.

Steps continued on the next page

Code Setup and Compilation Steps continued

6: Delphi - Activate Menu Item: File → New → Form

Save the new form as mainwindowunit.pas to the pp4_14 folder. Enter the source code for the mainwindowunit.pas file. Remove the following line of code found in the CBI: 4-14.1.1.3 code block:

```
Application.CreateForm(TForm1, Form1);
```

Change the following line of code found in the CBI: 4-14.1.1.3 code block:

From

```
Application.CreateForm(TloMainWindow, loMainWindow);
```

To

```
Application.CreateForm(TMainWindow, loMainWindow);
```

7: Open the mainwindowunit.dfm file, right-click on the form and then activate the "View as Text" menu item. Enter the appropriate source code for the mainwindowunit.dfm file.

8: Create the phase.ico image file according to the instructions in Appendix O. Copy the image file to the pp4_14 folder.

9: Delphi - Activate Menu Item: File → New → Other

Select "Text" from the "Other Files" item category and then activate the "OK" button. Enter the source code for the resource.rc file and then save the text file as resource.rc in the pp4_14 folder.

10: Open a command prompt and chance directories to the pp4_14 folder. Enter the following in the pp4_14 folder:

```
brcc32.exe resource.rc
```

This command generates the resource.res file referenced in the pp4_14.dpr file.

11: Remove any code that has been automatically added above the Reserved code block of the pp4_14.dpr file.

12: Delphi - Activate Menu Item: File → Save All

13: Delphi - Activate Menu Item: Project → Build pp4_14

Program Execution

- Execute Program

```
Delphi - Activate Menu Item: Run → Run
```

- Debug Program

```
Delphi - Activate Menu Item: Run → Step Over
```

Program Phase 4-15

C++ ▪ QT4 ▪ Multi-Platform

GUI Based Program with Main Window

- Program Phase Task 4 is implemented in Program Phase 4-15 using the C++ programming language and the QT4 library.

- Program Phase 4-15 contains four source code files: pp4_15.cpp, mainwindow.h, mainwindow.cpp, and resource.qrc. In addition, an icon image file called phase16x16.png is used as the window icon for the main window. On the Windows platform, the application icon is implemented with the resource.rc text file and phase.ico image file. The phase.icns image file is used on the Mac OS X platform for the application icon.

Code Block Features

The Program Phase 4-15 code blocks illustrate the following programming features using the C++ programming language and the QT4 library:

- **Create a Resizable Main Window for a GUI Based Application**

- **Set the Main Window Caption**

- **Set the Main Window Menu**

- **Set the Main Window Background Color and Mouse Cursor**

- **Prompt to Exit the Application when the Main Window is Closed**

C++ QT4
Create a Resizable Main Window for a GUI Based Application

- The MainWindow class is based on the QMainWindow class and is defined in the mainwindow.h header file. The QApplication object is used for managing system resources in a GUI based application. After the QApplication object is created, the main window is created with a new instance of the MainWindow class.

- The default border style of a QMainWindow instance is resizable. If a fixed border style is desired, the setFixedSize() method can be called to set the fixed width dimensions of the window.

- The showMaximized() method of the MainWindow instance is called to maximize and display the main window.

- The event loop is started by calling the exec() method of the QApplication instance. This prevents the main() function from ending until the main window is closed.

test1.pro: Test1 Project File

```
TEMPLATE = app
TARGET =
DEPENDPATH += .
INCLUDEPATH += .

# Input
HEADERS += mainwindow.h
SOURCES += test1.cpp
```

mainwindow.h: C++ QT4 MainWindow Class Definition for test1.cpp

```
#ifndef MAINWINDOW_H
#define MAINWINDOW_H

#include <QMainWindow>

class MainWindow : public QMainWindow
{};
#endif
```

test1.cpp: C++ QT4 Create a Resizable Main Window for a GUI Based Application

```
#include <QApplication>
#include "mainwindow.h"

int main(int tnArgc, char *taArgv[])
{
   QApplication loApplication(tnArgc, taArgv);

   MainWindow *loMainWindow;

   // Create the main window
   loMainWindow = new MainWindow();
   //loMainWindow->setFixedSize(640,480);

   // Maximize and display the main window
   loMainWindow->showMaximized();

   // Start the event loop
   loApplication.exec();

   return 0;
}
```

C++ QT4
Set the Main Window Icon and Caption

- The main window icon is set by calling the setWindowIcon() method of the MainWindow instance. The icon file is stored in a file called phase16x16.png. This file is referenced in a file called resource.qrc, and the resource.qrc file is referenced in the test2.pro project file.

- On the Windows platform, the application icon is stored in a file called phase.ico and is referenced in the resource.rc text file. The resource.rc file is referenced in the test2.pro text file. The phase.icns image file is used as the application icon on the Mac OS X platform.

- The setWindowTitle() method of the MainWindow instance is called to set the caption of the main window.

test2.pro: Test2 Project File

```
TEMPLATE = app
DEPENDPATH += .
INCLUDEPATH += .

# Input
HEADERS += mainwindow.h
SOURCES += test2.cpp
RESOURCES = resource.qrc
```

mainwindow.h: C++ QT4 MainWindow Class Definition for test2.cpp

```
#ifndef MAINWINDOW_H
#define MAINWINDOW_H

#include <QMainWindow>

class MainWindow : public QMainWindow
{};
#endif
```

resource.qrc: QT Resource File for test2.cpp

```
<!DOCTYPE RCC><RCC version="1.0">
<qresource>
    <file>phase16x16.png</file>
</qresource>
</RCC>
```

test2.cpp: C++ QT4 Set the Main Window Icon and Caption

```
#include <QApplication>
#include <QtGui>
#include "mainwindow.h"

int main(int tnArgc,char *taArgv[])
{
   QApplication loApplication(tnArgc, taArgv);
   MainWindow *loMainWindow;

   // Create the main window
   loMainWindow = new MainWindow();

   // Set the main window icon
   loMainWindow->setWindowIcon(QIcon(":/phase16x16.png"));

   // Set the main window caption
   loMainWindow->setWindowTitle("Hello World!");

   // Maximize and display the main window
   loMainWindow->showMaximized();

   // Start the event loop
   loApplication.exec();

   return 0;
}
```

C++ QT4
Set the Main Window Menu

- The following example creates a "File" menu with a "Hello World!" menu item and "Exit" menu item:

test3.pro: Test3 Project File

```
TEMPLATE = app
DEPENDPATH += .
INCLUDEPATH += .

# Input
HEADERS += mainwindow.h
SOURCES += test3.cpp mainwindow.cpp
```

mainwindow.h: C++ QT4 MainWindow Class Definition for test2.cpp

```
#ifndef MAINWINDOW_H
#define MAINWINDOW_H

#include <QMainWindow>
#include <QtGui>
#include <QAction>

class QAction;
class QMenu;

class MainWindow : public QMainWindow
{
   Q_OBJECT
   private slots:
      void MenuItem1_Click();
      void MenuItem2_Click();
};
#endif
```

mainwindow.cpp: C++ QT4 MainWindow Class Implementation for mainwindow.h

```
#include "mainwindow.h"

void MainWindow::MenuItem1_Click()
{
   QMessageBox::information(0,"Program Phase 4-15","test",
                            QMessageBox::Ok,QMessageBox::NoButton,
                            QMessageBox::NoButton);
}

void MainWindow::MenuItem2_Click()
{
   this->close();
}
```

test3.cpp: C++ QT4 Set the Main Window Menu

```
#include "mainwindow.h"
#include <QApplication>
#include <QtGui>
#include <QAction>
```

test3.cpp continued on the next page

test3.cpp: C++ QT4 Set the Main Window Menu continued

```
int main(int tnArgc,char *taArgv[])
{
   QApplication loApplication(tnArgc,taArgv);

   MainWindow *loMainWindow;
   QMenu *loFileMenu;
   QAction *loMenuItem1;
   QAction *loMenuItem2;

   // Create the main window
   loMainWindow = new MainWindow();

   // File menu
   loFileMenu = loMainWindow->menuBar()->addMenu(MainWindow::tr("&File"));

   // Hello World! menu item
   loMenuItem1 = new QAction("&Hello World!",loMainWindow);


   loMainWindow->connect(loMenuItem1,SIGNAL(triggered()),loMainWindow,
                         SLOT(MenuItem1_Click()));

   loMenuItem1->setShortcut(MainWindow::tr("Ctrl+H"));
   loFileMenu->addAction(loMenuItem1);

   // Exit menu item
   loMenuItem2 = new QAction("E&xit",loMainWindow);

   loMainWindow->connect(loMenuItem2, SIGNAL(triggered()),loMainWindow,
                         SLOT(MenuItem2_Click()));

   loMenuItem2->setShortcut(MainWindow::tr("Ctrl+X"));
   loFileMenu->addAction(loMenuItem2);

   // Assign the menu to the main window
   // A menubar is automatically created and assigned to a QMainWindow window.

    // Maximize and display the main window
   loMainWindow->showMaximized();

   // Start the event loop
   loApplication.exec();

   return 0;
}
```

C++ QT4
Set the Main Window Background Color and Mouse Cursor

- The following example sets the main window background color and mouse cursor:

test4.pro: Test4 Project File

```
TEMPLATE = app
DEPENDPATH += .
INCLUDEPATH += .

# Input
HEADERS += mainwindow.h
SOURCES += test4.cpp
```

mainwindow.h: C++ QT4 MainWindow Class Definition for test4.cpp

```
#ifndef MAINWINDOW_H
#define MAINWINDOW_H

#include <QMainWindow>

class MainWindow : public QMainWindow
{};
#endif
```

test4.cpp: C++ QT4 Set the Main Window Background Color and Mouse Cursor

```
#include "mainwindow.h"
#include <QApplication>

int main(int tnArgc, char *taArgv[])
{
   QApplication loApplication(tnArgc, taArgv);

   MainWindow *loMainWindow;
   QColor loWindowBackColor;
   QPalette loPalette;

   // Main window mouse cursor
   QCursor loMouseCursor;

   // Create the main window
   loMainWindow = new MainWindow();

   // Set the main window background color
   loWindowBackColor.setRgb(255,255,255);
   loPalette.setColor(QPalette::Background, loWindowBackColor);

   loMainWindow->setAutoFillBackground(true);
   loMainWindow->setPalette(loPalette);

   // Set the main window mouse cursor
   loMouseCursor.setShape(Qt::ArrowCursor);
   loMainWindow->setCursor(loMouseCursor);

    // Maximize and display the main window
   loMainWindow->showMaximized();

   // Start the event loop
   loApplication.exec();

   return 0;
}
```

C++ QT4
Prompt to Exit the Application when the Main Window is Closed

- The closeEvent() member function is implemented for the MainWindow class. This method is automatically called when the window is closed.

- A Boolean variable called "lFlag" is created for the MainWindow class and is assigned a value of "false" if the main window is closed as a result of the "Exit" menu item being activated. The specifications for Program Phase Task 4 call for the user to be prompted to exit the program when the main window is closed in any way that does not include activating the "Exit" menu item. If the "lFlag" variable is "true" in the closeEvent() function, the user is not prompted to continue closing the main window.

test5.pro: Test5 Project File

```
TEMPLATE = app
DEPENDPATH += .
INCLUDEPATH += .

# Input
HEADERS += mainwindow.h
SOURCES += mainwindow.cpp test5.cpp
```

mainwindow.h: C++ QT4 MainWindow Class Definition for test5.cpp

```
#ifndef MAINWINDOW_H
#define MAINWINDOW_H

#include <QMainWindow>
#include <QtGui>
#include <QAction>

class MainWindow : public QMainWindow
{
   Q_OBJECT

   public:
      MainWindow();

   protected:
      void closeEvent(QCloseEvent *event);

    private:
      bool lFlag;
};
#endif
```

mainwindow.cpp: C++ QT4 MainWindow Class Implementation for mainwindow.h

```
#include "mainwindow.h"

MainWindow::MainWindow()
{
   lFlag = true;
}

void MainWindow::closeEvent(QCloseEvent *toEvent)
{
   int lnResult;

   if (this->lFlag == true)
   {
      // Prompt the user to continue closing the main window
      lnResult = QMessageBox::question(this,"test","Close the main window?",
                                       QMessageBox::Yes,QMessageBox::No,
                                       QMessageBox::NoButton);

      if (lnResult == QMessageBox::No)
      {
         toEvent->ignore();
      }
      else
      {
         toEvent->accept();
      }
   }
```

mainwindow.cpp continued on the next page

mainwindow.cpp: C++ QT4 MainWindow Implementation for mainwindow.h continued

```
   else
   {
      toEvent->accept();
   }
}
```

test5.cpp: C++ QT4 Prompt to Exit the Application when the Main Window is Closed

```
#include "mainwindow.h"
#include <QApplication>
#include <QtGui>
#include <QAction>

int main(int tnArgc, char *taArgv[])
{
   QApplication loApplication(tnArgc, taArgv);

   MainWindow *loMainWindow;

   // Create the main window
   loMainWindow = new MainWindow();

    // Maximize and display the main window
   loMainWindow->showMaximized();

   // Start the event loop
   loApplication.exec();

   return 0;
}
```

Source Code Files

- Text files: pp4_15.pro, pp4_15.cpp, mainwindow.h, mainwindow.cpp, resource.qrc
- Image files:

  phase.ico (Multi-image icon file, Appendix O, page O1)

  phase16x16.png (Single-image icon file, Appendix O, page O8)

  phase.icns (Multi-image icon file, Appendix O, page O7)

pp4_15.pro: pp4_15 Project File

```
TEMPLATE = app
TARGET =
DEPENDPATH += .
INCLUDEPATH += .

# Input
HEADERS += mainwindow.h
SOURCES += mainwindow.cpp pp4_15.cpp
RESOURCES = resource.qrc
RC_FILE = resource.rc
```

pp4_15.cpp: Program Phase 4-15 Source Code

```
//******************************************************************************
// Program Phase 4-15 C++ QT4 Main Window with File Menu                       *
// Programming Tasks Illustrated: QT4 GUI based application                    *
//                                Main window                                  *
//                                Window icon                                  *
//                                Window caption                               *
//                                Window menu with hotkeys                     *
//                                Window background color                      *
//                                Window mouse cursor                          *
//                                User sizable window                          *
//                                Message box input/output                     *
//******************************************************************************

//******************************************************************************
// File: pp4_15.cpp                                                            *
// Reserved                                                                    *
//******************************************************************************

#include "mainwindow.h"
#include <QApplication>
#include <QtGui>
#include <QAction>
#include <QColor>
#include <QCursor>


//******************************************************************************
// Program Phase 4-15 Main                                                     *
// Define the Entry Point of Execution (EPE) for Program Phase 4-15            *
// CBI:  4-15.1.1.1                                                            *
//******************************************************************************

int main(int tnArgc, char *taArgv[])
{
   QApplication loApplication(tnArgc, taArgv);


//******************************************************************************
// Program Phase 4-15 Main                                                     *
// Declare the local variables for the "main" program                          *
// CBI:  4-15.1.1.2                                                            *
//******************************************************************************

   // Main window
   MainWindow *loMainWindow;

   // Main window menu
   QMenu *loFileMenu;
   QAction *loMenuItem1;
   QAction *loMenuItem2;

   // Main window background color
   QColor loWindowBackColor;
   QPalette loPalette;

   // Main window mouse cursor
   QCursor loMouseCursor;


//******************************************************************************
// Program Phase 4-15 Main                                                     *
// Create the main window                                                      *
// CBI:  4-15.1.1.3                                                            *
//******************************************************************************

   loMainWindow = new MainWindow();
```

pp4_15.cpp continued on the next page

pp4_15.cpp: Program Phase 4-15 Source Code continued

```
//*************************************************************************
// Program Phase 4-15 Main                                                *
// Set the icon for the main window                                       *
// CBI:  4-15.1.1.4                                                       *
//*************************************************************************

   loMainWindow->setWindowIcon(QIcon(":/phase16x16.png"));


//*************************************************************************
// Program Phase 4-15 Main                                                *
// Set the caption of the main window                                     *
// CBI:  4-15.1.1.5                                                       *
//*************************************************************************

   loMainWindow->setWindowTitle("Program Phase 4-15   |  "
                                "Platform:  Multi-Platform  |  "
                                "Programming Language:  C++  |  "
                                "GUI API:  QT4");


//*************************************************************************
// Program Phase 4-15 Main                                                *
// Create the menu for the main window                                    *
// CBI:  4-15.1.1.6                                                       *
//*************************************************************************

   // File menu
   loFileMenu = loMainWindow->menuBar()->addMenu(MainWindow::tr("&File"));

   // Hello World! menu item
   loMenuItem1 = new QAction("&Hello World!",loMainWindow);

   loMenuItem1->setShortcut(MainWindow::tr("Ctrl+H"));

   loMainWindow->connect(loMenuItem1, SIGNAL(triggered()),loMainWindow,
                         SLOT(MenuItem1_Click()));

   loFileMenu->addAction(loMenuItem1);

   // Exit menu item
   loMenuItem2 = new QAction("E&xit",loMainWindow);
   loMenuItem2->setShortcut(MainWindow::tr("Ctrl+X"));

   loMainWindow->connect(loMenuItem2,SIGNAL(triggered()),loMainWindow,
                         SLOT(MenuItem2_Click()));
   loFileMenu->addAction(loMenuItem2);

   // Assign the menu to the main window
   // A menubar is automatically created and assigned to a QMainWindow window.


//*************************************************************************
// Program Phase 4-15 Main                                                *
// Set the background color of the main window                            *
// CBI:  4-15.1.1.7                                                       *
//*************************************************************************

   loWindowBackColor.setRgb(255,255,255);
   loPalette.setColor(QPalette::Background, loWindowBackColor);

   loMainWindow->setAutoFillBackground(true);
   loMainWindow->setPalette(loPalette);
```

pp4_15.cpp continued on the next page

pp4_15.cpp: Program Phase 4-15 Source Code continued

```
//*****************************************************************************
// Program Phase 4-15 Main                                                    *
// Set the mouse cursor displayed when positioned over the main window        *
// CBI:  4-15.1.1.8                                                           *
//*****************************************************************************

   loMouseCursor.setShape(Qt::ArrowCursor);
   loMainWindow->setCursor(loMouseCursor);


//*****************************************************************************
// Program Phase 4-15 Main                                                    *
// Allow resizing of the main window                                          *
// CBI:  4-15.1.1.9                                                           *
//*****************************************************************************

 // A QMainWindow's default behavior is to allow for the border to be resized.
 // To set a fixed size window with a non sizable border, use:

      //loMainWindow->setFixedSize(640,480);


//*****************************************************************************
// Program Phase 4-15 Main                                                    *
// Maximize and display the main window                                       *
// CBI:  4-15.1.1.10                                                          *
//*****************************************************************************

   loMainWindow->showMaximized();


//*****************************************************************************
// Program Phase 4-15 Main                                                    *
// Start the event loop                                                       *
// CBI:  4-15.1.1.11                                                          *
//*****************************************************************************

   loApplication.exec();


//*****************************************************************************
// Program Phase 4-15 Main                                                    *
// Cleanup the resources used by the main window                              *
// CBI:  4-15.1.1.12                                                          *
//*****************************************************************************

   return 0;
}
```

mainwindow.h: MainWindow Class Definition for pp4_15.cpp

```
//*****************************************************************************
// File: mainwindow.h                                                         *
// Reserved                                                                   *
//*****************************************************************************

#ifndef MAINWINDOW_H
#define MAINWINDOW_H

#include <QMainWindow>
#include <QtGui>
#include <QAction>
#include <QColor>
#include <QCursor>
```

mainwindow.h continued on the next page

mainwindow.h: MainWindow Class Definition for pp4_15.cpp continued

```
class QAction;
class QMenu;

class MainWindow : public QMainWindow
{
   Q_OBJECT

   public:

      MainWindow();

   protected:

      void closeEvent(QCloseEvent *event);

   private slots:

      void MenuItem1_Click();
      void MenuItem2_Click();

    private:
      bool lFlag;
};

#endif
```

mainwindow.cpp: MainWindow Class Implementation for mainwindow.h

```
//****************************************************************************
// File: mainwindow.cpp                                                      *
// Reserved                                                                  *
//****************************************************************************

#include "mainwindow.h"

MainWindow::MainWindow()
{
   lFlag = true;
}


//****************************************************************************
// Callback Functions                                                        *
// Implement the callback function for the Hello World! menu item            *
// CBI:  4-15.1.2.1                                                          *
//****************************************************************************

void MainWindow::MenuItem1_Click()
{
   QMessageBox::information(0,"Program Phase 4-15","Hello World!",
                            QMessageBox::Ok,QMessageBox::NoButton,
                            QMessageBox::NoButton);
}


//****************************************************************************
// Callback Functions                                                        *
// Implement the callback function for the Exit menu item                    *
// CBI:  4-15.1.3.1                                                          *
//****************************************************************************

void MainWindow::MenuItem2_Click()
{
```

mainwindow.cpp continued on the next page

mainwindow.cpp: MainWindow Class Implementation for mainwindow.h continued

```
   this->lFlag = false;

   // Exit the program if the user activates the Exit menu item
   this->close();
}


//**********************************************************************
// Callback Functions                                                  *
// Implement the callback function that fires when the main window is closed *
// CBI:  4-15.1.4.1                                                    *
//**********************************************************************

void MainWindow::closeEvent(QCloseEvent *toEvent)
{
   int lnResult;

   if (this->lFlag == true)
   {
      // Prompt the user to continue closing the main window
      lnResult = QMessageBox::question(this,"Program Phase 4-15",
                                       "Close the main window?",
                                       QMessageBox::Yes,QMessageBox::No,
                                       QMessageBox::NoButton);

      if (lnResult == QMessageBox::No)
      {
         toEvent->ignore();
      }
      else
      {
         toEvent->accept();
      }
   }
   else
   {
      toEvent->accept();
   }
}
```

resource.qrc: QT Resources File for pp4_15.cpp

```
<!DOCTYPE RCC><RCC version="1.0">
<qresource>
    <file>phase16x16.png</file>
</qresource>
</RCC>
```

Windows Code Setup and Compilation

- Tools: Mingw compiler and the QT4 library (Appendix E)

Windows Code Setup and Compilation Steps

1: Create a folder called pp4_15 that will store the source code files.

2: Using a text editor, enter the source code for the pp4_15.cpp file and then save it in the pp4_15 folder. Also, create the mainwindow.h, mainwindow.cpp, and resource.qrc source code files in the pp4_15 folder and then enter the appropriate source code.

Steps continued on the next page

Windows Code Setup and Compilation Steps continued

3: Open a QT 4 command prompt and then change directories to the pp4_15 folder.

4: Enter the following command:

```
qmake -project
```

5: Create the phase.ico image file according to the instructions in Appendix O. Copy the image file to the pp4_15 folder.

6: Create the phase16x16.png image file according to the instructions in Appendix O. Copy the image file to the pp4_15 folder.

7: Create a new text file called resource.rc and save it in the pp4_15 folder with the following contents:

```
IDI_ICON1 ICON "phase.ico"
```

8:

Edit the pp4_15.pro file that has been generated. Include the following entries:

```
TEMPLATE = app
TARGET =
DEPENDPATH += .
INCLUDEPATH += .

# Input
HEADERS += mainwindow.h
SOURCES += mainwindow.cpp pp4_15.cpp
RESOURCES = resource.qrc
RC_FILE = resource.rc
```

9: After editing the pp4_15.pro file, save and close it and then enter the following commands:

```
qmake pp4_15.pro
make
```

The qmake command creates a file called Makefile, and the make command compiles the program. The steps detailed here create a release executable file that accesses the QT4 library in a shared dll.

Linux Code Setup and Compilation

- Tools: GNU GCC (Appendix B), QT4 Library (Appendix E)

Linux Code Setup and Compilation Steps

1: Create a folder called pp4_15 that will store the source code files.

2: Using a text editor, enter the source code for the pp4_15.cpp file and then save it in the pp4_15 folder. Also, create the mainwindow.h, mainwindow.cpp, and resource.qrc source code files in the pp4_15 folder and then enter the appropriate source code.

3: Open a terminal window and then change directories to the pp4_15 folder.

Steps continued on the next page

Linux Code Setup and Compilation Steps continued

4: Enter the following command:

```
qmake -project
```

5: Create the phase16x16.png image file according to the instructions in Appendix O. Copy the image file to the pp4_15 folder.

6: Edit the pp4_15.pro file that has just been generated. Include the following entries:

```
TEMPLATE = app
TARGET =
DEPENDPATH += .
INCLUDEPATH += .

# Input
HEADERS += mainwindow.h
SOURCES += mainwindow.cpp pp4_15.cpp
RESOURCES = resource.qrc
```

7: After editing the pp4_15.pro file, save and close it and then enter the following commands:

```
qmake pp4_15.pro
make
```

The qmake command creates a file called Makefile, and the make command compiles the program. The steps detailed here create a release executable file that accesses the QT4 library in a shared dll.

Mac OS X Code Setup and Compilation

- Tools: Xcode (Appendix C), QT4 Library (Appendix E)

Mac OS X Code Setup and Compilation Steps

1: Create a folder called pp4_15 that will store the source code files.

2: Using a text editor, enter the source code for the pp4_15.cpp file and then save it in the pp4_15 folder. Also, create the mainwindow.h, mainwindow.cpp, and resource.qrc source code files in the pp4_15 folder and then enter the appropriate source code.

3: Open a terminal window and change directories to the pp4_15 folder.

4: Enter the following commands to create an Xcode project for Program Phase 4-15:

```
qmake -project
qmake -spec macx-xcode
```

5: Create the phase16x16.png image file according to the instructions in Appendix O. Copy the image file to the pp4_15 folder.

6: Start the Xcode IDE program.

Steps continued on the next page

Mac OS X Code Setup and Compilation Steps continued

7: Xcode - Activate Menu Item: File → Open

Select the pp4_15.xcodeproj project file and then activate the "Open" button.

8: Create the phase.icns icon file according to the instructions found in Appendix O.

9: Xcode - Activate Menu Item: Project → Add to Project

Select the phase.icns file and then activate the "Add" button.

10: Xcode - Activate Menu Item: Project → Edit Active Target "pp4_15"

On the "Properties" tab, enter phase.icns for the "Icon File".

11: Xcode - Activate Menu Item: Build → Clean

12: Compile the program by activating the "Build" button.

Windows Program Execution

- To execute the pp4_15 program from a command prompt, change directories to pp4_15\release folder and then enter the following command:

```
pp4_15.exe
```

Linux Program Execution

- To execute the pp4_15 program from a terminal window, change directories to pp4_15/release folder and then enter the following command:

```
./pp4_15
```

Mac OS X Program Execution

- Execute Program

  To execute the pp4_15 program from the Xcode IDE, activate the "Build/Go" button.

- Debug Program

  To debug the pp4_15.cpp file one line at a time, place the cursor at the first line of code in the CBI: 4-15.1.1.3 code block and then create a breakpoint.

```
   Xcode 2.4 - Activate Menu Item: Debug → Add Breakpoint at Current Line
   Xcode 3 - Activate Menu Item: Run → Manage Breakpoints → Add
Breakpoint at Current Line
```

  After the break point has been created, the program can be debugged.

```
   Xcode - Activate Menu Item: Build → Build and Debug
```

Program Phase 4-16

C++ ▪ wxWidgets ▪ Multi-Platform

GUI Based Program with Main Window

- Program Phase Task 4 is implemented in Program Phase 4-16 using the C++ programming language and the wxWidgets library.

- Program Phase 4-16 contains a main source code file named pp4_16.cpp. In addition to the pp4_16.cpp text file, an icon image file called phase16x16.xpm is used as the window icon for the main window. On the Windows platform, the main window and application icons are implemented with the resource.rc text file and phase.ico image file.

Code Block Features

The Program Phase 4-16 code blocks illustrate the following programming features using the C++ programming language and the wxWidgets library:

- **Create a Resizable Main Window for a GUI Based Application**

- **Set the Main Window Icon and Caption**

- **Set the Main Window Menu**

- **Set the Main Window Background Color and Mouse Cursor**

- **Prompt to Exit the Application when the Main Window is Closed**

C++ with wxWidgets
Create a Resizable Main Window for a GUI Based Application

- The main window is created from a class based on the wxFrame class found in the wxWidgets library.

- The border of the main window is set to be resizable by calling the SetWindowStyle() method with the "wxDEFAULT_FRAME_STYLE" parameter. This style includes all of the following styles:

```
   wxMINIMIZE_BOX | wxMAXIMIZE_BOX | wxRESIZE_BORDER | wxSYSTEM_MENU |
wxCAPTION | wxCLOSE_BOX | wxCLIP_CHILDREN
```

- Returning a Boolean "true" value from the OnInit() method will start the event loop for the program. This loop prevents the program from automatically exiting. The event loop exits when the main window wxFrame instance is closed since no more wxFrame windows are visible. The main window wxFrame object is destroyed in the following example when the window is closed.

test1.cpp: C++ wxWidgets Create a Resizable Main Window for a GUI Application

```
#include "wx/wx.h"

class pp4_16 : public wxApp
{
public:
    virtual bool OnInit();
};

class MainWindow : public wxFrame
{
public:
    MainWindow();
};

IMPLEMENT_APP(pp4_16)

bool pp4_16::OnInit()
{
   MainWindow* loMainWindow;

   // Create the main window
   loMainWindow = new MainWindow();
   loMainWindow->SetWindowStyle(wxDEFAULT_FRAME_STYLE);

   // Maximize and display the main window
   loMainWindow->Maximize(true);
   loMainWindow->Show(true);

   // Start the event loop
   return true;
}

MainWindow::MainWindow() : wxFrame(NULL, wxID_ANY, wxT(""))
{
}
```

C++ wxWidgets
Set the Main Window Icon and Caption

- The wxICON() macro is used along with the wxIcon class to create an icon object that is assigned to the main window using the SetIcon() method of the main window wxFrame instance. On the Windows platform, the wxICON() macro returns a value appropriate for referencing the phase.ico file specified in the resource.rc file. On the Linux platform, the wxICON() macro returns a value appropriate for accessing the icon defined in the phase16x16.xpm image file.

- Instructions for creating the phase16x16.xpm (renamed to phase.xpm for Program Phase 4-16) and phase.ico file are found in Appendix O.

- The SetTitle() method of the main window wxFrame object is used to set the caption of the main window.

test2.cpp: C++ wxWidgets Set the Main Window Icon and Caption

```
#include "wx/wx.h"
#include "phase.xpm"

class test2 : public wxApp
{
```

test2.cpp continued on the next page

test2.cpp: C++ wxWidgets Set the Main Window Icon and Caption continued

```
public:
    virtual bool OnInit();
};

class MainWindow : public wxFrame
{
public:
    MainWindow();
};
IMPLEMENT_APP(test2)

bool test2::OnInit()
{
   MainWindow* loMainWindow;
   wxIcon loIcon(wxICON(phase));

   // Create the main window
   loMainWindow = new MainWindow();
   loMainWindow->SetWindowStyle(wxDEFAULT_FRAME_STYLE);

   // Set the main window icon
   loMainWindow->SetIcon(loIcon);

   // Set the main window caption
   loMainWindow->SetTitle(wxT("Hello World!"));

   // Maximize and display the main window
   loMainWindow->Maximize(true);
   loMainWindow->Show(true);

   // Start the event loop
   return true;
}

MainWindow::MainWindow() : wxFrame(NULL, wxID_ANY, wxT(""))
{
}
```

resource.rc: Resource File for the phase.ico Icon File

```
phase ICON phase.ico
```

C++ wxWidgets Set the Main Window Menu

- The following example creates a "File" menu with a "Hello World!" menu item and "Exit" menu item:

test3.cpp: C++ wxWidgets Set the Main Window Menu

```
#include "wx/wx.h"
#define IDM_MENUITEM1 100
#define IDM_MENUITEM2 wxID_EXIT

class test3 : public wxApp
{
public:
    virtual bool OnInit();
};
```

test3.cpp continued on the next page

test3.cpp: C++ wxWidgets Set the Main Window Menu continued

```
class MainWindow : public wxFrame
{
public:
    MainWindow();
    void MenuItem1_Activate(wxCommandEvent& event);
    void MenuItem2_Activate(wxCommandEvent& event);

private:
    DECLARE_EVENT_TABLE()
};

IMPLEMENT_APP(test3)

BEGIN_EVENT_TABLE(MainWindow, wxFrame)
    EVT_MENU(IDM_MENUITEM1,MainWindow::MenuItem1_Activate)
    EVT_MENU(IDM_MENUITEM2,MainWindow::MenuItem2_Activate)
END_EVENT_TABLE()


bool test3::OnInit()
{
   MainWindow* loMainWindow;
   wxMenuBar* loMenuBar;
   wxMenu* loFileMenu;

   // Create the main window
   loMainWindow = new MainWindow();
   loMainWindow->SetWindowStyle(wxDEFAULT_FRAME_STYLE);

   // Menu bar
   loMenuBar = new wxMenuBar();

   // File Menu
   loFileMenu = new wxMenu;
   loMenuBar->Append(loFileMenu,wxT("&File"));

   // Hello World! Menu Item
   loFileMenu->Append(IDM_MENUITEM1,wxT("&Hello World\tCtrl-H"),
                      wxT("Show Hello World!"));

   // Exit Menu Item
   loFileMenu->Append(IDM_MENUITEM2,wxT("E&xit\tCtrl-X"),
                      wxT("Quit this program"));

   // Assign the File menu to the main window
   loMainWindow->SetMenuBar(loMenuBar);

   // Maximize and display the main window
   loMainWindow->Maximize(true);
   loMainWindow->Show(true);

   // Start the event loop
   return true;
}

MainWindow::MainWindow() : wxFrame(NULL, wxID_ANY, wxT(""))
{
}

void MainWindow::MenuItem1_Activate(wxCommandEvent& toEvent)
{
   wxMessageBox(wxT("Hello World!"),wxT("test"),
               wxOK | wxICON_INFORMATION,this);
}
```

test3.cpp continued on the next page

test3.cpp: C++ wxWidgets Set the Main Window Menu continued

```
void MainWindow::MenuItem2_Activate(wxCommandEvent& toEvent)
{
   this->Destroy();
}
```

C++ wxWidgets
Set the Main Window Background Color and Mouse Cursor

- The following example sets the main window background color and mouse cursor:

test4.cpp: C++ wxWidgets Set the Main Window Background Color and Mouse Cursor

```
#include "wx/wx.h"

class test4 : public wxApp
{
public:
    virtual bool OnInit();
};

IMPLEMENT_APP(test4)

class MainWindow : public wxFrame
{
public:
    MainWindow();
};

bool test4::OnInit()
{
   MainWindow* loMainWindow;
   wxColour* loWindowBackColor;
   wxCursor* loMouseCursor;

   // Create the main window
   loMainWindow = new MainWindow();
   loMainWindow->SetWindowStyle(wxDEFAULT_FRAME_STYLE);

   // Set the main window background color
   loWindowBackColor = new wxColour(255,255,255);
   loMainWindow->SetBackgroundColour(*loWindowBackColor);

   // Set the main window mouse cursor
   loMouseCursor = new wxCursor(wxCURSOR_ARROW);
   loMainWindow->SetCursor(*loMouseCursor);

   // Maximize and display the main window
   loMainWindow->Maximize(true);
   loMainWindow->Show(true);

   // Start the event loop
   return true;
}

MainWindow::MainWindow() : wxFrame(NULL, wxID_ANY, wxT(""))
{
}
```

C++ wxWidgets
Prompt to Exit the Application when the Main Window is Closed

- The MainWindow::MainWindow_Closing() callback function is assigned to the main window wxFrame instance by using the EVT_CLOSE() macro in the event table declaration.

- The wxMessageDialog class is used to prompt the user to continue closing the main window. If the user selects the "Yes" button, the Destroy() method of the main window wxFrame instance is called. If the user selects the "No" button, the Veto() method of the event object is called, causing the main window to remain visible.

test5.cpp: C++ wxWidgets Prompt to Exit the App. when the Main Window is Closed

```
#include "wx/wx.h"

class test5 : public wxApp
{
public:
    virtual bool OnInit();
};

class MainWindow : public wxFrame
{
public:
    MainWindow();
    void MainWindow_Closing(wxCloseEvent& event);

private:
    DECLARE_EVENT_TABLE()
};

IMPLEMENT_APP(test5)

BEGIN_EVENT_TABLE(MainWindow, wxFrame)
    EVT_CLOSE(MainWindow::MainWindow_Closing)
END_EVENT_TABLE()

bool test5::OnInit()
{
   MainWindow* loMainWindow;

   // Create the main window
   loMainWindow = new MainWindow();
   loMainWindow->SetWindowStyle(wxDEFAULT_FRAME_STYLE);

   // Maximize and display the main window
   loMainWindow->Maximize(true);
   loMainWindow->Show(true);

// Start the event loop
   return true;
}

MainWindow::MainWindow() : wxFrame(NULL, wxID_ANY, wxT(""))
{
}

void MainWindow::MainWindow_Closing(wxCloseEvent& toEvent)
{
   wxMessageDialog* loMessageBox;
   int lnResult;
```

test5.cpp continued on the next page

test5.cpp: C++ wxWidgets Prompt to Exit when the Main Window is Closed continued

```
   // Prompt the user to continue closing the main window
   loMessageBox = new wxMessageDialog(this,"Close the main window?",
                                      "test",wxYES_NO);

   lnResult = loMessageBox->ShowModal();
   loMessageBox->Destroy();

   if (lnResult == wxID_YES)
   {
      this->Destroy();
   }
   else
   {
      if (toEvent.CanVeto() == false)
      {
         this->Destroy();
      }
      else
      {
         toEvent.Veto();
      }
   }
}
```

Source Code Files

- Text files: pp4_16.cpp, resource.rc
- Image files:

    phase.ico (Multi-image icon file, Appendix O, page O1)

    phase16x16.xpm (Single-image icon file, Appendix O, page O6)

pp4_16.cpp: Program Phase 4-16 Source Code

```
//***************************************************************************
// Program Phase 4-16 C++ wxWidgets Main Window with File Menu             *
// Programming Tasks Illustrated: wxWidgets GUI based application          *
//                                Main window                              *
//                                Window icon                              *
//                                Window caption                           *
//                                Window menu with hotkeys                 *
//                                Window background color                  *
//                                Window mouse cursor                      *
//                                User sizable window                      *
//                                Message box input/output                 *
//***************************************************************************

//***************************************************************************
// File: pp4_16.cpp                                                         *
// Reserved                                                                 *
//***************************************************************************

#include "wx/wx.h"
#include "phase.xpm"

#define IDM_MENUITEM1 100
#define IDM_MENUITEM2 wxID_EXIT

class pp4_16 : public wxApp
{
```

pp4_16.cpp continued on the next page

pp4_16.cpp: Program Phase 4-16 Source Code continued

```
public:
    virtual bool OnInit();
};

class MainWindow : public wxFrame
{
public:
    MainWindow();
    void MenuItem1_Activate(wxCommandEvent& event);
    void MenuItem2_Activate(wxCommandEvent& event);
    void MainWindow_Closing(wxCloseEvent& event);

private:
    DECLARE_EVENT_TABLE()
};

DECLARE_APP(pp4_16)
IMPLEMENT_APP(pp4_16)

BEGIN_EVENT_TABLE(MainWindow, wxFrame)
    EVT_MENU(IDM_MENUITEM1,MainWindow::MenuItem1_Activate)
    EVT_MENU(IDM_MENUITEM2,MainWindow::MenuItem2_Activate)
    EVT_CLOSE(MainWindow::MainWindow_Closing)
END_EVENT_TABLE()


//***********************************************************************
// Program Phase 4-16 Main                                               *
// Define the Entry Point of Execution (EPE) for Program Phase 4-16      *
// CBI:  4-16.1.1.1                                                      *
//***********************************************************************

bool pp4_16::OnInit()
{


//***********************************************************************
// Program Phase 4-16 Main                                               *
// Declare the local variables for the "main" program                    *
// CBI:  4-16.1.1.2                                                      *
//***********************************************************************

   // Main window
   MainWindow* loMainWindow;

   // Main window icon
   wxIcon loIcon(wxICON(phase));

   // Main window caption
   wxString lcWindowCaption;


   // Main window menu
   wxMenu* loFileMenu;
   wxMenuBar* loMenuBar;

   // Main window background color
   wxColour* loWindowBackColor;

   // Main window mouse cursor
   wxCursor* loMouseCursor;
```

pp4_16.cpp continued on the next page

pp4_16.cpp: Program Phase 4-16 Source Code continued

```
//****************************************************************************
// Program Phase 4-16 Main                                                   *
// Create the main window                                                    *
// CBI:  4-16.1.1.3                                                          *
//****************************************************************************

   loMainWindow = new MainWindow();


//****************************************************************************
// Program Phase 4-16 Main                                                   *
// Set the icon for the main window                                          *
// CBI:  4-16.1.1.4                                                          *
//****************************************************************************

   loMainWindow->SetIcon(loIcon);


//****************************************************************************
// Program Phase 4-16 Main                                                   *
// Set the caption of the main window                                        *
// CBI:  4-16.1.1.5                                                          *
//****************************************************************************

   lcWindowCaption = wxT("Program Phase 4-16  |  "
                         "Platform:  Windows  |  "
                         "Programming Language:  C++  |  "
                         "GUI API:  wxWidgets");

   loMainWindow->SetTitle(lcWindowCaption);


//****************************************************************************
// Program Phase 4-16 Main                                                   *
// Create the menu for the main window                                       *
// CBI:  4-16.1.1.6                                                          *
//****************************************************************************

   // Menu bar
   loMenuBar = new wxMenuBar();

   // File Menu
   loFileMenu = new wxMenu;
   loMenuBar->Append(loFileMenu,wxT("&File"));

   // Hello World! Menu Item
   loFileMenu->Append(IDM_MENUITEM1,wxT("&Hello World\tCtrl-H"),
                      wxT("Show about dialog"));

   // Exit Menu Item
   loFileMenu->Append(IDM_MENUITEM2,wxT("E&xit\tCtrl-X"),
                      wxT("Quit this program"));

   // Assign the File menu to the main window
   loMainWindow->SetMenuBar(loMenuBar);


//****************************************************************************
// Program Phase 4-16 Main                                                   *
// Set the background color of the main window                               *
// CBI:  4-16.1.1.7                                                          *
//****************************************************************************

   loWindowBackColor = new wxColour(255,255,255);
   loMainWindow->SetBackgroundColour(*loWindowBackColor);
```

pp4_16.cpp continued on the next page

pp4_16.cpp: Program Phase 4-16 Source Code continued

```
//****************************************************************************
// Program Phase 4-16 Main                                                   *
// Set the mouse cursor displayed when positoned over the main window        *
// CBI:  4-16.1.1.8                                                          *
//****************************************************************************

   loMouseCursor = new wxCursor(wxCURSOR_ARROW);
   loMainWindow->SetCursor(*loMouseCursor);


//****************************************************************************
// Program Phase 4-16 Main                                                   *
// Allow resizing of the main window                                         *
// CBI:  4-16.1.1.9                                                          *
//****************************************************************************

   loMainWindow->SetWindowStyle(wxDEFAULT_FRAME_STYLE);


//****************************************************************************
// Program Phase 4-16 Main                                                   *
// Maximize and display the main window                                      *
// CBI:  4-16.1.1.10                                                         *
//****************************************************************************

   loMainWindow->Maximize(true);
   loMainWindow->Show(true);


//****************************************************************************
// Program Phase 4-16 Main                                                   *
// Start the  event loop                                                     *
// CBI:  4-16.1.1.11                                                         *
//****************************************************************************

   return true;


//****************************************************************************
// Program Phase 4-16 Main                                                   *
// Cleanup the resources used by the main window                             *
// CBI:  4-16.1.1.12                                                         *
//****************************************************************************

}


//****************************************************************************
// Callback Functions                                                        *
// Implement the callback function for the Hello World! menu item            *
// CBI:  4-16.1.2.1                                                          *
//****************************************************************************

void MainWindow::MenuItem1_Activate(wxCommandEvent& toEvent)
{
   wxMessageBox(wxT("Hello World!"),wxT("Program Phase 4-16"),
                wxOK | wxICON_INFORMATION,this);
}


//****************************************************************************
// Callback Functions                                                        *
// Implement the callback function for the Exit menu item                    *
// CBI:  4-16.1.3.1                                                          *
//****************************************************************************
```

pp4_16.cpp continued on the next page

pp4_16.cpp: Program Phase 4-16 Source Code continued

```
void MainWindow::MenuItem2_Activate(wxCommandEvent& toEvent)
{
   this->Destroy();
}

//****************************************************************************
// Callback Functions                                                        *
// Implement the callback function that fires when the main window is closed *
// CBI:  4-16.1.4.1                                                          *
//****************************************************************************

void MainWindow::MainWindow_Closing(wxCloseEvent& toEvent)
{
   wxMessageDialog* loMessageBox;
   int lnResult;

   loMessageBox = new wxMessageDialog(this,"Close the main window?",
                                      "Program Phase 4-16",wxYES_NO);

   lnResult = loMessageBox->ShowModal();

   loMessageBox->Destroy();

   if (lnResult == wxID_YES)
   {
      this->Destroy();
   }
   else
   {
      if (toEvent.CanVeto() == false)
      {
         this->Destroy();
      }
      else
      {
         toEvent.Veto();
      }
   }
}

MainWindow::MainWindow() : wxFrame(NULL, wxID_ANY, wxT(""))
{}
```

resource.rc: Resource File for Creating the resource.res File (Windows only)

```
phase ICON phase.ico
```

Windows – Code Setup and Compilation

- Tools: Microsoft Visual Studio 2008 Express Edition (msdn.microsoft.com), wxWidgets library (Appendix D)

Windows Code Setup and Compilation Steps

1: Start the Visual C++ 2008 Express Edition program.

Steps continued on the next page

Windows Code Setup and Compilation Steps continued

2: VC++ EE - Activate Menu Item: File → New → Project

For the "Project type", select "Win32" and then select the "Win32 Console Application" template. Enter pp4_16 as the project "Name". Enter the appropriate folder as the "Project Location". Make sure that the "Create directory for solution" check box is not checked. Activate the "OK" button to proceed with the "Win32 Application Wizard".

3: Activate the "Next" button of the "Win32 Application Wizard".

4: Verify that a "Console Application" is selected and also check the "Empty project" check box. Activate the "Finish" button of the "Win32 Application Wizard".

5: VC++ EE - Activate Menu Item: Project → Add New Item

On the "Add New Item" dialog window, select the "Visual C++ → Code" category and then select the "C++ File" template. Enter pp4_16.cpp for the file "Name" and then activate the "Add" button.

6: Enter the source code for the pp4_16.cpp file.

7: Create the phase.ico file according to the instructions found in Appendix O. Save the image file to the pp4_16 folder.

8: Using a text editor, create the resource.rc file and then enter the appropriate source code. Copy the resource.rc file to the pp4_16 folder.

9: VC++ EE - Activate Menu Item: Project → Add Existing Item

Select the resource.rc file in the pp4_16 folder.

10: Create the phase16x16.xpm file according to the instructions in Appendix O. Copy the file to the pp4_16 folder and then rename it to phase.xpm. Open the phase.xpm file with a text editor and then change the string value in the text file from phase16x16.xpm to phase.xpm.

11: VC++ EE - Activate Menu Item: Build → Configuration Manager

Select "Release" or "Debug" for the Active solution configuration. This setting needs to match the setting specified when the wxWidgets library was compiled (Appendix D).

12: VC++ EE - Activate Menu Item: Project → pp4_16 Properties

Enter the following settings:

Configuration Properties → General → Character Set

For ANSI Configuration:

```
"Use Multi-Byte Character Set"
```

For Unicode Configuration:

```
"Use Unicode Character Set"
```

Configuration Properties → C/C++ → General → Additional Include Directories

```
"$(wxwin)\lib\vc_lib\msw";"$(wxwin)\include"
```

Steps continued on the next page

Windows Code Setup and Compilation Steps continued

13: Continue entering settings on the "pp4_16 Property Pages" window.

Configuration Properties → C/C++ → Preprocessor → Processor Definitions

```
For Release Configuration:  WIN32;__WXMSW__;_WINDOWS;NOPCH

For Debug Configuration:  WIN32;__WXMSW__;_WINDOWS;__WXDEBUG__;NOPCH
```

Configuration Properties → C/C++ → Code Generation → Runtime Library

For Release Configuration:

```
Multi-threaded (/MT) or Multi-threaded DLL (/MD)
```

For Debug Configuration:

```
Multi-threaded Debug /MTd or Multi-threaded Debug DLL (/MDd)
```

This setting needs to match the setting specified when the wxWidgets library was compiled (Appendix D).

Configuration Properties → Linker → General → Additional Library Directories

```
"$(wxwin)\lib\vc_lib"
```

Configuration Properties → Linker -> Input → Additional Dependencies

For Release Configuration:

```
wxmsw28_core.lib wxbase28.lib comctl32.lib rpcrt4.lib
```

For Debug Configuration:

```
wxmsw28d_core.lib wxbase28d.lib comctl32.lib rpcrt4.lib
```

Substitute the appropriate version number in the file name to match the version of the wxWidgets library installed on your computer.

Configuration Properties → Linker → System → SubSystem

```
Windows (/SUBSYSTEM:WINDOWS)
```

14: Close the "pp4_16 Property Pages" by activating the "OK" button.

15: VC++ EE - Activate Menu Item: Build → Build pp4_16

Windows Command Prompt Compilation Steps

1: From a Visual Studio 2008 command prompt, enter the following command:

For Release Configuration:

```
cl.exe /I "C:\Program Files\Microsoft SDK's\Windows\v6.0A\Include"
/I "c:\wxWidgets-2.8.6\lib\vc_lib\msw"
/I "c:\wxWidgets-2.8.6\include"
/D "WIN32"
/D "__WXMSW__"
/D "_WINDOWS"
/MT /Fo"Release\\" /EHsc /c pp4_16.cpp
```

Steps continued on the next page

Windows Command Prompt Compilation Steps continued

For Debug Configuration:

```
cl.exe /I "C:\Program Files\Microsoft SDK's\Windows\v6.0A\Include"
/I "c:\wxWidgets-2.8.6\lib\vc_lib\msw"
/I "c:\wxWidgets-2.8.6\include"
/D "WIN32"
/D "__WXMSW__"
/D "__WXDEBUG__"
/D "_WINDOWS"
/MTd /Fo"Debug\\" /EHsc /c pp4_16.cpp
```

The preceding commands need to be entered on a single line.

2: Compile the resource file into the resource.res file.

```
rc.exe resource.rc
```

3: To create the pp4_16.exe file, the pp4_16.obj and resource.res files must be linked.

For Release Configuration:

```
link.exe /OUT:"pp4_16.exe" /INCREMENTAL:NO
/LIBPATH:"c:\wxWidgets-2.8.6\lib\vc_lib"
/LIBPATH:"C:\Program Files\Microsoft SDK's\Windows\v6.0A\Lib"
/SUBSYSTEM:WINDOWS
wxmsw28_core.lib wxbase28.lib winmm.lib comctl32.lib rpcrt4.lib
wsock32.lib oleacc.lib  kernel32.lib user32.lib gdi32.lib winspool.lib
comdlg32.lib advapi32.lib shell32.lib ole32.lib oleaut32.lib uuid.lib
.\release\pp4_16.obj resource.res
```

For Debug Configuration:

```
link.exe /OUT:"pp4_16.exe" /INCREMENTAL:NO
/LIBPATH:"c:\wxWidgets-2.8.6\lib\vc_lib"
/LIBPATH:"C:\Program Files\Microsoft SDK's\Windows\v6.0A\Lib"
/SUBSYSTEM:WINDOWS
wxmsw28d_core.lib wxbase28d.lib winmm.lib comctl32.lib rpcrt4.lib
wsock32.lib oleacc.lib  kernel32.lib user32.lib gdi32.lib winspool.lib
comdlg32.lib advapi32.lib shell32.lib ole32.lib oleaut32.lib uuid.lib
.\debug\pp4_16.obj resource.res
```

The preceding commands need to be entered on a single line.

Linux – Code Setup and Compilation

- Tools: GNU GCC, KDevelop (Appendix B), wxWidgets library (Appendix D)

Linux Code Setup and Compilation Steps

1: Update the LD_LIBRARY_PATH variable and then start the KDevelop program.

```
export LD_LIBRARY_PATH=/usr/local/lib:$LD_LIBRARY_PATH
kdevelop &
```

2: KDevelop - Activate Menu Item: Project → New Project

Select the "C++ → Simple Hello world program" template and then activate the "Next" button. Set the "Application name" to pp4_16. Set the "Location" to the appropriate folder. Activate the "Next" button four times and then activate the "Finish" button.

Steps continued on the next page

Linux Code Setup and Compilation Steps continued

3: KDevelop - Activate Menu Item: Project → Build Configuration → debug

4: Enter the appropriate source code for the pp4_16.cpp file.

5: Create the phase16x16.xpm file according to the instructions found in Appendix O. Copy the file to the pp4_16/src folder and then rename it to phase.xpm. Open the phase.xpm file with a text editor and then change the string value in the text file from phase16x16_xpm to phase_xpm.

6: Before compiling the source code files, additional settings for accessing the wxWidgets library need to be entered into the KDevelop project. From a terminal window, enter the following:

```
For Release Configuration:

   wx-config --unicode=no --debug=no --static=yes --cxxflags >
cxxresults.txt

For Debug Configuration:

   wx-config --unicode=no --debug=yes --static=yes --cxxflags >
cxxresults.txt
```

The above settings need to match the settings specified when the wxWidgets library was compiled (Appendix D). This causes the output of the wx-config command to be stored in the text file called cxxresults.txt.

7: Next, run this command:

```
For Release Configuration:

  wx-config --unicode=no --debug=no --static=yes --libs > libresults.txt

For Debug Configuration:

  wx-config --unicode=no --debug=yes --static=yes --libs > libresults.txt
```

The above settings need to match the settings specified when the wxWidgets library was compiled (Appendix D). This command results in the output being stored in the libresults.txt file.

8: KDevelop - Activate Menu Item: Project → Project Options

Click on the "Configure Options" item in the left pane. Select the "debug" configuration. Click on the "C++" tab. Here you will see the "Compiler flags" textbox. The results of running the wx-config utility stored in the cxxresults.txt file must be copied and pasted here. Next, click on the "General" tab and then paste the contents of the libresults.txt file in the "Linker flags" textbox. You may be prompted to "Re-run configure". Select the "Do Not Run" button.

9: KDevelop - Activate Menu Item: Build → Run automake and friends

10: KDevelop - Activate Menu Item: Build → Run Configure

11: KDevelop - Activate Menu Item: Build → Build Project

If you get a message concerning no Makefile, activate the "Run Them" button.

```
Linux Command Prompt Compilation
```

```
For Release Configuration:

g++ pp4_16.cpp `wx-config --unicode=no --debug=no --static=yes --libs`
`wx-config --unicode=no --debug=no --static=yes --cxxflags` -o pp4_16

For Debug Configuration:

g++ pp4_16.cpp `wx-config --unicode=no --debug=yes --static=yes --libs`
`wx-config --unicode=no --debug=yes --static=yes --cxxflags` -o pp4_16
```

The preceding commands should be entered on a single line inside the source code folder (pp4_16/src). The command line settings need to match the settings specified when the wxWidgets library was compiled (Appendix D).

- Mac OS X code setup and compilation steps can be found at the following URL:

  `http://www.wxwidgets.org/wiki/index.php/Getting_started_on_OS_X`

Windows – Program Execution

- Execute Program

  ```
  VC++ EE - Activate Menu Item: Debug → Start Without Debugging
  ```

- Debug Program

  To debug the pp4_16.cpp file one line at a time, set the "Generate Debug Info" entry in the "pp4_16 Property Pages" to "Yes". This setting is found in the "pp4_16 Property Pages" under the "Configuration Properties → Linker → Debugging" entry. After this has been set, the program can be debugged.

  ```
  VC++ EE - Activate Menu Item: Debug → Step Into
  ```

Linux – Program Execution

- Execute Program

  ```
  KDevelop - Activate Menu Item: Build → Execute Program
  ```

- Debug Program

  ```
  KDevelop - Activate Menu Item: Project → Project Options
  ```

  Click on the "Configure Options" item. Select the "debug configuration" and then enter "--enable-debug=full" in the "Configure arguments" field on the "General" tab. Close the "Project Options" dialog window.

  Select the debug configuration for the project.

  ```
  KDevelop - Activate Menu Item: Project → Build Configuration
  ```

  Set the cursor position in the source file to the first line of code in the CBI: 4-16.1.1.3 code block. Create a breakpoint.

  ```
  KDevelop - Activate Menu Item: Debug → Toggle Breakpoint
  KDevelop - Activate Menu Item: Debug → Start
  ```

Program Phase 4-17

C ▪ Carbon ▪ Mac OS X

GUI Based Program with Main Window

- Program Phase Task 4 is implemented in Program Phase 4-17 using the C programming language and the Carbon API.
- Program Phase 4-17 contains a single source code file named pp4_17.c. In addition to the pp4_17.c text file, an image file called phase.icns is used to represent the icon for the application.

Code Block Features

The Program Phase 4-17 code blocks illustrate the following programming features using the C programming language and the Carbon API:

- **Create a Resizable Main Window for a GUI Based Application**
- **Set the Main Window Caption**
- **Set the Main Window Menu**
- **Set the Main Window Background Color and Mouse Cursor**
- **Prompt to Exit the Application when the Main Window is Closed**

C with Carbon
Create a Resizable Main Window for a GUI Based Application

- The Carbon CreateNewWindow() function is used to create the main window.
- The first parameter to the CreateNewWindow() function indicates the window class from which the window is created. The "kDocumentWindowClass" parameter value indicates that a standard document window is created. Additional window features are specified in the second parameter to the CreateNewWindow() function in the form of window attributes. The "kWindowResizableAttribute" can be specified in the second parameter to the CreateNewWindow() function or it can be set with the ChangeWindowAttributes() function. The initial dimensions of the window are specified in a "rect" structure passed as the third parameter to the CreateNewWindow() function. The last parameter to the CreateNewWindow() function is a variable that holds a reference to the created main window.
- The GetRegionBounds() function, along with the GetGreyRgn() function, is called to retrieve the size of the desktop. The ZoomWindowIdeal() function uses this information to maximize the main window. The window is made visible with the ShowWindow() function.

- The RunApplicationEventLoop() function starts the event loop for the application. This prevents the program from automatically exiting until the "Quit" menu item is activated from the automatically created application menu.

- The application does not exit automatically when the main window is closed. Most Mac OS X applications will continue running with an application menu being displayed even when the main window is closed.

test1.c: C with Carbon Create a Resizable Main Window for a GUI Based Application

```
#include <Carbon/Carbon.h>

int main(int argc, const char *argv[])
{
   WindowRef loMainWindow = NULL;
   Rect loRect;
   Point loIdealSize;
   OSStatus lnError = noErr;

   loRect.left = 0;
   loRect.right = 640;
   loRect.top = 60;
   loRect.bottom = 560;

   // Create the main window
   lnError = CreateNewWindow(kDocumentWindowClass,
                             kWindowCloseBoxAttribute |
                             kWindowFullZoomAttribute |
                             kWindowCollapseBoxAttribute |
                             kWindowStandardHandlerAttribute,
                             &loRect,&loMainWindow);

   if (lnError != noErr || loMainWindow == NULL)
   {
      return EXIT_FAILURE;
   }

   // Set the window to be resizable.
   ChangeWindowAttributes(loMainWindow,kWindowResizableAttribute,NULL);

   // Maximize and display the main window
   GetRegionBounds(GetGrayRgn(),&loRect);
   loIdealSize.h = loRect.right - loRect.left;
   loIdealSize.v = loRect.bottom - loRect.top;
   ZoomWindowIdeal(loMainWindow,inZoomOut,&loIdealSize);
   ShowWindow(loMainWindow);

   // Start the event loop
   RunApplicationEventLoop();

   return EXIT_SUCCESS;
}
```

C with Carbon
Set the Main Window Icon and Caption

- Program Phase 4-17 does not implement an icon for the main window. An icon is set for the application. See the Code Setup and Compilation instructions for more information concerning the application icon.

- The kWindowStandardDocumentAttributes constant includes the following: kWindowCloseBoxAttribute, kWindowFullZoomAttribute, kWindowCollapseBoxAttribute., and kWindowResizableAttribute.

- The SetWTitle() function is called to set the caption of the main window.

test2.c: C with Carbon Set the Main Window Caption

```
#include <Carbon/Carbon.h>

int main(int argc, const char *argv[])
{
   WindowRef loMainWindow = NULL;

   Rect loRect;
   Point loIdealSize;
   OSStatus lnError = noErr;

   loRect.left = 0;
   loRect.right = 640;
   loRect.top = 60;
   loRect.bottom = 560;

   // Create the main window
   lnError = CreateNewWindow(kDocumentWindowClass,
                             kWindowStandardDocumentAttributes |
                             kWindowStandardHandlerAttribute,
                             &loRect,&loMainWindow);

   if (lnError != noErr || loMainWindow == NULL)
   {
      return EXIT_FAILURE;
   }

   // Set the main window caption
   SetWTitle(loMainWindow,"\p Hello World");

   // Maximize and display the main window
   GetRegionBounds(GetGrayRgn(),&loRect);
   loIdealSize.h = loRect.right - loRect.left;
   loIdealSize.v = loRect.bottom - loRect.top;
   ZoomWindowIdeal(loMainWindow,inZoomOut,&loIdealSize);
   ShowWindow(loMainWindow);

   // Start the event loop
   RunApplicationEventLoop();
   return EXIT_SUCCESS;
}
```

C with Carbon
Set the Main Window Menu

- The following example creates a "File" menu with a "Hello World!" menu item and "Exit" menu item:

test3.c: C with Carbon Set the Main Window Menu

```
#include <Carbon/Carbon.h>

static pascal OSStatus MyAppEventHandler (EventHandlerCallRef myHandlerChain,
                                          EventRef event, void* userData);

int main(int argc, const char *argv[])
{
   WindowRef loMainWindow = NULL;
   Rect loRect;
   Point loIdealSize;
   OSStatus lnError = noErr;
```

test3.c continued on the next page

test3.c: C with Carbon Set the Main Window Menu continued

```
   MenuRef loMenuBar;
   MenuRef loFileMenu;


   MenuItemIndex loMenuItemIndex1;
   MenuItemIndex loMenuItemIndex2;
   MenuItemIndex loFileMenuIndex;

   loRect.left = 0;
   loRect.right = 640;
   loRect.top = 60;
   loRect.bottom = 560;

   // Create the main window
   lnError = CreateNewWindow(kDocumentWindowClass,
                             kWindowStandardDocumentAttributes |
                             kWindowStandardHandlerAttribute,
                             &loRect,
                             &loMainWindow);

   if (lnError != noErr || loMainWindow == NULL)
   {
      return EXIT_FAILURE;
   }

  EventTypeSpec laAppEventList[] = {{kEventClassCommand,kEventCommandProcess}};

   InstallApplicationEventHandler(NewEventHandlerUPP(MyAppEventHandler),1,
                                  laAppEventList,0,NULL);

   // Menu bar
   CreateNewMenu(0,0,&loMenuBar);

   // File menu
   CreateNewMenu(1,0,&loFileMenu);
   SetMenuTitleWithCFString(loFileMenu,CFSTR("File"));
   AppendMenuItemTextWithCFString(loMenuBar,NULL,0,0,&loFileMenuIndex);
   SetMenuItemHierarchicalMenu(loMenuBar,loFileMenuIndex,loFileMenu);

   // Hello World! menu item
   AppendMenuItemTextWithCFString(loFileMenu,CFSTR("Hello World!"),0,100,
                                  &loMenuItemIndex1);

   SetItemCmd(loFileMenu,loMenuItemIndex1,'H');

   // Exit menu item
   AppendMenuItemTextWithCFString(loFileMenu,CFSTR("Exit"),0,101,
                                  &loMenuItemIndex2);

   SetItemCmd(loFileMenu,loMenuItemIndex2,'X');

   // Assign the menu bar to the main window
   SetRootMenu(loMenuBar);

   // Maximize and display the main window
   GetRegionBounds(GetGrayRgn(),&loRect);
   loIdealSize.h = loRect.right - loRect.left;
   loIdealSize.v = loRect.bottom - loRect.top;
   ZoomWindowIdeal(loMainWindow,inZoomOut,&loIdealSize);
   ShowWindow(loMainWindow);

   // Start the event loop
   RunApplicationEventLoop();
   return EXIT_SUCCESS;
}
```

test3.c continued on the next page

test3.c: C with Carbon Set the Main Window Menu continued

```
static pascal OSStatus MyAppEventHandler(EventHandlerCallRef toHandlerChain,
                                         EventRef toEvent, void* toUserData)
{
   UInt32 lnEventKind;
   HICommand loCommandStruct;
   short lnResult;
   AlertStdAlertParamRec loParamRec = {};
   WindowPtr loWindowPtr;

   lnEventKind = GetEventKind(toEvent);

   switch (lnEventKind)
   {
      case kEventCommandProcess:

         GetEventParameter(toEvent,kEventParamDirectObject,typeHICommand,NULL,
                           sizeof(HICommand),NULL,&loCommandStruct);

         switch (loCommandStruct.commandID)
         {
            case 100:

               loParamRec.defaultText = "\pOK";
               loParamRec.cancelText = nil;
               loParamRec.defaultButton = kStdOkItemIndex;
               loParamRec.position = kWindowAlertPositionParentWindowScreen;

               StandardAlert(kAlertStopAlert,"\pHello World!","\ptest",
                             &loParamRec,&lnResult);
               break;

            case 101:

               loWindowPtr = FrontWindow();


               if (loWindowPtr != nil)
               {
                  DisposeWindow(loWindowPtr);
               }

               ExitToShell();
               break;

            default:
               break;
         }

         break;

      default:
         break;
   }
   return eventNotHandledErr;
}
```

C with Carbon
Set the Main Window Background Color and Mouse Cursor

- The following example sets the main window background color and mouse cursor:

test4.c: C with Carbon Set the Main Window Background Color and Mouse Cursor

```
#include <Carbon/Carbon.h>

int main(int argc, const char *argv[])
{
    WindowRef loMainWindow = NULL;
    Rect loRect;
    Point loIdealSize;
    OSStatus lnError = noErr;
    RGBColor loWindowBackColor;

    loRect.left = 0;
    loRect.right = 640;

    loRect.top = 60;
    loRect.bottom = 560;

    // Create the main window
    lnError = CreateNewWindow(kDocumentWindowClass,
                              kWindowStandardDocumentAttributes |
                              kWindowStandardHandlerAttribute,
                              &loRect,
                              &loMainWindow);

     if (lnError != noErr || loMainWindow == NULL)
     {
         return EXIT_FAILURE;
     }

    // Set the main window background color
    loWindowBackColor.red = 0xFFFF;
    loWindowBackColor.green = 0xFFFF;
    loWindowBackColor.blue = 0xFFFF;

    SetWindowContentColor(loMainWindow,&loWindowBackColor);

    // Set the main window mouse cursor
    SetThemeCursor(kThemeArrowCursor);

    // Maximize and display the main window
    GetRegionBounds(GetGrayRgn(),&loRect);
    loIdealSize.h = loRect.right - loRect.left;
    loIdealSize.v = loRect.bottom - loRect.top;
    ZoomWindowIdeal(loMainWindow,inZoomOut,&loIdealSize);
    ShowWindow(loMainWindow);

    // Start the event loop
    RunApplicationEventLoop();

    return EXIT_SUCCESS;
}
```

C with Carbon
Prompt to Exit the Application when the Main Window is Closed

- When the user attempts to close the main window, an event handler allows the "close" event to be processed. The user is prompted with a message box to continue closing the main window. If the "OK" button is selected, the DisposeWindow() function is called to close the main window and then the ExitToShell() function is called to exit the application.

test5.c: C with Carbon Prompt to Exit the App. when the Main Window is Closed

```
#include <Carbon/Carbon.h>

static pascal OSStatus MyWindowEventHandler(EventHandlerCallRef myHandler,
                                            EventRef event, void* userData);

int main(int argc, const char *argv[])
{
   WindowRef loMainWindow = NULL;
   Rect loRect;
   Point loIdealSize;
   OSStatus lnError = noErr;

   loRect.left = 0;
   loRect.right = 640;
   loRect.top = 60;
   loRect.bottom = 560;

   // Create the main window
   lnError = CreateNewWindow(kDocumentWindowClass,
                             kWindowStandardDocumentAttributes |
                             kWindowStandardHandlerAttribute,
                             &loRect,&loMainWindow);

  if (lnError != noErr || loMainWindow == NULL)
   {
      return EXIT_FAILURE;
   }

   EventTypeSpec laWindowEventList[] = {{kEventClassWindow,kEventWindowClose}};

   InstallWindowEventHandler(loMainWindow,
                             NewEventHandlerUPP(MyWindowEventHandler),
                             1,laWindowEventList,0,NULL);

   // Maximize and display the main window
   GetRegionBounds(GetGrayRgn(),&loRect);
   loIdealSize.h = loRect.right - loRect.left;
   loIdealSize.v = loRect.bottom - loRect.top;
   ZoomWindowIdeal(loMainWindow,inZoomOut,&loIdealSize);
   ShowWindow(loMainWindow);

   // Start the event loop
   RunApplicationEventLoop();

   return EXIT_SUCCESS;
}

static pascal OSStatus MyWindowEventHandler(EventHandlerCallRef toMyHandler,
                                            EventRef toEvent,void* toUserData)
{
   UInt32 lnEventKind;
   WindowPtr loWindowPtr;
   SInt16 lnResult;
   AlertStdAlertParamRec loParamRec = {};

   GetEventParameter(toEvent,kEventParamDirectObject,typeWindowRef,
                     NULL,sizeof(loWindowPtr),NULL,&loWindowPtr);

   lnEventKind = GetEventKind(toEvent);

   switch (lnEventKind)
   {
      case kEventWindowClose:

         loParamRec.defaultText = "\pYes";
         loParamRec.cancelText = "\pNo";
```

test5.c continued on the next page

test5.c: C with Carbon Prompt to Exit when the Main Window is Closed continued

```
         loParamRec.defaultButton = kStdOkItemIndex;
         loParamRec.cancelButton = kStdCancelItemIndex;
         loParamRec.position = kWindowAlertPositionParentWindowScreen;

         StandardAlert(kAlertStopAlert,"\pClose the main window?",
                       "\pProgram Phase 4-17",&loParamRec,&lnResult);


         if (lnResult == kAlertStdAlertOKButton)
         {
            if (loWindowPtr != nil)
            {
               DisposeWindow(loWindowPtr);
               ExitToShell();
            }
         }
         else
         {
            return false;
         }
         break;

      default:
         break;
   }

   return eventNotHandledErr;
}
```

Source Code Files

- Text files: pp4_17.c
- Image files: phase.icns (Appendix O)

pp4_17.c: Program Phase 4-17 Source Code

```
//*************************************************************************
// Program Phase 4-17 C Carbon Main Window with File Menu                 *
// Programming Tasks Illustrated: Carbon GUI based application            *
//                                Main window                             *
//                                Window icon                             *
//                                Window caption                          *
//                                Window menu with hotkeys                *
//                                Window background color                 *
//                                Window mouse cursor                     *
//                                User sizable window                     *
//                                Message box input/output                *
//*************************************************************************

//*************************************************************************
// File: pp4_17.c                                                         *
// Reserved                                                               *
//*************************************************************************

#include <Carbon/Carbon.h>

#define idm_menuitem1 102
#define idm_menuitem2 103

static pascal OSStatus MyWindowEventHandler(EventHandlerCallRef myHandler,
                                            EventRef event, void* userData);
```

pp4_17.c continued on the next page

pp4_17.c: Program Phase 4-17 Source Code continued

```
static pascal OSStatus MyAppEventHandler (EventHandlerCallRef myHandlerChain,
                                          EventRef event, void* userData);


//*****************************************************************************
// Program Phase 4-17 Main                                                    *
// Define the Entry Point of Execution (EPE) for Program Phase 4-17           *
// CBI:  4-17.1.1.1                                                           *
//*****************************************************************************

int main(int argc, const char *argv[])
{


//*****************************************************************************
// Program Phase 4-17 Main                                                    *
// Declare the local variables for the "main" program                         *
// CBI:  4-17.1.1.2                                                           *
//*****************************************************************************

   // Main window
   WindowRef loMainWindow = NULL;
   Rect loRect;
   Point loIdealSize;
   OSStatus lnError = noErr;

   // Main window menu
   MenuRef loMenuBar;
   MenuRef loFileMenu;
   MenuItemIndex loMenuItemIndex1;
   MenuItemIndex loMenuItemIndex2;
   MenuItemIndex loFileMenuIndex;

   // Main window back color
   RGBColor loWindowBackColor;


//*****************************************************************************
// Program Phase 4-17 Main                                                    *
// Create the main window                                                     *
// CBI:  4-17.1.1.3                                                           *
//*****************************************************************************

   loRect.left = 0;
   loRect.right = 640;
   loRect.top = 60;
   loRect.bottom = 560;

   lnError = CreateNewWindow(kDocumentWindowClass,
                             kWindowCloseBoxAttribute |
                             kWindowFullZoomAttribute |
                             kWindowCollapseBoxAttribute |
                             kWindowStandardHandlerAttribute,
                             &loRect,
                             &loMainWindow);

   if (lnError != noErr || loMainWindow == NULL)
   {
      return EXIT_FAILURE;
   }

   EventTypeSpec  laApplicationEventList[] =
   {
      {kEventClassCommand,kEventCommandProcess}
   };
```

pp4_17.c continued on the next page

pp4_17.c: Program Phase 4-17 Source Code continued

```
   EventTypeSpec laWindowEventList[] =
   {
      {kEventClassWindow, kEventWindowClose}
   };

   InstallApplicationEventHandler(NewEventHandlerUPP(MyAppEventHandler),
                                  1,laApplicationEventList,0,NULL);

   InstallWindowEventHandler(loMainWindow,
                             NewEventHandlerUPP(MyWindowEventHandler),
                             2,laWindowEventList,0,NULL);


//*************************************************************************
// Program Phase 4-17 Main                                                *
// Set the icon for the main window                                       *
// CBI:  4-17.1.1.4                                                       *
//*************************************************************************

// The main window icon is not set in Program Phase 4-17.
// See the Code Setup and Compilation steps for setting the application icon.


//*************************************************************************
// Program Phase 4-17 Main                                                *
// Set the caption of the main window                                     *
// CBI:  4-17.1.1.5                                                       *
//*************************************************************************

   SetWTitle(loMainWindow,"\p Program Phase 4-17  |  "
                          "Platform: Mac OS X  |  "
                          "Programming Language C  |  "
                          "GUI API: Carbon");


//*************************************************************************
// Program Phase 4-17 Main                                                *
// Create the menu for the main window                                    *
// CBI:  4-17.1.1.6                                                       *
//*************************************************************************

   // Menu Bar
   CreateNewMenu(0,0,&loMenuBar);

   // File Menu
   CreateNewMenu(1,0,&loFileMenu);
   SetMenuTitleWithCFString(loFileMenu,CFSTR("File"));
   AppendMenuItemTextWithCFString(loMenuBar,NULL,0,0,&loFileMenuIndex);
   SetMenuItemHierarchicalMenu(loMenuBar,loFileMenuIndex,loFileMenu);

   // Hello World! Menu Item
   AppendMenuItemTextWithCFString(loFileMenu,CFSTR("Hello World!"),0,
                                  idm_menuitem1,&loMenuItemIndex1);

   SetItemCmd(loFileMenu,loMenuItemIndex1,'H');

   // Exit Menu Item
   AppendMenuItemTextWithCFString(loFileMenu,CFSTR("Exit"),0,
                                  idm_menuitem2,&loMenuItemIndex2);

   SetItemCmd(loFileMenu,loMenuItemIndex2,'X');

   // Assign the File menu to the main window
   SetRootMenu(loMenuBar);
```

pp4_17.c continued on the next page

pp4_17.c: Program Phase 4-17 Source Code continued

```
//****************************************************************************
// Program Phase 4-17 Main                                                   *
// Set the background color of the main window                               *
// CBI:  4-17.1.1.7                                                          *
//****************************************************************************

   loWindowBackColor.red = 0xFFFF;
   loWindowBackColor.green = 0xFFFF;
   loWindowBackColor.blue = 0xFFFF;
   SetWindowContentColor(loMainWindow,&loWindowBackColor);


//****************************************************************************
// Program Phase 4-17 Main                                                   *
// Set the mouse cursor displayed when positoned over the main window        *
// CBI:  4-17.1.1.8                                                          *
//****************************************************************************

   SetThemeCursor(kThemeArrowCursor);


//****************************************************************************
// Program Phase 4-17 Main                                                   *
// Allow resizing of the main window                                         *
// CBI:  4-17.1.1.9                                                          *
//****************************************************************************

   ChangeWindowAttributes(loMainWindow,kWindowResizableAttribute,NULL);


//****************************************************************************
// Program Phase 4-17 Main                                                   *
// Maximize and display the main window                                      *
// CBI:  4-17.1.1.10                                                         *
//****************************************************************************

   GetRegionBounds(GetGrayRgn(),&loRect);
   loIdealSize.h = loRect.right - loRect.left;
   loIdealSize.v = loRect.bottom - loRect.top;

   ZoomWindowIdeal(loMainWindow,inZoomOut,&loIdealSize);
   ShowWindow(loMainWindow);


//****************************************************************************
// Program Phase 4-17 Main                                                   *
// Start the event loop                                                      *
// CBI:  4-17.1.1.11                                                         *
//****************************************************************************

   RunApplicationEventLoop();


//****************************************************************************
// Program Phase 4-17 Main                                                   *
// Cleanup the resources used by the main window                             *
// CBI:  4-17.1.1.12                                                         *
//****************************************************************************

   return EXIT_SUCCESS;

}
```

pp4_17.c continued on the next page

pp4_17.c: Program Phase 4-17 Source Code continued

```
// Callback Functions

static pascal OSStatus MyAppEventHandler(EventHandlerCallRef toHandlerChain,
                                          EventRef toEvent, void* toUserData)
{
   UInt32 lnEventKind;
   HICommand loCommandStruct;
   short lnResult;
   AlertStdAlertParamRec loParamRec = {};
   WindowPtr loWindowPtr;
   lnEventKind = GetEventKind(toEvent);

   switch (lnEventKind)
   {

      case kEventCommandProcess:

         GetEventParameter (toEvent,
                            kEventParamDirectObject,
                            typeHICommand,
                            NULL,
                            sizeof(HICommand),
                            NULL,
                            &loCommandStruct);

         switch (loCommandStruct.commandID)
         {


//******************************************************************************
// Callback Functions                                                          *
// Implement the callback function for the Hello World! menu item              *
// CBI:  4-17.1.2.1                                                            *
//******************************************************************************

            case idm_menuitem1:

               loParamRec.defaultText = "\pOK";
               loParamRec.cancelText = nil;
               loParamRec.defaultButton = kStdOkItemIndex;
               loParamRec.position = kWindowAlertPositionParentWindowScreen;

               StandardAlert(kAlertStopAlert,
                             "\pHello World!","\pProgram Phase 4-17",
                             &loParamRec,&lnResult);
               break;


//******************************************************************************
// Callback Functions                                                          *
// Implement the callback function for the Exit menu item                      *
// CBI:  4-17.1.3.1                                                            *
//******************************************************************************

         case idm_menuitem2:

               loWindowPtr = FrontWindow();

               if (loWindowPtr != nil)
               {
                  DisposeWindow(loWindowPtr);
                  ExitToShell();
               }

               break;
```

pp4_17.c continued on the next page

pp4_17.c: Program Phase 4-17 Source Code continued

```
            default:

               break;
         }

         break;

      default:

         break;
   }
   return eventNotHandledErr;
}

static pascal OSStatus MyWindowEventHandler(EventHandlerCallRef toMyHandler,
                                            EventRef toEvent,
                                            void* toUserData)
{
   UInt32 lnEventKind;
   WindowPtr loWindowPtr;
   SInt16 lnResult;
   AlertStdAlertParamRec loParamRec = {};

   GetEventParameter(toEvent,kEventParamDirectObject,
                     typeWindowRef,NULL,sizeof(loWindowPtr),
                     NULL,&loWindowPtr);

   lnEventKind = GetEventKind(toEvent);

   switch (lnEventKind)
   {


//****************************************************************************
// Callback Functions                                                        *
// Implement the callback function that fires when the main window is closed *
// CBI:  4-17.1.4.1                                                          *
//****************************************************************************

      case kEventWindowClose:

         loParamRec.defaultText = "\pYes";
         loParamRec.cancelText = "\pNo";
         loParamRec.defaultButton = kStdOkItemIndex;
         loParamRec.cancelButton = kStdCancelItemIndex;
         loParamRec.position = kWindowAlertPositionParentWindowScreen;

         StandardAlert(kAlertStopAlert,
                       "\pClose the main window?",
                       "\pProgram Phase 4-17",
                       &loParamRec,&lnResult);

         if (lnResult == kAlertStdAlertOKButton)
         {
            if (loWindowPtr != nil)
            {
               DisposeWindow(loWindowPtr);
               ExitToShell();
            }
         }
         else
         {
            return false;
         }

         break;
```

pp4_17.c continued on the next page

pp4_17.c: Program Phase 4-17 Source Code continued

```
        default:

            break;
    }

    return eventNotHandledErr;
}
```

Code Setup and Compilation

- Tools: Xcode (Appendix C), Carbon API

Code Setup and Compilation Steps

1: Start the Xcode program.

2: Xcode - Activate Menu Item: File → New Project

3: Select "Application → Carbon Application" and then activate the "Next" button. Set the "Project Name" to pp4_17. Set the "Project Directory" to the appropriate folder. Activate the "Finish" button.

4: Delete the main.c and main.nib files that have been automatically added to the project.

5: Xcode - Activate Menu Item: File → New File

Select "Empty File in Project" and then activate the "Next" button. Name the file pp4_17.c and set the "Location" to the pp4_17 folder. Activate the "Finish" button.

6: Enter the source code for the pp4_17.c file and then save the file.

7: Create the phase.icns icon file according to the instructions found in Appendix O.

8: Select the Resources group in the project.

9: Xcode - Activate Menu Item: Project → Add to Project

Select the phase.icns file and then activate the "Add" button.

Xcode - Activate Menu Item: Project → Edit Active Target "pp4_17"

On the "Properties" tab, enter phase.icns for the "Icon File".

10: Xcode - Activate Menu Item: Build → Clean

11: Compile the program by activating the "Build" button.

Command Prompt Compilation

Open a terminal window and then change directories to the pp4_17 folder. Inside the pp4_17 folder, enter the following:

```
xcodebuild
```

Program Execution

- Execute Program

  To execute the pp4_17 program, activate the "Build/Go" button in the Xcode IDE.

- Debug Program

  Place the cursor in the CBI: 4-17.1.1.3 code block

```
   Xcode 2.4 - Activate Menu Item: Debug → Add Breakpoint at Current Line
   Xcode 3 - Activate Menu Item: Run → Manage Breakpoints → Add
Breakpoint at Current Line

   Xcode - Activate Menu Item: Build → Build and Debug
```

Program Phase 4-18

Objective-C ▪ Cocoa ▪ Mac OS X

GUI Based Program with Main Window

- Program Phase Task 4 is implemented in Program Phase 4-18 using the Objective-C programming language and the Cocoa Foundation framework.

- Program Phase 4-18 contains a single source code file named pp4_18.m. In addition to the pp4_18.m text file, an image file called phase.icns is used to represent the icon for the application.

Code Block Features

The Program Phase 4-18 code blocks illustrate the following programming features using the Objective-C programming language and the Cocoa Foundation framework:

- **Create a Resizable Main Window for a GUI Based Application**

- **Set the Main Window Caption**

- **Set the Main Window Menu**

- **Set the Main Window Background Color and Mouse Cursor**

- **Prompt to Exit the Application when the Main Window is Closed**

Objective-C with Cocoa
Create a Resizable Main Window for a GUI Based Application

- The program begins by first creating an NSAutoreleasePool object, which is used by the Cocoa garbage collector. After the NSAutoreleasePool object is created, a special global Cocoa application object called NSApplication is created. Each Cocoa application needs a single NSApplication instance.

- The Cocoa NSWindow class is used to represent the main window for the application.

- The initWithContentRect() method is called to initialize the main window. The first parameter is a "rect" structure that indicates the initial dimensions of the main window. The second parameter allows various style settings to be applied to the main window. The third parameter indicates how the window drawing is buffered by the internals of the Cocoa Foundation framework. The "NSBackingStoreBuffered" setting indicates that the drawing in the window takes place in a buffer and then is flushed to the screen. The fourth parameter indicates whether or not a Cocoa window device is created immediately or is created when the window is moved on the screen. A value of "NO" indicates that the window device is created immediately for the main window.

- The performZoom() method is used to maximize the main window. The makeKeyAndOrderFront() method is called to make the main window visible.

- The run() method of the global NSApp object is called to begin the event loop for the application. This event loop prevents the program from automatically exiting until a stop message has been sent by activating the "Quit" menu item from the application menu.

- The application does not exit automatically when the main window is closed. Most Mac OS X applications will continue running with an application menu being displayed even when the main window has been closed. To close the program, right-click on the application icon in the Dock and then activate the "Quit" menu item.

test1.m: Objective-C w/ Cocoa Create a Resizable Main Window for a GUI Based App.

```
#import <Cocoa/Cocoa.h>

int main(int argc, const char **argv)
{
   NSAutoreleasePool * loPool = [[NSAutoreleasePool alloc] init];
   NSApp = [[NSApplication alloc] init];

   NSWindow *loMainWindow;
   NSRect  loRect;

   loRect = NSMakeRect(100,350,800,600);

   // Create the main window
   loMainWindow = [[NSWindow alloc]
                initWithContentRect: loRect
                          styleMask: NSTitledWindowMask |
                                     NSClosableWindowMask |
                                     NSMiniaturizableWindowMask |
                                     NSResizableWindowMask
                            backing: NSBackingStoreBuffered
                              defer: NO];

   // Maximize and display the main window
   [loMainWindow performZoom:NSApp];
   [loMainWindow makeKeyAndOrderFront: nil];

   // Start the event loop
   [NSApp run];

   [NSApp release];
   [loPool release];
   return(EXIT_SUCCESS);
}
```

Objective-C with Cocoa
Set the Main Window Icon and Caption

- Program Phase 4-18 does not implement an icon for the main window. The application icon is displayed for the pp4_18.app file in the Finder window and is also displayed in the Dock when the application is running. The application icon is also shown in any message box windows displayed by the application. See the Code Setup and Compilation instructions for more information concerning the application icon.

- The setTitle() method of the NSWindow instance is called to set the caption of the main window.

- To close the test2.m program, right-click on the application icon in the Dock and activate the "Quit" menu item.

test2.m: Objective-C with Cocoa Set the Main Window Icon and Caption

```
#import <Cocoa/Cocoa.h>

int main(int argc, const char **argv)
{
   NSAutoreleasePool * loPool = [[NSAutoreleasePool alloc] init];
   NSApp = [[NSApplication alloc] init];

   NSWindow *loMainWindow;
   NSRect  loRect;
   loRect = NSMakeRect(100,350,800,600);

   // Create the main window
   loMainWindow = [[NSWindow alloc]
                   initWithContentRect: loRect
                             styleMask: NSTitledWindowMask |
                                        NSClosableWindowMask |
                                        NSMiniaturizableWindowMask |
                                        NSResizableWindowMask
                               backing: NSBackingStoreBuffered
                                 defer: NO];

   // Set the main window icon
   // There is no main window icon for Program Phase 4-18

   // Set the main window caption
   [loMainWindow setTitle:@"Hello World!"];

   // Maximize and display the main window
   [loMainWindow performZoom:NSApp];
   [loMainWindow makeKeyAndOrderFront: nil];

   // Start the event loop
   [NSApp run];

   [NSApp release];
   [loPool release];
   return(EXIT_SUCCESS);
}
```

Objective-C with Cocoa
Set the Main Window Menu

- The test3.m example creates a "File" menu with a "Hello World!" menu item and "Exit" menu item. In addition, an Apple menu is created that contains menu items common to most Mac OS X applications.

test3.m: Objective-C with Cocoa Set the Main Window Menu

```
#import <Cocoa/Cocoa.h>

@interface WindowView : NSView{}
@end

@interface AppDelegate : NSObject{}
- (void) MenuItem1_Activate:(id)sender;
@end

int main(int argc, const char **argv)
{
```

test3.m continued on the next page

test3.m: Objective-C with Cocoa Set the Main Window Menu continued

```
    NSAutoreleasePool * loPool = [[NSAutoreleasePool alloc] init];
    NSApp = [[NSApplication alloc] init];

    NSWindow *loMainWindow;
    NSView *loWindowView;
    NSRect  loRect;
    NSObject *loAppDelegate;
    NSMenu *loMenuBar;
    NSMenuItem *loMenuBarItem1;
    NSMenuItem *loMenuBarItem2;
    NSMenu *loFileMenu;
    NSMenu *loAppleMenu;
    NSMenu *loServicesMenu;
    NSMenuItem *loServicesBarItem;
    NSMenuItem *loHideOthersMenuItem;

    loAppDelegate = [AppDelegate new];
    [NSApp setDelegate: loAppDelegate];

    loRect = NSMakeRect(100,350,800,600);

    // Create the main window
    loMainWindow = [[NSWindow alloc]
                    initWithContentRect: loRect
                              styleMask: NSTitledWindowMask |
                                         NSClosableWindowMask |
                                         NSMiniaturizableWindowMask |
                                         NSResizableWindowMask
                                backing: NSBackingStoreBuffered
                                  defer: NO];

    loWindowView = [[[WindowView alloc] initWithFrame:loRect] autorelease];
    [loMainWindow setContentView:loWindowView];
    [loMainWindow setDelegate:loWindowView];

    // Menu bar
    loMenuBar = [[[NSMenu alloc] initWithTitle:@""] autorelease];

    // File menu
    loMenuBarItem2  = [[[NSMenuItem alloc] initWithTitle:@""
                                                  action:nil
                                           keyEquivalent:@""] autorelease];

    loFileMenu = [[NSMenu alloc] initWithTitle:@"File"];
    [loMenuBarItem2 setSubmenu:[loFileMenu autorelease]];

    // Hello World! menu item for the File menu
    [loFileMenu addItemWithTitle: @"Hello World!"
                          action: @selector(MenuItem1_Activate:)
                   keyEquivalent: @"h"];

    // Exit menu item for the File menu
    [loFileMenu addItemWithTitle: @"Exit"
                          action: @selector(stop:)
                   keyEquivalent: @"x"];

    // Apple menu
    loMenuBarItem1 = [[[NSMenuItem alloc] init] autorelease];
    loAppleMenu = [[[NSMenu alloc] initWithTitle:@"Apple Menu"] autorelease];
    [loMenuBarItem1 setSubmenu:loAppleMenu];

     // Services menu
    loServicesBarItem = [[[NSMenuItem alloc]
                          initWithTitle:@"Services"
                                 action:nil
                          keyEquivalent:@""] autorelease];
```

test3.m continued on the next page

test3.m: Objective-C with Cocoa Set the Main Window Menu continued

```
   loServicesMenu = [[NSMenu alloc] initWithTitle:@""];
   [loServicesBarItem setSubmenu:[loServicesMenu autorelease]];

   // Standard menu items for the Service menu
   [NSApp setServicesMenu:loServicesMenu];

   // Services menu item for the Apple menu
   [loAppleMenu addItem:loServicesBarItem];

   // Separator menu item for the Apple menu
   [loAppleMenu addItem:[NSMenuItem separatorItem]];

   // Hide menu item for the Apple menu
   [loAppleMenu addItemWithTitle: @"Hide"
                          action: @selector(hide:)
                   keyEquivalent: @""];

   // Hide Others menu item for the Apple menu
   loHideOthersMenuItem = [[[NSMenuItem alloc]
                            initWithTitle:@"Hide Others"
                                   action:@selector(hideOtherApplications:)
                            keyEquivalent:@"h"] autorelease];

   [loHideOthersMenuItem setKeyEquivalentModifierMask:
                                (NSAlternateKeyMask|NSCommandKeyMask)];

   [loAppleMenu addItem:loHideOthersMenuItem];

   // Show All menu item for the Apple menu
   [loAppleMenu addItemWithTitle: @"Show All"
                          action: @selector(unhideAllApplications:)
                   keyEquivalent: @""];

   // Separator menu item for the Apple menu
   [loAppleMenu addItem:[NSMenuItem separatorItem]];

   // Quit menu item for the Apple menu
   [loAppleMenu addItemWithTitle: @"Quit pp4_18"
                          action: @selector(terminate:)
                   keyEquivalent: @"q"];

   // Assign the menu bar items to the menu bar
   [loMenuBar addItem:loMenuBarItem1];
   [loMenuBar addItem:loMenuBarItem2];

   // Assign the menu bar to the main window
   [NSApp setMainMenu:loMenuBar];

   // Assign the Apple menu to the main window application menu
   [NSApp setAppleMenu:loAppleMenu];

   // Maximize and display the main window
   [loMainWindow performZoom:NSApp];
   [loMainWindow makeKeyAndOrderFront: nil];

   // Start the event loop
   [NSApp run];

   [NSApp release];
   [loPool release];
   return(EXIT_SUCCESS);
}

@implementation AppDelegate : NSObject

- (void) MenuItem1_Activate:(id)sender
```

test3.m continued on the next page

test3.m: Objective-C with Cocoa Set the Main Window Menu continued

```
{
   NSRunAlertPanel(@"test",@"Hello World!",@"OK",nil,nil);
}
@end

@implementation WindowView
-(void)windowWillClose:(NSNotification *)notification
{
   [NSApp terminate:self];
}

-(void)resetCursorRects
{
   [self discardCursorRects];
   [self addCursorRect:[self visibleRect] cursor:[NSCursor arrowCursor]];
}

@end
```

Objective-C with Cocoa
Set the Main Window Background Color and Mouse Cursor

- The test4.m example sets the main window background color and mouse cursor. To close the test4.m program, right-click on the application icon in the Dock and then activate the "Quit" menu item.

test4.m: Objective-C with Cocoa Set the Main Window BG Color and Mouse Cursor

```
#import <Cocoa/Cocoa.h>

@interface WindowView : NSView{}
-(void)resetCursorRects;
@end

int main(int argc, const char **argv)
{
   NSAutoreleasePool * loPool = [[NSAutoreleasePool alloc] init];
   NSApp = [[NSApplication alloc] init];

   NSWindow *loMainWindow;
   NSRect  loRect;
   NSColor *loWindowBackColor;
   NSView   *loWindowView;

   loRect = NSMakeRect(100,350,800,600);

   loMainWindow = [[NSWindow alloc]
                    initWithContentRect: loRect
                              styleMask: NSTitledWindowMask |
                                         NSClosableWindowMask |
                                         NSMiniaturizableWindowMask |
                                         NSResizableWindowMask
                                backing: NSBackingStoreBuffered
                                  defer: NO];

   loWindowView = [[[WindowView alloc] initWithFrame:loRect] autorelease];

   [loMainWindow setContentView:loWindowView];
   [loMainWindow setDelegate:loWindowView];
```

test4.m continued on the next page

test4.m: Obj-C with Cocoa Set the Main Window BG Color and Mouse Cursor continued

```
    // Set main window background color to red
    loWindowBackColor = [NSColor colorWithDeviceRed: (255 + 1)/256
                                              green: (255 + 1)/256
                                              blue:  (255 + 1)/256
                                              alpha: 1.0];

    [loMainWindow setBackgroundColor:loWindowBackColor];
    [loMainWindow performZoom:NSApp];

    [loMainWindow makeKeyAndOrderFront: nil];
    [NSApp run];

    [NSApp release];
    [loPool release];

    return(EXIT_SUCCESS);
}

@implementation WindowView

-(void)resetCursorRects
{
    [self addCursorRect:[self visibleRect] cursor:[NSCursor arrowCursor]];
}

@end
```

Objective-C with Cocoa
Prompt to Exit the Application when the Main Window is Closed

- An interface based on the NSView class is instantiated and assigned as the content view for the main window by calling the SetContentView() method.

- The NSView instance is assigned to be a delegate of the main window by calling the setDelegate() method. The delegate allows callback functions to be automatically called when specific window events occur for the main window.

- The windowShouldClose() callback function is automatically called when the main window is about to close. The NSRunAlertPanel() function is called to prompt the user to continue closing the main window. If the constant "NO" is returned from the windowShouldClose() function, the main window is not closed.

- The windowWillClose() callback function is automatically called when the main window is closed after the windowShouldClose() function has been called and has returned the constant "YES". The terminate() method of the NSApp object is called to exit the application when the main window is closed.

test5.m: Objective-C with Cocoa Prompt to Exit when the Main Window is Closed

```
#import <Cocoa/Cocoa.h>

@interface WindowView : NSView{}

-(BOOL)windowShouldClose:(NSWindow *)sender;
-(void)windowWillClose:(NSNotification *)notification;

@end
```

test5.m continued on the next page

test5.m: Obj-C with Cocoa Prompt to Exit when the Main Window is Closed continued

```
int main(int argc, const char **argv)
{
   NSAutoreleasePool * loPool = [[NSAutoreleasePool alloc] init];
   NSApp = [[NSApplication alloc] init];

   NSWindow *loMainWindow;
   NSRect  loRect;

   NSView   *loWindowView;

   loRect = NSMakeRect(100,350,800,600);

   loMainWindow = [[NSWindow alloc]
                    initWithContentRect: loRect

                              styleMask: NSTitledWindowMask |
                                         NSClosableWindowMask |
                                         NSMiniaturizableWindowMask |
                                         NSResizableWindowMask
                                backing: NSBackingStoreBuffered
                                  defer: NO];

   loWindowView = [[[WindowView alloc] initWithFrame:loRect] autorelease];

   [loMainWindow setContentView:loWindowView];
   [loMainWindow setDelegate:loWindowView];

   [loMainWindow performZoom:NSApp];
   [loMainWindow makeKeyAndOrderFront: nil];
   [NSApp run];


   [NSApp release];
   [loPool release];
   return(EXIT_SUCCESS);
}

@implementation WindowView

-(BOOL)windowShouldClose:(NSWindow *)sender
{
   int lnResult;

   lnResult = NSRunAlertPanel(@"test",@"Close the main window?",
                              @"Yes",@"No",nil);

   switch (lnResult)
   {
      case NSAlertDefaultReturn:

          return YES;

        default:

          return NO;
   }
}

-(void)windowWillClose:(NSNotification *)notification
{
    [NSApp terminate:self];
}

@end
```

Source Code Files

- Text files: pp4_18.m
- Image files: phase.icns (Appendix O)

pp4_18.m: Program Phase 4-18 Source Code

```
//****************************************************************************
// Program Phase 4-18 Objective-C Main Window with File Menu                 *
// Programming Tasks Illustrated: Cocoa GUI based application                *
//                                Main window                                *
//                                Window icon                                *
//                                Window caption                             *
//                                Window menu with hotkeys                   *
//                                Window background color                    *
//                                Window mouse cursor                        *
//                                User sizable window                        *
//                                Message box input/output                   *
//****************************************************************************

//****************************************************************************
// File:  pp4_18.m                                                           *
// Reserved                                                                  *
//****************************************************************************

#import <Cocoa/Cocoa.h>

@interface WindowView : NSView{}
@end

@interface AppDelegate : NSObject{}
- (void) MenuItem1_Activate:(id)sender;
@end


//****************************************************************************
// Program Phase 4-18 Main                                                   *
// Define the Entry Point of Execution (EPE) for Program Phase 4-18          *
// CBI:  4-18.1.1.1                                                          *
//****************************************************************************

int main(int argc, const char **argv)
{
   NSAutoreleasePool * loPool = [[NSAutoreleasePool alloc] init];
   NSApp = [[NSApplication alloc] init];


//****************************************************************************
// Program Phase 4-18 Main                                                   *
// Declare the local variables for the "main" program                        *
// CBI:  4-18.1.1.2                                                          *
//****************************************************************************

   NSObject *loAppDelegate;
   NSWindow *loMainWindow;
   NSView   *loWindowView;
   NSRect  loRect;
   NSColor *loWindowBackColor;
   NSMenu *loMenuBar;
   NSMenuItem *loMenuBarItem1;
   NSMenuItem *loMenuBarItem2;
   NSMenu *loFileMenu;
   NSMenu *loAppleMenu;
   NSMenu *loServicesMenu;
```

pp4_18.m continued on the next page

pp4_18.m: Program Phase 4-18 Source Code continued

```
   NSMenuItem *loServicesBarItem;
   NSMenuItem *loHideOthersMenuItem;


//****************************************************************************
// Program Phase 4-18 Main                                                   *
// Create the main window                                                    *
// CBI:  4-18.1.1.3                                                          *
//****************************************************************************

   loAppDelegate = [AppDelegate new];
   [NSApp setDelegate: loAppDelegate];

   loRect = NSMakeRect(100.0, 350.0, 800.0, 600.0);

   loMainWindow = [ [NSWindow alloc] initWithContentRect: loRect
                                  styleMask: NSTitledWindowMask |
                                             NSClosableWindowMask |
                                             NSMiniaturizableWindowMask |
                                             NSResizableWindowMask
                                    backing: NSBackingStoreBuffered
                                      defer: NO];

   loWindowView = [[[WindowView alloc] initWithFrame:loRect] autorelease];
   [loMainWindow setContentView:loWindowView];
   [loMainWindow setDelegate:loWindowView];


//****************************************************************************
// Program Phase 4-18 Main                                                   *
// Set the icon for the main window                                          *
// CBI:  4-18.1.1.4                                                          *
//****************************************************************************

// The main window icon is not set in Program Phase 4-18.
// See the Code Setup and Compilation steps for setting the application icon.


//****************************************************************************
// Program Phase 4-18 Main                                                   *
// Set the caption of the main window                                        *
// CBI:  4-18.1.1.5                                                          *
//****************************************************************************

    [loMainWindow setTitle:@"Program Phase 4-18  |  Platform:  OSX  |  "
                           "Programming Language:  Objective-C  |  "
                           "GUI API:  Cocoa"];


//****************************************************************************
// Program Phase 4-18 Main                                                   *
// Create the menu for the main window                                       *
// CBI:  4-18.1.1.6                                                          *
//****************************************************************************

   // Menu bar
   loMenuBar = [[[NSMenu alloc] initWithTitle:@""] autorelease];

   // File menu
   loMenuBarItem2  = [[[NSMenuItem alloc] initWithTitle:@""
                                               action:nil
                                        keyEquivalent:@""] autorelease];

   loFileMenu = [[NSMenu alloc] initWithTitle:@"File"];

   [loMenuBarItem2 setSubmenu:[loFileMenu autorelease]];
```

pp4_18.m continued on the next page

pp4_18.m: Program Phase 4-18 Source Code continued

```
   // Hello World! menu item for the File menu
   [loFileMenu addItemWithTitle: @"Hello World!"
                         action: @selector(MenuItem1_Activate:)
                  keyEquivalent: @"h"];

   // Exit menu item for the File menu
   [loFileMenu addItemWithTitle: @"Exit"
                         action: @selector(stop:)
                  keyEquivalent: @"x"];

   // Apple menu
   loMenuBarItem1 = [[[NSMenuItem alloc] init] autorelease];
   loAppleMenu = [[[NSMenu alloc] initWithTitle:@"Apple Menu"] autorelease];
   [loMenuBarItem1 setSubmenu:loAppleMenu];

    // Services menu
   loServicesBarItem = [[[NSMenuItem alloc]
                         initWithTitle:@"Services"
                                action:nil
                         keyEquivalent:@""] autorelease];

   loServicesMenu = [[NSMenu alloc] initWithTitle:@""];
   [loServicesBarItem setSubmenu:[loServicesMenu autorelease]];

   // Standard menu items for the Service menu
   [NSApp setServicesMenu:loServicesMenu];

   // Services menu item for the Apple menu
   [loAppleMenu addItem:loServicesBarItem];

   // Separator menu item for the Apple menu
   [loAppleMenu addItem:[NSMenuItem separatorItem]];

   // Hide menu item for the Apple menu
   [loAppleMenu addItemWithTitle: @"Hide"
                          action: @selector(hide:)
                   keyEquivalent: @""];

   // Hide Others menu item for the Apple menu
   loHideOthersMenuItem = [[[NSMenuItem alloc]
                            initWithTitle:@"Hide Others"
                                   action:@selector(hideOtherApplications:)
                            keyEquivalent:@"h"] autorelease];

   [loHideOthersMenuItem setKeyEquivalentModifierMask:
                                   (NSAlternateKeyMask|NSCommandKeyMask)];

   [loAppleMenu addItem:loHideOthersMenuItem];

   // Show All menu item for the Apple menu
   [loAppleMenu addItemWithTitle: @"Show All"
                          action: @selector(unhideAllApplications:)
                   keyEquivalent: @""];

   // Separator menu item for the Apple menu
   [loAppleMenu addItem:[NSMenuItem separatorItem]];

   // Quit menu item for the Apple menu
   [loAppleMenu addItemWithTitle: @"Quit pp4_18"
                          action: @selector(terminate:)
                   keyEquivalent: @"q"];

   // Assign the menu bar items to the menu bar
   [loMenuBar addItem:loMenuBarItem1];
   [loMenuBar addItem:loMenuBarItem2];
```

pp4_18.m continued on the next page

pp4_18.m: Program Phase 4-18 Source Code continued

```
    // Assign the menu bar to the main window
    [NSApp setMainMenu:loMenuBar];

    // Assign the Apple menu to the main window application menu
    [NSApp setAppleMenu:loAppleMenu];


//*************************************************************************
// Program Phase 4-18 Main                                                *
// Set the background color of the main window                            *
// CBI:  4-18.1.1.7                                                       *
//*************************************************************************

    loWindowBackColor = [NSColor colorWithDeviceRed: (255 + 1)/256
                                              green: (255 + 1)/256
                                              blue:  (255 + 1)/256
                                              alpha: 1.0];

    [loMainWindow setBackgroundColor:loWindowBackColor];


//*************************************************************************
// Program Phase 4-18 Main                                                *
// Set the mouse cursor displayed when positioned over the main window    *
// CBI:  4-18.1.1.8                                                       *
//*************************************************************************

    // This is done in the resetCursorRects event.

//*************************************************************************
// Program Phase 4-18 Main                                                *
// Allow resizing of the main window                                      *
// CBI:  4-18.1.1.9                                                       *
//*************************************************************************

    // This is set in CBI: 4-18.1.1.3 with the NSResizableWindowMask setting.

//*************************************************************************
// Program Phase 4-18 Main                                                *
// Maximize and display the main window                                   *
// CBI:  4-18.1.1.10                                                      *
//*************************************************************************

    [loMainWindow makeKeyAndOrderFront: nil];
    [loMainWindow performZoom:NSApp];


//*************************************************************************
// Program Phase 4-18 Main                                                *
// Start the event loop                                                   *
// CBI:  4-18.1.1.11                                                      *
//*************************************************************************

     [NSApp run];


//*************************************************************************
// Program Phase 4-18 Main                                                *
// Cleanup the resources used by the main window                          *
// CBI:  4-18.1.1.12                                                      *
//*************************************************************************

     [NSApp release];
     [loPool release];
     return(EXIT_SUCCESS);
}
```

pp4_18.m continued on the next page

pp4_18.m: Program Phase 4-18 Source Code continued

```
// Callback Functions

//*************************************************************************
// Callback Functions                                                     *
// Implement the callback function for the Hello World! menu item         *
// CBI:  4-18.1.2.1                                                       *
//*************************************************************************

@implementation AppDelegate : NSObject

- (void) MenuItem1_Activate:(id)sender
{
   NSRunAlertPanel(@"Program Phase 4-18",@"Hello World!",@"OK",nil,nil);
}

@end


//*************************************************************************
// Callback Functions                                                     *
// Implement the callback function for the Exit menu item                 *
// CBI:  4-18.1.3.1                                                       *
//*************************************************************************

// There is no callback function for the Exit menu item.  A stop message is
// sent when the Exit menu item is activated.


//*************************************************************************
// Callback Functions                                                     *
// Implement the callback function that fires when the main window is closed  *
// CBI:  4-18.1.4.1                                                       *
//*************************************************************************

@implementation WindowView

-(BOOL)windowShouldClose:(NSWindow *)sender
{
   int lnResult;

   lnResult = NSRunAlertPanel(@"Program Phase 4-18",
                              @"Close the main window?",
                              @"Yes",@"No",nil);
   switch (lnResult)
   {
      case NSAlertDefaultReturn:

             return YES;

          default:

             return NO;
   }
}

-(void)windowWillClose:(NSNotification *)notification
{
    [NSApp terminate:self];
}

-(void)resetCursorRects
{
   [self discardCursorRects];
   [self addCursorRect:[self visibleRect] cursor:[NSCursor arrowCursor]];
}

@end
```

Code Setup and Compilation

- Tools: Xcode (Appendix C), AppKit

Code Setup and Compilation Steps

1: Start the Xcode IDE program.

2: Xcode - Activate Menu Item: File → New Project

3: Select "Application → Cocoa Application" and then activate the "Next" button. Set the project name to pp4_18 and set the project directory to the appropriate folder. Activate the "Finish" button.

4: Right-click on the main.m file that has been automatically added to the project and then activate the "Delete" menu item on the displayed context sensitive menu. Select delete references and files. Right-click on the MainMenu.nib file that has been automatically added to the project and then activate the "Delete" menu item on the displayed context sensitive menu. Select delete references and files.

5: Xcode - Activate Menu Item: File → New File

Select "Empty File in Project" and then activate the "Next" button. Set the file name to pp4_18.m and set the destination folder to the pp4_18 folder. Activate the "Finish" button.

6: Enter the source code for the pp4_18.m file and then save the file.

7: Create the phase.icns icon file according to the instructions found in Appendix O.

8: Select the Resources group in the project.

9: Xcode - Activate Menu Item: Project → Add to Project

Select the phase.icns file and then activate the "Add" button.

10: Xcode - Activate Menu Item: Project → Edit Active Target "pp4_18"

On the "Properties" tab, enter phase.icns for the "Icon File".

11: Xcode - Activate Menu Item: Build → Clean

12: Compile the program by activating the "Build" button.

Command Prompt Compilation

Open a terminal window and then change directories to the pp4_18 folder. Inside the pp4_18 folder, enter the following:

```
xcodebuild
```

Program Execution

- Execute Program

  To execute the pp4_18 program, activate the "Build/Go" button in the Xcode IDE.

- Debug Program

  Place the cursor in the CBI: 4-18.1.1.3 code block and then activate the following menu items:

```
   Xcode 2.4 - Activate Menu Item: Debug → Add Breakpoint at Current Line
   Xcode 3 - Activate Menu Item: Run → Manage Breakpoints → Add
Breakpoint at Current Line

   Xcode - Activate Menu Item: Build → Build and Debug
```

Program Phase 4-19

C ▪ GTK+ ▪ Linux

GUI Based Program with Main Window

- Program Phase Task 4 is implemented in Program Phase 4-19 using the C programming language and the GTK+ library.

- Program Phase 4-19 contains a single source code file named pp4_19.c. In addition to the pp4_19.c text file, an icon image file called phase16x16.xpm is used as the window icon for the main window.

Code Block Features

The Program Phase 4-19 code blocks illustrate the following programming features using the C programming language and the GTK+ library:

- **Create a Resizable Main Window for a GUI Based Application**

- **Set the Main Window Caption**

- **Set the Main Window Menu**

- **Set the Main Window Background Color and Mouse Cursor**

- **Prompt to Exit the Application when the Main Window is Closed**

C with GTK+
Create a Resizable Main Window for a GUI Based Application

- The gtk_init() function is called before any other GTK function is called. It prepares the GTK+ toolkit, so other GTK+ functions can be called. If the gtk_init() function fails, the program automatically terminates. There is an alternative function called gtk_init_check() that does the same thing as the gtk_init() function except that it returns a Boolean "false" value if the function fails.

- The gtk_window_new() function is called with the "GTK_WINDOW_TOPLEVEL" constant, passed as the only parameter to create the main window for the application.

- The gtk_window_set_resizable() function is called to make the main window resizable.

- The g_signal_connect() function is used to tell the application to call the gtk_main_quit() function when the main window is closed.

- The main window is maximized with the gtk_window_maximize() function and made visible with the gtk_widget_show() function.

- The event loop is started with the gtk_main() function. This loop prevents the program from automatically exiting. When the main window is closed, the gtk_main_quit()

function is automatically called, which causes the end of the event loop.

test1.c: C with GTK+ Create a Resizable Main Window for a GUI Based Application

```
#include <gtk/gtk.h>

int main(int argc,char *argv[])
{
   GtkWidget *loMainWindow;

   gtk_init(&argc, &argv);

   // Create a resizable main window
   loMainWindow = gtk_window_new (GTK_WINDOW_TOPLEVEL);
   gtk_window_set_resizable(GTK_WINDOW(loMainWindow),1);

   g_signal_connect (G_OBJECT (loMainWindow),"destroy",
                     G_CALLBACK (gtk_main_quit),NULL);

   // Maximize and display the main window
   gtk_window_set_default_size(GTK_WINDOW(loMainWindow),640,480);
   gtk_window_maximize(GTK_WINDOW(loMainWindow));
   gtk_widget_show(loMainWindow);

   // Start the event loop
   gtk_main();
   return 0;
}
```

C with GTK+ Set the Main Window Icon and Caption

- The window icon object is created from the phase16x16.xpm file using the gdk_pixbuf_new_from_file() function. The icon object is assigned to the main window by using the gtk_window_set_icon() function.
- The gtk_window_set_title() function is used to set the caption of the main window.

test2.c: C with GTK+ Set the Main Window Icon and Caption

```
#include <gtk/gtk.h>

int main(int argc,char *argv[])
{
   GtkWidget *loMainWindow;
   GdkPixbuf *loIcon;
   GError *loError;

   gtk_init(&argc, &argv);

   // Create a resizable main window
   loMainWindow = gtk_window_new (GTK_WINDOW_TOPLEVEL);
   gtk_window_set_resizable(GTK_WINDOW(loMainWindow),1);

   g_signal_connect (G_OBJECT (loMainWindow),"destroy",
                     G_CALLBACK (gtk_main_quit),NULL);

   // Set the main window icon
   loError = NULL;
   loIcon = gdk_pixbuf_new_from_file("phase16x16.xpm",&loError);
```

test2.c continued on the next page

test2.c: C with GTK+ Set the Main Window Icon and Caption continued

```
    gtk_window_set_icon(GTK_WINDOW(loMainWindow),loIcon);

    // Set the main window caption
    gtk_window_set_title(GTK_WINDOW(loMainWindow),"Hello World!");

    // Maximize and display the main window
    gtk_window_set_default_size(GTK_WINDOW(loMainWindow),640,480);
    gtk_window_maximize(GTK_WINDOW(loMainWindow));
    gtk_widget_show(loMainWindow);

    // Start the event loop
    gtk_main();

    return 0;
}
```

C with GTK+ Set the Main Window Menu

- The following example creates a "File" menu with a "Hello World!" menu item and "Exit" menu item:

test3.c: C with GTK+ Set the Main Window Menu

```
#include <gtk/gtk.h>
#include <gdk/gdkkeysyms.h>

static void MenuItem1_Click (gchar *);
static void MenuItem2_Click (gchar *);

int main(int argc,char *argv[])
{
    GtkWidget *loMainWindow;
    GtkWidget *loMenuBar;
    GtkWidget *loMenu;
    GtkWidget *loSubMenu;
    GtkWidget *loMenuItem1;
    GtkWidget *loMenuItem2;
    GtkWidget* loVbox;
    GtkAccelGroup* loAccelGroup;

    gtk_init(&argc, &argv);

    // Create a resizable main window
    loMainWindow = gtk_window_new (GTK_WINDOW_TOPLEVEL);
    gtk_window_set_resizable(GTK_WINDOW(loMainWindow),1);

    g_signal_connect (G_OBJECT (loMainWindow),"destroy",
                      G_CALLBACK (gtk_main_quit),NULL);

    // Menu Bar
    loMenuBar = gtk_menu_bar_new();
    loAccelGroup = gtk_accel_group_new();
    gtk_window_add_accel_group(GTK_WINDOW(loMainWindow),loAccelGroup);

    // File menu
    loSubMenu = gtk_menu_new();
    loMenu = gtk_menu_item_new_with_label("");

    gtk_label_set_text_with_mnemonic(GTK_LABEL(GTK_BIN (loMenu)->child),"_File");
    gtk_menu_item_set_submenu(GTK_MENU_ITEM(loMenu),loSubMenu);
    gtk_widget_show (loMenu);
```

test3.c continued on the next page

test3.c: C with GTK+ Set the Main Window Menu continued

```
   gtk_menu_shell_append(GTK_MENU_SHELL(loMenuBar),loMenu);

   // Hello World! menu item
   loMenuItem1 = gtk_menu_item_new_with_label("");

   gtk_label_set_text_with_mnemonic(GTK_LABEL (GTK_BIN (loMenuItem1)->child),
                                    "_Hello World!");

   gtk_menu_shell_append(GTK_MENU_SHELL(loSubMenu),loMenuItem1);

   g_signal_connect_swapped(G_OBJECT (loMenuItem1),"activate",
                            G_CALLBACK (MenuItem1_Click),
                             (gpointer) g_strdup ("Hello World!"));

   gtk_widget_show (loMenuItem1);

   gtk_widget_add_accelerator(loMenuItem1,"activate",loAccelGroup,
                              GDK_H,GDK_CONTROL_MASK,GTK_ACCEL_VISIBLE );

   // Exit menu item
   loMenuItem2 = gtk_menu_item_new_with_label("");

   gtk_label_set_text_with_mnemonic(GTK_LABEL(GTK_BIN(loMenuItem2)->child),
                                    "E_xit");

   gtk_menu_shell_append(GTK_MENU_SHELL(loSubMenu),loMenuItem2);

   g_signal_connect_swapped(G_OBJECT (loMenuItem2),"activate",
                            G_CALLBACK (MenuItem2_Click),
                             (gpointer) g_strdup ("Exit"));

   gtk_widget_show (loMenuItem2);

   gtk_widget_add_accelerator(loMenuItem2,"activate",loAccelGroup,GDK_X,
                              GDK_CONTROL_MASK,GTK_ACCEL_VISIBLE );

   // Assign the File menu to the main window
   loVbox = gtk_vbox_new(FALSE,0);
   gtk_container_add (GTK_CONTAINER (loMainWindow),loVbox);
   gtk_widget_show (loVbox);
   gtk_box_pack_start(GTK_BOX(loVbox),loMenuBar,FALSE,FALSE,2);
   gtk_widget_show (loMenuBar);

   // Maximize and display the main window
   gtk_window_set_default_size(GTK_WINDOW(loMainWindow),640,480);
   gtk_window_maximize(GTK_WINDOW(loMainWindow));
   gtk_widget_show(loMainWindow);

   // Start the event loop
   gtk_main();

   return 0;
}

static void MenuItem1_Click(gchar *tcString)
{
   GtkWidget* loMessageBox;

   loMessageBox = gtk_message_dialog_new(NULL,
                                         GTK_DIALOG_DESTROY_WITH_PARENT,
                                         GTK_MESSAGE_INFO,
                                         GTK_BUTTONS_OK,
                                         "Hello World!");

   gtk_dialog_run (GTK_DIALOG(loMessageBox));
   gtk_widget_destroy(loMessageBox);
```

test3.c continued on the next page

test3.c: C with GTK+ Set the Main Window Menu continued

```
}

static void MenuItem2_Click(gchar *tcString)
{
   // Exit the program if the user activates the Exit menu item
   gtk_main_quit();
}
```

C with GTK+ Set the Main Window Background Color and Mouse Cursor

- The following example sets the main window background color and mouse cursor:

test4.c: C with GTK+ Set the Main Window Background Color and Mouse Cursor

```
#include <gtk/gtk.h>

int main(int argc,char *argv[])
{
   GtkWidget *loMainWindow;
   char lcBackColor[1 + 6 + 1];
   GdkColor loBackColor;
   GtkStyle *loStyle;

   // Main window mouse cursor
   GdkCursor *loMouseCursor;

   gtk_init(&argc, &argv);

   // Create a resizable main window
   loMainWindow = gtk_window_new (GTK_WINDOW_TOPLEVEL);
   gtk_window_set_resizable(GTK_WINDOW(loMainWindow),1);

   g_signal_connect (G_OBJECT (loMainWindow),"destroy",
                     G_CALLBACK (gtk_main_quit),NULL);

   // Set the main window background color
   loStyle = gtk_widget_get_style(loMainWindow);

   sprintf(lcBackColor,"#%02x%02x%02x",255,255,255);
   gdk_color_parse (lcBackColor,&loBackColor);
   gtk_widget_set_style(loMainWindow,loStyle);
   loStyle->bg[GTK_STATE_NORMAL] = loBackColor;

   // Set the main window mouse cursor
   gtk_widget_realize(loMainWindow);
   loMouseCursor = gdk_cursor_new(GDK_LEFT_PTR);
   gdk_window_set_cursor(loMainWindow->window,loMouseCursor);

   gdk_cursor_destroy(loMouseCursor);

   // Maximize and display the main window
   gtk_window_set_default_size(GTK_WINDOW(loMainWindow),640,480);
   gtk_window_maximize(GTK_WINDOW(loMainWindow));
   gtk_widget_show(loMainWindow);

   // Start the event loop
   gtk_main();

   return 0;
}
```

C with GTK+
Prompt to Exit the Application when the Main Window is Closed

- The MainWindow_Delete() callback function is assigned as the delete event for the main window object using the g_signal_connect() function. This causes the MainWindow_Delete() function to be called automatically when the main window is about to be closed. Returning a Boolean "true" value from this event causes the main window to remain visible.

test5.c: C with GTK+ Prompt to Exit the App. when the Main Window is Closed

```
#include <gtk/gtk.h>

static gboolean MainWindow_Delete(GtkWidget *toWidget,GdkEvent *toEvent,
                                  gpointer toData );

int main(int argc,char *argv[])
{
   GtkWidget *loMainWindow;

   // Main window mouse cursor
   GdkCursor *loMouseCursor;

   gtk_init(&argc, &argv);

   // Create a resizable main window
   loMainWindow = gtk_window_new(GTK_WINDOW_TOPLEVEL);
   gtk_window_set_resizable(GTK_WINDOW(loMainWindow),1);

   g_signal_connect(G_OBJECT (loMainWindow),"delete_event",
                    G_CALLBACK (MainWindow_Delete),NULL);

   g_signal_connect (G_OBJECT (loMainWindow),"destroy",
                     G_CALLBACK (gtk_main_quit),NULL);

   // Maximize and display the main window
   gtk_window_set_default_size(GTK_WINDOW(loMainWindow),640,480);
   gtk_window_maximize(GTK_WINDOW(loMainWindow));
   gtk_widget_show(loMainWindow);

   // Start the event loop
   gtk_main();

   return 0;
}

static gboolean MainWindow_Delete(GtkWidget *toWidget,GdkEvent *toEvent,
                                  gpointer toData)
{
   GtkWidget* loMessageBox;
   gint lnResult;

   // Prompt the user to continue closing the main window
   loMessageBox = gtk_message_dialog_new(NULL,
                                         GTK_DIALOG_DESTROY_WITH_PARENT,
                                         GTK_MESSAGE_QUESTION,
                                         GTK_BUTTONS_YES_NO,
                                         "Close the main window?");

   lnResult = gtk_dialog_run (GTK_DIALOG(loMessageBox));
   gtk_widget_destroy (loMessageBox);
```

test5.c continued on the next page

test5.c: C with GTK+ Prompt to Exit when the Main Window is Closed continued

```
   if (lnResult == GTK_RESPONSE_NO)
   {
      return TRUE;
   }

   return FALSE;
}
```

Source Code Files

- Text files: pp4_19.c
- Image files: phase16x16.xpm (Appendix O)

pp4_19.c: Program Phase 4-19 Source Code

```
//**************************************************************************
// Program Phase 4-19 C GTK+ Main Window with File Menu                    *
// Programming Tasks Illustrated: GTK+ GUI based application               *
//                               Main window                               *
//                               Window icon                               *
//                               Window caption                            *
//                               Window menu with hotkeys                  *
//                               Window background color                   *
//                               Window mouse cursor                       *
//                               User sizable window                       *
//                               Message box input/output                  *
//**************************************************************************

//**************************************************************************
// File: pp4_19.c                                                          *
// Reserved                                                                *
//**************************************************************************

#include <gtk/gtk.h>
#include <gdk/gdkkeysyms.h>

static void MenuItem1_Click (gchar *);
static void MenuItem2_Click (gchar *);

static gboolean MainWindow_Delete(GtkWidget *toWidget,GdkEvent *toEvent,
                               gpointer toData );


//**************************************************************************
// Program Phase 4-19 Main                                                 *
// Define the Entry Point of Execution (EPE) for Program Phase 4-19        *
// CBI:  4-19.1.1.1                                                        *
//**************************************************************************

int main(int argc,char *argv[])
{


//**************************************************************************
// Program Phase 4-19 Main                                                 *
// Declare the local variables for the "main" program                      *
// CBI:  4-19.1.1.2                                                        *
//**************************************************************************

   // Main window
   GtkWidget *loMainWindow;
   GtkWidget* loMessageBox;
```

pp4_19.c continued on the next page

pp4_19.c: Program Phase 4-19 Source Code continued

```
   // Main window icon
   GdkPixbuf *loIcon;
   GError *loError;

   // Main window menu
   GtkWidget *loMenuBar;
   GtkWidget *loMenu;
   GtkWidget *loSubMenu;
   GtkWidget *loMenuItem1;
   GtkWidget *loMenuItem2;
   GtkWidget* loVbox;
   GtkAccelGroup* loAccelGroup;

   // Main window background color
   char lcBackColor[1 + 6 + 1];
   GdkColor loBackColor;
   GtkStyle *loStyle;

   // Main window mouse cursor
   GdkCursor *loMouseCursor;


//*************************************************************************
// Program Phase 4-19 Main                                                *
// Create the main window                                                 *
// CBI:  4-19.1.1.3                                                       *
//*************************************************************************

   gtk_init(&argc, &argv);

   loMainWindow = gtk_window_new (GTK_WINDOW_TOPLEVEL);

   g_signal_connect (G_OBJECT (loMainWindow),"delete_event",
                 G_CALLBACK (MainWindow_Delete),NULL);

   g_signal_connect (G_OBJECT (loMainWindow),"destroy",
                  G_CALLBACK (gtk_main_quit),NULL);


//*************************************************************************
// Program Phase 4-19 Main                                                *
// Set the icon for the main window                                       *
// CBI:  4-19.1.1.4                                                       *
//*************************************************************************

   loError = NULL;
   loIcon = gdk_pixbuf_new_from_file("phase16x16.xpm",&loError);

   if(loIcon == 0)
   {
      loMessageBox = gtk_message_dialog_new(NULL,
                                      GTK_DIALOG_DESTROY_WITH_PARENT,
                                      GTK_MESSAGE_ERROR,
                                      GTK_BUTTONS_OK,
                                      "The gdk_pixbuf_new_from_file() "
                                      "function failed.");

      gtk_dialog_run (GTK_DIALOG(loMessageBox));
      gtk_widget_destroy (loMessageBox);
   }

   gtk_window_set_icon(GTK_WINDOW(loMainWindow),loIcon);
```

pp4_19.c continued on the next page

pp4_19.c: Program Phase 4-19 Source Code continued

```
//*************************************************************************
// Program Phase 4-19 Main                                                *
// Set the caption of the main window                                     *
// CBI:  4-19.1.1.5                                                       *
//*************************************************************************

   gtk_window_set_title(GTK_WINDOW(loMainWindow),"Program Phase 4-19  |  "
                                              "Platform:  Linux  |  "
                                              "Programming Language:  C"
                                              "  |  GUI API:  Gtk");


//*************************************************************************
// Program Phase 4-19 Main                                                *
// Create the menu for the main window                                    *
// CBI:  4-19.1.1.6                                                       *
//*************************************************************************

   // Menu Bar
   loMenuBar = gtk_menu_bar_new();
   loAccelGroup = gtk_accel_group_new();
   gtk_window_add_accel_group(GTK_WINDOW(loMainWindow),loAccelGroup);

   // File menu
   loSubMenu = gtk_menu_new();
   loMenu = gtk_menu_item_new_with_label("");

   gtk_label_set_text_with_mnemonic(GTK_LABEL(GTK_BIN (loMenu)->child),
                                    "_File");

   gtk_menu_item_set_submenu(GTK_MENU_ITEM(loMenu),loSubMenu);
   gtk_widget_show (loMenu);
   gtk_menu_shell_append(GTK_MENU_SHELL(loMenuBar),loMenu);

   // Hello World! menu item
   loMenuItem1 = gtk_menu_item_new_with_label("");

   gtk_label_set_text_with_mnemonic(GTK_LABEL(GTK_BIN(loMenuItem1)->child),
                                    "_Hello World!");

   gtk_menu_shell_append(GTK_MENU_SHELL(loSubMenu),loMenuItem1);

   g_signal_connect_swapped(G_OBJECT (loMenuItem1),"activate",
                            G_CALLBACK (MenuItem1_Click),
                            (gpointer) g_strdup ("Hello World!"));

   gtk_widget_show (loMenuItem1);

   gtk_widget_add_accelerator(loMenuItem1,"activate",
                              loAccelGroup,GDK_H,
                              GDK_CONTROL_MASK,GTK_ACCEL_VISIBLE );
   // Exit menu item
   loMenuItem2 = gtk_menu_item_new_with_label("");

   gtk_label_set_text_with_mnemonic(GTK_LABEL(GTK_BIN(
                                    loMenuItem2)->child),
                                    "E_xit");

   gtk_menu_shell_append(GTK_MENU_SHELL(loSubMenu),loMenuItem2);

   g_signal_connect_swapped(G_OBJECT (loMenuItem2),"activate",
                            G_CALLBACK (MenuItem2_Click),
                            (gpointer) g_strdup ("Exit"));

   gtk_widget_show (loMenuItem2);
```

pp4_19.c continued on the next page

pp4_19.c: Program Phase 4-19 Source Code continued

```
   gtk_widget_add_accelerator(loMenuItem2,"activate",
                              loAccelGroup,GDK_X,
                              GDK_CONTROL_MASK,GTK_ACCEL_VISIBLE);

   // Assign the File menu to the main window
   loVbox = gtk_vbox_new(FALSE,0);
   gtk_container_add (GTK_CONTAINER (loMainWindow),loVbox);
   gtk_widget_show (loVbox);
   gtk_box_pack_start(GTK_BOX(loVbox),loMenuBar,FALSE,FALSE,2);
   gtk_widget_show (loMenuBar);


//***************************************************************************
// Program Phase 4-19 Main                                                  *
// Set the background color of the main window                              *
// CBI:  4-19.1.1.7                                                         *
//***************************************************************************

   loStyle = gtk_widget_get_style(loMainWindow);
   sprintf(lcBackColor,"#%02x%02x%02x",255,255,255);
   gdk_color_parse (lcBackColor, &loBackColor);
   gtk_widget_set_style(loMainWindow,loStyle);
   loStyle->bg[GTK_STATE_NORMAL] = loBackColor;


//***************************************************************************
// Program Phase 4-19 Main                                                  *
// Set the mouse cursor displayed when positioned over the main window      *
// CBI:  4-19.1.1.8                                                         *
//***************************************************************************

   gtk_widget_realize(loMainWindow);
   loMouseCursor = gdk_cursor_new(GDK_LEFT_PTR);
   gdk_window_set_cursor(loMainWindow->window,loMouseCursor);
   gdk_cursor_destroy(loMouseCursor);


//***************************************************************************
// Program Phase 4-19 Main                                                  *
// Allow resizing of the main window                                        *
// CBI:  4-19.1.1.9                                                         *
//***************************************************************************

   gtk_window_set_resizable(GTK_WINDOW(loMainWindow),1);


//***************************************************************************
// Program Phase 4-19 Main                                                  *
// Maximize and display the main window                                     *
// CBI:  4-19.1.1.10                                                        *
//***************************************************************************

   gtk_window_set_default_size(GTK_WINDOW(loMainWindow),640,480);
   gtk_window_maximize(GTK_WINDOW(loMainWindow));
   gtk_widget_show(loMainWindow);


//***************************************************************************
// Program Phase 4-19 Main                                                  *
// Start the event loop                                                     *
// CBI:  4-19.1.1.11                                                        *
//***************************************************************************

   gtk_main();
}
```

pp4_19.c continued on the next page

pp4_19.c: Program Phase 4-19 Source Code continued

```
//Callback functions

//*****************************************************************************
// Callback Functions                                                         *
// Implement the callback function for the Hello World! menu item             *
// CBI:  4-19.1.2.1                                                           *
//*****************************************************************************

static void MenuItem1_Click(gchar *tcString)
{
   GtkWidget* loMessageBox;

   loMessageBox = gtk_message_dialog_new(NULL,GTK_DIALOG_DESTROY_WITH_PARENT,
                                         GTK_MESSAGE_INFO,GTK_BUTTONS_OK,
                                         "Hello World!");

   gtk_dialog_run (GTK_DIALOG(loMessageBox));
   gtk_widget_destroy(loMessageBox);
}

//*****************************************************************************
// Callback Functions                                                         *
// Implement the callback function for the Exit menu item                     *
// CBI:  4-19.1.3.1                                                           *
//*****************************************************************************

static void MenuItem2_Click(gchar *tcString)
{
   gtk_main_quit ();
}


//*****************************************************************************
// Callback Functions                                                         *
// Implement the callback function that fires when the main window is closed  *
// CBI:  4-19.1.4.1                                                           *
//*****************************************************************************

static gboolean MainWindow_Delete(GtkWidget *toWidget,GdkEvent *toEvent,
                                  gpointer toData)
{
   GtkWidget* loMessageBox;
   gint lnResult;

   loMessageBox = gtk_message_dialog_new(NULL,GTK_DIALOG_DESTROY_WITH_PARENT,
                                         GTK_MESSAGE_QUESTION,
                                         GTK_BUTTONS_YES_NO,
                                         "Close the main window?");

   lnResult = gtk_dialog_run (GTK_DIALOG(loMessageBox));
   gtk_widget_destroy (loMessageBox);

   if (lnResult == GTK_RESPONSE_NO)
   {
      return TRUE;
   }

   return FALSE;
}
```

Code Setup and Compilation

- Tools: GNU GCC, KDevelop (Appendix B), GTK+-2 (Appendix L)

Code Setup and Compilation Steps

1: Start the KDevelop program.

2: KDevelop - Activate Menu Item: Project → New Project

Select "C → Simple Hello world program". Set the "Application name" to pp4_19. Set the "Location" to the appropriate folder.

3: Activate the "Next" button four times and then activate the "Finish" button.

4: KDevelop - Activate Menu Item: Project → Build Configuration → debug

This results in the executable file being placed in the debug/src folder under the pp4_19 source code folder.

5: Enter the source code for the pp4_19.c file and then save and close the file.

6: Before compiling the pp4_19.c source code file, additional settings for accessing the GTK+ library need to be entered into the KDevelop project. From a terminal window, enter the following:

```
pkg-config --cflags gtk+-2.0 > cflags.txt
```

This causes the output of the pkg-config command to be stored in the text file called cflags.txt. Be sure to check the contents of the cflags.txt file for any errors. Next, run this command:

```
pkg-config --libs gtk+-2.0 > libresults.txt
```

This command results in the output being stored in the libresults.txt file. Check the libresults.txt file for any errors.

7: KDevelop - Activate Menu Item: Project → Project Options

Click on the "Configure Options" item in the left pane. Select the "debug" configuration. Click on the "C" tab. The results of running the pkg-config utility stored in the cflags.txt file must be pasted into the "Compiler flags" textbox. Next, click on the "General" tab and paste the contents of the libresults.txt file in the "Linker flags" textbox. You may be prompted to "Re-run configure". Select the "Do Not Run" button.

8: KDevelop - Activate Menu Item: Build → Run automake and friends

9: KDevelop - Activate Menu Item: Build → Run Configure

10: KDevelop - Activate Menu Item: Build → Build Project

If prompted about a missing Makefile, choose the "Run Them" button.

Steps continued on the next page

Code Setup and Compilation Steps continued

11: Create the phase16x16.xpm image file according to the instructions in Appendix O. Copy the image file to the folder in which the executable file was created.

For Debug Configuration:

```
pp4_19/debug/src
```

For Optimized Configuration:

```
pp4_19/optimized/src
```

Command Prompt Compilation

Enter the following command on a single line in the pp4_19/src folder:

```
g++ pp4_19.c -o pp4_19 `pkg-config --cflags gtk+-2.0` `pkg-config --libs
gtk+-2.0` -I.
```

Program Execution

- Execute Program

```
KDevelop - Activate Menu Item: Build → Execute Program
```

- Debug Program

```
KDevelop - Activate Menu Item: Project → Project Options
```

Click on the "Configure Options" item. Select the "debug" configuration and then enter "--enable-debug=full" in the "Configure arguments" field on the "General" tab. Close the "Project Options" dialog window.

Select the debug configuration for the project.

```
KDevelop - Activate Menu Item: Project → Build Configuration
```

Set the cursor position in the source file to the first line of code in the CBI: 4-19.1.1.3 code block. Create a breakpoint.

```
KDevelop - Activate Menu Item: Debug → Toggle Breakpoint
```

After the breakpoint has been created, the program can be debugged.

```
KDevelop - Activate Menu Item: Debug → Start
```

Client Side JavaScript ▪ Multi-Platform

GUI Based Program with Main Window

- Program Phase Task 4 is implemented in Program Phase 4-20 using client side JavaScript and HTML. The program is executed in a web browser.
- Two source code files are used in Program Phase 4-20. A launcher file called launchpp4_20.html is used to start the pp4_20.html file. The icon for the web page is stored in a single-image icon file called phase16x16.ico

---

Code Block Features

The Program Phase 4-20 code blocks illustrate the following programming features using the JavaScript programming language and HTML:

- **Create a Resizable Main Window for a GUI Based Application**
- **Set the Main Window Caption**
- **Set the Main Window Menu**
- **Set the Main Window Background Color and Mouse Cursor**
- **Prompt to Exit the Application when the Main Window is Closed**

Client Side JavaScript
Create a Resizable Main Window for a GUI Based Application

- When implementing Program Phase Task 4 with client side JavaScript in a web browser, the concept of creating a main window does not directly translate. The web browser is the main window. In order to get more control over the web browser, the main window is implemented as a web page opened by a separate JavaScript launcher program.
- The launchtest1.html example illustrates a file launcher, which launches the test1.html file as the main window for the test1 program.
- The window.open() method is called to open the test1.html file. The main browser window is set to be resizable by specifying "resizable=yes" in the third parameter to the open() method.
- The DNS name or IP address for the web server can be substituted with the appropriate value in the launchtest1.html example file.
- The window.resizeTo() method is used to resize the web browser that represents the main window. The maximize code is not included in the remaining sample programs.
- The following example outputs the text "Test1" in the web browser:

launchtest1.html: JavaScript Create a Resizable Main Window for a GUI Based App.

```
<HTML>
<BODY>

   <BUTTON onclick="Launchtest1()">Launch Test1</BUTTON>

</BODY>
</HTML>

<SCRIPT TYPE="text/javascript">

function Launchtest1()
{
   var loMainWindow;

   // The main window is created here.
   loMainWindow = window.open("http://127.0.0.1/test1.html",
                              null,
                              "resizable=yes,menubar=no,location=yes");
}

</SCRIPT>
```

test1.html: HTML File that Becomes the Main Window Opened by launchtest1.html

```
<HTML>
<BODY>

   Test1

</BODY>

<SCRIPT TYPE="text/javascript">

   // Maximize and display the main window
   window.moveTo(0,0);
   window.resizeTo(screen.availWidth,screen.availHeight);

</SCRIPT>
</HTML>
```

Client Side JavaScript
Set the Main Window Icon and Caption

- The "LINK" tag with the "rel" attribute set to the value of "SHORTCUT ICON" and the "href" attribute set to the path to the icon image file allows the browser icon to be set.

- The icon is displayed in the address bar of the web browser.

- The main window caption is specified by setting the "title" property of the document object.

- The following example can be launched by the launchtest1.html file with the test2.html file specified in the window.open() method:

test2.html: JavaScript Set the Main Window Icon and Caption

```
<HTML>
<HEAD>

   <!-- Set the main window icon -->
   <LINK rel="SHORTCUT ICON" href="phase16x16.ico">

</HEAD>

<BODY>
<SCRIPT TYPE="text/javascript">

   // Set the main window caption
   document.title = "Hello World!";

</SCRIPT>
</BODY>
</HTML>
```

Client Side JavaScript
Set the Main Window Menu

- The main window menu is implemented with Dynamic HTML (DHTML). The styles for the HTML menu items are set in the test3.css cascading style sheet file.

- The "DOCTYPE" of the test3.html page is set to HTML 4.01 Transitional.

- The "File" menu is implemented as an HTML table that contains a single row.

- Inside the only cell of the single row table, a division (DIV) is created for grouping the menu items. Inside the "DIV" tag, an additional table is created that contains two rows with a single column. Inside each of the cells in the table row, an "A" element HTML tag is created that corresponds to the links for each of the menu items. Each of these links is set to call the MenuItem1_Click() and MenuItem2_Click() callback functions respectively.

- The JavaScript onmouseover() event is used to change the class name of the table data and division to the string "DisplayMenuClass" when the mouse pointer is positioned over the first enclosing table with the class "MenuBar". When the class name of the table data and division are set to "DisplayMenuClass", the styles specified in the test3.css cascading style sheet cause the menu items to be visible. When the mouse moves away from the "MenuBar" table, the onmouseout() event fires, which sets the class name of the division and table data back to "HideMenuClass". When the class name of the division and table data are set to "HideMenuClass", the styles defined in the test3.css cascading style sheet cause the menu items to be hidden.

- The callback functions for the menu items are implemented by using JavaScript functions. The window.close() method is called in the MenuItem2_Click() function. The call to close the window by using the window.close() method works because the window is initially opened with a call to the window.open() function.

- The keyboard shortcuts are set by specifying a value for the "accesskey" attribute in the link for the menu items. The keyboard shortcuts are activated by pressing the "Alt-Shift-Key" combination when using the FireFox web browser. For the Safari web browser, the keyboard shortcuts are activated by using the "Ctrl-Key" combination. When an "accesskey" is activated in the Internet Explorer web browser with the "Alt-Key" sequence, the link is not activated, but rather it is set to have the keyboard focus. The keyboard shortcuts implemented for Program Phase 4-20 do not function properly in Internet Explorer.

- The following example can be launched by the launchtest1.html file with the test3.html file specified in the window.open() method:

test3.html: JavaScript Set the Main Window Menu

```
<!DOCTYPE HTML PUBLIC "-//W3C//DTD HTML 4.01 Transitional//EN"
"http://www.w3.org/TR/html4/loose.dtd">

<HTML>

<HEAD>
 <LINK rel="StyleSheet" href="test3.css">
</HEAD>

<BODY>

<!-- Menu Bar -->
<TABLE class="MenuBar">
<TR>

   <!-- File Menu -->
   <TD class="HideMenuClass" onmouseover="DisplayMenuItems(this);"
                             onmouseout="HideMenuItems(this);" >
      <P>File</P>

        <!-- Division tag used for grouping the menu items. -->
        <DIV class="HideMenuClass">

        <!-- Additional table that holds the menu items -->
        <TABLE class="MenuItems" cellpadding="0" cellspacing="0"  >

            <!-- Hello World! menu item -->
            <TR><TD class="MenuItem"  >
      <A class="MenuItem" href="#" accesskey="h" onClick="MenuItem1_Click()">
                 Hello World!
              </A>
            </TD></TR>

   <!-- Exit menu item -->
            <TR><TD class="MenuItem" >
      <A class="MenuItem" href="#" accesskey="x" onClick="MenuItem2_Click()">
                 Exit
              </A>
            </TD></TR>

        </TABLE>
        </DIV>
   </TD>

</TR>
</TABLE>
</BODY>
</HTML>

<SCRIPT TYPE="text/javascript">
```

test3.html continued on the next page

test3.html: JavaScript Set the Main Window Menu continued

```
function DisplayMenuItems(toTableData)
{
   var loDivItem;

   loDivItem = toTableData.getElementsByTagName("DIV").item(0);
   toTableData.className = "DisplayMenuClass";

   loDivItem.className = "DisplayMenuClass";
}

function HideMenuItems(toTableData)
{
   var loDivItem;

   loDivItem = toTableData.getElementsByTagName("DIV").item(0);

   toTableData.className = "HideMenuClass";
   loDivItem.className = "HideMenuClass";
}

function MenuItem1_Click()
{
   alert("Hello World!");
}

function MenuItem2_Click()
{
   window.close();
}

</SCRIPT>
```

test3.css: Cascading Style Sheet for the Main Window Menu

```
/*  If this is not set, there is a gap between the          */
/*   File menu and menu items when displayed in IE and FF   */
P
{
   margin:0;
}

/*  If this is not set, there is a gap between the   */
/*   File menu and menu items when displayed in IE   */
table.FileMenu
{
   vertical-align: bottom;
}

/*  When the loDivItem.className is set to            */
/*   HideMenuClass, this entry sets the display to    */
/*   none for the Division which causes the dropdown  */
/*   menu to be hidden.                               */

div.HideMenuClass
{
   display: none;
}

/*  When the loDivItem.className is set to DisplayMenuClass,  */
/*   this entry sets the display to inline for the Division   */

div.DisplayMenuClass
{
   display: inline;
}
```

test3.css continued on the next page

test3.css: Cascading Style Sheet for the Main Window Menu continued

```
/*  When the mouse cursor hovers over the menu items,  */
/*   the menu item is formatted properly.              */

a.MenuItem:hover
{
   text-decoration: none;
   color: black;
   background-color: lightgreen;
   display: block;
}

/*  This entry prevents the menu items from being  */
/*   displayed as underlined hyperlinks.           */

a.MenuItem
{
   text-decoration: none;
   color: black;
   display: block;
}
```

Client Side JavaScript
Set the Main Window Background Color and Mouse Cursor

- The "bgColor" property of the document object allows the background color of the web page to be set.
- The "style" attribute is set in the HTML tag to the value "min-height: 100%". This allows the mouse cursor to be set for the entire web page viewed in the web browser.
- An alternate method for setting the mouse cursor is to edit the <HTML> tag directly.

```
<HTML style="min-height:100%;cursor:default">
```

test4.html: JavaScript Set the Main Window Background Color and Mouse Cursor

```
<HTML style="min-height:100%">

<BODY>
</BODY>

<SCRIPT TYPE="text/javascript">

   var lnRed;
   var lnGreen;
   var lnBlue;

   lnRed = 255;
   lnGreen = 255;
   lnBlue = 255;

   document.bgColor= "#" + lnRed.toString(16).toUpperCase() +
                     lnGreen.toString(16).toUpperCase()  +
                     lnBlue.toString(16).toUpperCase();

   document.getElementsByTagName("html")[0].style.cursor='default';

</SCRIPT>
</HTML>
```

Client Side JavaScript
Prompt to Exit the Application when the Main Window is Closed

- The "onbeforeunload" attribute of the "BODY" tag is set to the name of a JavaScript function, which is automatically called when the browser main window is closed or navigated to a different web page. If the "event.returnValue" property is set to any string value, the user is prompted to continue with the current operation of closing or navigating. This feature is supported in the Internet Explorer web browser and does not work in FireFox or Safari.

test5.html: JavaScript Prompt to Exit the App. when the Main Window is Closed

```
<HTML>
<BODY onbeforeunload="Page_BeforeUnload()">

</BODY>

<SCRIPT TYPE="text/javascript">

function Page_BeforeUnload()
{
   event.returnValue = "";
}

</SCRIPT>
</HTML>
```

Source Code Files

- Text files: launchpp4_20.html, pp4_20.html, menu.css

- Image files: phase16x16.ico (Single-image icon file, Appendix O)

launchpp4_20.html: Launcher Program for the pp4_20.html File

```
<!--*********************************************************************-->
<!--* File: launchpp4_20.html                                           *-->
<!--* Reserved                                                          *-->
<!--*********************************************************************-->

<HTML>
<BODY>

   <BUTTON onclick="Launchpp4_20()">Launch Program Phase 4-20</BUTTON>

</BODY>
</HTML>

<SCRIPT TYPE="text/javascript">

function Launchpp4_20()
{
   var loMainWindow;

   // The main window is created here.
   loMainWindow = window.open("http://127.0.0.1/pp4_20.html",null,
                              "resizable=yes,menubar=no,location=yes");
}

</SCRIPT>
```

pp4_20.html: Program Phase 4-20 Source Code

```
<!--*********************************************************************-->
<!--* Program Phase 4-20 JavaScript Main Window with File Menu          *-->
<!--* Programming Tasks Illustrated: Browser based application          *-->
<!--*                                Browser Main window                *-->
<!--*                                Window icon                        *-->
<!--*                                Window caption                     *-->
<!--*                                Window menu with hotkeys           *-->
<!--*                                Window background color            *-->
<!--*                                Window mouse cursor                *-->
<!--*                                User sizable window               *-->
<!--*                                Message box input/output           *-->
<!--*********************************************************************-->

<!--*********************************************************************-->
<!--* File: pp4_20.html                                                 *-->
<!--* Reserved                                                          *-->
<!--*********************************************************************-->

<!DOCTYPE HTML PUBLIC "-//W3C//DTD HTML 4.01 Transitional//EN"
"http://www.w3.org/TR/html4/loose.dtd">

<HTML style="min-height:100%">

<HEAD>
 <LINK rel="StyleSheet" href="menu.css">
 <LINK rel="SHORTCUT ICON" href="phase16x16.ico">
</HEAD>

<BODY onbeforeunload="Page_BeforeUnload()">

<SCRIPT TYPE="text/javascript">

   glExitMenuItemClicked = 0;


//***********************************************************************
// Program Phase 4-20 Main                                              *
// Define the Entry Point of Execution (EPE) for Program Phase 4-20     *
// CBI:  4-20.1.1.1                                                     *
//***********************************************************************

   // The first line of text in the pp4_20.html file is the EPE for the
   // program.


//***********************************************************************
// Program Phase 4-20 Main                                              *
// Declare the local variables for the "main" program                   *
// CBI:  4-20.1.1.2                                                     *
//***********************************************************************

   var lnRed;
   var lnGreen;
   var lnBlue;


//***********************************************************************
// Program Phase 4-20 Main                                              *
// Create the main window                                               *
// CBI:  4-20.1.1.3                                                     *
//***********************************************************************

   // The main window for the program is the browser window displaying
   // html output.
```

pp4_20.html continued on the next page

pp4_20.html: Program Phase 4-20 Source Code continued

```
//****************************************************************************
// Program Phase 4-20 Main                                                   *
// Set the icon for the main window                                          *
// CBI:  4-20.1.1.4                                                          *
//****************************************************************************

   // The address bar icon for the pp4_20.html page is set in the
   // Reserved code block.


//****************************************************************************
// Program Phase 4-20 Main                                                   *
// Set the caption of the main window                                        *
// CBI:  4-20.1.1.5                                                          *
//****************************************************************************

   document.title = "Program Phase 4-20  |  " +
                    "Platform:  Web Browser  |  " +
                    "Programming Language:  JavaScript  |  " +
                    "GUI API:  DHTML";
</SCRIPT>


<!--*********************************************************************-->
<!--* Program Phase 4-20 Main                                           *-->
<!--* Create the menu for the main window                               *-->
<!--* CBI:  4-20.1.1.6                                                  *-->
<!--*********************************************************************-->

<!-- Menu Bar -->
<TABLE class="MenuBar">
<TR>

   <!-- File Menu -->
   <TD class="HideMenuClass" onmouseover="DisplayMenuItems(this);"
                             onmouseout="HideMenuItems(this);" >
      <P>File</P>

        <!-- Division tag used for grouping the menu items. -->
        <DIV class="HideMenuClass">

        <!-- Additional table that holds the menu items -->
        <TABLE class="MenuItems" cellpadding="0" cellspacing="0"  >

            <!-- Hello World! menu item -->
            <TR><TD class="MenuItem"  >
       <A class="MenuItem" href="#" accesskey="h" onClick="MenuItem1_Click()">
                Hello World!
             </A>
            </TD></TR>

            <!-- Exit menu item -->
            <TR><TD class="MenuItem" >
      <A class="MenuItem" href="#" accesskey="x" onClick="MenuItem2_Click()">
                Exit
             </A>
            </TD></TR>

        </TABLE>
        </DIV>
   </TD>
</TR>
</TABLE>
</BODY>
</HTML>
```

pp4_20.html continued on the next page

pp4_20.html: Program Phase 4-20 Source Code continued

```
<SCRIPT type="text/javascript">


//*****************************************************************************
// Program Phase 4-20 Main                                                    *
// Set the background color of the main window                                *
// CBI:  4-20.1.1.7                                                           *
//*****************************************************************************

   lnRed = 255;
   lnGreen = 255;
   lnBlue = 255;

   document.bgColor= "#" + lnRed.toString(16).toUpperCase() +
                     lnGreen.toString(16).toUpperCase()  +
                     lnBlue.toString(16).toUpperCase();


//*****************************************************************************
// Program Phase 4-20 Main                                                    *
// Set the mouse cursor displayed when positioned over the main window        *
// CBI:  4-20.1.1.8                                                           *
//*****************************************************************************

   document.getElementsByTagName("html")[0].style.cursor='default';


//*****************************************************************************
// Program Phase 4-20 Main                                                    *
// Allow resizing of the main window                                          *
// CBI:  4-20.1.1.9                                                           *
//*****************************************************************************

   // This is specified in the third parameter to window.open()
   // in the launchpp4_20.html file.


//*****************************************************************************
// Program Phase 4-20 Main                                                    *
// Maximize and display the main window                                       *
// CBI:  4-20.1.1.10                                                          *
//*****************************************************************************

   window.moveTo(0,0);
   window.resizeTo(screen.availWidth,screen.availHeight);


//*****************************************************************************
// Program Phase 4-20 Main                                                    *
// Start the event loop                                                       *
// CBI:  4-20.1.1.11                                                          *
//*****************************************************************************

   // The web browser implements the event loop.


//*****************************************************************************
// Program Phase 4-20 Main                                                    *
// Cleanup the resources used by the main window                              *
// CBI:  4-20.1.1.12                                                          *
//*****************************************************************************
```

pp4_20.html continued on the next page

pp4_20.html: Program Phase 4-20 Source Code continued

```
// Callback Functions

function DisplayMenuItems(toTableData)
{
  var loDivItem;

  loDivItem = toTableData.getElementsByTagName("DIV").item(0);
  toTableData.className = "DisplayMenuClass";
  loDivItem.className = "DisplayMenuClass";
}

function HideMenuItems(toTableData)
{
   var loDivItem;

   loDivItem = toTableData.getElementsByTagName("DIV").item(0);
   toTableData.className = "HideMenuClass";
   loDivItem.className = "HideMenuClass";
}


//****************************************************************************
// Callback Functions                                                        *
// Implement the callback function for the Hello World! menu item            *
// CBI:  4-20.1.2.1                                                          *
//****************************************************************************

function MenuItem1_Click()
{
   alert("Hello World!");
}

//****************************************************************************
// Callback Functions                                                        *
// Implement the callback function for the Exit menu item                    *
// CBI:  4-20.1.3.1                                                          *
//****************************************************************************

function MenuItem2_Click()
{
   glExitMenuItemClicked = 1;
   window.close();
}

//****************************************************************************
// Callback Functions                                                        *
// Implement the callback function that fires when the main window is closed *
// CBI:  4-20.1.4.1                                                          *
//****************************************************************************

// This function has been assigned to be the onbeforeunload() event in the
// <BODY> tag.  The onbeforeunload() event is only supported on IE.

function Page_BeforeUnload()
{
   if (glExitMenuItemClicked == 0)
   {
      event.returnValue = "";
   }
}
</SCRIPT>
```

menu.css: Cascading Style Sheet for the Main Window Menu

```
/*  If this is not set, there is a gap between the          */
/*   File menu and menu items when displayed in IE and FF   */

P
{
   margin:0;
}

/*  If this is not set, there is a gap between the    */
/*   File menu and menu items when displayed in IE    */

table.FileMenu
{
   vertical-align: bottom;
}

/*  When the loDivItem.className is set to             */
/*   HideMenuClass, this entry sets the display to     */
/*   none for the Division which causes the dropdown   */
/*   menu to be hidden.                                */

div.HideMenuClass
{
   display: none;
}

/*  When the loDivItem.className is set to DisplayMenuClass,  */
/*   this entry sets the display to inline for the Division   */

div.DisplayMenuClass
{
   display: inline;
}

/*  When the mouse cursor hovers over the menu items,  */
/*   the menu item is formatted properly.              */

a.MenuItem:hover
{
   text-decoration: none;
   color: black;
   background-color: lightgreen;
   display: block;
}

/*  This entry prevents the menu items from being  */
/*   displayed as underlined hyperlinks.           */

a.MenuItem
{
   text-decoration: none;
   color: black;
   display: block;
}
```

Code Setup and Compilation

- Tools: IIS or Apache (Appendix N), Internet Explorer, FireFox, Safari

Code Setup and Compilation Steps

1: Using a text editor, create the launchpp4_20.html, pp4_20.html, and menu.css files and enter the appropriate source code.

2: The launchpp4_20.html and pp4_20.html files can be copied to the default wwwroot folder of IIS. On most systems, this folder is found in C:\Inetpub\wwwroot.

3: The launchpp4_20.html and pp4_20.html files can be copied to the DocumentRoot folder of the Apache web server installation. This folder is specified in the httpd.conf text configuration file for the Apache installation.

```
Windows

   C:\Program Files\Apache Software Foundation\Apache2.2\htdocs

Linux

   Debian, Ubuntu ,Mepis, Mint:      /var/www or /var/www/apache2-default
   OpenSUSE:                         /srv/www/htdocs
   PCLinuxOS, Fedora Core, Mandriva:    /var/www/html

Mac OS X

   /Library/WebServer/Documents
```

4: Create the phase16x16.ico image file according to the instructions found in Appendix O. Save the icon file to the root folder of the web server.

5: After copying the launchpp4_20.html, pp4_20.html, menu.css and phase16x16.ico files to the web server, open a web browser and then open the launchpp4_20.html file by typing the following in the address bar of the web browser:

```
http://127.0.0.1/launchpp4_20.html
```

Replace "127.0.0.1" with the IP address or DNS name and path of the web server that stores the source code files.

Program Execution

- When the launchpp4_20.html file is opened, the following is displayed in the web browser:

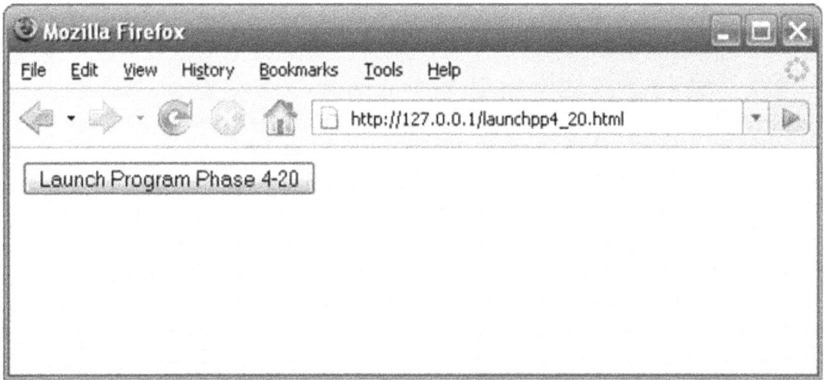

When the Launch Program Phase 4-20 button is activated, the following main window web page is displayed in a new browser window:

The "File" menu contains the "Hello World!" menu item and the "Exit" menu item. The prompt to exit when the main window is closed is only implemented on the IE platform.

- See Appendix P for information concerning debugging client side JavaScript programs.

Appendix

A - Java Installation

B - GNU GCC and KDevelop Installation

C - Xcode Installation

D - wxWidgets Source Code Setup

E - QT4 Source Code Setup

F - Komodo Installation

G - Python Installation

H - Perl/Tk Installation

I - Ruby Installation

J - PHP CLI and PHP-GTK Installation

K - Tcl/Tk Installation

L - GTK+-2 Installation

M - Delphi Installation

N - Internet Information Server and Apache Installation

O - Main Window and Application Icons

P - Client Side JavaScript Debugging

Q - Update the Path

R - ASCII Table

S - Window and Mouse Constants

Appendix A
Java Installation

Java SDK Installation

- The Java SE Development Kit (JDK) software can be used to compile and execute Program Phase 1-1, 2-1, 3-1, and 4-1. In addition, The Netbeans IDE can be used to edit, compile, execute, and debug the Java source code files. As of this writing, the JDK and Netbeans IDE were available as a single file installation at the following URL:

  ```
  http://java.sun.com/javase/downloads/index.jsp
  ```

- The JDK and Netbeans software can be installed on Linux without root privileges by specifying the home folder as the destination for the file installation. To start the install program on Linux, enter the following commands:

  ```
  chmod 744 jdk-6u1-nb-5_5-linux-ml.bin
  ./jdk-6u1-nb-5_5-linux-ml.bin
  ```

  Substitute the appropriate file name for the downloaded file.

- The Java JDK is included with Mac OS X.

Appendix B
GNU GCC and KDevelop Installation

Installation of GNU GCC and KDevelop on the Linux platform

- The GNU Compiler Collection (GCC) source code is available at the following URL:

  ```
  http://gcc.gnu.org
  ```

- GCC source code compilation and installation instructions are available at the following URL:

  ```
  http://gcc.gnu.org/install/
  ```

- KDevelop binaries and source code are available for many popular Linux distributions at the following URL:

  ```
  http://www.kdevelop.org
  ```

- The source code for the KDevelop program can be downloaded from the KDevelop web site. Compiling the source code requires the installation of several dependency programs. Compilation and installation instructions for KDevelop are detailed at the KDevelop web site.

- The following commands can be issued to install GCC and KDevelop on various Linux distributions:

- **Debian, Ubuntu, Mint:**

  ```
  apt-get update
  apt-get install gcc g++ kdevelop libtool gdb automake konsole
  ```

  Mepis:

  ```
  apt-get update
  apt-get install gcc g++ kdevelop3 libtool gdb automake konsole
  ```

  To start KDevelop on Mepis, issue the command "kdevelop3".

  PCLinuxOS:

  ```
  apt-get update
  apt-get install gcc kdevelop libtool gdb automake1.4
  ```

  OpenSUSE:

  ```
  yast -i gcc libtool gdb automake kdevelop3
  ```

  Fedora:

  ```
  yum install gcc gcc-c++ kdevelop kdebase
  ```

  Mandriva:

  ```
  urpmi gcc gcc-c++ libtool automake kdevelop konsole
  ```

Appendix C
Xcode Installation

Steps to install the Xcode Tools on the Mac OS X platform

- The Xcode program is available from the following URL:

  `http://developer.apple.com`

`Xcode Installation Steps`

1: After downloading the Xcode disk image file from the Apple developer web site, double-click on the file. This will open a window with the contents of the disk image being displayed in the "Xcode Tools" window.

2: Double-click on the XcodeTools.mpkg file in the "Xcode Tools" window. This will start the installation tool for the Xcode program.

3: Activate the "Continue" button in the "Install Xcode Tools" window to continue with the installation. Follow the prompts to finish the installation of the Xcode Tools.

Appendix D

wxWidgets Source Code Setup

Steps to compile the wxWidgets source code

Windows Compilation

- The wxWidgets library is available at the following URL:

  `http://www.wxwidgets.org`

  The wxMSW source archive contains an installer for the Windows platform. This needs to be installed before proceeding with the Source Code Compilation steps.

- The Microsoft Windows SDK for Visual Studio 2008 needs to be installed in order to compile the wxWidgets library. The SDK should automatically be installed when the Visual C++ 2008 Express Edition program is installed.

Windows wxWidgets Source Code Compilation Steps

1: Start the Visual C++ 2008 Express Edition program.

2: Open the wxWidgets workspace file by navigating to the wxWidets installation folder and then selecting the wx.dsw file found in the build\msw folder. When opening this workspace with the Microsoft Visual C++ 2008 Express Edition IDE, you may be prompted to convert the projects to a newer format. Select "yes to all" to convert all of the projects in the workspace file.

3: For non-debug applications, select either the "Release" or "Unicode Release" configuration. If you would like to create a build of wxWidgets that allows for debugging, select either the "Debug" or "Unicode Debug" configuration.

4: Control-click on each of the projects under the wx Solution until all of the projects are highlighted. Right-click on the highlighted projects and then activate the "Properties" menu item from the context sensitive popup menu. This allows the settings for all of the projects to be modified at one time.

5: On the "Property Pages" dialog window, expand the "Configuration Properties → C/C++ → Code Generation" item. For the "Runtime Library" setting, select the appropriate value. The setting that you specify here also needs to be specified for the project properties for each of the Program Phases that accesses the wxWidgets library. Activate the "OK" button to close the "Project Properties" window.

6: To build the wxWidgets library, activate the "Build Solution" menu item from the "Build" menu.

Steps continued on the next page

Windows wxWidgets Source Code Compilation Steps continued

7: Windows - Activate Menu Item: Start → Settings → Control Panel

8: Activate the "System" icon in the "Control Panel"

9: On the "System Properties" window, select the "Advanced" tab and then activate the "Environment Variables" button.

10: Create a new "User" or "System" environment variable called "wxwin" with the following string value:

```
c:\wxWidgets-2.8.6
```

Substitute the appropriate path for the version of the wxWidgets library installed.

Linux Compilation

The wxWidgets library is available in multiple configurations for Linux. The wxGTK configuration is detailed in this book and is suitable for compiling the examples presented. The wxGTK library source code is available at the following URL:

```
http://www.wxwidgets.org
```

The Linux wxWidgets Source Code Compilation steps are adapted from the instructions found at the following URL:

```
http://www.wxwidgets.org/wiki/index.php/Compiling_and_getting_start
ed
```

Linux wxWidgets Source Code Compilation Steps

1: Install GNU GCC (Appendix B) and GTK+-2 (Appendix L).

2: Download the wxGTK version of the wxWidgets library. Extract the downloaded file with the following command:

```
tar xzvf wxGTK-2.8.4.tar.gz
```

The preceding command should be substituted with the name of the particular file that has been downloaded from the wxWidgets web site.

3: After the file has been extracted, change directories to the folder containing the source code for the wxWidgets library, substituting for the actual version of the wxWidgets file that has been downloaded.

```
cd wxGTK-2.8.4
```

4: Create a folder called build-release inside the wxGTK-2.8.4 folder.

```
mkdir build-release
cd build-release
```

Steps continued on the next page

Linux wxWidgets Source Code Compilation Steps continued

5: Before compiling the wxWidgets library, it can be configured with various options. The following settings set up an ANSI release build that provides for static linking:

```
../configure --disable-unicode --disable-debug --disable-shared
```

6: After the configure command is executed, enter the following command:

```
make
```

7: After make has successfully executed, enter the following command:

```
make install
```

- Note that the "make install" command requires root privileges. The above commands result in the wxGTK library being installed without Unicode, debug, and shared library support. If you would like to use different features of the wxGTK library in your program, create the appropriate folder along side the build-release folder (build-debug for a debug configuration) and then from this folder, run the configure command again with the appropriate settings and then run make and make install. This results in multiple configurations of the wxGTK library being installed in the /usr/local/lib folder (destination folder when make install is executed). It is possible to select which configuration is used at compile time, so it is ok to have multiple configurations of the wxGTK library installed at the same time. This is done by using the wx-config utility to specify configuration options for the project.

Appendix E

QT4 Source Code Setup

Steps to compile the QT4 source code

- The open source version of QT4 is available as a free download and provides a license for creating applications suitable for personal and educational use. If you wish to distribute a QT4 application using the open source version of QT4, the distribution of the program must include the source code and adhere to the GNU General Public License (GPL). If you wish to distribute your application without the source code, the commercial edition of QT4 can be used.

  The QT4 framework can be downloaded from the following URL:

  ```
  http://www.trolltech.com
  ```

Windows Installation

- QT4 can be installed from a pre-compiled binary file on the Windows platform. To install the open source edition of the QT4 framework and the Mingw compiler, download the latest QT/Windows open source edition from the following URL:

  ```
  http://www.trolltech.com
  ```

  Example

  ```
  qt-win-opensource-4.1.4-mingw.exe
  ```

  Be sure to select for the Mingw compiler to be installed. After installation, update the system path to include the Qt bin folder.

  `Example`

  ```
  PATH = C:\Qt\4.1.4\bin;$PATH
  ```

  See Appendix Q for information about updating the path permanently.

Linux Compilation

- The QT4 framework source code can be compiled on the Linux platform.

`Linux QT4 Source Code Compilation Steps`

1: Download the qt-x11-opensource-src-4.1.4.tgz file (or newer version) to a temporary folder on your computer.

2: Open a terminal window and change directories to the download folder. Extract the source file with the following command substituting for the appropriate file name:

```
tar xzvf qt-x11-opensource-src-4.1.4.tar.gz
```

`Steps continued on the next page`

Linux QT4 Source Code Compilation Steps continued

3: Change directories to the folder containing the source code for the QT4 library, substituting for the actual version of the QT4 file that has been downloaded.

```
cd qt-x11-opensource-src-4.1.4
```

4: In the source code folder, enter the following commands:

```
./configure
make
make install
```

5: The path to the QT4 framework binary files needs to be set.

Bash

```
export PATH=/usr/local/Trolltech/Qt-4.1.4/bin:$PATH
```

C and TC shell

```
setenv PATH /usr/local/Trolltech/Qt-4.1.4/bin:$PATH
```

See Appendix Q for information about updating the path permanently.

Mac OS X Compilation

- The Xcode IDE can be used to compile C++ QT4 applications on Mac OS X. (Appendix C).
- In addition to the Xcode IDE, the QT4 library must be setup properly.

Mac OS X QT4 Source Code Compilation Steps

1: Download the QT4 library source code for Mac OS X. After the source file has been downloaded, it must be extracted. From a terminal window, change directories to the download folder and then enter the following:

```
tar xzvf qt-mac-opensource-src-4.1.4.tar.gz
```

Substitute the appropriate name for the downloaded file.

2: Change directories to the folder containing the source code for the QT4 library, substituting for the actual version of the QT4 file that has been downloaded.

```
cd qt-mac-opensource-src-4.1.4
```

3: In the source code folder, enter the following commands:

```
./configure
make
sudo make install
```

4: The path to the QT4 framework binary files needs to be set.

Example

```
export PATH=/usr/local/Trolltech/Qt-4.1.4/bin:$PATH
```

See Appendix Q for information about updating the path permanently.

Appendix F

Komodo Installation

Steps to install the Komodo IDE on multiple platforms

- The Komodo IDE program is available at the following URL:

  `http://downloads.activestate.com/Komodo`

- A Komodo license file needs to be purchased and installed in the appropriate location. Purchased license files can be downloaded from the Activestate web site in the "My Downloads" section.

- Komodo Edit (free) can be used instead of Komodo IDE for program editing and execution. Komodo Edit cannot be used for debugging.

`Windows Komodo Installation Steps`

1: Download the Komodo installation file for the Windows platform.

Example

```
Komodo-IDE-4.2.1-283000.msi
```

2: Double-click on the downloaded installer file to begin the installation.

3: Download the Windows license from the "My Downloads" area of the Activestate web site. The license file on the Windows platform will look something like this:

```
Komodo_IDE_Windows_XXXXXXXXXX.exe
```

After downloading the executable license file, double-click on it to install the license.

`Linux Komodo Installation Steps`

1: Download the Komodo installation file for the Linux platform.

Example

```
Komodo-IDE-4.2.1-283000-linux-libcpp5-x86.tar.gz
```

2: Extract the installation file substituting for the appropriate file name.

```
tar zxvf Komodo-IDE-4.2.1-283000-linux-libcpp5-x86.tar
```

3: Change directories to the Komodo-IDE-4.2.1-283000-linux-libcpp5-x86 folder and then launch the install.sh installer script.

```
cd Komodo-IDE-4.2.1-283000-linux-libcpp5-x86
./install.sh
```

Substitute the appropriate name for the file downloaded. You may need root or sudo privileges to properly execute the install.sh script.

`Steps continued on the next page`

Linux Komodo Installation Steps continued

4: If you get an error about libstdc++.so.5 missing, the libstdc++.so.5 file needs to be installed.

Debian, Ubuntu

```
apt-get install libstdc++5
```

Fedora

```
yum install compat-libstdc++-33
```

5: Download the Linux license from the "My Downloads" area of the Activestate web site. The license file on the Linux platform will look something like this:

```
Komodo_IDE_Linux_x86_XXXXXXXXXX.bin
```

The license file can be made executable with the following command:

```
chmod 744 Komodo_IDE_Linux_x86_XXXXXXXXXX.bin
```

Execute the following command to install the license:

```
./Komodo_IDE_Linux_x86_XXXXXXXXXX.bin
```

Substitute the appropriate name for the file name.

6: To start the program, enter the following in a terminal window:

```
~/Komodo-IDE-4.2/bin/komodo &
```

Substitute the appropriate path for the Komodo version installed.

Mac OS X Komodo Installation Steps

1: Download the Komodo installation file for the Mac OS X platform.

Example

```
Komodo-IDE-4.2.1-283000-macosx-x86.dmg
```

2: Double-click on the downloaded disk image file to proceed with the installation.

3: Download the Mac OS X license from the "My Downloads" area of the Activestate web site. The license file on the Mac OS X platform will look something like this:

```
Komodo_IDE_Mac_OS_X_Intel_XXXXXXXXXX.zip
```

After downloading the executable license file, double-click on it to extract the "ActiveState License Installer". Double-click on the "ActiveState License Installer" to install the license.

Appendix G

Python Installation

Steps to install the Python Interpreter on multiple platforms

- Windows binary installers for Python are available at the following URL:

  ```
  http://www.python.org
  ```

  In addition, Activestate provides Widows binary distributions of Python.

  ```
  http://www.activestate.com
  ```

  The default installation folder for Python 2.5 on Windows is c:\Python25.

- Python and Tk can be installed on various Linux distributions.

  Debian, Ubuntu, Mepis, Mint:

  ```
  apt-get install python python-tk
  ```

  PC Linux OS:

  ```
  apt-get install python tkinter
  ```

  Fedora:

  ```
  yum install python python-tools
  ```

  OpenSuse:

  ```
  yast -i python python-tk
  ```

  Mandriva:

  ```
  urpmi python-base python tkinter
  ```

- Python comes pre-installed on Mac OS X 10.4 and 10.5. To execute Program Phase 3-9 and Program Phase 4-9, the Tk module needs to be installed (Appendix H).

- The Komodo IDE program can be used to edit, debug, and launch Python programs on the Windows, Linux, and Mac OS X platforms.

Komodo IDE Setup Steps

1: Start the Komodo IDE program.

2: Windows and Linux – Komodo - Activate Menu Item: Edit → Preferences

Mac OS X – Komodo - Activate Menu Item: Komodo → Preferences

3: Expand the "Languages" category on the left side of the dialog window and then select the "Python" entry. The interpreter should be set to "Find on Path". When the Python distribution is installed on the Linux and Mac OS X platforms, it is usually installed in the /usr/bin folder, which is normally in the search path. See Appendix Q for information about updating the search path.

Appendix H
Perl/Tk Installation

Steps to install the Perl Interpreter and Tk module on multiple platforms

- Windows binary installers for Perl are available at the official Perl website.

  ```
  http://www.perl.com
  ```

  In addition, Activestate provides binary distributions of Python.

  ```
  http://www.activestate.com
  ```

  The default installation folder for Perl on Windows is c:\perl\bin. The Perl programs in this book have been tested with Activestate Perl 5.8.x which includes the Tk module. The Tk module is not included with Activestate Perl 5.10.x. The Tk module can be installed from a command prompt with the following command after Activestate Perl 5.10.x has been installed:

  ```
  ppm install Tk
  ```

- Perl and Tk can be installed on various Linux distributions.

  Debian, Ubuntu, Mepis, Mint:

  ```
  apt-get install perl libtk-perl
  ```

  PC Linux OS:

  ```
  apt-get install perl perl-Tk
  ```

  Fedora:

  ```
  yum install perl perl-Tk
  ```

  OpenSuse:

  ```
  yast -i perl perl-Tk
  ```

  Mandriva:

  ```
  urpmi perl perl-Tk
  ```

- Perl comes pre-installed on Mac OS X 10.4 and 10.5. The Tk module is not included. The Tk module can be compiled from source. To compile the Tk module source code, install the Apple developer tools including Xcode and the X11 SDK. See Appendix C for information on installing Xcode. The Tk module source code can be downloaded from the following URL:

  ```
  http://search.cpan.org/~ni-s/Tk-804.027/
  ```

  Install the X11 program from the Mac OS X installation cd. From an X11 xterm terminal window, enter the following commands to compile and install the Perl Tk module:

  ```
  tar xzvf Tk-804.027.tar.gz
  cd Tk-804.027
  perl Makefile.PL
  ```

```
make
make test
sudo make install
```

Substitute the appropriate file name for the downloaded version of Tk. A Perl program that uses the Tk module on the Mac OS X platform must be launched from an X11 xterm terminal window.

- The Komodo IDE can be used to edit, debug, and launch Perl programs on the Windows, Linux, and Mac OS X platforms.

Komodo IDE Setup Steps

1: Start the Komodo IDE program.

2: Windows and Linux – Komodo - Activate Menu Item: Edit → Preferences

Mac OS X – Komodo - Activate Menu Item: Komodo → Preferences

3: Expand the "Languages" category on the left side of the dialog window and then select the "Perl" entry. The interpreter should be set to "Find on Path". When the Perl distribution is installed on the Linux and Mac OS X platforms, it is usually installed in the /usr/bin folder, which is normally in the search path. See Appendix Q for information about updating the search path.

4: Activate the "OK" button to close the "Preferences" window.

Appendix I

Ruby Installation

Steps to install the Ruby Interpreter on multiple platforms

- A binary installer for Ruby on the Windows platform is available at the official Ruby website at the following URL:

  ```
  http://www.ruby-lang.org
  ```

  The default installation folder for Ruby on Windows is c:\ruby\bin. To use the Tk library with Ruby, the proper Tk library files need to be installed. The Activestate Tcl distribution includes the required Tk library. See Appendix K for information about installing Tcl.

- The source code for Ruby can be downloaded at the following URL:

  ```
  http://www.ruby-lang.org
  ```

  Ruby can be installed on various Linux distributions.

  Debian, Ubuntu, Mepis, Mint:

  ```
  apt-get install ruby libtk-ruby
  ```

  PCLinuxOS:

  ```
  apt-get install ruby ruby-tk
  ```

  Fedora:

  ```
  yum install ruby ruby-tcltk
  ```

  OpenSuse:

  ```
  yast -i ruby ruby-tk
  ```

  Mandriva:

  ```
  urpmi ruby ruby-tk
  ```

- Ruby comes pre-installed on Mac OS X 10.4 and 10.5. To execute Program Phase 3-12 and Program Phase 4-12, the Tk module needs to be installed. Appendix H contains installation instructions for the Tk module on the Mac OS X platform.

- The Komodo IDE can be used to edit, debug, and launch Ruby programs on the Windows, Linux, and Mac OS X platforms.

Komodo IDE Setup Steps

1: Start the Komodo IDE program.

2: Windows and Linux – Komodo - Activate Menu Item: Edit → Preferences

Mac OS X – Komodo - Activate Menu Item: Komodo → Preferences

3: Expand the "Languages" category on the left side of the dialog window and then select the "Ruby" entry. The interpreter should be set to "Find on Path". When the Ruby distribution is installed on the Linux and Mac OS X platforms, it is usually installed in the /usr/bin folder, which is normally in the search path. See Appendix Q for information about updating the search path.

4: Activate the "OK" button to close the "Preferences" window.

Appendix J

PHP CLI and PHP-GTK Installation

Steps to install PHP CLI and PHP-GTK on multiple platforms

- The GNOPE distribution of PHP comes configured for GTK. A Windows binary installer for GNOPE is available from the following URL:

  ```
  http://www.gnope.org
  ```

- PHP CLI can be installed on various Linux distributions.

  Debian, Ubuntu,Mepis, Mint:

  ```
     apt-get install php5-cli php5-dev php5-gd pkg-config
  libglib2.0-dev libgtk2.0-dev

     *** Proceed to the PHP-GTK Installation Section
  ```

  PCLinuxOS:

  ```
     apt-get install php-cli php-devel php-gd pkgconfig
  libglib2.0_0-devel libgtk+2.0_0-devel

     *** Proceed to the PHP-GTK Installation Section
  ```

  Fedora:

  ```
     yum install php-cli php-devel php-gd

     *** Proceed to the PHP-GTK Installation Section
  ```

  OpenSuse:

  ```
     yast -i php5 php5-devel php5-gd pkgconfig autoconf gcc
  glib2-devel gtk2-devel

     *** Proceed to the PHP-GTK Installation Section
  ```

  Mandriva:

  ```
     urpmi php-gd php-gtk2

  edit the php.ini file and add the following settings:

     extension=gd.so
     extension=php_gtk2.so
  ```

- PHP-GTK Installation - All Linux Distributions (excluding Mandriva)

  Download php-gtk from http://gtk.php.net and then install with the following commands substituting the appropriate file name:

  ```
  tar -xvzf php-gtk-2.0.0beta-2_8.tar.gz
  cd php-gtk-2.0.0beta
  ./buildconf
  ./configure
  make
  make install
  ```

Edit the php.ini file and add the following settings:

```
extension=gd.so
extension=php_gtk2.so
```

- More information for installing on the Linux platform can be found at the following URL:

  `http://gtk.php.net/manual/en/tutorials.installation.php`

- Instructions for installing PHP-GTK on the Mac OS X platform can be found at the following URL:

  `http://gtk.php.net/manual/en/tutorials.installation.macosx-stepbystep.php`

Komodo IDE Setup Steps

1: Start the Komodo IDE program.

2: Windows and Linux – Komodo - Activate Menu Item: Edit → Preferences

Mac OS X – Komodo - Activate Menu Item: Komodo → Preferences

3: Expand the "Languages" category on the left side of the dialog window and then select the "PHP" entry. The item selected for "Use this interpreter" can be set to "Find on Path", or an absolute path to the php (php.exe on Windows) executable file can be specified. If "Find On Path" is selected, make sure that the php executable file is in the search path. See Appendix Q for information about updating the search path.

4: Activate the "Debugger Config Wizard" button and then activate the "Next" button.

5: In the "Setup this installation" textbox, enter the full path to the php executable file and then activate the "Next" button.

6: The "INI file to be copied" textbox needs to contain the full path to the php.ini file being used by your PHP-CLI installation. The "Put debug version of ini at" textbox should be set to a folder called debug found in the same folder that contains the php executable file. Activate the "Next" button. If an error occurs that says, "You have chosen a destination for the debug ini file that does not exist.", create a folder called debug inside the folder where your php executable file is found. The "Use this extensions directory" textbox needs to be set to the extensions directory usually called ext inside your php-cli installation folder. Activate the Next button twice and then activate the Finish button.

Appendix K
Tcl/Tk Installation

Steps to install Tcl/Tk on multiple platforms

- Windows binary installers for Tcl are available from the Activestate website at the following URL :

  ```
  http://www.activestate.com
  ```

  The Activestate Tcl distribution comes with the Tk library.

- Tcl and Tk can be installed on various Linux distributions.

  Debian, Ubuntu, Mepis, Mint:

  ```
  apt-get install tclx8.3-dev tk8.3-dev
  ```

  PC Linux OS:

  ```
  apt-get install tcl tk
  ```

  Fedora:

  ```
  yum install tcl tk-devel
  ```

  OpenSuse:

  ```
  yast -i tcl tk
  ```

  Mandriva:

  ```
  urpmi tcl tk
  ```

- Tcl comes pre-installed on Mac OS X 10.4 and 10.5. To execute Program Phase 3-13 and Program Phase 4-13, the Tk module needs to be installed. Appendix H contains installation instructions for the Tk module on the Mac OS X platform.

- XOTcl (Extended Object Tcl) support is required for executing Program Phase 3-13. More information is available from the XOTcl web site found at:

  ```
  http://media.wu-wien.ac.at/download.html
  ```

  The following is an overview of some of the installation options:

  Windows

  ```
  1) ActiveTcl binary distribution (http://www.activestate.com)
  ```

  Linux

  ```
  1) ActiveTcl binary distribution (http://www.activestate.com)
  2) Install from RPM file (http://media.wu-
  wien.ac.at/download.html)
  3) Compile from source (http://media.wu-wien.ac.at/download.html)
  ```

  Mac OS X

  ```
  1)  ActiveTcl binary distribution (http://www.activestate.com)
  ```

- The Komodo IDE can be used to edit, debug, and launch Tcl programs on the Windows, Linux, and Mac OS X platforms.

```
Komodo IDE Setup Steps
```

1: Start the Komodo IDE program.

2: Windows and Linux – Komodo - Activate Menu Item: Edit → Preferences

Mac OS X – Komodo - Activate Menu Item: Komodo → Preferences

3: Expand the "Languages" category on the left side of the dialog window and then select the "Tcl" entry. The interpreter should be set to "Find on Path". When the Tcl distribution is installed on the Linux and Mac OS X platforms, it is usually installed in the /usr/bin folder, which is normally in the search path. See Appendix Q for information about updating the search path.

4: Activate the "OK" button to close the "Preferences" window.

Appendix L

GTK+-2 Installation

Steps to install the GTK+-2 development library

- GTK+-2 can be installed on various Linux distributions.

Debian, Ubuntu, Mepis, Mint:

```
apt-get install libgtk2.0-dev
```

PCLinuxOS:

```
apt-get install libgtk+2.0_0-devel
```

Fedora:

```
yum install gtk2-devel
```

OpenSuse:

```
yast -i gtk2-devel
```

Mandriva:

```
urpmi libgtk+2-devel
```

Appendix M
Delphi Installation

Steps to install the Turbo Delphi Explorer IDE on the Windows platform

- The Turbo Delphi Explorer program is available at the following URL:

  `http://www.codegear.com/downloads/free`

`Turbo Delphi Explorer IDE Installation Steps`

1: Download the Turbo Delphi Explorer installation file and install the software.

2: Register to obtain a free serial number and authorization key.

3: Enter the serial number and authorization key to activate the Turbo Delphi Explorer program.

Appendix N

IIS and Apache Installation

Steps to install Internet Information Server and Apache

- Internet Information Server (IIS) is included with Windows XP and can be installed with the "Add or Remove Programs" item in the Windows Control Panel.

- Windows binary installers for Apache are available from the following URL:

  ```
  http://httpd.apache.org
  ```

- Apache can be installed on various Linux distributions.

  Debian, Ubuntu, Mepis, Mint:

  ```
  apt-get install apache2
  ```

  PC Linux OS:

  ```
  apt-get install apache-base
  ```

  Fedora:

  ```
  yum install httpd
  ```

  OpenSuse:

  ```
  yast -i apache2
  ```

  Mandriva:

  ```
  urpmi apache
  ```

- Apache comes pre-installed on Mac OS X 10.4 and 10.5.

Appendix O

Main Window and Application Icons

Steps to create the icons for Program Phase Task 4

- Each of the Program Phases that implements Program Phase Task 4 uses a particular file format for the main window icon and/or the application icon. The following icon image types are used in this book:

```
.ico
.gif
.xpm
.icns
.png
```

- The GNU Image Manipulation Program (GIMP) can be used to create the .ico, .gif, xpm and .png image files used in this book. The GIMP image editor is a free program and is available for multiple platforms, including Windows, Linux, and Mac OS X. The GIMP is available as a free download from the following URL:

```
http://www.gimp.org
```

  The GIMP can be used to create all of the image file formats presented except for the .icns files created for Program Phase 4-17 and Program Phase 4-18.

- The Icon Composer application can be used to create the .icns file for Program Phase 4-17 and Program Phase 4-18 on the Mac OS X platform. The Icon Composer application is available as a part of the Xcode tools, which can be downloaded from the following URL:

```
http://developer.apple.com
```

---

phase.ico – multi-image icon file

- A multi-image icon file called phase.ico is used in the following Program Phases for the main window and application icon:

```
Program Phase 4-2
Program Phase 4-3
Program Phase 4-4
Program Phase 4-5
Program Phase 4-6
Program Phase 4-7
Program Phase 4-8
Program Phase 4-14
Program Phase 4-15
Program Phase 4-16 (Windows)
```

- The multi-image phase.ico icon file contains two images in one file. The first image is a 16 x 16 pixel representation of the icon image. A 32 x 32 pixel icon image is also created and stored in the phase.ico file. When the phase.ico icon file is assigned to be the main window icon, the 16 x 16 pixel image will be displayed. On the Windows platform, when the phase.ico file is assigned as the application icon, the icon will be displayed when the executable file is viewed in Windows Explorer. Depending on the current view in Windows Explorer, either the 16 x 16 pixel or the 32 x 32 pixel image will be displayed.

The GIMP phase.ico Multi-Image File Creation Steps

1: Start the GIMP program.

2: GIMP - Activate Menu Item: File → New

3: On the "Create a New Image" dialog window, make sure that no template is selected and set the width and height of the image to 32 x 32 pixels. Expand the "Advanced" options and then specify that the "Color Space" is set to "RGB Color" and the "Fill With" setting is set to "Background color". Activate the "OK" button to proceed.

4: GIMP - Activate Menu Item: View → Zoom → 800%

5: Click on the "Fill with a Color or Pattern" icon (looks like a tipping paint can) in the GIMP program. Select "FG color fill" for the "Fill Type". "Affected areas" should be set to "Fill whole selection". Select the appropriate color and then click on the image to fill the image.

6: Change the current color to a different color and then click on the GIMP icon "Paint hard edged pixels" (looks like a pencil). Select "Circle (01)" as the "Brush". Edit the image appropriately.

7:

8: GIMP - Activate Menu Item: Layer → New Layer

9: On the New Layer dialog window, set the width and height to 16 x 16 pixels and set the "Layer fill type" to "Background color". Activate the "OK" button to proceed.

10: Click on the "Fill with a Color or Pattern" icon (looks like a tipping paint can) in the GIMP program. Select "FG color fill" for the "Fill Type". "Affected areas" should be set to "Fill whole selection". Select the appropriate color and then click on the image to fill the screen with the desired color. To use the color picker to select a color from the first layer, switch to the 32 x 32 layer by activating the "Stack → Select Bottom Layer" menu item from the "Layer" menu. Use the color picker to select the appropriate color used in the 32 x 32 pixel image. Now switch back to the 16 x 16 pixel image layer by activating the "Stack → Select Next Layer" menu item from the "Layer" menu. Use the fill tool to fill the image with the appropriate color. To go back to editing the 32 x 32 pixel image, the "Stack → Bottem Layer" menu item in the "Layer" menu can be used to place the 32 x 32 pixel image above the 16 x 16 pixel image.

Steps continued on the next page

The GIMP phase.ico Multi-Image File Creation Steps continued

11: Change the current color to the appropriate color and then click on the GIMP icon "Paint hard edged pixels" (looks like a pencil). Select "Circle (01)" as the "Brush". Edit the image appropriately.

12: GIMP - Activate Menu Item: File → Save

On the "Save Image" dialog window, make sure that the "Select File Type" setting is set to "By Extension". Enter phase.ico as the file name and then activate the "Save" button.

13: The "GIMP Windows Icon Plugin" window should appear. Select "4 bpp, 1-bit alpha, 16-slot palette" for each of the layers and then activate the "OK" button.

---

phase16x16.ico – single image icon file

- A single image icon file called phase16x16.ico is used in the following Program Phases for the main window:

```
Program Phase 4-9
Program Phase 4-12
Program Phase 4-13
Program Phase 4-20
```

- The phase16x16.ico image file contains a single 16 x 16 pixel image.

The GIMP phase16x16.ico Single Image File Creation Steps

1: Start the GIMP program.

2: GIMP - Activate Menu Item: File → New

3: On the "Create a New Image" dialog window, make sure that no template is selected and then set the width and height of the image to 16 x 16 pixels. Expand the "Advanced" options and then specify that the "Color Space" is set to "RGB Color", and the "Fill With" setting is set to "Background color".

4: GIMP - Activate Menu Item: View → Zoom → 800%

Steps continued on the next page

The GIMP phase16x16.ico Single Image File Creation Steps continued

5: Click on the "Fill with a Color or Pattern" icon (looks like a tipping paint can) in the GIMP program. Select "FG color fill" for the "Fill Type". "Affected areas" should be set to "Fill whole selection". Select the appropriate color and then click on the image to fill the image.

6: Select the appropriate color and then click on the "Paint hard edged pixels" icon (looks like a pencil). Select "Circle (01)" as the "Brush". Edit the icon appropriately.

7: GIMP - Activate Menu Item: File → Save

On the "Save Image" dialog window, make sure that the "Select File Type" setting is set to "By Extension". Enter phase16x16.ico as the file name and then activate the "Save" button.

8: On the "Windows Icon Plugin" window, select 4 bpp, 1-bit alpha, 16-slot palette and then activate the "OK" button.

---

phase16x16.gif

- A single image icon file called phase16x16.gif is used in the following Program Phases for the main window (not the application icon):

  Program Phase 4-1

- The phase16x16.gif image file contains a single 16 x 16 pixel image.

The GIMP phase16x16.gif Single Image File Creation Steps

1: Start the GIMP program.

2: GIMP - Activate Menu Item: File → New

3: On the "Create a New Image" dialog window, make sure that no template is selected and then set the width and height of the image to 16 x 16 pixels. Expand the "Advanced" options and then specify that the "Color Space" is set to "RGB Color" and the "Fill With" setting is set to "Background color". Activate the "OK" button.

4: GIMP - Activate Menu Item: View → Zoom → 800%

5: Click on the "Fill with a Color or Pattern icon" (looks like a tipping paint can) in the GIMP program. Select "FG color fill" for the "Fill Type". Affected areas should be set to "Fill whole selection". Select the appropriate color and then click on the image to fill the image.

Steps continued on the next page

The GIMP phase16x16.gif Single Image File Creation Steps continued

6: Select the appropriate color and then click on the "Paint hard edged pixels" icon (looks like a pencil). Select "Circle (01)" as the "Brush". Edit the icon appropriately.

7: GIMP - Activate Menu Item: File → Save

On the "Save Image" dialog window, make sure that the "Select File Type" setting is set to "By Extension". Enter phase16x16.gif as the file name and then activate the "Save" button.

8: If the "Export File" dialog window is displayed, select "Convert To Indexed using default settings" and then activate the "Export" button. On the "Save as GIF" dialog window, do not select "Interlace" and then activate the "Save" button.

---

phase32x32.gif

- A single image icon file called phase32x32.gif is used in the following Program Phases for the main window:

  ```
  Program Phase 4-10
  ```

- The phase32x32.gif image file contains a single 32 x 32 pixel image.

The GIMP phase32x32.gif Single Image File Creation Steps

1: Start the GIMP program.

2: GIMP - Activate Menu Item: File → New

3: On the "Create a New Image" dialog window, make sure that no template is selected and set the width and height of the image to 32 x 32 pixels. Expand the "Advanced" options and specify that the "Color Space" is set to "RGB Color" and the "Fill With" setting is set to "Background color".

4: GIMP - Activate Menu Item: View → Zoom → 800%

5: Click on the "Fill with a Color or Pattern" icon (looks like a tipping paint can) in the GIMP program. Select "FG color fill" for the "Fill Type". "Affected areas" should be set to "Fill whole selection". Select the appropriate color and then click on the image to fill the image.

6: Select the appropriate color and then click on the "Paint hard edged pixels" icon (looks like a pencil). Select "Circle (01)" as the "Brush".

Steps continued on the next page

The GIMP phase32x32.gif Single Image File Creation Steps continued

7: GIMP - Activate Menu Item: File → Save

On the "Save Image" dialog window, make sure that the "Select File Type" setting is set to "By Extension". Enter phase32x32.gif as the file name and then activate the "Save" button.

8: If the "Export File" dialog window is displayed, select "Convert To Indexed using default settings" and then activate the "Export" button. On the "Save as GIF" dialog window, do not select "Interlace" and then activate the "OK" button.

---

phase16x16.xpm

- A single image icon file called phase16x16.xpm is used in the following Program Phases for the main window:

```
Program Phase 4-11
Program Phase 4-16 (Linux)
Program Phase 4-19
```

- The phase16x16.xpm image file contains a single 16 x 16 pixel image.

The GIMP phase16x16.xpm Single Image File Creation Steps

1: Start the GIMP program.

2: GIMP - Activate Menu Item: File → New

3: On the "Create a New Image" dialog window, make sure that no template is selected and set the width and height of the image to 16 x 16 pixels. Expand the "Advanced" options and then set the "Color Space" to "RGB Color" and the "Fill With" setting to "Background color". Activate the "OK" button.

4: GIMP - Activate Menu Item: View → Zoom → 800%

5: Click on the "Fill with a Color or Pattern" icon (looks like a tipping paint can) in the GIMP program. Select "FG color fill" for the "Fill Type". "Affected areas" should be set to "Fill whole selection". Select the appropriate color and then click on the image to fill the image.

Steps continued on the next page

The GIMP phase16x16.xpm Single Image File Creation Steps continued

6: Select the appropriate color and then click on the "Paint hard edged pixels" icon (looks like a pencil). Select "Circle (01)" as the "Brush". Edit the icon appropriately.

7: GIMP - Activate Menu Item: File → Save

On the "Save Image" dialog window, make sure that the "Select File Type" setting is set to "By Extension". Enter phase16x16.xpm as the file name and then activate the "Save" button.

---

phase.icns

- A multi-image icon file called phase.icns is used in the following Program Phases for the application icon:

```
Program Phase 4-17
Program Phase 4-18
```

- The phase.icns file can be created by using the Icon Composer application. The phase.icns file can contain four images. The following image resolutions are supported:

```
16 x 16
32 x 32
48 x 48
128 x 128
```

Icon Composer phase.icns Multi-Image File Creation Steps

1: Create the phase32x32.png file according to the instructions found on page O8.

2: Open the phase32x32.png image with the GIMP program.

GIMP - Activate Menu Item: Image → Scale Image

Change the width and height to 128 x 128 and for Interpolation select "None". Activate the "Scale" button. Save the file as phase128x128.png.

3: On the Mac OS X platform, start the Icon Composer program found in the Developer/Applications/Utilities folder.

4: When the program starts, a blank icns file is automatically created.

5: Drag the phase128x128.png image file to the Thumbnail 128 x 128 square.

Steps continued on the next page

Icon Composer phase.icns Multi-Image File Creation Steps continued

6: Assign the phase128x128.png image to the remaining image sizes. "Select Use Scaled Version" after selecting the phase128x128.png image for each of the remaining images by dragging the 128x128 image to the remaining image boxes. Select "Extract mask" for each of the remaining images. The 1bit mask is used to determine the clickable area of each scaled image. Program Phase 4-17 and Program Phase 4-18 do not use the images found in the phase.icns file as clickable images, so this value is not important.

7: Icon Composer - File → Save

Save the multi-image icon file as phase.icns.

---

phase16x16.png

- A single image icon file called phase16x16.png is used in the following Program Phases for the main window:

  Program Phase 4-15

- The phase16x16.png image file contains a single 16 x 16 pixel image.

The GIMP phase16x16.png Single Image File Creation Steps

1: Start the GIMP program.

2: GIMP - Activate Menu Item: File → New

3: On the "Create a New Image" dialog window, make sure that no template is selected and then set the width and height of the image to 16 x 16 pixels. Expand the "Advanced" options and then set the "Color Space" to "RGB Color" and the "Fill With" setting to "Background color".

4: GIMP - Activate Menu Item: View → Zoom → 800%

5: Click on the "Fill with a Color or Pattern" icon (looks like a tipping paint can) in the GIMP program. Select "FG color fill" for the "Fill Type". "Affected areas" should be set to "Fill whole selection". Select the appropriate color and then click on the image to fill the image.

6: Select the appropriate color and then click on the "Paint hard edged pixels" icon (looks like a pencil). Select "Circle (01)" as the "Brush". Edit the icon appropriately.

7: GIMP - Activate Menu Item: File → Save

On the "Save Image" dialog window, make sure that the "Select File Type" setting is set to "By Extension". Save the file as phase16x16.png

Appendix P

Client Side JavaScript Debugging

JavaScript Debugging

- Instructions are provided for debugging JavaScript by using FireFox with the Venkman Extension.
- The JavaScript "debugger" keyword is used to create a breakpoint.
- The Venkman Javascript debugger extension is available at the following URL:

  `https://addons.mozilla.org/en-US/firefox/addon/216`

`FireFox with the Venkman Extension Debugging Steps`

1: Start the FireFox web browser.

2: FireFox - Activate Menu Item: Tools → JavaScript Debugger

3: When the JavaScript file is opened in FireFox, the script debugger will launch and break at the "debugger" command. At this point, the script can be stepped through one line at a time.

Appendix Q
Update the Path

Steps to update the program search path

- The following examples illustrate how to update the search path for the QT4 library:

- Linux Bash

```
export PATH=/usr/local/Trolltech/Qt-4.1.4/bin:$PATH
```

Linux C and TC shell

```
setenv PATH /usr/local/Trolltech/Qt-4.1.4/bin:$PATH
```

For the Bash shell, the path can be updated permanently by editing the .bash_profile, .bashrc, or .profile text file in the user's home folder. For the C and TC shell, the path can be updated permanently by editing the .cshrc text file found in the user's home folder.

- Mac OS X Bash

```
export PATH=/usr/local/Trolltech/Qt-4.1.4/bin:$PATH
```

For the Bash shell, the path can be updated permanently by editing the .profile text file in the user's home folder.

- Windows

```
PATH = C:\Qt\4.1.4\bin;$PATH
```

Windows Path Permanent Update Steps

1: Windows - Activate Menu Item: Start → Settings → Control Panel

2: Activate the "System" icon in the "Control Panel"

3: On the "System Properties" window, select the "Advanced" tab and then activate the "Environment Variables" button.

4: Update the path in the "User" or "System" Path environment variable.

Appendix R

ASCII Table

Dec	Hex	Bin	ASCII	Keyboard
0	00	0000 0000	NUL	<CTRL><1>, Null
1	01	0000 0001	SOH	<CTRL><A>, Start of Heading
2	02	0000 0010	STX	<CTRL><B>, Start of Text
3	03	0000 0011	ETX	<CTRL><C>, End of Text
4	04	0000 0100	EOT	<CTRL><D>, End of Transmission
5	05	0000 0101	ENQ	<CTRL><E>, Enquiry
6	06	0000 0110	ACK	<CTRL><F>, Acknowledge
7	07	0000 0111	BEL	<CTRL><G>, Bell
8	08	0000 1000	BS	<CTRL><H>, Backspace
9	09	0000 1001	HT	<CTRL><I>, Horizontal Tab
10	0A	0000 1010	LF	<CTRL><J>, Line Feed
11	0B	0000 1011	VT	<CTRL><K>, Vertical Tab
12	0C	0000 1100	FF	<CTRL><L>, Form Feed
13	0D	0000 1101	CR	<CTRL><M>, Return
14	0E	0000 1110	SO	<CTRL><N>, Shift Out
15	0F	0000 1111	SI	<CTRL><O>, Shift In
16	10	0001 0000	DLE	<CTRL><P>, Data Link Escape
17	11	0001 0001	DC1	<CTRL><Q>, Device Control 1
18	12	0001 0010	DC2	<CTRL><R>, Device Control 2
19	13	0001 0011	DC3	<CTRL><S>, Device Control 3
20	14	0001 0100	DC4	<CTRL><T>, Device Control 4
21	15	0001 0101	NAK	<CTRL><U>, Negative Acknowledge
22	16	0001 0110	SYN	<CTRL><V>, Synchronous Idle
23	17	0001 0111	ETB	<CTRL><W>, End Transmission Block
24	18	0001 1000	CAN	<CTRL><X>, Cancel
25	19	0001 1001	EM	<CTRL><Y>, End of Medium
26	1A	0001 1010	SUB	<CTRL><Z>, Substitute
27	1B	0001 1011	ESC	Esc, Escape
28	1C	0001 1100	FS	<CTRL></\>, File Separator
29	1D	0001 1101	GS	<CTRL></]>, Group Separator
30	1E	0001 1110	RS	<CTRL></=>, Record Separator
31	1F	0001 1111	US	<CTRL></->, Unit Separator
32	20	0010 0000	SP	Spacebar
33	21	0010 0001	!	!
34	22	0010 0010	"	"
35	23	0010 0011	#	#
36	24	0010 0100	$	$
37	25	0010 0101	%	%
38	26	0010 0110	&	&
39	27	0010 0111	'	'
40	28	0010 1000	(	(
41	29	0010 1001	)	)
42	2A	0010 1010	*	*
43	2B	0010 1011	+	+
44	2C	0010 1100	,	,
45	2D	0010 1101	-	-
46	2E	0010 1110	.	.
47	2F	0010 1111	/	/
48	30	0011 0000	0	0
49	31	0011 0001	1	1

Dec	Hex	Bin	ASCII	Keyboard
50	32	0011 0010	2	2
51	33	0011 0011	3	3
52	34	0011 0100	4	4
53	35	0011 0101	5	5
54	36	0011 0110	6	6
55	37	0011 0111	7	7
56	38	0011 1000	8	8
57	39	0011 1001	9	9
58	3A	0011 1010	:	:
59	3B	0011 1011	;	;
60	3C	0011 1100	<	<
61	3D	0011 1101	=	=
62	3E	0011 1110	>	>
63	3F	0011 1111	?	?
64	40	0100 0000	@	@
65	41	0100 0001	A	A
66	42	0100 0010	B	B
67	43	0100 0011	C	C
68	44	0100 0100	D	D
69	45	0100 0101	E	E
70	46	0100 0110	F	F
71	47	0100 0111	G	G
72	48	0100 1000	H	H
73	49	0100 1001	I	I
74	4A	0100 1010	J	J
75	4B	0100 1011	K	K
76	4C	0100 1100	L	L
77	4D	0100 1101	M	M
78	4E	0100 1110	N	N
79	4F	0100 1111	O	O
80	50	0101 0000	P	P
81	51	0101 0001	Q	Q
82	52	0101 0010	R	R
83	53	0101 0011	S	S
84	54	0101 0100	T	T
85	55	0101 0101	U	U
86	56	0101 0110	V	V
87	57	0101 0111	W	W
88	58	0101 1000	X	X
89	59	0101 1001	Y	Y
90	5A	0101 1010	Z	Z
91	5B	0101 1011	[	[
92	5C	0101 1100	\	\
93	5D	0101 1101	]	]
94	5E	0101 1110	^	^
95	5F	0101 1111	_	_
96	60	0110 0000	`	`
97	61	0110 0001	a	a
98	62	0110 0010	b	b
99	63	0110 0011	c	c
100	64	0110 0100	d	d
101	65	0110 0101	e	e
102	66	0110 0110	f	f
103	67	0110 0111	g	g
104	68	0110 1000	h	h

Dec	Hex	Bin	ASCII	Keyboard
105	69	0110 1001	i	i
106	6A	0110 1010	j	j
107	6B	0110 1011	k	k
108	6C	0110 1100	l	l
109	6D	0110 1101	m	m
110	6E	0110 1110	n	n
111	6F	0110 1111	o	o
112	70	0111 0000	p	p
113	71	0111 0001	q	q
114	72	0111 0010	r	r
115	73	0111 0011	s	s
116	74	0111 0100	t	t
117	75	0111 0101	u	u
118	76	0111 0110	v	v
119	77	0111 0111	w	w
120	78	0111 1000	x	x
121	79	0111 1001	y	y
122	7A	0111 1010	z	z
123	7B	0111 1011	{	{
124	7C	0111 1100	|	|
125	7D	0111 1101	}	}
126	7E	0111 1110	~	~
127	7F	0111 1111	Del	Delete

Appendix S

Window and Mouse Constants

Constants and Functions for Window State, Window Border, and Mouse Cursor

- **Java - JFrame**

```
Window State

   JFrame.NORMAL, JFrame.ICONIFIED, Jrame.MAXIMIZED_HORIZ,
   JFrame.MAXIMIZED_VERT, JFrame.MAXIMIZED_BOTH

Border Style

   setResizable(true), setResizable(false),
   Use JWindow instead of JFrame for borderless window

Mouse Cursor

   CROSSHAIR_CURSOR, CUSTOM_CURSOR, DEFAULT_CURSOR, E_RESIZE_CURSOR
   HAND_CURSOR, MOVE_CURSOR, N_RESIZE_CURSOR, NE_RESIZE_CURSOR
   NW_RESIZE_CURSOR, S_RESIZE_CURSOR, SE_RESIZE_CURSOR,
   SW_RESIZE_CURSOR, TEXT_CURSOR, W_RESIZE_CURSOR, WAIT_CURSOR
```

- **Visual FoxPro**

```
Window State

   0 - Normal, 1 - Minimized, 2 - Maximized

Border Style

   0 - No Border, 1 - Fixed Single, 2 - Fixed Dialog, 3 - Sizable

Mouse Cursor

   0 - Object Determined, 1 - Arrow, 2 - Cross, 3 - I beam,
   4 - Icon, 5 - Size, 6 - Size NE SW, 7 - Size NS, 8 - Size NW SE
   9 - Size WE, 10 - Up arrow, 11 - Hourglass, 12 - No drop,
   13 - Hide pointer, 14 - Arrow, 15 - Hand, 16 - Down arrow,
   99 - Custom
```

- **C - Win32**

```
Window State

   SW_SHOWNORMAL, SW_SHOWMINIMIZED, SW_SHOWMAXIMIZED

Border Style

   Resizable - WS_OVERLAPPEDWINDOW
   Fixed - WS_BORDER | WS_MAXIMIZEBOX | WS_MINIMIZEBOX | WS_SYSMENU
| WS_CAPTION

Mouse Cursor

   IDC_APPSTARTING, IDC_ARROW, IDC_CROSS, IDC_HAND, IDC_HELP,
   IDC_IBEAM, IDC_ICON, IDC_NO, IDC_SIZE, IDC_SIZEALL, IDC_SIZENESW
   IDC_SIZENS, IDC_SIZENWSE, IDC_SIZEWE, IDC_UPARROW, IDC_WAIT
```

- **Visual Basic 6**

```
Window State

   vbNormal, vbMinimized, vbMaximized

Border Style

   vbBSNone, vbFixedSingle, vbSizable, vbFixedDouble,
   vbFixedToolWindow, vbSizableToolWindow

Mouse Cursor

   vbDefault, vbArrow, vbCrosshair, vbIbeam, vbIconPointer,
   vbSizePointer, vbSizeNESW, vbSizeNS, vbSizeNWSE, vbSizeWE,
   vbUpArrow, vbHourglass, vbNoDrop, vbArrowHourglass,
   vbArrowQuestion, vbSizeAll, vbCustom
```

- **C++ MFC**

```
Window State

   SW_SHOWNORMAL, SW_SHOWMINIMIZED, SW_SHOWMAXIMIZED

Border Style

   Resizable - WS_OVERLAPPEDWINDOW
   Fixed - WS_BORDER | WS_MAXIMIZEBOX | WS_MINIMIZEBOX | WS_SYSMENU
| WS_CAPTION

Mouse Cursor

   IDC_ARROW, IDC_IBEAM, IDC_WAIT, IDC_CROSS, IDC_UPARROW,
   IDC_SIZE, IDC_SIZEALL, IDC_ICON, IDC_SIZENWSE, IDC_SIZENESW,
   IDC_SIZEWE, IDC_SIZENS
```

- **C# - .NET Framework – Mono**

```
Window State

   FormWindowState.Normal, FormWindowState.Minimized,
   FormWindowState.Maximized

Border Style

   FormBorderStyle.None, FormBorderStyle.FixedSingle,
   FormBorderStyle.Fixed3D, FormBorderStyle.FixedDialog,
   FormBorderStyle.Sizable, FormBorderStyle.FixedToolWindow,
   FormBorderStyle.SizableToolWindow

Mouse Cursor

   Cursors.None, Cursors.No, Cursors.Arrow, Cursors.AppStarting,
   Cursors.Cross, Cursors.Help, Cursors.IBeam, Cursors.SizeAll,
   Cursors.SizeNESW, Cursors.SizeNS, Cursors.SizeNWSE,
   Cursors.SizeWE,  Cursors.UpArrow, Cursors.Wait, Cursors.Hand,
   Cursors.Pen,  Cursors.ScrollNS, Cursors.ScrollWE,
   Cursors.ScrollAll, Cursors.ScrollN, Cursors.ScrollS,
   Cursors.ScrollW, Cursors.ScrollE, Cursors.ScrollNW,
   Cursors.ScrollNE, Cursors.ScrollSW, Cursors.ScrollSE,
   Cursors.ArrowCD
```

- **Visual Basic.NET**

Window State

```
FormWindowState.Normal, FormWindowState.Minimized,
FormWindowState.Maximized
```

Border Style

```
FormBorderStyle.None, FormBorderStyle.FixedSingle,
FormBorderStyle.Fixed3D, FormBorderStyle.FixedDialog,
FormBorderStyle.Sizable, FormBorderStyle.FixedToolWindow,
FormBorderStyle.SizableToolWindow
```

Mouse Cursor

```
Cursors.None, Cursors.No, Cursors.Arrow, Cursors.AppStarting,
Cursors.Cross, Cursors.Help, Cursors.IBeam, Cursors.SizeAll,
Cursors.SizeNESW, Cursors.SizeNS, Cursors.SizeNWSE,
Cursors.SizeWE,  Cursors.UpArrow, Cursors.Wait, Cursors.Hand,
Cursors.Pen,  Cursors.ScrollNS, Cursors.ScrollWE,
Cursors.ScrollAll, Cursors.ScrollN, Cursors.ScrollS,
Cursors.ScrollW, Cursors.ScrollE, Cursors.ScrollNW,
Cursors.ScrollNE, Cursors.ScrollSW, Cursors.ScrollSE,
Cursors.ArrowCD
```

- **C++ - .NET Framework**

Window State

```
FormWindowState::Normal, FormWindowState::Minimized,
FormWindowState::Maximized
```

Border Style

```
FormBorderStyle::None, FormBorderStyle::FixedSingle,
FormBorderStyle::Fixed3D, FormBorderStyle::FixedDialog,
FormBorderStyle::Sizable, FormBorderStyle::FixedToolWindow,
FormBorderStyle::SizableToolWindow
```

Mouse Cursor

```
Cursors::None, Cursors::No, Cursors::Arrow,
Cursors::AppStarting, Cursors::Cross, Cursors::Help,
Cursors::IBeam, Cursors::SizeAll, Cursors::SizeNESW,
Cursors::SizeNS, Cursors::SizeNWSE, Cursors::SizeWE,
Cursors::UpArrow, Cursors::Wait, Cursors::Hand,
Cursors::Pen,  Cursors::ScrollNS, Cursors::ScrollWE,
Cursors::ScrollAll, Cursors::ScrollN, Cursors::ScrollS,
Cursors::ScrollW, Cursors::ScrollE, Cursors::ScrollNW,
Cursors::ScrollNE, Cursors::ScrollSW, Cursors::ScrollSE,
Cursors::ArrowCD
```

- **Python - Tk**

Window State

```
newstate="normal", newstate="zoomed" (Windows Only),
newstate="iconic"
```

Border Style

```
resizable(1,1) - Resizable Window, resizable(0,0) - Fixed
```

Mouse Cursor

```
X_cursor, arrow, based_arrow_down, based_arrow_up, boat,
bogosity, bottom_left_corner, bottom_right_corner, bottom_side,
bottom_tee, box_spiral, center_ptr, circle, clock, coffee_mug,
```

```
cross, cross_reverse, crosshair, diamond_cross, dot, dotbox,
double_arrow, draft_large, draft_small, draped_box, exchange,
fleur, gobbler, gumby, hand1, hand2, heart, icon, iron_cross,
left_ptr, left_side, left_tee, leftbutton, ll_angle, lr_angle,
man, middlebutton, mouse, pencil, pirate, plus, question_arrow,
right_ptr, right_side, right_tee, rightbutton, rtl_logo,
sailboat, sb_down_arrow, sb_h_double_arrow, sb_left_arrow,
sb_right_arrow, sb_up_arrow, sb_v_double_arrow, shuttle, sizing,
spider, spraycan, star, target, tcross, top_left_arrow,
top_left_corner, top_right_corner, top_side, top_tee, trek,
ul_angle, umbrella, ur_angle, watch, xterm
```

- **Perl - Tk**

Window State

```
newstate="normal", newstate="zoomed" (Windows Only),
newstate="iconic"
```

Border Style

```
resizable(1,1) - Resizable Window, resizable(0,0) - Fixed
```

Mouse Cursor

```
X_cursor, arrow, based_arrow_down, based_arrow_up, boat,
bogosity, bottom_left_corner, bottom_right_corner, bottom_side,
bottom_tee, box_spiral, center_ptr, circle, clock, coffee_mug,
cross, cross_reverse, crosshair, diamond_cross, dot, dotbox,
double_arrow, draft_large, draft_small, draped_box, exchange,
fleur, gobbler, gumby, hand1, hand2, heart, icon, iron_cross,
left_ptr, left_side, left_tee, leftbutton, ll_angle, lr_angle,
man, middlebutton, mouse, pencil, pirate, plus, question_arrow,
right_ptr, right_side, right_tee, rightbutton, rtl_logo,
sailboat, sb_down_arrow, sb_h_double_arrow, sb_left_arrow,
sb_right_arrow, sb_up_arrow, sb_v_double_arrow, shuttle, sizing,
spider, spraycan, star, target, tcross, top_left_arrow,
top_left_corner, top_right_corner, top_side, top_tee, trek,
ul_angle, umbrella, ur_angle, watch, xterm
```

- **PHP-CLI - Gtk**

Window State

```
GtkWindow::unmaximize() - Normal,
GtkWindow::iconify() - Minimized,
GtkWindow::maximize() - Maximized
```

Border Style

```
set_resizable(0) - Resizable Window, set_resizable(1) - Fixed
```

Mouse Cursor

```
Gdk::X_CURSOR, Gdk::ARROW, Gdk::BASED_ARROW_DOWN,
Gdk::BASED_ARROW_UP, Gdk::BOAT, Gdk::BOGOSITY,
Gdk::BOTTOM_LEFT_CORNER, Gdk::BOTTOM_RIGHT_CORNER,
Gdk::BOTTOM_SIDE, Gdk::BOTTOM_TEE, Gdk::BOX_SPIRAL,
Gdk::CENTER_PTR, Gdk::CIRCLE, Gdk::CLOCK, Gdk::COFFEE_MUG,
Gdk::CROSS, Gdk::CROSS_REVERSE, Gdk::CROSSHAIR,
Gdk::DIAMOND_CROSS, Gdk::DOT, Gdk::DOTBOX, Gdk::DOUBLE_ARROW,
Gdk::DRAFT_LARGE, Gdk::DRAFT_SMALL, Gdk::DRAPED_BOX,
Gdk::EXCHANGE, Gdk::FLEUR, Gdk::GOBBLER, Gdk::GUMBY, Gdk::HAND1,
Gdk::HAND2, Gdk::HEART, Gdk::ICON, Gdk::IRON_CROSS,
Gdk::LEFT_PTR, Gdk::LEFT_SIDE, Gdk::LEFT_TEE, Gdk::LEFTBUTTON,
Gdk::LL_ANGLE, Gdk::LR_ANGLE, Gdk::MAN, Gdk::MIDDLEBUTTON,
Gdk::MOUSE, Gdk::PENCIL, Gdk::PIRATE, Gdk::PLUS,
Gdk::QUESTION_ARROW, Gdk::RIGHT_PTR, Gdk::RIGHT_SIDE,
Gdk::RIGHT_TEE, Gdk::RIGHTBUTTON, Gdk::RTL_LOGO, Gdk::SAILBOAT,
```

```
Gdk::SB_DOWN_ARROW, Gdk::SB_H_DOUBLE_ARROW, Gdk::SB_LEFT_ARROW,
Gdk::SB_RIGHT_ARROW, Gdk::SB_UP_ARROW, Gdk::SB_V_DOUBLE_ARROW,
Gdk::SHUTTLE, Gdk::SIZING, Gdk::SPIDER, Gdk::SPRAYCAN,
Gdk::STAR, Gdk::TARGET, Gdk::TCROSS, Gdk::TOP_LEFT_ARROW,
Gdk::TOP_LEFT_CORNER, Gdk::TOP_RIGHT_CORNER, Gdk::TOP_SIDE,
Gdk::TOP_TEE, Gdk::TREK, Gdk::UL_ANGLE, Gdk::UMBRELLA
Gdk::UR_ANGLE, Gdk::WATCH, Gdk::XTERM, Gdk::LAST_CURSOR,
Gdk::CURSOR_IS_PIXMAP
```

- **Ruby - Tk**

```
Window State

   normal, zoomed (Windows Only), iconic

Border Style

   resizable(1,1) - Resizable Window, resizable(0,0) - Fixed

Mouse Cursor

   X_cursor, arrow, based_arrow_down, based_arrow_up, boat,
   bogosity, bottom_left_corner, bottom_right_corner, bottom_side,
   bottom_tee, box_spiral, center_ptr, circle, clock, coffee_mug,
   cross, cross_reverse, crosshair, diamond_cross, dot, dotbox,
   double_arrow, draft_large, draft_small, draped_box, exchange,
   fleur, gobbler, gumby, hand1, hand2, heart, icon, iron_cross,
   left_ptr, left_side, left_tee, leftbutton, ll_angle, lr_angle,
   man, middlebutton, mouse, pencil, pirate, plus, question_arrow,
   right_ptr, right_side, right_tee, rightbutton, rtl_logo,
   sailboat, sb_down_arrow, sb_h_double_arrow, sb_left_arrow,
   sb_right_arrow, sb_up_arrow, sb_v_double_arrow, shuttle, sizing,
   spider, spraycan, star, target, tcross, top_left_arrow,
   top_left_corner, top_right_corner, top_side, top_tee, trek,
   ul_angle, umbrella, ur_angle, watch, xterm
```

- **Tcl - Tk**

```
Window State

   normal, zoomed (Windows Only), iconic

Border Style

   resizable . 1 1 - Resizable Window, resizable . 0 0 - Fixed

Mouse Cursor

   X_cursor, arrow, based_arrow_down, based_arrow_up, boat,
   bogosity, bottom_left_corner, bottom_right_corner, bottom_side,
   bottom_tee, box_spiral, center_ptr, circle, clock, coffee_mug,
   cross, cross_reverse, crosshair, diamond_cross, dot, dotbox,
   double_arrow, draft_large, draft_small, draped_box, exchange,
   fleur, gobbler, gumby, hand1, hand2, heart, icon, iron_cross,
   left_ptr, left_side, left_tee, leftbutton, ll_angle, lr_angle,
   man, middlebutton, mouse, pencil, pirate, plus, question_arrow,
   right_ptr, right_side, right_tee, rightbutton, rtl_logo,
   sailboat, sb_down_arrow, sb_h_double_arrow, sb_left_arrow,
   sb_right_arrow, sb_up_arrow, sb_v_double_arrow, shuttle, sizing,
   spider, spraycan, star, target, tcross, top_left_arrow,
   top_left_corner, top_right_corner, top_side, top_tee, trek,
   ul_angle, umbrella, ur_angle, watch, xterm
```

- **Delphi**

```
Window State

   wsNormal, wxMaximized, wsMinimized

Border Style

   bsDialog, bsNone, bsSingle, bsSizeable, bsSizeToolWin,
   bsToolWindow

Mouse Cursor

   crAppStart, crArrow, crCross, crDefault, crDrag, crHandPoint,
   crHelp, crHourGlass, crHSplit, crIBeam, crMultiDrag,
   crNo, crNoDrop, crSizeAll, crSizeNESW, crSizeNS, crSizeNWSE,
   crSizeWE, crSQLWait, crUpArrow, crVSplit
```

- **C++ - QT4**

```
Window State

   showNormal, showMaximized, showMinimized

Border Style

   setFixedSize(640,480) - Fixed

Mouse Cursor

   Qt::ArrowCursor, Qt::UpArrowCursor, Qt::CrossCursor,
   Qt::IBeamCursor, Qt::WaitCursor, Qt::BusyCursor
   Qt::ForbiddenCursor, Qt::PointingHandCursor,
   Qt::WhatsThisCursor, Qt::SizeVerCursor, Qt::SizeHorCursor,
   Qt::SizeBDiagCursor, Qt::SizeFDiagCursor, Qt::SizeAllCursor,
   Qt::SplitVCursor, Qt::SplitHCursor, Qt::OpenHandCursor,
   Qt::ClosedHandCursor
```

- **C++ - wxWidgets**

```
Window State

   Maximize(true), Iconize(true)

Border Style

   wxDEFAULT_FRAME_STYLE
   wxDEFAULT_FRAME_STYLE & ~ (wxRESIZE_BORDER | wxRESIZE_BOX |
wxMAXIMIZE_BOX)

Mouse Cursor

   wxCURSOR_ARROW, wxCURSOR_RIGHT_ARROW, wxCURSOR_BLANK,
   wxCURSOR_BULLSEYE, wxCURSOR_CHAR, wxCURSOR_CROSS
   wxCURSOR_HAND, wxCURSOR_IBEAM, wxCURSOR_LEFT_BUTTON
   wxCURSOR_MAGNIFIER, wxCURSOR_MIDDLE_BUTTON, wxCURSOR_NO_ENTRY,
   wxCURSOR_PAINT_BRUSH, wxCURSOR_PENCIL, wxCURSOR_POINT_LEFT
   wxCURSOR_POINT_RIGHT, wxCURSOR_QUESTION_ARROW,
   wxCURSOR_RIGHT_BUTTON, wxCURSOR_SIZENESW, wxCURSOR_SIZENS,
   wxCURSOR_SIZENWSE, wxCURSOR_SIZEWE, wxCURSOR_SIZING
   wxCURSOR_SPRAYCAN, wxCURSOR_WAIT, wxCURSOR_WATCH,
   wxCURSOR_ARROWWAIT
```

- **C - Carbon**

```
Window State

   inZoomIn, inZoomOut

Border Style

   kWindowResizableAttribute

Mouse Cursor

   kThemeArrowCursor, kThemeCopyArrowCursor,
   kThemeAliasArrowCursor, kThemeContextualMenuArrowCursor,
   kThemeIBeamCursor, kThemeCrossCursor, kThemePlusCursor,
   kThemeWatchCursor, kThemeClosedHandCursor, kThemeOpenHandCursor,
   kThemePointingHandCursor, kThemeCountingUpHandCursor,
   kThemeCountingDownHandCursor, kThemeCountingUpAndDownHandCursor,
   kThemeSpinningCursor, kThemeResizeLeftCursor,
   kThemeResizeRightCursor, kThemeResizeLeftRightCursor
```

- **Objective-C - Cocoa**

```
Window State

   performMiniaturize:NSApp, performZoom:NSApp

Border Style

   NSResizableWindowMask

Mouse Cursor

   arrowCursor, IBeamCursor, crosshairCursor, closedHandCursor,
   openHandCursor, pointingHandCursor, resizeLeftCursor,
   resizeRightCursor, resizeLeftRightCursor, resizeUpCursor,
   resizeDownCursor, resizeUpDownCursor, disappearingItemCursor
```

- **C - GTK+**

```
Window State

   gtk_window_iconify(GTK_WINDOW(loMainWindow)),
   gtk_window_maximize(GTK_WINDOW(loMainWindow))

Border Style

   gtk_window_set_resizable(GTK_WINDOW(loMainWindow),1),
   gtk_window_set_resizable(GTK_WINDOW(loMainWindow),0)

Mouse Cursor

   GDK_X_CURSOR, GDK_ARROW, GDK_BASED_ARROW_DOWN,
   GDK_BASED_ARROW_UP, GDK_BOAT, GDK_BOGOSITY,
   GDK_BOTTOM_LEFT_CORNER, GDK_BOTTOM_RIGHT_CORNER
   GDK_BOTTOM_SIDE, GDK_BOTTOM_TEE, GDK_BOX_SPIRAL,
   GDK_CENTER_PTR, GDK_CIRCLE, GDK_CLOCK, GDK_COFFEE_MUG,
   GDK_CROSS, GDK_CROSS_REVERSE, GDK_CROSSHAIR, GDK_DIAMOND_CROSS,
   GDK_DOT, GDK_DOTBOX, GDK_DOUBLE_ARROW, GDK_DRAFT_LARGE,
   GDK_DRAFT_SMALL, GDK_DRAPED_BOX, GDK_EXCHANGE, GDK_FLEUR
   GDK_GOBBLER, GDK_GUMBY, GDK_HAND1, GDK_HAND2, GDK_HEART,
   GDK_ICON, GDK_IRON_CROSS, GDK_LEFT_PTR, GDK_LEFT_SIDE
   GDK_LEFT_TEE, GDK_LEFTBUTTON, GDK_LL_ANGLE, GDK_LR_ANGLE,
   GDK_MAN, GDK_MIDDLEBUTTON, GDK_MOUSE, GDK_PENCIL, GDK_PIRATE,
   GDK_PLUS, GDK_QUESTION_ARROW, GDK_RIGHT_PTR, GDK_RIGHT_SIDE,
   GDK_RIGHT_TEE, GDK_RIGHTBUTTON, GDK_RTL_LOGO, GDK_SAILBOAT,
   GDK_SB_DOWN_ARROW, GDK_SB_H_DOUBLE_ARROW, GDK_SB_LEFT_ARROW,
   GDK_SB_RIGHT_ARROW, GDK_SB_UP_ARROW, GDK_SB_V_DOUBLE_ARROW,
   GDK_SHUTTLE, GDK_SIZING, GDK_SPIDER, GDK_SPRAYCAN, GDK_STAR,
```

```
GDK_TARGET, GDK_TCROSS, GDK_TOP_LEFT_ARROW, GDK_TOP_LEFT_CORNER,
GDK_TOP_RIGHT_CORNER, GDK_TOP_SIDE, GDK_TOP_TEE, GDK_TREK,
GDK_UL_ANGLE, GDK_UMBRELLA, GDK_UR_ANGLE, GDK_WATCH,
GDK_XTERM, GDK_LAST_CURSOR, GDK_CURSOR_IS_PIXMAP
```

- **JavaScript**

```
Window State

   Maximize

      window.moveTo(0,0);
      window.resizeTo(screen.availWidth,screen.availHeight);

   Minimize (IE7, FireFox, Safari)

      window.resizeTo(150,250);
      window.moveTo(screen.width,screen.height);

Border Style (IE Only)

   window.open("http://127.0.0.1/test1.html",null,resizable=yes")
   window.open("http://127.0.0.1/test1.html",null,resizable=no")

Mouse Cursor

   auto, crosshair, default, e-resize, hand, help, move, n-resize,
   ne-resize, nw-resize, pointer, s-resize, se-resize, sw-resize
   text, w-resize, wait
```